FRONTIER CONTACT BETWEEN CHOSŎN KOREA AND TOKUGAWA JAPAN

Focusing on the period 1600–1900, this ground-breaking work presents Korean history as a tension between structures and agents. It examines economy, demography, and mentalities and focuses on Korean and Japanese attitudes towards each other, forged at their point of contact on the frontier. The book argues that frontier contact in the pre-modern world was at least as important for the formation of cultural perceptions and historical memory as the writings of intellectuals far away in national centres. It raises questions about pre-modern self-perceptions and the processes by which perceptions were formed of other peoples. The book also links local history with transnational relations and presents East Asian pre-modern history in a completely new light.

James B. Lewis is the Korea Foundation University Lecturer in Korean Studies, Director of the Korean Studies Programme, and Fellow of Wolfson College, University of Oxford. Current projects include *The Kōrim Teisei, an Eighteenth-century Japanese View of Korea*; *The Imjin Waeran – Hideyoshi's Invasion of Korea: Problems and Perspectives*; and *An Economic History of Korea, 1400–1930*.

FRONTIER CONTACT BETWEEN CHOSŎN KOREA AND TOKUGAWA JAPAN

James B. Lewis

Routledge
Taylor & Francis Group

LONDON AND NEW YORK

First published 2003
by Routledge
2 Park Square, Milton Park, Abingdon, Oxon, OX14 4RN

Simultaneously published in the USA and Canada
by Routledge
270 Madison Ave, New York NY 10016

Routledge is an imprint of the Taylor & Francis Group

Transferred to Digital Printing 2010

© 2003 James B. Lewis

Typeset in 10/12pt Goudy by Graphicraft Limited, Hong Kong

British Library Cataloguing in Publication Data
A catalogue record for this book is available
from the British Library

Library of Congress Cataloging in Publication Data
Lewis, James Bryant.
Frontier contact between choson Korea and
Tokugawa Japan / James B. Lewis.
p. cm.
Includes bibliographical references and index.
1. Korea – Relations – Japan.   2. Japan – Relations – Korea.
3.   Korea – History – 1637–1864.   4. Japan – History – Tokugawa period,
1600–1868.   I. Title.
DS910.2.J3L48 2003
327.519052'09'03–dc21   2003041582

ISBN10: 0-7007-1301-8 (hbk)
ISBN10: 0-415-60006-5 (pbk)

ISBN13: 978-0-7007-1301-1 (hbk)
ISBN13: 978-0-415-60006-4 (pbk)

CONTENTS

CONTENTS

FIGURES

MAPS

TABLES

ACKNOWLEDGMENTS

A man can never count all his blessings, no matter how hard he tries. There are simply too many conversations, patient answers to questions, extensive attempts to teach one something, and chance encounters that went into the following pages. My interest in Korea goes back to the late 1970s, when I was a student in Japan. Eighth-century Nara fascinated me, and I spent every spare moment visiting the temples and museums around Kansai. Either no-one mentioned Korea or I was oblivious to the connections. When I visited Seoul on vacation in the winter of 1977, I found myself one cold morning in the National Museum with my head reeling as I stood in front of the display cases. There were the very same material remains I had been studying in connection with early Japan, only these were "Korean" relics. Everyone deserves an epiphany, however small, and I guess that I had mine that cold morning in the museum. Suddenly, Japan had a context for me. I had to know all about relations between the two peoples, which meant I had to know all about Korea. Little did I know how difficult that would prove to be.

I dabbled with the legal position of the Korean minority in Japan just before the fingerprint movement of the early 1980s began, and imposed myself on a host of good people in the Korean community in Ikuno Ward for nearly a year. They taught me more than they will ever know about courage and dignity. Someday, I hope to repay them, but I had to give up that line of contemporary study, because it seemed too politicized and too recalcitrant of resolution.

I went to Korea and while there became interested in pre-modern Korean–Japanese relations. While visiting Roy Hanashiro in Fukuoka, I met Saeki Kōji, who is now the Professor of Medieval Japanese history at Kyūshū University. He introduced me to Tanaka Ryūji, who was then studying at Yonsei University, and with whom I took up the study of Amenomori Hōshū's *Kōrin teisei*. Tanaka has since become an expert on colonial relations, but he had just finished an undergraduate thesis on the *Kōrin teisei*. Also at that time I was reading Professor Tashiro Kazui's articles and book in Japanese and Professor Ronald Toby's book in English. As fortune would have it, Tashiro and Toby visited Korea in 1984. Tashiro's book (*Kinsei Ni-Chō tsūkō bōekishi no kenkyū*) had been out a few years and Toby's book (*State and Diplomacy in Early Modern Japan*) had just come out. I trace the germ of this study to a morning conversation with Professor Toby in 1983 at Yonsei University's Guest House.

Back in Hawai'i, Professor Ch'oe Yŏng-ho encouraged me in a thousand ways, even suggesting the document base, and patiently offered incisive criticism as I struggled with a focus. He was the first to open my eyes to the rich document base of the Korean past. Professor Hugh Kang exhibited unflagging encouragement and has counseled me in many ways over the years. By some miracle unknown to me, the Japanese Monbushō agreed to fund my studies on Korean history at Kyūshū University under the direction of Professor Osa Masanori. I arrived in Hakata in 1987 just in time to join the mourners at Professor Osa's funeral. Professor Nakamura Tadashi became my teacher for Japanese documents and my mooring when the untimely death of Professor Osa put my ship adrift. Alas, he passed away before he could review the finished study. He and his students lent their patient wisdom, vast historical knowledge, and ability to read grass writing at critical moments.

Osa Masanori's teaching assistant – Shirakawa Yutaka – and students at Kyūshū University in 1987 – Rokutanda Yutaka, Nakanishi Takeshi, Tada Yukio, Tsurusaki Satoshi, Kuwano Eiji, Fujiishi Takayo, Katsubei Hajime, Azuma Chikusa, and Tahara Yasuiyuki – supplied living testimony to the scholarly, collegiate, and moral ideals of their deceased master, guiding me through days of research and nights of debriefing over *yakitori* and *shōchū*. Many of them have become leaders in the study of Korean history and culture in Japan. Shirakawa Yutaka has become the Professor of Korean Literature at Kyūshū Sangyō University. Rokutanda Yutaka held appointments at Kurume University, Kyūshū University, and is now a Professor of Korean History at Tōkyō University. Kuwano Eiji was a teaching assistant at Kyūshū University and is now the Professor of Korean History at Kurume University. Fujiishi Takayo is the Professor of Korean Literature and Language at Niigata University. As I studied with them at Kyūdai, my interest in Tsushima deepened, and I am grateful to both Professor Izumi Chōichi of Kansai University and Professor Osa Setsuko of Kyūshū Sangyō University for sharing their time with me. Both have given generously of their instruction, counsel, and personal warmth over the years.

While on a research trip to the Kyujanggak, I carried a letter of introduction from Rokutanda Yutaka to Professor Yi T'ae-jin. Rokutanda had been Yi's student while studying at the Chŏngsin Munhwa Yŏn'guwŏn. Professor Yi, in turn, introduced me to a young scholar who had been recently appointed to Chŏlla Pukto University. When I saw his face, I realized that I had met him a couple of years earlier at Kyūshū University. To my great benefit, Professor Ha Woo Bong became intrigued by this young American who was carrying away several boxes of photocopied manuscripts on Korean relations with Japan. Ha Woo Bong has led modern research on Chosŏn-era relations with Japan through his own work and by inspiring a new generation of scholars whom I am fortunate to count as my friends. Dr. Han Munjong taught me much about medieval relations and has recently become a Professor of Korean History at Chŏlla Pukto University. Dr. Hong Sŏng-dŏk is a colleague in the study of early-modern relations and has worked to translate and annotate certain key documents, such as the *Chŭngjŏng kyorinji* that appears so often in the following pages. Dr. Chang Sun-sun has recently obtained her doctorate with an important study that focuses on the creation and maintenance of the Waegwans. Her excellent study came to me at a late stage, and I was unable to incorporate it here, but I list it in the bibliography. I hope she will forgive my many mistakes.

During my visits to Korea, I also came to know Dr. Yi Hun of the Kuksa P'yŏnch'an Wiwŏnhoe and Professor Chŏng Sŏng-il, formerly of the Kuksa P'yŏnch'an Wiwŏnhoe and now a Professor of Korean History at Chŏlla Namdo University. Both Dr. Yi and Professor Chŏng share responsibility with Professor Ha for inspiring young Korean scholars (and numerous foreign students). Their work on castaways and trade undergirds numerous parts of the present study.

Many others have contributed to my work in countless ways. Professor Kim Ŭi-hwan took an interest in my studies, offered inspiration, and even invited me to travel with him one spring to survey sites in Korea. It saddens me that he left this earth before I could show him this study. He would have been amused. Mr. Nagasato Kazu, resident of Izuhara, provided a similar example with the unflagging energy he has thrown into his studies of the history of Tsushima. Professor Hamada Kosaku, the Professor of Korean History at Kyūshū University and successor to Osa Masanori, has tolerated my frustrations and outbursts over the years with great patience. Dr. Miyazaki Katsunori of Kyūshū University helped me re-write the chapter on prostitution for publication in Japan, and I committed the unforgivable sin of not acknowledging that help when the study was first published. Mr. Ch'oe Chae-pok of the Chŏngsin Munhwa Yŏn'guwŏn and Mr. Chi Young-hae of the University of Oxford helped me re-write the same chapter for publication in Korea, and Mr. Chi Young-hae also helped me re-write the chapter on riots for publication in Korea. He has suffered greatly at my insistences over the years. Professor Hamada Kosaku, Professor Rokutanda Yutaka, and Ms. Shibata Sachiko struggled doggedly with a stubborn author on a very early version of Chapter 4 that was written in Japanese. The kind editors of the journal Chihōshi patiently put up with my extensive, even abusive pre-publication corrections to the tables that underpin Chapter 5. Dr. Jun Seongho of Sŭnggyungwan University and recently of the Chŏngsin Munhwa Yŏn'guwŏn provided the expertise in economic history that finally broke the hold on Chapter 4. He has become both a good friend and a collaborator. Professor Kenneth Robinson of International Christian University in Tōkyō, another good friend, has given me sage advice on many things, including this study, and I am grateful, even when I ignore that advice. Dr. James McMullen of the University of Oxford read an early draft and suggested the additions on demography that became Chapter 3. Mr. Kang Han-Rog (University of Oxford) was the key to obtain permission to use the map on the cover. Professor Chung Ku-Bok (Academy of Korean Studies) and Mr. Sim Chae-u (The National Museum of Korea) kindly helped me get permission to reproduce Map 2.4. I would like to express my deep appreciation to Ms. Rosemary Morlin for her patient attention to the multitude of mistakes in my manuscript and to Ms. Jo Jacomb for shepherding this book to final production. Despite the enormous help of these great and good people, the study that follows is filled with errors,all my own and all unintentional.

Finally, this work is dedicated to the late Professor Osa Masanori, a man who, even in death, has done so much to bring Koreans and Japanese together; a man I almost knew.

A note on transliteration

Korean and Japanese transliterated terms are given in parentheses usually following K: (for Korean) or J: for Japanese. The romanization system for Korean is the McCune-Reischauer system; Hepburn for Japanese; and Pinyin for Chinese. All East Asian names are given as surname followed by given names.

1

INTRODUCTION

Reconstructing the past and constructing the future

> Although many speak of sincere relations, the great majority do not
> understand the meaning of the word. Sincerity [means], with a true
> heart, avoid deception, avoid strife, and engage each other with the
> truth. This is sincerity. If you were actually to consider practicing
> sincere relations with Korea, then you would completely stop sending
> envoys. It is impossible to speak of true sincerity when [my lord] is
> constantly a burden on that country. If we were to look at that country's
> books, then this fundamental idea would be clear. Nevertheless,
> achieving [sincerity by ceasing to be a burden, i.e. by changing things]
> is not easily done. Because [Korea] may not be expected to speak easily
> of changing the way things have been done up to now, practice
> [religiously] the customs as they have come to be. [In that way] I hope
> that [my lord] will not lose any more sincerity [than has already
> been lost].
>
> (Amenomori Hōshū, 1728)[1]

In May of 1990, the former President of the Republic of Korea, Roh Tae-woo, followed
in the footsteps of his predecessor, Chun Doo-hwan, and visited Japan as a guest of
the Japanese state, banqueting with the Japanese Emperor. During his speech to the
assembled notables of Japan's political, economic, and social worlds, President Roh
Tae-woo welcomed the new Japanese era, Heisei, as a time when the Cold War had
ended and Korea and Japan had a particular leadership role to play for the new age.
But, he cautioned, Japan had to re-assess realistically its own history to appreciate
the sentiment of its neighbors. As an example of sensitivity towards others, particularly Japanese sensitivity towards Korea, the President recounted the following:

> [Some] two hundred and seventy years ago, Amenomori Hōshū, concerned
> with Korean relations, left to [you], as an article of faith, [the injunction to
> practice] "sincere relations [with Korea.]" His opposite number in Korea,
> Hyŏn Tŏk-yun, built the Sŏngsin-dang (Hall of Truth and Sincerity) in
> Tongnae and entertained Japanese Envoys. Similarly, with that sort of mutual
> respect and understanding, the relations between our two countries hereafter
> should develop [based on] the identification of mutual ideals and interests.[2]

Roh's olive branch was perfectly expressive of a Confucian view of history, capable
of locating a golden age in the past sparkling with potential for present and future
emulation. Roh was thereby able to capture the Japanese popular mind, which has

been desperate to find some form of relations that neither disparages Korea nor demands incessant Japanese expressions of breast-beating guilt. The style of the early modern period answers that need. Moreover, Roh was able to deliver his message by drawing on a bit of Japanese history not known to most Japanese, thereby demonstrating the breadth and depth of his knowledge (or his advisors') about Japan and the history of Korea–Japan relations. The suggestion of a golden age as a metaphor for the present and the future was a diplomatic coup.

The Japanese public was stunned, since Hōshū was then known to but a few Japanese. A sudden boom in studies of Hōshū's "cosmopolitanism" ensued. Most of these popular works were didactic in nature and concerned more with what modern Japanese can learn from Hōshū's attitude towards foreigners and less with what marked Hōshū as a man of the early eighteenth century. Usually, they were even less concerned with what concrete problems Hōshū had to face as Confucian advisor to the Sō lords of Tsushima. The most famous in this genre is Kamigaito Kenichi's *Amenomori Hōshū: Genroku Kyōhō no kokusaijin* ("Amenomori Hōshū: a cosmopolitan of the Genroku and Kyōhō eras, 1688–1735"), publication of which actually preceded Roh's visit by six or seven months, but which quickly experienced an enormous sales boost and numerous reissues.[3] Hōshū quickly became the officially preferred interpreter for Korean–Japanese past, present, and future relations.

Roh Tae-woo's message came at a time when the Japanese academy was ready. Over the period from the late 1970s to the present, the traditional scholarly position that Japan was "isolated" during the Edo period has been nearly universally rejected. Even those scholars who still use the *sakoku* model spend their ink discussing how it worked in practice to regulate trade and contact with the outside, rather than how it excluded that contact. Trade and contact with the outside was never actually denied; but what is now passing for consensus is that previous estimates of the range and depth of the contacts have been too conservative. In particular, information on the magnitude of the Korean connection, ignored or even suppressed by Imperial Japan, is now flooding the academies and the museums with new questions about the extent of Edo-period Japan's intercourse with the outside world. Such intercourse was economic, political, and cultural-intellectual. The extensive revision of views on Edo-period contacts with Korea is one way for modern Japan to re-join Asia with a respectable history of relations that requires no apologies. From the Korean point of view, early-modern contacts serve to remind Japanese of the grand civilization of Chosŏn Korea and of its "civilizing" mission towards the Japanese islands.

In sum, the end of the twentieth century and the beginning of the twenty-first century saw the initiation of a slow healing process possible only through the creation of a common discourse. For a Korean leader to identify a good Japanese is a significant step, but the genius was to find him in a period removed yet close, in a time before international complexities intruded on a stable, cordial, equal relationship. Chosŏn–Tokugawa relations were just such a period. Chauvinistic nationalism had yet to rear its ugly head. Imperialism, fueled by technology, capitalism, and some specious civilizing mission, was in the future. From 1600 to the 1870s Japan did not prey upon Korea militarily or economically, and the Confucian ideal of a self-sufficient, communal society pursuing the arts of civilization stood dominant in East Asia. We can only applaud the new discourse inaugurated by Roh Tae-woo for the diplomatic and historical creativity it revealed and the plain desire in Korea and Japan to put the twentieth century in some sort of perspective and to find common cause for the future based on a vision of a dignified past.

Politicians have immediate agendas and cannot be concerned with the complexities and ambiguities of historical moments. They have time only to loot the past for the materials to create visions of the future. Historians have different concerns. We would ask, what then characterized the mental apparatus of this so-called golden age of relations? To write the "biography of an idea," as Arthur O. Lovejoy puts it, is to skate on the near edge of disaster, since one's enterprise may "easily degenerate into a species of merely imaginative historical generalization . . ."[4] Lovejoy enjoins us with several principles to guide such a dangerous undertaking and the one we should particularly look to here demands that our "specific unit-ideas" be a "part of the stock of many minds," not just something held to be true by a "small number of profound thinkers or eminent writers."[5] We cannot assume the Platonic and metaphysical existence of ideas, but neither can we assume that a common idea exists only for a fleeting moment at the chance intersection of two subjectivities. The obvious problem that emerges is to demonstrate an idea's wide dissemination. Ideally, we should find our theme in many texts and discourses: literary, philosophical, scientific, and artistic. For example, Jacob Burkhardt surveyed politics, scholarship, education, literature, art, society, and religion from the thirteenth to the sixteenth century in Italy and argued that the modern world began with the rediscovery of the individual.[6] Lucien Febvre focused on Rabelais to argue that sixteenth-century France had no concept of atheism.[7] Erwin Panofsky argued that the central tenets of High Scholasticism, such as clarification and homology, were expressed in High Gothic cathedral architecture.[8] Since our concern will be to discuss mentalities, our "problem," to borrow Febvre's favorite methodology, is: what did the Koreans think about the Japanese during this relatively harmonious period? We can identify four sites of production of the Korean mentality regarding the Japanese: the ideas elaborated by Korean intellectuals, the reports left by the Korean Embassy to Edo, the treatment of castaways, and the Korean experiences surrounding the Japan House in Pusan. Information on the last three can only be found in the impressions and ideas formulated by direct experience and are our concern.

The writings of Korean intellectuals take us into realms beyond the scope of this study. To examine Korean intellectual discourse on Japan would, by necessity, require that we concern ourselves more with the minutiae of the intellectuals themselves than with the minutiae of Korea–Japan relations. We would have to pose broad questions, such as what they thought constituted civilization, what they thought constituted a reasonably functional society and/or polity, or what philosophical congruences or influences existed between Korean intellectuals and Japanese intellectuals. Since few of the writings left to us by Korean intellectuals betray a first-hand knowledge of direct contact with the Japanese, to pursue intellectual discourse would take us rather far from our main concern.

Moreover, there are a number of good studies of this intellectual discourse. Ha Woo Bong has offered us an excellent, comprehensive study of the *sirhak* scholars' views of Japan.[9] Abe Yoshio, Kang Chae-ŏn, Mark Setton, Willem Jan Boot, and others have offered us approaches to philosophical congruences and influences.[10] Moreover, Etsuko Hae-jin Kang has attempted to summarize and to interpret the ideological prejudices of Korean and Japanese intellectuals.[11] Although Etsuko Kang goes the farthest in claiming the effects of intellectual discourse on the actual workings of relations, she ignores trade and frontier contact in favor of analyzing the symbolic diplomacy between Hansŏng and Kyoto or Edo. Kang's study reifies the writings of capital intellectuals with the result that interpretive schema seem designed to find the origins of late nineteenth- and twentieth-century "national" views in the fifteenth through eighteenth centuries. In order to find these origins, the pluralism of agents, ideas, levels of interaction, and spatial considerations are set aside.

The power of ideas, though, seems undeniable, and it would be naive to dismiss a concern with "national" views or nationalism. The hot and cold industrial wars of the twentieth century were, in many ways, confrontations of nationalisms and abstract ideas, and these industrial wars depended on the mass mobilization of troops and laborers.[12] Mobilization was made easier by ideas that constructed national identities. Of course, nation building in Europe relied on identity construction from before the twentieth century, but large-scale industrial war proved its virulence. We have conventionally referred to identity construction as the central project of nationalism, and lately, debate has raged over whether identities are ancient (primordialists) or constructed (instrumentalists).[13]

Anthony Smith, representative of the primordialist school, seeks the roots of national identity in a plethora of continuous identities that link pre-modern agricultural societies, even ancient societies, to modern industrial societies.[14] Smith argues that almost all successful nations have clear ethnic identities that have allowed them to mobilize vast numbers of people in the industrial age and form nation-states. The nation-state is a recent phenomenon, Smith concedes, but the pre-existence of ethnic identity allowed it to emerge and that pre-existing or latent ethnic identity was often the necessary condition for the success or failure of the nation-state.

Ernest Gellner and Benedict Anderson represent approaches from modernist and materialist perspectives, and they emphasize the development of new technologies and colonial expansion as creators of new social arrangements and world-views.[15] The shift of industrial production towards "semantic" or literate labor and print capitalism threw up discontinuities between the agricultural and industrial worlds. Industry needed literate labor. Mass education and the creation of a market for the mass circulation of newspapers, magazines, and books enabled an elite culture – a cult of particularity – to be established as the measure of identity. The rising use of vernaculars in combination with print capitalism allowed the creation of common time and a sense of common destiny. In short, industrial production created both the need and the means for the mass production and consumption of intellectual conformity, something that had been the monopoly of a narrow elite. Gellner concedes that some nations have ancient ethnic identities while others have none, but he strenuously argues against Smith and asserts that the vast majority of nation-states have invented identities because the conditions of modernity require this. For Gellner and Anderson, mentalities arise from the material conditions of the modern world: industrial production, mass literacy, mass markets, and colonial models that affect the metropole society.

Thongchai Winichakul offers a similar approach that focuses on the conceptual moment and the technological means of national construction.[16] Like much of

Southeast Asia, pre-modern Siam had frontiers but lacked boundaries. To preserve its integrity from the predations of European imperialism, the Siamese court was forced to adopt a geographical or topographical world-view that constructed space using a European cosmology based on mathematics. The technology was cartography and the result was the map with meridian lines. Such a map matched European constructions and implied a full and even exercise of sovereignty over the land between specified boundaries, a view that nineteenth-century Europe was also developing. With this, the "nation" as territory could be visually presented, thereby legitimating all the necessities of a "modern" defense of those borders.

Liah Greenfeld separates national identity from any system of production or technology and focuses on political history and the literary production of capital elites caught in various crises of identity.[17] Individual states of mind – dissatisfied states of mind – led to action that created social structures and ideas, which produced further states of mind, which produced new social structures, and so on. For example, in the English case, the original dissatisfied state of mind was the desire by English elites to separate England from Catholic Christendom, the identification of Protestantism with nation, and the loyalty of newly created social groups to the opportunities for social mobility opened by the Tudor seizure of Church estates. Dissatisfied and newly emergent literate elites were the creators of mentalities. Nationalism appeared first in the English form as "individualistic-libertarian" and then later in the French, Russian, and German forms as "collectivistic-authoritarian". In all situations, the appearance of a national consciousness elevated the entire (literate) populace to become the possessors of legitimate sovereignty and that created the basis of modern democratic governance. This is modernity, and it was created by literate urban elites.[18]

These few paragraphs are nothing more than brief notes on a few recent approaches to the question of identity construction and maintenance, but they serve to illustrate a problem common to such discussions: they discuss the development of political, economic, and cultural cores by assuming that the boundaries and frontiers of countries were passive and receptive vessels.[19] Cores do mobilize wealth and power and seek self-definition, but cores inevitably have peripheries and frontiers; some of them are interior and some of them abut other countries. In addition to focusing on developments at the cores, be they cartographical (Thongchai), technological (Anderson), social (Gellner), or intellectual (Greenfeld and Smith), we might also consider the boundaries and frontiers for expressions of identity. Here, the core's "mode of production" or the "orthodox discourse" takes second place to the day-to-day interactions of one people with another. Fredrik Barth's paradigmatic essay on ethnic groups and boundaries focuses squarely on engagement at the boundary in contrast to abstracted thinking from the remove of the center. Barth writes, "I would argue that people's categories are for acting, and are significantly affected by interaction rather than contemplation."[20]

Barth is concerned with ethnicity. He separates ethnicity from culture and concentrates on ascription to an ethnic category. He argues that what usually passes for a discussion of culture is really no more than a catalogue of traits. These traits or institutional forms change over time and they change with ecological niche. Therefore, ethnic groups are best thought of as groups that *identify* themselves to be different and groups that *are identified* by other groups as different. In both cases, the purpose of identification is to engage in interaction with other groups. The cultural content that identifies ethnic groups is composed of "overt signals" (dress, language, food, life-style) and "basic value orientations: the standards of morality and excellence by which performance is judged." The main activity that ensures continuity of the ethnic group, the activity that gives it its existence, is the maintenance of the boundary or the structured and rigid practice of overt signals and the application of standards to judge the performance of its constituency. The boundary defines the group, "not the cultural stuff that it encloses." Finally, boundaries are maintained between groups by interaction that is structured to allow the persistence of difference. This implies rigidity of interaction, but it also allows for the permeability of ascription. If one acts in accordance with the group's value orientations and adopts the group's institutional forms, then one can claim membership. Of course, this also implies that two groups will accent their differences for easy mutual recognition. In short, at the boundaries we can expect to find the clearest definition of group membership, since it is there that differences matter the most.

Barth was unconcerned with the state, and his theoretical template has been employed most often to examine the metaphorical borders of de-territorialized postmodern identities. By contrast, Thomas Wilson and Hastings Donnan are unconcerned with metaphorical borders and focus on the dialectic between states and their borders: "The anthropological study of the everyday lives of border communities is simultaneously the study of the daily life of the state. . . ."[21] Because the border and the center are in a dialectic, the border is valuable for what it can tell us about the "interplay between nation and state . . . an anthropology of borders sits squarely within the wider anthropology of nationalism."[22]

The seminal historical study on frontiers was perhaps Lucien Febvre's essay on the meaning of the word *frontière*.[23] Febvre discusses "frontier" in terms that mean a territory in depth on both sides of a boundary. In his 1928 essay, we find many germs of the ideas mentioned here and examined in the following pages. His concern was chiefly with sovereignty, and we will turn to that question in Chapters 5 and 6. Most importantly, he saw the frontier in a dialectical relationship to the center, specifically, to the state.

More recently, Peter Sahlins' study of the boundary between France and Spain in the Pyrenees has creatively approached the interaction between frontiers and cores.[24] Sahlins takes the usual assertion that modern nations were built from the center outwards and then reverses it: "The Cerdanya is a case where the nation appeared on the periphery before it was built by the center. . . ."[25] Between 1659 (France and Spain divided the valley by the Peace of the Pyrenees) and 1868 (the Treaty of Bayonne stipulated the laying of stones to mark the boundary), the frontier between France and Spain collapsed from a jurisdictional patchwork into a territorialized border. Over these two centuries, the people in this Catalan valley developed national identities and a national boundary – a line. Identities and a boundary were not imposed from the outside. "Foreigner" originally referred to a landowner who lived elsewhere or the inhabitant of another village. Local residents maintained a variety of boundaries and usufruct rights and paid rents and taxes according to the identity of the official, not his spatial location: "Jurisdictional sovereignty was above all a relation between king and subject, not between king and territory."[26] The territorialization of the Cerdanya came with the imposition from Spain of a territorial property tax on the villages in 1717 and a cadastral survey in 1732. The new revolutionary government in France took a similar step in 1791 followed by a cadastral survey in the 1820s. From the late eighteenth century, the villagers began to look to the national centers for patrons to be enlisted in local claims over land and water use. For example, in 1777, the French King found himself in receipt of a petition from the French Cerdanya requesting aid to limit "Spaniards" in their use of pastures. By 1825, local disputes over pastureland and water rights turned violent and involved clear assertions of "French" and "Spanish" nationality. Without giving up their Catalan and Cerdanya identities, the local villagers acquired Spanish and French identities as a way to appeal to the centers. Pleas to define the boundary composed a large part of their petitions.

Among Sahlins' many contributions to this problem of boundaries is his clarification of concepts.[27] The word "frontier" carries a zonal connotation and "boundary" and "border" carry a linear connotation. Michiel Baud and Willem van Schendel offer different definitions of the terms frontier, boundary, and border. They argue that "boundary" has a diplomatic usage and is used to indicate the division between cultures or peoples.[28] "Border" has been used to refer to psychological differences and regions. "Frontier" implies territorial expansion of nations or civilizations. Rather than these terms, Baud and van Schendel prefer the term "borderlands" to indicate,

> . . . broad scenes of intense interactions in which people from both sides work out everyday accommodations based on face-to-face relationships. In this way, the study of border regions implies a critique of state-centered approaches that picture borders as unchanging, uncontested, and unproblematic.[29]

For our purposes, we will use "frontier" to refer to a zone or region bisected by a legal "boundary" where the peoples on either side of the boundary interact with each other.

Frontiers can be intellectual conceptions as well as actual places, but to qualify as a frontier for the purposes of this study, they must be the sites of actual contact. Roh Tae-woo's use of Hōshū was powerful, because Hōshū is an authentic voice. Hōshū was an interested participant/observer on the frontier. In the milieu between Korea and Japan, identity construction and maintenance were products of the functional aspects of relations, of politics, economy, and law. The following chapters will try to reconstruct the frontier between early modern Korea and Japan in the port of Pusan. Before launching into that project, we should briefly comment on the other points of direct contact, the Korean Embassy to Edo and the castaways.

T'ongsinsa

The T'ongsinsa (J: Tsūshinshi) or Korean Embassy to Edo, was a highly staged affair that sent gifted Korean literati and professional diplomats to Japan for the better part of a year. From 1607 to 1811 they visited Japan twelve times, but the last embassy (1811) never went beyond Tsushima. The embassy was an intensive exposure to Japanese, both high and low, of some of Korea's best attempts at civilizing its neighbor. Many diaries written by the Korean participants have been preserved but only a few have been studied.

7

For Koreans and Japanese at that time (and even the present) the Embassy was a very flattering event. The T'ongsinsa was the apotheosis of cultural exchange; it epitomized the notion that relations between Korea and Japan, stretching from the end of the Hideyoshi invasions to the Meiji Restoration, were peaceful, cultural exchanges. As research expands, we can begin to appreciate the numerous roles played by the Korean Embassy to Edo in the consciousness formation of Koreans and Japanese. Japanese literati of the Tokugawa period eagerly wished for contact with the Embassy. They requested embassy members to brush forwards to their collections of Chinese verse or reveled in exchanges of poetry and brushwork with the envoys, either along the way or at the embassy's lodgings in Edo. Arai Hakuseki had his talent in prose and poetry recognized by the Embassy in 1682 and with that endorsement he was able to enter Kinoshita Jun'an's academy and so launch his career.[30] We can see by this example that the embassy played the role of literary critic in early-modern Japanese letters.

The passage of an embassy left much in its wake: by sea from Pusan via Tsushima and the Inland Sea to Ōsaka, and then overland to Edo and back, usually in less than a year. Numbering up to 500 Koreans and including nearly 1,500 Japanese as escorts and baggage carriers, the entourage easily vied with the largest *daimyō* retinue.[31] Japanese elites vied with each other to lay on lavish entertainment along the route and in the capital. In Edo, the Korean Embassy's equestrians delighted high officials of the *bakufu*.[32] Members of the embassy met with leaders of Japanese letters and politics and exchanged courtesies.

Shin Ki-su and others have pointed out that ordinary Japanese had a great interest in and, despite official prohibitions, actual contact with the embassy's entourage. The number of personal recollections, written exchanges, and art on the Japanese side that survives has yet to be fully revealed. Pieces of representational art continue to surface, having been ignored, mislabeled, or their original intent either forgotten or suppressed. Peasants and townspeople along the embassies' route incorporated the styles and forms of the entourage into regional festivals; some of this performance art was suppressed during the Meiji period but has been revived in contemporary times. One particular medium often commissioned for all sorts of commemorative or devotional reasons by peasants, fishermen, and ordinary villagers was a painting on a wide, rectangular or square board called an *ema*. Ronald Toby has found an example of certain individuals substituting the Korean Embassy train for the Buddhist icon Amida and his entourage in an *ema* version of Amida's Descent from the Western Paradise. This particular painting was completed nearly a century after either those who commissioned it or the artist could have possibly witnessed the passage of a Korean Embassy, indicating a long popular memory.[33] Given its exotic foreign flavor, the Korean Embassy of the Edo period provided an incomparable display of splendor and pomp that attracted the attention of all levels of Japanese society. The envoys' diaries were the intellectual impact of the embassies on Korean consciousness, but below, we will mention no more than the embassies' economic impact.

We can only welcome the fact that a broad spotlight of popular interest and research has fallen on the Korean Embassy. The image of the Korean Embassy as exemplifying peaceful, refined cultural exchange plays a large role in the development of contemporary relations between Japan and the Republic of Korea. For this reason, the Korean Embassy has nearly become the sum total of early-modern Korea–Japan relations, and the study of those relations has popularly come to mean the study of the Korean Embassy. There are many amateur historians and politicians in Korea and Japan who speak of the embassy and this period for the purpose of resurrecting in the present a sort of ideal relationship they believe to have existed in the past. The name "T'ongsinsa" itself was a Korean designation from the fifteenth century and literally meant: "Embassy to transmit sincerity."

The belief that early modern Korea–Japan relations were marked by peaceful, refined cultural exchanges arises from a closure of interest around the Korean Embassy, an activity that occurred in Japan. The purpose of this study is to open the discussion to include the Japan House (K: *Waegwan*), or the Japanese trading post in Korea. Just as the Korean Embassy was a manifestation of Korean culture in Japan, the Japan House was a manifestation of Japanese culture in Korea. Just as various Japanese espied the Korean Embassy and formulated ideas about Koreans, many Koreans looked upon the Japanese at their trading post and formulated judgments about the people of Tsushima and about Japanese in general. Therefore, investigations of the various problems related to the Waegwan will reveal to us the actual circumstances of the Japan House as well as the impressions and views of Koreans directly in contact with the Japanese on a daily basis. Before we turn to the Japan House, we should consider the other site of direct contact between Korea and Japan: shipwrecks and the problems of repatriating castaways.

Castaways

The secondary work on Koreans and Japanese castaways is yet scarce despite the enormous amount of documentary data available. One obvious problem lies in choosing appropriate analytical approaches to elicit meaning from the data. Two young researchers working in Korea and Japan have recently presented us with good initial research efforts. A brief discussion of their work will give us some idea of the questions, approaches, and findings thus far.

Yi Hun has been looking through the details of handling castaways to create an understanding of Korea–Tsushima and Korea–Japan relations.[34] She is attempting to formulate a model of the structure of diplomacy that governed Korea–Tsushima and Korea–Japan relations after Hideyoshi by analyzing the functional aspects of castaway repatriation. She is consciously attempting to revise a particular statist model that has existed since the Meiji period: the *sakoku* model and its most recent re-interpretation by Tashiro Kazui, Ronald Toby, and Arano Yasunori.[35]

The *sakoku* model of a closed Japan assumes a strong *bakufu* capable of enforcing its will over all domains in Japan. In the 1630s, this *bakufu* was able to sever relations with the outside, primarily for reasons of its own political and economic consolidation against outside threats, one being Christianity. A small window on the outside was maintained in Nagasaki where the Dutch were allowed to call. Until the 1850s, Japan was closed to the world, with near disastrous results if it had not been for the open door policies of the new Meiji government.

Arano Yasunori and others since the 1980s have retained the image of a hegemonic *bakufu*, able to impose its will to monopolize foreign contact but have reinterpreted the motivations and results of the policies laid out in the 1630s. In their revision, Japanese relations with the outside were not severed but regularized and brought under control to bolster the *bakufu* politically. Japan never cut relations with its neighbors in Northeast Asia, but joined them in a shared vision of carefully regulated foreign contact; rather than isolation after Hideyoshi's adventure, Japan rejoined East Asia, albeit in the same ambiguous position to the Chinese sphere it had always held. The Dutch connection in Nagasaki falls from its favored position as the most important foreign connection to one among many: Korea through Tsushima, Ezo through Matsumae, Ryūkyū through Satsuma, and the Chinese and Dutch in Nagasaki under a *bakufu* magistrate.

Nevertheless, Tashiro, Toby, Arano, and other revisionists share the same statist assumptions as the model they were revising. Control over foreign relations was one of the defining features of the so-called *bakuhan* system, often explained as a system of feudal domains under the hegemony of the Tokugawa *bakufu*. The English shorthand for this system is "centralized feudalism." Major aspects of the "centralized" in centralized feudalism were the monarchical ambitions of the *bakufu* to extend central control over foreign affairs. The other activity we moderns associate with central power – taxation – did not apply, since the *bakufu* had no direct taxation powers over the domains.

In the earlier *sakoku* version of the statist model, the Tokugawas drove foreigners, particularly Europeans, out of Japan and retreated into isolation. In the more recent version of the statist model, isolation has been re-interpreted as a creative and positive imposition of order over chaos, of course, to Tokugawa advantage. But Yi Hun questions the statist model by a close examination of Tsushima's role in repatriating castaways.

Under the Tokugawa order, argues Yi, Tsushima was charged with numerous diplomatic duties towards Korea. Yi borrows Tanaka Takeo's list of Tsushima's duties: defense against attack from Korea, intelligence gathering on foreign affairs, conduct of diplomacy, and repatriation of castaways. While other domains were charged with merely "defense,"[36] Tsushima was charged with all the above duties as "national civilian duties,"[37] making the actual relations between Korea and Japan or between the Chosŏn court and the Tokugawa *bakufu* less clear than the views from centers would have us believe.

Since Tsushima actually handled the working aspects of the relationship between the Chosŏn government and the Tokugawa *bakufu*, what did this mean for Tokugawa hegemony? Moreover, when we consider that Tsushima presented Korean castaways in Pusan in a context of tribute relations, then Tsushima's role as mere agent for the Tokugawa becomes untenable. Moreover, since Tsushima's tribute relations with Korea had no bearing on the *bakufu*'s relations with Chosŏn, we have yet another wrinkle in the fabric. Thus the statist model of Korea–Japan relations, which supposes a Japanese "nation,"[38] however loosely construed, becomes an obstacle to our understanding of the conduct of affairs between Tsushima and Chosŏn Korea. A concrete study of castaways, in particular Koreans repatriated from Japan, reveals the inner workings of Korean relations with Tsushima as tribute bearer and vassal to both Hanyang and Edo. In most of her work on castaways, Yi Hun examines the details of this question of Tsushima's position as intermediary.

The revisionists are probably correct when they argue that the *bakufu* was not recoiling from the previous century of freewheeling foreign contact and seeking to close the country; no, the *bakufu* was creatively instituting order over disorder and in fact becoming more like its closest neighbors. Yi Hun, then, gives us an excellent case study of the gap between what the *bakufu* thought it controlled and what actually occurred. Her perspective is critically important and is the same perspective taken in this study. Rather than considering relations from the center, an approach that carries a strong statist bias, we must consider relations from the frontier where business actually transpired. If we wish to take special note of the castaways themselves, for this purpose, she supplies us with an excellent historical summary for the period in the form of tables. Using the archives of the Kuksa P'yŏnch'an Wiwŏnhoe in Kwach'ŏn, together with well-known standard works, she has confirmed that Tsushima repatriated Koreans from 1606 (*Sillok* entry) to 1870 (Sō clan archives in Kwach'ŏn), incidentally indicating that Tsushima played a special role past the Meiji Restoration.

In her first article on the subject, Yi Hun prepared four statistical tables based on the *Pyŏllye chibyo* (entries from 1627 to 1824). In them, we find 385 cases of Korean castaways on Japanese shores but only 77 cases of Japanese shipwrecks in Korea, no doubt due to the prevailing south to north-east currents.[39] Most Korean castaways appeared in Japan between 1691 and 1740. She hypothesizes that the large number of reported repatriations at this time was probably related to efforts on Tsushima's part to make up for losses from a general decline in trade, since the Tsushima envoy bearing the castaways received goods and supplies as gifts and per diem. Most of the Koreans were fishermen or traders and slaves, including runaway slaves.

Yi Hun's tables also reveal the geographical distribution of shipwrecks in Korea and Japan. Most Korean castaways came from Cheju Island, Ulsan, Kyŏngju, Changgi, and Tongnae, in that order. They wrecked on the shores of Tsushima, Chōmon (Yamaguchi), Iwami (Tottori), Hizen (Saga, Iki), and Chikuzen (Fukuoka). Most Japanese castaways came from Satsuma (Kagoshima), Tsushima, Sesshū (Hyōgo), Osaka, Izumi (Ōsaka), and Kaga (Ishikawa), in that order. They usually ended up in Ulsan, Kyŏngju, Tadae-p'o (Tongnae) in Kyŏngsang Province, and Cheju Island in Chŏlla Province. We have entries for 59 sites of origin or landing in Korea and 34 sites in Japan. Sites in Korea are concentrated in Chŏlla and Kyŏngsang Provinces while sites in Japan stretch the entire length of the Japan Sea coast, from Hokkaido to Kyūshū, with concentrations in Kyūshū and Yamaguchi.

Compared to the scant records for the early Chosŏn period, which mention only Cheju Island, the late Chosŏn records give us a much fuller account. These repatriation records once again reinforce the image that the post-Hideyoshi period in Korea–Japan relations was a time of peaceful intercourse with widespread official and non-official concern for the lives of other nationals. Compared to previous periods when castaways might have become slaves in Japan, or compared to later periods such as the Meiji, when ships or salvageable baggage were sold to pay repatriation expenses, the generosity of the Tokugawa period stands out as a time when Korean castaways' board and transport were paid out of pocket by Japanese authorities. It is a well known fact that the repatriation of castaways and prisoners of war by Tsushima was the chief method used to show post-war Chosŏn that Tsushima was again worthy of trust, and prompt castaway repatriation figured prominently in negotiations to normalize Korea–Tsushima relations in 1607.

In 1993, Kibe Kazuaki[40] contributed a short but interesting study on Korean castaways in Japan, written from the perspective of a historical anthropologist. Unlike

Yi Hun, he is less concerned with the political structure of relations and more concerned with the extra-structural problems and questions presented by the case studies. Kibe argues that most research on early-modern Japan–Korea relations has been concerned with the T'ongsinsa, and we must look to other contacts as well to begin understanding the views and attitudes of more ordinary Japanese. The problem of castaways offers itself as an "unofficial history" (*yashi*, K: *yasa*) to the "official history" (*seishi*, K: *chŏngsa*) of the T'ongsinsa.[41]

Although Kibe focuses on Chōshū domain (modern-day Yamaguchi), his points are general. First, the system of repatriation required all castaways to be sent to Nagasaki, where the Nagasaki *bugyō* (Magistrate) would investigate the foreign sailors and turn them over to Tsushima authorities for repatriation through the Waegwan. Kibe cites an entry in the *Koji ruien* that makes clear that the repatriation of Koreans was something the Tokugawa *bakufu* institutionalized in the spirit of peace and *seishin* (K: *sŏngsin*)[42] or "sincerity," the term and sentiment invoked by President Roh in his greetings to the Japanese Emperor. Before the Tokugawa hegemony was established, repatriation was practiced by regional authorities, increasingly routed through Tsushima as the fifteenth century progressed, but not by any national Japanese authority. Kibe dates the Tokugawa practice from 1641.

An entry in the 1716 *Kiyō gundan* (A Multitude of Discussions on Kiyō [Nagasaki])[43] by a Nagasaki Magistrate corroborates Kibe's findings and gives us some details. Magistrate Ōoka explains that Koreans usually shipwrecked on Japanese shores, particularly Chikuzen and Chōmon (Fukuoka and Yamaguchi), from the end of fall to the end of spring. When a shipwreck was discovered, reports were made to both Nagasaki and Tsushima, the latter report being an early notification to help speed the Koreans on their way home.

Korean sailors were returned overland from Chōshū to Nagasaki and by sea from Chikuzen. Their ship and/or baggage were sent by sea in both cases. From the site of the shipwreck to Nagasaki, the burden of provisions was borne by local authorities with re-imbursement from the *bakufu*. Tsushima was reimbursed in silver for necessary provisions but nothing is stated specifically about re-imbursements for other domains.

The Tsushima *daimyō* had officials and interpreters in Nagasaki to aid in the investigation. The investigators particularly sought any official papers from the Korean government carried by the survivors and also had them trample a *fumie* (a small bronze relief portrait of Christ or the Virgin Mary) as well as answer questions about Buddhism to ascertain that the castaways were not Christians. Japanese returning from Korea likewise had to pass through *bakufu* offices either in Nagasaki or Ōsaka for interrogation and *fumie* trampling. Magistrate Ōoka mentions that an escort was assigned to the castaways and "to avoid problems and answer [their] questions when in custody."[44]

That is, when they could communicate with each other. Kibe elaborates on the problem of communication by looking for information on Korean language interpreters locally available in Chōshū. He discusses a few cases, but notes that their absence is more to be noticed than their presence. Of course, when the Korean sailors could read and write Chinese, conversations could be conducted through a Japanese Confucianist, much as conversations were conducted with the members of the T'ongsinsa. Usually, however, Korean fishermen were illiterate in Chinese and the spoken word was important. One interpreter in the early 1640s was a Korean kidnapped in the Hideyoshi invasion. Another from the early eighteenth century was a Tsushima man. But there was at least one other, Hayashi Fujiuemon, from the 1850s, origin unknown, whose Korean was evidently useful. Wondering how Hayashi acquired his knowledge leads us to reconsider the presumed insularity of ordinary Japanese at the time. A general lack of interpreters gives Kibe an explanation as to why Korean castaways occasionally ran riot and caused disturbances.

The "language barrier" was formidable and too much for most Korean fishermen to be expected to overcome. Direct action got attention, but sometimes it got too much attention. In at least one case, formal complaints were filed with the Tongnae Magistrate that resulted in arrests after repatriation and a beheading of the leader for fomenting "contempt"[45] among Japanese for Koreans. The importance of language is illustrated by an early nineteenth-century incident in which the Korean castaways were at loggerheads with their escort and resorted to violence. A man was produced from the market place who, with a few words, calmed them down. Kibe hypothesizes that he was a merchant, an amateur scholar, or a merchant from Tsushima.

Who were these occasional interpreters? Where did they obtain their learning? What impression did the occasional riotous Koreans leave on the minds of ordinary Japanese? These are the questions to which Kibe returns over and over. The point is simple and clear. There was an entire world of sensibilities and impressions among ordinary Japanese engendered by contact with shipwrecked Koreans. That world has gone virtually unexamined while efforts have focused on the erudite glories of the central elites. We believe that the reverse of the coin is equally important: what impressions did Korean castaways carry back home? Such questions must await further research.[46]

The Waegwan

The present study is in the same vein as the approaches taken above by Yi Hun and Kibe Kazuaki. The following pages will examine working-level structures to establish context and use case studies to find the edges of those structures. We need to broaden the base of knowledge about early-modern Korea–Japan relations by looking into the circumstances of a little known institution: the Japan House in Pusan during the late Chosŏn kingdom. A number of articles on the Japan House already exist which have been very helpful in describing the institution.[47]

This study differs from previous studies in that we will explore Korean–Japanese relations with the view that the area from Kyŏngsang Province to Tsushima island was a frontier region. The great degree of interpenetration and interaction within this region gave many Koreans and Japanese direct experience with each other. The records left to us offer some of the most authentic avenues of investigation into early-modern Korean–Japanese relations. The following chapters will re-construct the structures that resulted from the presence of Japanese in post-1600 Korea. These structures were only partially visible to the peoples of the time, but occasionally Clio helps us reveal them with her long views. At the same time, our concern is with perceptions, images, or the mentalities born from the experience of frontier contact. Here we follow one basic principle. We will privilege the voices from the frontier: the Tongnae Magistrate, the Master of the Japan House, the Japanese envoys,

Tsushima-based commentators, lower samurai in the Japan House, Korean slave women, and others. They were most intimate with their own reality.

Chapter 2 considers Tsushima's identity as perceived by Hansŏng and Edo and discusses a few aspects of how it was affected by its proximity to Korea. In connection with Korean influence, we will briefly consider Tsushima's adoption of a Korean-style accounting method for benefices, Tsushima's unusual adoption of a system of slavery, and the deployment of Koreans as part of the invading Japanese forces under Tsushima in the Hideyoshi invasions. Turning from Tsushima to its outpost in Korea, we offer a description of the post-Hideyoshi Japan House, its history, facilities, and officials. Our purpose in Chapter 2 is to cast more doubt on the veracity of the statist model by showing that Tsushima, although Japanese, was truly an ambiguous entity between Korea and Japan.

In Chapter 3, we turn to the first of the problems from the Korean perspective. The deeper structures of southeast Korea must be set out at the beginning to understand the wider stage of our dramas. The frontier with Japan was heavily populated, and it is necessary to dissect population distribution and look for its causes. Southeast Korea was part of a wider maritime world in which the Japanese were but one part. The same weather and ocean currents that bring devastating typhoons to Korea also bring it fish. The sea's riches undoubtedly attracted many Chosŏn-era Koreans as it had been doing since pre-historical times. But, were Koreans also attracted to the southeast for the Japan trade, and did they come in sufficient numbers to register a demographic anomaly? In the Chosŏn period, limitations were put on foreign travel, but the Japanese connection tied Korea to regional and even global trading networks and supplied Korea with certain necessary goods in addition to elite luxuries. Chapter 3 outlines the demographics of the southeast maritime world, explains the general trading order with the Japanese, and goes in search of Korean merchants.

In Chapter 4, we consider the Japanese role in Kyŏngsang Province's economic structure. To assess the relative economic role of the Japanese connection poses particular problems, since notions of what constituted a loss or a gain must be clarified. Where did diplomacy end, and where did trade begin? By assessing the amounts of goods in the official trade at the Waegwan – not luxury goods but basic commodities such as cotton and rice – we can then begin to address larger questions such as loss and gain to Korea from the Japan trade and the role of the Japan trade in the political economy of Chosŏn. The first step, though, is an accurate assessment of amounts, a clear formulation of expenditure categories and accounting style, and some idea of expenditure sourcing. Here again, since we are primarily concerned with mental structures, we will introduce as our problem the gap between the general Korean rhetoric regarding expenses associated with the Japanese and what we believe to be a fairly accurate estimation of those actual expenses. Ultimately, what the Japanese actually cost Korea is secondary to what the Koreans said relations cost them, but the appearance of a gap leads to many other questions in economic and cultural history and deserves emphasis. For example, trade relations with Tsushima and the Korean attitudes towards those relations offer a case study of Chosŏn-period attitudes toward trade and economy. These attitudes are often said to have been disparaging of trade, that it was a loss to a self-sufficient agricultural economy. We will see that the Korean perspective on Japanese trade did relegate trade to a losing activity even while acknowledging needs and benefits. The dominant moral economy was tempered by practical necessity, but these Korean views stood diametrically opposed to the Japanese mercantilist approach.

In Chapter 5, we will see extensive evidence of a Japanese impact on the politics of the Tongnae Magistrate and consider the peculiar problems presented to the only Korean magistracy that had to handle Japanese. By examining the liability of the Tongnae Magistrate to uncontrollable Japanese behaviors, we can see that the Magistrates' careers were affected by the presence of the Japanese. Where Chapter 4 outlines the Korean perspective on the economic structures governing the Waegwan, Chapter 5 outlines the political structures for the same. Chapter 5 also serves as a transitional step from structures to individuals. It introduces the plight of the County Magistrate in attempting to govern the Japanese, but really goes no farther than a statistical analysis of that plight and a few illustrative examples of problems. Chapters 6 and 7 examine thematically two particularly difficult problems faced by the magistrates: rioting and prostitution. Their common thread is the Magistrate's fight to impose his power over the frontier in Pusan.

In Chapter 6, we focus on several cases of political confrontation between the Tongnae Magistrate and the Waegwan Japanese. Political will was and is often expressed successfully only when one can claim authority and then invoke sufficient power to induce or coerce others to obey a will they would otherwise freely choose to ignore. The problem was simple. Could the Tongnae Magistrate impose Korean rules over the movements of the Waegwan Japanese or not? It was to Korea's advantage to contain the movement of Japanese outside the Waegwan compound. It was to Japanese advantage to use riotous behavior outside the Waegwan as a means of applying pressure in negotiations with the Koreans. We will see that, by the beginning of the eighteenth century, the Tongnae Magistrate obtained what he considered a legally binding agreement to limit Japanese movements. We will observe how he employed that agreement to final Korean advantage, thereby successfully imposing his power and authority. We will also consider the development of popular Korean perceptions of changing power relations between Koreans and Japanese.

In Chapter 7, we examine Korean attempts to impose Korean authority over a particularly vexing problem created by the Japanese presence – prostitution. The Waegwan provided a market for prostitution and smuggling and a magnet for other problems such as thievery. Again, Korean resolve hardened towards the end of the seventeenth century and in 1711 an agreement with Tsushima was concluded that specified punishments for the Japanese involved in buying women. We consider the case of prostitution and attempt to deconstruct Korean and Japanese differences regarding the propriety of Korean women visiting the Japan House for the sex trade. Aside from the moral overtones of the problem, we hypothesize that the Korean resolve to eliminate prostitution at the Waegwan came from the desire to contain Japanese immigration and settlement, and to prevent a dilution of political loyalty in the frontier.

The frontier between Korea and Japan in Pusan was a site of identity maintenance and power negotiation. It was also a site of production for Korean mentality regarding the Japanese. The production was not abstract but came out of the structures and contexts that formed and controlled contact. Cross-cultural and intra-regional contact was extensive and complex. Pointing out the large role Kyŏngsang Province played in Tsushima's economy and society is consistent with all past scholarship. But we must go further and examine the role Tsushima played in the economy, politics, and society of Kyŏngsang Province. Moreover, we must ask how that role was perceived in Korea, since Korean perceptions of Tsushima generalized to Korean perceptions of Japan. Tsushima was, as it often insisted to the *bakufu* when applying for special loans and favors, Japan's diplomatic face to Korea, Japan's antechamber for Korean visitors, and Japan's first line of defense towards the peninsula and the continent. But Tsushima was more than that. It was also the conductor, if not the actual creator, of Japanese relations with Korea for the better part of half a millennium. We have chosen to focus on only the latter half of that vast span.

2

TSUSHIMA'S IDENTITY AND THE POST-IMJIN WAERAN JAPAN HOUSE

[The Koreans] always say that if support was withdrawn and the market closed, it would be tantamount to taking the babe, Tsushima, away from the teat.

(Amenomori Hōshū, 1728)[1]

Tsushima is an island roughly 70 kilometers long, some 53 kilometers from the southern tip of Korea and about 90 kilometers from Kyūshū. It has been known by that name since before the third century A.D., when it appeared in the *Weizhi* (c.A.D. 297).[2] The island is extremely mountainous with peaks falling precipitously to valleys sunken below sea level. Tsushima's people have always been seafarers, because agricultural production is difficult. Asō bay ("shallow reed bay") divides the island into a southern and northern half and offers safe anchorage as do Waniura ("crocodile bay") in the north and Izuhara ("stern field") in the south.

In antiquity, Tsushima played a key role in the thalassocracy suggested by Gari Ledyard, which stretched from southern Korea to Kyūshū and the Inland Sea.[3] In the period from the late thirteenth-century Mongol invasions of Japan to the end of the Koryŏ kingdom in 1392, Tsushima was an important base for the infamous *Waegu* (J: *Wakō*) pirates who ravaged Korean and Chinese coastlines and helped bring down the Koryŏ kingdom.[4]

Because of the *Waegu* pirates, Tsushima developed a reputation for outlawry by the time Yi Sŏng-gye, the founder of the Chosŏn kingdom, took the throne in 1392. In 1389, a Koryŏ navy of 100 ships attacked Tsushima, destroying 300 Japanese ships and repatriating more than 100 Korean captives. Tsushima, as a famous pirate enclave, was viewed with great suspicion by the court and became a target of Chosŏn policies designed to suppress piracy. In the twelfth month of 1396, there was another attack.[5] In 1419, the fourth king, Sejong, dispatched 16,000 troops to attack pirates on Tsushima.[6] The brief invasion was the last instance of the Chosŏn kingdom militarily moving against Tsushima. The court preferred to offer the prospect of trade to the pirates and spent most of the fifteenth century establishing regulations to govern their contact with Korea. Policies to legalize and regularize trade were very successful in converting Tsushima to a respectable role as intermediary between Japan and Korea, a role it continued to play until 1873, despite being used as a reluctant staging ground for the firestorms of the Imjin Waeran or the Hideyoshi invasion from 1592 to 1598.

Tsushima's contact with Korea was most immediate at the open ports and the Japan Houses. It was there that Korea focused its civilizing mission on the Japanese from Tsushima, and it was there that Tsushima drew its sustenance. The history of the Japan Houses from the fifteenth to the nineteenth centuries is a large part of the history of early-modern Korean daily contact with the Japanese. Nearly 450 years of contact at the ports prior to the intrusion of the West inscribed on the minds of the Koreans raw impressions about conducting business with their neighbors. That business and those impressions are the concern of Chapters 3 through 6, but we must first set the stage.

This chapter addresses the question of Tsushima's identity, primarily during the period from about 1600 to 1870. We will begin with a general survey of Chosŏn–Tsushima relations from the founding of the Chosŏn kingdom in 1392. Our survey will bring us up to 1635 when a major forgery scandal put Tsushima under close scrutiny by the Edo *bakufu*. We will briefly consider the result of the forgery scandal as it defined Tsushima's identity in the Tokugawa *bakuhan* state system. Next, we will mention an aspect of the Korean view on Tsushima's identity – was the island actually Korean territory temporarily occupied by Japanese? Then, we will examine three aspects of Tsushima's early-modern institutions and history that suggest the island's ambiguous position between Korea and Japan. Finally, we will turn to Tsushima's post-1600 trading post on Korean soil, the early-modern Waegwan or Japan House in Pusan, and we will introduce the Japanese *dramatis personae* in Pusan. We will introduce their Korean counterparts in Chapter 5.

Tsushima's identity: the view from Edo

Chosŏn kingdom relations with Japan took several forms: state to state relations as represented by the T'ongsinsa or the Korean Embassy to Japan, direct trade relations with prominent Kyūshū and western Honshū lords, and tribute relations with lesser lords of Kyūshū, Iki, and Tsushima. Early Chosŏn policy towards Japan was codified and clarified by the compilation of Sin Suk-chu's *Haedong chegukki* ("Records of Lands in the Eastern Sea") in 1471, which listed all recognized Japanese envoys and defined their statuses for reception purposes. For information prior to the time of the *Haedong chegukki*, specifics must be pieced together from the Chosŏn Veritable Records and elsewhere. There are four good, modern guides to early Korean–Japanese relations and the diplomatic structures that regulated those relations: Nakamura Hidetaka, Kim Yong-uk, Yi Hyŏn-jong, and Kenneth Robinson.[7] Much of the following discussion is indebted to these scholars' works.

After the founding of the Chosŏn kingdom in 1392, and as a method of co-opting pirates, Japanese traders and envoys were allowed to land anywhere in Korea, but from 1407, traders were restricted to Ungch'ŏn County's Che Harbor (or Chep'o, also known as Naeip'o; *p'o* means harbor) and Tongnae County's Pusan Harbor (Pusanp'o). Envoys were still allowed to land anywhere. From the same year, Korean documents (*haengjang*) issued by Chosŏn authorities were required of Japanese traders.[8] From 1418, copper seals (*tosŏ*) were also required. Sejong invaded Tsushima to suppress piracy in 1419 and also requested the help of powers in western Japan and Kyūshū in regulating Japanese traders. From 1426, Ulsan County's Yŏm Harbor (Yŏmp'o) was added to ports open to traders, making three open ports (see Map 2.1). From about the same time, envoys as well were restricted to the three ports. As ports were opened, controls were increased to staunch the flow of excessive trade and unregulated contacts.[9]

18

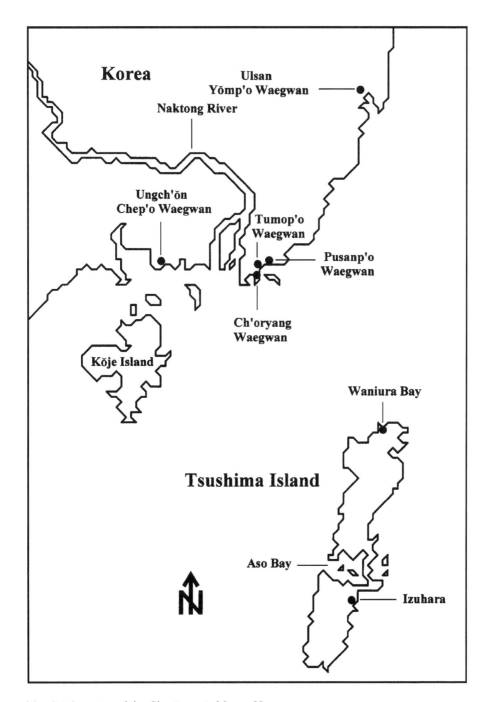

Map 2.1 Location of the Chosŏn-period Japan Houses

During the early decades of the fifteenth century, Japanese documents were issued to traders and envoys from Kyūshū in the form of letters (K: sŏgye) from the Kyūshū Governor (*Tandai*) in Dazaifu and the Shibukawa lords in Hakata. The Sō on Tsushima issued sŏgye for those from Tsushima. The Governor in Dazaifu, although ostensibly the shogun's Deputy in Kyūshū, was, in fact, eliminated politically in 1425, and his right to issue sŏgye was divided among the great lords of Kyūshū. Sō on Tsushima seized the opportunity to press his case with Korea for a monopoly on sŏgye issuance. From 1436, the Chosŏn kingdom gave Sō Sadamori a monopoly on issuing sealed documents of passage (now called *mun'in*) to Tsushima people, and from 1438, Sadamori's monopoly was extended to all Japanese. From 1439, exceptions to Sadamori's grip were made for powerful lords from Kyūshū (e.g. Kikuchi), western Japan (e.g. Ōuchi), and the home provinces in the Kinai,[10] but for the most part, Tsushima became the gatekeeper for all Japanese going to Korea. The model for these diplomatic structures was taken from domestic Korean controls over travel, not from a Chinese model of international relations.[11] Their destinations were the overseas Japanese settlements in the Three Ports (Chep'o, Pusanp'o, and Yŏmp'o). These particular ports were chosen for reasons of proximity to Japan and ease of security arrangements. Pusan Harbor contained the Left Naval Headquarters for Kyŏngsang Province and the other ports contained lesser naval installations.

Formal "Agreements" (K: *yakjo*) with Tsushima and royal edicts governed the conduct of trade at the ports. We need mention only three such Agreements that generally governed Tsushima's access to Korea for most of the Chosŏn period: the Agreements of 1443, 1512, and 1609.[12] The 1443 Agreement established an annual stipend for the lord of Tsushima – 200 *sŏk* of rice and soybeans – and permitted him 50 ships annually with additional special envoys. Later Agreements were increasingly restrictive. Given the high degree of access to the Three Ports and the amount of traffic during this period, in addition to the liberal Agreement of 1443 with Sō, the fifteenth century can be considered the peak of peaceful Japanese contact with Korea prior to the end of the twentieth century. In 1471, the *Haedong chegukki* was completed as a compilation of various regulations issued over the preceding 70 years that had proven their value in governing Japanese contact with Chosŏn and testifies to the vast extent of contacts. The large number of entries for licensed Japanese traders is partly a product of the Ōnin War and the clamor in Japan to trade with Korea to obtain funds and supplies for war and so represents the greatest number of recognized envoys and traders.

The Korean government established reception centers for Japanese ("Japan Houses" or Waegwan) in the open ports and in Hansŏng, the capital. Up the Naktong River, about 20 kilometers to the northwest of Taegu, there was also a depot for Japanese traveling to Hansŏng at a river landing that still bears the name Waegwan, although this was only a reception and trans-shipment point for Japanese. In Hansŏng there was the Hall of Great Peace (Taep'yŏng-gwan) for Chinese envoys, the Hall of Northern Peace (Pukp'yŏng-gwan) for Jurchen envoys, and the Hall of Eastern Peace (Tongp'yŏng-gwan) for Japanese envoys.[13]

We can see maps of the Three Ports with the location of the Waegwans in the frontispieces to the 1471 *Haedong chegukki*. From initial attempts to separate envoys from traders, particularly resident traders, these Waegwans had evolved over the more than 70 years since the founding of the kingdom. During Sejong's attack on

Tsushima in 1419, the Japanese in Chep'o and Pusan were arrested and enslaved and all structures were razed. Nevertheless, from 1419 to 1510, the Japanese returned to create overseas towns. From 1423, government warehouses were established in Chep'o and Pusan to supply the Japanese, and, as mentioned above, from 1427, Yŏmp'o in Ulsan was added as a port of call. From 1438, fences were erected around the Waegwans to separate them from the resident Japanese as a measure to stop the draining of provisions intended only for envoys.[14] The number of Japanese residents in Korea increased to over 3,100 by 1494 and the growth of "Japan Towns" drew particular attention from Korean authorities. By the end of the fifteenth century, the Japanese population in the ports had swelled to more than 3,000 people.[15] Korean government attempts to tax and control the Japanese sparked the revolt in 1510, known as the Revolt of the Three Ports.

The 1512 Agreement followed the 1510 revolt. The island lord's stipend was halved to 100 *sŏk*; his annual ships were reduced to 25; their lengths and crew sizes were specified (e.g. nine "large" ships with a crew of 40, etc.); his special envoys were eliminated; his son's annual ships were limited to three; limitations were put on his niece and people who had received investiture from the Chosŏn kingdom, and certain Japanese who had been invested by the Chosŏn kingdom were now refused receptions. Most importantly, Japanese were forbidden residence in Korea. All Japanese envoys and traders were restricted to the Japan House compounds. From 1512, Japanese were restricted to Chep'o. In 1521, Pusan was added to Chep'o, making two ports available.[16] In 1544, the Waegwan in Chep'o was shut down after yet another Japanese revolt, the largest since 1510.[17] In 1547, there was another, smaller riot in the ports, and thereafter the Japanese were restricted to only Pusan. From 1547 to the Kanghwa Treaty of 1876, Japanese access to Korea was limited to Pusan.

During all periods, Japanese bona fides were confirmed at the harbors on landing, as were the size of the boats, the number of crew, and the number of ships (yearly limits). The crew and envoy were then housed and fed in the Japan House. Before the Imjin Waeran, an envoy and a few selected officials were conducted to the capital, where they were given a royal audience. Afterwards, Japanese could not leave the Pusan Japan House without official permission and no access to anywhere outside the area of Pusan Harbor was granted. Official and private trade occurred both in the ports (or port depending on the period) and in the capital before the Imjin Waeran, but only in Pusan afterwards. Smuggling took place where it could. There was one exception to Japanese traveling in Korea after the Imjin Waeran. After much wrangling, in the early seventeenth century, a few Japanese from Tsushima were conducted to the Chosŏn capital of Hansŏng.[18] Since our focus is on the later Chosŏn period, we should now turn to a closer examination of the diplomatic history behind the establishment of the post-Imjin Waeran Japan House.

Hideyoshi's megalomaniac ambition to conquer China and perhaps even India resulted in a devastating war for Korea and shattered the previous arrangements for Japanese ships calling in Korea. In 1599, Yanagawa Shigeoki, a leading vassal of the Sō house, was, according to Tsushima records, instructed by Tokugawa Ieyasu to establish peace with Korea. For this purpose, envoys were dispatched. After a few false starts, Tsushima's efforts with prisoner repatriation paid off, and in 1605, Tokugawa Ieyasu met an unofficial Korean envoy at Fushimi Castle in Kyōto. In 1607, the first Korean "Reply and Prisoner Repatriation Envoy," not an actual

Korean Embassy to Edo (K: *T'ongsinsa* or "Communication Envoy"), visited Hidetada in Edo and then called on Ieyasu at Sunpu. Negotiations began in earnest between Tsushima and the Chosŏn kingdom for trading rights and eventuated in the *Kiyu* (J: *Kiyū*, after the sexagenary cycle) Agreement of 1609, which again legitimated and defined Sŏ's access to Korea.[19]

The 1609 Agreement, or Kiyu Agreement, has received a good deal of attention from scholars.[20] The 1609 Agreement governed basic Korea–Tsushima relations until the Kanghwa Treaty of 1876 and was the most restrictive to that time, not surprising since this Agreement followed Hideyoshi's invasion of 1592–1598. The Kiyu Agreement limited the island lord to 20 ships, including special envoys. He subsequently evaded this restriction by sending Irregular Envoys (K: *ch'awae*). Time in port for various envoys was specially limited. Sŏ's subsidy was again affirmed at 100 *sŏk*, where it had fallen in 1512, and was never to rise thereafter. Ships' lengths and crew numbers were again specified. Amnesties for participating in Hideyoshi's invasions were issued. All envoys had to carry Sŏ's *mun'in* or writ of passage, a consistent policy from 1436 to 1876, or risk being labeled a pirate.[21] Other miscellaneous provisions issued a seal to Sŏ, specified per diem for traveling expenses, and abrogated all previous agreements.[22] The only port opened was Pusan (Table 2.1). The freewheeling Tsushima diplomacy that led to the 1609 Agreement also led to a significant political change in Tsushima's position in relation to Edo. In Chapter 3, we will consider the economic significance of these changes.

Yanagawa Shigeoki was able to open negotiations for the dispatch of the Korean 1607 envoy by producing a letter from Ieyasu (forged) together with two men alleged to have robbed Korean royal tombs during the invasions, the two conditions demanded by Korea. Yanagawa's ruse was accepted by Korea for reasons of expediency; an official envoy was dispatched to Japan in 1607, and the finalization of the Kiyu Agreement followed in 1609. Yanagawa's forgery of state letters was too successful from this early point, however, since once precedents in diplomatic language, although forged, had been established, they had to be repeated for the 1617 and 1624 embassies. Korea required documents signed by the "King" of Japan, but the Edo *bakufu* refused to use "King" to refer to the shogun. Hence the form of address of all letters had to be re-written.[23]

The fraud went on until 1634 when Yanagawa Kagenao sued Sŏ Yoshinari to become a *hatamoto* or a direct vassal of the shogun and the forgeries became public knowledge. Kagenao foolishly mentioned the practice to *bakufu* officials and it was exposed. The *bakufu* tried Kagenao, his lord Yoshinari, and others for treason. The decision stripped Kagenao of all positions and property and exiled the priest-diplomat involved, Kihaku Genpō, but confirmed Yoshinari in his position as lord of Tsushima. In addition, the *bakufu* established a rotating system of priests from the Gozan temples of Kyōtō to reside on Tsushima at the Itei Hermitage (*Iteian rinban*). Their responsibility was to oversee all diplomatic correspondence between the *bakufu* and Korea and prevent a recurrence of forgeries.[24]

Korea may have been satisfied that, at last, the Chosŏn kingdom was dealing with the actual rulers of Japan and that their communications would pass untampered, since in 1636, the first T'ongsinsa of the post-Hideyoshi period was sent to Japan. The previous several envoys had actually been "Reply and Repatriation Envoys," but a "Communication Envoy" (*T'ongsinsa*) signified that relations had been "normalized"

Table 2.1 Vicissitudes of the Chosŏn-period Waegwans

Period	Site(s)	Year established	Number of years in or out of operation	Notes
Multiple Waegwans	Pusanp'o; Chep'o (or Naeip'o) First closure	T'aejong 8 (1408) Sejong 1 to 8 (1419–1426)	12 8	Attack on Tsushima to suppress piracy Period of Three Ports
	Pusanp'o (from 1423); Chep'o; Yŏmp'o (from 1427)	Sejong 8 (1426)	85	
	Second closure	Chungjong 5 to 7 (1510–1512)	3	Japanese revolt in the Three Ports
Single Waegwan	Chep'o	Chungjong 7 (1512)	9	
Multiple Waegwans	Pusanp'o (from 1521) added to Chep'o		24	
	Third Closure	Chungjong 39 (1544) – Myŏngjong 2 (1547)	4	Chep'o closed permanently as result of 1544 incident
Single Waegwan	Pusanp'o	Myŏngjong 2 (1547)	45	
	Fourth closure	Sŏnjo 25 to 34 (1592–1601)	10	Imjin Waeran (Hideyoshi invasion)
	Temporary Waegwan on Chŏlyŏng Island in Pusan Harbor	Sŏnjo 34 to 40 (1601–1607)	7	
	Pusan Tumop'o (Old Waegwan)	Sŏnjo 40 (1607)	72	
	Pusan Ch'oryang (New Waegwan)	Sukjong 4 (1678)	199	
Abolition	Pusan Ch'oryang Japanese Concession	Kojong 13 (1876)		Kanghwa Treaty (Chosŏn–Meiji Japan)

Source: Adapted from Yi Wan-yŏng, "Tongnae-bu mit Waegwan ŭi haengjŏng soko," Hangdo Pusan, 2 (1963): 51.

to the extent that Korea ostensibly initiated the communication. Its purpose was to bear Korean felicitations and re-affirm relations based on sincere trust, an expanded translation of the envoy's title.[25]

The outcome of the Yanagawa Affair situated Tsushima within the *bakuhan* system. The critical changes imposed from Edo began with the establishment of the Iteian rotational system of Gozan monks as overseer priests for diplomatic documents. Tsushima's monopoly over relations with Korea was confirmed and strengthened. Tsushima became the only domain allowed to send their people to a foreign port during a period when foreign travel was ordinarily met with capital punishment (unless we consider Naha to have been "foreign"). Tsushima was retained as the official guide for all Korean envoys when they visited Japan. Tsushima was specially guaranteed selected Southeast Asian goods imported by Chinese and Dutch ships into Nagasaki. These goods, and specially minted silver, purchased Korean ginseng and Chinese silk in Pusan. Tsushima was given the Korean ginseng monopoly and was relied on to ship massive amounts of silk and silk thread from Korea to the markets of Kyōtō and Ōsaka. In the *bakumatsu* period, Tsushima and a few other select domains were extended loans by a near-bankrupt *bakufu* to maintain the island's economic viability since it was the intermediary with Korea.

Even before the *bakufu* collapsed, it was a Tsushima man, Ōshima Tomonojō, who made common cause with Katsu Kaishū over the idea that Japan was vulnerable to a foreign attack launched from Korean soil and that Tsushima could provide the first line of defense. This geopolitical argument was later to germinate into a significant part of the infamous *Seikanron*, or "Conquer Korea Thesis."[26] Finally, at the dawn of the modern period, the newly established Gaimushō or Foreign Office of the Meiji government took Tsushima's Japan House in Pusan in 1872 as its first foreign legation.

Thus, Tsushima's identity in the eyes of the Edo *bakufu* was clear. The island was intermediary and trading partner with the sole foreign regime that maintained official intercourse with Japan from the earliest years of Tokugawa Ieyasu's rule to the arrival of Perry. The islanders supplied the Japanese markets in Osaka, Kyōto, and Edo with precious and rare commodities from Korea and China and in turn received special dispensation to export Japanese silver and copper. Eventually, from the late eighteenth century, Tsushima required special subsidies and loans from the *bakufu* to stay solvent.

Tsushima's identity: the view from Hansŏng

From Korea's perspective, Tsushima's identity was more complex. Prior to the Chosŏn period, Tsushima's identity is a mystery, since we have little mention of the island in the Korean classics. The only mention of Tsushima in the *Samguk sagi* reads:

> In the second month of the seventh year of [King] Silsŏng (408), the king heard that the Wae had established an installation on Tsushima and were laying in weaponry and supplies in a plot to invade our [country].[27]

The passage reveals nothing about sovereignty or possession and may even imply that the island was uninhabited. Parenthetically, we should note that this particular passage has figured rather prominently in historians' debates over whether the Wae were from a northern Kyūshū kingdom or from a powerful kingdom located in the Kinki region of Japan. As we can see, though, the passage itself gives no clues to an answer.[28] There are no entries about Tsushima in the *Samguk yusa*. A cursory survey of entries concerning Tsushima in the *Koryŏsa* and the *Chŭngbo munhŏn pigo* indicates no entries claiming possession.

The oft-repeated Korean belief that Tsushima was Korean territory in antiquity seems to be an idea that originated during the Chosŏn period. We see what may be the origin of the idea in the *Sejong sillok*, where T'aejong speaks on the eve of the attack on Tsushima in 1419, mounted during Sejong's reign, to suppress piracy:

[T'aejong] discoursed on domestic and foreign matters, saying, "the abuse of military power is a concern to confident sages, and to punish the guilty [by] mobilizing troops is not the wish of Emperors and Kings. [Nevertheless], in antiquity, Cheng Tang (c.1700 B.C., founder of the Shang dynasty) gave up the harvest to attack the Xia [dynasty]. Xuan Wang (11th sovereign of the Zhou) took six months [from his duties] and chastised the Xian Yun (a savage tribe to the north). In these examples, although there are differences [depending on the case], they all promoted [the principle of] punishing the guilty. In that, they were the same; there is nothing more to be said. *Tsushima is an island and originally it was our land.* Merely because it was cut off and secluded, confined and squalid did we allow the Japanese bastards (*Waenom*) to set themselves up there, but they are scheming curs and thieving rats with plots to steal [from us]."[29] (emphasis added)

Although there is no entry in the *Sejong sillok chiriji* for Tsushima, T'aejong's opinion became orthodoxy and was repeated and elaborated in the *Sinjŭng tongguk yŏji sŭngnam*, first compiled in 1481.[30] The same statement appears almost verbatim in Ŏ Suk-kwŏn's (1525–1554) *P'aegwan chapki*:

A long time ago Tsushima was subordinate to Kyerim (archaic name for Kyŏngju, the capital of Silla). It is unknown when it was occupied by the Wae. The island is divided into eight counties . . .[31]

The idea that Tsushima was Silla's territory carried over into the later Chosŏn period as well. Ŏ Suk-kwŏn's passage is quoted in the widely read, late eighteenth-century *Yŏllyŏsil kisul*, which we will examine further in Chapter 3.[32] The passage from the *Sinjŭng tongguk yŏji sŭngnam* is repeated verbatim in the *Tongnae-bu ŭpchi* (1759, 1832, and 1871) or the Gazetteers for Tongnae County, which included Pusan Harbor.[33]

The Koreans did not hesitate to voice this belief about Tsushima's identity to Japanese as evidenced by Suyama Donō's (1657–1732) *Taikan zakki* (Miscellany on Korea). Here, Suyama was reporting statements by the Korean *Hundo*, a Korean liaison official, when he recorded the *Hundo* as saying, "Tsushima was originally within the [county] of Kyerim of Kyŏngsang Province."[34]

A similar idea appears in the court debate over Arai Hakuseki's request to the Korean court to change the address of the letter carried by the 1711 Korean Embassy to Edo. From 1636, the Japanese had established *Taikun* (K: *Taegun*) or "Great

Prince" as the official diplomatic term for the shogun, but Arai had monarchical ambitions for the shogunate and requested that the Koreans re-write the letter and address it to the King of Japan.[35] During the Korean court debate, Sŏ Chong-t'ae states, "The lord of Tsushima was as much a vassal of our country as of Japan."[36] Sŏ Chong-t'ae is referring to his times but his point is consistent with the widespread belief that Tsushima was a Korean dependency and probably had been since antiquity.

Finally, a small curiosity in protocol deserves mention for what it reveals about Tsushima's ambiguous situation. In the wake of the Yanagawa Affair in the mid-1630s, the Edo *bakufu* sought to gain control of the communication channel to Korea and establish its preferred diplomatic conventions in official correspondence. The most famous reform of conventions was to forbid use of the term "King" to refer to the shogun and to request that Korea use the use the term "Taikun," which became the shogun's moniker in foreign relations until the late nineteenth century and was also transformed into the English word tycoon. Ming reign names for dating were dropped and dates were to be indicated only in terms of the sexagenary cycle, thereby avoiding consideration of China. Finally, the term for "tribute" from Tsushima to the Korean throne, *chinsang*, was changed to *pongjin*. Why the *bakufu* changed this term for Tsushima's tribute to Korea has yet to be clarified but suggests a conscious concern in Edo over Tsushima's identity.

From a survey of the usage of *chinsang* and *pongjin* in the Veritable Records, it seems that they were used almost interchangeably for what the Korean government got from the Japanese, the Kingdom of the Ryūkyūs, the Jurchen; what it got from its own provinces,[37] and to describe its presentation of items to China. If the terms for domestic and foreign contacts were completely interchangeable, then why did the *bakufu* insist on a change? The difference between the terms appears to be that *chinsang* was a verb which was used in routine situations, merely to indicate "presentation" from an inferior to a superior, but *pongjin* seems to have elevated the statement in tone, perhaps indicating a gift that was not particularly usual or that required special attention. The *pong* in *pongjin*, of course, refers to some kind of formally agreed, ritual relationship between two parties that clearly designates the giver as inferior and beholden to the receiver. For example, the gloss on *pongjin* in the Ch'ŏphae sinŏ (J: *Shōkai shingo*),[38] the Japanese-language primer used to train Korean interpreters to negotiate with the Japanese, describes *pongjin* as meaning various goods which were offered up (to the Korean court) and for which a return ritual gift and letter were issued by the court. This falls within the ritualistic meaning of tribute trade and implies something more than a distant, domestic province offering tribute to the court. *Pongjin* then seems to imply a more formal, tributary relationship. If the formality added distance, then the intention of the *bakufu* in insisting on *pongjin* might have been to distance Tsushima from Chosŏn and to clarify the international tributary relationship at the expense of any implications that put Tsushima in a closer, more subordinate, perhaps even domestic and routine position vis-à-vis Korea.

The Chosŏn government accepted the change in terms, but only in part, and this is where the tale becomes a bit stranger. The *Chŭngjŏng kyorinji* (an administrative handbook on Japanese relations compiled in 1802) and the *Tongnae-bu saye* of 1868 (Ledger of Tongnae County) use *pongjin* (foreign tribute) only in the passages referring to receptions for the envoys from Tsushima. The goods that these envoys brought to offer to the Chosŏn court are referred to as *chinsang* (domestic tribute).[39] It appears that the envoy was recognized as foreign while the goods he brought for tribute were regarded as domestic. By implication, Tsushima's territory was regarded as part of Korea, while the people who lived there were clearly foreigners. In short, in the eyes of Koreans, Tsushima was Korean land under foreign occupation.

Tsushima's identity: a dependent island economy

We should now examine three topics that suggest Korean influence on Tsushima and emphasize the island's ambiguous position between Korea and Japan. We will shortly see that Tsushima was dependent on the Korean economy. Less certain but highly likely was the effect of the Korean political economy and social models on Tsushima. That is, the method of measuring agricultural production was strikingly similar to the Korean model. In addition, Tsushima's practice of enslaving criminals, although unusual in Japan at that time, may have been influenced by Korean law. Finally, Tsushima's ambiguous position is nowhere clearer than in the fact that the lord of Tsushima appears to have been in the extraordinary position of leading Koreans against Koreans in the Imjin Waeran.

Tsushima and Kyŏngsang Province, together, formed a single economic sphere. Chapter 3 will explore this question from the Korean side, but we should first consider Tsushima's point of view. Tsushima had various expenses but we will concern ourselves with the two major parts of its economic requirements: support of the island economy and support of its installation in Edo, generally referred to as the Edo mansion (*yashiki*). Of interest to us are the twin questions: how was Tsushima's income apportioned between these two expenses and how much of that income derived from Korea?

Table 2.2 ("Tsushima's Agricultural Income and Korea's Role") offers a rough view of Tsushima's income: island production, mainland Kyūshū production, and Korean rice. The Tashiro holdings in northern Kyūshū (Hizen), also known as Kiyabu (13,000 *koku*), were awarded to Sō Yoshitoshi, lord of Tsushima, in 1599 for service in the Korean campaign. In 1605, an additional 2,800 *koku* was added in reward for re-establishing the Korean connection. As a result of the Yanagawa Affair of 1635–1636, some of these holdings were taken back by the *bakufu*.[40] Since income from the private trade is missing from this scheme, the actual values of income derived from Korea would probably be higher. We will concern ourselves only with income from the official trade with Korea. Again, Chapter 4 will supply further details on official trade.

The "total" in Table 2.2 is the sum of all commodity revenue sources. We have data for only a few instances, so the conclusions are general and indicative, not conclusive. Under Kyūshū production, "rice on hand" indicates the actual production amount, not the assessed, theoretical value of the land, usually referred to as *kokudaka*. The "total for island use only" is a calculation of what was left after deducting expenses for the Edo mansion, usually the Kyūshū production.

In 1651, Sō requested that Korea exchange a portion of his official trade cotton for rice, pleading that the Hizen (Kyūshū) income all went to support the Edo mansion. If such was true, then island expenses were met with a combination of island production and Korean rice. When we enquire after the relative importance of total grain revenues derived from Korea, we estimate that in 1830, nearly

Table 2.2 Tsushima's agricultural income and Korea's role

	1636[a]	1830[b]	1840[c]
(A) Tsushima island production	Unhulled barley 6,273.5 *koku* = rice: 5,018.8 *koku*[d]	2,470 *koku* (after conversion of barley to rice)[e]	Unhulled barley 5,000 *koku* = rice: 4,000 *koku*[d] and rice: 300 *koku*
(B) Kyūshū production	Holdings valued at 11,837 *koku*	14,711 *koku* (after deducting for local personnel)[f]	Rice on hand: 6,800 *koku* (all to Edo Mansion)[g]
(C) Korean rice		6,250 *koku*[h]	10,056 *sŏk* (5,921 Japanese *koku*)[i]
Total (A) + (B) + (C)	Rice on hand: 16,855.8 *koku*	23,431 *koku* (27% from Korea)	17,021 *koku* (35% from Korea)
Total for island use only (A) + (C)	Rice on hand: 5,018.8 *koku* (after deducting for Edo mansion: 11,837 *koku*?)	8,720 *koku* (72% from Korea) (after deducting 14,711 *koku* for the Edo mansion)	10,221 *koku* (58% from Korea) (after deducting 6,800 *koku* for the Edo mansion)

Notes:

a Figures for 1636 Tsushima island production and Hizen production come from the Nagasaki Kenshi. See "Tsushima han," in Nagasaki kenshi hensan iinkai, ed., *Nagasaki kenshi hansei hen* (Tōkyō: Yoshikawa Kōbunkan), 1973: 856 ff. Following the Yanagawa Affair of 1635, Sō was given Yanagawa's holdings in Hizen.

b Tashiro Kazui, *Kinsei Ni-Chō tsūkō bōekishi no kenkyū* (Tōkyō: Sōbunsha), 1981: 164, who reports the 1830 figures for Tsushima, Kyūshū, and Korean sources from the *Goshutsuiri tsumori utushi* (Tenri daigaku toshokan shozō), thought to have been a record written by Karō (elder) Sugimura, dated 1830.

c The figures for Tsushima and Kyūshū production come from *Chōsen koku kōbōeki aitodokori on kattemuki on nanjū no omomuki oyobi go naii sōrō tokoro okane ichi man ryō on haishaku narabi nennen hannō kin on sashihiki no kiroku* (MS B30/154 in Kyūshū daigaku bungakubu Kyūshū bunkashi kenkyū shisetsuko, folio 5a). The figures for Korean rice come from Tashiro Kazui, *Kinsei Ni-Chō tsūkō bōekishi no kenkyū*, pp. 153–154.

d This is the "rice on hand" (*genmai*) and has been calculated from the "total possible yield" (*kokudaka*) in unhulled barley (*aramugi*): 6,273.5 *koku*. One *koku* of barley was calculated into rice at the rate of 1 *koku* of barley = 8 *to* of rice or 0.8 *koku*. See *Nagasaki kenshi, hansei hen*, p. 857, which quotes the following passage from *Tsushima [no] uchi go kenchi no oboe* (1636): "Item, the total barley is 6,273 *koku* 5 *to*, and when we [calculate] barley into rice, we subtract 20%." Thus, the unhulled barley to rice calculation reads: 6273.5 *koku* × 80% = rice 5018.8 *koku*. The same calculation was done for the barley figure for 1840.

e The conversion rate reported by Tashiro is 1 koku of rice = 2 koku of barley. See Tashiro Kazui, *Kinsei Ni-Chō tsūkō bōekishi no kenkyū*, p. 164, note 9.

f The details are as follows:

Hizen Tashiro operating expenses (*shomumai*)	8,000 *koku*
Hizen Matsuura, Chikuzen, Ito-gun operating expenses (*shomumai*)	6,600 *koku*
Yashū operating expenses (*shomumai*)	111 *koku*
	14,711 *koku*

g Hizen koku, Kiyabu-gun.

h No conversion rate is reported. Moreover, it is not clear if this figure is the total received from Korea before deducting for Waegwan consumption or if this is the total shipped to Tsushima after deducting for Waegwan consumption. The Total and Total for Island Use Only are calculated as if this was the rice shipped to Tsushima in Japanese *koku*. According to a "mid nineteenth-century" document reported by Tashiro, about 60% of the rice received from Korea at the Waegwan was shipped on to Tsushima. See Tashiro Kazui, *Kinsei Ni-Chō tsūkō bōekishi no kenkyū*, pp. 154–155.

i Tashiro Kazui, "Tsushima han no Chōsenmai yunyū to 'Wakan masu': Sō-ke kiroku *Masu ikken oboegaki* kara mita Chōsenmai no keiryōhō," *Chōsen gakuhō*, 124 (1987.7): 25 gives the following exchange rate between Korean and Japanese rice for the early eighteenth century: 1 Korean *sŏk* = 0.54427 Japanese *koku*. However, the numbers used here for Korean rice are converted at 1 Korean *sŏk* = 0.5889 Japanese *koku*. For the latter conversion rate, see Tashiro Kazui, *Kinsei Ni-Chō tsūkō bōekishi no kenkyū*, pp. 154–155. A further problem is the dating for these numbers. Tashiro merely refers to them as "mid-nineteenth century."

27 percent of Tsushima domain's total revenues in grains came from Korea and 72 percent of the grain consumed on Tsushima came from Korea. In 1840, nearly 35 percent of Tsushima's net grain income was from Korea, while 58 percent of the grain consumed on Tsushima was Korean. Of course, not all of the grain received at the Waegwan went back to Tsushima. "Korean rice" consisted of cotton converted to rice plus other supplies and payments. Tashiro Kazui estimates that about 60 percent of the rice obtained at the Waegwan was shipped back to Tsushima in the mid-nineteenth century.[41] These figures are very rough and indicate only the range of Tsushima's dependence on Korean grains in the mid-nineteenth century. Nevertheless, they are clear in their general message: about two-thirds (and probably more) of the grains consumed on Tsushima came from Korea.

According to the *Nagasaki kenshi* (Nagasaki Prefectural History), the Tokugawa-era situation was the following:

> The policy governing appropriations of stipends derived from Korea to retainers was one of trusting to providence; when Korea experienced harvest shortfalls, then naturally it became impossible to support rice stipends on Tsushima.[42]

In truth, Korean "poor harvests" were a life or death matter for Tsushima. Amenomori Hōshū (1668–1755), Confucian advisor to the Tsushima lord, summed up Tsushima's vulnerability in his *Kōrin teisei*:

> [The Koreans] always say that if support was withdrawn and the market closed, it would be tantamount to taking the babe, Tsushima, away from the teat. I think this is the best way [for them] to inflict a heavy blow on us.[43]

The Zen priest Kihaku Genpō (diplomat and foreign policy advisor to Sō in the early seventeenth century) is reputed to have said, "Our people depend on Korea for food; although our bodies are here, we are the same as them."[44]

Not everyone on Tsushima considered such a situation healthy. Suyama Donō (or Totsuan, 1657–1732), one of Tsushima's more illustrious Confucian scholars, policy advisor, and prolific essayist on agricultural economics, is said to have reacted negatively to assertions of Tsushima's dependence on Korea. Donō registered his opposition by refusing grains from Korea and living on Tsushima-grown barley, rice, and vegetables. Donō is best remembered on Tsushima as the man who rid the island of wild boars.

In 1840, when Tsushima quietly requested the *bakufu* to loan it 10,000 *ryō* of gold, the following reasons were given:

> . . . [in 1834], due to poor harvests [in Korea] and the destruction by fire of the [Korean] palace, our income in gold through trade reached roughly 71,800 *ryō*; [because of] a gradual worsening of our situation, and through discreet discussions, we were issued a loan of a mere 10,000 *ryō*.[45]

In the same negotiations for a loan, Tsushima stated the following to the *bakufu* regarding its traditional role as defender of Edo's interests to Korea:

... [W]ith the present insufficiency in our estates of 10,000 *koku*, it is very difficult to act in our role as your agent and first line of defense. Times when we [should] concern ourselves with the dignity of your government [may find us] not up to the task. Such will force you to make inquiries.[46]

We can see that Tsushima knew how to exploit the center's concern with its own prestige. In other words, Tsushima was dependent on Korean rice, but when that was insufficient, they pleaded with the *bakufu* for loans while holding Edo's prestige abroad as hostage.

Tsushima's identity: institutional borrowings from Korea

Tsushima's dependence on Korean rice seems to have had effects in other areas as well. Tsushima's *kanshaku* law (first promulgated in 1636) was unique to Tsushima and expressed the productive capabilities of land in *kan, shaku, sun, bu, rin,* and *mō*,[47] or in terms used for surface area. Korean land measurement for taxation also used a measure of productive capability (*kyŏlbu*) expressed in surface area. It is yet unclear whether Tsushima was affected by Korean law. To help clarify this question, we might first determine the similarities between Tsushima's *kanshaku* law and Korea's *kyŏlbu* system. A comparative study of their applications does not yet exist, so our comments are merely suggestive.

Both Korean law and the Tsushima system calculated finances in a similar fashion. For example, on Tsushima, rights to the production of land were issued to retainers in *kan*, a term usually reserved for surface area measurement, but which had the meaning of production. One *kan* of land always produced a certain average amount of grain (113.15412 bushels of barley) and/or other commodities, but since no two pieces of land are ever equivalent in quality, piece A may be only 5 square meters while piece B is 7 square meters. Since both piece A and piece B are graded at one *kan*, piece A is obviously of a higher grade than piece B and so requires less surface area for the same production. Tsushima had roughly 12 grades of land; the lower down we go, from paddy to dry field to slash-and-burn field, the larger the surface area required for the same production.[48] This system was virtually identical to the Korean system, which, by the sixteenth century, had about 6 grades of land.

The more typical Japanese *kokudaka* system made reference only to the amount of grain either assessed or actually produced (*toridaka*). *Koku* is a dry measure (4.9629 bushels) and *daka*, in this case, means number. Literally translated, *kokudaka* means "number of dry measures." Tsushima authorities may have found their *kanshaku* system conveniently vague, since it allowed stipends to be calculated in commodities besides grains, such as fish. By contrast, the *kokudaka* system made explicit reference to grains.

The *kanshaku* system was strikingly similar to the Korean *kyŏlbu* system. The *kyŏl* was often given as a unit of surface area, 10,000 square *ch'ŏk* (land survey feet, 9,121.25 square meters or 1 hectare or 1 acre),[49] but in reality, it was an expression of production value, a fixed production value that meant the required surface area was variable. It was less ambiguous than the Tsushima *kanshaku* system in that the *kyŏlbu* system almost always referred to a grain: rice, beans, and millet. Moreover, the *kyŏlbu* system was designed for tax assessment; tax disbursements were given in dry measures. For example, government stipends are indicated in *sŏk* (a dry measure of 144 kg. in modern times) in the *Kyŏngguk taejŏn* or the National Code, compiled between the 1460s and the 1480s. By contrast, the *kanshaku* system was designed for disbursing feudal stipends. Whatever the differences, the idea to generalize various commodities under the rubric of surface area on Tsushima was probably borrowed from Korea. Since, in all of Japan, only Tsushima employed the *kanshaku* system, is it mere coincidence that it closely resembles the Korean *kyŏlbu* system?

The matter of unfree labor on Tsushima also implies Korean influence. "Unfree labor," often called slavery, is a difficult term to define and we will not attempt a new definition here. We use the word "slave," since the English translation of Yi Ki-baek's *A New History of Korea* uses the word.[50] Ellen Salem Unruh defines slavery as "a non-kinship relationship in which one individual is subject to the will of another individual or group to the extent that he can be bought or sold."[51] Such a definition comes rather close to the situation of Tsushima's "slavery" as described by Higaki Motokichi.[52]

Higaki's description is based on a number of studies of crime on Tsushima done at Kyūshū University's Kyūshū Bunkashi Kenkyūjo (Research Center for Kyūshū Cultural History). He depicts enslavement on Tsushima as a system that made certain men and their families the property of the samurai feudal class. Higaki explains that the lord awarded criminals to his retainers like chattel. In Higaki's view, the slave on Tsushima was an integral part of the feudal political economy, being, in fact, one means of production. Higaki attributes the origins of slavery on Tsushima to the material necessities of a difficult productive situation in which a large consuming class (roughly two samurai for every three commoners) sought to maintain itself by enslaving members of the producing class. Higaki does not discuss the buying and selling of people, nor does he mention the possibility that Korean models may have been influential.

Although approaching the question from a similar materialist perspective, Yasukōchi Hiroshi differs somewhat in that he finds similarities with, if not influence from, the Korean example.[53] Yasukōchi does not discuss the ability to buy and sell people either, so strictly speaking, use of the term "slave" in Unruh's sense to describe the Tsushima situation may be strained. Nevertheless, Higaki and Yasukōchi use *nuhi* (K: *nobi*), commonly translated into English as "slave".

According to Yasukōchi, slavery existed in Japan from antiquity and was codified in the Ritsuryō system. During the Nara and Heian periods, slaves never exceeded 5 percent of the population and the institution disappeared in most religions in the mid-Heian period. Slavery was practiced in Kyūshū up to the end of the sixteenth century. Korean captives from Hideyoshi's invasion were sold on to European traders, although Hideyoshi banned slavery in 1590. The Edo *bakufu* did indeed prescribe enslavement of the immediate family of executed criminals in Article 17 of the *Gotōke reijō* (Tokugawa House Laws), but the practice never became common. The *Gotōke reijō* was promulgated in 1711 and compiled from over 600 statutes issued from 1597 to 1696.

Other domains besides Tsushima, which show some evidence of enslavement, were domains in present-day Miyagi (Sendai *han*), Ibaraki (Mito *han*), Ishikawa (Kanazawa *han*), and Fukushima (Nakamura *han*) prefectures, but in general, Yasukōchi asserts, the evidence from other domains is fragmentary or infinitesimal. Tsushima, by contrast, practiced slavery from the Muromachi to the early Meiji, and from the early Edo period enslavement became the principal form of punishment.

Tsushima's practice originated in the Muromachi period with grants of slaves to retainers from the domainal lord (*c*.1441–1443). Criminals, commoners, and non-officials were bequeathed as gifts. Nevertheless, from the Kanbun (1661–1672) period, slavery became primarily a device for punishment. From the Genroku–Shōtoku (1688–1715) period, "country slaves" (*inaka yakko*), one category of penal servitude, surpassed "household slaves" (*go kechū yakko*). "Term-limit slaves" (*nengiri yakko*) appeared from the Shōtoku (1711–1715) period and "public service slaves" (*kōeki yakko*) appeared thereafter. Evidently, some were enslaved for crimes committed at the Waegwan in violation of Korean law.[54]

Yasukōchi argues that Tsushima's slave system was based on Korean examples from the Koryŏ and Chosŏn periods. Enslavement in China was almost solely meted out to rebels, while Korean practices expanded enslavement to cover a wide variety of criminal activities: forgery, absconding, robbery, and others. According to Yasukōchi, Tsushima also expanded its use to the point where enslavement became the principal penalty.

Other similarities point to a strong connection as well. Major criminals and their families in Korea were enslaved in border regions for fixed terms or indefinitely. Tsushima practiced fixed-term enslavement and the "country slaves" were likewise internal exiles. The Chinese characters for the Tsushima term for permanent enslavement were nearly identical to the Korean usage.[55] Yasukōchi makes no mention of self-enslavement or slave enterprises on Tsushima, both noted by Ellen Unruh as characteristics of Koryŏ-period slavery.[56] Since enslavement and manumission were the sole prerogatives of the Tsushima *daimyō*, Yasukōchi argues that, particularly in the Edo period, Tsushima slaves should be considered "government slaves" (*kan nuhi*). On this point of self-enslavement, Tsushima's practice differs from the Korean model.

Tsushima's identity: war

Leaving slavery aside, we should finally note an unusual piece of information from the Hideyoshi invasions that draws into question many assumptions we moderns hold dear about the sanctity of national boundaries and the strength of identity. Nakamura Tadashi uncovered an interesting document on Sō Yoshitoshi's (1568–1615) troop dispensations as of the fourth month of 1592, the eve of the Hideyoshi invasion. According to the *Chōsen gorin ondomo no jinrui* (Various Followers and Comrades in the Korean [Campaign]), Yoshitoshi was unable to meet the required 5,000 troops, fielding a total of only some 4,271 men. Some of these were interpreters (93) and the others were warriors and porters. Thirty of the interpreters and 1,000 porters were referred to separately as *tōjin*. We will return to this term in Chapter 7, but suffice it to say here that the term was used on Tsushima as a general term for other Asians and in particular for people from the peninsula. The *tōjin* translators were described in the *Chōsen gorin ondomo no jinrui* as "men provided by Yūtani Kōhiro [who] are to be guides." The 1,000 *tōjin* porters were "to be used as coolies and, in Kim Han-sei's plan (name in *katakana*), will assist Yanagawa Kennosuke (or Yanagawa Shigenobu). They are to be quartered in Pusan." Nakamura deduces that Kim Han-sei was a Korean in Sō's employ, leaving us with the distinct impression that Sō was employing Koreans to aid the Japanese war effort.[57] After the invasion began, many Koreans were dragooned into providing porterage for Hideyoshi's forces, but here we have an instance before the event of Yoshitoshi naming a labor broker and specifying the number of able-bodied Koreans available to assist in an invasion of their own country.

We might consider that the 1,030 *tōjin* may have existed only on paper or that they were unaware of the dark purpose of their employ. What we should note, however, is that Yoshitoshi included their number (or their theoretical number) in official plans, perhaps thereby indicating his ability to recruit as many as 1,000 Koreans from Kyŏngsang Province. Tsushima truly seems to have occupied, to borrow Ronald Toby's phrase, a "zone of ambiguous boundary qualities"[58] between Korea and Japan, defying easy categorization as one or the other. Who populated such a zone? Murai Shōsuke has proposed the term "marginal man" to refer to the Japanese settling in Korea prior to 1510. These people were essentially the result of a diaspora from the Japanese archipelago to the coastal areas of Korea, Southeast Asia, and the Chinese coast.[59] Their identity may have been "new" or different from any of the better-known identity signifiers used here: "Korean" or "Japanese," or more likely, simply overlapped with numerous other identities. The differences obviously come from the special circumstances of the frontier.[60] To elaborate on Murai's "marginal man" is beyond the scope of this study, since it would require a detailed study of fourteenth- and fifteenth-century relations. It seems, however, that the essential ambiguities suggested by Murai survived until the late 1500s. In Chapter 7, we will return to the significance of identity ambiguity and the threat it posed to the Korean state.

What the people of Tsushima considered themselves to have been, Japanese or Korean, is possibly an unanswerable question; in fact, it is probably a non-question. The language was a Japanese dialect, and the politics, economics, social structure, and most daily customs were predominantly Japanese in that similarities with other parts of the islands outweighed similarities with peninsular models. Edo-period Tsushima documents refer to Korea as *kano-kuni* (that country), *kano-tokoro* (that place), *wataru-tokoro* (the place we cross over to), or simply as Korea (J: *Chōsen*, K: *Chosŏn*).[61] Tsushima documents never refer to Korea as *waga-kuni* (our land or country) or *kono-tokoro* (this place), terms reserved for references to Tsushima and the other Japanese islands. The prose of Tsushima documents is a standard Japanese epistolary style common to all bureaucratic writings in the archipelago at the time and not classical Chinese or Korean *idu*, the prose styles in use in Korea at the time. The most important political questions for Tsushima involved the Tokugawa *bakufu*; but many of the most important economic questions involved Korea.

Nevertheless, as is apparent from the above, Korean models influenced Tsushima. Tsushima's accounting system for its vassals seems to have been borrowed from Korea. Tsushima's penal code of enforced slavery was also probably borrowed from Korea. But most curious of all was the fact that, in 1592, Tsushima could marshal over 1,000 *tōjin* to assist it in invading Korea with Hideyoshi. Certainly, Tsushima's institutional structures show strong Korean influences at work, and this is not surprising considering its frontier existence.

Japanese historians have been debating a restructuring of the medieval Japanese worldview, and the problem of Tsushima's self-identity will probably be more fruitfully addressed in the future. Approaches to this problem might start from the assumption that the question of "did people on Tsushima think of themselves as Korean or as

Japanese" is a non-question. Aside from a few elites, Tsushima people most likely did not identify with nor did they concern themselves with the interests of Kyōto, Edo, or Hansŏng, unless forced to do so. They concerned themselves with their own interests, and they identified themselves as being people from Tsushima or some part of Tsushima, since customs varied across the island. Considering that the Sō established themselves on Tsushima during the Kamakura period and were displaced during the Meiji, a span of about 500 years, the people of Tsushima did and still do consider themselves unique, with particular connections, interests, and a certain savvy regarding Korea. Eighteenth-century Tsushima authorities demanded and received *bakufu* relief from currency devaluation with the argument that they would be unable to supply Korean products to the Japanese market with degraded silver. Nineteenth-century authorities argued to the *bakufu* that their position as the *bakufu*'s diplomat to Korea necessitated special consideration for loans, which Tsushima received when others were refused. In the first half of the twentieth century, Tsushima residents preferred Pusan for shopping, entertainment, and health care. Fukuoka was too distant. Given a choice, many would do the same in the early twenty-first century.

Korean authorities may have considered the island as theirs, but the people were thought of as foreigners; they were the *Wae* (islanders or "Japanese") who inhabited Tsushima. When we discuss the Waegwan in Pusan Harbor, we must keep in mind this tension in Tsushima's ambiguous position. Was the Waegwan an outpost of Japan or an outpost of Tsushima? Did Koreans generalize to all Japanese the impressions they garnered from the islanders in the Waegwan or did they retain a conscious, or even unconscious, distinction? As the corollary to Tsushima's ambiguous position, we will, particularly in Chapters 3 and 4, be concerned with the question of the extent of the Waegwan's impact on Kyŏngsang Province's economy and politics and argue that Kyŏngsang Province was deeply affected by its connection with Tsushima. Did Kyŏngsang Province also occupy a "zone of ambiguous boundary qualities"?

The Japan House of the later Chosŏn period

The final task of this chapter is to describe, physically and administratively, the Pusan Japan House, this extension of Tsushima onto Korean soil. We will limit ourselves to the post-Hideyoshi period and return to our story of early negotiations to establish the Kiyu Agreement of 1609.

The first problem for post-war negotiators was the site of the Japanese residence in Pusan Harbor, since the former Pusan Waegwan had been absorbed into the Pusan Castle built by Hideyoshi's troops. The Japanese Pusan Castle was later used as the Korean Pusan Garrison after the war, but such close proximity to the Japanese was, no doubt, difficult to imagine and difficult to endure for the Koreans. Tsushima envoys from 1601 to 1607 were lodged in a temporary Japan House on Chŏlyŏng Island (present-day Yŏngdo Island) in Pusan Harbor. In 1607, a permanent compound was built at Tumo, 5 *li* to the west of the Garrison.[62] The Tumo Waegwan was 126 *po* (one *po* was about 2 meters)[63] by 63 *po* or 7,938 square *po* (34,449 square meters). Its eastern flank faced the sea. A wall enclosed the south, north, west, and part of the east sides. Directly outside the East Gate was a river. It was divided into east and west areas with the Banquet Hall in the middle. The eastern half was slightly broader, but open to the southerly winds.[64]

34

Almost immediately after construction discussion began within the Korean government to move the site. The Left Naval Command was then billeted in the Pusan Garrison and found the proximity of the Japanese uncomfortable. Negotiations were opened with the Japanese to move them back to Chŏlyŏng Island, but the Japanese declined and the matter was dropped.[65] Shortly thereafter the Japanese began to complain that the mooring at the Tumo site was unsafe, since the eastern side was buffeted by a south wind. They requested, beginning in 1640, that the Waegwan be removed to a more convenient location. In 1640, they first requested re-admission to Pusan Castle; later (1671) they asked for a removal to Ungch'ŏn (site of the old Chep'o Waegwan).[66] Negotiations were opened eight times by either the Korean or Japanese side over a change from Tumo (1611, 1640, 1658, 1668, 1669, 1671, and 1672). None of these succeeded.

The Korean government, wishing to put the Japanese at arm's length for security reasons, struck an agreement with them in 1673 over the Ch'oryang site, quite removed from the Pusan Garrison (about 4.2 kilometers distant), yet still within Pusan Harbor (see Maps 2.2 and 2.3).[67] From 1678, the Pusan Waegwan remained at

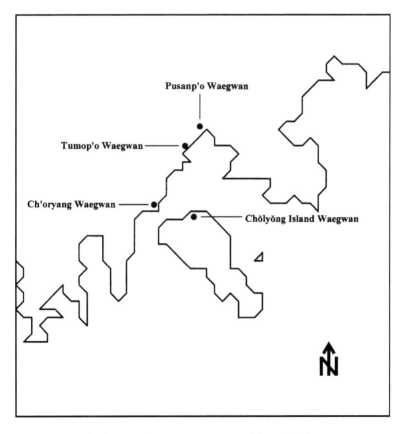

Map 2.2 Location of the historical Japan Houses around Pusan Harbor
Source: Adapted from Kim-Ŭi-hwan "Fuzan wakan bōeki no kenkyū: 15 seki kara 17 seki ni kakete no bōeki keitai o chūshin ni" *Chōsen gakuhō*, 127 (1988): 49.

Map 2.3 Japanese Imperial Army map of Pusan Harbor (1875)
Source: Adapted from *Chōsen zendo, Bufu, Rikugun Sambō-kyoku* (1875).

Ch'oryang until it became Meiji Japan's first overseas consulate as a result of the 1876 Kanghwa Treaty.[68]

The area of the Ch'oryang Waegwan may have been nearly ten times the size of the Tumo Waegwan.[69] The new enclosure contained two hills, one of which was stripped away by port construction in the early twentieth century. Yongdu-san (Dragon Head Mountain), once in the center of the Waegwan, remains today and serves as the focus of Yongdu Mountain Park and the base for Pusan Tower. Reference to Maps 2.4, 2.5, and 2.6 will make the discussion clearer.[70] Map 2.4 was painted

Map 2.4 The Waegwan-do (1783)
Source: Preserved by The National Museum of Korea, Seoul.

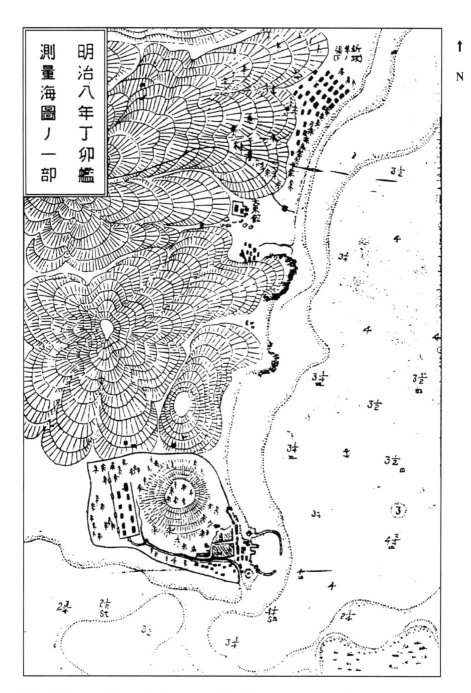

N

Map 2.5 Japanese Imperial Army map of the Ch'oryang Waegwan (1875)
Source: Adapted from Oda, Seigo, "Pusan no Wakan no setsumon ni tuite," *Chōsen*, 125 (1926): 160.

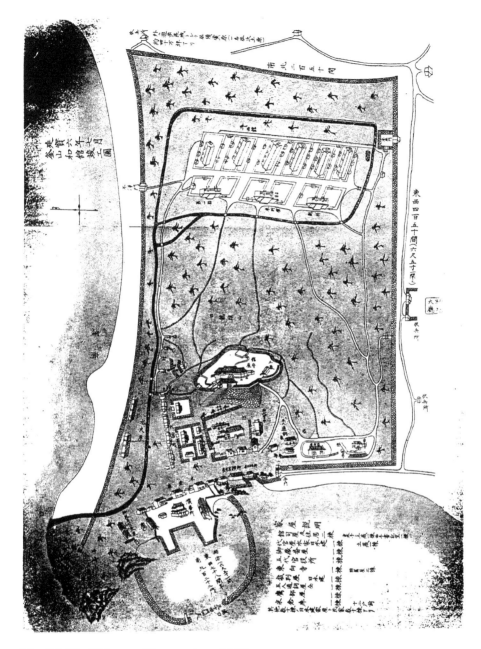

Map 2.6 The Ch'oryang Waegwan (post 1742)
Source: Adapted from Takahashi, Shonosuke, *Sōke to Chōsen* (Keijō: Hokunai Insatsusho), 1920.

by Pyŏn Pak and is preserved in The National Museum of Korea. Here we can see the general layout of the compound. Map 2.5 is clearly a nautical map, dated 1875, the eve of the Kanghwa Treaty of 1876. Map 2.6 is yet unclear, but judging from internal evidence (to be discussed below), it could not have been produced prior to 1742. None of the Waegwan remains today, but if one ascends Pusan Tower, one can see in the street patterns below the extent of the walls of the Waegwan, since the modern avenues were laid out skirting the edges of those walls. Map 2.7 is a composite of modern Pusan's city streets with an overlay of the probable location of the Waegwan.[71] The cost of construction (over 6,000 yang of silver and over 9,000 sŏk of rice)[72] was borne by the Korean government on the grounds, as explained by the modern scholar Ch'oe Yŏng-hŭi, that "a great land is merciful to a lesser land."[73]

As we can see from Maps 2.4, 2.5, and 2.6, there were two jetties offering break-waters and a quiet anchorage. We can also see that the Waegwan was divided into an eastern part and a western part. The east was for trade and the west was for diplomacy where envoys carrying official documents were housed. In front of the main gate (Sumun) just north of the anchorage was where the morning fish and vegetable market was held. Outside the compound to the north was the Yŏn[hyang] Taech'ŏng (see Map 2.6) or Banquet Hall for envoys. Also to the north off Map 2.6 were the Sŏngsin-dang (Hall of Truth and Sincerity), the Hundo and Pyŏlch'a's residences, and the Yuwŏn'gwan (Hall of Graciousness to Strangers or the Lodge for Korean Interpreters attending banquets). The name of the Yuwŏn'gwan indicates "Korean civility towards foreign, backward types."[74] We also do not see in Map 2.6, the Kaeksa where Japanese envoys paid obeisance to mortuary tablets of the Chosŏn kings.[75] There were numerous other structures and gates in the area as well, among which we should note the Ch'ulsa Ch'ŏng, which provided accommodation for the personnel of the Munwihaeng (K.) or the Tōkai Yakkanshi or simply Yakkanshi (J.). These were the Korean interpreters appointed from Hansŏng and elsewhere who visited Tsushima as envoys.[76]

A 2-meter high wall enclosed the compound (originally earthen, but rebuilt in stone in 1709),[77] and as we can see in Map 2.6, there were at least five structures around the perimeter where guards (Pokbyŏngso) were posted. Three guardhouses are clearly labeled and two similar structures are unlabeled. There were originally three and this number was doubled in 1739; here we have one piece of internal evidence to date Map 2.6 as after 1739, since Map 2.6 seems to show at least five guard posts.[78] Tashiro Kazui points out that Map 2.6, obviously a Tsushima product, also contains a building for five interpreters, an office established in 1742, and also dates Map 2.6 from after this time.[79] Map 2.4 shows the main gate (sumun).

In the fourth month of 1677, the Master of the Japan House led some 454 Japanese from the "old" Tumo Waegwan to the "new" Ch'oryang Waegwan.[80] "Old" and "new" are commonly used in documents of the period to indicate the two installations. The Japanese population of the Pusan Waegwans was probably around 500 and never exceeded 1,000 men[81] or about 2.53 percent of Tsushima's population, calculated from a peak island population of 39,455 in 1699.[82] The longest continuous resident, either the Chaep'an (J: Saihan, a special liaison official for the Sō), or the Master of the Japan House, was appointed for a two- to three-year period and occasionally re-appointed.[83] Lying only a day's sailing from Tsushima, the Pusan

Map 2.7 Outline of the Ch'oryang Waegwan overlaid on modern Pusan
Source: Adapted from *Pusan chikhal-si kaepal chehan kuyŏk-do* (Seoul: Chung'ang Chido Munhwa-sa), 1988.

Waegwan was the only instance of Japanese legally residing abroad during the Edo period. Satsuma officials resided in Naha and Ryukyuans resided in China, but what were the Ryūkyū Islands from the seventeenth century, a foreign territory or a Satsuma satrapy? Their identity was indeed even much more ambiguous than Tsushima's.

The Waegwan: offices and documents

To conclude our survey of the Waegwan, we must finally turn to consider the Japanese administrative structure that managed it. A discussion of Tongnae County officials responsible for the Waegwan can be found in Chapter 5. By considering the Japanese players, we can appreciate more fully the various dramas described in Chapters 6 (riots) and 7 (prostitution).

In 1968 Osa Masanori published a highly informative article[84] on the Japanese offices of the "new" Ch'oryang Waegwan and the extant documents produced by these offices. Osa discusses in brief the offices of: (1) Kanshu (K: Kwansu, House Master); (2) Daikan (K: Taegwan, daimyō deputy for trade affairs); (3) Wakan (K: Waegwan) constables; (4) Tōkōji (K: Sŏsŭngwae, Zen monk scribe); and (5) Saihan (K: Chaep'an, Special Liaison). Let us consider these offices in turn and the major archival collections kept by them.

The Kanshu or House Master was a direct appointee by the lord of Tsushima. The post originated in 1637 in the wake of the Yanagawa forgery scandal and the second Manchu invasion of Korea when Uchino Kenbeei was appointed. With the second appointee from 1639, the Korean government recognized the position. Such was indicated by the institutionalization of a special rice and bean stipend for the House Master. Korean records also record the office originating in 1639. The Korean government referred to the Kanshu (K: Kwansu) with the same Chinese characters.

Appointments were for two years and House Masters were chosen from among the Bangashira (Captains of the Guard) of the Umamawari class, or the highest class of three classes of Sō retainers. The Umamawari were originally mounted perimeter guards of a general's field unit and in the Edo period formed the core of a feudal lord's battle deployment. A newly appointed House Master would be given one physician and one interpreter who would accompany him to Pusan. Upon arrival he would present his credentials with gifts to the Board of Rites, the Tongnae Magistrate, and the Commander of the Pusan Garrison. The Magistrate and Garrison Commander would greet the new House Master with a "ship-landing" banquet and a "tea ceremony." The Koreans regularly supplied the House Master, and after his tour finished, he was given a "ship boarding" banquet.

The single most inclusive annal kept by the Japanese at the Japan House was the [Wakan] mainikki (or "Japan House Diary"). The Japan House diaries served a parallel function to and were kept in like fashion with diaries at Izuhara and at the Tsushima mansion in Edo. In the National Diet Library in Tōkyō we have diaries from 1687 to 1870 without significant breaks. Bibliographies for Izuhara, seat of the Tsushima government, and the Kuksa P'yŏnch'an Wiwŏnhoe in Kwach'ŏn, south of Seoul, reveal no significant additions. The Kanshu nikki (House Master's Diary) from 1726 to 1866 is also extant. The bulk is in Tōkyō with a few items in Izuhara and Kwach'ŏn.[85]

We should note and keep in mind that a major difficulty in using Tsushima documents is the fact that they are scattered between two countries and nearly three times as many archives.[86] Japan House documents generally ended up in the National Diet Library in Tōkyō and many are on microfilm. The new Meiji government's Ministry of Foreign Affairs took over the Japan House in 1872 and came into possession of the records stored there. In 1894, these documents were given to the Imperial Library, which became the National Diet Library after the Pacific War.

Japan House documents and a variety of other documents important for research on Korean–Japanese relations also exist in Kwach'ŏn at the Kuksa P'yŏnch'an Wiwŏnhoe. During the colonial era, the Chōsen Sōtokufu purchased a number of documents from Tsushima and elsewhere, which remained in Korea following Liberation in 1945.[87] The Kwach'ŏn holdings are completely catalogued and many items are now on microfilm.[88]

If the House Master was overseer of the compound and chief author of the *Wakan mainikki* and the *Kanshu nikki*, the officials in charge of trade, both official and private were the *Daikan* (deputies of the lord of Tsushima, the Sō). In the *bakufu* government, these officials fell under the offices in charge of revenue, i.e. in charge of agricultural taxation, and in similar fashion, we see them in the Tsushima government fulfilling the role of revenue accumulation on behalf of the Tsushima *daimyō*. The earliest appearance of the *Daikan* in the post-1600 context is in a Korean record dated 1612. The number of *Daikan* varied depending on the period. Prior to 1635, we see 12; from 1635 to 1684, there were 20, and thereafter ten. The increase in the number in the wake of the Yanagawa Incident led Osa to hypothesize that this was one result of the Sō wresting control of the Japan House away from the Yanagawa clan, since the Yanagawa had something of a lock on the office of *Daikan*. Salaries for the top two *Daikan* reached a high of 200 *koku*. A large proportion of the lower *Daikan* were merchants. There are a few extant *Daikan* diaries.[89] The Korean government knew them by the same Chinese characters used in Japanese records (K: *Taegwan*). The Japan House staff also included some twenty or so constables (known as *yokome* and *metsuke* to the Japanese and *kŭmtowae* to the Koreans).

The Waegwan boasted a Zen monk charged with mundane religious duties and the critical job of writing Chinese letters to Korean officials. The monk was called *Tōkōji* (after the name of the temple) by the Japanese and *Sŏsŭngwae* ("Wae monk scribe") by the Koreans. Monks from Tsushima were rotated through this post in a similar fashion to the Iteian Rotational System set up in Izuhara by order of the *bakufu* after the 1635 forgery scandal. Correspondence coming from Tsushima or from Edo bound for Korean officials had already been rendered into Chinese by the Iteian monks to prevent forgeries, but documents coming from Korea passed through the hands of the Japan House monk first. Also, any Japanese documents returned by Korea as unacceptable were first reviewed by the Japan House monk and theoretically could have been altered with the collusion of the House Master. In short, the Iteian system of *bakufu* oversight for diplomatic correspondence was not airtight. The *Tōkōji* or *Sŏsŭngwae* was not from the Iteian in Izuhara, Tsushima's castle town, but arrived at the Japan House at the pleasure of lord Sō. One does not want to make too much of the possibilities of circumvention, but such a private negotiation track between the Japan House and the Tongnae Magistrate undoubtedly was beneficial to Tsushima, since it offered one more means of hiding from *bakufu* oversight Tsushima's actual conduct of Korean relations. The origin of the post of *Tōkōji* is obscure since the oldest extant record of post-1609 correspondence is from the very late year of 1654. Although the rotational period was understood by the Koreans as three years, actual appointments were from one to two years in length.

The documents produced by the *Tōkōji* monks at the Japan House are called the *Ryōkoku ōfuku kakiutsushi* (Record of Correspondence Between the Two Countries). In Tōkyō, we have records from 1654 to 1869 with a few gaps, and there are a few records on Tsushima.[90] The *Ryōkoku ōfuku kakiutsushi* parallels the *Honpō Chōsen ōfukusho*[91] (Record of Correspondence Between Our Land and Korea) kept by the resident monks of the Iteian in Izuhara.

Finally, perhaps the most critical Japanese official at the Waegwan was the *Saihan* (K: *Chaep'an*) or Special Liaison from the Tsushima *daimyō*. The Japanese and the Koreans knew this officer by the same Chinese characters. The *Saihan* was a *Soch'awae* (Minor Irregular Envoy) in the Korean scheme. In other words, he carried letters addressed to the *Ch'am'ŭi* (Upper Sr. 3) or the Third Minister in the Board of Rites to whom Sō addressed his correspondence. By contrast, *Taech'awae* (Great Irregular Envoys) carried letters addressed to the *Ch'amp'an* (Jr. 2) or the Second Minister, to whom the *bakufu* addressed its regular correspondence. The economic costs of the Minor Irregular Envoys and the Great Irregular Envoys are examined in detail in Chapter 4. The concern here is the nature of the *Saihan*'s duties. Although the Great Irregular Envoys were empowered to negotiate at higher levels, in fact, their status was purely formal, and they were nothing more than couriers. For matters ranging from Japan House affairs to the dispatch of a Korean Embassy to Edo, the *Saihan* and the House Master handled the actual negotiations with Korean authorities. It comes as no surprise then that a *Saihan* was always in residence and changed every two to three years, making him occasionally the longest residing senior Japanese official, since the House Master's tour was two years.

The post of *Saihan* predates the Hideyoshi invasion of 1592, but information on the earlier period is scant. The early *Saihan* were said to have been merchants, but following the invasion and from the appointment of Tachibana Chishō, recruitment generally shifted to the warrior class. This same Tachibana appears frequently in Korean records in connection with the initial negotiations for normalization after Katō Kiyomasa's withdrawal in 1598, and he continues to appear up to and beyond the successful negotiations that secured the 1605 unofficial Korean envoy, the 1607 Response and Prisoner Repatriation Envoy, and the successful conclusion of the Kiyu Agreement in 1609. Aside from Tachibana, one of the more famous men to have served as *Saihan* was Amenomori Hōshū, a Confucian advisor to the Tsushima *daimyō* in the early eighteenth century and a man whose insights concerning Tsushima relations with Korea appear throughout this study.

Osa Masanori calls the *Saihan* the "cornerstone" or the "rivet" of diplomacy with Korea. Given the heavy responsibilities of the post and the necessity of tapping able men, we still see appointments after 1600 from the merchant class. *Saihan* were usually given a personal interpreter in like fashion with the House Master. The four main diplomatic jobs of the *Saihan* were the following. One, the *Saihan* escorted the *T'ongsinsa* from Pusan to Tsushima and from Tsushima to Pusan on the return trip. Two, the *Saihan* escorted the *Munwihaeng* or *Tōkai Yakkanshi* (the Interpreter Embassies) from Pusan to Tsushima and back. Three, the *Saihan* was responsible from 1651 for re-negotiating every five years additional grants of permission to convert cotton to rice (see Chapter 4) and other matters related to the quality and timing of the delivery of official trade goods. Four, the *Saihan* was responsible for negotiations when problems arose over such miscellaneous affairs as daily provisions issued every five days and exchange rates for the ginseng given Japanese in return for tribute goods. He was also a prominent actor in the dramas we will examine in Chapters 6 and 7. We are fortunate to have in Tōkyō, Kwach'ŏn, and Izuhara a good number of extant *Saihan kiroku* or the daily diaries kept by the *Saihan*. In Tōkyō we have the longest run of *Saihan kiroku* from 1705 to 1868.[92]

Since Japanese officials and others needed reference tools – convenient collections of precedents arranged thematically – we should note a secondary document base of extreme importance. The *Bunrui kiji daikō* (Classified Collected Articles), a Japan House document in the National Diet Library Collection that covers the period from 1651 to 1712 and arranges excerpts from the various *Mainikki* in chronological order under topics. Such types of collections not only indicate the concerns of the times, but since they act as something of an annotated index and provide a chronology for the other documents of the period, they aid research enormously and have been extensively used for this study.

Conclusion

The geographical "core" of the present study is Kyŏngsang Province, Tsushima Island, and the waters in between, best thought of as a single region that straddled numerous boundaries and possessed a single economy and an interactive political culture. While Tsushima was economically dependent on Korea for rice, we will demonstrate in following chapters that the demographics, economy, politics, and society of Kyŏngsang Province were affected by Tsushima's demands and the volatility of the 500 Japanese in the Pusan Japan House.

In this chapter we briefly considered the identity of Tsushima. Located over the horizon from Kyūshū and visible from Pusan, Tsushima was undoubtedly Japanese territory in the eyes of the Edo *bakufu*, although for practical purposes Tsushima had to be given a great amount of latitude in its dealings with Korea. When Tsushima's forgery of diplomatic correspondence threatened the *bakufu*'s ostensible hegemonic monopoly over foreign relations, reforms were made in 1635; but the Tsushima *daimyō* was left in place and supported in later periods with special dispensations for the export of precious metals, when Nagasaki traders could not, and special loans, when others were denied. Although the people of Tsushima were Japanese in speech and customs, various early modern socio-economic institutions owe a great deal to Korean influence. Much remains to be examined in this regard.

From the Korean perspective, Tsushima went generally unnoticed in antiquity except as a staging ground for attacks. Such an image was amply corroborated in the medieval period when Tsushima became a pirate's lair and base for the *Waegu*. The Chosŏn policies to suppress piracy involved a mixture of legalized trade and diplomacy that eventually gave Tsushima a monopoly over contacts with Korea. Sejong's attack on Tsushima in 1419 was a police action against pirates and left no administration on the island. On the eve of the assault, Sejong's father, T'aejong, referred to Tsushima as Korean territory in antiquity. This notion became orthodoxy for the remainder of the Chosŏn period, even finding an echo in the post-1945 First Republic bellicosity of Syngman Rhee who claimed Tsushima as a territory of the

Republic of Korea. Diplomatic language used to describe the tribute goods brought by Tsushima envoys also reflected this idea.

Japanese landed at several ports in Korea up to 1510 when a disturbance known as the Riot of the Three Ports convinced the Koreans that stronger controls were necessary. From the middle of the sixteenth century, Pusan became the only port open to the Japanese. Following Hideyoshi, controls were made even stricter and residence was restricted to the Japan House Compound in Pusan Harbor. After prolonged negotiations, a mutually acceptable structure was built at Ch'oryang in 1678 that served as the Japan House until the modern period. The trade conducted there by Tsushima people formed the lifeline for the island's economy.

Finally, having considered the establishment of Tsushima's presence on Korean soil, we should now turn to our central concern, which is to determine how the Japan House affected Korea. Beginning with Chapter 3, we will look at the Japan House from the Korean perspective and consider what sorts of problems it posed for Korea. We will see that the Japanese had many more far-reaching effects on seventeenth-, eighteenth-, and nineteenth-century Korea than has heretofore been acknowledged. Chapter 3 examines the demographic impact on Korea of the Japan House. Chapter 4 describes the economic support structure for the Japan House as a budgetary item for Tongnae County, Kyŏngsang Province, and the country as a whole. Chapter 5 considers the political structure governing the Japan House and the impact on the office of Tongnae Magistrate posed by the presence of the Japanese. Chapter 6 offers a case study of the struggle faced by the Tongnae Magistrate in extending his authority and power over the Japanese residents and Japanese methods of violent negotiation. Chapter 7 is a case study of the outer limit of Japanese penetration into the Korean social body and discusses prostitution at the Waegwan.

3

THE DEMOGRAPHIC
SIGNIFICANCE OF THE
JAPAN HOUSE

In search of a maritime economy

[Tongnae] produces: cod, herning, skate, shad . . .
(Tongnae-bu ŭpchi, 1759)

The surest way to test our received hypotheses about various things "national" – identities, economy, society, and polities – is to examine local documents and write histories that pursue the extent of local integration with larger regions, even with other countries.[1] In doing this, we must be open to the idea that localities and regions of the Chosŏn period may not be bound in ways familiar to us. For example, trade structures can deeply involve a region of one country with a region of another country.[2] In such a situation, what is the meaning of "the economy of Chosŏn"? Or, the natural diversity of agricultural production can produce regional economies with various social structures.[3] In that case, what is meant by "the society of Chosŏn"? Or, the presence of foreign nationals can have a long-term profound impact on local, even regional politics.[4] How, then, are we to understand "the politics of Chosŏn"?

One task of historians is to design methodologies to identify and define regions within various time frames (geologic, environmental, and human), on various geographic and economic scales, and at many social and political levels. Certainly, we should consider regions above and below the "national" level and across what we may think of as national boundaries. Here we focus on the southeastern corner of the Korean peninsula. In geologic terms, Korea is the edge of the East Asian continent, but the southeastern part of the peninsula has much in common with western Honshū and northwestern Kyūshū and is "the transition to the Pacific rim."[5] The "southeastern part" of the peninsula refers to an oval area that includes Taegu to the northwest, Kyŏngju and Ulsan to the northeast, Pusan to the southeast, and Masan to the southwest. It is an area of evenly distributed sedimentary rock, but during the late Cretaceous period, when flowering plants were developing and dinosaurs were disappearing, the area saw extensive volcanic activity, during which subsidence occurred and produced a circular fault that now defines the region. Below ground, magma consolidated to form igneous rock. Granite porphyry flows and granite intrusions, such as we see exposed near Kyŏngju and Pulguk Temple, formed an arc-shaped dike around the northeastern part of the circular fault, giving us the oval definition apparent today. During the 1930s, Japanese geologists referred to this area as part of the Tsushima basin. The basin was said to encompass the western side of a single

47

stratigraphical region that stretched to western Japan and had Tsushima at its center.[6] Hermann Lautensach, writing in the late 1930s, referred to the region as the Naktong Basin.[7] Modern geologists call it the Pusan–Taegu Volcanic-Tectonic Depression.[8]

In the times inhabited by man, the southeastern corner of the peninsula has been drained by the Naktong River and has acquired a temperate, monsoon climate strongly affected by the sea. It has four distinct seasons with no extreme changes in temperature. This study narrows its geographic focus to the pre-modern county of Tongnae, commonly known from the late nineteenth century as Pusan. The central and eastern parts of modern Pusan contain plains divided by mountains rising 500 meters. The T'aebaek mountain range, the peninsula's spinal column, ends in Pusan.[9] The western part of the contemporary municipality was formed in recent decades: the eastern part of the Naktong alluvial plain was incorporated from Kimhae County to the west into the Pusan municipal area in 1978 and the remaining western part followed in 1989. This area is a low alluvial plain at the mouth of the Naktong River, rarely reaching five meters above sea level.[10] (See Map 3.1: Modern Pusan Metropolitan Area.)

With these acquisitions, Pusan came to include the mouth of the Naktong River; at 525 kilometers, it is the second longest river on the peninsula after the Yalu (813 km.). The Naktong flows north to south in the Kyŏngsang basin between the T'aebaek and the Sobaek mountain ranges. In the 1930s, it was navigable by riverboat up 340 kilometers or to just beyond the mouth of the Naesŏng River.[11] Upstream, it

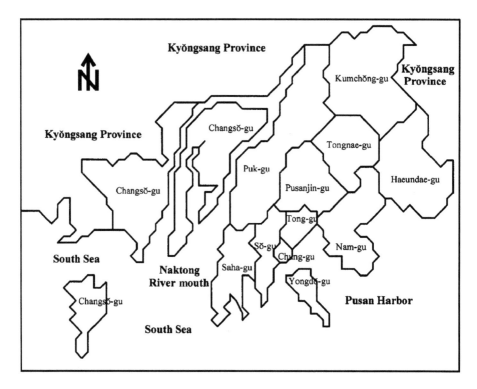

Map 3.1 Modern Pusan metropolitan area
Source: Adapted from O Kŏn-hwan, "Chise," in Pusan chikhal-si sa p'yŏnchan wiwŏnhoe, ed., *Pusan-si sa* (Pusan: Pusan Chikhal-si, 1989): 42.

is swift flowing between high valley walls. Midstream, the inclination of the beds has been eroded, the speed of the current is slower, and the river meanders. Downstream, the current slows even more, sand and earth accumulate, and the river becomes a "river of heaven's wells" (*ch'ŏn chŏng ch'ŏn*). As the river approaches the sea, it widens rapidly and deposits rich silt on the land and into the surrounding sea. The Naktong River has, from at least the beginning of our Holocene era, been the staging area for the cultures of the Yŏngnam region[12] and the "maritime gateway to the land bridge of the Korean peninsula."[13] Modern Pusan is a world center of sea-borne trade and the center of marine production in southeastern Korea.[14] This, then, is our geologic and geographic frame.

Our temporal bounds stretch from the late Koryŏ-early Chosŏn period to the Kanghwa Treaty of 1876; our economic frame is a pre-modern maritime regional community centered on fishing and trade. Our methodology is historical and demographic. We will ascertain relative differences among counties within Kyŏngsang Province and among townships within the single county of Tongnae. We will see a concentration of population in coastal areas of Kyŏngsang Province, especially in Tongnae, and we will see an unusual concentration of men in the coastal areas of Tongnae County. These results suggest a more extensive maritime economy than heretofore explored. In short, we will attempt to map a region and indicate the "traces"[15] of a community, only part of which is found in the southern coastal area of the Korean peninsula.

We might sketch our model of this pre-modern maritime region in the following terms. The southern and western Korean coasts are rich in marine resources and have been the focus of intensive fishing by peninsular peoples probably for as long as the past 10,000 years. At least from the past millennium, an interactive trading region developed that stretched from the southern Korean coast, through the Japanese archipelago, to Southeast Asia and presented itself on the Korean peninsula as the ports open to the Japanese. Trade was sanctioned in the open ports by the Chosŏn government and was progressively limited to Japan Houses. The ports and the Japan Houses were permanent or semi-permanent manifestations of a wider sea-borne community. Because so little research has been done on the Chosŏn maritime economy in general, it is still difficult to define, but we could turn to various topics to gauge its geographic reach away from the peninsula: patterns of castaway incidents, trading networks, fishing patterns, and the routes of diplomats. We will not look away from the land, but focus on unusual concentrations of people on the coast. In other words, we are looking for traces of the demographic impact of a maritime economy on southeastern Chosŏn society. We are searching for patterns of Korean population concentration that suggest the importance of fishing and trading to the larger Chosŏn economy and society. Along the way, we will consider the variety and complexity of the southern counties, suggest methodological approaches to problems of locality, touch on activities of a maritime community (fishing and trading), and raise questions about the social economy of a coastal area profiting from lucrative foreign trade.

Tongnae's relative position in Kyŏngsang Province

This chapter considers Tongnae County's relative demographic position in Kyŏngsang Province and the relative demographic peculiarities of Tongnae's townships (*myŏn*).

First, we are looking for any indication that Tongnae was demographically and perhaps economically unusual in Kyŏngsang Province. Second, we will investigate the internal demographics of the county to pinpoint any unusual aspects of the townships in and around the location of the Japan House. We are not concerned as much with the absolute size of populations or the same for the agricultural base as we are with any discernable relative differences between different areas.[16] The comparisons will be both synchronic (Tongnae's relative position in Kyŏngsang Province and the relative position of Tongnae's townships) and diachronic (changes in relative positions over time). Province-level data come from 1432/1454, 1759, and 1832. County-level data come from 1740, 1789, and 1867. We will be able to compare Tongnae County with other counties of Kyŏngsang Province before and after the Imjin Waeran, but because demographic data from before the eighteenth century for Tongnae's townships has not survived, we will not be able to assess the internal demographics of the county from before 1740.

Fifteenth century

Yi Ho-ch'ŏl's study of early Chosŏn agriculture can help us first to consider larger questions at the national level. His general conclusion is that the early Chosŏn period was characterized by the extensive farming of dry fields and that management was manorial. To show this, he points to the length of the handle of the most common farming tool – the hoe – and to the large numbers of men working individual farms. During the early Chosŏn, the larger number of men per household, together with the use of long-handled hoes, indicated the presence of extensive, cooperative farming. For example, the manorial character of extensive farming is suggested by the fact that the early Chosŏn period saw a greater ratio of men to household than the later Chosŏn. Nationally, Kyŏngsang Province came last of the eight provinces with 6.035 men per household and Chŏlla came first with 15.863 men per household.[17] Ownership was in the hands of the ruling class (royalty, yangban, and government clerks) and labor was largely supplied by unfree labor or slaves.

Tongnae was unusual in its relatively low number of men per household. In the fifteenth century, the county generally had four men per household. This low number in a province already identified as being at the low end nationally indicates an early shift towards intensive farming. Through the sixteenth century, the national population rose,[18] and the number of runaway slaves increased. In the seventeenth century, land productivity outstripped labor productivity. These changes led to a style of agriculture characterized by intensive farming, managed by landlords, and worked by tenants. Such changes are reflected in even fewer men per household during the later Chosŏn. For example, in 1759, Kyŏngsang Province had 1.87 men per household and Tongnae had two men per household.

The national position of Kyŏngsang Province in 1759 cannot be discussed here because of space, but in general, we can say that its position within the larger scheme had always been unusual and characterized as "constricted land, large population" (chich'ak minjung). Yi Ho-ch'ŏl's national-level comparison of provinces demonstrates that Kyŏngsang Province, even from the early Chosŏn period, had the smallest scale of agricultural management, while Chŏlla Province was just the opposite. Relatively speaking, then, Kyŏngsang Province was leading the trend towards intensive cultivation, but we must not assume that all of its land was becoming paddy. Yi convincingly argues that both Chŏlla and Kyŏngsang Provinces were generally characterized by dry fields and large-scale agriculture before 1592 and even into the seventeenth century and beyond.[19] Leaving Yi's national-level conclusions aside, what concerns us is Kyŏngsang Province's reputation for population concentration, or, as we will call it, person per *kyŏl* or *kyŏl* per person.[20] A *kyŏl* was the unit used throughout the Chosŏn period to indicate the productive value of land. To join *kyŏl* and population in ratios is to identify a working definition of population concentration or the number of people who had to live on a certain unit of agricultural production. The *kyŏl* used in this chapter are the *kyŏl* indicated in pre-1600 records as *kanjŏn* and in post-1600 records as *wŏnjangbu* or the assessment of arable land. Actual production (*sigi kyŏl* or *sil kyŏl*) varied annually and might fluctuate widely. The arable land assessment was quite stable over centuries.[21]

The calculations done in this chapter for person per *kyŏl* were done independently of Yi Ho-ch'ŏl's work but agree with his findings. Yi gathered and analyzed an enormous amount of agricultural economic data for national-level comparisons of provinces, setting a standard for comprehensiveness and sophistication of analysis regarding agricultural and demographic data. After analyzing the *Sejong sillok chiriji*, he concludes that the average *kyŏl* per man ratio for the entire province was 1.501.[22] This is the lowest for all the eight provinces and indicates the intensive use of land or a high concentration of men on arable land. Kyŏnggi Province had the highest ratio at 4.096 *kyŏl* per man, and no other province dropped below 2 *kyŏl* per man.

These figures demonstrate Kyŏngsang Province's relative character in favor of small-scale farming as well as the province's relatively high population concentration. The average figure for Kyŏngsang Province arrived at in this chapter is 0.72 *kyŏl* per person. Population figures from the *Sejong sillok chiriji* are only men, but the *Kyŏngsang-do chiriji* gives numbers of women as well. Since my figure is based on men and women and Yi is counting only able-bodied men, we should double my number of *kyŏl* per person, giving us 1.44 *kyŏl* to one able-bodied man, close to Yi's figure of 1.501. The difference between 1.44 and 1.501 derives from my usage of the 1432 *Kyŏngsang-do chiriji* as the primary source for population data. The *Kyŏngsang-do chiriji* figures used here are preferable to the 1454 *Sillok* population figures used by Yi, because greater detail is usually a good indication of greater accuracy. Yi was unable to use the *Kyŏngsang-do chiriji*, because he needed a common database for all provinces and the *Sejong sillok chiriji* is the only comprehensive extant database. Our needs require a common database for Kyŏngsang province only.

The following discussion will reverse the ratio and discuss person per *kyŏl* rather than *kyŏl* per person. The reason my calculations are for person per *kyŏl* rather than *kyŏl* per person, as Yi has done, is because the emphasis here is on concentration of population, whereas Yi's emphasis is on concentration of land. When we reverse my ratio of 0.72 *kyŏl* per person, we have 1.48 people per *kyŏl*, according to the *Kyŏngsang-do chiriji*. This view of people per agricultural unit is the view that will be taken in all the following discussion.

Because we still lack good, national data, we will leave aside comparisons among provinces and go inside Kyŏngsang Province to consider Tongnae County among counties. From a rough survey of the *Kyŏngsang-do chiriji* and the 1454 *Sejong sillok chiriji*,[23] we can see that Tongnae County was in the fiftieth place in a field of 70 in

1. Songju (19,557)
2. Kyongju (17,146)
3. Andong (15,441)
4. Chinju (15,254)
5. Kimhae (14,204)
50. Tongnae (2,416)
68. Koje (945)

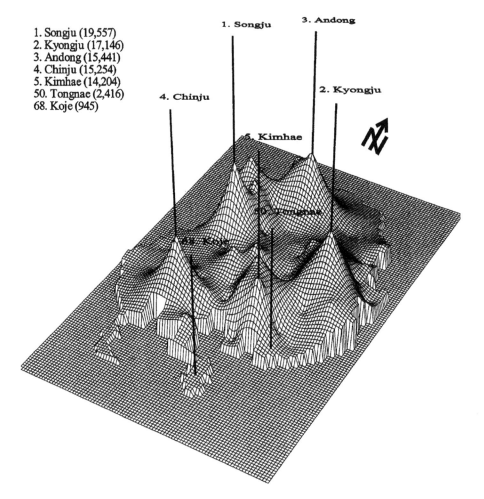

Figure 3.1 Kyŏngsang-do population 1432 and 1454 amalgamated
Sources: Provincial boundaries for this and all other provincial plots were taken from the *Ch'onggu sŏnp'yo-do* (c.1834) by Kim Chŏng-ho; population figures were taken from the *Kyŏngsang-do chiriji* (c.1432) and the *Sejong sillok chiriji* (1454).

population (see Figure 3.1) and forty-seventh in a field of 60 in the absolute size of its arable land (dry and paddy fields) as measured in *kyŏl* (see Figure 3.2). In other words, Tongnae was in the bottom third of all counties in Kyŏngsang Province in absolute demographic and agricultural terms.

When we combine demographic and agricultural data (person per *kyŏl*), we can discuss Tongnae's relative concentration of population. The purpose is to determine if Tongnae's concentration of people on top of land resources was typical or atypical. If it was atypical, we want to know if the concentration was heavy or light. A light concentration would indicate an under-population relative to available land resources. A heavy concentration would indicate over-population. In 1432/1454, Tongnae's person to *kyŏl* ratio was 1.402 people per *kyŏl* (thirty-third in a field of 60, see Figure 3.3). As mentioned above, the provincial average was 1.48 people per

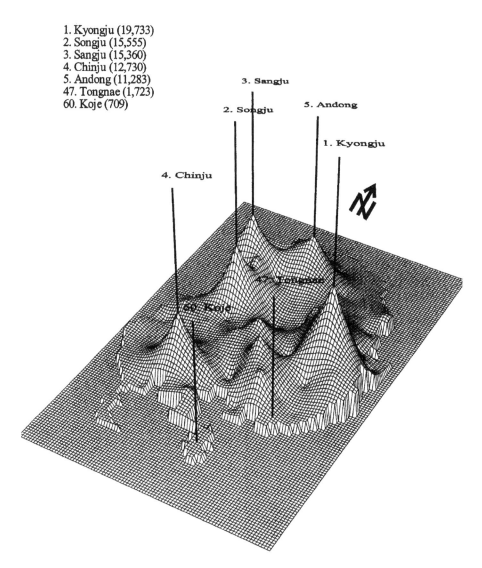

1. Kyongju (19,733)
2. Songju (15,555)
3. Sangju (15,360)
4. Chinju (12,730)
5. Andong (11,283)
47. Tongnae (1,723)
60. Koje (709)

3. Sangju

2. Songju

5. Andong

1. Kyongju

4. Chinju

Figure 3.2 Kyŏngsang-do arable land 1454
Source: Sejong sillok chiriji (c.1454).

kyŏl, and Tongnae fell just below that or only 0.078 away from the mean, indicating a typical concentration of people on land resources.[24] Figure 3.4 indicates Tongnae's position relative to the average. The middle dotted line is the average; one standard deviation above and below that is also indicated by dotted lines. Note the locations of Tongnae (far right, x = 71) and Kŏje Island (left center, x = 16). Kŏje's significance will be discussed in a moment. Both Tongnae and Kŏje are within one standard deviation or within the mainstream, and both indicate a lighter than average concentration of people on available land resources. Tongnae's concentration of paddy land was 62.5 percent, the quality of its land was rated *pi* or "bountiful," and its

53

1. Chinhae (2.492)
2. Ye'an (2.282)
3. Onyang (2.271)
4. Chiye (2.197)
5. Ch'angwon (2.186)
33. Tongnae (1.402)
40. Koje (1.333)

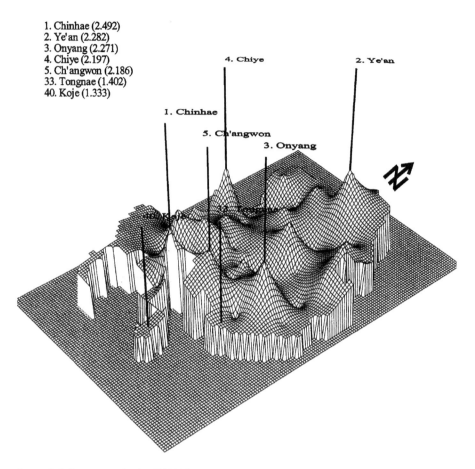

Figure 3.3 Person per *kyŏl* 1432/1454
Sources: Kyŏngsang-do chiriji (c.1432) and *Sejong sillok chiriji* (c.1459).

climate was *nan* or "warm."[25] According to Yi Ho-ch'ŏl's national survey, Tongnae was one of only 30 counties, out of a national total of 335 counties, with more than 55 percent of its land in paddy land. Surrounding coastal counties did not rival it, with only 35 percent to 55 percent of their lands in paddy.[26] In fact, Tongnae had about 62.5 percent of its land in 1454 in paddy, 67 percent in 1759, and 68 percent in 1832. Being in the top 9 percent nationally, Tongnae was well blessed with highly productive land, and a lighter than average concentration of population. This characterization will be our baseline to judge later changes.

Eighteenth century

Between the *Sejong sillok chiriji* (1454) and 1740, we have no extant gazetteers on Tongnae and not until c.1759 (*Yŏji tosŏ*) do we have a collection of county gazetteers for the entire province allowing us to compare Tongnae's position with other counties. The *Yŏji tosŏ*, which contains 1759 data for Kyŏngsang Province,[27] tells us that in a

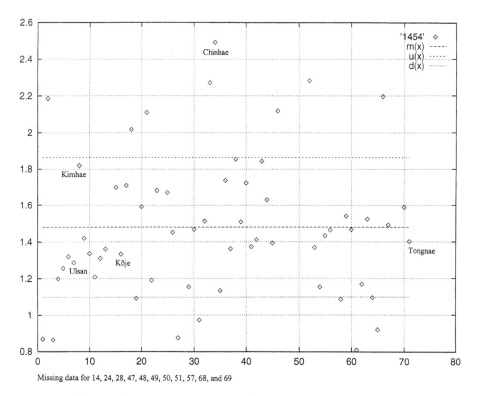

Figure 3.4 Relative distribution of Kyŏngsang-do magistracies in terms of person per *kyŏl* ratios (1432/1454)
Sources: Kyŏngsang-do chiriji (c.1432) and *Sejong sillok chiriji* (c.1459).

field of 71, Tongnae advanced to twentieth place in population (see Figure 3.5) and thirty-fourth place in the absolute size of its arable land holdings (Figure 3.6). The *Tongnae-bu ŭpchi* (1759), prepared as the *Yŏji tosŏ*'s section on Tongnae, reveals that the county's person to *kyŏl* ratio was 7.81 people per *kyŏl* (see Figure 3.7). The provincial mean was 4.86 people per *kyŏl*, meaning that Tongnae's population had become denser between 1432/1454 and 1759; in fact, the county had advanced from thirty-third place in 1454 to become the third densest spot after Kŏje (8.23) and Chiye (7.85) in people to unit of arable land by 1759. The standard deviation for all cases was 1.3973, indicating that Tongnae now lay beyond two standard deviations and had clearly become an outlier with a heavy concentration of people to land resources. Figure 3.8 indicates Tongnae's position relative to the average. Note the locations of Tongnae (far right, x = 71) and Kŏje (left center, x = 16). The radical rise in Tongnae's density may have been attributable to a growth in fishing and the presence of trade with the Japanese, but this will be discussed below.

Nineteenth century

When we examine the 1832 *Kyŏngsang-do ŭpchi*, we see corroboration that Tongnae had risen considerably in population and arable land between the mid-fifteenth

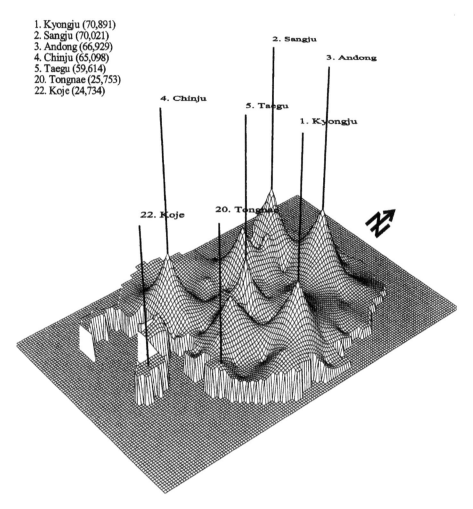

1. Kyongju (70,891)
2. Sangju (70,021)
3. Andong (66,929)
4. Chinju (65,098)
5. Taegu (59,614)
20. Tongnae (25,753)
22. Koje (24,734)

2. Sangju

3. Andong

4. Chinju

5. Taegu

1. Kyongju

22. Koje

20. Tongnae

Figure 3.5 Kyŏngsang-do population 1759
Source: *Yŏji tosŏ (c.1759).*

century and the mid-eighteenth century. By 1832, Tongnae had become fourteenth in absolute population (see Figure 3.9) and thirty-fourth (see Figure 3.10) in the absolute size of its arable land base, changes consistent with the data from 1759. Tongnae's person to *kyŏl* ratio was 9.94 people per *kyŏl*, again significantly different from the provincial mean of 4.95 people per *kyŏl* (see Figure 3.11 and Figure 3.12). The standard deviation in 1832 was 1.82, indicating that Tongnae's population density relative to arable land had become even more unusual. In 1759, Tongnae lay beyond two standard deviations, and by 1832, it was almost at three standard deviations from the mean.

To summarize, the 1432/1454 data give Tongnae a person to *kyŏl* ratio of 1.402 and a relative position in the province of thirty-third place in terms of population concentration on available land resources. The 1759 data give Tongnae a ratio of

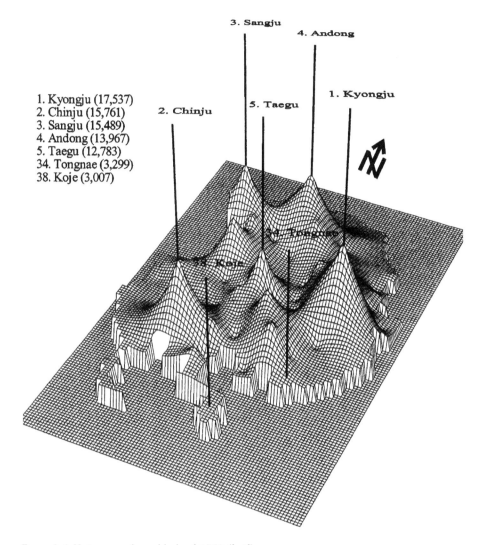

1. Kyongju (17,537)
2. Chinju (15,761)
3. Sangju (15,489)
4. Andong (13,967)
5. Taegu (12,783)
34. Tongnae (3,299)
38. Koje (3,007)

Figure 3.6 Kyŏngsang-do arable land 1759 (*kyŏl*)
Source: *Yŏji tosŏ* (c.1759).

7.81 people per *kyŏl* and a relative position of third place. The 1832 data give Tongnae a ratio of 9.94 people per *kyŏl* and a relative position of second place. In addition, the relative position of Tongnae, in amount of arable land, improved from the fifteenth to the eighteenth century (from forty-seventh to thirty-fourth place by 1759), and the relative size of its population radically increased (from fiftieth to twentieth place by 1759). These figures are summarized in Table 3.1.

While considering Table 3.1, we should pause to consider the reliability of the available data. More will be said below, but in the specific cases of 1759 and 1832, we should note that the 1832 figure for total arable land in *kyŏl* is identical to the 1740 figure and probably derives from it. If population figures rise but the size of the

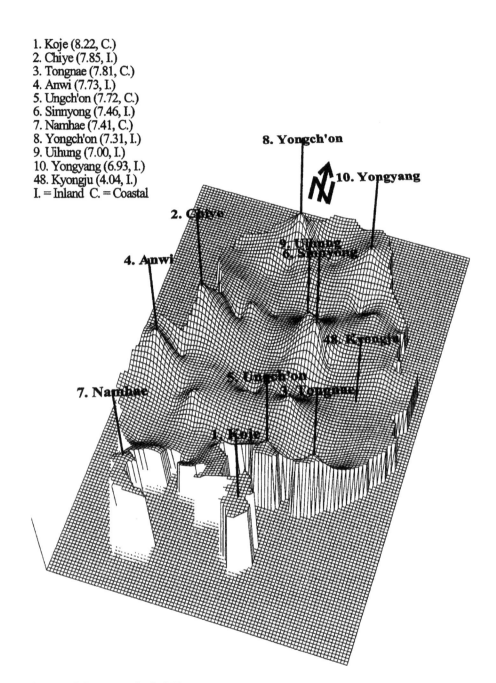

1. Koje (8.22, C.)
2. Chiye (7.85, I.)
3. Tongnae (7.81, C.)
4. Anwi (7.73, I.)
5. Ungch'on (7.72, C.)
6. Sinnyong (7.46, I.)
7. Namhae (7.41, C.)
8. Yongch'on (7.31, I.)
9. Uihung (7.00, I.)
10. Yongyang (6.93, I.)
48. Kyongju (4.04, I.)
I. = Inland C. = Coastal

Figure 3.7 Person per *kyŏl* 1759
Source: *Yŏji tosŏ* (c.1759).

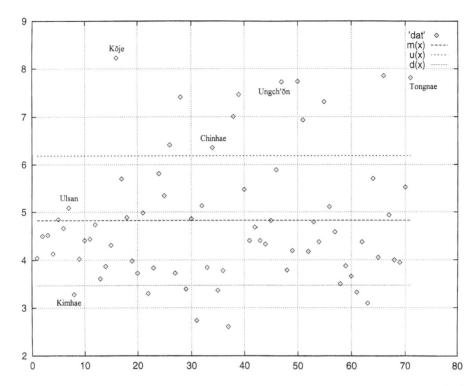

Figure 3.8 Relative distribution of Kyŏngsang-do magistracies in terms of person per *kyŏl* ratios (1759)
Source: Yŏji tosŏ (c.1759).

arable land figure stays the same or even falls, as it did between 1759 and 1832, then the ratio of people to land becomes skewed higher. The 1832 figure for population per *kyŏl* probably is, therefore, somewhat less trustworthy than the 1759 figure.

Finally, other information (1868, 1871, and 1895) is provided in Table 3.1 only for informational purposes and falls outside our analysis. It is included to warn the reader of the dangers inherent in the data. For example, the 1868 *Tongnae-bu saye* gives us a ratio of 8.5 people per *kyŏl* (also recording the 1740 *kyŏl* figure for arable land); the 1871 gazetteer tells us there were a bit over eight people per *kyŏl*, and the 1895 gazetteer records slightly over six people per *kyŏl*. Reasons for excluding these are that the 1868 figures are not comparable, like the 1740 figures, because we lack data from other counties (hence the NA in brackets). The coverage of other counties by the 1871 figures is too sparse to make it reliably comparable to the 1759 and 1832 figures. The 1895 figures were compiled during a period of rapid historical change: dynastic decline, sweeping social change, and the opening of Pusan harbor after 1876. Moreover, important counties useful for comparison are missing from the 1895 data. For example, the 1895 figures omit information about Kyŏngju County, a traditional leader in population and land. The recording of obsolete numbers and incomplete records should remind us of the tentative nature of the conclusions drawn thus far. Fifteenth-century and eighteenth-century data were used in the

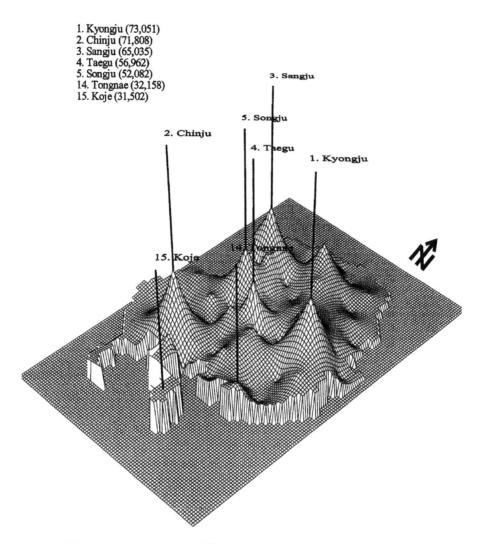

1. Kyongju (73,051)
2. Chinju (71,808)
3. Sangju (65,035)
4. Taegu (56,962)
5. Songju (52,082)
14. Tongnae (32,158)
15. Koje (31,502)

Figure 3.9 Kyŏngsang-do population 1832
Source: Kyŏngsang-do ŭpchi (c.1832).

above discussion, because they offer the most complete records and the best possibility for analysis and not because they offer hard certainty.

To summarize at this point, when we take the relationship between arable land and population into account in terms of people per *kyŏl*, we see dramatic changes in Tongnae's relative standing from the fifteenth century to the eighteenth century. From the first third of the fifteenth century to the mid-eighteenth century, Tongnae became relatively larger in population, relatively larger in the size of its arable land base or tax base, and strikingly denser in the number of people per unit of arable land. We can surmise that Tongnae's relative importance demographically and economically increased. Obviously, its favorable agriculture helped to power the change, but can we hypothesize that maritime connections had any impact? Let us suggest

60

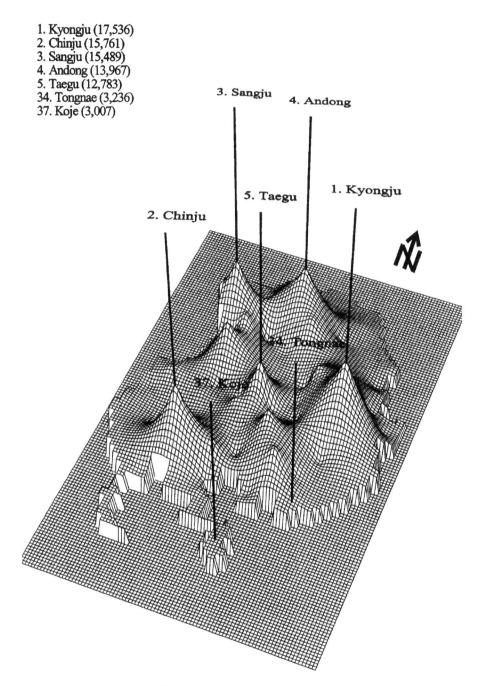

1. Kyongju (17,536)
2. Chinju (15,761)
3. Sangju (15,489)
4. Andong (13,967)
5. Taegu (12,783)
34. Tongnae (3,236)
37. Koje (3,007)

3. Sangju

4. Andong

1. Kyongju

5. Taegu

2. Chinju

Figure 3.10 Kyŏngsang-do arable land 1832
Source: *Kyŏngsang-do ŭpchi* (c.1832).

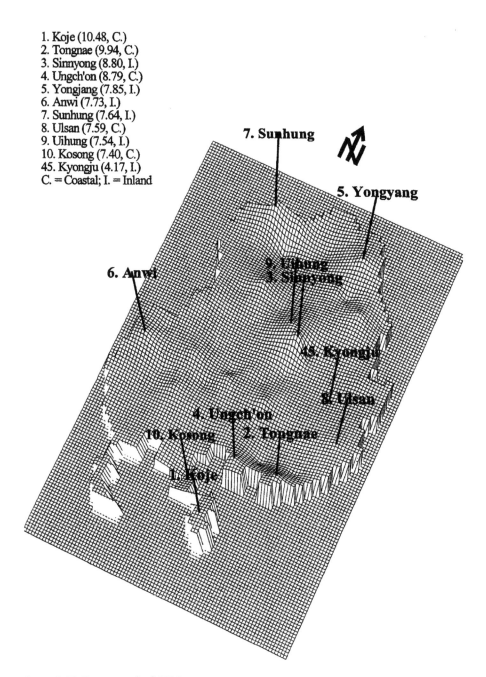

1. Koje (10.48, C.)
2. Tongnae (9.94, C.)
3. Sinnyong (8.80, I.)
4. Ungch'on (8.79, C.)
5. Yongjang (7.85, I.)
6. Anwi (7.73, I.)
7. Sunhung (7.64, I.)
8. Ulsan (7.59, C.)
9. Uihung (7.54, I.)
10. Kosong (7.40, C.)
45. Kyongju (4.17, I.)
C. = Coastal; I. = Inland

7. Sunhung

5. Yongyang

6. Anwi

9. Uihung
3. Sinnyong

45. Kyongju

8. Ulsan

4. Ungch'on

10. Kosong   2. Tongnae

1. Koje

Figure 3.11 Person per *kyŏl* 1832
Source: *Kyŏngsang-do ŭpchi* (c.1832).

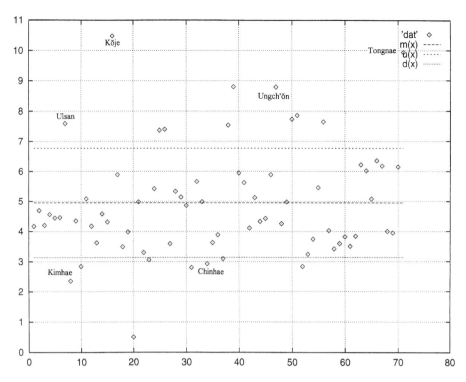

Figure 3.12 Relative distribution of Kyŏngsang-do magistracies in terms of person per *kyŏl* ratios (1832)
Source: *Kyŏngsang-do ŭpchi* (c.1832).

Table 3.1 Summation of information on Tongnae

Year	Population (position in field)	Kyŏl (position in field)	Population/Kyŏl (position in field)	Provincial Mean (standard deviation)
1432/1454	2,416 (50 in 70)	1,723 (47 in 60)	1.402 (33 in 60)	1.48 (0.38)
1740	19,099 [actual count: 21,241] (NA)	3,236 (NA)	6.00 (NA)	(NA)
1759	25,753 (20 in 71)	3,299 (34 in 71)	7.81 (3 in 71)	4.86 (1.40)
1832	32,158 (14 in 71)	3,236 (34 in 71) (same as 1740)	9.94 (2 in 71)	4.95 (1.82)
1868	27,449 (NA)	3,236 (NA) (same as 1740)	8.50 (NA)	(NA)
1871	27,329 (13 in 61)	3,364 (23 in 58)	8.12 (4 in 57)	5.10 (1.64)
1895	20,356 (21 in 51)	3,318 (22 in 47)	6.13 (10 in 41)	5.32 (2.22)

Sources: Sejong sillok chiriji (1432/1454); *Kyŏngsang-do chiriji* (1432/1454); *Tongnae-buji* (1740); *Yŏji tosŏ* (1759); *Tongnae-bu ŭpchi* (1759); *Kyŏngsang-do ŭpchi* (1832); *Tongnae-bu saye* (1868); *Tongnae-bu ŭpchi* (1871); *Tongnae-bu ŭpchi* (1895). For details, see text.

for the moment that there was a connection between fishing and foreign trade and the relative shifts in Tongnae's demographic and economic importance. How might we elaborate such a hypothesis? First, let us consider the *longue durée* of fishing and the general maritime economy and then later go on to the question of the role of trade. By first establishing the environmental circumstances that would enable maritime wealth creation and cataloguing the means of production, we will be in a better position to assess the significance of Tongnae's unique asset, its connection to Japanese trade.

A glimpse of the coastal maritime economy

Three currents flow around southeast Korea and create rich fishing grounds: the northward moving Kuroshio and at least two southward moving colder currents. The Kuroshio originates from a westward-moving, warm, equatorial current that divides at the Philippines, branches northwards along the east coasts of Luzon and Taiwan and divides again at Kyūshū. The main current continues into the north Pacific along the Pacific side of the Japanese archipelago where it meets the less saline Oyashio. A smaller branch heads northwest towards the southern part of the Korean peninsula. Part of this smaller branch flows northward through the Korea/ Tsushima Straits into the Korean East Sea or the Sea of Japan and becomes this sea's major inflow. It is commonly called the Tsushima Current or the East Korea Warm Current. These warm flows on the surface heading north interact with or help to create colder flows moving south, such as the seasonal current from the Yellow Sea and the currents from the East Sea.[28]

Before the transition from the Pleistocene epoch (the last ice age) into our Holocene epoch, or around 10,000 B.P., the Yellow Sea was an exposed part of the Chinese mainland. In fact, the old Yellow River bed is still identifiable, although submerged. The Yellow Sea was flooded with the onset of the Holocene epoch and is today a shallow continental shelf. It is covered on its western side with silt from the Yellow River. The silt overlays an older and deeper sandy layer that extends up to the Korean peninsula. Wintertime water temperatures and the salinity of shallow and deep layers are both generally uniform. Spring and summer bring warmth to the surface, and fresh water from the Chinese rivers dilutes the surface salinity. Deep layers remain cold and saline. The warm northward currents stir the deeper, stagnant, cold water in the summer, and it advances southwards attracting commercial bottom fishes at its leading edge.

On the other side of the peninsula, the Korean East Sea or Sea of Japan resembles the Mediterranean for being connected to adjacent seas by shallow straits. The continental shelf of the Korean East Sea composes about one fifth of its area and is around 200 meters deep, while the deepest parts of the Japan Basin reach 4,049 meters. The southern end of the Korean East Sea has two straits that straddle the island of Tsushima: the Korea Straits between Tsushima and the Korean peninsula and the Tsushima Straits between the island and the Japanese archipelago. Depths in the straits fall to around 100 meters on either side of Tsushima with one small area off the northwest of the island reaching 200 meters. The straits are about 180 kilometers wide at the narrowest point between Honshū and Korea. Tsushima's northern tip is a mere 50 kilometers from Pusan and its southern tip is 80 kilometers from Kyūshū.

64

The southern end of the Korean East Sea receives the Tsushima Current through the straits. These warm, saline waters flow northwards and eventually out of the semi-enclosed sea through the La Perouse Straits and the Tsugaru Straits. The warm current from the south, the formation of deep, cool layers in the Japan, Yamato, and Tsushima basins, and the seasonal heating and cooling of surface waters produce a counterclockwise movement of colder, less saline, oxygen-rich waters. These currents circulate southwards and are known as the Liman Current, the North Korea Cold Current, and the Central Japan Sea Currents.

In short, the colder, deeper waters of the Yellow Sea and the Korean East Sea are laden with oxygen and nutrients. They are pushed southwards by warmer surface currents coming from the south and appear around the shallow, nutrient-rich southern coast of the Korean peninsula to produce rich fishing grounds.[29] If we consider pre-Korean War data that allows a comparison of the entire peninsula's catches, we have few sources, but Lautensach provides 1925 data that identifies the "South Coast Zone" of Kyŏngsang Province and Chŏlla Province as producing 45.2 percent of the Korean catch. The "Japan Sea Zone" (Hamgyŏng Province to North Kyŏngsang Province) came next with 37.5 percent, and the Yellow Sea Zone (North Chŏlla Province to North P'yŏng'an Province) came last with 17.3 percent.[30]

Large ocean currents are not the only conditions that produce good fishing. Sea depths in the interior of Pusan harbor begin around 5 meters and drop to 10 and 20 meters at the mouths of the harbor on the northern and southern sides of Chŏlyŏng Island (modern-day Yŏng Island). Such shallows characterize the coast from Pusan south and west with extensive shallows of 5 meters extending outwards from the mouth of the Naktong River. Pusan is at the northeastern end of a long stretch of southern shallows.[31] Despite the shallows, the coast from Ulsan to Masan does not suffer from the high tidal range of the Yellow Sea coast, and with almost no tidal flats, landings are easy and ports plentiful,[32] characteristics that enabled fishermen to land catches easily and that made the coastline particularly attractive to Japanese traders.

Currents and shallows produce a wide variety of marine resources. For example, the seas around Pusan currently carry around 1,800 different types of invertebrates (including eels and flatfish), about 190 types of seaweed, and 12 types of commercial marine products including: anchovies, croakers, mackerel, squid, octopus, abalone, oysters, crabs, and sea mustard.[33] We can assume that these conditions have existed for some time into the past, possibly as far back as the early Holocene epoch when the Yellow Sea plain was submerged. Prehistoric petroglyphs from the Ulsan area clearly show extensive whaling activity with distinct depictions of different species of whale.[34] Fish and marine mammals were well known, but the oldest known Japanese literary reference to the Kuroshio current is no older than the early nineteenth century.[35] We know that fish stocks were more plentiful prior to industrialized fishing, because herring and cod were commonly caught, but by the late twentieth century, they have either disappeared altogether or have become very rare.[36]

Hints of the importance of the sea to the pre-modern people of Tongnae are legion. One clue is found in the name of the first Buddhist temple listed in the gazetteers: Pŏm'ŏsa, loosely translatable as the "Temple of the Brahma Fish." Many other place names in Tongnae carry dragon and turtle in their names, indicating a close association with the dragon king of the sea and the turtle god of the Naktong

River. Haeundae's Pyŏl-sin *kut* and sacrifices to the God of the Southern Sea (Namhae-sin) also reflect popular concern with the ocean's resources.[37]

Evidence of maritime activity appears in the list of local products in the gazetteers from 1740 to 1871 where we see 32 of 46 products listed as coming from the sea: 15 kinds of fish, five kinds of shell fish, sea cucumber, seaweed, seaweed products (agar-agar), and other marine products.[38] If we compare these records to records from the early Chosŏn period, there is a large expansion in the numbers and types of marine products listed as tribute or local products. This probably indicates a growth in marine production over the entire period. Chi Tu-hwan argues that in the early Chosŏn period, the state viewed marine production as a supplement to farming, but in the late Chosŏn period, the sea took on a larger role. Chi states that the number of house-holds specializing in marine activities rose, the number and amount of the means of production (boats and gear) increased, outside labor was hired, and "capitalist" management appeared to a certain extent.[39] The 1832 and 1871 gazetteers mention fishing boats, salt tubs, and weirs by township. Table 3.2 illustrates the numbers of boats, salt pans, and weirs by year and township (see Map 3.2 for township locations).

In Table 3.2 we can see either a rapid rise in the means of production or innova-tions in recording information. Specifically, in just four decades, the number of "wide" boats rises nearly four times and the number of small boats nearly doubles.[40] The number of salt pans and weirs does not appreciably change between these two years. When compared with early Chosŏn, there is also remarkable consistency, at least in the number of salt pans, for which there is data. The 1425/1432 *Kyŏngsang-do chiriji* lists 40 pans for Tongp'yŏng-hyŏn and 25 for Tongnae-hyŏn, for a total of 65 or exactly the number recorded by the 1871 gazetteer.[41] This is a curious fact, since the higher populat-ion would have been expected to demand and consume more salt. Perhaps, unrecorded private pans proliferated, or production became more efficient.[42] Finally, since fishing boats are not recorded in early Chosŏn documents, a comparison is not possible.

Information on "ownership" of the means of production is sketchy, but we do have information on taxation.[43] Chi Tu-hwan describes a long-running tension between state and private interests for control of salt and fishing. In 1299, King Ch'ungyŏl established a tax on salt and seized private operations from royal clans, temples, and powerful lords. Salt was sold at a fixed price to county offices, leaving the state responsible for management and transport. By the end of the Koryŏ period, the state system had broken down and private interests were again at the fore. In 1394, salt was brought back under state control and sold at market prices for rice or hemp. Private pans and flats were also allowed. Official operations used sailors or commoners who had effectively been reduced to official slavery.[44] Their corvée was fixed, and they had to produce large quotas. After the Imjin Waeran, royal clans and *yangban* acquired salt rights as private interests, but in 1750, King Yŏngjo effectively nation-alized all salt operations and forbade private ownership as an aspect of the Equal-Service Law (*Kyunyŏkbŏp*).[45]

Fixed fishing operations had a similar history. King T'aejo nationalized all fish weirs in his accession speech in 1392. In 1398, they were registered and taxed. Under King Sejo (1455–1468), royals and the ruling class acquired extensive private holdings. The 1485 *Kyŏngguk taejŏn* required the registry of weirs and salt pans and prescribed punishment for private ownership. After the Imjin Waeran, royals rapidly

Table 3.2 Boats, salt pans, and weirs by year

Township	1832 Boats[a] Small	1832 Boats[a] Wide	1832 Salt pans	1832 Weirs (river)	1868 Boats Small	1868 Boats Wide	1868 Salt pans	1868 Weirs[b]	1871 Boats Small	1871 Boats Wide	1871 Salt pans	1871 Weirs (river)
Tong-myŏn	12		23	9					15		23	9
Pusan	39		4	49					65	1	4	49
Upper Sach'ŏn		12								13		
Lower Sach'ŏn	22		7	92					43	13	7	92
Namch'on	19		38	39					47	2	31	39
Kyesŏ[c]										16		
Subtotal	92	12			180	49			170	45		
Total	104		72	189	229		69	212	215		65	189

Sources: Tongnae-bu ŭpchi (1832) in Kim Tong-ch'ŏl, ed., Tongnae saryo, 2, p. 279; Tongnae-bu ŭpchi (1871) in Kim Tong-ch'ŏl, ed., Tongnae saryo, 2, pp. 387–388; and Tongnae-bu saye (1868) (Kyujanggank MS 4272) in Kim Tong-ch'ŏl, ed., Tongnae saryo, 2 (Seoul: Yŏgang Ch'ulp'ansa, 1989): 521–523.

Notes:

a Small boats were sea-going vessels, and wide boats were for the river. See: "Tongnae-bu saye" (1868): 521.

b For 1868, "weirs" included 54 river weirs and 158 sieve nets. Ch'a Mun-sŏp, "Kyunyŏkpŏp ŭi silsi," in Kuksa p'yŏnch'an wiwŏnhoe, ed., Hanguksa, 13 (Seoul: Kuksa p'yŏnch'an wiwŏnhoe, 1984): 250, explains the difference among haejang (boat fishing), haejo (sieves), and pangyŏm (river weirs).

c Kyesŏ Township appears only in the 1871 gazetteer and has only four villages. Its location is unclear. See: Tongnae-bu ŭpchi (1871) in Kim Tong-ch'ŏl, ed., Tongnae saryo, 2, p. 372.

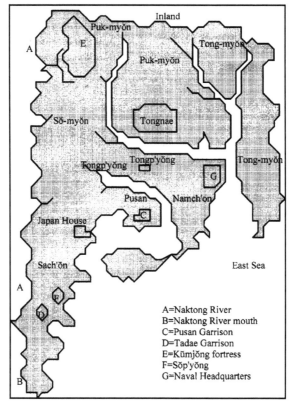

A=Naktong River
B=Naktong River mouth
C=Pusan Garrison
D=Tadae Garrison
E=Kŭmjŏng fortress
F=Sŏp'yŏng
G=Naval Headquarters

Map 3.2 Tongnae townships
Source: Adapted from *Tongnae-bu ŭpchi* (1871).

Table 3.3 1774 duty roster for Tongnae

Classification	Number of people
Military cloth tax	3,322
Subject to military service in the Signal Corps, Messenger Corps, or as stable boys	2,426
Merit subjects descendents' administration; shamans; temple slaves	66
Left naval H.Q. and sailors attached to each garrison	3,391
Tax transport; cloth tax for artisans and musicians	919
Station attendants and gate keepers for schools and academies	649
Servants for banquets at the Japan House	160
Officers and soldiers attached to the county seat	1,197
Petty officials	220
Total	12,450[a]

Source: Chŏngjo sillok, 2:40a–41a (1776.9.22).

Note:
a The actual arithmetic count is 12,350.

seized fishing, salt, and fuel rights, but in 1750, King Yŏngjo declared private usurpa-tion null and void. The actual practice of the maritime economy seems to have worked around commoners "borrowing" (leasing) fishing grounds from the state or from the well-placed "private owners" mentioned above. Local officials controlled most salt operations and administered grounds directly, using *kongch'ŏn* (a class of people often treated as official slaves) as labor and "loaning" some areas to commoners.[46]

To summarize at this point, the southeastern and southern seas were rich fishing grounds, because of a confluence of warm and cold currents. The populace of Tongnae responded to the opportunities offered by fishing and salt manufacture. The Koryŏ and Chosŏn courts also craved these assets as it fought with the expansion of private interests to keep the means of production available for taxation. We can surmise that marine resources supplemented the diets and the economy of the people of Tongnae, but was the bounty of the sea sufficient to explain the concentration of people? We now need to return to the question of Tongnae's monopoly on the trading connection with Japan from 1544 to consider the international dimensions of Tongnae's population concentration.

Was Tongnae's population concentration unusual?

From the early fifteenth century to the mid-eighteenth century, Tongae's relative demographic position in the province grew dramatically. Exactly when or why the shift occurred is unknown, but the timing of the shift and its possible reasons should be discussed together. Let us first consider a population shift prior to 1600. There are two related possibilities. First, population growth may have begun in the last half of the fifteenth century, prior to the 1510 Japanese revolt in the Three Ports. The 1510 revolt closed off all Japanese trading access to Chosŏn until 1512 and access to Pusan until 1544. In connection with this hypothesis, we should keep in mind the general situation of coastal populations in the early Chosŏn period. Namely, as a result of pirate depredations in the fourteenth century, populations fled coastal areas. How long it took people to return is yet unclear, but by 1510, the coasts had enjoyed over a century of peace and the flourishing Japanese port trade in Chep'o (Che Harbor), Pusanp'o (Pusan Harbor), and Yŏmp'o (Yŏm Harbor) probably offered attractions. Until 1510, Japanese carrying proper documentation called primarily at these three ports, but others made landfall almost anywhere they pleased along the coast. From 1510 to 1512, all three ports were closed. From 1512 to 1547, Chep'o was opened, and from 1547 to 1876, Pusanp'o was the sole permissible Japanese landfall in Korea.

When the *Kyŏngsang-do chiriji* (1425/1432) and the *Sejong sillok chiriji* (1454) were being compiled in the fifteenth century, Pusan Harbor was under Tongnae County, Che Harbor under Kimhae County, and Yŏm Harbor under Ulsan County. Since most of this chapter is devoted to Tongnae, let us set Tongnae aside for the moment and consider the situation of the only other officially permitted landfalls, Chep'o (first under Kimhae and from *c.*1450 under Ungch'ŏn County) and Yŏmp'o (Ulsan County). The question is whether the presence or absence of Japanese had any discernable impact on population concentration.

At the time of the compilation of Sejong's *Chiriji*, Che harbor was under Ungsin, which was a subcounty (*sokhyŏn*) of Kimhae County.[47] Since Chep'o was very popular among the Japanese, that may have been a factor pushing Kimhae up to a position as eleventh in 1454 in person to *kyŏl* ratios. The suggestion is that people gathered and lived on other income than agricultural production, i.e. on trade with the Japanese. By 1759, Kimhae had dropped to sixty-eighth position and to seventieth position by 1832. We can see Kimhae's fall in Figures 3.4, 3.8, and 3.12 ($x = 8$). One might conclude that the presence of Japanese in the mid-fifteenth century pushed Kimhae up the relative scale (people gathered to trade with the Japanese) and the later absence of the Japanese pushed it down, but the real reason was that the harbor went out of Kimhae's jurisdiction and so disappeared from its demographic data.

Ungsin, which was a part of Kimhae in the mid-fifteenth century, became Ungch'ŏn County under King Munjong (between 1450 and 1452), but it is absent from Sejong's *Chiriji* as an independent county. By the time we reach the data for 1759, Ungch'ŏn had long been invested as a county and Chep'o was under its jurisdiction. In 1759, Ungch'ŏn was fifth on the relative scale (high concentration), and in 1832, it was fourth highest in concentration of population ($x = 47$ in Figures 3.8 and 3.12).

One might argue that the flourishing Japanese presence in the fifteenth century might explain the high concentration of people in Kimhae, as it appears in the *Kyŏngsang-do chiriji* and *Sejong sillok chiriji*, but Ungch'ŏn's high position in 1759 and 1832 would contradict that assertion. If the Japanese in Chep'o had been such a decisive factor for Kimhae County in the mid-1400s, which is still a possibility, then their absence in 1759 and 1832 should have had the reverse effect and should have driven Ungch'ŏn County down in the ranks in the 1700s. The fact that whichever county possessed Chep'o Harbor remained high in the rankings or, in other words, remained relatively densely populated, means that other factors in addition to a Japanese presence were working to concentrate people around the harbor. Further evidence that the ports attracted people for a variety of reasons can be found in the case of Yŏm Harbor and Ulsan County.

Yŏm Harbor was under Ulsan County throughout the Chosŏn period. In Sejong's *Chiriji*, Ulsan ranked forty-third in person to *kyŏl* ratios, perhaps unusually low if the Japanese had been an important factor in concentrating population. Or, since Yŏmp'o opened to the Japanese only in 1426/1427, perhaps the recorded data precedes the opening.[48] In any event, by 1759, Ulsan had risen to twenty-second place, and by 1832, Ulsan had risen dramatically to eighth place (total field of 71), all in a period when Japanese had presumably not been to Ulsan since the sixteenth century. We can track Ulsan's movements in Figures 3.4, 3.8, and 3.12 ($x = 7$). But do not let simple comparisons mislead us. The data for Ulsan are suspect for 1759 and 1832. Total arable land went unreported for 1759, 1832, 1871, and 1895. The last figure available or the figure used for land in this chapter is from 1454. The population reported in 1832 was identical to 1759, so any apparent changes over the period were relative to the rise and fall of other places. Even with this caveat about obsolete data, Ulsan's rise without the Japanese would suggest that other factors, again perhaps in addition to the Japanese presence, concentrated population.

To sum up at this point, Kimhae County's early high ranking (Che Harbor) may have been partly due to the Japanese presence. Ungch'ŏn County inherited Che Harbor between 1450 and 1452 and Ungch'ŏn displays a rise in population concentration in the 1759 and 1832 data, but the Japanese were not there at that time. Ulsan County (Yŏm Harbor) did not seem to benefit in the early period from the presence of the Japanese, since it was ranked low in the early Chosŏn, when the

Japanese should have been there, and high in the later Chosŏn, when they were not. Of course, Ulsan's data may precede the 1426/1427 opening of Yŏm Harbor to Japanese traders. In short, we must conclude from these cases that the maritime world available to coastal populations was complex and that there were other factors besides trading with the Japanese that concentrated people in the three, old, open ports.

Lest we assume that all coastal areas saw an increasing concentration of people, we should also consider the case of Chinhae County (Figures 3.4, 3.8, and 3.12, x = 34). Chinhae started out as the most concentrated place in 1454, dropped to thirteenth by 1759 and fell to sixty-sixth by 1832. Like Kimhae, Chinhae's fall indicates a relative fall in the number of people concentrated on arable land and stems from a rapid population drop. Between 1759 and 1832, some 27 counties in Kyŏngsang Province saw a drop in population. For example, Kimhae recorded the fourth largest drop in absolute numbers and the seventh largest drop in percentages; it lost 27 percent of its population. Chinhae recorded the tenth largest drop in absolute numbers and the second largest drop in percentages; it lost 54 percent of its population. Such rapid falls beg the investigation of epidemics, famines, forced relocations, and of course administrative changes in recording population, such as Ungsin sub-county being split off from Kimhae and becoming Ungch'ŏn County. By contrast, Ulsan, Tongnae, Kŏje, and whichever county had Che Harbor (Kimhae or Ungch'ŏn from c.1450), all saw their absolute populations grow between 1759 and 1832. Again, we are confronted with evidence showing us complexity and diversity among even geographically close localities.

Like Tongnae, Kŏje County (x = 16) also demonstrated highly unusual growth, moving from fortieth position in 1454 to first in 1759 and 1832 in person to *kyŏl* ratios. Such a rise in the concentration of population may have been partly attribut-able to central government policies to re-populate the offshore islands[49] and partly attributable to the attractions of the maritime economy. If we chiefly credit the attractions of the sea, then Kŏje's dramatic rise among the coastal counties, like that of Ulsan and Ungch'ŏn, indicates that Tongnae's rise was not entirely unusual. Since Tongnae was not unique among coastal counties in its growth, its trend toward population concentration must have been supported by a variety of attractions on offer from the maritime world.

Politically, Tongnae was elevated in the mid-sixteenth century as a result of its designation as the sole Japanese landfall in Korea. The Japan House was shifted from Chep'o to Pusanp'o in 1544, and the Tongnae Magistrate's post was elevated from District Magistrate (*Hyŏllyŏng*, Jr. 5) to Regional Military Commander (*Tohobusa*, Jr. 3) in 1547 in connection with entertaining the Japanese.[50] As Regional Military Commander, the Tongnae Magistrate shared oversight of the Left Naval Headquarters. Politics seems to have followed a concentration of diplomacy, demographics, and trade wealth.

Let us summarize comparisons at this point. Kŏje County and Ungch'ŏn County serve as control variables for the data on Tongnae. Considering that Kŏje and Ungch'ŏn also had high ratios of people to arable land, but had no Japanese element, the attraction of fishing and economies heavily dependent on marine products were probably the most likely reasons for population concentration in these two counties.[51] Could Tongnae's population concentration also be largely hypothecated, as in these other cases, from the lure of fishing, radical improvements in agricultural techniques, a rapid expansion in paddy land, or all of these? We saw above that Tongnae possessed an unusually high concentration of paddy land, higher than nearby coastal counties, and we have seen that the bounty of the sea was available (although contested and controlled). But what of trade and the Japanese? Luckily, we have internal, county-level demographic data for Tongnae that do reveal a concentration of men along the seaside. The concentration may well have been for military and trading reasons associated with the Japan House, but the data is limited to the late Chosŏn period, so we cannot get a "before Japanese" and "after Japanese" snapshot. We turn now to a consideration of the internal demographics of Tongnae County, again in search of traces of a maritime community of fishermen and traders.

Inside Tongnae County: inland and coast

Specific demographic data for Tongnae down to the household level is not extant.[52] Here, we will use general figures found in the Tongnae gazetteers and the *Hogu ch'ongsu* (1789). These sources indicate population data at the township (*myŏn*) level but do not go down to the village level. Depending on the period, there were eight or nine townships. We will refer to eight, since the ninth was never given a separate name but was formed by dividing the largest township (Sach'ŏn) in half.[53] Four of these faced the sea and four were inland. The four which faced the sea were: Sach'ŏn (which contained the Ch'oryang Japan House), Pusan, Namch'on, and Tong-myŏn. The four inland townships were: Tongp'yŏng, Sŏ-myŏn, Puk-myŏn, and Tongnae. Please refer to "Map 3.2: Tongnae Townships."

We have data for three different years: 1740, 1789, and 1867. The 1740 *Tongnae-buji* only mentions numbers of households for each township and offers a baseline for the later information. In the 1789 *Hogu ch'ongsu*, we find population totals for each province from 1395 to 1789, but without any sub-provincial breakdowns, except for 1789. The 1868 *Tongnae-bu saye* has data for 1867.

Table 3.4 Population data to accompany Figure 3.13 and Figures 3.20 to 3.24 (1740)

Township	Households	Population
Inland		
Tongnae	115	. . .
Tongp'yŏng	209	. . .
Sŏ-myŏn	333	. . .
Puyk-myŏn	452	. . .
Subtotal/average	2,109/527	. . .
Coastal		
Tong-myŏn	533	. . .
Pusan	759	. . .
Sach'ŏn	1,064	. . .
Namch'on	998	. . .
Subtotal/average	3,354/839	. . .
Total/average	**5,463/683**	19,099[a] (actual count 21,471)

Source: "Tongnae-buji" in *Tongnae saryo*, 2 (Seoul: Yŏgang Ch'ulp'ansa, 1978): 34–35.

Note:
a Men 9,616 with 230 monks; women 11,625.

Table 3.5 Population data to accompany Figures 3.14, 3.16, 3.18, 3.19, and Figures 3.20 to 3.24 (1789)[a]

Township	Households	Population[b]	Households per village	Population per village	Men	Women	Women/men ratio	Population per household	Men per household	Women per household
Tongnae	1,414	5,946	64.3	270.3	2,775	3,171	+6.66	4.2	1.96	2.24
Tongp'yŏng	254	1,126	42.3	187.7	474	652	+15.81	4.4	1.87	2.57
Sŏ-myŏn	491	1,915	49.1	191.5	925	990	+3.39	3.9	1.88	2.02
Puyk-myŏn	584	2,464	58.4	246.4	1,116	1,348	+9.42	4.2	1.91	2.31
Tong-myŏn	725	3,417	48.3	227.8	1,520	1,897	+11.03	4.7	2.1	2.62
Pusan	972	3,696	97.2	369.6	1,851	1,845	−0.2	3.8	1.90	1.90
Sach'ŏn	1,242	4,949	82.8	334.4	2,428	2,521	+1.88	3.98	1.95	2.03
Namch'on	1,325	5,351	82.8	329.9	2,524	2,827	+0.56	4.0	1.90	2.13
Total/average	Total: 7,007	Total: 28,864	Average: 65.65	Average: 269.7	Total: 13,613	Total: 15,251	Average (%): 6.07	Average: 4.15	Average: 1.93	Average: 2.23

Source: *Hogu ch'ongsu* (Seoul: Seoul Taehakkyo Ch'ulp'anbu, 1971): 276.

Notes:
a 8 townships; 104 villages.
b 13,613 men; 15,251 women.

1 Tongnae-myon (1,115)
2 Sach'on-myon (1,064)
3 Namch'on-myon (998)
4 Pusan Garrison (Pusan-myon: 759)
5 Tong-myon (533)
6 Puk-myon (452)
7 So-myon (333)
8 Tongp'yong-myon (209)
9 Left Naval Headquarters
10 Tadae Garrison
11 Japan House

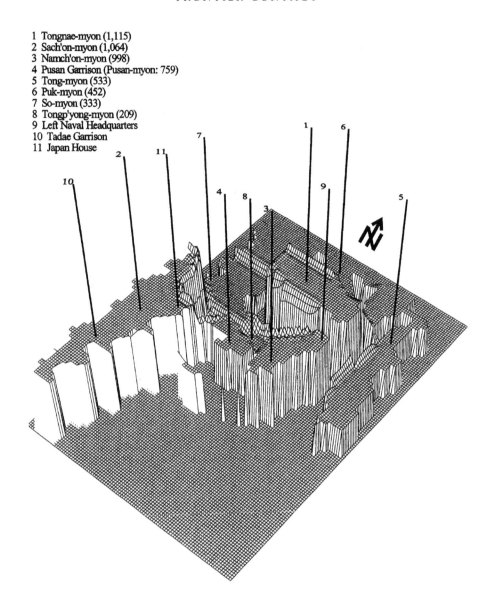

Figure 3.13 Households by township 1740
Source: Tongnae-bu chi (1740).

If we begin with the only available variable for all three years (households by townships, Figures 3.13, 3.14, and 3.15), there is no appreciable comparative difference among the three years. Tongnae and Sach'ŏn townships consistently lead as first and second, followed by Namch'on (third) and Pusan (fourth) for all three years. Three of the four coastal townships and the township where the county seat was located (Ŭp-myŏn or Tongnae-myŏn) contained the largest concentration of households.

Population data (Figure 3.16 and Figure 3.17) confirm the concentration of people around the county seat and in the coastal townships. In 1789, Tongnae led, followed

1 Tongnae-myon (1,414)
2 Sach'on-myon (1,325)
3 Namch'on-myon (1,242)
4 Pusan Garrison (Pusan-myon 972)
5 Tong-myon (725)
6 Puk-myon (584)
7 So-myon (491)
8 Tongp'yong-myon (254)
9 Left Naval Headquarters
10 Tadae Garrison
11 Japan House

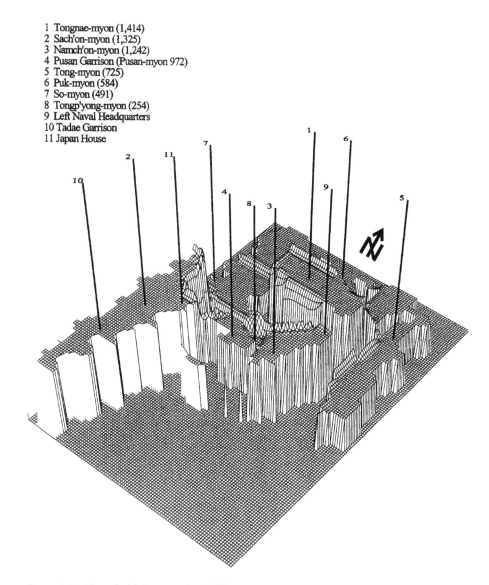

Figure 3.14 Households by township 1789
Source: *Hogu ch'ongsu* (1789).

by Sach'ŏn, Namch'on, Pusan, and Tong-myŏn. In 1867, Sach'ŏn led, followed by Tongnae, Namch'on, Pusan, and Tong-myŏn.

Both household and population data point to a coastal concentration of people. After reviewing the data for 1789, the most detailed available, we can confirm that the county was demographically composed of two parts: an inland area (Puk-myŏn, Sŏ-myŏn, Tongp'yŏng, and Tongnae) and a coastal area (Namch'on, Pusan, and Sach'ŏn). Tong-myŏn, although geographically coastal, seems to have had more in common with the inland area than with the coastal area. Specific differences make

75

1 Tongnae-myon (1,597)
2 Sach'on-myon (1,468)
3 Namch'on-myon (1,049)
4 Pusan Garrison (Pusan-myon 1,047)
5 Tong-myon (738)
6 Puk-myon (668)
7 So-myon (659)
8 Tongp'yong-myon (211)
9 Left Naval Headquarters
10 Tadae Garrison
11 Japan House

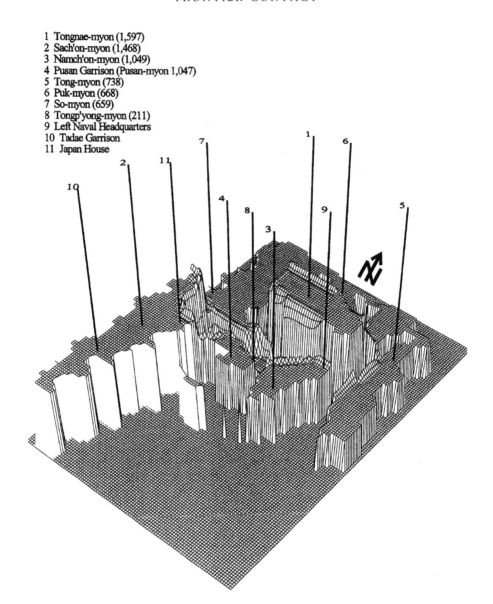

Figure 3.15 Households by township 1868
Source: Tongnae-bu saye (1868).

this general statement true. Noticeable differences between the two areas appear first in the number of households per village (see Figure 3.18). The coastal area of Pusan, Sach'ŏn, and Namch'on tended to have villages from 30 percent to 100 percent larger than inland areas. Consequently, the population of individual coastal villages was similarly larger (20 percent to 90 percent). A startling difference also appears in the relative sizes of the female/male populations. While the inland villages had from 3.39 percent to 15.81 percent more women, the coastal villages never increased

1 Tongnae-myon (5,946)
2 Sach'on-myon (5,351)
3 Namch'on-myon (4,949)
4 Pusan Garrison (Pusan-myon 3,696)
5 Tong-myon (3,417)
6 Puk-myon (2,464)
7 So-myon (1,915)
8 Tongp'yong-myon (1,126)
9 Left Naval Headquarters
10 Tadae Garrison
11 Japan House

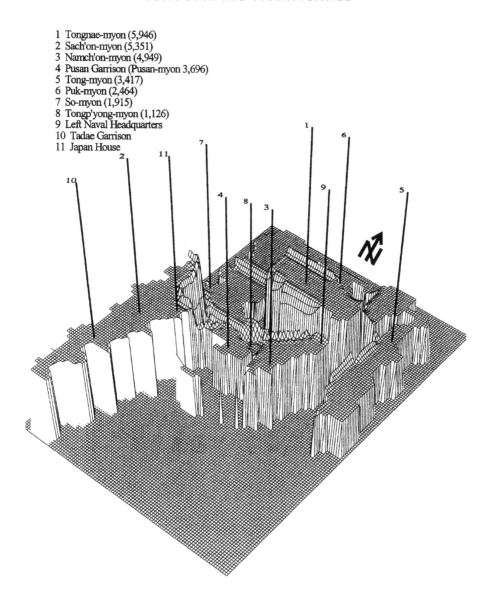

Figure 3.16 Population by township 1789
Source: *Hogu ch'ongsu* (1789).

beyond 1.88 percent more women than men. These findings probably indicate concentrations of soldiers and fishermen as well as traders. Figure 3.19 shows the relative
distribution of female:male ratios and the concentration of the women away from
the coast. In short, coastal townships had large villages and many more men.

Finally, let us briefly consider absolute figures for households (see Figures 3.20,
3.21 and 3.22) to see where growth occurred within Tongnae County. When we
compare the 1740 *Tongnae-buji*, the 1789 *Hogu ch'ongsu* and the 1868 *Tongnae-bu
saye*, we can see a general growth in the number of households in all townships

77

1 Sach'on-myon (6,422)
2 Tongnae-myon (4,663)
3 Namch'on-myon (3,914)
4 Pusan Garrison (Pusan-myon 3,714)
5 Tong-myon (2,920)
6 So-myon (2,715)
7 Puk-myon (2,167)
8 Tongp'yong-myon (924)
9 Left Naval Headquarters
10 Tadae Garrison
11 Japan House

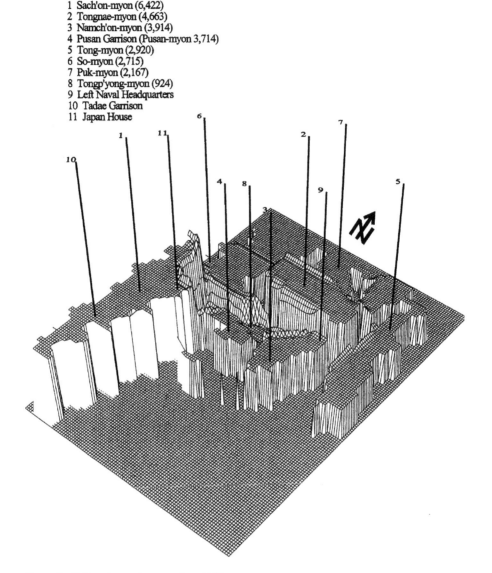

Figure 3.17 Population by township 1868
Source: Tongnae-bu saye (1868).

except Tongp'yŏng (inland) and Namch'on (coastal) (Figures 3.20 and 21). These two townships adjoin each other and Namch'on opens on the eastern part of the harbor. Why these two townships did not grow is unknown. We can also see that overall population, indicated by the number of households, was concentrated in the coastal areas (Figure 3.22).

When we look at percentages of change in households among the townships, Sŏ-myŏn clearly leads in growth (average 40.8 percent). Namch'on clearly lags in growth (average 4.45 percent) and most other townships fall in a band, averaging

Table 3.6 Population data to accompany Figures 3.15, 3.17 and Figures 3.20 to 3.24 (1867)

Township	Households	Population	Population per household
Tongnae	1,597	4,663	2.92
Tongp'yŏng	211	924	4.38
Sŏ-myŏn	659	2,715	4.12
Puyk-myŏn	668	2,167	3.24
Tong-myŏn	738	2,920	3.96
Pusan	1,047	3,714	4.54
Sach'ŏn (Upper)	460	1,825	3.97 (4.37)[b]
Sach'ŏn (Lower)	1,008	4,597	4.56 (4.37)[b]
Namch'on	1,049	3,914	3.73
Total/average	Total: 7,437	Total: 27,449[a]	Average: 3.82 (3.78)[c]

Source: "Tongnae-bu saye" in *Tongnae saryo*, pp. 455–457.

Notes:

a The stated figure is 27,439, but the actual additional is 27,449.

b Sach'ŏn is divided into Upper and Lower in this document, but is listed as a single township in other documents and is so considered in this study. When we take the "Population per household" for the combined Upper and Lower Sach'ŏn, we have the figure in parentheses: 4.37.

c When we combine Upper and Lower Sach'ŏn, we have an overall average "Population per household" of 3.78.

from 17.7 percent to 21.8 percent (see Figures 3.23 and 3.24). We might hypothesize that Tongnae Township probably grew as a result of the demands of government installations; Sŏ-myŏn and Puk-myŏn probably grew as a result of land reclamation from the Naktong River delta or river access to the sea, and Sach'ŏn and Pusan's growth was probably due to expanded fishing and trade with the Japanese in the Japan House.

Our statements on demography are tentative and included here primarily to suggest the general demographic complexion of Tongnae County. We have, as yet, no data to give us an economic map of the county, since the most detailed economic document on the county, the 1868 *Tongnae-bu saye*, does not indicate its tax income by township. Furthermore, until other coastal counties are subjected to a similar type of analysis of comparing townships, we will remain uncertain as to the typicality of Tongnae's population dispersion. Of 14 candidate counties briefly examined, most lack the necessary detailed information to determine township outlines, which would enable geographic comparisons. Thus far, only Chinhae and Ulsan counties offer some promise for analysis, and a rough, preliminary examination reveals the following. In 1759, Chinhae's population was concentrated in the two coastal townships. Women predominated in these two townships, by about 8 percent in the most populous township and by about 28 percent in the other. Men predominated by about 6 percent in the sole inland township. In 1759, Ulsan's population was concentrated in the coastal townships or those townships along the southern banks of the T'aehwa River. Among Ulsan's 11 townships, women predominated by large margins in all except two, which were coastal townships, but these two were among the three least populated.[54] Our tentative conclusion, based on this cursory comparison of Tongnae, Chinhae, and Ulsan, is that population does concentrate in coastal areas of seaside counties, but large numbers of men may not follow that concentration. The large concentration of men in the most populous

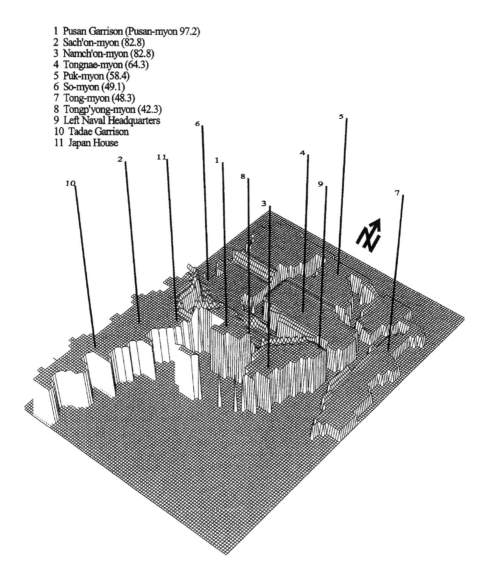

1 Pusan Garrison (Pusan-myon 97.2)
2 Sach'on-myon (82.8)
3 Namch'on-myon (82.8)
4 Tongnae-myon (64.3)
5 Puk-myon (58.4)
6 So-myon (49.1)
7 Tong-myon (48.3)
8 Tongp'yong-myon (42.3)
9 Left Naval Headquarters
10 Tadae Garrison
11 Japan House

Figure 3.18 Households by village 1789
Source: Hogu ch'ongsu (1789).

townships seems to be an unusual aspect of Tongnae. The fact that Tongnae's coastal townships either contained or were near the Japan House suggests that the men were concentrated for trade or administration connected with the Japanese.

Reliability of data

We have, so far, taken little consideration of the reliability of available data. Rather than scatter comments throughout the text, I have gathered most questions of reliability here to aid the reader. Many doubts remain and much work has yet to be done.

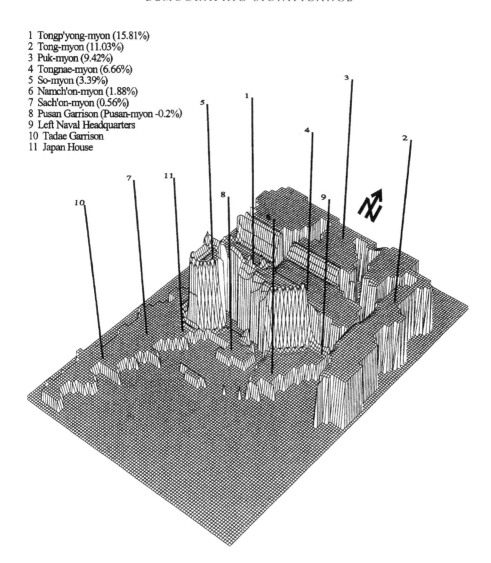

1 Tongp'yong-myon (15.81%)
2 Tong-myon (11.03%)
3 Puk-myon (9.42%)
4 Tongnae-myon (6.66%)
5 So-myon (3.39%)
6 Namch'on-myon (1.88%)
7 Sach'on-myon (0.56%)
8 Pusan Garrison (Pusan-myon -0.2%)
9 Left Naval Headquarters
10 Tadae Garrison
11 Japan House

Figure 3.19 Concentration of women 1789
Source: Hogu ch'ongsu (1789).

All of the province-wide data may be impossible to compare synchronically because of uneven reporting. For example, some figures may represent 80 percent of what actually existed and others only 50 percent. Under-reporting of information associated with taxation (e.g. able-bodied men or land holdings or land production) can be generally assumed, since it seems to be a fact that peoples everywhere and at all times seek to avoid taxation, but it is impossible to assume that the degree of under-reporting was consistent across the province. The provincial data used above assumes comparability, but there is no certainty of this. Nevertheless, the consistency of Tongnae's relative position at different points in time indicates that there must have been some consistency in reporting. For example, the similarity of relative positions

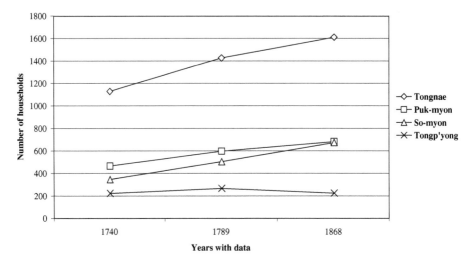

Figure 3.20 Inland households
Sources: *Tongnae-buji* (c.1740), *Hogu ch'ongsu* (c.1789) and *Tongnae-bu saye* (c.1868).

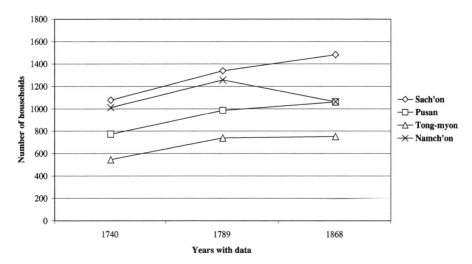

Figure 3.21 Coastal households
Sources: *Tongnae-buji* (c.1740), *Hogu ch'ongsu* (c.1789) and *Tongnae-bu saye* (c.1868).

in 1759 and 1832 indicates a degree of consistency in reporting across the province, but we still do not know if some counties reported only 50 percent while others reported as much as 80 percent or even 100 percent.

Two problems relate to comparing diachronically fifteenth-century land tax data with eighteenth- and nineteenth-century land tax data. The first is semantic and the second is historical. First, the data from the fifteenth century was referred to as *kanjŏn*, whereas the data from the eighteenth and nineteenth centuries was called *wŏnjangbu kyŏl*. *Kanjŏn* is taken to mean arable land. The *Sejong sillok chiriji* gives us the *kanjŏn* figure as the only figure for land and supplies notes to indicate what portion was

82

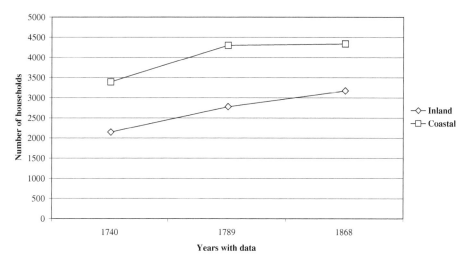

Figure 3.22 Number of households: inland and coast
Sources: Tongnae-buji (c.1740), *Hogu ch'ongsu* (c.1789) and *Tongnae-bu saye* (c.1868).

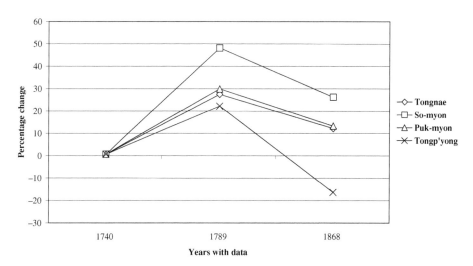

Figure 3.23 Inland household growth
Sources: Tongnae-buji (c.1740), *Hogu ch'ongsu* (c.1789) and *Tongnae-bu saye* (c.1868).

paddy land. If *kanjŏn* and *wŏnjangbu kyŏl* are essentially the same in meaning[55] – at least, that is how they are treated here – then certain general statements are possible. For example, a comparison of fifteenth-century paddy-land figures with eighteenth-century paddy-land figures shows an increase, county-by-county, of from 51 *kyŏl* to 3,601 *kyŏl* or an average, province-wide increase in paddy land of 788 *kyŏl*. We have data for 64 counties, of which 56, or 88 percent, increased their paddy-land holdings. Further examination of these cases would shed light on questions related to changing land use and the distribution of improvements in agricultural techniques between the fifteenth and eighteenth centuries.

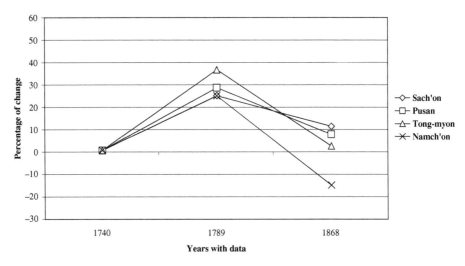

Figure 3.24 Coastal household growth
Sources: *Tongnae-buji* (c.1740), *Hogu ch'ongsu* (c.1789) and *Tongnae-bu saye* (c.1868).

The second problem is historical: can we make province-wide comparisons between the fifteenth century and the eighteenth and nineteenth centuries and ignore the changes in taxation as a result of the Tribute Tax Law (*Kongbŏp*) of 1444 and the Law of Uniform Land Tax (*Taedongbŏp*) from the seventeenth century? The comparisons presented here take no account of any changes to the basic land figures that may have derived from the imposition of a complex system of land ranking and the assessment of regional tribute goods as was imposed with the *Kongbŏp* of 1444. Nor does the analysis consider the post-Imjin Waeran substitution of grains for those same regional tribute goods as a result of the imposition of the *Taedongbŏp* from the seventeenth century. For these reasons, it is not clear if the comparison of fifteenth-century data with eighteenth- and nineteenth-century data is a viable comparison and requires further consideration. Invalidation of the comparison would nullify the chief finding of this chapter: Tongnae's population underwent a process of concentration. If the data is not comparable, then we do not know if Tongnae's population became denser and a search for the causes of the concentration becomes pointless. The analysis above is based on the assumption that a diachronic comparison is valid, because the data does not come from the transition period when the new policies were being unevenly applied but from periods either before implementation (1432) or after complete implementation (1740, etc.). This does not assure comparability across time, but it does argue for consistency across the province. Again, we must remember that the degree of Tongnae's population concentration was determined by its relative position vis-à-vis other counties. For a relative comparison to be valid, all data must be affected by the same policies, and, as pointed out above, to be reported in the same way. In sum, the data was probably affected by the same policies, but we cannot be sure that all counties reported their data with the same degree of accuracy.

Finally, mention must be made of the difficulties encountered in trying to draw the boundaries of townships for Chosŏn-era counties, such as has been done here for Tongnae. Pre-modern gazetteers often carry maps with the names of major sites, townships, and even villages, but the maps never have jurisdictional lines indicated for those townships, merely the names inscribed somewhere on the map, presumably in the general area where the township was located. The accompanying gazetteer text is usually careful to mention township names but rarely lists village names underneath the townships. Thus, drawing the boundaries of a township can never be precise. It is essential to know the boundaries of townships in order to plot the demographics of a county, as has been done for Tongnae, because demographic data is occasionally available for townships but not for villages. Since local magistrates must have needed to know precise jurisdictional lines, presumably, accurate lines can someday be drawn based on county records. For some sixteen coastal counties in Kyŏngsang Province, quickly usable matches of township (demographics) with village names (geographic extent) are available for only three counties: Tongnae, Ulsan, and Chinhae, or the three mentioned above. Of these three, only Tongnae has been examined in detail in this study. Eventually, accurate jurisdictional lines may be drawn for other counties, and Chosŏn's southeastern seaboard will more clearly emerge.

Estimates of the number of Korean officials

Another approach to the question of the Japan House's impact on the demographics of Tongnae might be to attempt to estimate the numbers of people directly associated with the Japanese presence, since we have information on officials connected to the Japan House. Yi Wan-yŏng gives us the highest estimates, which he derives from the *Fuzan-fu shi genkō*, a history of Pusan written sometime in the colonial period in Japanese.[56] Yi suggests a range of from 3,000 to 5,000 civil and military officials connected with the Japan House,[57] but Kim Ŭi-hwan points out that the *Fuzan-fu shi genkō* gives no citation for its information.[58] If we consider Yi's numbers for officials as a part of the population, we have a range of from 10.4 percent to 17.3 percent of the total population of the entire county. For the townships, we have a range of from 33.2 percent to 55.3 percent for Sach'ŏn and Pusan, and from 56.1 percent to 93.4 percent for just Sach'ŏn. If we calculate for dependents as well,[59] Yi's 3,000 to 5,000 officials grows to from 11,460 to 20,750 people or from 39.7 percent to 71.9 percent of the total population of Tongnae in 1789. His figures are certainly too high, since he does not distinguish between military personnel stationed in Tongnae, because of the general security concerns associated with defending the coast, such as is represented by the Left Naval Headquarters (*Sugun'yŏng*), and those there to manage the trade associated with the Japan House.

Kim Ŭi-hwan estimates that about 150 Korean officials were directly attached to the Japan House or up to 1,000 people if one includes dependents.[60] When we add up the officials actually mentioned by Kim, we have 135. When we calculate for dependents, we have a total population (officials plus family) of from 515.7 to 560.25 or, for simplicity's sake, we could say 600 people. The estimate of 600 people is 2.1 percent of the total population (28,864) of Tongnae in 1789.[61] Those 600 would have formed 6.6 percent of the population of Pusan and Sach'ŏn Townships combined (9,047) or 11.2 percent of just Sach'ŏn's population (5,351) in 1789. In general, then, Kim's estimate means that from the eighteenth century to the mid-nineteenth century, about one person in 50 in all of Tongnae was directly and officially connected to the Japan House. Kim's figures, however, are probably too low, since he makes no mention of military personnel stationed in Tongnae because of the Japan House.

Fortunately, we have a rather detailed breakdown of the corvée tax roster that clarifies government personnel in the county. In 1774, Tongnae Magistrate Yu Tang memorialized the throne requesting changes in the categories for duty taxes and the remission of taxes to ease the burden on Tongnae's populace. In the course of his memorial, he listed the various categories of service required in the county and the specified number of people for each category. His problem was that the county lacked a sufficient population to bear the burden. The categories and personnel numbers in his report are listed in Table 3.3.

Of the military personnel mentioned, it is impossible to conclude which category was directly related to the presence of the Japan House. There were several garrisons in the county aside from the Left Naval Headquarters, but as with all coastal defense, their presence was related to the general defense and not necessarily related to the trade with Japan. Signal officers and messengers might report the arrival of Japanese ships. The Japan House was probably located in Pusan Harbor because of the presence of the Left Naval Headquarters and not the other way around. The broader defensive capabilities of the Left Naval Headquarters were designed to counter Japanese piracy or invasions launched from Tsushima or Kyūshū and coincidentally related to the actual presence of Japanese traders. The only category directly connected to the Japan House appears to be that of 160 servants for banquets, a category not mentioned by Kim Ŭi-hwan.

If we combine this number of 160 with Kim Ŭi-hwan's figures, then we might be able to estimate those directly associated with the Japan House. In short, 160 servants plus 135 civil officials is 295 government personnel. When we consider their households, we have from 1,127 to 1,224 people. If we take the average of these two estimates (1,175), we can estimate that about 4 percent of the entire county's population was officially connected to the Japan House in 1789: 13 percent of Pusan and Sach'ŏn townships' population and 22 percent of Sach'ŏn's population. In general, perhaps one in ten persons in the general vicinity of the Japan House was connected to its affairs in an official capacity.

Both Yi Wan-yŏng and Kim Ŭi-hwan's estimates are inconclusive, even after we introduce Yu Tang's memorial, because data are yet insufficient. Moreover, there is another element in the population for which we still do not even have estimates. Namely, how many Korean merchants were in Tongnae as a direct consequence of the Japan House?

Trade with the Japanese

We should now return to the central question of this chapter: when and why did Tongnae's population become so concentrated as to make Tongnae one of the densest counties in Kyŏngsang Province? Above, we considered growth in the fifteenth and sixteenth centuries in connection with the ports open to Japanese traders. Comparing Tongnae to other counties, it seems apparent that the presence of Japanese traders was but one part of a maritime economy and possibly not decisive as a lure. When we then turned to the internal demographics of the county, the division between inland and coastal townships became clear, but the Japanese presence still did not loom out as the main factor that concentrated people. We can estimate the numbers of officials needed to cope with the Japanese, but these numbers are not great. Let us now consider the seventeenth to nineteenth centuries and attempt to estimate the impact on local society of the trade with the Japanese.

Our second hypothesis for population growth in Tongnae would place the population expansion in the seventeenth century, deriving in part from the encampment of Hideyoshi's troops and the logistics and supply demands of a foreign army and navy. After the war, Pusan again became the only port open to the Japanese and trading operations created new demands. In the post-invasion period, the private trade recovered quickly. At that time, Pusan probably attracted people for trade, for government provisioning operations in connection with the Japan House, and for defense and security reasons related to the Left Naval Headquarters and the presence of the Japanese. We have discussed officials, and now we should turn to merchants. In order to discuss merchants, we must explain the trading regime.

Yi Wŏn-kyun describes late Chosŏn commerce as generally depressed. The primitive state of agriculture, transport, and currency conspired with general self-sufficiency and conscious anti-mercantile government policies to suppress merchant activities. However, in Tongnae, there were few anti-mercantile *yangban* (in our discussion of the social position of merchants, we will return to the question of mercantilistic elites), and the presence of the Japan House produced a prosperous trade that sparked the local economy. From the seventeenth century, there were at least three separate markets aside from those connected with the Japan House where local people exchanged agricultural goods, handicrafts, or traded with itinerant peddlers.[62] Since the largest trading opportunities were connected to the Japan House, we should turn to that topic and sketch the form and content of the trade. We will also look at the current state of the debate over trade volume, what that can tell us about the relative significance of the trade, and conclude with a discussion of Korean merchants.

Trade at the Japan House occurred in four forms: tribute, official, private, and illegal trade (smuggling). A number of scholars have examined in detail the system and goods associated with tribute, official, and private trade, and their studies provide the basis of the following discussion. Due to the complicated nature and dearth of studies on smuggling, we will set that problem aside for future consideration.

Many scholars have described the conduct of pre-1600 trade and hinted at its scope; all have made reference to Asian trading spheres.[63] Trading routes connecting Korea, Japan, and China have existed from antiquity. Koreans have always had a land route to China, but Japanese have always had to cross water to reach the continent. Many famous Japanese monks made pilgrimages from Japan through Korea to China, but it might be more to our point to consider traders. Famous among these, from the Japanese monk Ennin's diary, is Kung-bok or Chang Po-go (*d*. 846), a sea-faring merchant admiral operating from the southwestern coast of Korea who linked Tang China, Silla Korea, and early Heian Japan. Other evidence of an extensive regional trading network spanning centuries comes from the marine excavation of a sunken vessel off the coast of Mokp'o at Sin'an, dating from about 1323. This find, in particular, is significant as it indicates that Chinese goods were being shipped to Japan via Korea aboard a Chinese ship manned by an international crew. Since our period is still later, we should now turn to an example of a Hakata trader, Sō Kin (d. 1454), active during the early fifteenth century to illustrate trading practices between Japan and Korea at that time. Following our discussion of Sō Kin's period, we will explain the post-1600 situation.

As revealed in the Ryūkyū *Rekidai Hōan*, Satsuma documents,[64] and the Chosŏn Veritable Records, there existed, at least by the early fifteenth century, several routes that intersected at Hakata in northern Kyūshū, connecting Korea to a wider trading world. One route stretched from Southeast Asia north through the Ryūkyūs to Satsuma in southern Kyūshū. From there, traders traveled north to the merchant city of Hakata and from Hakata headed east through Akamagaseki (Shimonoseki) to enter the Inland Sea for Hyōgo and the Kinai region. Another route also came from the south through the Ryūkyūs and Satsuma to Hakata but then extended on to Tsushima and finally to Korea. A third route directly connected Hakata with Ming China. The direct route to the Ming was most vulnerable to the vagaries of international diplomacy and consequently was the least traveled (only 19 known instances in contrast to over 200 known trading embassies through the southern route).[65]

The case of Sō Kin, a Hakata merchant of the fifteenth century, illustrates many important points concerning early Chosŏn period relations with Japan.[66] We will consider his case for what it can tell us about the conduct and content of the trade, but first we should ask who he was and how he was able to trade. Sō Kin's social identity is the subject of some debate. Arimitsu Yasushige refers to him as a merchant. Tanaka Takeo and Ueda Junichi suggest that he was a Zen monk. The picture is complicated by Song Hŭi-gyŏng's diary of his embassy to Japan in 1419–1420. Herein, Song refers to Sō Kin as a monk,[67] but Song used the word monk rather indiscriminately for any Japanese who had taken the tonsure. At the time, the tonsure was popular among the Japanese warrior class as an expression of personal grief. Saeki Kōji believes that, considering Sō Kin's wide circle of acquaintants, extensive travels, and knowledge of Inland Sea pirate customs, Sō Kin was possibly a secular monk and definitely a rich Hakata merchant with very good connections, who, through those connections, was able to expand his business to include the Korea trade. In 1455, the Chosŏn court heard a posthumous report on Sō Kin and this constitutes the most detailed information we have. He was described as a very rich man who was able to avoid losing everything in the conflict between the Ōuchi and the Kyūshū Tandai, the Shōni, when they fought for control of Hakata.[68] The shogun (unidentified in the *Sillok*) liked Sō Kin and gave him a writ that ensured his warm welcome everywhere. He died in the eighth month of 1455 leaving four sons.[69]

In a world where trade was dependent on diplomacy, we naturally see Sō Kin as an active diplomat. He aided the Korean embassy to Kyoto, led by Song Hŭi-gyŏng, to negotiate their way through the pirate world of the Inland Sea in 1419–1420, and he visited Korea for the first time in 1420, probably in exchange for his services to the Korean embassy.[70] By the end of 1425, Sō Kin had visited Korea five times, accompanying the Kyūshū Tandai's retainers and the Ashikaga envoys or "Envoys of the King of Japan" (Nihon kokuō-shi). Although the *Sillok* is not specific, Sō Kin probably carried the Tandai's letter (sŏgye), since the Tandai was then resident in Hakata. In 1425, Shibukawa (the Kyūshū Tandai) was eliminated by Shōni and Kikuchi,[71] and in the same year, on his fifth trip to Korea, Sō Kin obtained his own copper seal (tosŏ). It may have been his service to Ambassador Song that got him his own seal; the *Sillok* simply states that he requested a seal and such was granted.[72] The possession of a seal entitled him or his representative to receive Korean receptions and provisions in the ports, travel to the capital for a state reception, including an audience with the king, and engage in official and private trade.[73] After 1425, Sō Kin's seal was used more than 30 times to visit Korea. Sō Kin was an important diplomat. He conveyed news of Ashikaga Yoshimochi's death in 1428 and informed the Chosŏn court of his younger brother's succession.[74] He advised the Korean court on the subject of whether to dispatch a Korean envoy to Kyoto at that time. At the same time, he suggested strengthening contacts with the western Japanese lords Ōtomo and Ōuchi,[75] possibly as a way to contribute to their cooperation in securing the safety of Korean envoys. In this same year an impostor envoy, posing as Sō Kin's man, was turned away, because his letter (*sŏgye*) from Sō Sadamori, governor of Tsushima, was irregular. It had no list of tribute items to accompany it, no seal imprint, and certain characters were irregular.[76] In 1430, Sō Kin went to Korea for the first time as an envoy for the shogun; in this case, it was Yoshinori (1394–1441),[77] who was anxious to re-establish trade ties with China and expand ties with Korea. Sō Kin was received despite that late in the previous year Sejong lamented before his ministers that Chosŏn need not send a T'ongsinsa, since the Japanese had not sent an embassy to inform the Chosŏn court of the previous shogun's death (1425) nor had they sent an embassy announcing the new accession (1429/3/15). The shogun's advisors (*shitsuji*) had merely sent Sō Kin to request gifts for celebration.[78] He also transmitted to Korea information on pirate activities via a representative in 1439.[79] After 1439/1440, envoys from Sō Kin presumably carried an access permit (*mun'in*) from the Tsushima governor (*shugo*), since it is from about this time that the Tsushima governor was established as the Korean gatekeeper for Kyūshū-based traders going to Chosŏn.[80] The added documentation from Tsushima (requiring some form of "taxation") would have cut into Sō Kin's profits. In 1447, he presented himself at court, made the proper bows and was praised by the Crown Prince: "You have come from afar after a long time; [we] approve of your sincerity."[81] Sō Kin died in 1454, and the Chosŏn court learned that his dying wish was to give his youngest son his seal.[82] This son's name appears in the *Haedong chegukki* (1471) as a sealholder with the explanation that he was given a seal in 1455.[83] In fact, in 1433, this same son sent a representative in his own name and there was discussion at the court whether to reject him because he lacked a patent of identification (*t'ongsin*). His defenders argued that his father was well known, had been of service, and was then in China.[84] The son was received. Another son was received as a shogunal envoy in 1475.[85] Sō Kin was so famous at the Chosŏn court that, in 1471, Hakata was described as "the place where Sō Kin lives."[86] Sō Kin was only one individual who moved in high, elite circles, even trading with Ming China.[87] Because of his high connections and fame, Sō Kin's case is not typical, but since we know of his activities in some detail, his history can be instructive of how trade was conducted and of what was traded between Korea and Japan in the early fifteenth century. If we turn to the content of the trade, Sō Kin's connections become apparent, and we can take reports of his cargo manifests as representative of the range of Korea–Japan trade at this time.

Saeki Kōji has classified Sō Kin's exports to Korea into three categories: Japanese products, Chinese products, and Southeast Asian goods. From Southeast Asia came:

rhino horn (Africa), turmeric (India), betony, garu-wood or lign aloes (India, Southeast Asia), and sappan wood (Sumatra and Cambodia), or spices, perfumes, medicines, and dye-stuffs. From China came camphor. From Japan came artisans' manufactures such as fans and swords and mined products such as copper, tin, and sulfur in addition to other items such as Japanese camphor and licorice root. Among these items, copper and sulfur dominated all others in sheer volume. Copper was taken from the Okayama area and sulfur from Kyūshū (Ōtomo and Shimazu). On most trips, Sō Kin or his envoys carried what are regrettably only referred to as "domestic products" (K: t'oŭi or t'omul) from Japan, about which we have no information. All of these records concerned tribute and official trade. From the Korean tribute trade, Sō Kin obtained hemp or linen, cotton, silk, ginseng, 25 percent grade alcohol, dogs (for Ōtomo), and the Buddhist Canon.[88] In Sō Kin's case, the largest return good from the tribute trade was hemp cloth (totals for 34 visits: 1,699 bolts of hemp, 150 bolts of cotton, 50 bolts of silk).[89] Of course, these figures represent only the return from the tribute and official trade. Private trade imports undoubtedly exceeded these amounts.

We have one indication of the private trade from 1428. Sō Kin's envoy brought 28,000 kŭn (16,800 kg.) of copper and iron and requested silk cloth (2,800 bolts) be delivered to their anchorage in Naeip'o and Pusanp'o. Since the size of the transaction was large, government approval was requested and granted.[90] Presumably, smaller transactions did not require government approval. Here we have a hint of the main items in transaction: Japanese metals for Korean cloth. In this case, the cloth is silk, but as the civil wars in Japan expanded, cotton became an important item obtained from Korea. No complete trade total is possible from the Sillok, since private trade, both in this period and the next, was only sporadically recorded. Nevertheless, indications are that the total volumes may have been quite large. For example, Kenneth Robinson reports that single trade retinues in the mid-fifteenth century transported nearly 17 metric tons to the Chosŏn capital, and more was usually left in the ports.[91] Considering the dense traffic between the archipelago and the peninsula and the volumes of trade, about which we will have more to say concerning the post-1600 situation, Robinson is right to speculate that "Seoul and the three open ports were among the busiest trade centers in northeast Asia in the fifteenth and sixteenth centuries."[92]

Sō Kin's case dates from the early 1400s, and the form and content of the trade during the next two centuries changed in that the Chosŏn government steadily imposed controls over Japanese access to the ports.[93] The Haedong chegukki of 1471 listed and codified contacts, constricting the flow of goods and people by setting quotas for categories of envoys. The Revolt of the Three Ports in 1510 resulted in constricting trade even further to a single port: Chep'o and later Pusan. In the sixteenth century, silver (from 1538)[94] and gold appeared in Japanese cargo manifests, but copper, tin, and various luxury goods from Southeast Asia remained prominent.[95] Copper appeared as a Japanese export from as early as 1417.[96] Throughout the 1500s, as the civil wars continued, Japanese continued to seek cloth goods, increasingly cotton, from Korea.

Following Hideyoshi's re-unification of Japan and his invasion of Korea in the last decades of the sixteenth century, we see a variety of changes in both the form and content of trade, but the broad outlines remained as they had been established in the early Chosŏn period. Most important among the changes was that the Korean trade became the complete monopoly of Tsushima. Before 1600, others had obtained diplomatic documents from Tsushima for access to Korea, but after 1600, only Tsushima traders were allowed to land. Trade was still conducted as tribute, official, and private. The special meaning of official trade will be discussed below and its economic significance will be examined in Chapter 4. In terms of volume, the tribute trade was clearly the least important of all. Chŏng Sŏng-il surveyed documents connected with the tribute trade from 1614 to 1699 and calculates that this trade composed about 10 to 20 percent of the entire official trade.[97] Japanese copper and tin with Southeast Asian goods dominated the tribute and the official trade, which went in exchange for Korean cotton. From the mid-seventeenth century, however, rice replaced about one-third of that cotton. The quality of Korean cotton declined and Tsushima traders could not market it in Japan. The remaining cotton was sold in the private market back to Korean merchants for rice. In essence, then, Korean cloth disappeared from returning Japanese cargoes and the official trade largely became Japanese metals for Korean rice. From the end of the sixteenth century through to the mid-eighteenth century, the private trade became Japanese silver in exchange for Chinese silks and Korean ginseng. From 1763, silver was banned as a Japanese export item.[98] Copper took its place only to become even more prevalent in Japanese exports, since it already played a large role in the official trade. As the domestic Japanese production of ginseng went forward in the eighteenth century,[99] the demand fell off, largely leaving Korean native products such as dried sea-slugs, cow-hides, cow horns and hooves, *Scutellaria lateriflora* (medicine),[100] and others, such as agar-agar jelly made from laver.[101] Let us now turn to a more detailed discussion of the form of the trade.

The number of seal ships authorized at the time of the Kiyu Agreement, or at least prior to the 1630s, was 30.[102] When we add in the escort and wood and water ships (12), the total reaches 42 ships. The goal of the Tsushima traders and the island lord was to add as many ships as possible to these numbers, thereby expanding the potential for trade.[103] (We will return to this point in Chapter 4.) Expansion of cargoes was possible only through the private trade, since the quantities in the official trade were fixed. In 1613, limits were placed on the size of tribute and official trade inventories, limits that remained in force until 1876. We should now turn to representative modern descriptions and analyses of the cross-straits private trade provided by Tashiro Kazui and Chŏng Sŏng-il.[104]

As mentioned above, three legitimate forms of trade took place at the Japan House after 1600: tribute trade, official trade, and private trade. Most researchers lump tribute trade and official trade together under the name "official trade," because the distinguishing criteria is the Korean trader himself, was he a government official or a merchant? Government officials conducted tribute and official trade; merchants conducted private trade.

Tribute trade was the oldest and most important component of the trade structure, not for its volume or content, but for its symbolism. Japanese brought items to "offer" to Korea and received in exchange "gifts" of higher value, since Korea was a greater land receiving supplicants. Koreans viewed tribute trade as a "burden" and a favor extended to needy islanders; the significance was diplomatic not economic. In the following chapter, we will examine the actual and perceived "burdens," since these will help us link economic structure to mentality. Chŏng Sŏng-il argues that a "medieval diplomatic order" was preserved in the tribute trade. Annual ships bore diplomatic documents (sŏgye) with addendums (pyŏlp'ok) listing tribute items (chinsang or pongjin from 1635) in expectation of receiving return gifts (hoesa). The Meiji government found this system a "humiliation" for Tsushima and sought its elimination.[105] Regardless of how they were viewed, tribute relations defined the general environment, that is, the Japanese visitor, from arrival to departure, was engaging his Korean host in a series of ceremonial exchanges to express his sincere wish to maintain cordial relations. Ancillary to and only as a secondary activity to the tributary exchanges, official and private trade were conducted. Let us consider a typical visit.

Sō's envoy arrived and immediately was conducted to a ceremonial meeting with the Tongnae Magistrate and the Commander of the Pusan Garrison called the "tea reception." In Robert Campbell's excellent translation of the Ch'ŏphae sinŏ (J: Shōkai shingo), the famous seventeenth-century Japanese language primer for Korean interpreters, we can read textbook conversations between Korean interpreters and Japanese envoys at the "tea reception."[106] Here the envoy proffered a letter (sŏgye) from the lord of Tsushima addressed to the Third Minister (Sr. 3) in the Board of Rites. Appended to the letter was a list of tribute goods. After several days, a reply was delivered with the "return gifts." Among these "gifts" was one category of "requested items," that the Tsushima letter had specifically mentioned. These goods and their amounts were fixed in 1612–1613. The Japanese offered pepper, alum (a desiccate useful for stanching wounds), and sappan wood (a red dyestuff) from Southeast Asia. In addition, and similar to the categories we discussed for the pre-1600 trade, we find Japanese manufactures: red dyestuff, makie (gold or silver lacquer ware) ink stone cases, makie round trays, red copper tea hearths, and figured paper. Tashiro notes that the increase in the number and variety of Japanese manufactures as compared to the Muromachi period bespeaks advances in the circulation of goods in Japan.[107] Nevertheless, the large number of Southeast Asian goods still stood in stark contrast to the return gifts from Korea, which were entirely Korean products or manufactures: ginseng, tiger skins, leopard skins, tiger meat, tiger gall bladder, dogs, hawks, white pongee, white ramie, black linen,[108] white silk thread, figured matting, thick oil paper, brushes, ink, ink stones, water droppers, swords, bamboo saddlebags, fans, combs, flatirons, (holy Buddhist) oil, honey, starch, small watermelon seeds, (Job's tears, coix lachryma-jobi, or pearl barley), juniper seeds (for oil used in red seal ink), hazel nuts, walnuts, chestnuts, and dates. Following the reorganization and rationalization of trade in 1635, the tribute trade was simplified, but we will discuss that below. Once the tribute trade had been initiated with the "tea ceremony," or once the envoy's credentials had been accepted, the envoy was recipient of numerous banquets while in port in addition to provisions while in country, travel per diem, and materials for ship repair and cargo handling (e.g. rope, masts, boards, hawsers, nails, and bags). As tribute trade and receptions were simplified from 1635, most of these items were converted to their grain cost equivalents and that was given to the Japanese together with other provisions.

With the credentials certified and decorum seen after, high volume trade began. Official trade now needs explanation, since the Chosŏn government was not ideologically predisposed towards mercantile activities. In short, official trade consisted of purchasing the remnants of Japanese tribute cargoes. The custom of the Korean government purchasing excess cargoes from Japanese traders had been around since the early 1400s. After 1600, the first record of this official trade appears even before (1608) the Kiyu Agreement of 1609.[109] The government's largess came as a result of the Japanese traders being unable to sell all of their goods, and rather than have potential pirates go away disgruntled, the government agreed to purchase the surplus. In the official trade, Japan exported copper, tin, sappan wood, and water buffalo horn. Amounts were fixed and repaid in Korean cotton. With the simplification of trade in 1635, the cotton, as well as the return gifts in the tribute trade, were calculated on an annual basis and given to Sō's deputies (K: *Taegwan*, J: *Daikan*) at the Japan House. While the private trade rose and fell, the tribute trade and its important offspring, the official trade, continued until the 1870s and helped to feed the people of Tsushima for over two and a half centuries. The size of the official trade will concern us in Chapter 4, and we should now turn to the lucrative but volatile private trade.

Most of Tashiro Kazui's work has been directed at the private trade, and it would be impossible to summarize all her findings in the short space here. The private trade was a complicated phenomenon, and more will be said on this point below, but we should give a brief outline of its content. Its form will be discussed shortly. The only items forbidden in the private trade by Korea were Korean gold, silver, copper coins, and leopard skins before 1600 and Ming court dress afterwards. The only Japanese ban was on the export of weapons.

Tashiro's study of the private trade's peak years from the latter half of the seventeenth century through the first half of the eighteenth century has become a standard interpretation, although some of her methods and conclusions have been questioned; the criticisms will be discussed below. Tashiro reports that during the seventeenth century, the most important Japanese exports (70–90 percent) were: silver, copper, tin, brass, and other metals.[110] Among these, silver dominated, commanding over 50 percent of the metal exports. Copper occupied only 10 percent to 20 percent of the private market exports at the time. Private trade imports from Korea during this peak period included: silk thread from China and Korean ginseng. The two together composed from 60 percent to 90 percent of Korean exports.[111] Moreover, as the market in Japan for Korean cotton began to disappear from the mid-seventeenth century, Korean cotton received by Tsushima in the private trade never left Korea but was re-exported to the Korean private market in exchange for rice.[112] Eventually, by the mid-eighteenth century, the Japanese market for Korean ginseng began to wither under pressure from Japanese domestic production and the private trade in ginseng fell off. During the nineteenth century, Japanese copper purchased dried sea slugs, cowhides, cow horns and hooves, and *Scutellaria lateriflora*.[113]

We should now turn to consider the trade reforms of the 1630s and their origins in internal Japanese politics (Tsushima in the *bakuhan* system). Political events in the 1620s and 1630s in Korea and Japan led to a re-vamping of the form of trade. The new atmosphere of Korean accommodation with Tsushima resulting from the Manchu invasion of 1627 and the simplification of trade that occurred following the Yanagawa Incident of 1635 set the framework for the next two centuries. Regarding the former, Chŏng argues that the Manchu crisis saw *bakufu* offers to Chosŏn of military support, offers which were entertained at the Chosŏn court but which only resulted in the 1629 Kihaku Genpō embassy to the capital Hansŏng. The close contacts in this connection set the stage for the establishment of the Chosŏn Inter-preter Embassies (*Munwihaeng*) to Tsushima from 1632, revision of the official trade structure from 1635, which we will discuss later, and reform of the Communication Embassy (*T'ongsinsa*) to Edo from 1636.[114] Chosŏn court willingness to talk came at an opportune coincidence with major developments on the Japanese side. In the 1630s, as the *bakufu* was completing a re-organization of its foreign policy and trade structures, loosely referred to as the *sakoku* edicts or the establishment of a structure that imposed tight controls over foreign travel and trade (usually referred to as *kaikin* by contemporary Japanese historians), an embarrassing incident erupted called the Yanagawa Affair. As a result of the scandal, the *bakufu* freshly scrutinized Tsushima's Korean contacts and made efforts to establish direct oversight. Tashiro refers to this period as a watershed that marked the transition from a "medieval" to an "early-modern" diplomatic and trading structure between Japan and Korea. As mentioned above, Chŏng believes that the "medieval" nature of a subservient Tsushima continued right up to 1876. We should consider Tashiro's point in more detail, but first, we must review the changes established in the 1630s in the structures that governed trade at the Japan House. Although the Yanagawa Incident has already been mentioned in Chapter 2, its main outlines bear repeating here to explain Tashiro's argument.

Chosŏn Korea naturally broke relations with Tsushima as a result of Hideyoshi's invasion. Following Hideyoshi's death and the withdrawal of Japanese forces, Tsushima diplomats, led by the Yanagawa clan, forged state letters between Korea and Japan to circumvent the Korean refusal to accept any letter not from the "king" of Japan and the Tokugawa unwillingness to use "king" in reference to the shogun. The forgeries succeeded in bringing Korean envoys to Japan on three different occasions and establishing the diplomatic framework within which Tsushima was able to re-establish trade with Korea in 1609. One result of the Yanagawa clan's active role in this high-level diplomacy was the ambition of the second generation. Yanagawa Shigeoki's son, Kagenao, wanted to be released from service to the Sō and accepted as a *hatamoto* (lower direct vassal) to the Tokugawa house. In the course of his appeal, Kagenao blundered before *bakufu* officials and mentioned the forgeries. The *bakufu* held a trial for all responsible parties and decided to dispossess the Yanagawa, banish the scribal diplomat-monk involved, and confirm Sō Yoshinari's monopoly over the Korea connection. The *bakufu* also took the opportunity to extend some form of central control over Korean relations. Among the resulting reforms, the *bakufu* decrees established the official title for the shogun in foreign correspondence (Taikun), dispatched an overseer to Tsushima for diplomatic letters (Iteian rotational system), and changed certain diplomatic language referring to the tributary gifts Sō sent to Korea.[115] These changes were a major link in the new diplomatic order the Tokugawa were erecting in the 1630s, commonly referred to as the *sakoku* system. At the same time, the Portuguese were being expelled and European and Chinese access to Japan was being monopolized under *bakufu* control in Nagasaki. Of course, this was also when Christianity was decisively outlawed. The 1636 Korean Embassy to Edo was the first since Hideyoshi to be called a *T'ongsinsa* or Communication Envoy and carried a letter addressed to the "Taikun" of Japan, indicating Korean acceptance of the new, unified, Japanese diplomatic order.

Specifically for Tsushima, the outcome of the Yanagawa Incident meant the destruction of individual contacts with Korea, such as contacts like the pre-1600 trader-diplomat Sō Kin. Like Sō Kin, many individuals in Kyūshū, Tsushima, and Iki had received seals from Korea giving them authorization to trade as individuals. After Hideyoshi, Yanagawa had emerged as the most powerful such private trader. With the destruction of the Yanagawa, the lord of Tsushima was able to monopolize all contact with Korea. The centralization of contacts and the elimination of private contacts was, to Tashiro, one of the major components, perhaps the main Japanese component, that defined the transition from "medieval" to "early-modern" in relations with Korea. The other was the simplification of the trading order that worked to separate diplomacy from trade.[116]

In 1635, Korea took the opportunity to negotiate a simplified reception-trading system with the Tsushima daimyo. The new system was called the *kyŏmdae* (J: *kentai*)[117] system and its purpose was to reduce the burden of tribute diplomacy on Korea. The new scheme theoretically retained the same number of annual ships and specially dispatched ships allotted to Sō under the 1609 Agreement, but collapsed the number of ships that would actually receive receptions down to five. As a result, the total number of ships requiring diplomatic receptions was reduced to eight or nine: the five directly given to Sō, one from the Banshōin, one from the Iteian, and one seal ship that was originally Yanagawa's but reverted to Sō. The Banshōin was the temple name for Sō Yoshitoshi and the name of a temple in Izuhara where the Sō lords from Yoshitoshi onwards (including Sadakuni, r. 1468–1492) are enshrined. A seal was given to the temple in appreciation for Yoshitoshi's good-will diplomacy following Hideyoshi's invasion. The Iteian was the overseer temple that accommodated the Gozan monks appointed by the *bakufu*. A Korean seal was given in appreciation for the monks Genso and Kihaku Genpō's good-will diplomacy following Hideyoshi's invasion. The occasional ninth ship carried seals issued to the Sō daimyo's heir apparent. In short, from 1635, Sō controlled Yanagawa's former ship and his heir's ship, giving him six to seven ships in addition to the rights to those seal ships (Regular Annual Envoys and Special Envoys) either retained or eliminated from receiving receptions. Simply because ships were eliminated from receiving the elaborate receptions of the tributary trade did not mean that they could not or did not call in Pusan for trade.

The new scheme worked in the following way. For the three Special Envoys from Sō, receptions for the Second and Third Special Envoys were collapsed into the First Special Envoy. That is, only the First Special Envoy was entertained at tea receptions and banquets, but the return gifts for all three envoys were converted to rice and presented to the First Special Envoy. For the 17 Annual Envoys from Sō, the fifth through seventeenth were similarly collapsed into the Fourth Annual Envoy, leaving only the First, Second, Third, and Fourth Annual Envoys to be officially received and entertained. The other seal ships mentioned above (Iteian, Banshōin, heir ship, and Yanagawa's former ship) were outside this new scheme and were individually received as before. All of the landing, provisioning, official trade items, and tribute trade items were gathered by the Korean government for bulk delivery to the *daikan* (K: *taegwan*), Sō's deputies at the Waegwan. The deputies claimed these goods with receipts (*sup'yo*) issued by the *Hundo* and *Pyŏlch'a*, the Korean liaison-interpreters. Miscellaneous items were converted to rice, and we find a list of conversion rates in the *Chŭngjŏng kyorinji*.[118] The advantage to Korea was to limit banqueting and reception expenses, thereby greatly reducing the burden of receiving individually 20 separate envoys. The burden of protocol was great. For example, for the First Annual Envoy, there were at least 15 reception or banquet ceremonies: the disembarkation tea reception (once), the disembarkation banquet (once), the additional banquet (once), the journey banquet (once), the feast days' banquets (four), the tea reception to present tribute goods (once), the tea reception to deliver return gifts (once), the embarkation banquet (once), the additional arrival and provisioning reception (twice) and the regular arrival and provisioning reception (twice).[119] In addition, Campbell reports a ceremony for the envoy to pay respects to the Korean royal lineage.[120] The only time the Japanese met the Tongnae Magistrate face to face was at these banquets and receptions. Negotiations to finalize the new kyŏmdae scheme took about two years, and the system did not actually come into full operation until the late spring of 1637. As a consequence, for their efforts, the Magistrate and the Korean Interpreter were given awards for meritorious service.

But, argues Tashiro, the result was not exactly what the Korean government had in mind. The ships still went, and they were not officially received, but no reception did not mean they could not land nor did it keep the Japanese from trading. As we should recall from our discussion above, the old order worked entirely within the framework of tributary relations: the envoy was greeted as a tribute bearer who, once his credentials were established and he had been received by the authorities in the "tea ceremony," could trade in the private market. The new system took a long step towards separating trade from diplomacy. Now, diplomatic duties were conducted by a select few Japanese (five envoys) whose service maintained the general tributary framework while freeing the remainder of the ships and their traders to focus their energies and resources on the private market. A ship, other than one of the five, needed to carry only its sŏgye (letter from Sō) and a list of tribute goods. These were presented to the Hundo and Pyŏlch'a who issued a receipt to the Daikan (K: Taegwan). The Daikan, acting on behalf of the Sō daimyo, claimed the commensurate cotton and rice, which was the return from the official trade. Thus, we see a near complete separation of trade and diplomacy. The private market expanded as the tributary aspect shrank. This shift, argues Tashiro, was a shift from a "medieval" structure to an "early-modern" structure. Chŏng's counter-point is that trade and diplomacy were not separated and the transition was not from "medieval" to "early-modern" but from "medieval" to "modern." Moreover, this transition did not take place until after 1876. The only reason official trade and private trade existed throughout the period from 1609 to 1876 was due to the continuance of tribute trade as the underlying framework. Chŏng's argument has merit when viewed from the perspective of the 1870s when the Meiji government intended to eliminate the obvious hierarchical relations symbolized by Tsushima's tribute trade. This was the "medieval" arrangement predicated on tribute trade. Regarding the 1870s, one might argue that the Meiji government wanted to do away with a "medieval" trade structure, but did not want to de-couple trade from diplomacy, rather trade was to be linked to a new type of diplomacy with a new set of symbolic relations.

If this was the content and the form, can we determine the significance of the trade? Absolute amounts would give us quantifiable reasons for Korean population concentration in Tongnae; amounts would give us a beginning for comparison with Chinese and Jurchen trade, and amounts would give us some idea of the relative importance of the Korean trade to western Japan and points farther east in the archipelago. Despite the vast amount of trade data gathered by Tashiro and Chŏng,[121] absolute amounts of trade goods are still incomplete.

Tashiro Kazui opened the debate in 1981 by taking as her problem for study the extent of the post-1600 private trade, so important to Tsushima, and arguing that post-Hideyoshi private trade peaked in the 1690s with profits that surpassed those obtained through the Nagasaki trade. With her detailed study of the Japan–Korea connection, Tashiro opened many questions concerning trade at the Japan House, but she has also drawn criticism regarding her calculations of the amounts involved. In the summer of 1992, Nakamura Tadashi, an economic historian of the Nagasaki trade, joined the debate with a rejection of Tashiro's thesis concerning the volume of Tsushima's exports and the extent of Tsushima's profits. Nakamura asserted that Tashiro had grossly over-estimated both volume and profits. Nakamura points out that Tashiro's figures lead one to conclude that in 1694, Tsushima's profits at the Japan House and in Kyoto surpassed 20,000 *kanme* of silver, compared to 7,000–8,000 *kanme* of profits made in Nagasaki. Nakamura argues that Tashiro is unclear as to where and how Tsushima derived a "profit," and that she makes the fundamental error of adding sales at both ends of a single trip and thereby ignoring buying-in and handling costs. Nakamura concludes that the ceiling for Tsushima's profits was 4,000 *kanme*.[122]

Chŏng Sŏng-il joined the debate in the early 1990s, and in early 2000, he summarized his findings and evaluated Tashiro's and Nakamura's arguments in light of his own extensive work on Tsushima documents. His conclusions are as follows. Tashiro did slightly overestimate the amounts of silver exported from Japan, but Nakamura's criticism that the volume is grossly exaggerated is itself an overstatement. Chŏng states that total trade averaged 6,000 *kanme* (22,500 kg.) between 1684 and 1710. Of this total trade value, the value of exports (Japanese goods or transshipped goods and Japanese silver) averaged a bit over 3,274 *kanme* and imports averaged a bit over 2,669 *kanme*.[123] The export numbers are slightly higher than those offered by Robert Innes, who compares his figures with the Nagasaki market and concludes that Tsushima's private trade never exceeded 50 percent of the Nagasaki market (years 1685–1706) and even when official trade by Tsushima is added in, the figures still range between 20 and 50 percent.[124] Chŏng agrees with Nakamura that Tashiro miscalculated profits.[125] Chŏng finds that in 1694, Tsushima profited up to about 3,800 *kanme* in silver and over the 1684–1710 period of Tashiro's focus averaged an annual profit of about 1,723 *kanme*, quite a bit less than the Nagasaki trade, but still substantial. He also explains that the various extant registers record the profit in two ways, equally valid as long as the reader understands that one type of entry is after costs are deducted and the other is an addition of sales at both ends of the same transaction.[126] Chŏng may have achieved a breakthrough in interpreting the data, but since the ledgers are single entry and cannot be balanced, much work remains to be done before conclusive statements are possible about profit and even volume.

Chŏng finds that the size of total trade (exports and imports) averaged nearly 6,000 *kanme* annually between 1684 and 1710, although from 1686, the *bakufu* had officially limited this to 1,080 *kanme* (raised to 1,800 *kanme* in 1700). The official limit for Satsuma trade with Ryūkyū was 120 *kanme*; the Dutch trade was limited to 3,000 *kanme*, and the Chinese trade was pegged at 6,000 *kanme*.[127] If the Nagasaki trade was tightly controlled and held to a total volume of 9,000 *kanme*, not an unreasonable assumption given that it was under the direct administration of a *bakufu* official (the Nagasaki *bugyō*), then the 6,000 *kanme* of the Tsushima trade with Korea clearly indicates that it was very significant in Japan's overall external trade, but never eclipsed the Nagasaki trade.

To summarize, the model for post-1600 private trade that we might derive from Tashiro, Nakamura, and Chŏng's studies would be something like the following. Tsushima traders collected Southeast Asian goods from Nagasaki (either from the *bakufu*'s "set-aside system" or from the open market) and combined these goods with Japanese goods and metals (copper, tin, and silver) for transport to Pusan. In exchanges in Pusan, Korean traders handed over silk thread, ginseng, and other goods.[128] When goods from Korea were sold in Japan, the original investment capital was recouped, profit realized, and buying-in or re-investment was begun for the next trip. According to Nakamura and Chŏng, Tashiro's mistake was to add the "profit" recorded at the Japan House to the "profit" taken in Japanese markets when Korean goods were sold, or ignoring costs and counting one transaction twice. According to Chŏng, Tashiro is correct in her calculation of the total size of the trade but mistaken in her estimates of the profit.

To describe how trade was conducted does not explain change over time. Chŏng's study goes much further than Tashiro and Nakamura's and gives us a dynamic and predictive model. By employing econometrics with an extensive examination of new documents, he is also able to conclude the following. The reason for the decline in private trade from 1698 was a gap that yawned between the price indices of Korean and Japanese goods. The gap developed because the *bakufu* devalued silver and that disturbed the market in Pusan. Korean exports (in particular, white silk thread) became too expensive.[129] However, Tsushima's worsening overall economy thereafter was not linked causally (although there may be a correlation) to the Japan House trade, since the trade continued to provide an income above its expenses. Despite there continuing to be some profit, the fact that the profit margin declined presented difficulties for the Tsushima *daimyō*. His government lost money and ran deficits when paying for its domestic costs and in maintaining an Edo compound.[130] Further, using correlation analysis and regression analysis on the prices and amounts of private trade goods, Chŏng is able to conclude that knowing the cost and amounts of a handful of particular goods allows the long-term prediction of trade volume and profit. For example, the amounts of high-grade copper ore, silver and zinc-coated plates (obtained in Nagasaki from the Dutch trade[131]) correlate to changes in total profit.[132] Establishing such correlations aids us greatly when faced with data that contain gaps.

Tashiro, Nakamura, and Chŏng are concerned with absolute amounts and profits, problems that relate directly to the questions raised here about a trans-border region encompassing southeast Korea and western Japan. To enlarge the question, Ronald Toby has employed Tashiro's findings to support his emphasis on the overlooked importance of the Korean connection to Tokugawa Japan as a whole.

> . . . But in the middle and late 1970s, Tashiro Kazui demonstrated through analysis of the records of Tsushima han, the monopoly trader with Korea, *that trade with Korea was a major factor in Japan's overall external trade in the seventeenth century* . . . Professor Tashiro was dealing only with the Korea

trade, and yet she showed that that trade was sufficient by itself to be a factor in the economy of Tokugawa Japan as a whole.[133]

(Emphasis added)

Even with Nakamura and Chŏng's adjustments to Tashiro's argument, Toby's conclusion that the Korea trade was a "factor" in the Tokugawa economy is true; Nakamura and Chŏng merely ask us to consider how "major" was that factor. Since the question raised by Tashiro and joined by Nakamura and Chŏng goes to the heart of the relative size of the trade, it behooves us to take their differences seriously.

The significance of the Korea trade reaches to the level of the global economy and the world trade in silver. Japan was the second largest producer of silver in the world after Spanish America in the period between 1560 and 1640 and competed with Spanish America for the world's largest silver market in China.[134] The Japanese exported silver through Nagasaki, Tsushima, and Satsuma and imported silk yarn. The export of Japanese silver was a result of many factors, not least of which was the propagation of a new smelting technique imported from Korea that allowed much higher extraction ratios from low-grade ore.[135] If we can determine the volumes going to Korea (ultimately destined for the Chinese market), then we can get closer to an accurate total for overall Japanese silver exports and assess the significance of the Korean route in global silver trade.

Regarding our description of trade, the reason why it has taken so long to construct export/import sequences (content) and even to describe the structures within which trade occurs (form) is because of the difficulties inherent in the documents we have. To assume that Korean and Japanese trade documents were written and compiled for the same purposes and can easily be compared is to court confusion. Japanese documents offer much more information about the practical operation of trade than Korean documents and were usually produced from the merchant's point of view. Nevertheless, accurate data on volumes of goods has been difficult to isolate, as indicated by the Tashiro–Nakamura controversy surrounding volume and profit. The nature of tribute trade and official trade differs from private trade in that, as an activity of the Chosŏn kingdom, there are government records for tribute and official trade but none for private trade. The T'ongmun'gwanji (1720) and the Chŭngjŏng kyorinji (1802) are but two examples of such records for the post-Hideyoshi period. The goods given to Japan and the goods taken from Japan under the official trade regime were included in the annual budgeted finances of the Chosŏn kingdom. The amounts requisitioned for transfer to the Japanese in the period after the early seventeenth century quickly became fixed and varied only insignificantly from year to year except in years of severe shortages and famine. In short, the basic view of the Korean documents is that there was little or no variation from year to year in production, requisition, and disbursement. Official trade will be the concern of Chapter 4.

The Tsushima documents reveal fluctuations and were governed by two principles. The first principle was that Tsushima documents reflected the activities of a commercial actor, not an agrarian actor such as in the Korean documents. Therefore the amount of commercial goods available from Nagasaki, the markets of Osaka or Kyoto, or the bakufu-controlled monopolies varied depending on the year. Since the economic premises are fluctuation (Tsushima) vs. stability (Korea), any comparison of Tsushima documents with Korean documents is fraught with difficulty. To determine the actual amounts of goods, one must examine Tsushima records on a year-by-year basis, since they assume a fluctuating source and reflect more closely the actual trade. Korean documents assume a stable source for Korean exports (and Japanese imports) and so are more of a plan for requisitions (either from the Korean countryside or from Japan) than a trade register. While Korean documents reflect expectations, Tsushima documents might be said to reflect reality. However advantageous Tsushima documents may appear as a source of trade information, a second principle intervenes which renders them difficult to approach at face value.

Tsushima's low grain production left it extremely vulnerable and dependent on trade between Korea and Japan. From long before 1600, Tsushima had practiced the art of survival between the Chosŏn government and whatever Japanese power it had to respect. Piracy, the forgery of diplomatic correspondence,[136] and duplicity in reporting its actual economic condition were but a few of the tools in its kit. Even after the re-unification of Japan in the late sixteenth century and the establishment of Tokugawa hegemony, Tsushima continued to practice forgery and duplicity, as revealed by the Yanagawa Incident of 1635–1636 mentioned above. This was a case of forging documents of the highest level (letters of state between the Chosŏn king and the Tokugawa shogun). After exposure, a closer eye was trained on Tsushima by the *bakufu*, and Tsushima authorities quickly found the need to keep elaborate records of its relations with Korea.[137] The chief reason must have been to prevent self-contradiction and subsequent exposure. Tsushima authorities, long used to playing intermediary between Korea and Japan, were very careful to prepare multiple documents depending on the readership. In particular, special care had to be taken with documents destined for the *bakufu* or documents that might be shown to the *bakufu*. Although its earlier, more free-wheeling days before the Yanagawa Incident were over, Tsushima could still conceal the actual state of trade to extract as much profit (e.g. specially minted high grade silver for silk or ginseng) and aid (e.g. *bakufu* loans[138]) as circumstances would allow. For example, Chŏng Sŏng-il's determination, after examining the exchange agreements (*myŏngmun*) between merchants in the great market at the Japan House, is that they do not reflect real market activities but were created for the purpose of producing acceptable documentation to satisfy the *bakufu* desire to know the details of Tsushima's Korean trade. Chŏng concludes that the chief utility of these documents to modern historians lies in the information they provide about individual merchants, not about transactions.[139] Such a situation burdens us with a major problem: since versions of records were kept for presentation to the *bakufu* and for actual record keeping, which documents reflect reality?

Finally, much attention has been given to private trade, but an attendant problem that has yet to be fully clarified is Tsushima's simultaneous practice of official and private trade. Whereas the Chosŏn government, particularly after 1592, took no interest in private trade, Tsushima's daimyo engaged in both simultaneously. Tsushima did keep records devoted to official trade, so a start can be made in determining how much of which goods were traded to the Korean government and under what category, but the situation is complex and not at all clear. Lastly, another difficulty has been the accessibility of documents. Only recently, with the third major archive of Tsushima documents being made available by the National Institute of Korean History (formerly Korea National History Compilation Committee), has it become possible to begin the cross-referencing necessary to appraise sources critically.

The issues are complex and much work remains to be done, but these beginnings clearly indicate the importance to the Japanese economy of the trade that went on in Pusan harbor. The task of this chapter is to make a small start towards indicating the significance of the trade to Korea by assessing the demographic impact of the trade. We must now return to the central question: when and why did Tongnae's population become concentrated and dense? The Japan trade was obviously extensive, but to link the Japan trade to Korean demography we must now turn to consider Korean merchants attracted by the trade.

Tongnae merchants

Tashiro Kazui and Nakamura Tadashi have tried to clarify the matter of private trade through Tsushima documents with an eye to answering certain questions germane to Japan's past,[140] and they have done a remarkable job in opening the discussion on relative size and importance. Kim Tong-ch'ŏl and Chŏng Sŏng-il have addressed matters from the Korean side with admirable competence, but up to now no one has fully addressed the significance of the trade with Japan for the economy of seventeenth- and eighteenth-century Korea. In the next chapter, we will link the Japanese connection to the wider Korean economy, but our concern in this chapter is with demography, and there are a host of economic questions that relate directly to demographic concentration. A thriving trade with Japan would have involved the Korean merchants who obtained the goods, the people who transported the goods, and of course, the people who used the goods for manufacturing or who otherwise consumed the imports. All of these people would have been involved in regional networks that are probably lurking in our demographic data.

Although space forbids further consideration, there are numerous questions to pursue if we follow Japanese imports into Korea. For example, over the period 1684 to 1710, Tashiro Kazui reports an average annual export from Japan of 256,598 *kin* (K: *kŭn*) (154 metric tons) for copper and 36,923 *kin* (about 22.2 metric tons) for tin.[141] The *T'ongmun'gwanji* (1720) records fixed annual copper imports of 29,373 *kŭn* (about 17.6 metric tons) and tin imports of 16,013 *kŭn* (about 9.6 metric tons). The *Chŭngjŏng kyorinji* (1802) records nearly the same numbers. For the period between 1846 and 1848, when the private trade was supposedly moribund, Chŏng reports 60,000 *kŭn* of copper was imported into Korea annually. Combine that with the 30,000 *kŭn* imported via official trade and we see nearly 54 metric tons of copper entering Korea in a single year.[142] Over the six-year period from 1844 to 1849, nearly 221 metric tons of copper entered the country in exchange for 121,000 cowhides, 831 sacks of cow horns, 489 sacks of *Scutellaria lateriflora*, and 691 racks of dried sea slugs.[143]

Where did the Japanese copper and tin go? Probably, the metals went into the domestic brass industry and for the production of coinage. Brass is composed of 50 to 95 percent copper and contains 5 to 50 percent zinc. Bronze was often used for coinage and is composed of copper and tin, harder than brass. If we set aside govern-ment needs for bronze coinage and consider the commonality of everyday life, brass utensils were used across Chosŏn for, among other things, the rituals to celebrate ancestors. Ansŏng County in Kyŏnggi Province was the industrial and commercial center for the manufacture and sale of brassware. It relied on copper from Suan, Yongsŏng (Kyŏnggi Province), Poŭn (Ch'ungch'ŏng Province), and tin, lead, and copper from Japan.[144] Brassware and gilding also need tin, "an item difficult and heavy to transport and circulate," but "decidedly a central item of import."[145] The connections between brassware and bronze coinage and the Japan trade throw serious doubt on Kim Ok-kŭn's assertion that the character of Korean–Japanese trade lay in the export of highly useful and important goods such as cotton and rice from Korea in exchange for Japanese luxury goods used only by the elite classes in Korean society.[146] Even if we consider that Japanese silver for Korean ginseng and Chinese silk may have been an example of the luxury trade, that also had an economy. We might note that the 1740 Tongnae gazetteer mentions one silversmith and 14 "grinders and polishers," the second largest group of craftsmen after bow makers.[147] Perhaps, some Japanese silver was re-cast in Tongnae before transport northwards where it was used by Korean embassies to China. Tashiro has pointed out that the importation of Japanese silver was linked to the departure of Chosŏn embassies for China. In short, Japanese silver was re-exported to China, thereby linking Korea to the pre-modern global trade in silver.[148] But we should return to the southeast coastal society of Tongnae and consider Korean merchants.

Until recently, studies of Tongnae merchants have been few, and no conclusive statements have been possible about their numbers, their identities, and their business.[149] Thanks to Korean and Japanese scholars such as Tashiro Kazui, Kim Tong-ch'ŏl, and Chŏng Sŏng-il, that ignorance is being dispelled.[150] We know that there were limitations on licensed merchants allowed into the Japan House to conduct trade. In 1678, the number was fixed at 20; in 1680, limits were abolished; and in 1691, the number was again fixed at 30. Ordinarily, the merchants are called Tongnae merchants but, at first, Seoul and Kaesŏng merchants were the key traders. Kim Tong-ch'ŏl states that the 1678 slate of 20 men were all capital merchants, but the 1691 slate of 30 were both capital and provincial merchants.[151] As time passed, merchants from the Tongnae area came to dominate but the time of transition is unclear.[152] Korean merchants were required to carry permits from the Board of Revenue and from the governor of their home province. Market days were on days with a three or an eight (3, 8, 13, 18, 23, and 28), making six market days a month. The Regular Annual Envoys were allowed to stay in port 85 days. The longest stay permitted an irregular envoy was 110 days, although most were not permitted beyond 55 days. The goods traded in the private market were subject to supply and demand, as well as political decisions in Japan on the export of currency.

Chŏng explains the markets for the private trade with the Japanese in the following way.[153] Private trade was literally conducted under the noses of Korean officials in the Chosŏn Great Hall within the Japan House compound. Six times monthly on days with a three or an eight, this "great" market was opened. Participants included not only the larger merchants (tojung) but also smaller merchants. There was also the daily morning market where the Japanese purchased fresh vegetables and fish and eventually wine, fruit, hand-crafted items, and even rice, which was banned from trade. In accordance with Japanese requests, a special market opened on the fifth of every month from 1665 to trade rice, but was discontinued by the central government from 1708 because of disturbances and the fear that national secrets would be leaked to the Japanese. Trade in rice was continued, but limited to the great market.

Although the government decided to tax private trade, these records have yet to see the light of day, if they exist. Chŏng Sŏng-il points out that the Board of

Taxation administered taxes in the great market, and the Tongnae Magistrate assumed this responsibility from 1763.[154] No-one has discovered extant receipts. The daily morning market was also taxed. From 1610, or almost as soon as the Japanese had returned to Pusan following the Imjin Waeran, the Tongnae Magistrate and local officials began taxing the morning market where the Japanese obtained daily necessities.[155] Chŏng hypothesizes that there were tensions between a central perspective wanting to keep activities to a minimum in hopes of preventing incidents and a local perspective wanting to expand small-scale trade in the morning market to benefit from greater taxes.[156]

The key question connecting the great market where high volumes of goods exchanged hands and the demography of Tongnae is whether the Japan House markets were specialist markets with little or no relation to the local economy or intimately connected with local markets. Even specialist markets would have required transport and handling and demanded labor and management. If further connections to the local economy and society can be established, then we can get even closer to judging the significance of the Japan trade for Tongnae's general populace. Let us first consider connections between international trade and local society by examining the linkages between the market openings for international trade and the market openings for the local economy. Afterwards we will compare merchant lists with the rosters of local officials.

Chŏng Sŏng-il has examined the rates of great market openings and presents the following findings. During the periods 1722–1726 and 1730–1732, the great market was convened at the high rate of 73.8 percent and 68.5 percent of its possible opening days. About a century later, that had fallen to 20 percent. In other words, by the 1820s and 1830s, the market opened only one-fifth of the time it could have. This probably meant a fall-off in private trade, but Chŏng has a different perspective. He argues that the lower rate of market opening does not, by itself, indicate a stagnation in private trade, but merely a curtailment of the opportunities for trade, a valid point but one that might imply either more volume on open days or the hidden presence of an alternative, unreported, and illegal market. The matter is still not clear.

More to the question of the connection between the Japan House great market and local county markets is Chŏng's data on opening days. An analysis by month indicates that the great market was just marginally more prone to be open between the tenth and the first months, therefore not clearly indicating a seasonal pattern, but a pattern does emerge when market openings are analyzed within a single month. Japan House market openings were concentrated on their scheduled days, and Chŏng argues that this regularity was consciously done on the Japan side to avoid overlapping with the regularly scheduled Tongae County markets. Chŏng asserts that a dovetailing of Waegwan great market openings and local county market openings establishes the close connection between international trade and the local or regional economy.[157]

If international trade and the local economy were closely connected, then can we pursue the significance of the trade for the local society by asking questions about the numbers, identity, status, and specialty of the Korean merchants? Kim Tong-ch'ŏl and Chŏng Sŏng-il have given us studies of Korean merchants in the nineteenth century. Chŏng supplies information on the trading activities of 13 large

Korean merchants (*tojung*) between 1844 and 1849 culled from Japanese records.[158] He discovers that positions were heritable, merchants can be ranked by the volumes they traded, and that the Korean government periodically re-drew the list of licensed traders.[159]

Kim Tong-ch'ŏl examined Korean documents for information on the suppliers to the licensed merchants who appear in the Japanese records examined by Chŏng. We might consider these suppliers as the next ring outwards from direct contact with the Japanese, since they were not licensed to enter the Waegwan. Kim discovered a list of 79 names for merchants of agar-agar between 1866 and 1875. Among the 79, in any given year, there were up to 48 active merchants (1866: 41, 1867: 42, 1875: 48).[160] From another list of merchants and shopkeepers handling unspecified items between 1871 and 1875, Kim has found 41 different names. Among these, 32 were merchants and 10 were shopkeepers. One individual was both merchant and shopkeeper. Both lists contain the names of monopoly merchants responsible for paying a fixed tax to the government. Kim has not only given us the full names of individuals (often not available in the Japanese records examined by Chŏng), but he has also collated these merchant lists with lists of local officials.[161] Only five of the 79 agar-agar merchants had some sort of government appointment, while 19 of the general merchants and two shopkeepers had appointments. Only two names from the total 120 names appear at the top of the local official scale (*hyangni*), but since the numbers of general merchants bunch up at the upper end of the scale underneath *hyangni*, and since *hyangni* were often appointed from these levels, Kim concludes that many upper-level local officials were active as merchants. In short, the local political status of the merchants was generally high. Their social position was also respectable as some ten from the total of 120 were inducted into the *Tongnae kiyŏnghoe* ("Tongae Council of Venerable Seniors").[162] Nine of these were general merchants; one was a shopkeeper, and no identifiable agar-agar merchant's name appears. The descending order of social status is clear: general merchants – shopkeepers – agar-agar merchants.[163] Herein, we can begin to glimpse the local societal role of merchants who dealt with the Japan trade, and find evidence for Yi Wŏn-kyun's assertion above that there were few *yangban* in Tongnae who opposed commerce.

Regarding numbers, these lists may be only fragmentary evidence, since agar-agar, in 1875, was eighth in a list of 35 separate items sold to Japanese traders. Judging by the results of Chŏng's study, one licensed merchant inside the Waegwan handled many goods and there were no monopolies.[164] According to Kim Tong-ch'ŏl, the suppliers to these licensed merchants held monopoly positions. If the lists presented by Kim are lists of monopoly merchants, then were there 35 other groups of merchants supplying the licensed merchants inside the Waegwan? We might also hypothesize that a merchant's name signifies more than a single person. At least, it represents a household and probably an extended household of servants and assistants or, in short, a corporate body or a trading house. For example, Chŏng's data from 1837 reveals one Chapŏm (pseudonym, full name unknown), the leading exporter of cowhides and leading importer of copper. His father was a licensed merchant (pseudonym Yunjung).[165] We know from Japanese records that he circulated around the capital and the provincial cities of Chŏnju and Taegu for business.[166] Considering that between 1844 and 1849, he exported between 25,000 and 30,000 cowhides and imported a little over 100,000 *kŭn* (60 metric tons) of copper,[167] it beggars belief that he could have conducted his trade alone. In short, nothing can yet be said about the total number of merchants who dealt with the Japan House, except that they numbered at least 150 and probably more. If we include immediate dependents, we have a range of from 573 to 623 people,[168] but mercantile operations are not known well enough to allow us to estimate the numbers represented by a single household head.

To summarize, we might borrow Kim Tong-ch'ŏl's model to describe the post-1600 private trade[169] and the role of the Tongnae merchants in that trade.[170] The main items handled by the Tongnae merchants were Chinese silks and Korean ginseng, which were exchanged for Japanese silver. From the 1680s, a variety of factors began to affect the supply of Chinese silks: direct trade between China and Japan was established; Chinese limits were imposed on the export of raw silk; Chinese raw silk prices rose, and competition for supply appeared from the British East India Company. Simultaneously, demand in Japan was being increasingly answered by the expanded domestic production of silk. Regarding ginseng, Korean production declined and Japanese domestic production started up in the mid-eighteenth century. By the 1740s, these changes began to have their effect on Korea's role as intermediary between China and Japan. Private trade declined, but did not disappear. Rather, the goods changed to Korean cowhides for Japanese copper. As yet, we have no information on Tongnae merchants prior to this transition period. We do have information on nineteenth-century merchants and that information reveals that a few licensed merchants were also local officials. This suggests the social respectability of commerce. We have much work yet to do on Tongnae merchants, but their activities deserve comparison with the merchants of Hansŏng, Kaesŏng, and Ŭiju.

After considering the extent of the Japanese trade and examining available studies on Tongnae merchants, we can make the following conclusions about the link between demographic concentration and trade. First, the volumes of commodities in the private trade with Japan were extensive. In the next chapter, we will see that official trade volumes were even larger. Second, high volumes of goods generated the usual transport and handling needs, and we can easily imagine that each commodity had a small economy of its own: producers, finishers/processors, suppliers, agents, carriers, warehouse operators, all behind the merchants we see in the market dealing with the Japanese. In short, it is hard to imagine that the trading circumstances in Pusan did not attract large numbers of Koreans.

Conclusion

Although there are grounds to question the demographic data, we should consider that the data were gathered and used by the people at that time to formulate and monitor government policies. If we generally accept the available data for Tongnae's position in Kyŏngsang Province, we can conclude the following. Tongnae's relative position in the province changed radically from early to late Chosŏn. Tongnae's population became highly concentrated on its available arable land. The problem above has been to determine what sustained that expanded population if it was so unusually concentrated on a relatively smaller land base. Were the resources of the land augmented by advances in agricultural technique (irrigation, fertilization, etc.)

that shifted the mode of production from extensive to intensive farming, or by trade with the Japanese, or by fishing, or by all of these and even some additional factors not yet identified? This chapter has asked if Tongnae County displays any unusual demographics that might be explained by an association with a wider maritime world of which the Japanese were a part. The basic assumption is that the Japanese would have required officials to administer them and would have attracted merchants to trade with them, and these concentrations, if significant, should have appeared in demographic records.

From the available data, we can detect signs that Tongnae was unusual within Kyŏngsang Province for its concentration of people, but in comparing coastal counties, all we can say is that people gathered close to the ocean to participate in a world that was probably dominated by fishing and other harvests from the sea. International trade played a part, but we cannot begin to see concentrations of people for trade until we look inside Tongnae County. Within the county, the coastal townships show a clear concentration of population and of men, unusual phenomena when compared with data from other counties. It is likely that this concentration of men was because of fishing and the trading opportunities offered by the Japanese presence. These reasons suggest that Tongnae was part of a wider maritime world of fishing and trade. Of fishing, we can say very little at the moment, but from what we know about trade, we can say that the population of Chosŏn-era Tongnae was actively involved with a trading world that stretched northwards to China, eastwards across the straits to the Japanese archipelago, and southwards to Southeast Asia.

Finally, the regional and local diversity uncovered in the course of our investigation (for example, certain coastal counties saw population declines while others saw rises) demands further work on local records to search for ecological, epidemiological, economic or other patterns and traces that may have been overlooked. The approach taken here has attempted to link maritime and trans-border activities to larger questions of Chosŏn demography. As we explore this linkage further and more accurately re-create the world of coastal residents, we will come to a fuller appreciation of the integration of Chosŏn, not as a singular, idealized system but as a set of dynamic regional structures interacting at different political, economic, intellectual, and social levels, all open in various ways to interaction across boundaries.

4

THE ECONOMIC SIGNIFICANCE
OF THE WAEGWAN

The entire island is covered by rocky mountains. The soil is rocky and
the people are poor. The people make their living by boiling salt
[water for the salt], catching fish, and trading.[1]

(from the descriptive comments on Tsushima
in the *Haedong chegukki*, 1471)

In the previous chapter we identified an unusual population concentration in Tongnae
and sought out reasons for this in fishing and trading. We sketched the maritime
world of the southeast and found much suggestive evidence for extensive fishing.
We outlined forms of trade, attempted to assess the volumes of the private trade, and
went in search of Korean merchants. The concern of this chapter is the movement
of official goods and what Koreans thought about that movement. In this connection, Michiel Baud and Willem van Schendel offer a few suggestions regarding
frontier economies. They point out that it is "important to treat the region on both
sides of the border as a single unit . . .". The reasons behind this are obvious: borderlands often connect two economic systems and states seek to control the movement
of goods. Since even short-term decisions have an immediate impact in the frontier,
decisions made on one side of the boundary lead to quick adaptation on the other.
Furthermore, frontier economic structures influence the center's view of the frontier.
For example, they assert that limitations on trade invite smuggling, and smuggling
gives the frontier economy "an air of stealth and subterfuge in the eyes of the state."[2]

The region – the frontier, the point of contact – has to be our focus because the
pre-modern centers rarely conducted any diplomacy or trade at all. Their distance
from each other allowed them to summarize relations in what we recognize as
ideological frameworks, and we often make the mistake of taking those ideological
frameworks as describing reality. The diplomatic and economic structures that formed
the architecture of relations were observed from afar by literate intellectuals at the
center. But the inside of these working structures should be our starting point to
understand pre-modern relations between Korea and Japan. Only by a close study of
port activities can we assess the accuracy of attitudes and contribute to a history of
mentalities. The sheer fact that a coherent and generally consistent, structured trade
regime was maintained between Chosŏn Korea and the Japanese archipelago for
nearly 500 years, with institutions that survived even the devastating Japanese invasion in the 1590s, testifies to the solidity of the structures built around Tongnae and
the deep-seated necessities that sparked them into life. But what did literate Koreans
think about the Japanese connection? We will be exploring an important part of the

Chosŏn-era Korean mentality regarding Japanese: they were a heavy burden on the economy and the society, consuming as much as half the production of one of the richest provinces in the country. Only by tying together material and mental structures can we begin to comprehend a regional history that includes the Korean peninsula, the Japanese archipelago, and beyond.

Below we will examine the volume of official trade and search for transaction costs or the costs of diplomacy at the site of contact. We will then determine Korean views on those costs. Contact was symbolic and ideological, but it was also material. By examining the working side of official trade between Chosŏn Korea and Tokugawa Japan, we can better judge the relevance of any ideological discourses deployed to interpret or to justify government action or inaction. By examining diplomatic costs, we can assess the level of resources sacrificed, and that will give us an idea of the commitment by Korean authorities to maintaining the Japanese connection.

Examining the economic structure of the Japan connection also affords us the opportunity to examine the workings of a Chosŏn-period county. A particular piece of county business – trade and diplomacy with the Japanese – concerns us here, but to examine a particular in detail offers a perspective on the whole. Official trade at the Waegwan leads directly to the local history of Tongnae County and to the regional history of Kyŏngsang Province.

The major state activity conducted at the open ports was the reception of Japanese, which, we have seen in the previous chapter, subsumed the activities of banqueting, entertaining, and provisioning, as well as a form of trade called official trade. Above, we examined private trade to argue that Koreans were attracted to the Japanese presence. Now, we will turn to official trade to expose attitudes towards that presence. By examining receptions and official trade, we are looking into the political economy of Chosŏn relations with Japan, and we will find concrete and quantifiable expressions of the Chosŏn government's willingness to engage with Japan and with Tsushima in particular.

The political economy of Chosŏn–Japan relations transcends the particularities of port activities. It leads to the political economy of Chosŏn itself and to the role of foreign connections in the kingdom's economy and consciousness. Relations with the Japanese were a serious concern and extensively documented. They offer us numerous cases to examine the symbols and activities of the state, the worldviews of the populace, and in this chapter, the structures of a regional economy and the mentality it created. Studies heretofore have addressed port activities and the official trade as separate activities from the economy of the kingdom. There has been little concern with accurately determining how many resources were consumed in the Japanese connection, where provisions and exports were sourced, how they were referred to and handled, and what happened to imports, much less with what Koreans said about these expenditures. Since we outlined the private trade above and other scholars have described what goods were traded, how and where,[3] these sorts of questions will be dealt with only in passing. We will focus on the connections between diplomacy, economy, and mentality.

The functions of Chosŏn diplomacy towards Tokugawa Japan were border control and civilizing a barbarian neighbor. The costs for Korea were great but not as great as the alternatives: piracy and even invasion. The Chosŏn state and its local representative in the Tongnae Magistrate were anxious to keep the lines open to Japan, since the Koreans needed intelligence on Japanese movement and intentions, and Japanese trade was useful. The functions of Japanese diplomacy towards Chosŏn Korea were devoted to keeping Tsushima alive and to the acquisition of prestige by both Tsushima and the *bakufu*. The costs to Japan were also great but the alternatives were starvation for Tsushima and a political loss of face for the *bakufu*.[4] In this chapter, we focus on Tsushima and Tongnae as the foundry for these greater projects.

Tsushima's vulnerability unquestionably made it dependent on Korea. Korean recognition of this vulnerability in the form of licensed trade and tributary diplomacy conducted at the Japan Houses, combined with military preparedness, offered a solution to the islanders' needs and suppressed the Waegu pirate problem. The cost of that solution meant turning raiders into traders, and those traders had to be accommodated within a diplomatic scheme, since from the Korean view, trade was viewed as no more than an unsightly adjunct to diplomacy and in this case as a necessary evil. Kenneth Robinson has examined the process by which Tsushima and other Japanese elites were incorporated into a Korean world order prior to 1600.[5] That process of incorporation is not our concern. Rather we are interested in the structures of that incorporation and their costs. The cogs in the machine were the large numbers of licensed envoys from many regions of Japan prior to 1609 and the reduction of those numbers to envoys from only Tsushima after 1609. The costs to Korea were monetary, political, and social.[6] In this chapter, we will limit ourselves to a consideration of monetary matters only and the worries they created. In later chapters, we will turn to politics and society.

Functions: exploitation of trading opportunities within a diplomatic framework

We have already explained that trade at the Japan House occurred in four forms in descending order of institutional importance: tribute, official, private, and illegal trade (smuggling). Tashiro Kazui lumps together tribute trade and official trade under the rubric "official trade." We will do the same, because our concern is not with the articles traded nor is it with the form of the trade. We are concerned with whether the trader was a government official or a merchant. The tribute and official trade was an official government concern and open to debate, not about its existence, but about its rationale and conduct. The private trade was a private concern.

At the risk of redundancy, a few key points bear repeating to explain the official trade. First, the official trade saw Japanese copper and tin, together with Southeast Asian goods, exchanged for Korean cotton. From the mid-1600s, rice began to replace cotton and very soon thereafter, as Japanese cotton production took off, Korean cotton was re-sold on the private market in Pusan for rice. In short, Tsushima's objective in the official trade became the acquisition of Korean rice.

Second, we should briefly review the Kiyu Agreement, because the 1609 Agreement governed basic Korea–Tsushima relations until the Kanghwa treaty of 1876 and was the most restrictive of all pre-modern arrangements for Japanese access to Korea.[7] It followed on from the Agreements of 1443, 1512, with amendments in the 1540s.[8] The Kiyu Agreement limited the island lord Sŏ to 20 ships, 17 Annual Ships and three Special Envoys. As we mentioned above, others on Tsushima were also granted seals. For example, those who contributed to peace negotiations during and after the Imjin Waeran got seals, and the heirs to the Tsushima lords occasionally received seals. The number of seal ships authorized, as of the early 1630s, was 30, although escort ships brought that to over 40. Amnesties for participating in Hideyoshi's invasions were issued.[9] All envoys had to carry Sō's mun'in or writ of passage, a consistent policy from 1436 to 1876, or risk being labeled a pirate.[10] The goal of the Tsushima traders and the island lord was to add as many ships as possible to the low limits set by the Agreement, thereby expanding their export and import cargoes. More ships arriving for diplomatic reasons meant more opportunities for private trade.[11] Sō worked to evade his restrictions by sending Ch'awae (J: Sawa) or "Irregular Envoys" to report on events in Japan or to conduct "extraordinary" business. These Irregular Envoys will be considered below for their economic impact.

From the Korean point of view, the Kiyu Agreement was designed to limit Japanese impact on the regional and national economy. In 1613, limits were placed on the size of tribute and official trade inventories, limits that remained in force until 1876. Sō's subsidy was re-affirmed at 100 sŏk, where it had fallen in 1512, and was never to rise thereafter. Ship sizes and crew numbers were again specified. Time in port for various envoys was specially limited. The Regular Envoys from Tsushima (Annual Envoys) were allowed to stay 85 days. The longest stay permitted an Irregular Envoy was 110 days, although most were not permitted beyond 55 days. Other miscellaneous provisions issued a seal to Sō, specified per diem for traveling expenses, and abrogated all previous agreements.[12] The only port opened was Pusan.

Official trade grew from tribute trade. Tribute trade was the oldest and most important component of the connection. As trade, the tribute exchange was probably a loss to Korea; the significance was not economic, but political. But the official trade was important, and we have already discussed the high volume of Japanese metals and their uses. Official and private trade, the real lucrative types of trade, were conducted as secondary and tertiary activities to tributary trade. In Chapter 3 we mentioned the form (procedures such as the tea reception that established the trading environment) and content (items and volumes) of the trade with Japan, but we now have to address the extent of the Waegwan's presence in the economy of seventeenth- and eighteenth-century Korea via an examination of the official trade. By examining the economic involvement of Chosŏn Korea with Tsushima, we can point out the deep links between diplomacy and trade. In addition, by examining how economic relations linked through diplomacy, we can quantify the cost to Chosŏn for its Japanese connection and that will give us a yardstick of sorts to assess how far the Chosŏn government was willing to go to maintain peaceful relations with the Japanese.

Costs: a re-construction of accounts related to Japan (eighteenth and nineteenth centuries)

Tsushima's trade with Korea was based on its diplomatic connections as outlined above. The problem is to determine the economy of that trade and diplomacy and its significance for Korea. "Significance" will be treated simply: what was the relative size of the economy associated directly with Japan? To answer this question, we will consider the tax revenues of Kyŏngsang Province and then we will compare that total to the amount of revenue devoted to the Japanese. In preparing data on the part of the government budget devoted to the Japanese, we will consider the two largest categories: official trade and receptions. Private trade was not a government activity. We will go on to consider the spatial impact on Kyŏngsang province in marshaling resources for the Japanese, or in other words, we will map the province's sources for the Waegwan. These assessments will give us the official or planned picture of the situation, but we will then gather together the few extant accounts for individual years for comparison. With the planned allotments and a few actual allotments, we can then be in a position to state the relative significance of the Japanese trading and diplomatic connection, at least as seen through Korean government documents. With such an assessment in hand, we can examine and judge the popularly held views of literate, Chosŏn-era Koreans.

In sum, the purpose of the study is two-fold. On the one hand, we want an objective determination of the size of Japanese involvement in the Korean economy, and on the other hand, we want to take stock of a major component of the Korean mentality towards Japan: remorse and frustration over the cost of that Japanese involvement. To begin, we must reconstruct Kyŏngsang Province's tax scheme after the Hideyoshi invasion, and in particular, after 1678, when a major tax reform was instituted.

Prior to 1600, Chosŏn taxation had been, generally speaking, composed of land tax (rice and beans) and tribute or the presentation of local specialties. After Hideyoshi's invasions, the tax system of Kyŏngsang Province changed greatly. That change was the establishment of the *taedong* tax reform in 1678 that procured rice in exchange for tribute goods. The *taedong* or "Great Equalizing" reform transmuted "tribute goods" to grain equivalents. Han Yong-guk, Kim Ok-kŭn, Rokutanda Yutaka, and James Palais have written extensively on the *taedong* tax,[13] and so we need not explain the new tax system in detail. Our task is to outline the overall tax revenues produced by Kyŏngsang Province, since that southeastern province had to provide the vast bulk of goods for the official trade with Japan. The general picture is presented in Table 4.1 ("A breakdown of post-1678 Kyŏngsang Province tax receipt categories").

The arrangement of Table 4.1 is based on Kim Ok-gŭn's *Chosŏn wangjo chaejŏngsa yŏn'gu* (A Study of the Financial History of the Chosŏn Kingdom).[14] Table 4.1 tells us the types of tax and what goods were usually provided in payment. Although Kim Ok-gŭn and others[15] have attempted to determine amounts paid in the various categories for selected years, these efforts are essentially useless. First, it has been impossible to find payment data for all categories of tax for even a single year. Second, agricultural production can vary greatly from year to year, so a few scattered, painstakingly reconstructed years may not be representative of a typical tax receipt for the province. Lastly, the payment of tax came in many forms: unhulled rice, cotton, cash, and even corvée labor and specialist commodities. Before we can speak of a "total" tax receipt, we must unify all the commodity values into a single item such as rice or cash. Exchange rates have yet to be clarified, and central and provincial accounts have yet to be analyzed, so attempts to convert everything to a single item are presently complex and difficult.

Rather, it is simpler to seek a general notion of tax receipts not in their payment but in their assessment. All of the categories of tax in Table 4.1 were assessed on the

Table 4.1 A breakdown of post-1678 provincial tax receipt categories[a]

Tax category	Goods for payment
Land tax (*chŏnse*)	Rice Beans Millet
Military training tax (*samsu-mi*)	Rice Millet
Taedong tax (*taedong-mi*)	Transferred to capital Sequestered in province Rice converted from cotton for official trade with Japan
Other [*taedong*] tax	Rice converted from cotton for official trade with Japan Beans converted from cotton for official trade with Japan Rice transferred to capital Beans transferred to capital Cotton transferred to capital
Cleared, dry field tax (*hwa-chŏnse*)	Cotton/millet
Reed field tax (low-lying fields beside rivers) (*no-chŏnse*)	Cotton (category applicable only in Hwanghae Province)
Additional tax on land (from 1750) (*kyŏlchak*)	Cash

Sources: *Mangi yoram, Chŭngbo munhŏn pigo, Yŏngnam taedong samok.*

Note:
a This table has been modeled on Kim Ok-kŭn's table for the same; see: Kim Ok-kŭn, *Chosŏn wangjo chejŏngsa yŏn'gu*, p. 8.

basis of land tax and land tax was assessed as *kyŏl* or the most commonly applied form of land measurement.[16] *Kyŏl*, as an area measurement, varied in size, because the objective was a specified amount of production and land of varying quality would produce varying amounts. For example, two hectares at site A might produce one *kyŏl*, but to obtain one *kyŏl* at site B, it might require 2.5 hectares of land. One *kyŏl* contained 10,000 *p'a* and one *p'a* was the amount of grain still on the stalk that a man could grasp in two hands. The *kyŏl* was used in the *T'akjijŏn pugo*, a record of eighteenth- and nineteenth-century accounts prepared by the central government to assess taxes for the entire country. The chief advantage of the *T'akjijŏn pugo* is that it offers us homogenous, standard records, a pre-requisite for compiling serial data.

Figure 4.1 has been prepared from the tax assessment in *kyŏl* for Kyŏngsang Province from 1744 to 1840.[17] Here, we can see the serialized data available to us in the *T'akjijŏn pugo*. Three of the categories are not as complete as the other two, but our concern is with the more complete "actual tax assessment" (*ch'ulse silgyŏl*). Other information in the table refers to the amount of arable land and tax relief and exemptions. The "total arable land" (*wŏnjangbu*) was recorded at ten-year intervals or from 1744 to 1834. The "tax relief for miscellaneous disasters" (*yunaejin chapt'al*) was recorded from 1776. The "tax exemption" (*myŏnse*) was recorded from 1776.

112

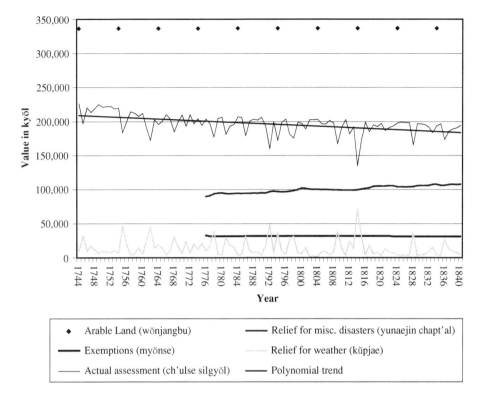

Figure 4.1 Kyŏngsang Province tax assessments (in *kyŏl*)
Source: *T'akjijŏn pugo* (c.1900).

The "relief for weather disasters" (*kŭpjae*) was recorded from 1744 to 1840 and mirrors the actual assessment. It is clear that total arable land, tax-exempt land, and relief for miscellaneous disasters hardly varied over this period. The land tax actually assessed and the relief given for bad weather varied greatly and operated in tandem clearly indicating that a "moral economy" based on the recognised needs of subsistence was at work.[18] Although there were obvious trends, we must set aside questions of long-term structural change until a more extensive national analysis has been completed. For the moment, all we need is a simple average of Kyŏngsang Province's actual land tax for the period covered by the data. The average for actual assessment over the period from 1744 to 1840 was 196,490.928 *kyŏl*.[19] This figure can be used as the rough tax value of Kyŏngsang Province from the mid-eighteenth to the mid-nineteenth centuries. We will return to this figure below many times.

Geographic extent of the Japanese connection

Now, we turn to a consideration of how much of these tax revenues were consumed in connection with the Japanese. First, we will examine the official understanding held by the central government regarding costs, and then we will turn to actual

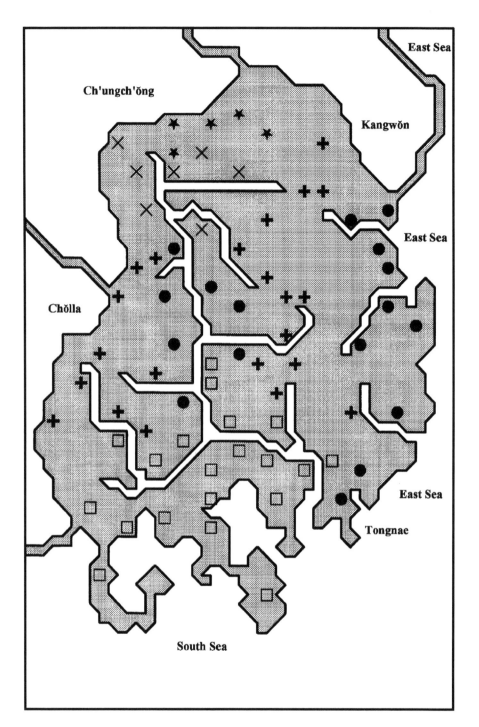

Map 4.1 Taxation zones in Kyŏngsang Province: areas specified by conversion since taxation in kind was difficult

Source: Sites from *T'akjijŏn pugo*; map adapted from *Ch'ŏnggu sŏnp'yo-do* (c.1800–1834) by Kim Chŏng-ho.

Notes:

● Yŏnhae (coastal counties, Waegwan supply)

+ San'gun (mountain counties, land tax converted to cotton)

X Yŏngjo (south of the mountains, land tax converted to cash)

★ Chug'yŏng (Chug'yŏng area, land tax converted to cash)

□ No listing (no conversions, shipped directly to center)

instances as recorded in central government documents and the Tongnae Magistrate's records. We will begin by analysing which counties of the province supplied the Waegwan and determine their relative portion within the provincial tax assessment.

Exactly which counties supplied the Waegwan in any given year is a question still under investigation, but the answer has two parts. We can easily determine the sources for official, centrally planned assessments, but the actual, year-on-year assessments varied, since local shortfalls had to be made good from neighboring counties. The 17 official supply counties reported in the *T'akjijŏn pugo* and the *Mangi yoram* represent policy, while the 50 counties mentioned in the *Puyŏk silch'ong* (1794) represent actual practice. The *T'akjijŏn pugo* and the *Mangi yoram* state that 17 counties along the "coast" had to send their land taxes to the Waegwan. The annual requirement was 721 *tong* 44 *p'il* of cotton and 16,000 *sŏk* of rice. If the counties could not fulfill this burden, then cotton was to be taken from the mountain counties (*san'gun*) and rice was to be taken from the *taedong* rice stores of nearby counties. The actual practice of supply ranged up to 50 counties for 1794 as reported in the *Puyŏk silch'ong*.[20] Map 4.1 ("Taxation zones . . .") presents the planned dispersal of taxation in Kyŏngsang Province according to the *Mangi yoram* and the *T'akjijŏn pugo*.[21] Here, we can see the geographic distribution of the 17 coastal counties indicated by a circle. These counties were responsible for sending their land tax to the Waegwan.

Map 4.2 ("Kyŏngsang Province taxation sites . . .") shows these same 17 counties and their actual tax assessments in scaled size for the year 1765.[22] Table 4.2 shows the actual amounts by county. The total tax assessment for the 17 in the year 1765

Table 4.2 Kyŏngsang Province taxation sites to support the Waegwan (1765)

County name	Amount in *kyŏl*
Kyŏngju	10,056.21
Taegu	8,676.13
Sŏngju	8,101.86
Sŏnsan	5,890.55
Indong	2,833.15
Tongnae	2,548.61
Kijang	2,488.84
Ch'ilgok	2,237.57
Ch'ogye	2,236.7
Hŭnghae	2,128.65
Koryŏng	2,005.81
Yŏng'il	1,776.37
Yŏngdŏk	1,211.69
Yŏnghae	904.02
Changgi	867.4
Ch'ŏngha	730.35
Ŭlsan	4,343[a]

Source: *Yŏji tosŏ.*

Note:
a Actual assessment (*sigi kyŏl*) not available, total arable land (*wŏnjangbu*) substituted.

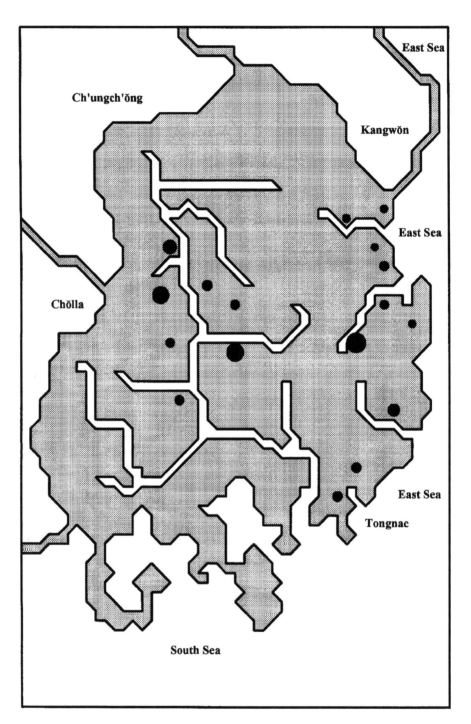

Map 4.2 Kyŏngsang Province taxation sites and relative proportion of actual tax receipts (*sigi kyŏl*) for 1765 support of the Waegwan

Source: Sites from *T'akjijŏn pugo* and amount in *kyŏl* from *Yŏji tosŏ* (1765); map adapted from *Ch'ŏnggu sŏnp'yo-do* (c.1800–1834) by Kim Chŏng-ho.

Notes:

Kyŏngju (10,056.21), Taegu (8676.13), Sŏngju (8101.86), Sŏnsan (5890.55), Indong (2833.15), Tongnae (2548.61), Kijang (2488.84), Ch'ilgok (2237.57), Ch'ogye (2236.7), Hŭnghae (2128.65), Koryŏng (2005.81), Yŏng'il (1776.37), Yŏngdŏk (1211.69), Yŏnghae (904.02), Changgi (867.4), Ch'ŏngha (703.35), Ulsan (*sigi kyŏl* not available, 4,343 for wŏnjangbu or arable land substituted).

was 59,036.91 *kyŏl*. If we calculate this against the average for actual assessment over the period from 1744 to 1840 or 196,490.928 *kyŏl*, we can obtain a rough idea of the officially planned impact of the Waegwan on Kyŏngsang Province's tax take. There are caveats to keep in mind. Since we have data for only 1765, we are unable to draw up a time series for the 17 supply counties to compare with the time series we have for the entire province (Figure 4.1). By using only 1765, we run the risk of misrepresentation, since this year may have been unusual for the 17 counties. The total provincial assessment for that year was 200,697 *kyŏl*, not an unusual total, so 1765 may have been a typical year in the 17 counties as well. In short, the central government's plans resulted in earmarking nearly 30 percent of the 1765 provincial tax assessment for the Waegwan.

Map 4.3 ("Waegwan supply sources") was compiled from the *Puyŏk silch'ong* (1794) and notes the 43 sites (from a total of 50 mentioned) from all over Kyŏngsang Province that supplied at least three *sŏk* of rice or the rough equivalent for support of the Waegwan. The main purpose of Map 4.3 is to show the geographic dispersion of support for the year 1794. Absolute amounts are only roughly known. The figures from the *Puyŏk silch'ong* are derived partly from conversion of commodities to rice and their accuracy is not certain. Until that accuracy can be confirmed, we are employing the map only to tell us various locales that supplied Tongnae, and presumably the Waegwan. The map specially notes the five principal sources: Kyŏngju (7,790 *sŏk*), Sŏngju (6,478 *sŏk*), Taegu (4,896 *sŏk*), Sŏnsan (4,062 *sŏk*), and Ulsan (3,195 *sŏk*). The rough total from the *Puyŏk silch'ong* is 43,860 *sŏk*. The total is not inconsistent with other figures that we will examine below, but we cannot compare it with certainty because of the problems associated with conversions. What is clear is that the Waegwan was actually supplied from a much wider number of locations than planning documents indicate.

In Tongnae County records we have detailed corroboration of external funds coming to Tongnae from other parts of Kyŏngsang Province. Although we do not know exactly where these funds came from, we can identify funds for both the Irregular Envoys (*taedong* taxes) and the regular, official trade (land tax from the 16 other counties). The actual accounts for Tongnae mention *taedong* tax funds entering the county and we can see that these were not extraordinary accounts by consulting provincial planning documents. The *Yŏngnamch'ŏng saye* (the section dealing with the Japanese was produced sometime between 1811 and 1825) is a record of the Yŏngnamch'ŏng (the office for the Yŏngnam or Kyŏngsang region) of the Sŏnhyech'ŏng (office in charge of the *taedong* tax), which gathered information on the structure and development of the *taedong* tax's operation in Kyŏngsang Province. Herein we can see an explanation of the *taedong* tax disbursed to the Waegwan,[23] and we can see what part of the total disbursement to the Waegwan was *taedong* tax rice. The amount of *taedong* rice included in the rice converted from cotton cloth was 2,666 *sŏk* 10 *tu* (or 40,000 *tu* with 15 *tu* per *sŏk*) and this amount was a planned minimum transfer to the Japanese annually from 1683 to 1811.

Table 4.3 has been created from the *Taedongsaek* entry of the *Tongnae-bu saye* (produced in 1868),[24] and shows *taedong* funds coming into Tongnae County. As we can see, the *taedong* tax rice imported from outside Tongnae was slightly more than 5,600 *sŏk*. In short, 75 percent of the *taedong* rice consumed in Tongnae was imported from other counties. This account was tied to the Japanese accounts for

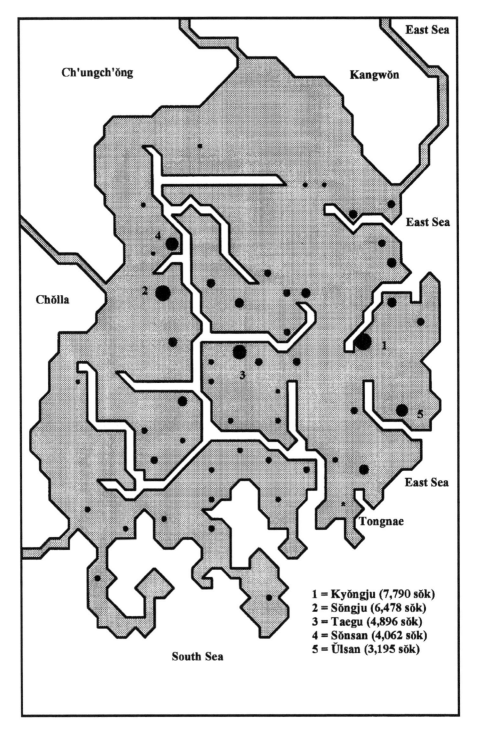

Map 4.3 Waegwan supply sources in Kyŏngsang-do, 1794
Source: Map adapted from Ch'ŏnggu sŏnp'yo-do (c.1800–1834) by Kim Chŏng-ho.
Notes:
Sites from Puyok silch'ong, books 6–8, Kyŏngsang-do (1794).

Table 4.3 Tongnae-bu saye's Taedong account (for the year 1867)[25]

A) Tongnae County	
1) Tax rice	1,767 sŏk 3 tu 8 sŭng 4 ch'ak
2) Sequestered rice	105 sŏk 5 tu 6 sŭng 4 hap 1 ch'ak
Sub-total from Tongnae	1,872 sŏk 9 tu 4 sŭng 4 hap 5 ch'ak
B) Other counties	
1) Spring harvest [rice]	5,607 sŏk 1 tu 8 hap 7 ch'ak
2) Banquet expenses	10 sŏk 6 tu 5 sŭng 5 hap
Sub-total from other counties	5,617 sŏk 7 tu 6 sŭng 3 hap 7 ch'ak
Total Rice (A + B)	7,490 sŏk 2 tu 8 hap 2 ch'ak

Source: See text.

Table 4.4 The Tongnae-bu saye's official trade conversion rice in the [Japanese] diplomatic account[26]

A) Two tu reduced sequestered rice:	627 sŏk 5 tu 2 sŭng 7 ch'ak
B) Received from other counties:	12,705 sŏk 14 tu 7 sŭng 9 hap 3 ch'ak
Total Rice (A + B)	13,333 sŏk

Source: See text.

the Irregular Envoys. We also see in Tongnae's records evidence of outside funds arriving for the official trade. For example, Table 4.4 clearly shows us an external account earmarked for the official trade. The portion labeled "Received from other counties" (ŭp) was over 12,700 sŏk. This account existed solely for the Japanese official trade. In sum, in 1867 Tongnae collected from other counties over 18,300 sŏk (Table 4.3: 5,617 sŏk plus Table 4.4: 12,705 sŏk) for the Japanese.

What is obvious from this discussion of the geographic extent for funding to supply the Waegwan is that the expenses at Tongnae for official trade and receptions involving the Japanese were not limited to revenues derived from within Tongnae County. The point has two significances. One is that the activities at the Waegwan had a direct economic effect on other areas outside of Tongnae in Kyŏngsang Province. The second significance is that since the Tongnae Magistrate managed an extraordinarily large budget for the Waegwan that drew from all over the province, the post of the Tongnae Magistrate must have been a relatively important post in Kyŏngsang Province.[27]

Having demonstrated the spatial reach of the Japanese connection, we must now return to its economic impact. "Economic impact" can only be understood as a relative statement and must be assessed in a similar fashion to the 30 percent figure already reached. In other words, we will compare central plans to actual accounts and to do this, we must disaggregate the accounts and we must convert tax assessment (kyŏl) into tax take (sŏk).

By using the unit of tax assessment, or the kyŏl, we have been able to unify our comparisons in a homogenous fashion and arrive at the conclusion that the central government planned to devote about 30 percent of Kyŏngsang Province's assessed tax base to the Waegwan. If we now turn to determine actual amounts in grain as *sŏk*, we enter a thicket of complexity. For example, the amount derived from the *Puyŏk silch'ong* (43,860 *sŏk*) is difficult to take as an absolute amount, since numerous commodities were converted to rice, and these conversion rates are still uncertain. If we take a simpler conversion, we could use the assessed 59,036.91 *kyŏl* for the 17 supply counties and convert that into unhulled tax rice using the rough guide provided in the *T'akjijŏn pugo*. The explanation provided there for taxation pegs the official rate of taxation for Kyŏngsang Province at 16 *tu* per *kyŏl*.[28] If we convert 59,036.91 *kyŏl* into *tu*, then the amount is 944,590.56 *tu*. Since the *sŏk* mentioned in connection with supplying the Waegwan were government *sŏk* or *p'yŏng sŏk*, they contained 15 *tu*.[29] When we convert *tu* to *sŏk*, we have 62,972.7 *sŏk*. If we convert this unhulled tax rice to milled rice (60% reduction rate), we have 25,189.08 *sok*. We can also use this same procedure to convert our average tax assessment for the entire province (196,490.928 *kyŏl*) into *sŏk*. In other words, the average land tax for Kyŏngsang Province from 1744 to 1840 was 3,143,854.8 *tu* or 209,590.32 (milled rice 83,836.13) government *sŏk* (15 *tu*) out of which 62,972.7 (milled rice 25,189.08) *sŏk* were transferred to Tongnae for the Waegwan. These conversions are based on *kyŏl* from Figure 4.1, so the ratio stays the same at about 30 percent. If we apply the same conversion to all data from Figure 4.1 (*kyŏl*), we can see the results in Figure 4.2. These conversions of planned supply to the Waegwan will become useful for comparison as we investigate actual amounts that went to the Waegwan.

Among the actual amounts that went to the Waegwan, we can identify two categories: official trade costs and reception costs in port. Later, we will also consider

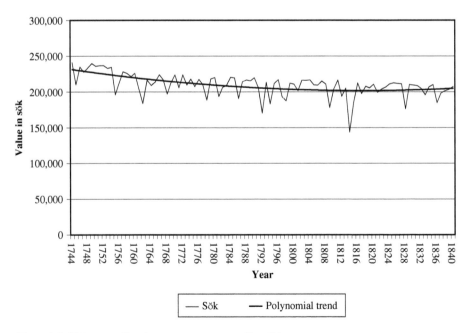

Figure 4.2 Kyŏngsang Province tax assessments (in *sŏk*)
Source: *T'akjijŏn pugo* (c.1900). Trendline is polynomial, order 2.

national diplomatic costs (Korean embassies to Tsushima and Edo that carried gifts). The following examines these costs in turn and then adds them up. If we can obtain an estimated actual total, then we can compare that with the official ceiling outlined above and compare the planned cost with the actual costs. Such a comparison will help us grasp the economic cost to Chosŏn Korea for the post-1600 Japanese connection.

Official trade costs

According to the *T'ongmun'gwanji* and the *Chŭngjŏng kyorinji*, after the Hideyoshi invasions, Korea began to accept goods as official trade from Tsushima and supplied in return 1,120 *tong* (one *tong* equals 50 bolts), 45 bolts, 17 *chŏk* (feet) of cotton cloth to the Waegwan with a small bit of that going to the Korean interpreters.[30] In the *Pyŏllye chibyo* we see the first post-Hideyoshi proposal concerning official trade, dated first month, 1608. In an entry dated twelfth month, 1612, we see that the Tongnae Magistrate, Yi Ch'ang-jŏng, determined official trade amounts of cotton fabric for each ship.[31] From 1651, 300 *tong* of that cotton cloth was, at Tsushima's request, converted to rice. Again from 1660, an additional 100 *tong* was added for conversion, totaling 400 *tong* of cotton that was converted to 16,000 *sŏk* of rice and supplied to the Waegwan.[32] One bolt of cloth was converted to 12 *tu* of rice, with 15 *tu* in one *sŏk*.[33] Permission for the cloth to rice conversion was granted in five-year installments and negotiating a renewal of the conversion agreement was the *Saihan* (K: *Chaep'an*)'s chief diplomatic duty. After 1660, the conversion was usually granted but only after negotiation. In sum, from 1660, 16,000 *sŏk* of rice (representing 400 *tong* of cotton) and 721 *tong* 44 bolts of cotton cloth were annually transferred from Tongnae to the Waegwan for official trade. These are the amounts specifically mentioned in the *T'akjijŏn pugo* for the 17 responsible counties in Kyŏngsang Province. According to Amenomori Hōshū's *Kōrin teisei*, that rice was viewed by the Japanese as *kaimai*, or "purchased rice."[34] If these amounts were the cost of official trade, how much did receptions cost?

Previous assessments of reception costs

Kim Ok-kŭn has written on the "burden" of receptions associated with the Waegwan at the end of the eighteenth and the beginning of the nineteenth centuries and argues the following in his study of the Chosŏn kingdom's finances:

> In the latter Chosŏn period, expenditures used for Japanese trade in the broadest sense – official trade and disbursements to Japanese envoys sent to Korea from all parts of Japan, beginning with Tsushima and the [Tokugawa] *bakufu* – when converted to annual rice expenditures, reached the enormity of from 70,000 to 80,000 *sŏk*.[35]

Kim Ok-kŭn seems to be ignorant of the diplomatic arrangements after 1609 that stripped non-Tsushima Japanese of permission to visit Korea, but the point is not this. The point is that his interest is the *taedong* tax and the tax burden on the peasantry, and in that connection, he rightly emphasizes the extraordinary tax burden placed on people around the port by the existence of the Waegwan in the Tongnae area.[36]

Nevertheless, Kim Ok-kŭn's method of calculation has one large mistake that results in inflating his figures: namely, his use of the conversion ratio of one bolt of cotton cloth to 12 *tu* of rice for the 721 *tong* of cotton left after the actual 400 *tong* was converted to rice. As mentioned above, the Chosŏn government agreed to convert 400 *tong* (20,000 *p'il* or bolts) of cotton to rice at the rate of 12 *tu* per bolt. The remaining 721 *tong* were given to the Japanese who then sold it on the Tongnae market for rice. Kim Ok-kŭn's purpose is to unify all expenditures into rice, but the special, official rate of one bolt to 12 *tu* of rice was most likely used only for the 400 *tong*, while another, market rate was used for the remaining 721 *tong*. Since the remaining 721 *tong* were sold to Tongnae merchants, it is hard to imagine that they would have paid an official rate.

Kim Ok-kŭn calculates the remaining 721 *tong* of cotton at the conversion rate for converted rice (1 bolt of cotton for 12 *tu* of rice), yielding 28,875 *sŏk*, 3 *tu*. However, in actuality, the 721 *tong* (1 *tong* contained 50 bolts) of cotton was probably converted at a rate of 1 bolt for 5 *tu* of rice. In a 1634 entry in the *Pongnae kosa*, we can see that the House Master negotiated the exchange of official trade cotton, some 30 *tong* (1500 bolts), for 400 to 500 *sŏk* of rice. Such an exchange would have been at a rate of one bolt for 4 or 5 *tu*. If we calculate the exchange of 721 *tong* of official trade cotton at 5 *tu* per bolt, we have about 12,017 *sŏk* of rice and not the 28,875 *sŏk* calculated by Kim Ok-kŭn.[37] The official trade cotton was taken into the Japan House and then sold on the private market without ever leaving Pusan.[38] Since the re-exported cotton went into the private market, one should not imagine that the merchants in Tongnae purchased the cotton at the exorbitant rate of 12 *tu* to one bolt. When the government wanted rice, it could force the peasantry to provide rice at the rate of 12 *tu* per bolt.[39] The transaction was inherently disadvantageous to the peasant, but he was powerless in this exchange. However, the parties to this transaction and the parties to the transaction at the Waegwan were different. At the Waegwan, the government gave the Japanese 721 *tong* of cotton, and the Japanese then sold that on the Tongnae market. The parties to that cotton-for-rice transaction were the Japanese and the Tongnae merchants. Since the Korean government was not a party to the final transaction, we find no discussion of the conversion of the remaining 721 *tong* of cotton to rice in any Korean government documents. In short, Kim Ok-kŭn's use of the same rate for the entire 1,121 *tong* of cotton exaggerates his calculations for the official trade category.

Also, within Kim's calculations is a 1781 estimate for Irregular Envoys given by Cho Si-jun, Governor of Kyŏngsang Province. The Governor complains about the shortfall in the *taedong* accounts and mentions 10,000 *sŏk* used for the Waegwan.[40] As mentioned above, the provincial *taedong* account was tapped for Irregular Envoys, and although 10,000 *sŏk* seems a bit high when compared with the 5,617 *sŏk* reported in Table 4.3, the difference may just be an annual fluctuation.

Another difference between Kim Ok-kŭn's work and the present study is his emphasis on the "burden" of Japanese expenses for the peasantry of Tongnae County and Kyŏngsang Province. He points to contradictions in a "feudal" society: with the rice and cotton extracted from the peasantry, all the goods purchased from Japan were luxury goods consumed by the upper classes. Kasuya Kenichi similarly states, "For the peasants of Kyŏngsang Province, the 'Neighborly Relations' [K: *kyorin*] with Japan were no more than something that brought them a burden they knew as a levy destined for provincial officials [rather than central officials]."[41]

Most assuredly these views are true, but they beg a question. Did Japanese trade also bring advantages? Costs in Japan to host the Korean Communication Envoy were also levies on the Japanese peasantry. The similarities are obvious, and we might say that elites always put the ultimate cost for diplomacy onto the peasantry, but the difference between diplomacy and trade must be borne in mind. For example, while the Korean Communication Envoy to Japan did not engage in trade of any significance, we should recall that Chosŏn imported from Japan some of the basic commodities (copper and tin) used to make brassware and bronze coinage.[42] Kim Ok-kŭn and Kasuya Kenichi aggregate official trade accounts with reception expenses, a view that tends toward viewing all the accounts as "costs" or "burdens" with no consideration of tangible benefits. The problem of "benefits" is beyond the reach of the present study, but to begin an answer one must start with an accurate consideration of the reception expenses and official trade expenses for the Japanese and attempt to disentangle diplomacy from trade.

Above we considered the size of the political economy associated with the Japanese from the point of view of what portion of the tax assessment was to have been sequestered for this purpose. Additionally, we considered the spatial reach into Kyŏngsang Province of the exports and supplies for the Waegwan. Now we are in a position to address actual cases of reception and trade expenses, which we will be able to compare with Kyŏngsang Province tax revenues.

Reception costs in port

Among the envoys sent by Tsushima were Regular and Irregular Envoys. The Regular Envoys were those specified by the Kiyu Agreement of 1609: yearly ships, seal-holding ships (*tosŏ-sŏn*), and ships from those who had appointments in the Korean government (*sujik'in-sŏn*). The Irregular Envoys were, in Tsushima documents, called *sanpanshi*, and in Korean documents, *ch'awae* or *pyŏlch'awae*. In similar fashion, the budget for the Waegwan had a regular and an irregular part.

Table 4.5 ("Categories and amounts of the Tongnae County budget to supply the Waegwan,") presents us with a picture of the local budget for four different years. The first thing we should note is the consistency. For the years with data, we can see that the Reception Warehouse, the Pusan Warehouse, and the Daily Warehouse expenditures did not change significantly. Moreover, the "Official Trade Converted Rice" was fairly constant. The "Official Trade Cotton Warehouse" category shows fluctuations, but the Official Trade Cotton amounts were all established by agreement with Tsushima and, in principle and aside from separate agreements, did not change.

For example, the Tongnae budget for the Waegwan in 1831 is as expected. The category of Official Trade Converted Rice saw a change from before. In 1811, Korea concluded a new agreement with Tsushima, which lowered the exchange rate between cotton and rice for the 400 *tong* of cotton specially set aside for this purpose. The rate went from 12 *tu* of rice to 10 *tu* of rice per bolt and is reflected here.

Table 4.5 Categories and amounts of the Tongnae County budget to supply the Waegwan

Warehouse	Year			
	1790[a]	1831[b]	1849[c]	1870[d]
Reception warehouse[e]		3,974 yang 3 chŏn 5 ri (rice 794 sŏk 13 tu)[f]		4,217 yang 2 chŏn 5 bun (rice 843 sŏk 7 tu)[f]
Official trade cotton warehouse	721 tong 44 p'il 32 ch'ŏk (rice 10,467 sŏk 5 tu)[g]	691 tong 46 p'il 21 ch'ŏk 3 ch'om (rice 10,032 sŏk 14 tu)[h]	665 tong 44 p'il 32 ch'ŏk 3 ch'om (rice 9,655 sŏk 5 tu)[i]	321 tong 44 p'il 32 ch'ŏk 3 ch'om (rice 4,667 sŏk 5 tu)[j]
Pusan warehouse[k]				
Per diem rice; sacks; ship repairs; firewood and charcoal[l]	2,672 sŏk 12 tu	2,670 sŏk 12 tu	2,670 sŏk 12 tu	2,670 sŏk 12 tu
Beans	822 sŏk 8 tu 6 sŭng (rice 548 sŏk 6 tu)[m]	822 sŏk 8 tu 6 sŭng (rice 548 sŏk 6 tu)	822 sŏk 8 tu 6 sŭng (rice 548 sŏk 6 tu)	822 sŏk 8 tu 6 sŭng (rice 548 sŏk 6 tu)
Daily warehouse				
Fish purchases	937 sŏk 7 tu	937 sŏk 7 tu	937 sŏk 7 tu	937 sŏk 7 tu
Hawk purchases		420 sŏk		420 sŏk
16 misc. items		91 sŏk 4 tu		91 sŏk 4 tu
Official trade converted rice				
Converted rice (from cotton) 1811 reduction[n]	16,000 sŏk	13,333 sŏk 5 tu[o]	13,333 sŏk	16,000 sŏk
Administrative rice	5,927 sŏk 11 tu			
Taedong warehouse		1,779 sŏk 2 tu[p]	5,419 sŏk	7,227 sŏk 6 tu[q]
Total	36,553 sŏk 11 tu	30,608 sŏk 3 tu	32,564 sŏk	33,406 sŏk 2 tu

Sources: Pyŏllye chibyo (1790 entry); Tongnae-bu ŭpchi (1832); Tongnae-bu kyenok (1849) entry; Tongnae-bu saye (1868).

Notes:

a Pyŏllye chibyo, fascicle 8, ha'nap chejŏl, 1790.6 entry. The document is Kyujanggak cat. no. 2089 and 2090. The Kuksa Pyŏnch'an Wiwŏnhoe published a typeset transcription in 1969. These figures are from the published transcription.

b Tongnae-bu ŭpchi (1832) also in the Kyujanggak (MS 666). For a published photolithographic reproduction of the original, see: Tongnae saryo, 2 (Seoul: Yŏgang ch'ulp'ansa), 1989.

c Tongnae-bu kyenok, 1849 entry, (Kyujanggak cat. no. 15105.) For a transcription, see: Pusansi-sa Pyŏnch'an Wiwŏnhoe, ed., Tongnae-bu kyenok (Pusan: Yŏngnam Inswaeso), 1964. See in particular: 1849/12/27 entry, pp. 41–42.

d *Tongnae-bu ŭpchi*, 1871, also in the Kyujanggak (MS 12173). For a published photolithographic reproduction of the original, see: *Tongnae saryo*, vol. 2.

e *Chiŭp-ko, Tongnae-bu saye*, 1868. This category is thought to include banquet costs (*sŏlyŏnpi*), which Kim Ok-kŭn lists as a separate item. See: Kim Ok-kŭn, *Chosŏn hugi kyŏngjaesa yŏn'gu* (Seoul: Sŏmundang, 1977): 65–66.

f The conversion rate from cash to rice is: 1 *sŏk* = 5 *yang* or one *yang* = rice 3 *tu*. See: *Mangi yoram*, chaeyong-p'yŏn, 2, suse, san'gun chŏnse changmok p'ojŏn: "changing to cash [is at the rate of] one *sŏk* of rice to five *yang*." See also the *T'akjijŏn pugo*, 1, suse. (Seoul: Yŏgang ch'ulp'ansa, 1986 photolithograph): 8 for same.

g The exchange rate from land tax rice to cotton was: one bolt = rice 4.35 *tu*. See: *T'akjijŏn pugo*, 1, suse, (Seoul: Yŏgang ch'ulp'ansa, 1986 photolithograph): 8: "Converting to cotton in every province is at the rate of tax rice one *sŏk* equals 3.5 bolts of cotton cloth." Another rate was one bolt = rice 5 *tu*. See: *Mangi yoram*, chaeyong-p'yŏn 5, kongmu, kongjangmi ha'nap: "tax rice one *sŏk* = converted cotton 3 bolts." The *T'akjijŏn pugo* rate is taken here as authoritative and all conversions are calculated at 1 bolt of cotton = rice 4.35 *tu*. Kim Ok-kŭn, *Chosŏn hugi kyŏngjaesa yŏn'gu*, pp. 68–70 calculates the exchange rate at one bolt = rice 12 *tu*, and the result is 28,875 *sŏk*. However, it is not clear why he uses this exchange rate. Perhaps, Kim Ok-kŭn's mistake stems from the following data in the *Hyŏnjong kaesu sillok*, 26:25b–26a (1672/10/24) entry: "[Kyŏngsang] Province's rice and cotton land tax [from] the lower half of the province is converted and given to the Wae. When we first converted rice to cotton, we converted cotton to rice, we converted at 12 *tu* to one bolt." This passage most likely refers to the 400 *tong* of specially converted cotton, not the remaining 721 *tong* of cotton that was given to the Japanese and which they then sold on the market in Tongnae at 5 *tu* to one bolt. For evidence of the ordinary exchange rate, see: *Pongnae kosa*, photolithographic reproduction in *Chōsen gakuhō*, 57 (1970.10) and 58 (1971.1), 1634/2 entry: "The House Master Taira Toshinasa requested [permission] to take 30 *tong* of cotton and buy 4–500 *sŏk* of rice and cereals [from] the government at cost." Such an exchange works at a rate of one bolt = 5 *tu* of rice. We can assume that when the Japanese acquired the remaining 721 *tong* of cotton and exchanged that with the Tongnae merchants, they traded at one bolt to 5 *tu* of rice. The extravagant rate of one bolt for 12 *tu* of rice was reserved for the 400 *tong* of *kongjangmi* or "cotton converted to rice." Since this burden was so heavy on the peasantry, in 1679, the rate was lowered to 10 *tu*, and again in 1843, it was lowered to 8 *tu*. See: *Mangi yoram*, chaeyong-p'yŏn 5, kongmu, kongjangmi ha'nap.

h This 691 *tong* is referred to as "actual disbursement to Wae" (*kwangūp Wae*). The "gross official cotton" (*wŏngongmok*) was 1,121 *tong* 44 *p'il* 32 *ch'ŏk* 3 *chŏn*; originally 400 *tong* of this was converted to rice (*kongjangmi*) for a limited period of five years, but such became relatively automatic, leaving more than 721 *tong* that was given to the Japanese as cotton. The specifics are:

Original allotment	721 *tong* 44 *p'il* 32 *ch'ŏk* 3 *ch'on*
1811: T'ongsinsa was canceled and ship refurbishment reduced the amount	−56 *tong*
	665 *tong* 44 *p'il* 32 *ch'ŏk* 3 *ch'on*
1825: A new annual envoy from Tsushima was accepted	+43 *tong* 42 *p'il* 24 *ch'ŏk*
	709 *tong* 37 *p'il* 21 *ch'ŏk* 3 *ch'on*
Due to a delay in the delivery of water buffalo horn	−17 *tong* 41 *p'il*
	691 *tong* 46 *p'il* 21 *ch'ŏk* 3 *ch'on*

i For a confirmation of this amount in a Japanese document, see: Tashiro Kazui "Bakumakki Ni-chō shi bōeki to Wakan bōeki shōnin: yunyū yon hinmoku no torihiki o chūshin ni," in *Tokugawa shakai kara no tenbō: hatten-kōzō-kokusai kankei –* (Tōkyō: Dōbunkan, 1989): 303.

j This 321 *tong* is also referred to as "actual disbursement to Wae" (*kwangūp Wae*). The specifics given are:

Gross Official Cotton (*wŏngongmok*)	1,121 *tong* 44 *p'il* 32 *ch'ŏk* 3 *ch'on*
In 1651, a certain portion was authorized to be converted to rice (*kongjangmi*)	−400 *tong*
	721 *tong* 44 *p'il* 32 *ch'ŏk* 3 *ch'on*
In recent years (1758 and 1774) because the Wae requested, the cotton was converted to cash to buy ginseng	−600 *tong*
Thus, actual disbursement to Wae	321 *tong* 44 *p'il* 32 *ch'ŏk* 3 *ch'on*
(Actual subtraction)	(121 *tong* 44 *p'il* 32 *ch'ŏk* 3 *ch'on*)

Table 4.5 (cont'd)

The actual subtraction gives us a figure 200 *tong* below that which appears in the budget (indicated in parentheses). The reason is yet unclear. In 1807, official trade cotton ceased to be converted to cash for the purchase of ginseng. The *Mangi yoram* gives us the following specifics on official cotton:

Annual official cotton	1,121 tong 44 p'il 32 ch'ŏk 3 ch'on
less portion for Korean translators (*Hundo, Pyŏlch'a*)	−49 p'il 15 ch'ŏk 3 ch'on
	1,120 tong 45 p'il 17 ch'ŏk
Actually given to Wae	−300 tong (one bolt = 12 *tu*)
1651 conversion to rice	−100 tong (one bolt = 12 *tu*)
1660 conversion to rice	−400 tong (40,000 *yang* for ginseng)
1758 conversion to cash	−200 tong (20,000 *yang* for ginseng)
1774 conversion to cash	+100 tong (10,000 *yang* for cotton)
1790 cash conversion to cotton	+100 tong (10,000 *yang* for cotton)
1795 cash conversion to cotton	+100 tong (10,000 *yang* for cotton)
1797 cash conversion to cotton	+300 tong (30,000 *yang* for cotton)
1806 cash conversion to cotton	(720 tong 45 p'il 17 ch'ŏk)

k The Pusan warehouse was located inside the Pusan Garrison. A brief explanation accompanies the itemized expenses: "Annually fixed provisions given to annual envoys and *pyŏlch'alwae* (irregular envoys)."

l The entry is "Provisions for Wae" (*Wae yomi*) and according to *Tongnae-bu saye*, Pusan ch'angŭp, this entry includes "sacks for rice and supplies for ship repairs" (*yungmul*) as well as "firewood and charcoal" (*sit'an*).

m The conversion rate is taken from: Yŏngnamch'ŏng *saye*, pongsang, wit'ae: "one *sŏk* of beans makes 10 *tu* of rice."

n According to an agreement between Korea and Tsushima in 1811, the official amount of rice converted from cotton (*kongangmi*) was reduced from 16,000 *sŏk* to 13,333 *sŏk* 5 *tu*. See: Yŏngnamch'ŏng *saye*, Waegwan soyong, kongiangmi: "[The Agreement] of 1811 [was that], since last year's Interpreter Envoy [to Tsushima] concluded an agreement that set one bolt of official [trade] cotton at 10 *tu* of polished official [trade] rice, this year [we will] supply official [trade] cotton and official [trade] rice at the reduced [levels]."

o In our source for 1831, we see the reduction agreed on in 1811, and the same reduction appears in our 1849 source as well. But it is absent from the 1870 source. The reason is unknown.

p Accompanying this entry is the following proviso: "The sequestered [for provincial use] rice is 1,779 *sŏk* 2 *tu* 2 *sŭng* 2 *hap* 1 *ch'ak*, and this was delivered in the winter of 1831. The annual plan prepares 8,500 *sŏk*, and this is fixed. But if [we] have not prepared [according to] the plan, or if the [disbursements] to the Wae are insufficient, then [we] make a request and increase the planned consumption of goods." According to this passage, we assume that requests from other warehouses to fill their quotas or requests derived from the unexpected arrival of irregular envoys were ideally held to a maximum of 8,500 *sŏk*. If requests exceeded that limit, then special requests had to be made.

q In our document for 1870, we see a similar statement as in Note p but without a mention of planned limits: "The sequestered [for provincial use] rice is 7,227 *sŏk* 5 *tu* 9 *sŭng* 7 *hap* 1 *ch'ak*, and this was delivered in the winter. If the [disbursements] to the Wae are insufficient, then [we] make a request and increase the planned consumption of goods."

Nevertheless, when looking at other years in the table, there are parts of budgets that differ from the prescriptions and are as yet unclear. For example, the 1870 budget ignores the Agreement of 1811 concerning the rice exchanged from cotton; again, the reason is unclear. All these prescribed and regular budgets were the lion's share of disbursements to the Waegwan. The problems arose with the arrival of Irregular Envoys bearing diplomatic messages. We must now consider how the Irregular Envoys were received, since budgets for them fluctuated.

As expected, we find fluctuations and irregularities among the line items charged with the Irregular Envoys (e.g. Taedong Warehouse). In this connection, the amounts from the Taedong Warehouse differ greatly depending on the year. Furthermore, under the category for the Taedong Warehouse, we find a note: "[If] the sequestered rice . . . is insufficient for the Wae, then file a request to increase the portion for consumption."[43] That is, since the reception expenses for the Irregular Envoys varied by year, when fixed disbursements from the Pusan Warehouse ("annual disbursement of provisions for Annual Envoys [Regular Envoys] and Pyŏlch'awae [Irregular Envoys] are fixed"[44]) were insufficient, then that insufficiency was to be disbursed from the Taedong Warehouse. For example, rice and soybean provisions for Japanese from the Pusan Warehouse had a ceiling of 2,672 sŏk, but when that ceiling was surpassed, petition was to be made to the Taedong Warehouse. Some Irregular Envoy dispersals were fixed because some "Irregular Envoys" such as the Saihan, or "Special Liaison," the Japan House Master, the Sō daimyō's financial deputies (Daikan), Japan House police, scribes, and interpreters, were quite regular, often resident, and their regularity allowed the Koreans to plan.

Theoretically, annual differences in the number of actual Irregular Envoys should appear as differences in the Taedong Warehouse amounts. But matters regarding the Taedong Warehouse were more complicated. To assume that the capacity of the Taedong Warehouse was devoted solely to Irregular Envoys is mistaken. According to the 1832 Tongnae Gazetteer, the Taedong Warehouse ceiling was 8,500 sŏk[45], some of which was to make up shortfalls in other expense categories. The taedong accounts were not only for the Waegwan but also for ceremonies and other functions in Tongnae.[46]

Perhaps, then, we should not include the Taedong Warehouse supplies in our overall addition. Nevertheless, since we want to point out how much of the Tongnae budget was set aside in preparation for the Japanese, in Table 4.5 we have included the amount for the Taedong Warehouse with the other expenses. Also Table 4.5's "Administrative Rice," in a similar fashion, seemed to have played some role in making up shortfalls together with the taedong rice, but we have no specific information. The purpose of including unclear accounts is to find whatever categories may have been used for the Japanese. As will become clear below, we should over-estimate, rather than under-estimate.

In Table 4.5 we are able to confirm the following two points. The first is the total budget (understood at the local level) devoted to the Waegwan for certain years (1790, 1831, 1849, and 1870). These total budgets included official trade accounts and reception expenses, and represent the total account for the Japanese, as known to Tongnae County. That ranged, for the scant number of years we know, from a high of 36,553 sŏk 11 tu (1790) to a low of 30,608 sŏk 3 tu (1831).

127

The second point is the standardization of that budget. At least for the nine-teenth century, when we have detailed records, most categories were fixed by agree-ments with Tsushima and the budgets for the years we know reflect little change. With the exception of a reduction in official trade cotton in 1811, and the fungible Taedong Warehouse accounts, all of the categories generally remained constant.

Table 4.5 gives us an overall picture of the Tongnae accounts devoted to the Waegwan from the Tongnae gazetteers, an often rough and ready record, but Table 4.6 shows us the part of those accounts for 1867 that were devoted to both Regular (First Special Envoy, First Annual Envoy, and Envoy using the Island Lord's juvenile name) and Irregular Envoys from an internal ledger, the *Tongnae-bu saye*. Again, the costs for these envoys were the direct cost of Chosŏn diplomacy with Tsushima and Japan. The total is a bit over 12,351 *sŏk*.

Table 4.7 gives us, again, an overall view of accounts devoted to the Waegwan from figures in the same internal ledger for 1867. What we should note is the general consistency between the totals derived from the 1867 ledger (Table 4.7: 35,955 *sŏk* 10 *tu* 1 *sŭng*) and the totals derived from the gazetteers (Table 4.5: 30,608 *sŏk* 3 *tu* to 36,553 *sŏk* 11 *tu*). If we step back from the county records, and look at the total accounts from the viewpoint of the capital (Table 4.8: 46,798 *sŏk* 14 *tu*), we still see a certain consistency, but we also see a larger figure in central government documents that included the cost of return presents, one of the key elements in the tribute trade. Obviously, Tongnae was not responsible for return presents, since nowhere in the county records do these expenses appear. If we consider the "Subtotal less presents," we drop back to 38,203 *sŏk* 14 *tu*, or roughly what our local documents also show.

The attitude of the Korean government towards the Irregular Envoys was rather negative, but resigned. We find the same explanation concerning the Irregular Envoys in the eighteenth-century text, the *T'ongmun'gwanji*, and in the nineteenth-century text, the *Chŭngjŏng kyorinji*. In short, according to the Kiyu Agreement of 1609, the number of annual Tsushima ships had been decreased compared to the situation before the Hideyoshi invasions, but Sŏ Yoshinari, the Lord of Tsushima, and Yanagawa Kagenao, his chief vassal, requested permission to dispatch extra envoys when unexpected problems arose. The Chosŏn court accepted Sŏ's petition in the 1630s and came to regret it.

> *Ch'awae* (Irregular Envoys) . . . We did not have the Irregular Envoy desig-nation in olden times. From the [time of the] Kiyu [Agreement of 1609, which] decreased [the number of] ships, if there were unusual requests, or requests to trade, [then they] specially sent some prominent Wae bearing a letter. [Since] the court saw them not as an Annual Envoy and in violation of the [Kiyu] Agreement, they were sent away. In like fashion, those who were repatriating prisoners of war and castaways, were also not permitted receptions, but supplied simply with provisions and meals. [And this is how affairs were conducted] until the Island Lord and [Yanagawa] Shigeoki (actually Kagenao) sued each other (i.e. the Yanagawa Affair). The circum-stances were unexpected, and the Court, in accordance with a request, changed its position and began to hold receptions [for Irregular Envoys]. It sincerely instituted [receptions] and gave a lot while getting a little.

Table 4.6 Tongnae-bu accounts devoted to supplying Japanese envoys (1867) according to the *Tongnae-bu saye*

Warehouse and type of supply	Envoy						
	Great irregular envoys	Envoy using the island Lord's juvenile name (Amyŏngwae)	Irregular envoy to repatriate [Japanese] castaways	Irregular envoy to repatriate [Korean] castaways	Chaep'an-wae (Special liaison, J: Saihan) 100 days	[Regular] first special envoy	[Regular] first annual envoy
Pusan warehouse							
Rice for supplies[a]	143 sŏk 6 tu 4 sŭng	69 sŏk 7 tu 6 sŭng	47 sŏk 7 tu 9 sŭng	47 sŏk 7 tu 9 sŭng	144 sŏk 13 tu 7 sŭng	206 sŏk 12 tu 2 sŭng	119 sŏk 11 tu 2 sŭng
Beans for supplies[a]	46 sŏk 2 tu 6 sŭng	9 sŏk 10 tu 1 sŭng	6 sŏk 8 tu 5 sŭng	6 sŏk 8 tu 5 sŭng	52 sŏk 3 tu 3 sŭng	58 sŏk 5 tu 5 sŭng	43 sŏk 13 tu 6 sŭng
Rice for banquets	15 sŏk 2 tu 7 sŭng	1 sŏk 9 tu 8 sŭng	1 sŏk 4 tu 2 sŭng		9 sŏk 4 tu 5 sŭng	16 sŏk 13 tu 8 sŭng	2 sŏk 8 tu 1 sŭng
Beans for banquets	4 sŏk 2 tu 4 sŭng				2 sŏk 7 tu 3 sŭng	2 sŏk 9 tu 3 sŭng	
Travel per diem			2 sŏk	2 sŏk	3 sŏk 8 tu		
Rice specially bestowed	3 sŏk						
Rice sacks	37 sŏk 5 tu	10 sŏk 10 tu	10 sŏk 10 tu	10 sŏk 10 tu	21 sŏk 5 tu		
Rice for bamboo and straw	13 sŏk 10 tu	4 sŏk 11 tu 5 sŭng	5 sŏk 2 tu 5 sŭng	5 sŏk 2 tu 5 sŭng	8 sŏk		
Rice from the Pusan Garrison	41 sŏk 10 tu		5 sŏk 11 tu 5 sŭng	5 sŏk 11 tu 5 sŭng	22 sŏk 4 tu 5 sŭng		
Rice for ships			40 sŏk	40 sŏk			
Daily warehouse							
Rice	258 sŏk 12 tu 4 sŭng	90 sŏk 4 tu 9 sŭng	59 sŏk 3 tu	61 sŏk 12 tu 4 sŭng	+284 sŏk 9 tu 6 sŭng subtotal for 100 days: 548 sŏk 10 tu 9 sŭng × 3.65 subtotal for one year: 2,002 sŏk 12 tu 8 sŭng	297 sŏk 4 tu 4 sŭng	81 sŏk 6 tu 5 sŭng
Rice for requested hawks		30 sŏk					
Rice for miscellaneous goods		3 sŏk 14 tu 1 sŭng					
Reception supplies warehouse							
Rice for banquets	148 sŏk 10 tu 2 sŭng	32 sŏk 2 tu 7 sŭng	19 sŏk 9 tu		90 sŏk 2 tu 7 sŭng (once on each arrival)		
Subtotal	712 sŏk 1 tu 7 sŭng	252 sŏk 10 tu 7 sŭng	197 sŏk 11 tu 6 sŭng	179 sŏk 7 tu 8 sŭng	2,093 sŏk 5 sŭng (365 days)	582 sŏk 2 sŭng	247 sŏk 9 tu 4 sŭng

Table 4.6 (cont'd)

Warehouse and type of supply	Envoy						
	Great irregular envoys	Envoy using the island Lord's juvenile name (Amyŏngwae)	Irregular envoy to repatriate [Japanese] castaways	Irregular envoy to repatriate [Korean] castaways	Chaep'an-wae (Special liaison, J: Saihan) 100 days	[Regular] first special envoy	[Regular] first annual envoy
Diplomatic accounts Official trade cotton[b]						50 tong (725 sŏk)	15 tong 31 bolts (226 sŏk 7 tu)
Cotton for return presents for tribute						16 tong 6 bolts (233 sŏk 11 tu)	16 tong 11 bolts (235 sŏk 3 tu)
Cotton converted to rice						3,333 sŏk 5 tu	3,333 sŏk 5 tu
Subtotal for Irregular Envoys: 3,435 sŏk 2 tu 3 sŭng	712 sŏk 1 tu 7 sŭng[c]	252 sŏk 10 tu 7 sŭng	197 sŏk 11 tu 6 sŭng	179 sŏk 7 tu 8 sŭng[d]	2,093 sŏk 5 sŭng	4,874 sŏk 1 tu 2 sŭng	4,042 sŏk 9 tu 4 sŭng
Total for Irregular Envoys; First Special Envoy; First Annual Envoy:	12,351 sŏk 12 tu 9 sŭng						

Source: Tongnae-bu saye.

Notes:

a The conversion of beans to rice: beans 1 sŏk = rice 10 tu. See: Yŏngnamch'ŏng saye, pongsang, wit'ae: "one sŏk of beans makes 10 tu of rice."

b The conversion of cotton to rice: cotton 1 bolt = rice 4.35 tu. See: T'akjijŏn pugo, 1, suse, (Seoul: Yŏgang ch'ulp'ansa, 1986 photolithograph): 8: "Converting to cotton in every province is at the rate of tax rice one sŏk equals 3.5 bolts of cotton cloth."

c One visit by a taech'awae costs 139 sŏk 8 tu 9 sŭng. According to this, the figure we have here (712 sŏk) probably represents either five different taech'awae or the same taech'awae visiting five times.

d One visit by a "Ch'awae to Repatriate [Korean] Castaways" costs 45 sŏk 12 tu 5 sŭng. According to this, the figure we have here (179 sŏk) probably represents four visits by that ch'awae.

Table 4.7 Total Japanese accounts for 1867 in the *Tongnae-bu saye*

Categories and goods	Amounts	Converted to rice
Cotton	664 *tong* 45 *p'il* 17 *ch'ŏk*	9,641 *sŏk* 1 *tu* 5 *sŭng*[a]
Rice converted from cotton	13,333 *sŏk* 5 *tu*	13,333 *sŏk* 5 *tu*
Ginseng	32 *kŭn* 8 *yang*	6,933 *sŏk* 5 *tu*[b]
Provisions – rice[c]		
Tongnae tax rice	737 *sŏk* 3 *tu* 7 *sŭng*	737 *sŏk* 3 *tu* 7 *sŭng*
Other counties	1,933 *sŏk* 8 *tu* 2 *sŭng* 7 *sŏk*	1,933 *sŏk* 8 *tu* 3 *sŭng*
Provisions – beans		
Tongnae tax beans	197 *sŏk* 9 *tu* 1 *sŭng*	131 *sŏk* 11 *tu* 1 *sŭng*[d]
Other counties	624 *sŏk* 14 *tu* 5 *sŭng*	416 *sŏk* 9 *tu* 7 *sŭng*
Daily supplies (fish, chicken eggs, misc.)	2,424 *sŏk* 1 *tu* 8 *sŭng*	2,424 *sŏk* 1 *tu* 8 *sŭng*
Diplomatic receptions (misc. trade goods and envoy receptions)	1,213 *yang* 8 *chŏn*	404 *sŏk* 9 *tu*[e]
Total		35,955 *sŏk* 10 *tu* 1 *sŭng*

Source: Tongnae-bu saye.

Notes:

a The conversion is one bolt = 4.35 *tu* of rice. See: *T'akjijŏn pugo*, 1, suse, (Seoul: Yŏgang ch'ulp'ansa, 1986 photolithograph): 8: "Converting to cotton in every province is at the rate of tax rice one *sŏk* equals 3.5 bolts of cotton cloth."

b The conversion rates were: ginseng 1 *kŭn* = cash 640 *yang*; cash 1 *yang* = rice 5 *tu*. This 32 *kŭn* 8 *yang* of ginseng is mentioned in the "Waegwan, official trade misc. items" (Waegwan, kong muyŏk chammul) section of the *Tongnae-bu saye*. For the ginseng to cash conversion, see *Tongnae-bu saye*, Waegwan, samjŏn: "[cash] 2,560 *yang* is the price of tax ginseng 4 *kŭn*" or 640 *yang* = tax ginseng 1 *kŭn*. Concerning the cash to rice exchange, see Note e below. The 32 *kŭn* 8 *yang* we see here agrees exactly with the figure we see in the *T'ongmun'gwanji*, but differs with the *Chŭngjŏng kyorinji* figure (30 *kŭn* 14 *yang*).

c In the Provisions – rice (*yomi*) and the Provisions – beans (*yok'ong*) are included all amounts for *pyŏlch'awae*, including straw, bamboo poles, and straw sacks. The cost of the five *pyŏlch'awae* listed was 824 *sŏk* 10 *tu*.

d The conversion of beans to rice was: one *sŏk* of beans = rice 10 *tu*. See: *Yŏngnamch'ŏng saye*, pongsang, wit'ae: "one *sŏk* of beans makes 10 *tu* of rice."

e The conversion rate for cash to rice was: 3 *yang* = 1 *sŏk* or 1 *yang* = 5 *tu*. See: *Tongnae-bu saye*, chidaeŭp: "one *sŏk* converts to 3 *yang*." Compare with the *Mangi yoram*, chaeyong-p'yŏn, 2, suse, san'gun chŏnse changmok p'ojŏn: "changing to cash [is at the rate of] one *sŏk* of rice to five *yang*."

[The Japanese] documents were abundant, therefore [we] supplied [them aplenty]. [Their ranks were] superior, therefore [we] bestowed [on them gifts] accordingly. In the midst of this [there was a] petition [from Sō] Yoshinari. Relying on the [1635] *kyŏmdae* (J: *kentai*) (Amalgamation of Ships') [Agreement], [Sō] cleverly made a list of the names [of the Irregular Envoys] who [now] repeatedly come and cannot be stopped. *The cost [of these Irregular Envoys] is much more than [that of] the [Regular] Envoys, and consequently [they] create incalculable difficulties.*[47]

(emphasis added)

Table 4.8 Expenses related to the Japan House and Japanese envoys in the *Mangi yoram* for 1807

Item	Amount	Converted to rice
Rice and official trade cotton		
Official trade cotton	721 *tong* 44 *p'il*	10,467 *sŏk* 4 *tu*[a]
Official trade rice; [Japan House] provisions and supplies[b]	25,630 *sŏk*	25,630 *sŏk*
Beans	820 *sŏk*	546 *sŏk* 10 *tu*[c]
Cash	800 *yang*	160 *sŏk*[d]
Transportation costs	900 *sŏk*	900 *sŏk*
Rice for receptions and provisions (of castaways)[e]	400–500 *sŏk*	500 *sŏk*
Subtotal less presents		38,203 *sŏk* 14 *tu*
Presents and return gifts for [regular and certain] irregular envoys[f]	42,975 *yang*	8,595 *sŏk*
Total		46,798 *sŏk* 14 *tu*

Source: Mangi yoram, chaeyong-p'yŏn 5, Wae yangnyo.

Notes:
a Cotton conversion rate is one bolt = 4.35 *tu* of rice. See: *T'akjijŏn pugo*, 1, suse, (Seoul: Yŏgang ch'ulp'ansa, 1986 photolithograph): 8: "Converting to cotton in every province is at the rate of tax rice one *sŏk* equals 3.5 bolts of cotton cloth." As mentioned in the text, Kim Ok-kŭn mistakenly converts this cotton at one bolt = 12 *tu*. At that conversion, the amount becomes 28,875 *sŏk* 3 *tu*. See: Kim Ok-kŭn, *Chosŏn hugi kyŏngjaesa yŏn'gu*, pp. 68–70.
b The specifics of this category are:

1) Provisions to the Waegwan	(the values of these three
2) Travel per diem	categories are not specified)
3) Rice for purchases of miscellaneous daily foods	
4) Annual subsidy to the Island Lord in rice and beans	100 *sŏk* (rice: 83 *sŏk*)
	7,180 *sŏk*
5) Cotton converted to rice	+16,000 *sŏk*
Total	23,180 *sŏk*

Although we can find specifics that add up to 23,180 *sŏk*, the *Mangi yoram* mentions a total of 25,630 *sŏk*, a difference of 2,450 *sŏk*, a sum for which we cannot yet account.
In addition to the above five categories, Kim Ok-kŭn includes charcoal and firewood (1,266 *sŏk*) and "sacks for rice and supplies for ship repairs" (*yungmul* 200 *sŏk*) as separate items, but according to the *Tongnae-bu saye* (1868), charcoal, firewood, and sacks for rice and supplies for ship repairs were included in "provisions and supplies." See: Kim Ok-kŭn, Note a above, pp. 62 and 65.
c The conversion of beans is one *sŏk* = rice 10 *tu*. See: *Yŏngnamch'ŏng saye*, pongsang, wit'ae.
d The conversion to cash is one *yang* = rice 3 *tu*. See: *Mangi yoram*, chaeyong-p'yŏn, 2, suse, san'gun chŏnse changmok p'ojŏn: "changing to cash [is at the rate of] one *sŏk* of rice to five *yang*."
e The explanation accompanying this figure is: "Many castaways from ships that come and go lodge in Ungch'ŏn and Kŏje counties, and [they] seek provisions (per diem travel expense). Therefore, annually, [we] take rice and budget it to these counties. This we call "entertain-Japanese per-diem travel-provision rice," and the amount is 400 to 500 *sŏk*." In short, this 400 to 500 *sŏk* is for castaways.
f Presents and return gifts for [regular and certain] irregular envoys include:

1) Presents and return gifts for regular annual envoys	cash 34,819 *yang*
2) Return gifts for the House Master and return gifts from the Tongnae [Magistrate] and [Commander of] Pusan [Garrison]	cash 2,477 *yang*
3) Return gifts for the *Chaep'an* (J: *Saihan*) and return gifts from the Tongnae [Magistrate] and [Commander of] Pusan [Garrison] [as well as] three banquets for the envoy, official in charge of trade and tribute goods, and the attendant	cash 5,679 *yang*
	cash 42,975 *yang*

Without citing a source, Kim Ok-kŭn treats "requests" (*kuch'ŏng*) in a separate category with a value of 8,000 *sŏk*. Here, we have assumed that "requests" were included in the category of return gifts, since there is no such separate account item. The conversion rate was one *yang* = rice 3 *tu*. Finally, as one *kŭn* of ginseng was worth cash 640 *yang*, 42,975 *yang* of cash would have purchased 67 *kŭn*, 2 *yang*, 4 *chŏn*, of ginseng.

We should recall that the Kyŏmdae Agreement of 1635 curtailed the number of official receptions for the 17 Regular Annual Envoys and the three Special Envoys. At the time, Sō obviously appealed for an alternative avenue to make sure that extraordinary messages (e.g. death of a shogun, designation of an heir apparent, etc.) could be properly transferred. Perusing the titles of these Irregular Envoys, we can easily see that they, in fact, were charged with carrying important messages. The Korean court acknowledged that Tsushima's argument was reasonable. Nevertheless, as we see in the passage above, the actual economic motives that Sō's request masked were, of course, realized in Korea and regretted.

Japanese diplomacy towards Chosŏn was Tsushima diplomacy. For Tsushima, diplomacy was the handmaiden to trade. The convenience of representing the Edo *bakufu* lent weight to requests to land and trade. Since the *bakufu* never sent an envoy to Korea, it can be said that, aside from the Korean Communication Embassy to Edo, Tsushima was Japan to late Chosŏn Korea. It can also be said that the function of Japanese diplomacy was to increase Tsushima's trade. Tsushima's Regular and Irregular Envoys carried important messages, but those messages were more often than not mere justification for landing privileges. In such a situation, ideological and diplomatic structures were little more than reasons put forward to enhance trade, at best rationales for ongoing and necessary activities if people were to eat, and at worst, nuisances to be got around with forgery.

How much did it all cost?

We can now finally turn to the question of what portion of Kyŏngsang Province's tax revenues during the seventeenth, eighteenth, and nineteenth centuries went to expenses connected with Japanese. First, we must re-consider our totals for Japanese expenses from two perspectives: the capital and Tongnae. The 46,798 *sŏk* 14 *tu* total in Table 4.8 represents the total expenses for the Waegwan in 1807 as recorded in the capital record, the *Mangi yoram*. This total was the approximate annual cost of the Waegwan in the eighteenth and the nineteenth centuries.

The total in Table 4.7, based on the *Tongnae-bu saye*, (35,955 *sŏk* 10 *tu* 1 *sŭng*) is less than the total in Table 4.8. In other words, from the capital, the expense looked greater, but the reasons were: (1) the Agreement of 1811 reduced the converted rice from cotton from 16,000 *sŏk* to 13,333 *sŏk* (concluded four years after the compilation of the *Mangi yoram*), and (2) certain items given to the Japanese envoys were not included in Tongnae's budget but were rather supplied by the central government. For example, in Table 4.7, ginseng is included, and the Tongnae Magistrate procured this ginseng. In Table 4.7, the amount of ginseng is 32 *kŭn* 8 *yang* (weight), but in Table 4.8 (see: Presents and return gifts), the cost is 42,975 *yang* (coinage) of money, about the value of 68 *kŭn* of ginseng or 32 *kŭn* 8 *yang* with other presents. In the latter half of the eighteenth century, about 60 *kŭn* of ginseng was supplied from Kanggye County (P'yŏng'an Province) in the far northwest.[48] Other goods, which would have fallen under this category (e.g. tiger skins, white silk thread, black sesame seed), came from the Board of Revenue and the Board of Rites of the central government, again, procured from the far reaches of the kingdom. For these reasons, the figures in the *Tongnae-bu saye* and the *Mangi yoram* should not agree. The difference is the goods supplied by the central government, which are included in

Table 4.9 Total cost of the Japan House as a percentage of Kyŏngsang Province tax revenues[49]

Mangi yoram's

$$\frac{\text{Japan House cost}}{\substack{\text{Kyŏngsang Province's} \\ \text{land tax revenues}}} = \frac{46,798.9 \; sŏk}{\substack{83,836.13 \; sŏk \\ \text{(milled)}}} \times 100 = 56\%$$

Tongnae-bu saye's

$$\frac{\text{Japan House cost}}{\substack{\text{Kyŏngsang Province's} \\ \text{land tax revenues}}} = \frac{35,955.67 \; sŏk}{\substack{209,590.32 \; sŏk \\ \text{(milled)}}} \times 100 = 43\%$$

Source: See text.

the *Mangi yoram* but not in the *Tongnae-bu saye*. Thus, the total recorded in the capital is greater than the total recorded at Tongnae.

Now we turn to the question of what portion of the tax revenue of Kyŏngsang Province was devoted to the accounts of the Waegwan. According to the calculations in Table 4.9, we can see that the entire cost (including central government expenses from the *Mangi yoram*) of the Waegwan exceeded half (56 percent) of the tax revenues of Kyŏngsang Province. In Table 4.9 we have also calculated that cost with the total from the *Tongnae-bu saye*, the counry ledger (43 percent). We assume that all payments were in milled rice.

If we reverse the position taken up to now – that reception costs and expenses associated with official trade are calculated together – and consider reception and trade separately, or in other words, consider that trade expenses are not a "burden" but a transaction with a benefit, what do we find? To answer this, we are considering only trade between Tsushima and the government, or official trade. The Chosŏn government received copper and tin in exchange for their official trade expenses. We might recall that Amenomori Hōshū, the Tsushima Confucianist, called the rice that Tsushima received for its copper and tin via the official trade "bought rice" (J: *kaimai*). The reason for this was that, when Tsushima and Chosŏn Korea exchanged goods within the official trade structure, Hōshū and the other inhabitants of Tsushima viewed the goods that Tsushima received as purchased goods. When viewed from Tsushima's perspective, only the grains expended on diplomatic receptions could have been considered a "burden" to Chosŏn; other grains, cotton, etc., were trade goods. But Tsushima got both and that was their fundamental purpose. Table 4.10 presents calculations concerning the cost of the Waegwan from a perspective that discriminates between trade and diplomacy. When we excise "Trade Related Accounts," the "cost" of the Waegwan to Chosŏn falls from 56 percent to 14 percent.

Chosŏn-era views on the function and costs of Japanese diplomacy

During the early Chosŏn period, *c*.1439, the notion that 100,000 *sŏk* was disbursed annually to Japanese envoys became the rhetorical "burden" of relations with Japan,

Table 4.10 Reception costs at the Waegwan as a percentage of Kyŏngsang Province tax revenues[a]

A *Waegwan cost*	46,798.9 *sŏk* (Table 4.8)	
B *Trade related accounts*	*Amount*	*Converted to rice*
Cotton	721 *tong* (50 bolts per *tong*)	10,467.3 *sŏk*
Converted cotton	16,000 *sŏk* (rice)	16,000 *sŏk*
Annual ships' presents (Table 4.8, note f1)	34,819 *yang* (cash)	6,964 *sŏk*
Return gifts for the House Master (Table 4.8, note f2)	2,477 *yang* (cash)	495 *sŏk*
Return gifts for the *Chaep'an* (J: *Saihan*) (Table 4.8, note f3)	5,679 *yang* (cash)	1,136 *sŏk*
$\dfrac{\text{Reception costs for the Japan House}}{\text{Kyŏngsang Province tax revenues}} = \dfrac{11,736.6 \ sŏk}{83,836.13 \ sŏk} \times 100 = 14\%.$ (milled)		

A – B = 11,736.6 *sŏk*

Source: See text.

relations which included the Japan Houses. The enormous figure of 100,000 *sŏk* was about 60 percent of tax revenues in Kyŏngsang Province at the time. When we consider the two components of the Japanese account: reception costs and the cotton trade, then we can get closer to actual, disaggregated figures. From 1471, when successful policies vis-à-vis the Japanese were gathered into the *Haedong chegukki*, the amounts disbursed to Japanese envoys for receptions were at least codified if not, in fact, somewhat curtailed. The amount for receptions alone could have reached a maximum of 22 percent of Kyŏngsang Province's tax revenues. When we include the cotton trade, we see an enormous leap. If 500,000 bolts left the country to Japan, then the figures soar beyond the 100,000-*sŏk* figure, actually reaching 203,666 *sŏk* 10 *tu* or 120 percent of 1439 provincial revenues. Other, more consistent, export figures of 100,000 bolts keep the estimated total around 41 percent of 1439 provincial revenues for receptions and the official cotton trade. Due to the Ōnin War, Japanese demand for Korean cotton was extraordinary, so occasional, large export volumes were possible.[50]

Although early Chosŏn period figures may be nothing more than estimates and calculations, later Chosŏn period figures are directly reported; at least, as seen so far, we have extant figures for the nineteenth century. We can say with a great degree of certainty that, in the later Chosŏn period, the accounts for Japanese envoys and the Waegwan were around 50 percent of Kyŏngsang Province's tax revenues. But if we change our perspective on these same figures, we can arrive at other conclusions. That is, if we subtract the official trade and consider only the costs of diplomatic receptions, then during the later Chosŏn period, the diplomatic "burden" may have been no more than about 14 percent of Kyŏngsang Province's tax revenues.

However crude our calculations, there is no doubt that the accounts connected with the Waegwan, whether they be seen as the price of diplomacy or as trade, played an enormous role in the economy of Kyŏngsang Province and, by extension, a significant role in the national economy. Although in Chapter 3 we mentioned some possible uses for Japanese imports, we are still left with important questions that are beyond this study. For example, where did the Japanese copper and tin go? Who used them to make what? How dependent was Korean coinage and brassware on Japanese imports?

Moreover, we did not discuss private trade since private trade was not a concern of the Korean state except when it turned to smuggling. The relative value of private trade depends on the period, but in general, we can say that the private trade was always subordinate to the official trade. Tsushima ate because of the official trade; it ate much better because of the private trade. If we ask about Japanese silver, we know something of its importation and re-export to China, thanks to the work conducted by Tashiro Kazui, but we do not yet know how that silver circulated within Korea.

Our focus on the regular and irregular costs associated with the Waegwan prevented a consideration of the costs of the entire Japanese connection to the Chosŏn kingdom. To determine that grand total, we must consider the outfitting of the Korean Embassy to Edo, a highly irregular expense, but a substantial irregular expense when one considers the over 200 *kŭn* of ginseng it usually carried. Here, as well, information is still scanty. Thus far, the only data available is in reference to the most valuable of the gifts taken: ginseng. The embassy's costs included the overland journey from Hansŏng to Tongnae: provisioning on the road and while awaiting departure in Tongnae, outfitting of the embassy both in livery and with gifts for the shogun, and the construction and outfitting of Korean vessels for the sea-leg of the trip. A consideration of ginseng addresses only a narrow aspect, albeit an important aspect, since ginseng was one of the most treasured gifts to the shogun. Table 4.11 ("Prices and amounts of ginseng carried by the Communication Embassy") summarizes the available information regarding ginseng.

We can attempt to gain a general perspective on some of these numbers by considering first the amount of ginseng mentioned: 187 *kŭn* to over 248 *kŭn*. In 1720, the Edo Ginseng Market (Edo Ninjin-za) sold a total of 550 *kŭn*. The Osaka market sold 4 *kŭn* and the Kyōtō market sold 9 *kŭn*. Thus, 563 *kŭn* of ginseng was officially sold in Japan in 1720; to present the shogun with a bit over 44 percent of that total or nearly half the ginseng sold in the country in a single year must have been quite a gift.[51]

The relative value of this gift within the Chosŏn economy is expressed in the conversion to rice. The size of these figures is startling. Ranging from 6,329 *sŏk* to 47,872 *sŏk*, at their upper end, they are comparable to the total operating costs for the Japanese to be supported at the Japan House, if that figure was somewhere between 35,955.67 *sŏk* (Table 4.7) and 46,798.9 *sŏk* (Table 4.8).

Bringing civilization to the barbarian was not an insignificant matter. Korean costs were local and national, but some of these "costs" were actually trade. Having assessed the accounts, and their widespread sourcing, it now remains to consider the ideas associated with the numbers in these accounts. We will see a consistency that can be called an aspect of the pre-modern Korean mentality regarding Japan. In other words, we are now in a position to understand the "burden" that Korea carried for Japan.

Table 4.11 Prices and amounts of ginseng carried by the Communication Embassy[52]

Communication Embassy	Ginseng			
	Complete roots	*Cuttings*	*Conversion to cash or rice*	*Comments*
1711	248 *kŭn* 5 *yang* 4 *chŏn*		Cash: 36,953 *yang*[a]; Rice: 7,390 *sŏk* 8 *tu*[b]	
1748	212 *kŭn* 11 *yang* 2 *chŏn*		Cash: 31,650 *yang* Rice: 6,329 *sŏk* 14 *tu*	
1763	233 *kŭn* 15 *yang* 5 *chŏn*	41 *kŭn* 3 *yang* 6 *chŏn*	Cash: 112,305 *yang* Rice: 22,461 *sŏk* Cash: 3,957 *yang* 6 *chŏn* Rice: 791 *sŏk* 8 *tu* Total Rice: 23,252 *sŏk* 8 *tu*	
1786	200 *kŭn*	40 *kŭn*	Cash: 134,400 *yang* Rice: 26,880 *sŏk* Cash: 18,240 *yang* Rice: 3,648 *sŏk* Total Rice: 30,528 *sŏk*	Expedition postponed
1802	187 *kŭn*		Cash: 239,360 *yang* Rice: 47,872 *sŏk*	

Source: Ch'im Sang-kyu, ed., *Mangi yoram*, chaeyong-p'yŏn 5, sinsam, (Seoul: Inmunhwa-sa, 1972): 761.

Notes:

a *Kanggyebu ŭpchi*, samsu, (Kyujanggak cat. no. 10948); MS reproduced in *Sasŏn ŭpchi* no. 53, P'yŏngan-do no. 9, (Seoul: Hanguk inmungwa hakwŏn, 1990): 227. According to the *Kanggyebu ŭpchi*:

1711 – *sam* 1 *kŭn* = 148 *yang* 8 *chŏn*	1786 – *ch'esam* 1 *kŭn* = 672 *yang*
1748 – *sam* 1 *kŭn* = 148 *yang* 8 *chŏn*	*misam* = 456 *yang*
1763 – *ch'esam* 1 *kŭn* = 480 *yang*	1802 – *sinsam* 1 *kŭn* = 1280 *yang*
misam 1 *kŭn* = 96 *yang*	

b According to the *Mangi yoram*, chaeyong-p'yŏn, 2, suse, san'gun chŏnse changmok p'ojŏn, the conversion rate was: one *yang* cash = rice 3 *tu*.

The burden stated by literate Koreans

Given the specificity of our particular idea – the cost of the Japanese connection to Chosŏn Korea – we are limited to those texts that make reference to foreign affairs or those texts that discuss state finances. When the Japanese are mentioned in reference to state finances we have what we seek, but then we must judge how widely the idea was disseminated. Among the few bits and pieces that have been gathered for consideration below are two references that we wish to give particular weight. These two references are drawn from one work (*Yongjae ch'onghwa*) from the early Chosŏn period and one work from the later Chosŏn period (*Ch'un'gwanji*). They first came to our attention, not in their original form, but as excerpts found in a very unusual collection of almost encyclopedic proportion, dating from the eighteenth century. It is, in fact, their appearance in the eighteenth-century *Yŏllyŏsil kisul* that we want to note.

The compiler/author of the *Yŏllyŏsil kisul*, Yi Kŭng-ik (1736–1806), a native of Chŏlla Province, denied himself an official career, probably in disgust at factional politics. His great uncle was accused of treason and imprisoned; his father was banished and died in exile. Kŭng-ik remained in seclusion his entire life and devoted his energies to historical study, leaving us a "monumental work"[53] in the form of a *yasa* or unauthorized history. There were many such *yasa*, but Yi Kŭng-ik's style and approach were extremely unusual. He employed a narrative style (*kisa ponmal ch'e*, literally, a record from beginning to end), instead of the two styles favored by official histories and other writers. Official histories employed the annal-biography style (*kijŏn ch'e*) seen in the *Samguk sagi* and the *Koryŏsa*. In contrast to the strict annalistic style (*p'yŏnnyŏn ch'e*) found in the *Tongguk t'onggam* and the *Koryŏsa chŏryo*, Yi Kŭng-ik used a style much like our modern historical style: he gathered information from over 400 sources and arranged it by subject. He neither paraphrased nor neglected to cite his sources. In fact, he left blanks and encouraged his readers to insert new data they might discover. Consequently, his work has been described as the most "scholarly," the easiest to understand, the most interesting,[54] and "one of the most useful histories of the Yi dynasty."[55] Of central importance to us, the *Yŏllyŏsil kisul* is said to have been "universally disseminated."[56]

These twentieth-century assertions of the quality and wide dissemination of an early nineteenth-century text beg for concrete studies of the use to which the *Yŏllyŏsil kisul* was put in its own society. We as yet have no information on its publication nor do we have record of its pedagogical use in the state or the private academies, two avenues that might place the *Yŏllyŏsil kisul* squarely in a popular context. For the moment, we must accept these assertions of its dissemination.

From a strict methodological point of view, we must also consider this text and others mentioned below as more than "objects whose distribution needs only to be catalogued or as entities with meanings that can be spoken of in universal terms."[57] They were read and understood by pre-modern Koreans in ways foreign to twenty-first-century readers. Through the explanation above, we can now historicize our reading of these texts and understand their usage of the terms "trade," "diplomacy," and specifically, "financial burden" and "reception."

Returning to our data, what we have are five corroborating statements, three of which were reported in the *Yŏllyŏsil kisul*. These three statements appeared in works that attracted their own fame, and being repeated in the *Yŏllyŏsil kisul* ensured an even wider dissemination. But to the point, the rhetorical similarity of all five reports suggests the existence of an idea, an idea to which we now turn.

Yi Kŭng-ik's *yasa*, the *Yŏllyŏsil kisul*, twice quantifies the "burden" of the Waegwan. The first mention was quoted from Sŏng Hyŏn's *Yongjae ch'onghwa* (fifteenth century):

> Since Tsushima's ground is rocky and there is a lack of soil, the five grains do not grow. Because only Chinese pink flowers can be planted, people pick the roots of arrowroot and fernbrake and eat them. The Island Lord lives on the taxes he receives from the Three Ports. [Some] of the island people have received [Korean] government titles and have become *hogun* (a generic term for two lower military titles). They come annually. Since never less than fifty ships arrive annually, stay for several months, and receive provisions with which they feed their families, *more than half* the grains from *lower* Kyŏngsang Province are lost to the costs of the Wae (Japanese).[58]
>
> (emphasis added)

Sŏng Hyŏn lived from 1439 to 1504 and was describing the burden of receiving and dealing with the Japanese during the fifteenth century. Sŏng Hyŏn came from a line of eminent scholars and officials, and his *Yongjae ch'onghwa* is a collection of miscellaneous writings on his interests and experiences. Being something of a literary prodigy, he held many high positions, at both central and provincial levels, and even traveled to China twice where his talents were recognized. The *Yongjae ch'onghwa's* purview is wide: stories from government offices, conversations with famous personages, comments on classics, painting, music, poetry, history, geography, customs, rituals, foreign relations, and women. Sŏng Hyŏn was not stuffy and turned his brush to ghost stories and comic tales as well. The *Yongjae ch'onghwa* was a literary achievement of the age. The *Yŏllyŏsil kisul* quotes Sŏng Hyŏn's *Yongjae ch'onghwa* faithfully.

Sŏng Hyŏn's understanding was not his alone. In the latter half of the fifteenth century, the court developed a concern with the rise in the Japanese population in the Three Ports.[59] In the *Veritable Records* for the fifth year of Sŏngjong (1474), we see the following passage:

> Yi Sŏ-chang, the Inspector-General (Jr.2), memorialized the throne. . . . Of the tax taken in Kyŏngsang Province *more than half* is used as expenditure for receiving the Wae. In various coastal towns, the granaries are completely empty. Presently, we move rice from regions and counties in the north of the province to make up the deficiency. Providing for the Wae will result in destitution.[60]

> (emphasis added)

Here we also see an assertion to the effect that "more than half" of the taxes are used for the reception of Japanese.

These two passages from the fifteenth century introduce the memory we wish to trace, but let us be careful. We should not lose sight of the qualification in Sŏng Hyŏn's first passage: "more than half of the grains from *lower* Kyŏngsang Province," which is missing in all other passages.[61] What significance it carries is yet unclear. This important qualifier deserves further investigation. Does "lower Kyŏngsang Province" mean only the coastal counties, and so half of the coastal counties' granaries were exhausted to support the Japanese? Furthermore, was this the state of affairs behind both Sŏng Hyŏn's "lower Kyŏngsang Province" and Yi Sŏ-chang's mention of the northern granaries supplying grain to the coast? If so, then the amount going to the Japanese was half of half the taxes of Kyŏngsang Province, or only some 25 percent. As will become clear from other such passages, 25 percent was not the transmitted memory; 50 percent was. Only Sŏng Hyŏn's statement explicitly mentions *lower* Kyŏngsang Province in connection with expenses for the Japanese, whereas Yi Sŏ-chang gives the clear impression that the Japanese ate half of the entire province's production. Yi Sŏ-chang's statement appears more authoritative for several reasons. First, it is consistent with all of our other data. Second, Yi Sŏ-chang's report in the *Sillok* was recorded at the highest forum of government debate, so it was probably scrutinized for ambiguity and clarity. His audience was the king and high ministers. Sŏng Hyŏn's passage was written later, in retirement, for a general audience, and cannot be read too literally. Finally, if detail suggests accuracy, then

Yi Sŏ-chang's statement, being more detailed regarding supplies and logistics, would carry greater weight. Yi Sŏ-chang mentions moving rice from the north of the province, because the coastal granaries were empty. If the coastal granaries were empty, then the lower half of the province was completely exhausted. That is, half of the province's tax grain was gone, not half of the coastal granaries' tax grain. Thus, for reasons of consistency, audience, and detail, we should take Yi Sŏ-chang's statement as authoritative. But is accuracy necessary when constructing rhetoric? Thus far we have considered the argument as one of accuracy or authority, but exactitude may not be necessary to convey the general rhetorical image we are actually seeking. What both passages, as well as the others presented below, point out is the enormity of the burden, and the consistent use of the word "half." This is the image we want to stress, since it was that simple statement "more than half" that was most widely disseminated. Our purpose is to emphasize the rhetorical image all these statements convey and to compare that image with an objective reality.

Leaving the fifteenth century behind, we move to the eighteenth and come across similar statements. Another passage from the *Yŏllyŏsil kisul* was taken from the *Ch'un'gwanji*, a text compiled by Yi Maeng-hyu at the behest of the king in 1744. That passage reads:

> [The *ch'awae* (J: *sawa* or irregular envoy) said that as] the lord of Tsushima has no other [productive capabilities] aside from the lands in Chikuzen (modern Fukuoka), [he] requests that [we] take 300 *tong* (of cotton) from among [the official trade cotton] and convert this to rice at the rate of 12 *tu* per bolt. [We] gave them special permission to convert [cotton to rice] for five years and drew up a mutually acceptable agreement. In the year *kyŏngja* (1660), the *ch'awae* again, since the cotton was restored, made statements, very selfishly getting angry and hoarse. The court increased the permitted [amount] by 100 *tong* making 400 *tong* converted to rice, altogether making 16,000 *sŏk* [of rice]. Cloth for official trade reached over 47,000 bolts. The financial strength of *half* of Kyŏngsang Province is all devoted to the needs of entertaining the Wae.[62]
>
> (emphasis added)

When we compare this statement to the fifteenth-century statements above, we can see that they are all virtually the same. Since the *Ch'un'gwanji* is a collection of case studies related to the Board of Rites, it is thought that Yi Maeng-hyu wrote the passage after referring to documents possessed by the Board of Rites. Since we can see references in the *Ch'un'gwanji* passage to rice specially converted from cotton (discussed above), it is clear that the passage refers to the latter Chosŏn period and the *kyŏngja* year is 1660. From 1651 to 1660, negotiations dragged on between Tsushima and Korea over Tsushima's request to convert a certain portion of Korea's official trade cotton to rice. The Korean court initially permitted 300 *tong* (15,000 bolts) for five years, but from 1660 the amount was raised to 400 *tong*. Thereafter, every five years, Tsushima re-negotiated an extension. Usually the five-year renewals were more-or-less automatic, but sometimes, renewal of the five-year grants required difficult negotiations.[63]

140

In a court debate, which appeared in the *Piguk tŭngnok* and was reported in the *Yŏllyŏsil kisul*, the issue was whether or not to give additional trade documents to the lord of Tsushima. Here, again, we find a familiar lament:

In 1709, the Japanese came to request a *tosŏ* (seal necessary for trade) in the name of the Tsushima lord's son whose name was Hikochiyo.[64] The king conferred with the State Council. All were of the opinion that, in the past, [we] issued seals bearing childhood names twice and refused also twice. In the time of [King] Injo [1595–r.1623–1649], since merit had accrued to Hikozō and Hikomitsu,[65] [we] employed special favor and permitted the bestowal [of seals], but afterwards the court directed that this action was not to establish a precedent. Afterwards, Ukyō [Sō Yoshitatsu] and Jirō[66] were designated heirs apparent to the Island Lord and pursued a request for trade seals in their childhood names. [Since] the refusal from the court at this time was just, these lords [of Tsushima] did not dare bring up the request again. Now, this [matter of] Hikochiyo's seal is again something not to be lightly permitted. Kim Chin-gyu [put up the] sharpest rebuttal, stating, "At present, *the [financial] strength of the people of Yŏngnam* (Kyŏngsang Province) has already been exhausted in entertaining the Wae. To permit [the issuance of another] seal in a casual fashion would add a ship and that would be an incalculable waste. In the end, we cannot permit this." In [1712], the Island Lord sent a letter again earnestly requesting [a seal], and the court had no choice but to issue permission.[67]

(emphasis added)

Here the burden is not quantified, but generalized to "the [financial] strength of the people of Yŏngnam (Kyŏngsang Province)."

Another eighteenth-century text, the *T'ongmun'gwanji*, goes even further in characterizing Japanese expenses as a drain on the country with no returns:

Again, because of the [Japanese invasion] in the *imjin* year (1592), we expelled [the Japanese]. In 1609, (the Japanese monk-diplomat) Genso came to negotiate. [We permitted] 20 ships; compared to the past, [we] reduced ship numbers by over half. Yet, [they] were provisioned and given gifts to take home. *The cost is not less than 100 times the old practice. A consideration of the* Haedong chegukki *reveals this.* Concerning official trade, although the *Kyŏngguk taejŏn* specifies the market price for return gifts [to the Japanese for their tribute], still whenever they come, [they] plead for a reduction of prices! After we fixed the prices, to our surprise, the evils multiplied. Gradually, [the situation] has amounted to this extreme. *They give us copper, tin, millet seed, pepper, and more, [but these] goods are of no profit to the country. [Their] expenses are what reduce the value [of their goods]. That is, in general, everything [they bring becomes] ten times [the price] relative to the private market.* Therefore, the annual supplies of cotton [given to the Japanese] amount to 60,000 bolts. Recently we have permitted cotton to be again converted to rice. That is, [return goods for Japanese goods] were at first supplied in cotton [bolts] of 8 *sŭng* (640 threads, indicating the width of the woof; one *sŭng* has 80 threads), 40 *chŏk* (feet) [long] with blue thread on each end. Accordingly, the Wae have made this the standard and [always] demand the same. We are unable to make everything the same. Gradually quality has declined to 5 *sŭng* (400 threads) [in width] and 35 *chŏk* [in length]. The irregular envoy's arrival brings a bitter fight every year.[68]

(emphasis added)

According to this passage, when one compares the cost that the Japanese pose to Korea in the later Chosŏn period with that cost explained in the *Haedong chegukki* for the early Chosŏn period, the later period exceeds the former period by 100 times. Moreover, the price of the goods brought by the Japanese as trade goods (copper, tin, etc.) is ten times the price of the private market, creating a loss in national expenditures.

Finally, we see the survival of the same rhetoric – Tsushima got half of Kyŏngsang Province's production – into the period after the new Meiji government initiated communications with the Chosŏn government. In the twelfth month of 1868, Tsushima sent an envoy to Pusan bearing news of the establishment of the new Meiji government. In the second month of 1869, the *Hundo*, An Tong-jun (1826–1875), citing irregularities in the documents, refused to accept the missive. Among the many irregularities of the documents (principally the use of Chinese characters for "emperor" and "imperial decree") was also the fact that the letter did not bear the seal issued by Korea to Tsushima. The Taewŏngun upheld the *Hundo*'s refusal to accept the Japanese documents and a deadlock ensued between Korea and Japan. In the eighth month of 1872, the Japanese Gaimushō took possession of the Waegwan, and in the third month of 1873, installed a Gaimushō official as House Master, changing the name of the Waegwan to *Tae-Il Konggwan* (J: *Dai Nihon Kōkan*).

With this situation developing, Pak Kyu-su (1807–1876) sent a letter to the Taewŏngun, dated 1874,[69] offering commentary on the foreign policy being conducted at Tongnae. Pak Kyu-su discussed the offensive Chinese characters and then went on to discuss the new seal used by the Japanese representatives. Pak Kyu-su's opinion probably carried some authority regarding the formulation of foreign policy, as he was Governor of P'yŏng'an Province when the General Sherman sailed up the Taedong River in the seventh month of 1866 and was destroyed with the loss of all hands.[70] He was also famous as a proponent of the advantages of foreign trade and later was a key player in the court's decision to negotiate with Japan for what became known as the Kanghwa Treaty of 1876.[71] Pak wrote:

The fact that they did not impress [their document] with the seal we gave them, but [rather] with a new stamp [means] our country's seal is superfluous. This is laughable. Giving [them] this seal [means that they] are our [political] servants! [It means] we have enfeoffed [them]! *[We] slice off half of the fat and blood of Kyŏngnam (Kyŏngsang Province) and offer it to them.* One seal made and given allows them [to take that]. All the universe laughs at this! [But] now they do not [even] use it. [They] use their new stamp. [This is just] too much to bear. Moreover, to abrogate agreements is shameful. Now, in [their] letter, if we want to establish our old Agreements, then we

142

ought to order [them to produce] a letter and a list [of tribute]. The en-
velope [must have] both stamp and [our] seal. It is appropriate [that they]
obey our command. This foolishness is a serious matter.[72]

(emphasis added)

Here, "they" obviously refers to Tsushima, traditional recipient of Yŏngnam's "fat
and blood," and "feudatory" of Korea. Pak Kyu-su does not quantify the exact amount
of "fat and blood" taken from Kyŏngsang Province but repeats the, by now dogmatic,
rhetorical "half."

All of the comments above originate from both the early and later Chosŏn
periods. When we consider that the broad quantifying statements from the *Yongjae
ch'onghwa* ("more than half from lower Kyŏngsang"), the *Veritable Records* ("more
than half"), the *Ch'un'gwanji* ("half"), and the general assessment of the *Piguk tŭngnok*
("strength of the people") appeared in their own rights and some of them were later
incorporated into the *Yŏllyŏsil kisul*, a product of the end of the eighteenth century
and the beginning of the nineteenth century, we can hypothesize what early and
late Chosŏn-era Koreans thought regarding the burden posed by the Waegwan.
In short, the rhetoric used by literate Koreans stated that over half of the government's financial resources from Kyŏngsang Province were being handed over to the
Japanese. Whether the rhetoric ultimately reflected popular belief is probably impossible to determine, but the power of this particular image was sufficient to have
dominated the literate discourse on the costs of the Japanese connection. Virtually
everywhere a literate Korean of the Chosŏn kingdom could have turned for information on the cost of the Japanese connection, he would have seen the word "half"
in connection with Kyŏngsang Province's revenues.

Finally, we might ask just why the Chosŏn dynasty accommodated the Japanese at
the Waegwan if literate opinion saw the Japanese as an exorbitant expense. We
have already raised the question above that Korea probably obtained certain goods
of value, that the Chosŏn kingdom may have had a real need for Japanese trade,
perhaps even one or more real dependencies on Japanese goods, but there were
other reasons, the ones which commonly appear in documents, the ones that seemed
to work in swaying court opinion. These were arguments both practical and moral.
The following passages from the early and late Chosŏn periods illustrate the practical application of a moral foreign policy. In short, Korean security came cheaper
when bought with trade. Withholding trade risked border disturbances and a re-
appearance of Japanese marauders. The first statement that follows was by none
other than Yi Hwang (T'oegye), a man widely considered to have been one of
Chosŏn Korea's foremost Confucian philosophers.

In the early Chosŏn period, T'oegye argued for the re-establishment of relations
with Tsushima in a 1545 memorial that presented the entire question as one of how
a civilized country should deal with barbarians who "hasten for aid to some great
country." Japanese had attacked and sacked the city of Saryang in 1544. Relations
were immediately severed, but by 1545 the court was debating a reversal of policy.
T'oegye opined:

... Now, the incident at Saryang, which the island barbarians [caused]
recently, was not worse than the thieving of dogs or mice. Since we have

already killed these brigands and thrown them back, and have wiped out the buildings where they stayed and expelled them, the might of our country has been shown, and the laws of the king have been put right again. . . . If [at this time], when the balance [of power] is favorable to us, we forget about this force [of circumstance] and treat them with frankness, they will certainly consider this as a great virtue and feel gladness in their hearts. And leading each other, they will submit to us. This is what is meant by "transforming them." And [when we have succeeded in transforming them], it is not even necessary to talk about "appeasing them."[73]

Appeasement referred to the threat of piracy that a hungry Tsushima might initiate.

The following is a snippet from a court debate on the five-year renewal of the cotton conversion element within official trade. It clarifies the practical view towards Tsushima's dependency.

In 1705, the Wae requested that we take cotton destined for them as a part of official trade and convert it to rice, giving them the rice instead of the cotton. We enquired of the State Council and Yun Chi-wan (1635–1718), a *Yŏngbusa* (*Yŏngjung ch'u pusa*, First Minister, Sr. 1 rank, Office of Ministers Without Portfolio), memorialized: "I went to Japan as an envoy (1682 Korean Embassy to Edo) some years ago. We returned to Tsushima [on the return journey to Korea], and after boarding ship, I noticed that the Japanese interpreter was very clever and asked him, '[since] there is no land on which to grow grains here on this isolated island, how do you get along?' To which he replied, 'before we obtained Korean grains, those with children could not endure seeing them grow up to starve to death and would summarily toss them into the sea. Now all children born [here] [can be] brought up. Because of this, the island prospers. Although the ordinary people have Japanese names, they differ not, in truth, from the peoples who live on the frontiers of Chosŏn.' This matter of permitting the conversion of [cotton] to rice, taken in light of the national budget, is, for the most part, mistaken. Nevertheless, since [King] Hyomyo's reign (Hyojong, r. 1649–1659) we have embarked down this path. Without [some clear] resolution [on our part], dare we not attach significance to [these precedents]. Whether to [answer] [Tsushima's] request for rice is the difference between having children and raising them or not. The circumstances [facing the island people] necessitate obstinate persistence at the risk of death. If [your majesty] turns toward a difficult border, and in the end, entertains no [requests] and grants no [favors], then we cannot avoid great losses to the nation [through pillage and raids]. Is it not best, in accordance with Ch'oe Sŏk-jŏng's [proposal], to limit the years and authorize a grant, since later, the principle of no new requests [can] be proclaimed in strict additions to agreements?" The king ordered forbearance for five years and permitted the disbursement of rice.[74]

Both passages reflect the same attitude, an attitude that needed little abstract rhetoric to communicate its force, that is, as long as one could recall Waegu pirates and Hideyoshi's invasion. The attitude naturally assumed Chosŏn's superiority to Tsushima, and by extension to Japan, but the attitude possessed other elements. We also find Confucian benevolence, even pity perhaps, and we certainly find pragmatism.

The rhetorical image carried by literate Koreans towards the Waegwan and its denizens depicted a heavy burden to the Chosŏn kingdom, a heavy burden tolerated first for reasons of border security and second for the generosity required of a great land towards its inferior. Enabling pirates to become peaceful traders was cheaper than fortifying the coasts. The poverty of Tsushima was seen clearly as the cause of their piracy and demanded generous understanding. In the end, we are still forced to admit a third reason. We can, as yet, pose this reason only in question form: What economic benefits did Chosŏn Korea derive from the Waegwan trade? Specifically, who used the imported metals and other goods to manufacture what goods, and how common to Chosŏn life were these goods?

Conclusion

Diplomacy with Japan tied up half of Kyŏngsang Province's revenues in the post-Hideyoshi period, an enormous and significant sum no matter how we view it. Whether Japanese accounts were reception expenses or trade accounts or some combination thereof, the Korean perception was one of loss and expense. When we disaggregate these accounts, we find actual reception expenses to have been low, but there is no doubt that the role of Japanese trade in the economy of the former and later Chosŏn periods was obviously significant. Tongnae had to source its requirements from all over Kyŏngsang Province. In a regional arrangement where Tsushima was so economically dependent, Kyŏngsang Province was affected in ways we are only beginning to see, if yet dimly. Undoubtedly, the economies of Kyŏngsang Province and Tsushima Island should be considered as a single entity.

The above takes a functional and material approach to consider the working diplomatic activities of the various envoys plying the straits between Korea and Japan. Our purpose in doing so is simple: the actual, day-to-day relations between pre-modern Korea and Japan have all too often been obscured by ideological rhetoric produced by intellectuals based in the capital cities. Only by building an economic and political context based on the realities of the frontier can we begin to judge the relevance of intellectual rhetoric. The size of the sums revealed above demonstrate the deep involvement of Chosŏn Korea, Tsushima, and Japan in each other's economies and polities and show that pre-modern Northeast Asia possessed the dynamics of a regional, integrated system.

5

THE POLITICAL SIGNIFICANCE OF THE WAEGWAN

> Furthermore, I am sending a letter to [Tsushima] remonstrating with the Island Lord; saying that you people have an untold excess of crimes. The [proper] way of receiving people from afar [does] not allow us to treat matters lightly. By all means, the law comes first.
>
> (From a report in the *Waein changna tŭngnok* dated 1690)[1]

In Chapter 4 we examined the extent of Tsushima's role in the economy of Kyŏngsang Province through official trade and receptions. We reconstructed accounts and compared those to what was commonly believed. We turn now to the Korean political-administrative structure governing Tongnae County and the Waegwan and ask: how much did the Japanese presence concern the local official in charge, the Magistrate of Tongnae County?[2] This chapter will provide an overview of the problems facing the Tongnae Magistrate in connection with the Japanese, and in the two chapters that follow, we will examine case studies – rioting and prostitution – to illustrate the volatile administrative challenge presented by the Waegwan.

In this chapter we will assess the political significance of the Waegwan. To judge "significance," we will describe the administrative apparatus and examine the types of concerns the Japanese raised for the Magistrate. We will approach the problem in two ways. First, we will look at the administrative history of Tongnae and describe the duties of the Tongnae functionaries, particularly those connected with the Waegwan. Second, we will statistically quantify the size of the Japanese presence as an administrative concern to the Tongnae Magistrate.[3]

Administrative history of the Tongnae Magistrate

The sixth sovereign of the Koryŏ kingdom, Sŏngjong (r. 981–997), divided the Korean peninsula into 12 provinces in 983. In 1018, the system was further refined, and at this time the circuit called Kyŏngsang Province was formed. The name derives from a combination of the first Chinese character in the names of the cities of Kyŏngju and Sangju, indicating a circuit that encompassed the two unified Silla administrative divisions centered on Kyŏngju (ancient Kŭmsŏng) and Sangju.

The National Code (*Kyŏngguk taejŏn*), promulgated under the Chosŏn monarch Sŏngjong in 1471, describes the basic administrative structure of Kyŏngsang Province for the period that concerns us. Prior to 1600, the provincial seat was Kyŏngju, where the Governor or *Kwanch'alsa* (Jr. 2) conducted business. From 1600 to 1895, the *Kwanch'alsa* was simultaneously appointed Magistrate of Taegu, which became the provincial seat.[4] Under him were the various county magistrates.[5] Tongnae was one of 66 counties in 1454 and one of 71 in 1832.[6]

King Sejong's Treatise on Geography (*Sejong sillok chiriji*) of 1454 set out the standard administrative history of Tongnae.[7] Tongnae first entered recorded history as Ko'hwangsan-guk ("Old Rough Mountain Country") or Naesan-guk ("Wild Herb Mountain Country"). In Naesan-guk we first see the *nae* (wild herb) in Tong*nae* (literally, "Eastern Wild Herb"). The Silla kingdom (A.D. ?–935) took the territory and called it Kŏch'ilsan-gun ("Residing in Lacquer Mountain" district). Under King Kyŏngdŏk (r. 742–765), ruler of unified Silla, the name was changed to Tongnae. King Hyŏnjong (r. 1009–1031) of the Koryŏ kingdom (918–1392) placed it under Ulju (Ulsan), a port city up the east coast to the north. Afterwards it was made an independent county magistracy (*Hyŏllyŏng*).

King T'aejo (r. 1392–1398), founder of the Chosŏn kingdom, established a garrison at Tongnae in 1397 governed by a military officer, a *Pyŏngmasa*, who was also a civil officer, a *P'anhyŏnsa*. The military officer was a Koryŏ kingdom official, Sr. 3 rank, first mentioned in 1176,[8] whose duties from King Ch'ungnyŏl's (r. 1275–1308) time included defense against Waegu.[9] The civil officer does not appear in the *Samguk sagi*, the *Koryŏsa*, or the *Kyŏngguk taejŏn*. Under King Sejong (r. 1418–1450), the garrison was moved to the sub-county, Tongp'yŏng, on the harbor. In connection with the 1419 attack on Tsushima, various high-ranking army and navy officers were stationed in Tongnae. Afterwards, a Magistrate (*Hyŏllyŏng*, civil Jr. 5) was again put in charge of Tongnae, thereby returning to the traditional division of civil and military. From 1547 to 1592, the Magistrate became a Town Magistrate (*Tohobusa*, Jr. 3). The promotion was directly associated with the re-location of the Waegwan from Chep'o, and the new responsibilities connected with Japanese relations. The promotion also subsumed the military garrisons under the Magistrate's direction and abolished the independent county status of Tongp'yŏng. After the fall of Tongnae to Hideyoshi's armies in 1592, Tongnae's status dropped back to *Hyŏllyŏng* until 1599, when it was again elevated to *Tohobusa* to receive a Ming general. It was not until 1604 that the post again became a civil appointment.[10] In 1895, as a part of the sweeping government reforms known as the Kabo Reforms, the post became a *Kunsu* (Great County Magistrate, Jr. 4), but towards the end of the Chosŏn period, *Kunsu* replaced not only *Tohobusa*, but *Moksa* (City Magistrate, Sr. 3), and *Hyŏn'gam* (Small County Magistrate, Jr. 6) as well.[11] The Tongnae Magistrate finally became a *Puyun* (old style: Special Capital Magistrate, Jr. 2) in 1896. In 1903, Tongnae-bu became Tongnae-gun and the Magistrate again became a *Kunsu* (Great County Magistrate).[12] By this time, the Japanese settlement in Tongnae, centered on the old Waegwan site, was becoming the trading, transport, and financial core of the modern metropolis of Pusan.

Tongnae County officials connected with the Waegwan

There were five major officials, a sub-group of lesser officials, and other service and military personnel posted in the area of the Waegwan.[13] Since we discussed the Japanese officials in Chapter 2, here we will consider only the Koreans: ceremonial officials, liaison officials, and military officials.

Ceremonial officials

We should recall from the discussion of trade in Chapter 3 that all contact was predicated on the tribute offered by Tsushima to Korea. The essence of tribute is ceremony and symbolism, so we must also start any discussion of Tongnae officials who handled the Japanese with a discussion of ceremonial officials. The Reception Official (*Chŏbwigwan*) was actually two officials, a Capital Reception Official (*Kyŏng Chŏbwigwan*), and a Provincial Reception Official (*Hyang Chŏbwigwan*). Capital Reception Officials were dispatched from the capital for the Great Irregular Envoys from Japan (*Taech'awae*)[14] and possessed a Sr. 3 rank; their status was equivalent to that of the three top officials who composed the Korean Embassy to Edo.[15] We should recall that the Great Irregular Envoys carried correspondence addressed to the *Ch'amp'an* (Jr. 2, Vice-minister) in the capital, the official in the Board of Rites, above the Reception Official (*Chŏbwigwan*), to whom the *bakufu* addressed its correspondence for routine matters. The Reception Officials had existed from before Hideyoshi and were then called *Sŏnwisa*; in 1629, however, this was changed to *Chŏbwigwan*.[16]

The Provincial Reception Official was ostensibly a *suryŏng* (generic term for local magistrate) dispatched from the Governor of the province.[17] In fact, the Tongnae Magistrate and the Commander of the Pusan Garrison simply assumed this title when they received and negotiated with Waegwan officials or Japanese envoys.[18] The Provincial Reception Official's responsibility was to entertain the Minor Irregular Envoys (*Soch'awae*) and the Tsushima Special Liaison (J: *Saihan*, K: *Chaep'an*) at the Yŏn[hyang] Taech'ong (banquet hall outside the north wall of the Waegwan). These envoys from Tsushima were bearing letters from the Tsushima *daimyō* to the *Ch'amŭi* (Sr. 3, Councillor), the capital official in the Board of Rites to whom the lord of Tsushima addressed his correspondence. Both the Capital and Provincial Reception Officials were responsible for handing over return gifts and replies to letters at the formal banquets for the Great and Minor Irregular Envoys from Tsushima.

Other ceremonial officials were two *Ch'abigwan* (Sr. 3) or Special Officials who advised the Provincial Reception Official. They were charged with handling tributary items and were temporarily appointed from among the *Yŏkkwan*, the Korean Interpreters employed in the Office of Interpreters (*Sayŏg'wŏn*) in the capital. As linguists, they functioned in a similar capacity as the *Hundo* and *Pyŏlch'a* (to be mentioned below) but were stationed in the Tongnae Magistrate's office.

We should note that there were a number of officials with a Sr. 3 rank who managed the tributary relations and this was the rank of the County Magistrate, the Pusan Garrison Commander, and the Commander of the Left Naval Garrison. Any of these men could, in theory, act as chief ceremonial official. The chief ceremonial official was usually the Tongnae Magistrate, which conveniently put the county's chief executive in charge of the basis of Tsushima's connection with Korea. When the magistrate needed to apply pressure, he could apply it at the core of relations by refusing to fulfill ceremonial duties. Without ceremony, trade was impossible.

Liaison officials

Below the ceremonial officials, the most important officials in functional daily contact with the Waegwan were the Liaison Officers with the Waegwan (*Imgwan*) and the Minor Interpreters (*Sot'ongsa*). "Liaison Officer" was actually one referent for two officials: *Hundo* (Jr. 9) and *Pyŏlch'a* (no rank). One of each was appointed to duties at the Waegwan. The *Hundo* for Japanese affairs was established sometime in the mid-fifteenth century as it appears in the *Kyŏngguk taejŏn*. Because of Hideyoshi and the severing of relations, the office was temporarily abolished in Tongnae and re-established after the invasion. There were 53 *Hundo* in all of Kyŏngsang Province, but only two *Hundo* in Japanese affairs (K: *Waehak*). They were appointed from the Office of Interpreters in the capital and dispatched to Pusan and Chep'o. The Chep'o *Hundo* generally handled castaways, and the Pusan *Hundo* oversaw Waegwan liaison with the Tongnae Magistrate, the Pusan Garrison Commander, and the Commander of the Left Naval Headquarters. The Pusan *Hundo* was also charged with conducting receptions for Japanese envoys, inspecting the frontier, and training interpreters. The pivotal position of the *Hundo* should not be forgotten, since this man was the face of the Korean government to the Japanese on a daily basis. Further evidence of the office's importance is to be found in the *Chŏphae sinŏ* (J: *Shōkai shingo*), the early seventeenth-century Japanese language primer used by Korean officials. Although Robert Campbell, the able translator of this text into English, leaves unresolved the question of exactly who is speaking in the dialogues for the Korean side, his suspicions fall heavily on the "chief interpreter," i.e. the *Hundo*.[19] Campbell's suspicions are correct, since corroborating evidence comes from Tsushima documents where the *Hundo* and the *Pyŏlch'a* appear consistently as the first line of daily contact between the Waegwan and Korean officialdom. The Pusan *Hundo*'s domicile was on the western side of a compound with the Sŏngsin-dang or "Hall of Truth and Sincerity," erected in 1727.[20] His tour of duty was 30 months or two and one-half years.

There was one other officer of rank with the *Hundo*, and that was the Foreign Ship Inspector (*Munjŏnggwan*), also from the Office of Interpreters. He was an Interpreter with Jr. 9 rank, equivalent to a *Hundo*, and was dispatched to investigate shipwrecks, interview the Japanese sailors, and issue vouchers for their necessary supplies until repatriation. He carried the same rights to horses and lodging as the official charged with greeting the Chinese ambassador at the Yalu and conducting him to the capital (*Munwigwan*).

The office of *Pyŏlch'a* was established in 1623 to assist the *Hundo* and develop an expertise in Japanese language, but possessed no rank. He was the most important interpreter at the local level and was recruited locally. He assisted the *Hundo* in managing daily relations with the Japanese and was charged with escorting Japanese when they left the "new" Ch'oryang Waegwan to visit graves of relatives in the vicinity of the "old" Tumo Waegwan at least twice a year (spring and fall). Until 1709, the *Pyŏlch'a* was also responsible for investigating shipwrecked Japanese, but this duty was given to the Foreign Ship Inspector. The *Pyŏlch'a*'s domicile[21] was also built in 1727 to the south of the Sŏngsin-dang. *Pyŏlch'a* were rotated annually.

The *Sot'ongsa* or Minor Interpreters were first among the local subordinates to the above officials. They were generally boys recruited locally from among the Attendants at Waegwan Banquets and Youths in Attendance on the *Hundo* and *Pyŏlch'a*. Originally numbering 16, they were at first called *Waehak* (Japanese affairs) Students. In 1703, their number was increased to 35, and in 1739, lowered to 30. They were assigned individually or in pairs to various activities and locales about the

Waegwan. The Minor Interpreters' domicile was to the east of the Sŏngsin-dang and was called the *T'ongsa-ch'ŏng* or Interpreters' Office.

There were other subordinate officials below the Minor Interpreters such as: *Sodong* (30 Youths in Attendance on the *Hundo, Pyŏlch'a, Munjŏnggwan,* and *Ch'abigwan*), *Kwanjik* (30 Attendants at Waegwan Banquets), *Yedanjik* (16 Ceremonial Attendants), *Kwabang* (15 Servants at the Tea Ceremony and Banquets), *Saryŏng* (four Runners for the *Hundo* and *Pyŏlch'a*), *Majik* (two Horse Attendants), *Sihan* (two Woodcutters for the *Hundo* and *Pyŏlch'a*), and *Palgun* (two Mounted Couriers). From the Minor Interpreters down to the Mounted Couriers all were subordinate to the *Hundo* and *Pyŏlch'a*. The Liaison Officials total 139 people at their maximum numbers.

Finally, we should say something about the symbolic geography of Korean official-dom's contact with the Japanese, although this really requires a separate study. We might note the orientation of the domiciles for the Liaison Officials. The Liaison Officials' quarters were arranged around the "Hall of Truth and Sincerity" (Sŏngsin-dang), just outside the Waegwan to the north. "Sincerity" was the highest principle in the pantheon of diplomatic rhetoric. The *Hundo* was to the west, the Minor Interpreters to the east, and the *Pyŏlch'a* to the south. Presumably, the Korean King or his representative, the Tongnae Magistrate symbolically occupied the north. Japanese officials were occasionally escorted to these quarters informally, but the symbolism of being located around the "Hall of Truth and Sincerity" was probably more for the Liaison Officers – to keep them focused on higher duties in the face of temptations to collude with the Japanese and turn a blind eye to smuggling.

Symbolic geography played a subtle role, but the form and content of ceremonies where people moved and said things was probably more efficacious in getting messages across. Above we merely noted that certain ceremonies established the framework for trade, but there were many other uses for ceremony that ranged into the creation of hierarchies and even cosmological positioning. One important point to note is that all ceremonies involving Korean officialdom took place outside the Waegwan. Perhaps this reflected the extraterritorial nature of the Waegwan? Japanese officials attended formal ceremonies (such as the 'tea ceremony' and other banquets mentioned above), where they were feted by the Tongnae Magistrate, but more importantly, accompanying some of these ceremonies, the Japanese offered tribute (*chinsang*) to the Korean King. Ceremonies took place in a structure outside the Waegwan to the north and towards the county seat called the Ch'oryang Kaeksa or Ch'oryang 'Guest House.' Like the symbolic geography of the Sŏngsin-dang, an analysis of the symbolism in these rituals is beyond our immediate concerns.

Military officials

We should recall that ceremony and trade were deployed to control piracy. If ceremony and trade were the carrots, a strong defense was the stick. The attack on Tsushima in 1419 and the forcible ejection of Japanese from the ports in 1510 demonstrated a Korean willingness to use force. The rout of Tongnae's defenses in 1592 shattered the superior Korean military image for Tsushima residents (not to mention Tokugawa-period Japanese), and created long-term problems for the control of Japanese in Pusan, as we shall see in Chapter 6. Nevertheless, Tongnae possessed a significant military presence that could be deployed against the Japanese.

All officials in the Tongnae County administration, including the *Hundo*, *Pyŏlch'a*, and the Foreign Ship Inspector, were subordinate to the Tongnae Magistrate. Army command as well came under the Tongnae Magistrate after 1544 when the post was raised to *Tohobusa* (Town Magistrate). According to Yi Wan-yŏng's findings, the Tongnae Magistrate officially commanded some 7,105 soldiers in five armies.[22] This figure has been difficult to verify.

In 1832, there were three garrisons in the county: Pusan, Tadae, and Chŏlyŏng Island.[23] The Pusan Garrison was commanded by a *Sugun Ch'ŏmjŏlchesa*, or Navy Deputy Commander (Sr. 3), who had under him 36 Military Officials in addition to others of lesser rank. We do not know exactly how many men of rank and file below Military Officials he actually commanded. The Tadae Garrison Commander held an identical rank but commanded only 14 Military Officials. In total, he commanded some 512 men. The Chŏlyŏng Island Garrison was under both Pusan and Tadae. The total number of men stationed at that garrison in 1898 numbered 437.[24] The Pusan Garrison Commander's specific duties towards the Waegwan were: monitoring Japanese shipping traffic, supplying firewood and charcoal, repairing structures, and suppressing riots.[25] In addition, he managed the supply of rice, cotton, ginseng, and even fish to the Japanese. The Pusan Garrison Commander reported to the Magistrate, the Governor of Kyŏngsang Province, and to the central government.

There were four smaller ports in the county and each had a *Sugun Manho* (Jr. 4) or Navy Sub-area Commander commanding eight or ten Military Officials at each station. All fell under the Left Naval Command for Kyŏngsang Province, which had been headquartered in Pusan Harbor from King T'aejo's time (1392–1398), but which seemed to have had no ordinary responsibilities for the Waegwan or county-level matters.[26] From Sejong's time (1418–1450), a *Sugun Chŏltosa*, or Navy Commander (Sr. 3), directed the Naval Command. Under him was a *Sugun Uhu* (Sr. 4) or Navy Inspector and various warships.

The Tongnae Magistrate and the Commander of the Pusan Garrison held ultimate responsibility in the county for Japanese matters. In previous chapters, we have considered the structural concerns (demographic and economic) surrounding the Japanese presence. We should turn now to the specific concerns of the local Korean officials. The remainder of this chapter examines the extent of the Japanese impact on the office of the Tongnae Magistrate and highlights the array of Japanese-related problems with which he had to contend. The direct responsibilities of the Tongnae Magistrate were open-ended regarding the Waegwan, and the discussions in Chapters 6 and 7 explore the challenges that such comprehensive responsibility entailed.

The Tongnae Magistrate and the Waegwan: a statistical analysis

In Chapters 3 and 4, we determined the impact of the Waegwan on Kyŏngsang Province's demography and economy. Aside from the uncontrollable variables of environment and war, the exchange of goods and the concentration of people were the two largest components of the socio-economic structures in which the Waegwan sat, and those were the circumstances that the Magistrate had to handle. Before we turn to case studies of the problems thrown up by these structures, we should attempt to assess the political significance of the Waegwan for Korea. In extraordinary times of war and upheaval, political significance can be measured in the terms preferred by Joseph Stalin, who is said to have answered his advisor's trepidations with the question: 'The Pope? How many tanks does the Pope have?' In ordinary times, political significance for the Chosŏn kingdom might be measured by the number of memorials put forward or the amount of time the court spent debating some issue, or the number and rank of officials purged. Political significance might also be measured by the damage an external problem can inflict on bureaucratic careers. The Japanese connection was an external matter, and the Tongnae Magistrate was the responsible official. The following attempts to quantify the impact on the careers of Tongnae Magistrates from the Japanese connection. In other words, we will attempt to determine the political significance of the Japanese presence by measuring the political costs associated with being responsible for the Japan House and its occupants. The structure of political liability is clear to us because we can survey centuries, but we have yet to find any comments by participants that might indicate Korean perceptions of the political bust or boom to be had from becoming a Tongnae Magistrate.

Extant gazetteers (ŭpchi) of Tongnae County give us information on individuals from Kim Hong-su, County Magistrate from 1506 to 1509, to Min Yŏng-don, Special Capital Magistrate from 1896 to 1897. Excluding the final two magistrates, Yi Chong-jik and Kim Kak-hyŏn, (we are given only their title: Puyun, with no notes), we have brief, succinct records for 285 officeholders from 1506 to 1897. In the shorter interval from 1599, when the Hideyoshi invasions finally reached a conclusion, to Min Yŏng-don (1896–1897), we have records for 223 individuals. If we examine subcategories of magistrates, then we see that from Kim Hong-su (1506–1509) to Min Yŏng-don (1896–1897), there were 27 Hyŏllyŏng (County Magistrate, Jr. 5), 255 Tohobusa (Town Magistrate, Jr. 3), two Kunsu (Great County Magistrate, Jr. 4), and three Puyun (Special Capital, Jr. 2).[27] All of these offices varied in rank but required roughly the same duties from the office-holder. Of course, after Pusan became the sole site of a Waegwan from 1544, the duties expanded to include diplomacy with the Japanese, and the magistrate was elevated to a Tohobusa as a direct result. The Tohobusa designation was the administrative designation most often carried by Tongnae, but for simplicity's sake, all titles referring to the chief executive officer of Tongnae County are rendered here as "Magistrate."

Tongnae County was only one of some 71 counties in Kyŏngsang Province in 1832. Moreover, Tongnae was only one of seven counties in the province that had a military commandery.[28] Tongnae was the only county in the entire country that hosted Japanese visitors from 1547 to 1876. The Magistrate was responsible for the Waegwan in addition to all the ordinary affairs of any county magistrate: tax collecting, adjudicating crimes, maintaining local shrines and festivals, and playing general exemplar for the local society. Above and beyond his ordinary duties, he conducted diplomacy with the Japanese, hosted envoys at tea receptions and banquets, coordinated the repatriation of castaways, both Korean and Japanese, and was responsible for all trade affairs.[29] Tongnae Magistrates were generally rotated into their positions every 18 to 24 months and usually held the official rank of junior third grade.

Through thumbnail sketches in the Tongnae Gazetteers we know something about 285 magistrates whose sequential tenures spanned almost 400 years. Despite the fact that the Tongnae Magistrate was the single most important responsible official for Japanese affairs during the Chosŏn period, we still lack an analysis of the post as the comptroller of daily relations. This study has been prepared to help remedy that problem. Our findings below statistically analyze the impact of the Japanese presence on the post of Tongnae Magistrate in, as yet, only the grossest terms: of all instances of official review for misconduct or controversial decisions, in how many instances do we find Japanese mentioned? The largest single group of Tongnae Magistrates transferred for "crimes" was the group held responsible when something went wrong in connection with the Japanese. When we include the six magistrates affected by uprisings or war (all connected with the Japanese), we find that one in six magistrates from 1506 to 1897 was directly and adversely affected as a result of the Japanese connection. We will see also that a concern for the Japanese presence seemed to play a critical role in re-appointments. From these bare facts, we know that the post was unique, difficult, and dangerous to the political careers and sometimes even the lives of the men who served.

Our data come from various sources; most important have been the Tongnae County gazetteers (ŭpchi) and the Veritable Records. The principal information was compiled from the Sŏnsaeng-an or "Role of Magistrates" in the gazetteers and analyzed for statistical purposes. The results are shown in Tables 5.1 through 5.4. The following discussion uses the conclusions drawn from these tables, points out particular case studies, examines discrepancies in the data, and provides a guide to the construction and context of the tables.

We will approach our data from three angles: responsibility, re-appointment, and promotion. The first perspective looks on the responsibility of the Tongnae Magistrate for incidents occurring within his jurisdiction. When an incident erupted, the Magistrate was investigated and judged. Aside from no action, the result could have been punishment, transfer to another post, or reward with a higher appointment.

Table 5.1 ("Instances of Tongnae Magistrates dismissed or transferred for crimes") is a general list of all Tongnae Magistrates transferred or punished for some incident or crime while in office, particularly including those punished for an incident related to the Japanese connection (section 12: "Matters related to Japanese"). As is apparent in Table 5.1, section 12, out of the total officeholders for whom we have records (285 people), 43 were punished for some incident involving Japanese.[30] These 43 men composed 15 percent of the total number of magistrates for whom we have records and 39 percent of the total number punished, the largest single group of those punished. Table 5.2 ("Magistrates affected by uprisings or war") enumerates all Tongnae Magistrates during the Chosŏn period affected by large-scale violence and offers statistics on those affected by uprisings or war. In all instances, the Japanese instigated the violence.

Table 5.3 ("Transfers and removals of Tongnae Magistrates due to matters related to Japanese") is a complete list of all magistrates whose careers were affected by the Japanese and contains direct translations ("Explanation of incident") from the gazetteers describing that particular magistrate's involvement with the Japanese. In Table 5.3, we see the magistrates' names, periods of tenure in office (the dates given are when the office was actually taken up and relinquished, not the date of appointment), whether they were Civil (C) or Military (M) officials, a translation of the gazetteer note following their names ("Explanation of incident"), the types of

Table 5.1 Instances of Tongnae Magistrates dismissed or transferred for crimes

Categories of transfers for crimes[a]	People	Percentage
1 Transferred due to criticisms filed by the Provincial Governor	14	13%
2 Misrule	2	2%
3 Loss of grazing horses	2	2%
4 Inadequate supervision and management of station horses	2	2%
5 Employment of unnecessary people; bringing one's family to the appointment; illegally visiting the place where one's family is located	3	3%
6 A discrepancy at the last appointment	3	3%
7 Arguments with or censure by army or naval officers	5	5%
8 Fiscal discrepancies	3	3%
9 Contents of reports were rude or inadequate	4	4%
10 Miscellaneous other	8	7%
11 Cause is unclear	20[b]	18%
12 Matters related to Japanese:[c]		
(1) Inability to prevent pillage and murder cases involving Japanese: Magistrates #5, #6, #7, #45	4	
(2) Japanese insulted officials or left the Waegwan and created disturbances: Magistrates #20, #21, #24, #30, #31, #49	6	
(3) Failure to investigate criminal merchants who had committed smuggling with Japanese: Magistrates #9, #10, #11, #41	4	
(4) Violations of public morals in relations between Korean women and Japanese: Magistrates #28, #48	2	
(5) Failure to re-write correspondence from the *Ch'awae* (irregular envoys): Magistrate #22	1	
(6) Altercation with Japanese from the Waegwan over formal obeisance (bowing): Magistrate #25	1	
(7) Failure to investigate the supplying of new building timber for the Waegwan by the Pusan Navy Deputy Commander, Jr.3: Magistrate #26	1	
(8) Allowed the *Chaep'an* (special liaison) to reside too long at the Waegwan: Magistrate #27	1	
(9) Lost castaway Japanese by the Pusan Garrison: Magistrate #29	1	
(10) Dispatched an answer to the Japanese before the Board of Rites could forward an answer, and Koreans attacked and entered the Waegwan three times: Magistrate #33	1	
(11) Accepted a [letter or gift] from the old *Kampaku* (K: *Kwanbaek*, Shogun) with the signature *Taitaikun* (K: *T'aedaekun*): Magistrate #35	1	
(12) Allowed a *Taech'awae* (great irregular envoy), not officially recognized in the regulations to enter (Pusan): Magistrate #39	1	
(13) Expulsion of a *Ch'awae* (irregular envoy): Magistrate #40	1	
(14) Failure to attend a banquet for the Japanese: Magistrate #42	1	
(15) Failure to enforce border prohibitions; failure to understand the frontier situation: Magistrates #44, #47	2	
(16) Disbursement of "new" silver before reporting: Magistrate #32	1	

Table 5.1 (cont'd)

Categories of transfers for crimes[a]	People	Percentage
(17) Prohibition of female entertainment at banquets (banquets for Japanese?): Magistrate #34	1	
(18) Argued with the Japanese over official trade rice, and violence ensued: Magistrate #23	1	
(19) Supplied the Japanese with Tongnae (?) ginseng and was consequently exiled to Haenam in Chŏlla Province: Magistrate #37	1	
(20) His reception of a Ming general was rude: Magistrate #18	1	
(21) Japanese violated regulations: Magistrate #36	1	
(22) Trouble arose involving official trade rice and the Chaep'an (special liaison) arrived over the matter: Magistrate #38		
(23) Trouble arose involving an official report about the Ch'awae (irregular envoy) for Castaways: Magistrate #43	1	
(24) Trouble arose involving the Japanese interpreter in Ok-p'o (Kŏje Island; Changsŭng Harbor): Magistrate #46	1	
(25) Japanese were being buried at their settlements (in Korea): Magistrate #1	1	
(26) Japanese filed a complaint: Magistrate #4	1	
(27) A smuggler broke out of jail: Magistrate #19	1	
(28) Transferred for some matter involving the Japanese: Magistrate #3	1	
(29) Disrespectful towards the people in his charge (failing to take up his post during the Hideyoshi invasion?): Magistrates #14, #15	2	
Total for matters relating to Japanese	43	39%
Total	109[d]	101%

Sources: Kyŏngsang Namdo Tongnaebu ŭpchi (1899), in Tongnae Saryo, 3 (Seoul: Yŏgang ch'ulp'ansa), 1989, and Yi Wŏn-kyun, "Chosŏn sidae ŭi suryŏngjik kyoch'ae silt'ae: Tongnae busa ŭi kyŏngu," Pusan sahak, 3 (1979.2): 61–86.

Notes:
a Categories and names were adapted from Yi Wŏn-kyun, "Chosŏn sidae ŭi suryŏngjik kyoch'ae silt'ae."
b Yi Wŏn-kyun lists 26 names in this category, but since he does not supply us with individual names, verification is impossible.
c For name, tenure in office, and further notes on the specific case, see the appropriate "Magistrate number" (#) in Table 5.3.
d Of the total number of Magistrates in this database of 285, 109 Magistrates compose 38% of the total number.

transfer (promotion, demotion, or lateral appointment as mentioned in the gazetteer note), an assessment by myself of the probable "source of the problem," and any supplementary "notes" or "relevant literature," aside from the gazetteer entries. Table 5.4 contains details on reappointments. We should now turn to consider an analysis of the data.

For example, let us turn to a case study of a Magistrate who was held responsible for Japanese activities. Yun Mun-kŏ (Table 5.3, Magistrate No. 21) took up the Magistrate's office in the eighth month of 1651. The reason given in the Gazetteer for his dismissal in the eleventh month of 1652 seems to be a pure fabrication, or at

Table 5.2 Magistrates affected by uprisings or war

Description	No. of People	Percentage of total number of Magistrates (285)
1 Magistrate #2 was promoted to Sr.3 rank and above as a result of services performed related to the Riot of the Three Ports of 1510.	1	
2 Magistrate #8 was transferred as a result of government findings regarding the Japanese uprising of 1555 in Chŏlla Province.	1	
3 Magistrate #12 died when the Tongnae Garrison fell to Hideyoshi's armies on 1592.4.15.	1	
4 Magistrate #13 died as a result of Hideyoshi's invasion while proceeding to his appointment at Tongnae.	1	
5 Magistrates #14 and #15 were dismissed for failing to take up their duty posts during the Hideyoshi invasion.	2	
Total	6	2.11%

Source: Same as Table 5.1.

Note:
Four magistrates compose 1.40% of the total 285 for whom we have information.

best too elliptical to understand. The Gazetteer carries a story about a fan being mistaken for an eagle or an eagle being mistaken for a fan and seems to have little relation to Yun Mun-kŏ's actual worries. The *Sillok* carries the following explanation of his case:

> At first, Tongnae County built a Waegwan and opened a market in the Taech'ŏng (Great Hall). The *Hundo*, *Pyŏlch'a*, and a tax assessor from the Board of Taxation were the directors of the market. They, with the *Taegwan* (J: *Daikan*) Wae sat facing each other from the east and the west. They put both countries' goods in the middle of the floor and traded. Everything was marked and [the traders] counted over lists. Such was our Agreement. From 1637 the law fell into disuse. The [Korean and Japanese] merchants scattered into individual rooms and dealt in secret. There appeared a hundred villainous artifices, [finally] resulting in the problem of [Korean merchants'] debt [to Japanese merchants]. The magistrate, Yun Mun-kŏ, wanted to return to the old rules. He reported [his desire] to the Pibyŏnsa and the Pibyŏnsa requested permission to do so. His majesty granted this [request]. Mun-kŏ then made an Agreement with the Wae to return to the old rules. The *Taegwan* Wae at first acceded but then abruptly changed and backed out. With the Island Lord in Edo, they were unable to act on their own authority. Mun-kŏ sent a [Korean] Interpreter (*Hundo*?) to dispute with them. The *Taegwan* and three Wae, suddenly led more than 90 of their charges out of the compound gate, brandishing cudgels and swords. The gate guards were unable to stop them. The Pusan Garrison was also unable

Table 5.3 Transfers and removals of Tongnae Magistrates due to matters related to the Japanese

No.	Name	Tenure	C/M[a] Rank[b]	Explanation of incident	Type of transfer, promotion or demotion[c]	Source of problem	Notes and relevant documents
1	Kim Hong-su	1506.8 1509.3 32 mos.	Hyŏllyŏng	The Magistrate [was] dismissed because Japanese were being buried at their settlements.	Dismissed	Japan	
2	Yun In-bok	1510.2 1510.4 2 mos.	Hyŏllyŏng	The Riot of the Three Ports occurred; [the Magistrate was] promoted to Sr.3; in 1512.1, transferred to Kosŏng.	Transferred and promoted	Japan	Riot of the Three Ports
3	Kwŏn Se-ho	1523.9 1525.2 17 mos.	Hyŏllyŏng	Transferred because of some matter related to Japanese.	Transferred	Unclear	
4	No Po-se	1525.4 1528.10 44 mos.	Hyŏllyŏng	Because of a Japanese complaint, [the Magistrate was] arrested and transferred.	Arrested and transferred	Japan	
5	Ha Sŏk-bŏm	1536.8 1536.11 3 mos.	Hyŏllyŏng	[Because] Japanese robbed a fishing boat and committed murder, [the Magistrate was] arrested and sent to military duty.	Arrested and demoted to military duty	Japan	
6	Kim Chŏn	1537.5 1537.12 7 mos.	Hyŏllyŏng	Transferred because a Japanese committed murder.	Transferred	Japan	
7	Kim P'aeng-jo	1540.2 1541.7 17 mos.	Hyŏllyŏng	Dismissed because the Japanese in the Japan House robbed and plundered the guard at Haeun Harbor.	Dismissed	Japan	
8	Cho Hŭi	1553.4 1555.5 25 mos.	Civil/Pusa	After a Japanese riot in Chŏlla Province, and due to the Provincial Governor's report to the throne, a military official was dispatched and the	Transferred	Japan	

Table 5.3 (cont'd)

No.	Name	Tenure	C/M[a] Rank[b]	Explanation of incident	Type of transfer, promotion or demotion[c]	Source of problem	Notes and relevant documents
				Magistrate was transferred.			
9	Kim Kŭk-hae	1559.7 1560.6 11 mos.	Military/ Pusa	Transferred since he was unable to stop smuggling.	Transferred	Japan ? Korea	
10	Yi To-nam	1561.6 1563.5 23 mos.	Civil/Pusa	Transferred since he was unable to stop smuggling.	Transferred	Japan ? Korea	
11	Yun Haeng	1563.6 1564.12 19 mos.	Civil/Pusa	Transferred since he was unable to stop smuggling.	Transferred	Japan ? Korea	
12	Song Sang-hyŏn	1591.8 1592.4 8 mos.	Civil/Pusa	He met the Japanese invasion; the castle fell; he died for the country, preserving his honor, and has a shrine dedicated to a loyal minister. [He was] awarded Jr.1 rank.	Posthumous promotion	Japan	Hideyoshi Invasion
13	Son In-gap	1592.9 0 mos.	Military/ Pusa	He was appointed, but before taking up his duties, he died in battle.	Death	Japan	Hideyoshi Invasion
14	Kim Ch'ung-min	1593.5 1594.6 14 mos.	Military/ Hyŏllyŏng	Reported to duty at Tongdo-sa (Tongdo Temple in Ulsan County) and in 1594.6, was dismissed for being disrespectful towards the people in his charge (for not taking up his post?).	Dismissed	Japan	Hideyoshi Invasion
15	Yi Tŏk-p'il	1595.1 1595.5 4 mos.	Military/ Hyŏllyŏng	The Pyŏngsagun took up his duties at Kyŏngju and in 1595.5 was dismissed for being disrespectful towards the people in his charge (for not taking up his post?).	Dismissed	Japan	Hideyoshi Invasion
16	Chŏng Kwang-ja	1595.7 1596.4 9 mos.	Military/ Hyŏllyŏng	[The Magistrate] took up his duties in Kyŏngju and in 1596.4 was transferred.	Transferred	Japan	Hideyoshi Invasion

No.	Name	Dates	Category	Description	Disposition	Japan	Hideyoshi Invasion
17	Yi Yu-sŏng	1596.4 1598.12 32 mos.	Military/ *Hyŏllyŏng*	[The Magistrate] took up his duties at Ulsan, and in 1598.12, the Japanese brigands crossed the sea (withdrew) and he [took up his duties] in Tongp'yŏng (inside Tongnae County) [where] he completed his tour and was transferred.	Transferred		Hideyoshi Invasion
18	Kim Chun-gye	1599.11 1600.8 9 mos.	Military/ *Pusa*	He was disrespectful in entertaining a [Ming] general and was dismissed.	Dismissed	Magistrate	
19	Yi Ch'ang-jŏng	1612.12 1613.5 5 mos.	Civil/*Pusa*	Ŏk-ji, a slave who smuggled, broke out of prison, fled, and hid. In 1613.5 the Magistrate was dismissed and [later] became a Provincial Governor.	Dismissed and later promoted	Japan ? Korea	
20	Min Ŭng-hyŏp	1646.10 1648.11 26 mos.	Civil/*Pusa*	The Tadae Garrison Commander (Jr. 3) was put in charge of repairing the Waegwan and was insulted. The Japanese made no [apology]. The throne was notified and the Magistrate was dismissed. He had a record of exemplary administration and [later] became an Inspector-General (Jr. 2).	Dismissed and later promoted	Magistrate	
21	Yun Mun-kŏ	1651.8 1652.11 15 mos.	Civil/*Pusa*	The Wae requested an eagle, but because [the Magistrate] mistakenly reported it as a round fan, he was dismissed. He had a record of exemplary administration and [later] was made an Inspector General (Jr. 2).[d]	Dismissed and later promoted (transferred)	Magistrate (Japan)	
22	Wŏn Man-sŏk	1656.12 1657.6 6 mos.	Civil/*Pusa*	He was Second Tutor to the Crown Prince (Sr. 4) and was promoted [to Tongnae Magistrate]. In 1657.6, the Ch'awae's (irregular envoy) letter was not re-written; the Magistrate was arrested, and dismissed, but since he had a record of exemplary administration, he [later] became a Royal Secretary (Sr. 3).	Arrested; dismissed and later promoted	Magistrate	

Table 5.3 (cont'd)

No.	Name	Tenure	C/M[a] Rank[b]	Explanation of incident	Type of transfer, promotion or demotion[c]	Source of problem	Notes and relevant documents
23	Yi Man-ung	1659.3 1659.11 8 mos.	Civil/*Pusa*	There was a dispute with a Wae over official trade rice. Violence was reported to the throne. [The Magistrate] was arrested and [later] became a Provincial Governor (Jr.2).	Arrested and later promoted	Magistrate	
24	Chŏng Sŏk	1669.7 1672.2 32 mos.	Civil/*Pusa*	After [Chŏng Sŏk] had finished his tour of duty, a *Ch'awae* (irregular envoy) recklessly left the [Japan House] without authorization. While the Magistrate was still in the garrison, he was re-appointed. On 1672.2.27, since a *Ch'awae* detained a *Chŏbwigwan* (Reception Official for Japanese), the Magistrate was arrested. [Later] a monument to his exemplary administration was erected, and he became a Second Minister (Jr. 2).	Arrested and later promoted	Japan	
25	Kwŏn Tae-jae	1674.6 1674.8 2 mos.	Civil/*Pusa*	Because Japanese in the compound quarreled over bowing (paying obeisance), the Magistrate was arrested and [later] became a Minister (Sr. 2).	Arrested and later promoted	Japan	
26	Ŏ Jin-ik	1674.8 1676.7 24 mos.	Civil/*Pusa*	He was formerly Second Censor (Jr. 3) (in the Office of the Censor-General), and was [Magistrate of Tongnae] until 1676.7.1. When the Pusan Garrison Commander (Jr. 3) supplied the [Wae]gwan with building timber, the Magistrate did not investigate and remonstrate with the officer; the Magistrate was arrested and [later] made a Provincial Governor.	Arrested and later promoted	Magistrate	

160

							Special liaisons
27	Yi Hang	1686.4 1688.1 22 mos.	Civil/*Pusa*	Since the *Chaep'an* (special liaison) was resident for a long time, the capital (?) dismissed [the Magistrate] in 1688.1, [but] erected a shrine for his veneration while he was still alive and a stele. He [later] became an Inspector-General (Jr. 2).	Dismissed and promoted	Japan	Furukawa Heibeii (1685–1687); Tobo Chuueimon (1687–1688)
28	Pak Sin	1689.4 1690.7 15 mos.	Civil/*Pusa*	Because a woman sneaked into the Japan House and was not immediately seized and expelled, the magistrate was arrested.	Arrested	Japan	*Waein Changma Tŭngnok*; *Kōkan Ikken*
29	Sŏng Kwan	1693.5 1694.4 11 mos.	Civil/*Pusa*	He was a Second Inspector (Jr. 3) [in the Office of Inspector Generals] and was promoted [to Tongnae Magistrate]. In 1694.4, because the Pusan Garrison lost some Japanese castaways, the Magistrate was arrested.	Arrested	Korea	
30	Yi Se-jae	1696.11 1698.1 15 mos.	Civil/*Pusa*	Because the Japanese rioted and went out [of the Waegwan] to the Sŏnam [Temple], in 1698.1, the Magistrate was arrested. He had a record of good administration and [later] became a Second Minister (Jr. 2).	Arrested and later promoted	Japan	
31	Pak Kwŏn	1698.1 1698.9 8 mos.	Civil/*Pusa*	Because a Japanese disguised himself and snuck into [Tongnae] town, in 1698.9, the Magistrate was arrested and later became a Minister (Sr. 2).	Arrested and later promoted	Japan	
32	Chŏng Ho	1699.7 1700.6 12 mos.	Civil/*Pusa*	Because the Magistrate made no report about the new silver and [hastily] accepted it, in 1700.6, he was arrested and [later promoted] to Chief State Councilor (Sr. 1).	Arrested and later promoted	Magistrate	

161

Table 5.3 (cont'd)

No.	Name	Tenure	C/M[a] Rank[b]	Explanation of incident	Type of transfer, promotion or demotion[c]	Source of problem	Notes and relevant documents
33	Pak T'ae-hang	1701.11 1703.4 18 mos.	Civil/Pusa	There was the matter of the Wae [having to] make repeated requests for their pottery production. There was the matter of the Magistrate directly supplying return gifts for the tribute trade [without petitioning the court]. There was the matter of [the shipwreck of the Korean Interpreter to Tsushima], the forced entry into the [Waegwan by the relatives of the deceased, [their attack on and injury of] three [Japanese], [and the Magistrate's inaction in prosecuting their crime]. In 1703.4, the Magistrate was arrested and later made a Minister (Sr. 2).[e]	Arrested and later promoted	Magistrate Korea	See: Waein kuch'ŏng tŭngnok
34	Kwŏn Su	1715.4 1715.9 5 mos.	Civil/Pusa	During a banquet [for the Japanese?], female entertainment was forbidden, and in a report to the throne, the Magistrate used a taboo posthumous name. In 1715.9, the capital ordered his dismissal; [later] he became a Minister (Sr. 2).	Dismissed and later promoted	Magistrate	See: Kōrin jikō; Sukjong Sillok[f]
35	Hong Chung-il	1746.8 1747.8 12 mos.	Civil/Pusa	Previously he was a First Tutor (Jr. 3) [in the Office of the Crown Prince Tutorial] and was promoted [to the Tongnae Magistracy]. In 1747.8, over the matter of [agreeing in negotiations to send] ceremonial gifts to the retired Shogun, the Taikun, (to accompany the 1748 T'ongsinsa) the Magistrate was arrested and interrogated before the king.[g]	Arrested and interrogated before the king	Magistrate	

36	Kim Sang-jung	1747.8 1747.12 4 mos.	Civil/*Pusa*	He was the *Moksa* (Special City Magistrate, Sr. 3) of Chinju, but was moved and appointed [to Tongnae]. In 1747.12, because the Japanese [broke] regulations, he was arrested.	Arrested (and dismissed?)	Japan
37	Sin Wi	1751.9 1753.4 19 mos.	Civil/*Pusa*	He was a Royal Secretary and assigned to [the Tongnae Magistracy]. Since it was reported to the throne by a secret inspector that he supplied the Japanese with Tong[nae?] ginseng, he was exiled to Haenam, Chŏlla Province, in 1753.4.	Exiled (but later promoted)[h]	Magistrate
38	Im Sang-wŏn	1754.1 1755.12 24 mos.	Civil/*Pusa*	He was the *Moksa* (Special City Magistrate, Sr. 3) of Hongju and was moved [to Tongnae]. In 1755.12, because of a problem involving the yearly limit on official trade rice [requiring] the dispatch of the *Chaep'an Ch'awae* (special liaison), [the Magistrate] was arrested and interrogated before the king.	Arrested and interrogated before the king (and later dismissed?)	Unclear
39	Yi Yu-sin	1755.12 1756.10 11 mos.	Civil/*Pusa*	He was the *Moksa* (Special City Magistrate, Sr. 3) of Kongju and was moved [to Tongnae]. In 1756.10, because [an envoy arrived and was entertained as] a *Taech'awae* (Great Irregular Envoy) in violation of regulations, and this was reported to the throne by a secret inspector, the Magistrate was arrested.	Arrested (and later dismissed?)	Japan
40	Hong Chung-hyo	1756.10 1757.7 9 mos.	Civil/*Pusa*	He was a Second Tutor (Sr. 4) who was promoted [to Tongnae]. In 1757.7, because he drove away a *Ch'awae* (irregular envoy) before the report reached the throne, he was banished to Kŏje, and arrested and interrogated before the king.	Arrested and interrogated before the king	Magistrate

Table 5.3 (cont'd)

No.	Name	Tenure	C/M[a] Rank[b]	Explanation of incident	Type of transfer, promotion or demotion[c]	Source of problem	Notes and relevant documents
41	Sim Pal	1759.1 1759.8 8 mos.	Civil/Pusa	He was a Royal Secretary and especially assigned [to Tongnae]. In 1759.8.8, since a smuggling operation was exposed after it was all over, he was arrested.	Arrested (and dismissed?)	Japan ? Korea	
42	Kwŏn To	1761.9 1762.9 13 mos.	Civil/Pusa	He had been a Royal Secretary who was assigned [to Tongnae]. On 1762.9.28, because he did not attend a Japanese banquet, he was arrested.	Arrested (and dismissed?)	Magistrate	
43	Yi Chŏng-jung	1778.10 1780.1 15 mos.	Civil/Pusa	Because of a report to the throne about the Ch'awae for castaways (the irregular envoy for castaways), the Magistrate was dismissed.	Dismissed	Unclear	
44	Yi Yang-jŏng	1782.7 1783.6 11 mos.	Civil/Pusa	Because the Magistrate did not enforce border regulations and a royal envoy reported [this], the Magistrate was first dismissed and later arrested.	Dismissed and later arrested	Unclear	
45	Hong Mun-yŏng	1786.2 1786.12 11 mos.	Civil/Pusa	The border situation had developed into a murder; because of a report by the Provincial Governor in his capacity as Military Inspector, the Magistrate was first dismissed and later arrested.[i]	Dismissed and later arrested	Unclear	
46	Yun Chang-yŏl	1795.4 1796.12 20 mos.	Civil/Pusa	Because of [a problem] involving the Japanese interpreter in Ok-p'o (Kŏje Island; Changsŭng Harbor), the Tongnae Magistrate was arrested and dismissed.	Arrested and later dismissed	Korea	

47	Sŏng Su-yŏn	1837.4 1838.11 20 mos.	Civil/*Pusa*	Because of the border situation, the Magistrate was dismissed over a Pibyŏnsa report, but he had an outstanding administrative record.	Dismissed	Unclear
48	Kim Sŏk	1859.1 1859.6 5 mos.	Civil/*Pusa*	Because of a report filed by the Provincial Governor, in his capacity as Military Inspector, concerning illicit sexual liaisons between Japanese and Koreans, the Magistrate was dismissed.	Dismissed	Japan Korea
49	Ŏm Sŏk-jŏng	1862.3 1863.3 13 mos.	Civil/*Pusa*	Because the Japanese in the Waegwan went out without authorization, and the Provincial Governor, in his capacity as Military Inspector, reported this, the Magistrate was dismissed.	Dismissed	Japan

Source: Hangukhak munhŏn yŏn'guso, ed., "[Tongnae] Bu Sŏnsaeng" (1895) in *Hanguk Chiriji Ŭpchi Ch'ongsŏ Ŭpchi Kyŏngsang-do* (Seoul: Asea Munhwasa), 1982: 159–166 and "[Tongnae] Bu Sŏnsaeng" (1899) in *Kyŏngsang Namdo Tongnaebu Ŭpchi* in *Tongnae Saryo*, 3 (Seoul: Yŏgang ch'ulp'ansa), 1989.

Notes:

a C = Civil Official; M = Military Official.

b Hyŏllyŏng: Jr.5; tenure 5 years; 1392–1547, 1592–1599
[Toho]Busa: Jr. 3 (Tangsanggwan); tenure 2.5 years; 1547–1592, 1597–1895
Kunsu: Jr. 4; during the end of the Chosŏn dynasty, Pusa, Moksa, Hyon'gam were abolished and these posts merged into Kunsu; 1895–1896
Puyun: Jr. 2; 1896–1899.

c *Kyoch'e* or *ch'ejik* were the general terms for transfer. Specifically, *kwach'e* meant transfer after completion of tour; *chŏch'e* meant transfer for violation; *sach'e* meant resignation and included the subcategories: *myŏnjik*: relieved of duty, *tangsang*: death, *sinbyŏng*: illness, and *sangb'i*: avoidance of conflict of interest. Dismissal is the translation of *p'ajik*. Promotion is the translation for *sŭng*. Arrest is the translation for *na* and *myŏng* is translated as "arrest and interrogation in the presence of the king." Exile is the translation for *t'ubi* and *ch'unggun* means "sent for military service." Re-appointment is *ingsa*.

d Yun Mun-kŏ's case is curious. The Gazetteers uniformly carry the translation given here, but the actual story appears in *Hyojong Sillok*, 9:17a–17b (1652/9/22).

e The Gazetteer is difficult to understand in this case, so recourse was made to the *Sukjong Sillok*, 38 sang:14b–16b (1703.3.5) for confirmation and elaboration. Corroborating details can also be found in the *Pibyŏnsa tŭngnok*, fascicle 53, pp. 132a–134a, (1703.3.7).

f *Sukjong Sillok po'gwŏl chŏngo*, 56:1b–1b (1715.6.29). Here we see mention of the taboo character, but nothing about female entertainers.

g Corroborating details can be found in the *Pyŏllye chibyo*, fascicle 18, entry 1747.5, p. 560.

h See the text below for a discussion of Sin Wi and his later promotion to Censor-General.

i For details, see: *Chŏngjo Sillok*, 22:50b–50b (1786.11.19). A Japanese killed a Korean who owed him money from trading.

Table 5.4 Re-appointment of Tongnae Magistrates

Name	Tenure	C./M. Rank	Circumstances	Transfer/Re-appointment	Comments
Yi Hong-mang	1632.12 1635.3 1635.10 Total: 35 mos.	Civil/*Pusa*	Yi completed his tour of duty and was re-appointed. In the tenth month, because of a report by a *Sunch'alsa* (Border Inspector, same as Governor, Jr. 2) of Yi's illness, Yi was dismissed. He had a record of excellent administration.	Re-appointment time was 7 mos.	
Chŏng Yang-p'il	1635.11 1638.4 1638.8 Total: 34 mos.	Civil/*Pusa*	Chŏng was re-appointed on 1638.4.1 and served until 1638.8.23. He was affectionately remembered for his service, and [later] became a Second Minister (Jr. 2).	Re-appointed in 1638.4; re-appointment time was 4 mos.	
Chŏng Sŏk (#20 in Table 5.3)	1669.7 1672.2 Total: 32 mos.	Civil/*Pusa*	After he had finished his tour of duty, a *Ch'awae* (irregular envoy) recklessly left the [Waegwan] without a pass. While the Magistrate was still in the garrison, he was re-appointed. On 1672.2.27, since a *Ch'awae* detained a *Chŏpwigwan* (Reception Official for Japanese) the Magistrate was questioned; a monument to his exemplary administration was erected and he [later] became a Second Minister (Jr. 2).	Time of re-appointment is unclear.	
Kang Ko	1863.3 1865.5 1866.5 Total: 39 mos.	Civil/*Pusa*	Kang was re-appointed in 1865.5 (intercalary) as a *Puch'ong-gwan* (Deputy Commander in the Five Military Commands, Jr. 2) with a special designation from the king. Kang finished his tour in 1866.5 and [later] became a Minister (Sr. 2).	Re-appointed in 1865.5; re-appointment time was 13 mos.	
Chŏng Hyŏn-dŏk	1867.6 1869.9 1869.12 1872.4 1874.1 Total: 82 mos.	Civil/*Pusa*	Chŏng served until 1869.9; was re-appointed in 1869.12 as a *Sŭngniui* (Third Minister in the Board of Personnel? Sr. 3); re-appointed in 1872.4; re-appointed; and in 1874.1, transferred up to Royal Secretary (Sr. 3).	Re-appointed three times; re-appointment time was 54 mos.	
Min Yŏng-don	1893.7 1894.11 (hiatus of four Magistrates) 1896.7 1897.2 Total: 23 mos.	Civil/*Pusa*/*Puyun* (for second appointment)	Min resigned on 1894.11.14. He was re-appointed to the same post on 1896.7.12, and on 1897.2.19, he [was made] a Secret Inspector General and a *Tobong* (title given to Provincial literati).	Re-appointed once; re-appointment time was 7 mos. Re-appointment came after hiatus of four other magistrates – only known case.	

Source: Same as Table 5.3.

166

to prevent the Wae from going directly to the County Seat (the magistrate's offices in Tongnae). First thing the next morning [the Japanese] were ordered to return to the compound. The Pusan Garrison Commander, Chŏng Ch'ŏk, the Tongnae Magistrate, Yun Mun-kŏ, and the Commander of the Left Naval Headquarters, Chŏng Pu-hyŏn, dispatched a report by mounted courier. The Provincial Governor, Yu Sim, requested the punishment of Yun Mun-kŏ and Chŏng Ch'ŏk for the crime of being unable to adapt to the situation and make the best of it. The King ordered the Board of Rites to deliberate on the matter. The Board of Rites requested the arrest, interrogation, and judicial investigation of the *Hundo* and *Pyŏlch'a* and the investigation and sentencing of Magistrate Yun Mun-kŏ and the Garrison Commander Chŏng Ch'ŏk before the throne. The king commanded this be done. As for the gate guards and the minor interpreters, [the Board of Rites requested] that they be arrested for investigation before the throne and that they be dispatched to a capital gaol. The Pibyŏnsa reported on the completion of its [investigation]. "The Pusan Garrison Commander, Chŏng Ch'ŏk, has long been unable to prevent [problems] or rectify [matters]. If it pleases your majesty, we will arrest him for investigation and decide matters in accordance with the law. Regarding the Tongnae Magistrate, Yun Mun-kŏ, he is being changed and [our] intent is to remove the problem. Because [we will] transfer him, it would be appropriate to go over any illegalities; we request an investigation." The king ordered that such be done.[31]

We will examine the Japanese use of violence in detail in Chapter 6, but we should note the following significant points about Yun Mun-kŏ's case.

First of all, he obviously had good intentions. He sought to eliminate a situation that led to Korean merchants incurring debt (advance payment for the delivery of goods) by returning to a transparent market. He may well have been lacking in diplomatic tact and the Provincial Governor's charge that Yun was unable to adapt to the situation certainly sounds as though this was the case. In the end, the magistrate was ultimately held responsible when the Japanese broke the peace.

Second, someone may have been sympathetic to Magistrate Yun, hence the Gazetteer's concoction about fans and eagles. The author of this record is unknown but the purpose seems to be to protect Yun's reputation. Obfuscation was not limited to the Gazetteers. We find reports on the same incident, even more detailed, in two different places in the *Pyŏllye chibyo*. One report is grouped with records of Japanese storming out of the Waegwan and is the fourth record of Japanese rioting after the re-establishment of relations between Korea and Tsushima in 1609. The incident involving Magistrate Yun was the largest up to 1652.[32] In another place in the *Pyŏllye chibyo*, we see the same incident again reported and a list of those who were dismissed for responsibility. Yun's name is absent from the punished, leaving no record of his personal responsibility. Needless to say, eagles and fans are nowhere to be seen.[33] Below, we will look at other cases, but Magistrate Yun serves as a typical example of the complexities faced by those posted to Tongnae. We should consider these complexities as career challenges. In this connection, we should look at tenure and rank, transfers, re-appointments, promotions, and conclude with examples of misunderstandings apparently stemming from cultural differences.

Tenure and rank

Over the nearly four centuries for which we have data, the tenure and ranks of the Magistrates maintained a general similarity. Until another county in Kyŏngsang province can be similarly analyzed, it is difficult to say that Tongnae was different, although more will be said on this point below. The mean length of time in office was about 15 months (standard deviation of 9.3 months).[34] The longest single appointment (1528.9–1533.8) was 61 months; the shortest was zero. After about 1620, the length of appointments falls off slightly.

Magistrates were either civil or military appointees. Entries indicating civil or military began with Chŏng Wŏn (1547.9–1548.12) who was a military official. There were 24 military officials appointed, 235 civil officials, and 26 indeterminate. Military officials were most frequently appointed up to 1573 (11) and during the period of 1592 to 1604 (10), when Hideyoshi invaded Korea.

Explanation of incident, source of problem, and type of transfer

The brief comments left for us in the gazetteers give us just enough information for a rough classification as represented in Tables 5.1 and 5.3. Where Table 5.1 ("Matters related to Japanese") paraphrases, Table 5.3 ("Explanation of incident") translates. Table 5.1 attempts a categorization of the details found in Table 5.3 (for matters related to Japanese), but the diversity of incidents makes most attempts at categorization nearly meaningless. The common thread is, of course, the Japanese presence, pointed out in Table 5.3 by the frequency with which we see "Japan" under the heading "Source of Problem."

Designating an origin of a particular problem or incident, although fraught with danger, is done simply to highlight the Japanese presence. For example, magistrates No. 9, No. 10, and No. 11 (Table 5.3) were transferred for being unable to stop smuggling. Since we can safely assume that the smuggling in question involved the Japanese, we designate the Japanese as the origin with a question mark, pending further investigation of the particulars.

We occasionally assume that merely the very presence of the Japanese made them ultimately responsible, but our entries try to avoid resorting to such a facile argument. Kim Chun-gye (Table 5.3, No. 18)'s case is the best example of reaching the outer edge of our argument in this fashion. Kim was disrespectful of a Ming general and was dismissed. Since the Ming army was in the country as a result of Hideyoshi's invasion; we include Kim Chun-gye. In fact, this particular incident seems to be primarily the personal responsibility of the magistrate and is so indicated in the column for "Source of the Problem." A similar type of incident, where the Japanese connection is incidental, is Yi Ch'ang-jong (No. 19), who was held responsible for the escape of a smuggler. Again, there were no other foreign traders allowed into Pusan, so the opposite party must have been a Japanese.

The point of including magistrates affected by seemingly tangential relations is to emphasize the context of the Tongnae Magistrate's full responsibilities. The Japanese presence was a large, unpredictable element in the political world of the Tongnae Magistrate and the multitude of connections cannot be overlooked. Of chief importance, however, is the fact that following each incident, regardless of its origin, the magistrate on duty was investigated.

According to the results of government arrest (*na*) and investigation (*myŏng*), the magistrate was dismissed (*p'ajik*), exiled (*t'ubi*), or transferred (*ch'ejik*), but many were eventually promoted (*sŭng*).[35] The long-term results of an investigation were not always bad. Among the 49 people listed in Table 5.3, at least 15 (30 percent) were eventually promoted. According to Yi Wŏn-kyun, the rate of Tongnae's Magistrates receiving official reprimands (about 40 percent) was lower than Kosŏng's (60 percent) and Sŏmch'ŏn's (45 percent).[36] At first glance the differences in reprimand rates would seem to indicate that the Tongnae Magistrate's post was not as dangerous as, and perhaps easier than, other posts. But when we consider that about 40 percent of the Tongnae Magistrates receiving official reprimands received these because of the Japanese presence, then we can say that the largest number of any difficulties met while managing Tongnae came from the Waegwan. If we excise the Japanese presence, then Tongnae's rate of reprimands falls to 24 percent. At 24 percent, Tongnae would have been a very low-hazard post, compared to Kosŏng and Sŏmch'ŏn. The low percentage of reprimands remaining after excluding the Japanese might indicate that the Tongnae Magistrates were handling their duties very well in all other cases. In other words, the quality of people sent to govern the county was probably high, and even the occasionally irascible Japanese, with whom these men had to contend, did not deter them from doing an excellent job.

Re-appointment

The Japanese impact on the re-appointment (*ingsa*) of magistrates is not conclusive, but a few details are listed in Table 5.4. As we can see there, at least three of the total of six reappointments were linked to the Japanese. It is most probable that Chŏng Yang-p'il (1635–1638) was re-appointed because he was a loyal purveyor of central policy during a rather delicate period with Japan. His tenure overlapped the Yanagawa Incident, during which the forgery of state documents between Korea and Japan was exposed (1634–1635). This was a particularly important period, after which post-Hideyoshi Korean-Japanese relations were normalized.

Chŏng Sŏk (1669–1672) received re-appointment at a critical time regarding the Japanese. We examine the period of the 1660s and the 1670s more fully in Chapters 6 and 7, but briefly stated, the Japanese were dissatisfied with the Tumo Waegwan, because it was small and the anchorage was poor. They wanted the Korean side to enter serious negotiations for a new location and were desperate to put pressure on the Korean authorities. The Gazetteer report suggests the explosive results of Japanese desperation, and links Chŏng Sŏk's re-appointment directly to the crisis:

> After [Chŏng Sŏk] had finished his tour of duty, an Irregular Envoy (*Ch'awae*) recklessly left the [Japan House] without authorization. While the Magistrate was still in the garrison, he was re-appointed. However, on 1672.2.27, since an Irregular Envoy detained a Reception Official (*Chŏbwigwan*), the Magistrate was arrested. [Later] a monument to his exemplary administration was erected, and he became a Second Minister (Jr.2).

Here we see that Chŏng Sŏk's re-appointment came as a result of a Japanese-inspired crisis that occurred in the 24th month of Chŏng Sŏk's term (1671.8) or at about the time his term should have ended. About one month after re-appointment, another incident erupted. An Irregular Envoy (Ch'awae), angered at the adulteration of rice, drew his sword and attacked a warehouse clerk, striking him on the head. Hōshū notes that rice was often squeezed out of the deliveries made to the Waegwan and the missing weight made up with waterlogged rice, sand, or gravel.[37] Although Chŏng Sŏk requested heavy punishment for the Japanese Irregular Envoy, the Waegwan authorities countered that if the matter had been personal, then severe punishment would be due, but since the trouble erupted over Japanese frustration with official business, there was no need for severe punishment, that is, if the warehouse clerk does not die. The king approved the dispatch of an Interpreter Envoy to Tsushima to take up the matter directly with the Island Lord,[38] evidently to no avail, since there is no known record of the Japanese being punished.

Chŏng Sŏk's troubles may have seemed endless, because just two months later (1671.11), a major crisis overtook the Waegwan. Other problems at the Waegwan must have quickly retreated into the shadows. On the night of the sixteenth day of the eleventh month, the Waegwan, all buildings, seven Japanese ships, clothes, utensils, everything, went up in a roaring conflagration. The court took pity and ordered the delivery of 200 sŏk of rice and 500 bolts of cotton to the Japanese in the compound.[39]

Finally, we come to the modern period and our examination of pre-modern relations must end, but there is one case on the cusp of the modern age that deserves special attention. Chŏng Hyŏn-dŏk's term of re-appointment (1867–1874) is unusually long (82 months). This is because of the high regard in which the Taewŏngun held Chŏng's diplomatic abilities with the Japanese.[40] Chŏng's case is rather unusual in that he, together with the Tongnae Hundo, An Tong-jun, and the Taewŏngun were the core of the diplomatic link with Tsushima and Japan during those critical years from the second month of 1869 to the eleventh month of 1873. In 1869, An Tong-jun refused to accept Tsushima's notification of the establishment of the Meiji government. In other words, An refused to recognize the new government and triggered the popular backlash in Japan later referred to as the Seikanron. Chŏng Hyŏn-dŏk, as Tongnae Magistrate, upheld his subordinate's position, a decision that reflected the Taewŏngun's distaste for modifying relations with Japan. Until the Taewŏngun's ouster in the eleventh month of 1873, Korea's position towards Tsushima and Japan was fixed and negotiations deadlocked. In 1874, Chŏng Hyŏn-dŏk and An Tong-jun were banished, and in 1875, An Tong-jun was beheaded.[41] Although Chŏng Yang-p'il, Chŏng Sŏk, and Chŏng Hyŏn-dŏk's re-appointments can be linked to the Japanese, the other cases of re-appointment are, as yet, undetermined.

Promotion

We conclude our statistical discussion of the Tongnae Magistrate's office with the question of promotion. As we can see in Table 5.3, a number of magistrates were investigated and promoted. At present, we lack data from other counties on promotions, so we cannot say if the Tongnae Magistrate's promotion rate was high, low, or average. With more province-wide data, we might be able to determine if the post of Tongnae Magistrate was a stepping-stone to higher office or if promotion from Tongnae was relatively difficult. Answering this question might reveal whether the Tongnae Magistracy was a career stepping-stone or a dead-end appointment.

For the interim, we might consider two cases that illustrate the peculiar difficulties of the posting and the apparent willingness of the central government to forgive mistakes and to later promote. First, we consider a case of exile, the most extreme punishment meted out to a Tongnae Magistrate, and the fact that, despite his exile, Sin Wi was later promoted (Table 5.3, #37).

In the Gazetteer, we see the following entry for Sin Wi:

> He was a Royal Secretary and assigned to [the Tongnae Magistracy]. Since it was reported to the throne by a secret inspector that he supplied the Japanese with Tong[nae?] ginseng, he was exiled to Haenam, Chŏlla Province, in 1753.4.[42]

The *Pyŏllye chibyo* gives us a general description of the incidents in the spring of 1753 that led to Sin Wi's exile.[43] This account is faithful to that found in the *Sillok* and although the *Pyŏllye chibyo* deletes some of Yŏngjo's rhetoric, the tone of outrage is preserved.[44]

In the first month of 1753, Sin Wi reported that a *Saihan* (K: *Chaep'an*), the Sō *daimyō*'s special liaison, had arrived in Pusan and requested new, fresh ginseng in exchange for the ginseng received from Korea through the tribute trade in the years 1751 and 1752. Magistrate Sin comments that such a request indicated a "profound greed" and requested instructions from the throne. The king retorted that this was a petty, administrative matter and ordered an administrative enquiry, presumably into Sin Wi's competence.

In the second month,[45] Magistrate Sin reported he had yet to receive about 40 *kŭn* of tributary ginseng, but of even greater import was the fact that last year's ginseng was adulterated, if not faked. There had even been a royal order concerning the use of real ginseng and the Japanese had cited this to question a delivery. The Magistrate ordered suspension of delivery. For legal clarification, Sin Wi proposed sending some of the fake ginseng he had received back to the Pibyŏnsa and awaiting direction from the court. The response from the capital was rather shrill. The magistrate was upbraided for the fact that the Japanese knew of this royal directive, although it had not been publicly promulgated. The interpreters were accused of egging on the Japanese in this matter, deceiving the magistrate, not valuing the tributary ginseng, and returning the ginseng without orders. They were to be banished to an island after making three complete tours with the bowman corps and receiving 50 strokes with a cudgel. Since the magistrate had stopped delivery and had not relied on his own initiative to manage affairs, presuming upon the court too much for minute matters, he was exiled to Haenam County in Chŏlla Province. For reasons as yet unclear, the previous magistrate, Cho Chae-min, was also ordered exiled to Haemi County for three years. The ginseng producers and others also received punishment. At the same audience, King Yŏngjo appointed the next Tongnae Magistrate. The *Sillok* makes clear that Sin Wi was named by an accuser, a secret inspector, even mentioned by the Gazetteer. But the Gazetteer is misleading in that

Sin Wi did not give the Japanese ginseng, rather he returned the ginseng sent down by the court, questioning its quality. Sin Wi's exile did not last very long. In the ninth month of 1753, only six months later, he was appointed Censor-General (Sr. 3) in the Office of the Censor-General,[46] perhaps for his abilities to detect fraud?

What is clear from this case is that, although the Magistrate incurred the king's ire with his inept administration, Sin Wi's abilities (or his backers' leverage?) were sufficient to retrieve him from exile. Sin Wi's offence sprang directly from the complexities of dealing not only with the Japanese but also with the internal corruption of the Chosŏn bureaucracy.

Having considered the most extreme punishment meted out to a Magistrate and its apparently short-lived consequences on Sin Wi's career, we might also consider the most illustrious magistrate, Chŏng Ho (1699.7–1700.6). Although cashiered in 1700, Chŏng Ho eventually rose to become State Councillor (Sr. 1) before his death in 1736. Chŏng Ho's problem was a bit complicated and requires a brief background explanation.

From 1695, the *bakufu* began to devalue its silver coinage as a means to increase the amount of money at its disposal. Silver was debased from 80 percent to 64 percent purity. The *bakufu* could enforce use of its debased coin inside Japan, but Tsushima faced problems in the Korea trade. For the interim, it used the old silver, but as bad money drives good from the market, the higher grade silver became difficult to obtain and eventually insufficient for trading purposes. On the eighteenth day of the fourth month of 1697, negotiations were opened with the Koreans to allow the use of the new silver. Korean negotiators were amenable to adding in a set rate to arrive at the previous grade of silver, but the Korean position was that the new silver was not 64 percent but 62 percent purity.[47]

In the seventh month of 1699, Chŏng Ho took up his appointment at Tongnae and thus became the central Korean negotiator. In the eighth and tenth months he reported on negotiations and expressed a distrust of the Japanese position, since they were yet able to supply the old, higher-grade silver.[48] In the twelfth month of 1699, an agreement was reached to admit the new silver at the rate of 63 percent recognized purity, requiring a weight ratio of 1:1.27 to equal the old 80 percent grade silver. That is, to equal the old silver (80 percent pure) at 1, the amount of the new silver would have to be 1.27.[49] Chŏng Ho was the central negotiator on the Korean side when the deal was struck. What then of his arrest because of this silver? In the Gazetteer, we see the following explanation:

> Because the Magistrate made no report about the new silver and [hastily] accepted it, in 1700.6, he was arrested and [later promoted] to Chief State Councilor (Sr.1).[50]

The *Sillok* gives us a few more details. On the twenty-ninth day of the fourth month of 1700, King Sukjong was informed that Chŏng Ho had, without approval, ordered the Tongnae merchants to accept over 120,000 *yang* of the new, debased silver from the Japanese. He did not require an assay and was accused of acting too hastily. The king approved the arrest of Chŏng Ho, the *Hundo*, and the *Pyŏlch'a*.[51] Nevertheless, in the second month of the following year, Chŏng Ho was appointed Special Capital Magistrate (*Puyun*, Jr. 2) for Kwangju, a higher position than Tongnae.

We must repeat that no general conclusion about promotion can be made from just two case studies, but we can draw a few conclusions about the magistrates in these cases that will help us to understand the complexity of their posting. Sin Wi seems to have been a capable and honest man if tactless enough to return to the capital fraudulent goods he had been given by the capital for delivery to the Japanese. Although details are lacking, Chŏng Ho seems to have lost his patience with the Tongnae merchants and simply told them to accept the new, debased Japanese silver. Both were punished; both were promoted at their next appointment. We can take that to mean that their talents were apparent or their backers were strong. From these cases and others examined below and in later chapters, we can see that the Tongnae Magistrate's post was exceptionally complex with a variety of dangers and difficulties that lay in wait.

Cultural collision

We should finally turn to a bit more of the flesh and blood lurking behind our statistics and again address the task of this study: how did the Japanese appear to the Koreans? That is, while supplying the Japanese with the necessities of life on a daily basis, what did the Tongnae officials think of their guests? We will briefly pick through our statistics once more for incidents involving a clash of customs or worldviews before going on to two large case studies in the following chapters.

In our data on the Tongnae Magistrate we find examples of cultural collision. The people of Kyŏngsang Province and Tsushima did not possess the same language and differed greatly in their social, intellectual, religious, and economic cultures, so naturally, conflicts appeared. When we analyze these conflicts in a detailed fashion, as in Chapters 6 and 7, we can glimpse what Koreans thought of Japanese and what Japanese thought of Koreans. Unfortunately, with few exceptions, these mutual views, ideas, and impressions born in the course of daily contact are not contained in neatly summarized statements. Instead they are woven into the fabric of daily life and existed as aspects of general mentalities.

Within the limitations of the documents left to us, all we can do is look for flashes of conflict or expressions of rapport in the transactions between the Tongnae Magistrate and the Japanese at the Waegwan. When two countries' economic, social, and political systems intersect, change occurs. In our suggestive comments on Korea's effects on Tsushima in Chapter 2, in our discussions of Chosŏn demography and economy in Chapters 3 and 4, and in our consideration of politics in this chapter, we have attempted to illuminate the structures of the frontier, the context, the stage on which human drama moves.

When we pity, laugh, or loathe, we enter the realm of human mores and custom or what Fredrik Barth has called "the basic value orientations: the standards of morality and excellence by which performance is judged."[52] We are not interested in abstractions drawn from afar, but in the accommodations, understandings, chauvinism, and even wisdom that can be born only at the point of direct daily contact between two different peoples. Many of the incidents briefly mentioned in Table 5.3 or examined in Chapters 6 and 7 arose from the clash between our protagonists, the Koreans, and our antagonists, the Japanese. From these incidents, the Koreans and Japanese constructed their understandings or confirmed their prejudices of one another. It is the insight available in observing the process of that construction or confirmation that makes the history of frontier contact rewarding.

For example, when looking at Table 5.3, it becomes apparent that the origin of a variety of incidents was the conflict between cultures. There were cases that turned on different notions of etiquette. The source of the incident for which Min Ŭng-hyŏp (#20, 1646–1648) received a reprimand was a problem involving an "insult." During Kwŏn Tae-jae's (No. 25, 1674) tenure, "bowing" surfaced as the core of the problem.

Let us consider these two cases in more detail. We can begin with Min Ŭng-hyŏp's problem with "insults." The Gazetteer reports the following on Magistrate Min:

> The Tadae Garrison Commander (Jr.3) was put in charge of repairing the Waegwan and was insulted. The Japanese made no [apology]. The throne was notified and the Magistrate was dismissed. He had a record of exemplary administration and [later] became an Inspector-General (Jr.2).[53]

Curiously, the *Pyŏllye chibyo* has no entry about Min Ŭng-hyŏp's "dismissal," but the *Sillok* gives us the details.

The Tadae Garrison Commander, Cho Kwang-wŏn, was dispatched to supervise reconstruction work at the Waegwan. The rear wall of the Tumo Waegwan compound was built very close in, although the Japanese had continually asked that it be more recessed. Pleas were made to the Tongnae Magistrate (Min Ŭng-hyŏp) who refused to permit changes. Cho Kwang-wŏn, himself, went to visit the site one day. When he refused to dismount his horse at one of the gates to the Waegwan, he was seized and beaten by the Japanese. Sin Yi, Commander of the Left Naval Headquarters demoted Cho.[54]

Four days after the throne heard this report, towards the end of the tenth month of Injo 26 (1648), decisions were made regarding the case. Since the Tadae Garrison Commander (Cho Kwang-wŏn) had been "disgraced" by the Japanese, Min Ŭng-hyŏp, the magistrate, was ordered dismissed. The *Hundo*, *Pyŏlch'a*, and others were detained for interrogation. Although Yi Si-man, the Sixth Royal Secretary (Sr. 3), rose to the magistrate's defense, the king retorted that the magistrate's administration had been inept from before and this case was but one more example. The King declared that Min Ŭng-hyŏp was not forceful enough in rejecting Japanese entreaties and should be held ultimately responsible for the mischief of the Japanese "bastards."[55]

Min Ŭng-hyŏp's case is interesting to us as the "insult" in question was the humiliation of being unable to prevent a government official from being publicly disgraced by foreigners. Cho Kwang-wŏn's culpability was in bringing the disgrace on himself, and this was recognized by his superior who demoted him. There does not seem to have been any serious discussion of why the Japanese wanted Cho to dismount at the gate, that is, Korean officialdom was completely unconcerned with Japanese sensibilities as to where one may ride a horse or with the Japanese perspective of having to look up at a mounted Korean military official.

Min Ŭng-hyŏp's period of magistracy spanned a time when reports reached the throne of discussions between the Shogun and the Tsushima *daimyō* about "borrowing a passage through Korea" to send reinforcements to support the Ming against the

Qing.[56] With Hideyoshi's invasion a mere 48 years in the past, the prospect of another invasion might have, one would have expected, made the magistrate and his subordinates more sensitive to Japanese sensibilities. Or, as was often the case with Tsushima's post-war dealings with Chosŏn, was this report of "borrowing a passage" merely another device by Tsushima to apply pressure on Tongnae with veiled threats and the Korean officials saw it as such?[57]

A quarter of a century later, Kwŏn Tae-chae (1674.6–1674.8) did not have an easy time of it either and was caught between the official concern for protocol and his own sympathy for the Japanese position. The Gazetteer gives us the following information on Magistrate Kwŏn:

> Because Japanese in the compound quarreled over bowing (paying obeisance), the Magistrate was arrested and [later] became a Minister (Sr.2).[58]

Neither the *Sillok* nor the *Pibyŏnsa tŭngnok* reveal anything about his case, but an entry in the *Pyŏllye chibyo* clarifies matters.

The *Pyŏllye chibyo* records Kwŏn's report to the capital and the response. The record makes no mention of just who in the capital handled this correspondence, but we might surmise that since the Magistrate usually addressed his reports to the Office of the Custodian of Foreign Visitors (*Chŏn'gaeksa*) in the Board of Rites, this report as well was directed to the same office.[59] In any event, the incident in question occurred, according to the *Pyŏllye chibyo*, in the following manner.

> In the seventh month of 1674, the House Master sent a message to the Magistrate stating, 'When I present tribute and pay obeisance (bow), [there is] raised a red, shade umbrella on the middle step. The interpreters (*Hundo* and *Pyŏlch'a*) stand in the hall, and I am made to bow from the courtyard. I apologize, but we will not do this again.'[60]

The Magistrate's gloss clarifies that the bow is not in question, nor the place from which the Japanese bow, but the fact that their red umbrella is only at the middle step while the receiving officials are in the hall. The red umbrella's exact significance is not clear, since it is not mentioned in Korean descriptions of the ceremony. Magistrate Kwŏn goes on to state his sympathy with the Japanese position: "I cannot say that [their objection] is completely groundless."[61]

The remainder of the report relates problems surrounding the tea reception for the Iteian Envoy from Tsushima, evidently the first formal instance of protocol after the House Master made his sentiments known and the first test of the House Master's resolve. Although the tea reception and the presentation of tribute goods were different, the tea reception offered the House Master an opportunity to clarify his objections, which he did. The Magistrate and the Commander of the Pusan Garrison arrived at the envoy's tea reception but the Japanese were not there. The *Hundo* and *Pyŏlch'a* were summoned and sent to rebuke the Japanese for their delay. The House Master held the two interpreters and would not release them. As nothing had been resolved by sunset, the Magistrate and the Garrison Commander retired.

The Board of Rites found fault with the magistrate's attitude. The protocol was intended to convey a particular message: the Japanese are on the middle step and the Koreans on the top. The Board of Rites argued that Magistrate Kwŏn's sympathy with the Japanese objection led to the humiliating fiasco of the Iteian Envoy's tea reception. Both Magistrate Kwŏn and the Commander of the Pusan Garrison were arrested and investigated.

Here, we have before us a clear display of the fine line trodden by the Magistrate. If he entertained any sympathy towards the Japanese position in a dispute over protocol, he ran the great risk of being humiliated by the Japanese and arrested by his own government. In short, as Magistrate Kwŏn's case demonstrates, the magistrate's role was not to question the order established by the center, and most certainly, he was never to take the Japanese position in a dispute.

Other cases sprang from chauvinistic biases and humiliating styles of negotiation. In the cases of Chŏng Sŏk (No. 24), Yi Se-jae (No. 30), and Ŏm Sŏk-chŏng (No. 49), we can see that Japanese committed acts of violence. What were the causes; why did relations decay to such a level; and why did the Japanese think that if they resorted to violence, the results would be to their favor? Some of these violent acts and Yi Se-jae's attempts to assert Korean political authority over the Waegwan Japanese will be examined in detail in Chapter 6.

Finally, we are attracted to cases that arose from problems of sex and power. Pak Sin (No. 28) and Kim Sŏk (No. 48) both received reprimands for incidents involving sexual crimes between Japanese and Koreans. Pak Sin's case is examined in detail in Chapter 7. Disputes over political authority and sexual relations, unlike rice, cotton, ginseng, and silver, were disputes over who obeys whom and whose morals are to prevail. An examination of the latter problem, as we shall see in Chapter 7, even takes us into the realm of morality as a political instrument.

Conclusion

The political cost of doing business with the Waegwan was great for the Tongnae Magistrate; in fact, statistically speaking, the Waegwan was the greatest of all his headaches. The unpredictability of the Japanese, the opportunities for crime involving the Japanese, and the compounding of ordinary administrative duties with the complexities of frontier diplomacy all made the post of Tongnae Magistrate extraordinarily delicate. From 1506 to 1897, the period for which we have records, one magistrate in six was affected by the connection with Japan. The worst punishment meted out to a magistrate for problems involving the Japanese was exile, and two magistrates were killed during war with Japan while attempting to carry out their duties. The meager comparative data suggests that the quality of the magistrates posted to Tongnae was unusually high. This would indicate that the central authorities paid particular attention to the frontier with Japan and dispatched some of their best people. Until we have more complete data on the relative ranks and career paths of Kyŏngsang Province county magistrates, we cannot make conclusive statements, but considering the level of resources devoted to the Japanese and the occasional serious nature of incidents at the Waegwan, it would be most surprising if the center did not dispatch some of its rising stars. If that was the case, then the Japanese impact on Korean politics went beyond the provincial level and affected politics at the center as well by affecting the career paths of some of the most capable men.[62]

6

LEAKY ROOFS AND
OTHER MATTERS

The riot as a Japanese negotiating tactic

> ...My county has direct contact with the Wae, [so] morning and
> night I [live in] anticipation of rebellion.[1]
>   (from Magistrate Yu Tang's memorial to the throne, 1776)

The Japanese in Pusan were, from 1512, clearly limited to their compound – the walls were the boundary. This chapter examines an aspect of the interaction of people inside and outside of these walls, and our chief concern is with the control of people's movements or the exercise of sovereignty.

Peter Sahlins also helps to clarify the concepts of sovereignty and territory. Sovereignty was jurisdictional, and in the Cerdanya valley, the patchwork of sovereignties slowly collapsed into a territorial definition of the national boundary.[2] In Chosŏn Korea, the land itself was territorialized vis-à-vis the Japanese, because of the sea and, from 1512, by the walls of the Japan House. Korean officials did not reside inside the compound from at least as early as 1607 and probably from before. Korean concerns with sovereignty in the ports were directed at the control of people, not of land. From the sixteenth century, land use was not at issue; people and their movements were.

Changing perceptions

In the winter of 1728–1729, a Confucian advisor to the Tsushima *daimyō*, Amenomori Hōshū, wrote an extended series of memos to his lord entitled *Kōrin teisei* ("Sober Advice on Relations with Korea"). In these memoranda Hōshū poses the thesis that Korean attitudes towards Japanese underwent change over the century and a quarter from the end of Hideyoshi's invasion to the early eighteenth century. Hōshū argues that from the end of Hideyoshi's campaigns in 1598 to about 1615, "fear" (*ojikeru*) dominated Korean attitudes towards Japan. From 1615 to 1657, fear changed to "avoidance" (*sakeru*), and from 1657 to the time of writing (c.1728), Koreans became "inured" (*nareru*) to Japanese bluster.[3] His dates derive from the reign dates of the successive Tsushima lords in the seventeenth century.

Hōshū warned that while Korean attitudes were changing, Japanese attitudes remained fixed. The Japanese believed their "prowess," their "power" (*yoi*), proven during the Hideyoshi invasions, still reverberated in the Korean consciousness. They entertained the notion that threats and blustering in negotiation with Koreans always resulted in success. In fact, argued Hōshū, from the time of the move to the new Waegwan at Ch'oryang in 1678, Japanese "power" had begun to evaporate before the eyes of the Koreans, although Japanese were not conscious of such.[4] Hōshū's point was to impress upon his lord a sense of the changed circumstances, which now required knowledge of Korean affairs where there had been ignorance, sensitivity to Korean customs and sensibilities where there had been bluster, and simple tact where there had been threats.

These last chapters offer case studies that examine Hōshū's thesis of changing circumstances from the late seventeenth century into the early eighteenth century. The Waegwan was more than the site of trade and diplomacy. It was also the site of contests over authority and power and the site of ethnic boundary maintenance. In both cases examined here, the Koreans prevailed, because ultimately they held the trump card: the flow of rice. But we must consider other questions that go beyond diplomatic, economic, and political concerns: can we find evidence for what would have constituted threats to Korea from the Waegwan Japanese? For where Koreans felt threatened or annoyed by Japanese actions on the level of day-to-day relations, we can glimpse attitudes about themselves in relation to others. In the problem cases, we will find indication of how Koreans thought their day-to-day relations with Japan should have functioned. By examining the aberrant cases, we can begin to grasp the boundaries of what constituted so-called "good relations" at the practical, working level of international relations. Without this knowledge, we are left with nothing more than the platitudes, hopes, and personal preferences of metropolitan political and intellectual figures at far remove from the working end of contact with another people. If we are truly lucky, we may even glimpse Korean self-conceptions.

We have thus far examined the economic and political contexts for the Waegwan; now we turn to the living texts of case studies and examine two types of incident that certainly got the attention of Korean authorities. In this chapter we consider the Japanese readiness to storm out of the gates of the Waegwan as a tactic to put pressure on their Korean keepers. In the following chapter, we examine the problem of prostitution at the Waegwan and its significance in the eyes of the Koreans.

The Pyŏllye chibyo (Collection of Border Precedents), edited in the capital by the Office of Custodian of Foreign Visitors (Chŏn'gaeksa) of the Board of Rites, devotes an entire chapter to the problem of Japanese leaving the Waegwan compound to wander about the Korean countryside without authorization. The Korean term for this was nanch'ul,[5] which literally meant "disorderly exiting" or "rioting and storming out." The fact that the Korean authorities would classify documents under such a category is significant. It reminds us of the complete loss of face and near destruction of the Chosŏn dynasty when it was unable to stop Hideyoshi's armies from ranging at will over the Korean peninsula. "Disorderly exiting" is the first of the Pyŏllye chibyo's problematic chapters connected with the Japanese; the others being: "Smuggling and miscellaneous crimes" (including prostitution); "Sea and Land Routes for Wae Castaways;" and "Miscellaneous Agreements" (including the Ullŭng Island–Takeshima problem). In these categories we have strong hints of what Koreans saw as threats to its southeastern frontier from the Japanese after about 1600: direct or indirect penetration of the country and outright seizure of territory. Direct penetration of Korea came as Japanese defiance of Korean power and unauthorized departures from the Waegwan to move around the countryside. It also came as impregnating Korean women. Indirect penetration, where Japanese were employing Korean agents, came as smuggling that corrupted both society and economy. Of course, the Japanese documents do not possess these particular designations. The Japanese document we will examine in this chapter on rioting survives to us as a miscellaneous document with no particular classification. Others examined in the following chapter on prostitution were also miscellaneous documents that usually carried no more of a title or classification than one that referred to the particular incident described. Perhaps we should not make too much of the way records are classified, but the concerns of the Koreans seem to be clear: keep the Japanese at bay.

Limitations on movement

Before examining the cases recorded in the *Pyŏllye chibyo*, we should clarify what regulations governed the movement of the Japanese and the Koreans at the Waegwan. First, let us consider the restrictions in force during the Tumo Waegwan period of 1607 to 1678. A 1646 Agreement in the *Pongnae kosa* is the first indication in the post-Hideyoshi period of passes being used for entry and exit to the Waegwan.[6] We find the same Agreement in the *Chŭngjŏng kyorinji*, but there it is dated 1653.[7] Both note that without "passes" Japanese were forbidden to come and go. All comings and goings were to be reported to the Japan House Master. Japanese without passes were considered "disorderly." The 1653 entry in the *Chŭngjŏng kyorinji* also stipulates that any Korean other than a Tongnae official or a Tongnae-issued pass-holder who entered the Waegwan was to be charged with criminal activities. Japanese leaving the compound did not have authorization to cross the river in front of the old Waegwan in Tumo, near the Pusan Garrison. Outside the gate Japanese were able to buy daily necessities at a morning market run by Korean fishmongers and greengrocers. This Agreement, like many others, possibly followed a particularly disputatious incident directly relevant to our topic of "disorderly exiting." In the ninth month of 1652, a smuggling ring was uncovered which involved collusion between Korean and Japanese merchants. The Tongnae Magistrate punished the Korean merchants and demanded punishment for the guilty Japanese. The Waegwan's *Daikan* (K: *Taegwan*, one of the Tsushima lord's deputies in charge of official trade at the Waegwan), arguing that the practices were, in fact, the norm, recruited 93 Japanese in the Waegwan, marched off to Tongnae, and demanded to negotiate directly with the Magistrate. Of course, to defy the chain of command in such an unprecedented and threatening manner was unacceptable to the Koreans. All complaints were to go first through the interpreters, the *Hundo* and *Pyŏlch'a*. The Tsushima *daimyō* eventually recalled the *Daikan* and his followers, most likely as a result of Korean complaints, in the twelfth month, and in the following year agreed to the restrictions listed above.[8]

A 1672 entry in the *Chŏpdae Waein saye* (Instances of Receiving Japanese) concerns itself with the prevention of smuggling by Korean locals under the responsibility of the Pusan Garrison Commander's Office (*Sugun Ch'ŏmjŏlchesa*). Although their entry and exit to the Waegwan could not be prevented, punishment for their crimes was to be heavily visited on the Garrison Commander.[9] In 1676, restrictions on entry by Koreans were re-stated: only those accompanied by officials or bearing

179

passes were allowed. Women were expressly forbidden. In the previous year, the earthen perimeter wall was re-built in stone.[10]

Turning now to the Ch'oryang Waegwan period of 1678 to 1873, we can see Korean authorities enforcing stricter and stricter controls. The exterior limit at the old Tumo Waegwan was the river. Since the new Ch'oryang Waegwan completed in 1678 was larger, less geographically defined, and farther from the Pusan Garrison, definite boundaries were necessary. From the Korean perspective, the construction of a new Waegwan in a new location offered the government an excellent opportunity to put more legal definition to the scope of Japanese movement.

A 1678 Agreement on the morning market includes limitations on the geographic extent of Japanese movement outside the walls of the new Waegwan. The details of that agreement are as follows: to the sea side, Japanese could not cross the harbor and go and come to Chŏlyŏng Island; to the west, Japanese could not go farther than the banquet hall (outside the northern wall);[11] to the east, Japanese could not go farther than the guest house (towards the Pusan Garrison).[12] For daily necessities, Japanese could buy fish and vegetables from villagers in front of the main gate, but could not go to the villagers' hamlet. Moreover, followers and attendants accompanying Japanese envoys to the Tongnae Magistrate's office could not fall behind the party or dally in the Korean hamlets and create mischief.[13]

A 1679 entry in the *Chŭngjŏng kyorinji* expands the geographic limits while at the same time more clearly defines them: to the east, Japanese could go some 300 paces to "Pine Hill;" to the west, Japanese could go about 80 paces to "West Hill;" to the southwest, Japanese could go about 100 paces towards Ch'oryang hamlet; to the south, Japanese could go 100 paces to the shore.[14] In 1683, the returning Korean Embassy to Edo struck an agreement while on Tsushima granting Japanese in the Ch'oryang Waegwan permission to visit ancestral graves near the old Waegwan at Tumo in the spring and fall and a few other days in the year, but the same agreement forbade Japanese to enter Korean houses along the way. In 1709, presumably because of a smuggling case, the court decreed that all Korean Interpreters going into the Waegwan and all Japanese from the Waegwan going to the residences for the *Hundo* and *Pyŏlch'a* had to be accompanied by two Korean officials.[15] Kim Yong-uk points out that mention of wall-jumping and Japanese going into local households in the second article of the new regulations indicates that the problem of illegal sexual liaison had superseded smuggling, an intriguing argument, but given the large number of incidents of small-scale smuggling reported in the *Pyŏllye chibyo*, it is difficult to state such conclusively.[16] The 1709 decree implied that the *Hundo* and *P'yŏlch'a* could be searched, but in 1736, body searches were abolished by the King as being too humiliating to Korean officials in front of the Japanese.[17] Most smuggling cases involved Korean ginseng for Japanese silver. In a 1738 report from the Tongnae Magistrate that appears in the *Chŭngjŏng kyorinji*, a long list of violations of the above regulations appears, making the point that access to the Waegwan was, despite controls to the contrary, virtually open. All of these regulations were primarily designed to thwart the free intermingling of Japanese and Koreans and were ostensibly designed to stop smuggling and sexual liaison. Violation of entry restrictions by Koreans constituted smuggling. Violation of exiting restrictions by Japanese constituted "disorderly exiting." Below we will examine Japanese violations, or "disorderly exiting," in detail. In Chapter 7, sexual liaison will be our concern.

Why Japanese rioted: exploding frustration or negotiating tactic?

The 19 or so cases listed in the *Pyŏllye chibyo* under "disorderly exiting" begin with a 1626 entry and end with an entry dated 1824, covering nearly two centuries. Fourteen cases occurred in the seventeenth century, three cases in the eighteenth century, and two cases in the nineteenth century.[18] In general, a change in the seriousness with which these incidents were treated in the Magistrate's reports appears in the 1690s. With the establishment of the new Waegwan at Ch'oryang in 1678, specific agreements defined the distances from the compound Japanese were allowed to roam. With these agreements, the Magistrate finally had a legal definition for infringements, which he could invoke to demand punishment for violators. Infringements after the 1678 Agreement could not be treated lightly, since the authority of the Tongnae Magistrate and behind him that of the Korean state were at stake.

Incidents prior to and after 1678 were of two general types. Either they were the activities of ordinary Japanese at the Waegwan or they were orchestrated and sometimes led by Japanese officials at the Waegwan. If ordinary traders and sailors left the compound to visit relatives' graves (1665.5, 1695.1), to watch ships (1665.6), to buy fish and vegetables (1708.2, 1710.3), or to demand the delivery of charcoal and firewood (1736.7), that was one thing. But when Japanese officials at the Waegwan, the very people who had enjoined themselves to enforce the regulations, became violators or even leaders, Korean authorities had "no-one to whom [they could] argue criminality," as Magistrate Yi Se-jae stated the problem in a report dated 1697.8.[19] Prior to the Agreement of 1678, we commonly see officials, notably the *Saihan*, the *Daikan*, and the House Master leading upwards of 100 men from the compound. After the 1678 Agreement, the reporting Magistrate singled out any officials among the violators for particular censure, and their punishment became a focus of the magistrate's communications with the Waegwan.

Another difference between the pre-1678 situation and the post-1678 situation was the physical distance the rioters had to go to make their protest. Prior to the Ch'oryang Waegwan, the Tumo Waegwan was just beyond the gates of the Pusan Garrison. Its proximity to the Pusan Garrison and the Tongnae Magistracy, just a little beyond, made exiting to lodge complaints easy, but the 4.5 kilometer remove of the Ch'oryang Waegwan meant complainants had to tramp across the Korean countryside before reaching the gates of either the Pusan Garrison or the county seat. Naturally, the embarrassment to the Korean government was magnified accordingly. Thus from 1678, not only did the Tongnae Magistrate have a diplomatic agreement to enforce (which worked to Korean advantage by explicitly forbidding Japanese from leaving the compound without authorization), but also any challenges to that agreement became more serious. After 1678, challengers had to create a larger, more sustained public display; this required more malice aforethought.

The purpose of rioting and marching out of the Waegwan was to address some complaint directly to the Tongnae Magistrate. The procedure for all communication with the Tongnae Magistrate or the Pusan Garrison Commander dictated that Japanese complaints or messages go through the *Hundo* and the *Pyŏlch'a*. Oftentimes, the Japanese thought these interpreter-liaison officials were not passing on their complaints to the Magistrate or the Garrison Commander and alternatives were necessary. Rioting and storming out of the Waegwan was one such alternative.

Amenomori Hōshū suggested another alternative in his *Kōrin teisei*. That was to break protocol at one of the official banquets or tea receptions and confront the Magistrate personally with some complaint.[20] But storming out of the Waegwan carried sufficient drama to catch the Magistrate's undivided attention.

From the Japanese perspective, marshalling a crowd and marching out of the gate to the Pusan Garrison or the county seat was designed to get the attention of authorities above the usual liaison officers and interpreters, but such bold action was also used to pressure a Magistrate whose attention one already had in negotiation. Below we will compare a particularly revealing Japanese document on this point with the Magistrate's reports, but to illustrate matters here, let us briefly examine a series of incidents in the early 1670s, during the tenure of Magistrate Chŏng Sŏk, whose re-appointment we discussed briefly in Chapter 5.

By 1671, the unfavorable anchorage and exposure of the Tumo Waegwan to strong winds made the site unbearable to the Japanese. In reaction to having yet another petition for relocation turned down, a *Ch'awae* (Japanese irregular envoy) from Tsushima led 100 men to the county seat in the eighth month and demanded revision of the Korean diplomatic note that had just been handed him rejecting Tsushima's request for a removal of the Waegwan. In the tenth month, he or another *Ch'awae* led 70 men to the county seat and withdrew after meeting with the Magistrate and the *Chŏbwigwan* (reception official).[21] Within a month, the Waegwan burned down, so temporary housing had to be found in village houses. A drunken House Master led several tens of men to demand that the Pusan Guest House (*Pusan Kaeksa*) be made available. Again in the same month (1671.11), a *Ch'awae* led 30 men to demand that something be done since the facility was gone.[22] The *Ch'awae* committed suicide in the twelfth month as all his efforts had met with failure: his negotiations to move the Waegwan and his threatening march on Tongnae. The *Sillok* refers to his death as being caused by illness.[23] In response, Korea sent Interpreters (*Yŏkkwan*) to Tsushima to negotiate directly with the Tsushima *daimyō*.[24] In the spring of 1672 (fourth month), the House Master led men to a Pusan village where they occupied villagers' homes. In the same month and repeatedly in the sixth month, the Japanese, complaining of cramped quarters, and "overcome with churlishness," wandered everywhere over the county.[25] Magistrates Chŏng Sŏk and Yi Ha were greatly perturbed, but negotiations for the new Waegwan at Ch'oryang went ahead, although none too quickly.

Kim Yong-uk tells us that between 1611 and 1675 negotiations to move the Waegwan occurred eight times. During this time, either by circumstance or design, the Tumo Waegwan managed to burn down no less than six times: 1621, 1667, 1671, 1672, 1674, and 1677.[26] Given the unusual frequency of fires in the 1670s, the rampaging about in 1671 and 1672 may have been tied to a convenient arson or two to push negotiations forward. Kim Yong-uk speculates arson was probably the case in the fire of 1671.[27] Doubt is thrown on this hypothesis by the *Sillok* description of the fire that destroyed the entire compound, seven Japanese ships, and forced the Japanese out of the compound with barely the clothes on their backs. If that fire was arson, then the court suspected nothing, since the throne ordered that Tsushima be given 200 *sŏk* of rice and 10 *tong* of cotton (500 bolts) as condolence.[28] In 1673, the Ch'oryang site was agreed, so a motive for arson after that date is difficult to imagine. The matter is yet inconclusive.

Japanese success with riots that spilled out of the compound in the early 1670s nearly saw a repeat in the 1690s, but the Agreement of 1678 that defined Japanese culpability intervened to Korean advantage. In the first month of 1695, six Japanese leaped a wall and visited Sŏn'am Temple[29] where they performed a religious ritual. They returned to the Waegwan without incident, but their crime was known. The House Master explained to the Korean authorities that they had been hawking and the birds got away; after the hawks went his men, unintentionally committing a crime. He reported to the Magistrate that they had been bound over to Tsushima for adjudication. Officials in Hansŏng demanded that their heads be put on pikes to deter others, since to let matters go would have gutted the new agreements.[30] By the second month, it became clear that the House Master had no intention of extraditing his former charges for certain death and stated that they had been banished. Although the court wanted capital punishment, since no Japanese officials had been involved, the Korean position was weak and Korean justice was forced to rely on Japanese prosecution, with unknown results.

In 1697, a wholly different situation developed. If bulk is any indication of the gravity of the 1697 incident, then we might note that nearly 40 percent of the chapter in the *Pyŏllye chibyo* on "disorderly exiting" is devoted to the events beginning in the eighth month of 1697. Fortunately, we also have a fairly detailed report from the Master of the Japan House about the same incident, giving us a chance to glimpse matters from the Japanese side.

The brief note in the Tongnae *ŭpchi* about Magistrate Yi Se-jae's tenure is taken up with a "revolt" by the Japanese and their unexcused exit from the Waegwan.

> Because the Japanese rioted and went out [of the Waegwan] to Sŏ'am [Sŏn'am Temple], in 1698.1, the Magistrate was arrested. He had a record of good administration and [later] became a Second Minister (Jr. 2).[31]

Because of this incident, Yi Se-jae was interrogated, but having a "record of good administration," he was eventually promoted. As we mentioned in Chapter 5, such promotions probably indicate an appreciation in the center for the difficulty of the frontier post.

When we turn to his reports in the *Pyŏllye chibyo*, we can easily understand the central government's appreciation. Yi Se-jae had a very difficult situation on his hands, but throughout the course of events, he maintained a clear grasp of the key issue: Waegwan officials had personally led their own men out of the Waegwan in complete contempt of the Agreement of 1678.

The problem began in the eighth month of 1697 (no day given), when the *Saihan* led 18 men to Sŏn'am Temple and back. When asked why he had done this, he complained that Korean merchants used to stay at market until the end of the day and returned home in the dark, but now they left early, and trade became difficult. In addition, he complained that a Tsushima request to revise diplomatic correspondence on Ullŭng Island had been ignored by the Magistrate and not forwarded to the capital.

The matter of Ullŭng Island deserves detailed treatment, but let us briefly review some of the developments at this point. In the previous fall and winter of 1696 a dispute over the ownership of Ullŭng Island had reached a conclusion. The issue was settled to Korean satisfaction when Tsushima officials reported in a letter to Magistrate Yi Se-jae in the first month of 1697 the conclusion reached by the shogun in the matter. He had asked the Lord of Tsushima whether *Takeshima* (K: *Ullŭng*) Island was Japanese or Korean territory, and the answer was that it is closer to Korea and therefore Korean, but both Koreans and Japanese went there for smuggling. The shogun ordered that Japanese be forbidden to visit Ullŭng Island.[32] The Korean authorities had responded with diplomatic notes affirming this situation. The Tsushima authorities, however, wanted the matter overturned and were pressing Tongnae to re-open negotiations on the matter. Yi Se-jae commented, "[these] people from afar were born stubborn."[33] The court agreed. To make clear that unauthorized exiting was strictly prohibited, the court directed Magistrate Yi to carve in stone the regulations governing the Waegwan and place this stone outside the Waegwan's main gate.

Again, in the eighth month of 1697 (no day given), the *Saihan*, after making daily entreaties to the *Pyŏlch'a* over Ullŭng Island, suddenly fell silent and after ten days led a group of 94 to Sŏn'am Temple stating that they wanted to view the fall landscape. Magistrate Yi saw clearly that he was the object of coercive pressure, and since the Japanese authorities themselves were orchestrating matters, he lamented having no one to whom he could argue criminality.[34]

Matters did not abate. Yet again in 1697.8, some 26 Japanese went out and returned. Then 132 left the compound with the purpose of obstructing the road between the Pusan Garrison and the Tongnae Magistrate's office. The activities of these 132 formed the critical core of the incident of 1697 and are described fully in the Japanese document on the incident discussed below. According to the Korean records, the "Wae" obstructed the road, brandished swords, and screamed and yelled. Two swords were lost, presumably in some sort of melee with Koreans. A group of 56 Japanese went to the exterior gate of the Pusan Garrison, demanding to see the Garrison Commander. The Garrison Commander sent a Military Official (K: *Kun'gwan*), Chŏn Yu-gwang, who chided them for being unreasonable. The Japanese overpowered Chŏn and the two servants with him and led them off. Soldiers from the Pusan Garrison attempted to rescue Chŏn and the others, but the Japanese succeeded in kidnapping them to the Waegwan. Negotiations with the House Master revealed the immediate Japanese demand: deliver the person who abducted the Japanese swords and the Military Official with the two servants will be released. Further negotiations between a Korean Interpreter Ch'oe Ŏk (*Yŏkkwan* and *P'ansa*, Jr. 5), the *Hundo* and *Pyŏlch'a*, and the *Saihan*, House Master, and *Daikan* revealed the entire gamut of reported grievances, and Magistrate Yi Se-jae recorded these.

The *Saihan* listed four complaints. He desired a revision of the diplomatic notes related to Ullŭng Island; undoubtedly, this meant a demand for Korean approval of Japanese visitations, that is, fishing in the area. The second complaint was that charcoal and firewood deliveries were insufficient. Third, he wanted the magistrate to relax his prohibitions on Korean merchants traveling after dark, so that the market could remain open longer. The *Saihan*'s last complaint was that deliveries of official trade rice (converted from cotton) had formerly been brought by two boats in lots of 200 *sŏk* per boat, but recently only one boat was operating. The decrease in services allowed deliveries of no more than 200 *sŏk* at a time. The reader should note at this point that none of the *Saihan*'s complaints touched on rice deliveries in arrears, but only on inadequate transport. Finally, the House Master pointed out that the West Hall leaked when it rained and that repairs were usually left undone. Satisfied that the Korean side had heard everything, the Japanese released the Military Official and promised not to storm out of the compound again. The two Korean servants remained under Japanese detention. There were a few token, light canings of Japanese in front of the main gate by Waegwan authorities, but Magistrate Yi was unconvinced of Japanese sincerity.[35]

As evidence of the vacuity of Japanese sincerity, Magistrate Yi pointed to a separate but revealing incident in the private trade market. A *Daikan* called Bangorō had created a disturbance by trying to use debased Japanese silver. Silver debasement was practiced under Shogun Tokugawa Tsunayoshi to shore up the *bakufu*'s finances, that is, to inflate itself out of debt. The former 80 percent purity of "Keichō" silver (names taken from reign names) dropped to 64 percent purity in 1695 and this was called "Genroku" silver in Japan. In 1711, long after the incident we are discussing, the quality dropped to 20 percent and was known as "Yotsuhō" silver. Afterwards there were further revaluations and devaluations.[36] Magistrate Yi refers to Genroku silver (64 percent purity). Negotiations about the silver debasement had opened in the fourth month of 1697, just four months prior to the incident under scrutiny here. In the midst of negotiations, the *Daikan* Bangorō had produced a threat to storm out of the Waegwan from his bag of negotiating tactics, a clear indication to Magistrate Yi that the Japanese side thought of such threats as but one more negotiating tactic, and that the Waegwan authorities felt no guilt or remorse for their violations of agreements with Korea.[37]

A directive from the capital accepted the Magistrate's position, shared his distrust, and introduced a new position. Capital officials ordered the Magistrate to discriminate the crimes of the Waegwan leadership from their underlings' transgressions and stop the provisions for the *Saihan*, who had obviously directed the affair, and for the First Special Envoy. Although the envoy was not seen as a ringleader, he was, with the *Saihan*, the highest-ranking participant. Supplies for the House Master and those below him were ordered delivered.

In a dispatch dated the ninth month of 1697, a month after the melee on the Pusan Garrison road, Magistrate Yi reported that the *Saihan* insisted on attending a tea reception given to an envoy from Tsushima. We should remember that these "tea receptions" as well as certain banquets for important envoys were the only opportunities the Japanese had to meet the Magistrate personally. As Hōshū mentioned, they were exploited as a forum to present direct appeals. On this occasion, the *Saihan* tendered a complete apology for the previous month's incidents and affirmed his pledge never to do such again. He then proceeded to his real business. He complained of a 5,000-*sŏk* shortfall in the delivery of official trade rice; he wanted to negotiate the conversion of official trade cotton to rice; and he was worried that the rate at which official trade cotton had been converted to rice (one bolt of cotton to 12 *tu* of rice) was to be reduced by one *tu*. Finally, he wished to discuss the sale of undelivered rice. The Magistrate assessed the *Saihan*'s display as one part apology and one part business. Mostly, however, he thought it pure opportunism.

Later dispatches from the Tongnae Magistrate in the same month testify to a House Master publicly castigating the *Saihan* for his offences in one breath and in another pleading that supplies be given to the First Special Envoy who was young, filled with visions of the beauties of Sŏn'am Temple, and who was easily led astray. The boy's life depended on receiving supplies. The House Master inveigled an invitation to a landing banquet for a Tsushima envoy and again broached the same items of business earlier presented by the *Saihan*. Here, we find a specific reply to the problem of the 5,000 missing *sŏk*. The *Hundo* explained that the shortfall was due to a bad harvest.

As with so many other incidents, this one had no real denouement. In the tenth month of 1697, Magistrate Yi Se-jae was ordered held for interrogation. As we know, his career did not falter, so the investigation evidently went to his advantage. The *Saihan* boarded ship for Tsushima in the third month of 1698, although a new *Saihan* did not take up appointment until 1699.7. Whether Takase Hachizaemon, the *Saihan* in question, ever returned during his period of appointment is yet unclear. According to Osa Masanori, Hachizaemon's appointment was from 1696.8 to 1699.7, and he was never re-appointed *Saihan*.[38] The matter of amending Korea's diplomatic notes on Ullŭng Island was again broached in the fourth month of 1698, and the First Special Envoy was still being seen about the Waegwan at the same time, his case still being championed by the House Master.

"We're going to give Tongnae hell"

If we now turn to a Japanese report on the core event of the 1697 incident, or that day when the military official and his servants were kidnapped, we can appreciate a fairly different perspective. One document in particular gives us a very detailed account of the incident including its origins and intent.[39] It is a report on a "fight" between Waegwan Japanese and Koreans while the Japanese were illegally passing on the road from Pusan to Tongp'yŏng, and was written by the House Master, Tōbō Shingorō, as a summary of the incident. According to Shingorō, in the spring of 1697, due to famine in Korea,[40] the customary 16,000 *sŏk* of official trade rice could not be delivered. Moreover, the visitation hours for Tongnae merchants were shortened, making private commerce as well as the purchase of fresh daily foodstuffs difficult. Another constant irritant at the Waegwan had also once again become acute: the lack of firewood and charcoal deliveries. Finally, the matter of Ullŭng Island (referred to in Japanese documents as Takeshima) still needed discussion. Although Shingorō was trying to communicate his dissatisfaction with all these matters to Magistrate Yi Se-jae, he became convinced that the liaison officials (the *Hundo* and the *Pyŏlch'a*) were not delivering his messages. Moreover, Shingorō suspected that this business of a famine was a hoax, since he had heard that there was some 20–30,000 *hyō* of rice in the Pusan Garrison warehouses.

Shingorō decided that the best way to get attention was to leave the Waegwan compound illegally and incite a riot, that is, to provoke the local authorities. The Magistrate and Pusan Commander would be sure to take notice, and then Shingorō would be able to deliver his petitions on these other matters. Thus decided, Shingorō sent out some 36 men to Tongpyŏng, a township within Tongnae, 10 *li* to the south of the county seat, and to Pusan, 21 *li* to the south of the county seat and closer to the Waegwan. Groups left the Waegwan on two occasions (seventeenth and twentieth of the eighth month) to stir up trouble, but they returned with no success.

On the twenty-first, Shingorō dispatched 40 men who were ambushed by a group of Koreans brandishing stones and bamboo pikes on the road in front of the Pusan Garrison. A skirmish ensued. Although we see no mention of Korean casualties, one Ichiuemon, an inspector and musketeer in the Japanese party was hit on the head, lost consciousness, and before he could recover, had his long and short swords stolen. The group went and found the "*jitō*" (headman?) of Pusan village and demanded the swords be given back along with the attacker so that Ichiuemon could exact his revenge and save his honor. The Japanese received nothing and no-one, and so took hostages on the spot, adding a threat to their demands. If the swords were not returned and the rock wielder not turned over, then the hostages would be cut down in his place and Japanese from the Waegwan would seize the Pusan Garrison. The swords were shortly returned but no Korean was turned over to the Japanese.

Undoubtedly feeling frustration at a bad plan gone awry, the Japanese side had seized two Korean bearers and a military official as hostages. The bearers were bound, but the military official was left without bonds to avoid "complications" at a later date.[41] The whole event had now reached a curious turn. Shingorō was willing to provoke armed conflict and threaten an escalation, but he and his men shied away from delivering an official of the Korean government to be bound and tied. Perhaps cooler heads had prevailed or perhaps Shingorō had reached some threshold of involvement beyond which he dare not go. Our source is not explicit.

On the twenty-second, a *P'ansa* (Jr. 5), an official outranking the usual liaison officers (Jr. 9) but subordinate to the Magistrate (Jr. 3), visited the Waegwan for negotiations and before nightfall the military official was released to the liaison officials. The *P'ansa* explained in negotiations, as had the headman on the previous day, that the attacker was one in a crowd, and so it would be impossible to determine the actual person. The House Master kept the two bearers until the twenty-fourth when they were released to the *Pyŏlch'a* who came bearing apologies. The rice for 1697 was never delivered; that year remained on Tsushima's books for decades as "delinquent accounts payable."[42]

A few points may be taken from this Japanese version of the incident. One, ordinary Koreans did not seek to "avoid" this group of armed Japanese but engaged them with nothing but rocks and bamboo pikes. In short, as Amenomori Hōshū argued at the beginning of this chapter, Japanese "power" had ceased to frighten Koreans by 1697 and an excessive display of the same "power" had actually resulted in the humiliation of a Japanese samurai. The right to wear swords was for many lower samurai their most cherished means of class distinction. The cliché is that a warrior without a sword was a warrior without a soul. Matters were even worse for Ichiuemon, since his opponents were peasants and not Korean military men.

Second, although brash, Shingorō maintained some sense of limits as evidenced by his decision not to bind up the military officer. A similar concern appears in Ichiuemon's recorded statement that is included in the report. Ichiuemon made it clear that he wanted to "cut down" any Korean of consequence to defend his stained honor but admitted this would be "stupid," bowed to his superiors, swallowed his pride, and promised to do nothing of the kind.

The most important point, however, is to take note of the Japanese willingness to employ violence as a negotiating tactic. The purposive character of rioting is demonstrated by House Master Tōbō Shingorō's moment of candor in his reports:

"we're going to give Tongnae hell."[43] From a more detached position, Hōshū criticizes rioting in the following terms.

> Understand that [Japanese storming out of the Japan House] and proceeding to Tongnae is tantamount to crossing swords with [the Magistrate]; [those who go] may not come back alive. . . . Thinking that [sending people] to Tongnae will put the [Korean] Interpreters in a very difficult position and get them into your hands and thereby settle matters is a calculated move that will certainly be ill-advised.[44]

From these two pieces of evidence in contemporary Japanese documents, we can state that "disorderly exiting" was a consciously applied negotiating technique.

Life at the Waegwan was undoubtedly difficult, since the daily necessities of food and fuel had to be supplied by the Korean government or local merchants. When supplies were cut off or delinquent, tempers naturally flared. In this case, the situation seems to have been compounded by a clash of personalities between the House Master, Tōbō Shingorō, and the Korean liaison officials. We can imagine that Shingorō's options were not so limited and that he may well have been able to get his concerns a hearing in Tongnae without resorting to rioting. Nevertheless, our purpose here is not to condemn any particular method but to emphasize the difficult unpredictability posed to the Tongnae Magistrate by the Japanese in the Waegwan. In the end, Shingorō expressed satisfaction that rice deliveries began again, although the Waegwan never did receive its 16,000 sŏk of rice for 1697.

When we compare the two versions of the incident left to us we find points of agreement and points of difference. The general outline of the incident is the same: Japanese left the compound; they fell into some kind of scuffle with Koreans; a Japanese had his swords taken; and with no immediate response to demands, a military official and two servants were taken as hostages by the Japanese to be released later. The Japanese account also corroborates Magistrate Yi Se-jae on two important points. One, Waegwan officials masterminded the entire incident. Two, the purpose was to put pressure on the Magistrate to accede to Japanese demands.

The largest difference is apparent in the comments on the importance and even size of the central Japanese complaint. Yi Se-jae saw the Japanese concerned above all else with the diplomatic notes on Ullŭng Island. The Tongnae Magistrate may have been overly sensitive to implicit Tsushima claims on Korean territory when he heard the House Master insist on re-opening negotiations over Japanese access to Ullŭng Island. The Waegwan House Master certainly begins his report with a discussion of the failure to have the notes re-written, but then goes on to discuss his other grievances, next being the fact that in recent years, annual rice transfers for official trade never exceeded 10,000 sŏk. In fact, the House Master thought he was being defrauded of rice owed to the Waegwan as a part of official trade. The House Master's report repeatedly returns to this problem and it becomes the centerpiece of his grievances. By contrast, the Magistrate's dispatches portray the issue of delinquent rice deliveries as an afterthought and denominate the shortfall at only 5,000 sŏk, reporting this figure as an amount mentioned by the Saihan.

The difference in identifying the central Japanese grievance may have arisen from various factors. To the House Master, the first concern was the delivery of rice, a key commodity not just for those in the Waegwan, but also very important to Tsushima, which was dependent on Korean rice. The Magistrate may have played down this complaint to avoid drawing attention to his own administration. Too close an investigation may have revealed corruption on the Korean side and the theft of rice before it got to the Japanese. Was the Magistrate directing the capital's attention elsewhere as a diversion, or do we simply have another example of miscommunication?

Later incidents

Shortages of food and fuel at the Waegwan are dominant themes in later incidents. In the third month of 1710, some 29 Japanese illegally left the Waegwan saying they were off to buy fish and vegetables. They returned after persuasion, but shortly thereafter 15 went out to the west. Women had been forbidden from attending the morning market and the number of vendors had fallen off. This problem was real enough to Magistrate Kwŏn Yi-jin, although not serious enough in his opinion to warrant unauthorized departures from the Waegwan.

The fire behind this particular smoke was a *Daikan* who had been "chattering" about a "full payment" of the official trade rice[45] and who had been making threats about rioting. Magistrate Kwŏn held the *Daikan* ultimately responsible and worked for his punishment and removal. When 57 more Japanese stormed out, the House Master finally made clear their grievances: fish, vegetables, and rice were in short supply. The House Master then became a target of punishment by the Magistrate. In accordance with the precedents established during the 1697 incident for selective withholding of provisions, Magistrate Kwŏn targeted the House Master's rations to make clear Korean displeasure with Japanese "disorderly exiting." By the eighth month, the House Master was "weeping and wailing" and the court advised re-supplying the official, since some limits had to be attached to the punishment. Otherwise, the court pointed out, the Japanese will cease to come and a "new," potentially dangerous situation may develop.[46] All Korean officials knew this meant a resort to piracy.

We should recall the Japanese concerns over deficient rice deliveries from the 1697 incident and here we see Magistrate Kwŏn considering this problem, if only obliquely, in a report from the third month of 1710.

> . . . I have detected the desires of the Wae. [They want] two years of official trade rice put together and paid in full. Afterwards, on top of this, they want the official trade rice for this year given to them in the fall. [But] first they storm out and then they make requests . . .[47]

Occasionally Korean policy met with success. In the seventh month of 1736, some 11 or 13 Japanese rioted and stormed out to Pusan demanding charcoal and firewood. Eleven Japanese were sent to Tsushima for punishment in the eighth month. Before the end of the year in the twelfth month, the House Master reported that the two leaders were sent to provincial areas as slaves in perpetuity.

In 1807, an odd affair occurred. A *Ch'awae* to request the dispatch of a T'ongsinsa led 110 men to press their request for the dispatch of a Korean Embassy to Edo. Five "flying ships" or small transports that worked the waters between Tsushima and

Pusan also participated, so the effect was riot by both land and sea. Large groups of 50 or so Japanese camped at the county seat. Magistrate O Han-wŏn reported no other demands, threw up his hands in despair and awaited a censure from the court that never came.

The cause behind the incident was probably simple. Tsushima's private trade began undergoing great changes from the mid- to late eighteenth century that saw a shift from high-value luxury commodities, such as ginseng, to lower-value, bulkier goods like laver and cow hides. The resulting fall off in the value of trade meant that the prospects of *bakufu* subsidies to host a Korean Embassy became steadily more attractive, and concerted efforts were marshaled to obtain Korean approval for the dispatch of another envoy to Edo. Actually, the final Korean Embassy of the pre-modern period left Pusan in 1811 but got no farther than Tsushima due to budget constraints in both Hansŏng and Edo. Both governments had settled on Tsushima as an acceptable site for diplomatic receptions, and Tsushima garnered its sought-after *bakufu* subsidies.

Finally, we have a report on an incident in 1824 during which Japanese broke into government offices in Tumo. No grievances are reported and there is not enough detailed information to hazard an analysis of the incident. This is the last Korean record.

Conclusion

Throughout the period following Hideyoshi's invasion, the Japanese employed rioting and storming out of the Waegwan as one more negotiating strategy to be turned on Tongnae. Prior to 1678 and the new Waegwan at Ch'oryang, Korean authorities had no mutually agreed legal standing from which they could demand punishment for offenders. After 1678 and the explicit agreements delimiting Japanese move-ment, the Tongnae Magistrate had a clear interest to uphold. Ordinary denizens of the Waegwan might be expected to wander out occasionally, but when the Waegwan authorities conspired to propel or even to lead their underlings out of the gate, matters became serious, as we saw in the first real test of this principle in 1697. As a practical way to handle the guilty, the court suggested ascertaining the complicity of any Japanese officials and then selectively withholding their support. Such a policy was appreciated by later Magistrates and employed. We must recall that, in Korean minds, the Japanese were the guests of the Korean state. For them to make demands and to riot was reprehensible. Magistrate after Magistrate used the word "cunning" to describe the Waegwan Japanese, since the Magistrates recognized "disorderly exiting" from the Waegwan as a tactic to apply pressure and obtain some further advantage from Korea.

The Japanese saw themselves as engaged in trade and diplomacy. Undelivered rice or diplomatic problems that turned not to one's favor were contestable matters. Official rice was a purchased commodity and the spoils of diplomacy were fair game for any means at hand, even limited violence. Occasionally, extreme means were necessary to pressure one's opposite number. But Hōshū was right. With the estab-lishment of the new Waegwan at Ch'oryang, the Korean government got agreements from Tsushima to limit Japanese movement, and they intended to enforce them. Thus, groups of Japanese running about waving swords carried no "power" or lingering aura of martial "prowess" left over from the time of Hideyoshi's invasion. Such displays had become unacceptable by common consent. True power now resided with the Tongnae Magistrate in the form of binding agreements. The problem for the Magistrate was that, although the Japanese had formally given their word to abide by their promise, their actions spoke otherwise.

Michiel Baud and Willem van Schendel offer a typology of political situations at boundaries: quiet, rebellious, or unruly.[48] A quiet borderland is either harmonious because it exists by mutual agreement or it is enforced by stalemated military forces. A rebellious borderland appears when local elites and the local populace take common cause against a state. An unruly borderland results when the structures of power are not clear or appear to be open for contestation. In these situations, the state is often exposed as weak. In Pusan we find the local representative of a centralized state seeking to impose his power and authority over unruly visitors. But Pusan society itself was a bit unruly: the local populace frequently engaged in smuggling with the Japanese, and as we will see, even procured women for the Japanese, all against the express wishes of the state and the local political elites. It is interesting that in the case of Ichiuemon and his lost sword, the local populace was not prepared to collude with the Japanese, but to make common cause with the Magistrate and help suppress the Japanese. Perhaps the Japanese sensed some sort of division between the populace and the Magistrate, and they sought to exploit it. We have no proof of this, but the Japanese certainly were testing the local representatives of the state by violently defying them. The Japanese were not recognizing Korean authority; they were not seeking ascription; they were adamantly rejecting absorption, and by so doing, they were making the ethnic boundary clear and the differences rigid. We might recall Fredrik Barth's definition of the ethnic boundary as that point where one set of moral standards and measures of excellence leaves off and another takes up.[49] In this sense, we can see that the Tongnae Magistrate was grappling with imposing his authority over the Japanese, and they were clearly resisting. In the frontier, where boundaries might become ambiguous, he was also struggling with imposing his authority over the local populace, and he was winning this battle. It might be difficult to say the same about the next issue we examine.

7

PÉNÉTRATION DU CORPS SOCIALE

Prostitution and the rivalry of power and culture at the Japan House in the eighteenth century

> ... We reached a place and leapt a wall [of the Japan House]. Although this was illegal entry, [it was only then that] I first became aware that I was being sold and tried to resist this evil, but Myŏng-wŏn pulled a dagger and threatened me. ...
>
> (Ae-gŭm confessing to the Magistrate of Tongnae how she was first coerced into entering the Waegwan in 1686.)[1]

Introduction

Around 500 Japanese lived in the Japan House between 1600 and the 1870s, and it was located in a country that has been labeled "the Hermit Kingdom." The Japanese lived there and came and went throughout a period that has been called the period of "the closed country" (*sakoku*) for Japan. Both "the Hermit Kingdom" and "the closed country" are European constructions and tell us little or nothing about Korean and Japanese self-conceptions. The Koreans and the Japanese saw themselves interacting with neighboring peoples within systems that were historically produced. It is our concern to know those historical conditions as a way to understand their forms of interaction. We have already discussed the diplomatic, economic, and political contexts, and in the previous chapter, we examined violent confrontations. In this chapter, we offer another case study of contact on the frontier.

Occasionally, "illicit sexual relations" became an issue at the Japan House, and the Tongnae Magistrate arrested the offenders and put their heads on pikes. Fortunately for our purposes, such incidents were not easily resolved and so were recorded in detail. Just as the records of the Inquisition help us to examine mentalities, worldviews, and popular religious beliefs in Europe, the records used here, kept by the local Korean magistrate, also give us insight into the world of ordinary contact between Koreans and Japanese. The sexual exchanges that are the concern of this chapter were not merely incidents of prostitution or even love; they were also shot through with cultural contradictions and power rivalries and introduce gender into the mix. By considering two well-recorded incidents of illicit sexual liaison, which arose in 1690 and 1708, we can better grasp the nature of pre-modern Korean–Japanese relations.

192

When frontier contact was for trade or diplomacy, sources are often highly explicit concerning motives. Where they are not, we can resort to arguments of economic logic, political power-brokering, or diplomatic decorum to explain the relation between cause and effect. When contact crossed sexual borders, we find ourselves in the quick of culture. Before us stretches a field of cross-cutting values and motives that make clear analysis difficult. Amid that morass, if we are lucky, glimmer archetypal values that, in their conflict, illumine the deeper structures of either culture.

Here we argue that sexual liaison, or penetration of the socio-political body at its core, was so highly feared by seventeenth-century Koreans, above the political and economic contacts already examined, that officials were prompted to enforce unusual punishments beyond what had been done in an earlier period and even beyond what the law required. This chapter focuses on two different but closely related incidents involving relations between Japanese men and Korean women: one was a case of prostitution; the other was perhaps a tragedy of love.

"Illicit sexual relations" and the control of resident Japanese in Korea

The Korean government was not predisposed to granting Japanese the right of residency in Korea before the Riot of the Three Ports in 1510, although Japanese did take up residence in Korea. Returning to the early decades of the Chosŏn kingdom, we find the following passage in the *Sillok* for King Taejong for the third month of 1418, just five months before Sejong ascended the throne and 14 months before Sejong's expedition left Korea to suppress pirates inhabiting Tsushima (6.1419). There are several points in the following passage that deserve notice, aside from the obvious fears of sexual liaison. Here we see Japanese classified into two general types: merchants and long-term residents who are referred to as "Wae", and "guests" (*kaek*) who are referred to as "Japanese." The former were a problem to be "cleaned out" and the latter were to be restricted to the Waegwans, the first mention in the *Sillok* of such structures outside the capital.[2]

> [The king] ordered that the Wae merchants in Kyŏngsang Province be segregated. The Board of War has received a report from the Deputy Pro-vincial Naval Commander (*Sugun Tojŏlchesa*, Jr. 3) in Kyŏngsang Province which states, 'The Wae who come and live in Pusan pursue trade or pro-stitutes. Japanese guests' and Wae merchant ships arrive and anchor. They assemble and buy in entertainment. Men and women mix with abandon. Guests who arrive to stay in other ports also come to buy spirits. They ask [to be allowed] to wait out bad winds, and they tarry for many days, spying on everything. They talk foolishness and cause trouble. [We] petition to [put them] in Yŏmp'o in Left [Kyŏngsang] Province and Kabaeryang (Kabaeryangsu in Kosŏng to the east of Chinhae) in Right [Kyŏngsang] Province. What if we build a Waegwan [in] each [port], clean out the resident Wae, and segregate their living [arrangements apart from locals]?' [The king] directed [Kyŏngsang] Province to segregate [the Wae into Waegwans] and not to disturb the people.[3]

According to the Deputy Provincial Naval Commander's report, the *"Waein"* had been coming to Pusan harbor for trade or prostitutes. In other ports as well, the *Wae* had been coming and staying for long periods, engaging in illicit sexual relations with Korean women, drinking, and spying on the Korean national situation. In the midst of this, he suggested the establishment of a Waegwan in Yŏmp'o Harbor for the accommodation of the Japanese. We can see that these Waegwan were first established in the ports as part of a policy to segregate the Japanese from ordinary Koreans, partly to suppress lewd behavior, partly to control financial drains on the state by clarifying the recipient of receptions, and partly for national security.

Not to mention piracy, the association of Japanese with licentious, even criminal, behavior by Koreans was firmly established early in the dynasty. Take for example the case of the commoner woman Ka-i. In 1428, King Sejong heard the following:

> The Board of Punishments memorialized: A commoner woman of Ch'ŏngsong (Northern Kyŏngsang), [by the name of] Ka-i, had illicit sexual relations in her youth with the private slave Pu-gum and had a child. The officials annulled [this] marriage between a commoner [woman] and a debased [man] and had her marry a Wae bastard [by the name of] Son-da (J: *Tadamasa?*). Ka-i, with Pu-gum and the neighbor, Yi nae-gŭn-nae, killed Son-da. Under law, Ka-i should be put to death by hacking her to pieces. However, from the first, she had suffered under the official's censure; she had been forced to give up the father of her child, and she had been married off to a Wae bastard. [However, her crimes of] being unable to stave off lust and murdering one's husband presents a precedent. We request adjudication by analogy with strangulation. [We ask for] Pu-gum to be beheaded and for Nae-gŭn-nae to be strangled. [The King] ordered a decrease [in punishment] for Ka-i by one degree and the remainder [to be handled] in conformance with the memorial.[4]

This brief account conjures up images of lust and murder worthy of the best brooding melodrama. The memorial accuses Ka-i of two crimes: viricide and promiscuity with a slave to the point of motherhood. Ordinarily, these crimes should have been punished by dismemberment until dead, but the mitigating circumstances were that the officials had forced her to divorce the father of her child and marry a Japanese. Presumably, the social status of the Japanese was above that of a slave, and that would have made the annulment and remarriage socially reasonable. It is difficult to say from this small scrap of information. It is obvious that Ka-i and her lover were not happy, and the victim got in the way. The Japanese may well have been a permanent resident or immigrant and may have had some influence over the officials involved to obtain a forced marriage. Again, we do not know. The "Wae bastard" seems a likely candidate for Murai Shōsuke's "marginal man" or a man of vaguely indeterminate identity who lived on the frontier between the archipelago, the peninsula, and the continent.[5] Immigrant, "bastard," or whatever, the victim was not considered beyond the pale of justice afforded by civilized law. Finally, we might note that the officials shied away from imposing death by hacking the murderess to pieces. Their plea to reduce the penalty derived from the extenuating circumstances, only one of which referred to the origins of the victim.

Later in the fifteenth century, we find a passage in the *Haedong chegukki* (1471) that discusses limitations on residency. Japanese residents were limited to only 60 households. The passage goes on to supply detail:

The following are expressly forbidden: those merchants [licensed through] earlier agreements who establish smuggling relations with permanent residents; those who [marry] and establish residences; and those who intentionally stay on [even] after they have finished trading.[6]

Despite these associations and state-administered controls, Japanese residing in Korea increased, and in 1510, they revolted in what is known as the Riot of the Three Ports, which centered on resident Japanese opposed to the toughening Korean position regarding taxation and access. Following that disturbance came profuse apologies from Tsushima with negotiations. The Chosŏn government eventually opened access to the peninsula again but limited Japanese landings to only Pusan from 1512. In 1521, residence in Yŏmp'o Harbor was permitted, but as a result of a piracy incident in 1544, relations between Tsushima and Chosŏn worsened, and the Chŏngmi Agreement of 1547 restricted all contact to the single port of Pusan.[7] Residence in Pusan was permitted for the stationing of envoys (K: *songsa*, J: *sōshi*) and "unlimited," long-term residence was strictly forbidden. The purpose was to avoid the lawlessness of earlier times and the social confusion that would result from an increase in Japanese residing in Korea and Koreans with Japanese fathers, something the Chosŏn government thought was the origin of the Riot of the Three Ports. At least, in 1710, such a historical memory was recorded in the *T'ongmun'gwanji*, and here we see a clear connection drawn between resident Japanese and revolt.

According to the *Chingbinok*, 'from the summer of 1591, Wae in the [Wae]gwan in Pusan gradually began slipping away in groups from ten to thirty and returning [to Japan], leaving the compound empty.' In 1598, a hurried and false memorial stated that, '[at the time of] the Riot [of the Three Ports in] 1510, a general was sent and he drove out all [the Wae]. Thereafter, under no circumstances, was [Japanese] residence permitted in the Three Ports; there were no Wae domiciles, and now 89 years have passed.' We are left with contradictory reports. [The truth is that] because of 1510, the Wae were driven out, [but] from 1512, [they] came [back] and were welcomed. [However, we] only permitted [Wae]gwan receptions for [their] envoys. Those who would be permanent residents [we] absolutely forbade. Because of the [mistaken] argument that there were Wae homes [in Korea] at that time, many false assertions have emerged. Some speak of Chŏlyŏng Island [in Pusan harbor], that there is the foundation of a Waegwan, but that building was razed without a trace, and there is no way to rely on [this information]. For a while, [movement on the matter must] await a thorough investigation.[8]

Here we see a snippet of the content of the debate surrounding the re-admission of Japanese to trade in Pusan Harbor after the Hideyoshi invasion. We should note the statements that explicitly forbade permanent residence and those that link permanent residence to the Riot of 1510. Prior to then, Japanese were mixing with Koreans in the ports, establishing households in Korea, and farming, trading, or fishing to support themselves.[9] Following the Riot of the Three Ports, the number of Japanese was "reduced," only a "Japan House" was left for the envoys, and according to the *Chingbinok*, just prior to Hideyoshi's invasion in 1592, the Japanese in Pusan were returning to Japan in obvious anticipation of the coming invasion.

In 1653, during the period of the Tumo Waegwan (1607–1678) – the Japan House established in the area called Tumo in Pusan Harbor – stricter controls were placed on entry and exit from the Japan House and these were tightened further by 1676. In 1675, an earthen wall was re-built with stone to stop people from leaping it. A contemporary (1675) passage in the *Sukjong sillok* bears witness to the concerns of the time.

> The Pibyŏnsa reported that 'a man in Tongnae, Ŏ Bu-dong, saw a Waein dallying with his wife, beat him to death and tossed the body in the sea. The witnesses were interrogated repeatedly, but without any evidence, we had to release him.' [The King] pardoned this [failure to prosecute]. These days, the frontier regulations have become slack. The [Japan] House Wae smuggle themselves in among the rural populace and have illicit intercourse with lewd women. Among the people of Tongnae and Pusan there are many Wae offspring. The people in the northwest (in reference to Ŭiju, on the Chinese border) are the same. Many have Mongol eyes and ears. [They] spy on national matters. This troubles those who know.[10]

Dalliance between Japanese men and Korean wives produced many Wae progeny, born as Japanese and Korean half-breeds among the Pusan populace. Here we see sexual liaison linked directly to spying, a national security concern of the state. We should note that, although we have a small hint of worry for something akin to racial purity, social morality and state security were the major concerns.[11]

At the dawn of the modern age, we still see mention of the Korean fear of Japanese men abducting Korean women and still the associations are with a loss of security. At the end of 1875, the Korean King Kojong reversed the Taewŏngun's foreign policy, which had declared that peaceful relations with western powers or the westernizing Japanese amounted to treason. In the second month of 1876, representatives of the Korean state concluded the Kanghwa Treaty with the Japanese Plenipotentiary Kuroda Kyotaka. The conservative Ch'oe Ik-hyŏn (1833–1906)[12] opposed this and wrote, "[n]ow, these Wae who come wear western clothes, use western cannon, and ride western ships – this is proof that the Wae and the westerners are one and the same." Ch'oe warned of awful results in giving Japanese access to Korea.

> They want to land [here], go and come, construct buildings, and reside. We have already discussed peace and have not spoken of refusing [these possibilities]. If we allow [them to come and go and live here,] then [it will mean] the plunder of [our] personal property and [our] women. Merely considering that which is being asked is the fourth reckless [road to] destruction.[13]

Ch'oe argued for the rejection of the treaty, stating that allowing access would lead to the plunder of personal property and women. The previous three roads to "reckless destruction" were: appeasing avariciousness from a position of weakness and thereby inviting limitless demands, trading Korea's useful goods for Japanese baubles and thereby courting national destruction, and thinking that heterodoxy will not flood the land, despite the obvious fact that the Japanese were now well and truly western-ized and fully capable of introducing such heresies as Christianity. The fifth and final act of "reckless destruction" was to make the mistake of negotiating peace with a people who know only materialism and not human principle; "such is like talking to a beast." Ch'oe's arguments had a long historical pedigree.

To summarize, from the fifteenth century, the Chosŏn kingdom had established and maintained contact with Japanese through the Japan House and had attempted to control Japanese residency. The need for control was great, since Japanese wanted permanent residency and engaged in various illegal activities. Perhaps most serious among these was "illicit sexual relations" with Korean women. Japanese residency was directly associated with the Riot of the Three Ports before Hideyoshi's invasion. After the invasion, the children born of Japanese men and Korean women were directly associated with threats to the security of the state. Recall our discussion of Tsushima's identity in Chapter 2: the 1,000 "tōjin" or "Koreans" fielded by the daimyō of Tsushima for Hideyoshi's invasion. After examining our case studies, we will return to the linkage between sexual union and state security. In short, it is clear that the Korean historical memory going back to the early fifteenth century saw Japanese in Korea as a source of crises.

Contact with Koreans

Before considering case studies of illicit sexual contact, let us briefly consider the means by which Japanese men might meet Korean women or Korean men who could act as procurers. Following the Riot of the Three Ports in 1510 and the strict imposition of Japanese segregation into Japan Houses, the likeliest means of contact with the local populace was in the daily food market that existed in the vicinity of the Waegwan.

From 1678, the Korean government moved the trading post to a site close to the hamlet of Ch'oryang in Pusan, which lay farther from the Pusan Garrison and possessed better anchorage. The principal site of Japanese–Korean exchange remained there until the modern period. The Ch'oryang Waegwan had a stone wall circumscrib-ing it on four sides (the Tumo Waegwan had a wall on three sides: south, north, west). The wall was some 1,630 kan 5 ch'ŏk long (about 2.965 kilometers) and about 2 meters high.[14] Entry and exit from the Waegwan was tightened up, primarily to control smuggling. Entry to the Waegwan by Korean women had been expressly forbidden in 1676 and, presumably, from long before in practice. It is still unclear even whether or not women had always been permitted near the Waegwan to sell daily foodstuffs.[15]

We do not have detailed information on this matter, but we do have two reports from the Magistrate's office dated 1710 and 1731, which mention women in the daily fish and vegetable market outside the main gate. In 1710, Japanese rioted and left the compound, citing as their reason for doing so the lack of fishmongers and vegetable dealers in the morning market. In reports on the riot, the Magistrate, Kwŏn I-jin, remarked that he had strictly forbade women from the morning market, leaving only men to handle the business. This move obviously created shortages, and

since Kwŏn identified the absence of women as the cause of the 1710 disturbance, possibly he allowed their re-entry into the market, but we do not know when
they had left the market prior to 1710.[16]

In 1731, Magistrate Chŏng Ŏn-sŏp left us a report explicitly linking women in
the morning market with prostitution.

> The morning market sees a daily assemblage of 20 or 30 old men and old
> women who sell to the Wae nothing beyond fish and vegetables. This is
> how the Wae take their morning and evening meals. Although we are
> unable to shut out [women] completely, old and younger women are mixed
> in [the group]. The Ch'oryang Village women are intimately acquainted
> with the Wae [because of] the morning market. The Wae promise to buy
> exclusively [from the women they know] such things as sandals and utensils
> and request their regular merchants to sew clothes for them. The Kam-ok
> incident of 1707 and the Kye-wŏl incident of 1716, both of which were
> crimes of illegal sexual liaison with Wae, stemmed from this intimate [market]
> situation. Although the women may be old, we especially forbid women
> from [participating in the market].[17]

Chŏng saw their presence, young or old, as a contributing factor to the prostitution
problem and concluded with a resolve to enforce their exclusion. The pressures to
allow women merchants to supply the Waegwan must have been enormous, considering that some 500 Japanese residents relied on only 20 to 30 suppliers for all
sorts of daily necessities.

Whatever the situation regarding female access to the morning market, when our
first case below opens in 1690, the inside of the Japan House at Ch'oryang was an
all-male environment and had been, implicitly, since 1512. Nevertheless, daily contact
with Korean women in the morning market was probably commonplace. Two of the
more famous cases of sexual liaison are presented below to illustrate developments
and thinking on both sides of the straits that eventually led to the 1711 Agreement
governing "illicit sexual liaison" at the Waegwan.

Case one: 1690

Ide Sōzaemon, one of the principles in our story, told the Master of the Japan House
that his problems began on the evening of the twenty-third of the second month
of 1690, when he was sweeping and dusting his kitchen. He heard a noise outside.
He went outside to see who was there, and discovered a Korean woman, who said
she had come to meet someone, but they had not come, and now that the dawn was
breaking, she could not leave. She prevailed on Sōzaemon to hide her until the
following night fell when she could leave. Night came and she did not leave.
Sōzaemon was thereupon discovered by the Japan House authorities to be hiding a
Korean woman.[18]

While Sōzaemon's troubles were just beginning, a separate incident was unraveling.
In the tenth month of 1689, Umeno Hisashiuemon gave 65 *monme* of silver to a
Korean he identified as "Chinsei" for pongee and cotton.[19] Osa Masanori identified
this type of transaction, providing money in advance for goods, as smuggling under

Korean law.[20] "Chinsei" did not reappear at the Japan House until the twentieth of the second month, 1690, some four months after he had received his advance. Not having the goods or the money, "Chinsei" offered a woman as collateral for four or five days until he could return with the silver. Here, in Umeno Hisashiuemon's confession, we see the close connection between smuggling and prostitution. By the night of the twenty-fourth, four days later, "Chinsei" had failed to return, and Hisashiuemon decided to put the woman out over the wall, but was discovered by the carpenter, Hidaka Riuemon. To keep Hisashiuemon's secret, Riuemon demanded the woman for four or five days and promised he would put her out over the wall himself. On the twenty-sixth, Hisashiuemon's fears came true when Riuemon was found to be still in possession of the woman.[21] Thus, by the end of the second month of 1690, the Japan House Master now had in custody two Korean women.

From the third to the sixth month of 1690, the Master of the Japan House replied to queries from the Magistrate of Tongnae that there were no women in the Japan House. The Magistrate was aware that they were inside, and he halted deliveries of rice and cooking fuel to the compound from the third month until the seventh month. For the Waegwan and Tsushima, dependent on Korean rice, a cessation of these deliveries was a serious blow.

On the eighth day of the seventh month, the two women, having been inside the Waegwan for about five months, were hidden under cotton in a small boat that put out from the Japan House quay. The Korean authorities arrested them after they went ashore near the "old" Japan House (Tumo Waegwan) and on the twenty-ninth day of the ninth month, beheaded three women: the two who had been caught escaping from the Waegwan and one other who had been apprehended earlier and charged with illegally entering the Waegwan. In addition, two men, the women's accomplices, were also beheaded. The executions took place in front of the Japan House and the heads were exposed on pikes. The Koreans gave no prior notification of the executions to the Waegwan authorities.[22] Of the women who had been in the Waegwan, one was 17 and the other was 29.[23] They were both "freeborn commoner women" (yangnyŏ), meaning that, by law, their legitimate sons could have sat for the state examinations.

The negotiating strategy of the Master of the Japan House throughout was simple: deny the presence of the women while awaiting an opportune moment to put them out of the compound and quietly return the Japanese involved to Tsushima to put them beyond the reach of the Tongnae Magistrate. The policy was designed to conceal criminal complicity by the Japanese involved. By denying the crime, the Master of the Japan House denied Japanese culpability and implicitly refused to turn over the Japanese involved for punishment under Korean law. Korean authorities were able to apprehend the Koreans involved, but faced with a flat denial from the Japanese, these same authorities were stymied in obtaining the Japanese involved. Danueimon, Master of the Waegwan, seemed to have carried the day, or so it appeared on Tsushima.[24]

Fortunately, we have a Korean record of the incident, and from the Korean side, matters appeared somewhat differently. The possibility of a prostitution ring first came to the attention of the Tongnae Magistrate on the twenty-fourth of the second month of 1690, just two days before the Master of the Japan House opened his investigation. Yi Myŏng-wŏn, attached to the Left Naval Headquarters, his wife, his daughter (Pun-i), his younger sister (Ch'ŏn-wŏl), two temple slaves from Pusan,

Yi Chin-su and Kwŏn Sang, and a signal-fire soldier, Sŏ Pu-sang, were identified as criminals involved in prostituting women to the Japanese.

The four men were arrested and interrogated. Yi Myŏng-wŏn pleaded that Yi Chin-su, probably Hisashiuemon's "Chinsei," and Kwŏn Sang had entangled Yi Myŏng-wŏn and his family since 1687 in prostitution. The temple slave Kwŏn Sang admitted that in the fourth month of 1687, Ide Sōzaemon, the Fourth *Daikan* (K: *Taegwan*), and two colleagues, one of whom was a Second *Daikan*, offered money to Yi Chin-su for women. Kwŏn Sang contacted Yi Myŏng-wŏn and from that time on the ring was formed. According to Yi Chin-su, Yi Myŏng-wŏn's wife later felt disgraced and ran off to an unknown location after having entered the compound only once. Yi Chin-su named one other man as a co-conspirator, Chŏng Ch'a-tol-i.

The signal-fire soldier Sŏ Pu-sang confessed that five to six years earlier (1684–1685), Yi Myŏng-wŏn's younger brother, Yi Chi-sŏk, who was now dead, had first come to him with a woman, Ae-gŭm, a private slave attached to the Naval Head-quarters, and a proposition to sell her to the Japan House. They sold Ae-gŭm to a Japanese in the Waegwan tavern. Chi-sŏk took her back there on four separate occasions, and each time he was paid three *yang* of silver.

Ae-gŭm and Chŏng Ch'a-tol-i were arrested. Ae-gŭm pleaded that she was taken at knife-point to the Japan House by Yi Myŏng-wŏn in 1686 and sold for six *yang* of silver. The Magistrate's report included Ae-gŭm's testimony.

> . . . A private slave, Ae-gŭm, who was 23, stated: '[I am a] woman, and when I was 19, in the eighth month of 1686, [I met] Yi Sam-sŏk [but] I did not know his elder brother Myŏng-wŏn. He deceived me by saying the Pusan *Hundo*'s office [had summoned me], and he would lead me there. On the way to Pusan, because [Myŏng-wŏn] had me change into men's clothing, I became alarmed, [thought it] strange, and resisted. Myŏng-wŏn told me that the *Hundo* wanted to conceal matters from others and that is why [he had me] change clothes. We reached a place and leapt a wall [of the Japan House]. Although this was illegal entry, [it was only then] I first became aware that I was being sold and tried to resist this evil, but Myŏng-wŏn pulled a dagger and threatened me. Still being a young and weak woman, I dared not disobey and resist, [and] with him, [we] illegally entered the tavern. [I] had illicit relations with the Waein bastard Uma-ōkami. Myŏng-wŏn was given six *yang* of silver. My clothes were taken away. What [they] did was awful. When the Waein were done, they passed me back to Sŏ Pu-sang. Afterwards, Pu-sang led me back there [many] times. I was given silver, and this was to atone [for everything]. The Waein who engaged in this illicit relation was a bastard called Uma-ōkami, who has now changed his name to Shikosamon, and the Fourth *Daikan* Shoku [Ji?]eimon, who has already returned [to Tsushima]. Since I have named these Waein, I beg you to be [merciful] in settling this matter.[25]

Six *yang* seems expensive, since at other times, the price fetched was two-and-a-half or three *yang*.[26] Late Chosŏn Korea did not use silver as a common currency, but the text clearly specifies silver. The silver was probably exchanged for negotiable currency, such as copper cash or rice, with Tongnae merchants, particularly the ginseng merchants, since they dealt in silver with the Japanese and had access to long-range trading networks that connected through Hansŏng and Kaesŏng to Ŭiju and the Chinese market.

When Chŏng Ch'a-tol-i's house was searched, Japanese goods appeared: a mottled short coat, a quilt, two scarves, two six-pint vessels of Japanese rice flour, one pair of Japanese scissors, and a Japanese fan. These goods were the possessions of Yi Ch'ŏn-wŏl, Yi Myŏng-wŏn's younger sister. Chŏng Ch'a-tol-i said that Yi Ch'ŏn-wŏl was first taken to the Japan House by Yi Chin-su and Kwŏn Sang, but Chŏng Ch'a-tol-i was not sure of the details. The last he saw her was on the fifth day of the eleventh month of 1689 when Yi Chin-su came and took her away. Chŏng Ch'a-tol-i asserted that Yi Ch'ŏn-wŏl was, at that moment, in the Waegwan.

In sum, the investigation netted everybody involved except Yi Ch'ŏn-wŏl and Yi Pun-i, who, the Magistrate deduced, were still inside the Japan House. He immediately set up a guard around the house and began negotiations with the Master of the Japan House for the extradition of the women. The Magistrate first feared that the Japanese involved might murder the women and his concern was to convince the House Master of the seriousness of the matter and have the House Master conduct a manhunt and extradite the women. The Magistrate, Pak Shin,[27] became convinced that the House Master was hiding something and took further steps. He cut off rice and cotton and proposed dispatching a letter to the lord of Tsushima.[28]

The court had the Board of Rites send a letter to Tsushima on the fifteenth day of the seventh month. The letter mentions Pun-i and Ch'ŏn-wŏl by name and accuses Japanese in the compound of having illegal relations with these women. It requests not only the women but also their clients. The letter also requests some sort of agreement to control this type of activity in the future.[29]

The Korean negotiators offered to withdraw the surrounding guard and a return to normalcy in exchange for the criminals, but to no avail. The Japanese side refused to admit any crime had been committed and maintained that women were not in the Japan House. The situation became clear to Magistrate Pak Shin: for the Master of the Japan House to seize the women and turn them over to the Tongnae Magistrate would be equivalent to implicating his subordinates, thus necessitating their seizure and prosecution. On the other hand, what alternatives did the Master of the Japan House have? Pak writes,

> ... I observed the mood. To seize and expel the women from the compound would mean that the Master of the Waegwan on down have committed crimes that are difficult to pardon, [so he] will secretly expel the women from the compound. Naturally, we will seize them. The chances for a lucky escape are small. This is truly taking up a sickle with blindfolded eyes; [it] is of no value to him to go 'round and 'round, prattling on and on, and being unable to bring the matter to a close.[30]

Judging from Japanese reports, Pak Shin was accurate with about half of his analysis. That is, the Master of the Japan House was at a loss as to what to do, but he was certain on one point: the Japanese involved must not be turned over to the Koreans, because they would face probable decapitation.[31] As for the fate of the women, the Master of the Japan House left no record of any intent to murder the women, as the Magistrate had feared, but neither did the Master seem to have been concerned with their fates once they were successfully secreted out of the compound. The Master's tactics were deception and evasion, hoping that the heat of Korean interest would dissipate.

One "Kim," a Censor of Criminal Activities (*Ubusŭngji*) of the Ministers without Portfolio (*Chungch'uwŏn*) or the Royal Secretariat (*Sŭngjŏngwŏn*, Sr. 3), is quoted in an attached memorial from the *Pibyŏnsa* commenting on Magistrate Pak Shin's report. He indicted Pak for several mistakes in handling the case. "Kim" points out that, regrettably, Yi Myŏng-wŏn and Yi Chin-su were caned while in shackles, and before sentencing could proceed, fell sick and died. "Kim" goes on to criticize Pak for a lax regime under which scoundrels such as Yi Myŏng-wŏn could appear and thrive. "Kim" calls for investigations of two other matters as well: the embargo of the Japan House and capital punishment for the criminals. Moreover, Kim lays part of the responsibility for Japanese intransigence on the heads of the *Hundo* and the *Pyŏlch'a*, the two senior liaison officials between the Tongnae Magistracy and the Japan House.[32]

The Provincial Governor echoed these charges, and on 1690.6.23, Magistrate Pak Shin and the liaison officers were ordered detained for interrogation. The following day, a new slate of personnel was recommended for the Tongnae Magistracy.[33] The King exonerated Pak on the thirtieth of the sixth month, and his successor, Nam Hu, was confirmed on the same day.[34] Nam took office on 1690.7.16.[35]

The execution was as the Japanese had described above. The Korean court received a report on the sixth day of the tenth month that Ae-gŭm, two other women (presumably Yi Pun-i and Yi Ch'ŏn-wŏl), together with Kwŏn Sang and Sŏ Pu-sang, were decapitated and their heads exposed outside the main gate of the Japan House.[36] The Koreans were never able to prosecute the Japanese involved, since they were never extradited.

Case two: 1708 and the Agreement of 1711

On the fifteenth of the first month of 1708, the court was informed that a village woman named Kam-ok had illicit sexual relations with a Japanese. In fact, the woman was described as feeling "sympathy" (K: *tongjŏng*),[37] dare we read love, for her Japanese partner. A letter to the Tsushima *daimyō* sent in the same year stated that a Korean woman called Kam-ok had voluntarily carried on in a "conjugal fashion" (K: *chumu*) with an unnamed Japanese at the Japan House.[38]

The Korean authorities negotiated for the extradition of Shiromizu Genshichi (?), the woman's paramour, for some time thereafter. On 1709.4.13, the court heard a report to the effect that Tsushima had refused to accept a letter demanding Shiromizu's extradition. Tsushima stated that Shiromizu had been banished, and moreover, if they were to accept such a letter, Edo would rebuke them.[39] From the Japanese point of view, the 1690 case was quietly settled and with this correspondence the 1708 case was also settled or, at least, that was what Tsushima thought.

The 1711 Korean envoys to Edo brought up the matter again, insisted on a firm agreement setting forth specific punishments for such activity, and even insisted on discussing the matter with the Shogun. Although the Tsushima lord and his retainers were thrown into consternation by the Korean envoys' tactics, Amenomori Hōshū provides us with a critical explanation for the strength of the Korean resolve by outlining the links between the 1690 case and the 1708 case – Amenomori's point being that an a-diplomatic, doctrinaire handling of all cases based on the apparent settlement of the 1690 case ignored fluid, diplomatic circumstances and thereby endangered Tsushima's dependent relationship with Korea. He argued that situations must be read at that time to determine what is best for negotiations, and as a general principle, Korean law should not be violated. The Koreans had not forgotten past incidents.[40] Rather, it was the Japanese who viewed these incidents as all separate and able to be settled by the kind of obstructionist tactics employed by the Master of the Japan House in the 1690 incident.

The second report on the 1690 incident by O Si-dae, Governor of Kyŏngsang Province, attests to Hōshū's assertion about a long Korean memory. Here we see O Si-dae's conclusions after reviewing similar incidents in 1661 and 1662. In these earlier cases, there was no extradition of the Japanese criminals, and the Korean authorities found themselves unable to control the situation. Since the Japanese are "cunning" (K: kyosa),[41] such an outcome was perhaps to be expected. Most important, concluded O Si-dae, was that Japanese prevarications resulted in sheltering the criminals and "staining" Korean rule.

> . . . when Yi Wŏn-chŏng [1661.4.21–1662.7) was made [Tongnae] Magistr-
> ate, commoner women and private slave women, altogether six [women],
> secretly had illicit relations with Waein. This became known, was investig-
> ated, and [the criminals] were punished appropriately. However, [we] were
> unable to enforce matters strictly (prevent the crime or obtain the guilty
> Japanese) and the people of the frontier (both Korean and Japanese?) saw
> the real situation. This was our shame. [The Japanese] illegalities must not
> stain [our] rule. . . .[42]

There seems to be a sting of embarrassment at the inability to control the Japanese. Such embarrassment was politically dangerous because it risked a loss of control over frontier society.

Let us return to the Korean Embassy's intention to broach the matter of illicit sexual liaison with the shogun himself. Before the 1711 Korean Embassy to Edo left Hansŏng, the King heard a debate on the principle that crimes by Koreans and Japanese should be prosecuted according to the same laws and that the 1711 Embassy should seek an Agreement containing this principle. The King lamented the fact that Korean heads were displayed, while the Japanese conducted no prosecu-tions. He commanded that an Agreement be established that would enshrine the principle of common criteria for guilt. Although murder was mentioned as a problem where common agreement had been reached, "crimes of a sexual nature" (K: pŏmgan) remained in limbo.[43] We might add that the principle of Japanese guilt for aiding and abetting smuggling had been established in 1683, so the problem of establishing common criteria should not have been a problem.[44]

Im Su-kan's Tongsa-ilgi reports on the envoy's negotiations in Edo. According to Im, negotiations with the lord of Tsushima went back and forth to no avail. The three envoys then decided to broach the matter directly with the shogun at their audience. They started to produce a draft agreement and discussed such with Tsushima officials. The Tsushima officials fell into an extreme "funk" (K: *hwanggŏp*) and immediately sat down and negotiated something that would conform to the envoy's demands. Within a short time, the agreement received the Tsushima lord's seal.[45]

This agreement can be seen in various Korean and Japanese sources from the period.[46] The Korean sources often carry an explanatory note: this agreement was established by the Korean envoy of 1711 to settle matters surrounding the decapitation of a Ch'oryang village woman for illicit liaisons with a Japan House man and subsequent Korean failure to obtain the Japanese involved for similar punishment.[47]

The provisions of the agreement were broken down into three types of cases. One, if a Japanese left the Japan House and raped a Korean woman, then that was a capital offense. Two, if a Japanese seduced a Korean woman without using force or if the crime was attempted rape, then the criminal was to be banished for life. Finally, if a Korean woman entered the Japan House of her own volition intending to conduct relations with a Japanese and he did not report her presence for detention and extradition, then the Japanese was to receive a lesser, unspecified punishment, presumably, a shorter period of banishment.[48] The provisions of the agreement covered only the actions of the Japanese men. According to a record dated 1712.5.5, the Tongnae Magistrate had the new agreement carved in stone and placed inside the Japan House.[49]

What of the Korean women involved? As evidenced by the results of the two cases examined above, any woman unlucky enough to have been involved and caught was beheaded. Such extreme punishment differed from the *Ming Code*, the common handbook of criminal law imported and used by the Chosŏn dynasty. The *Ming Code* did not punish the victim.[50] In our cases, the Korean women who had been coerced into entering the Japan House (Ae-gŭm in Case 1: 1690) or who had been possibly seduced by a Japanese (Kam-ok in Case 2: 1708) were decapitated. Even Myŏng-wŏn's 17-year-old daughter's head went onto a pike, although she had first been taken into the Waegwan as a girl of 13 by her own father.

The new agreement, however, seemed to ameliorate matters somewhat. In a 1716 case, the heads of the Korean procurers were taken and the Japanese clients were punished: one was returned to Tushima, two were banished, and two disappeared. The Magistrate wrote of the "extreme pain inflicted on *sŏng*" (sincerity) by the "cunning" Japanese.[51] The woman involved was described as a victim of coercion, escorted into a "beguiling snake-pit."[52] The central government had suspicions as to whether the case really was one of coercion, but because the woman confessed, her execution was pardoned and she was exiled. King Sukjong confirmed the justice of executing the Korean male procurers in 1717.[53] In cases in 1726 and 1738, the Korean procurers were beheaded; the women and the Japanese banished.[54] In the *Pyŏllye chibyo* records on a 1786 incident, we see a mention of statutes regarding women: "if she was seduced and prostituted herself, she should receive 100 strokes and banishment according to the *Taejŏn t'ongp'yŏn* statutes." The *Taejŏn t'ongp'yŏn*, although finished c.1785, quotes this statute verbatim from the 1744 *Sok taejŏn*, an earlier, similar compilation.[55] In this 1786 case, the woman was judged to have been enticed into the crime and noting that she confessed everything, she was spared a caning, banished, and her enticer was beheaded.[56] We should note that 100 strokes with a cane were sufficiently severe to rival the death penalty. Hendrick Hamel, castaway in Korea from 1653 to 1666, wrote after his escape, "one hundred strokes bring death."[57]

Perhaps since the Korean side had finally extracted a law to govern the Japanese, women no longer needed to be sacrificed on the altars of national security and state morality. With the Japanese side having formally agreed that Korean–Japanese unions were illegal, the Korean anxiety over the political threats that such unions posed apparently subsided, at least regarding the women involved, but procurers were still treated sternly. According to the *Sinbo sugyo chimnok* (compiled *c*.1743), we find the following royal "intention" included.

> [Among] deceitful people on the frontier, those who secretly receive Waein bribes, smuggle women into the [Wae]gwan, and bring about illicit sexual relations with Wae, as well as those who covet a few pieces of silver and give their beautiful wives to the crafty Wae, these people will have their heads displayed outside the [Wae]gwan gate.
>
> (1717 Royal Decree)[58]

Note that the King's wrath is wholly directed at those who procure women.

Previous studies

The relevant question is why did the Korean authorities take such a dim view of Korean women consorting with Japanese men? Two earlier studies have answered this question by reference to Confucian morality. Kim Ŭi-hwan and Son Sŭng-ch'ŏl mention male–female relations at the Waegwan as violating the norms of Confucian morality. Kim Ŭi-hwan writes:

> The Korean government at the time established the realization of a Neo-Confucian ideal as its supreme political objective, and illicit sexual behavior would have stained such beautiful and good customs. Therefore they were impermissible. . . . Japan, at the time, with its prosperous urban culture, had harlots everywhere and practiced free sexual behavior. Here we can grasp the society and politics of Korea under a Neo-Confucian order. We must always keep this in mind when thinking of the Korea of that time.[59]

In short, Kim accuses Japanese culture of the Tokugawa period of having been sexually promiscuous, at best, and states that "illicit sexual relations" with Japanese violated Korean customs or, we might say, they were immoral, and that is why the Chosŏn government banned them. Son Sŭng-ch'ŏl also explains the anger of Koreans towards sexual relations at the Waegwan from the same point of view.

> It is common knowledge that the Chosŏn kingdom adopted Confucianism as a national policy, and as a country with a [consciously] constructed social discipline, possessed very strict norms, especially concerning the morals [governing] male–female relations. Nevertheless, these norms were, at times, broken by the *Waein* [Japanese], who resided for long periods at the Waegwan. Violations were more than a simple problem of man–woman relations; they were an enormous problem that threatened the basic values of Korean society and inflamed diplomatic problems between the two countries.[60]

Both state that the banning of sexual relations at the Waegwan by the Chosŏn government was because they ran counter to Confucian morality. This was undoubtedly true.

However, when viewed historically, sexual relations between Japanese and Koreans inflamed much more than moral outrage. Moral concerns ultimately shaded into political concerns. Confucian morality, established as a political ideal in Korean elite society from the fifteenth century onwards, was enforced through statutory laws that saw no division between public and private. In other words, there was no division between morality and politics.[61] Individual moral actions were taken as the starting point to preserve the stability of society and state.[62] Both Kim and Son explain the counter-measures taken by the Chosŏn government against sexual relations with Japanese largely from a moral dimension, but here we are exploring the problem from its political dimension. In short, actions taken as counter-measures against sexual relations with Japanese, to protect women's bodies from the "Wae," occupied the same ground as actions taken to protect the state. The identification of this line of defense had a history, which means that the concerns of the state changed over time. Moral concerns may have changed as well, or perhaps the change we see was the process of imposing elite morality on lower and lower social groups at further and further spatial reaches within the kingdom in an attempt to protect the state.

As historians, we are interested in change over time; we cannot assume moral or philosophical positions to be static. Our emphasis on the political dimension comes from the fact that under different political circumstances, the state's countermeasures were different. Prior to 1510, Japanese men resided in Korean port towns, and there they farmed the land and took Korean women as their wives. The sexual relations in the port towns from that time were seen as a nuisance for the local societies and measures were devised to control contact between Japanese and local residents, but it was not until the period following Hideyoshi's invasion that even stricter controls were applied. The change was connected with the invasion and the fact that Hideyoshi's armies nearly destroyed the dynasty. As we pointed out in another context, among the 1,000 "tōjin" under the Sō lord, deployed as guides or coolies for the Korean invasion, many or even all were probably the mixed blood of Japanese and Koreans. Functioning as guides and interpreters, we can imagine that they had a significant impact on the success or failure of the Korean invasion. The problem of allowing the populace to become too close to the Japanese was not just an abstract problem of Confucian morality or a violation of local custom, but a problem of state policy and a threat to the existence of the state, which was a threat to the existence of Korean society. After Hideyoshi, popular contact was more than a mere nuisance for local communities; it was subversive. In other words, for not controlling sexual liaison in the ports, the state came to face larger and larger problems: the 1510 Revolt of the Three Ports and Hideyoshi's invasion beginning in 1592. Following each, we can see a tightening of control over frontier society. Until 1711 and Japanese acknowledgment of the necessity to punish the Japanese clients of sexual liaison, the Korean government response to incidents in the post-Hideyoshi period was severe and capital punishment was routinely meted out to violators. Following 1711, we again see a change in the application of punishment to target the male procurers.

In this sense, sexual relations between Koreans and Japanese were not simply a moral problem; they were a political problem, but not in the narrow sense of political as commonly understood in the post-Enlightenment, secular West. Illicit sexual relations were political within a spectrum that extended from metaphysics to moral philosophy to law and custom to politics to military force. If one approaches the problem, as Kim and Son have done, from the metaphysical end of the spectrum, then the concern over illicit sexual relations appears as a heightened moral sensitivity, but if one approaches the problem from the military end of the spectrum, then illicit sexual relations with the Japanese after 1592 carried the specter of Hideyoshi's invading hordes guided by half-breed Japanese-Koreans.

Culture

Up to this point, we have examined rivalries of authority and power, questions of jurisdiction and punishment. At a certain level, as suggested above, who controlled female reproductive capacity on the frontier was a matter of power and authority, but if we leave the discussion now, all we have is the Korean view of what was politically and morally acceptable and that may indict the Japanese as immoral or intentionally subversive of Korean society. We must finally consider the rivalry of culture that flowed through these incidents, because that will give us a glimpse of the Japanese view, which considered itself to be at least pragmatic, perhaps even moral, and not at all subversive.

We have argued that the Korean push to define sexual liaison as illegal and to specify harsh punishments for the Japanese stemmed from outrage at the impropriety of extramarital sexual relations, but a deeper source was the drive to police sexual liaison as a way of keeping the frontier from being populated by people of dubious loyalty. Ultimately, it was a problem of power, loyalty, and authority. The Chosŏn administration was willing to violate their own domestic law and behead the women involved to make their point clearly understood to the Japanese and to the local society under the Tongnae Magistrate. The Korean mode of argument with the Japanese allowed for no compromise and sounded dogmatic to the islanders.

Controls over the sexual activities of foreign guests was not an alien concept to Tokugawa Japan; what was alien was the Korean unwillingness to recognize that such activities would naturally happen and that these activities would be more controllable through management than suppression. Given that one might realistically expect sexual relations to go on in ports where foreign merchants drop anchor, the Japanese pragmatically thought it best to monitor and license such relations. Let us recall that Tokugawa Japan was extremely xenophobic regarding the ideological threat posed by Christianity. Despite this concern, Japanese authorities allowed the Chinese and the Dutch to trade in Nagasaki. Moreover, permanent establishments were built and the officials overseeing the Chinese and Dutch factories in Nagasaki condoned the coming and going of Japanese courtesans.[63]

That the Tsushima authorities were aware of the Nagasaki situation is evident by a point of negotiation in 1708 from the Master of the Japan House preserved in Korean records. The Waegwan Master informed the Koreans in the ninth month of 1708 that Japanese women consort with "foreigners."[64] Although the site of this consorting was not specified, the Master was undoubtedly referring to the Chinese compound (Tōjin Yashiki) and the Dutch factory (Deshima), both in Nagasaki, and the licensing of Japanese courtesans to enter these two compounds. Although the argument seemed relevant to the House Master, there is no evidence that the Koreans did anything other than ignore his point. Perhaps, the fact that "foreign barbarians" (i.e. the Japanese)[65] condoned such an immoral and potentially subversive activity must not have been too surprising and required no comment.

Finally, we should recall that, for similar reasons as in Korea, the Japanese authorities did not condone children as a result of courtesan liaisons with foreigners. The export to Batavia of children from Hirado is famous in this connection, but that particular cruelty was involved with the suppression of Christianity, a religion that the *bakufu* deemed to be ideologically and politically threatening. So, in the end, Korean concerns could not have been too alien to the Japanese in the Waegwan.

Conclusion

The 1711 Agreement with Tsushima obtained Japanese recognition of the illegality of Korean–Japanese sexual relations. The agreement was the culmination over centuries of a Korean desire to prevent Japanese from permanently settling on the peninsula. That desire was articulated before the 1510 Riot of the Three Ports and then codified in policies following 1510. Hideyoshi's invasion strengthened Korean resolve and strictures became even tighter. In 1711, the Korean side finally won Japanese cooperation in keeping Japanese out. Specifically, the 1711 Agreement got a pledge from Tsushima to punish those inside the Japan House guilty of having sexual relations with Korean women. To obtain the acquiescence of Tsushima authorities to formulate such an agreement, the Koreans had to resort to threats that they would negotiate directly with the shogun and embarrass the Lord of Tsushima. At that point, the Tsushima position quickly became pliable.

In negotiating the 1690 incident with the Japan House Master, Tongnae Magistrate Pak Shin thought he might have been dealing with someone in disarray. The Magistrate was only partly correct in his assessment. Fukami Danueimon, Master of the Japan House,[66] certainly wanted to protect his subordinates; the best way he found to do this was by simply denying all culpability and waiting for a moment to expel the women quietly. For such handling of the case, Danueimon was congratulated on Tsushima.[67] When a similar policy was adopted in 1708, Korean pressure again receded, but this time only to wait for an opportune moment to re-emerge. As Hōshū argued, the Koreans remembered everything and the Japanese learned nothing. They seem to have been puzzled by the severity of the Korean concern, because they recalled the Nagasaki courtesans who visited the Dutch and the Chinese but forgot the reasons for their own strictures in Nagasaki.

One might argue that the Koreans had been trying to civilize their Japanese charges from antiquity and here we have just one more example of the *ka-i* (civilized-versus-barbarian) Korean worldview and its condescension towards the Japanese.[68] That is partly true, but we must consider what was actually at stake and not limit our consideration to abstract cultural projects put together by capital intellectuals. If a strict moralistic Korean view had always been paramount, why do we have a progressive tightening of residency requirements? There is more here than morality; there is a conflict of power and a struggle over who will populate and control the frontier. The post-1600, prophylactic measures to contain sexual liaison stand in contrast to earlier periods, and they even contradict the flourishing trade relations after 1600. The dark specters of espionage and immigration must have loomed large after Hideyoshi demonstrated what the islanders were capable of doing. Beyond these worries perhaps lay even deeper Korean concerns, visceral concerns about interbreeding, the barbarization of blood, and the mongrelization of society, but we have found precious little evidence for this. There was certainly a deep fear of losing control over Korean female bodies on the frontier and the subversive threat that posed. Korean authorities developed an adamant opposition to intermingling because it was distasteful and immoral, but more importantly, they feared it because it was associated with riots and invasion. Particularly after 1598, Korean authorities drew a clear boundary beyond which they would not allow foreign intercourse with their society, but it took them another 110 years to wring acknowledgment from the Japanese.

8

CONCLUSION

This study has been concerned with two major projects: one overt and one covert. The overt project has been to examine Korean ideas about Tsushima and Japan generated from direct Korean contact with the Japanese at the Japan House, with particular emphasis on the later Chosŏn period. Direct, first-hand contacts at the frontier clarify values and produce authentic voices. The covert project has been to explore the connections between structures, institutions, and mentalities. Demographic, economic, political, and diplomatic structures and institutions reflect or produce moments of contact. Structures also refer to the environmental and ecological givens on which human institutions are erected. They produce types of contact that span long periods of time and, in many ways, establish frameworks within which institutions and ideas emerge. As these ideas become widespread, recurring, and habitual, they become mentalities.

Throughout the Chosŏn period, Kyŏngsang Province and Tsushima Island formed a single frontier region where "Korea" and "Japan" overlapped. Looking from the Korean side, we sketched the common environmental elements of the frontier and then examined human interaction. Within that single region all parties were forced to examine their own values, accommodate themselves to the other party, and develop explanations to explain their own and the other's behavior.

Our approach has been to privilege the view from the frontier, the site of daily contact, rather than to view the frontier from the centers. Chapter 1 introduced the problem as a revision of more traditional approaches to international relations. Chapter 2 pointed out Tsushima's economic dependence on Chosŏn Korea and suggested other political-economic and social influences Korea had on Tsushima. After mentioning Korea's effects on Tsushima, we then turned to examine the effects of Tsushima's dependence on Korea. Chapters 3, 4, and 5 addressed the demographic, economic, and political influences of the Japan House on Kyŏngsang Province, Tongnae County, and the Tongnae Magistrate. Then we went in search of individuals living and working in the frontier. Chapters 6 and 7 were case studies of the political and social problems thrown up by the presence of the Japanese. The following comments summarize the conclusions of each chapter and pose remaining questions for further research.

Chapter 1 mapped the broad approach and the field of inquiry. We began by arguing that countries and their relations with each other work on at least two levels. There is the core with its state and its capital city. In the capital, political authority and legitimacy are established, information is gathered, personnel from near and far are recruited, armies are financed and trained, elite views are created, and policy is formulated. All these activities are designed to impose control over the capital area and various other parts of the country. The purpose of the control is to draw in resources to the capital and to preserve the position of the ruling elite.

There is the frontier. It is there that we find people who identify with some or all of the core's interests and have contact with other people, different from themselves, who do not share the same values and interests. The cores are naturally vain and slow to acknowledge the interests of the frontier, because where the territory of the country ends and the sovereignty of the core ceases to be effective depend in the first instance on the people who live in the frontier. For the core to admit this obvious element in national construction draws into question the authority, legitimacy, and self-styled primacy of the core, so the dominant discourse in central records is loath to admit the role of the frontier in its own self-definition. This is to be expected, but we moderns are doubly blinded by mobilizing states. We have all been trained to look first to capitals for direction, and so we are prone to overlook the dynamics of the frontier as the other half of the dialectic that creates a nation. The frontier is not more important than the center in this activity, but it is certainly the center's partner or foil and cannot be ignored. Our overt project has been to put the frontier into the foreground and leave the core aside as much as possible. This does not mean that the prerogatives of the core are insignificant. It means that they deserve a separate study, of which there have been aplenty.

In Chapters 1 and 2, we attempted to define the pre-modern frontier between Korea and Japan. Following the Hideyoshi invasion, its failure, and the establishment of the Tokugawa *bakufu*, Tsushima was again left to play intermediary between Korea and Japan. For the next two-and-a-half centuries, peaceful relations transpired on an equal basis between the Chosŏn court and the Tokugawa *bakufu*. The Republic of Korea and the post-war Japanese state have recently enshrined this relationship as the model of good relations. Central to those good relations were three, actually four, points of contact between Korea and Japan: the Korean Embassy to Edo (T'ongsinsa); the repatriation of castaways; and the Japan House. The fourth, which we did not mention, but which might be considered within the diplomatic category, were the embassies of Korean Interpreters to Tsushima dispatched for face-to-face diplomatic relations with the Lord of Tsushima in Izuhara.

Among these points of direct contact, the Korean Embassy to Edo, because of its glorious display in Japan of some of the finest of Korean culture, has received the most scholarly and popular attention. Calling forth the interest, awe, and respect of the great and the small of Tokugawa-period Japanese, the embassy has been adopted by the contemporary governments of the Republic of Korea and Japan as the preferred metaphor for their present and future relations.

But other points of contact existed, not to be overlooked or dismissed. In fact, these other points of contact, concerned as they were with the day-to-day affairs of international relations, are, in many ways, more revealing of attitudes and the ideas that shaped the working relationship. An examination of castaways suggests many serious questions about the assumptions held regarding both the extent of *bakufu* control over foreign contact and the extent of ordinary Japanese ignorance of foreign lands and languages. Korean castaways and their circumstances in Japan reveal

Japanese attitudes towards Koreans. It is their accidental character that can uncover so much that remained unspoken. By contrast, the institution of the Japan House, as a Japanese outpost on Korean soil from the fifteenth century, can reveal the explicit structures and mentalities of Korean–Japanese relations. That is why we focused on the Japan House in Pusan Harbor. Given the long span of time and the vast materials available, the focus narrowed to the period from 1600 to 1870.

Chapter 2 explored the ambiguous identity of Tsushima between Korea and Japan. We outlined Edo's view of the island and noted that the *bakufu* regarded Tsushima as an important intermediary and its representative to Chosŏn Korea. The Korean view of Tsushima's identity depicted the land as Korean territory from antiquity but currently under Japanese occupation. We reiterated Tsushima's dependence on Korea for grains and trade goods, hypothesized that such dependency resulted in Korean influences on the island's economy, politics, and society. Specifically, these influences can be seen in a Korean style of disbursing feudal dues and a slave system unique to Tsushima among Japanese territories of the period but having elements in common with Chosŏn Korea. Finally, we introduced the physical plant of the Japan House and its complement of Japanese officials.

Chapter 3 turned to the influence on Korea by the Japanese or, more specifically, by the Tsushima, connection. Chapter 3 mentioned a few of the dominant structures that defined the frontier. Primary among these were fishing and trade or the two most important elements of the pre-modern maritime world. The Japanese appeared to the Koreans as an aspect of the maritime world, so it would have been misleading to isolate the Japanese from the larger forces at work. To glimpse the power of those forces, we looked at a few demographic elements of the coast and tried to gauge the significance of the Japanese presence and its power to draw Koreans. We found that the maritime economies of the southern coast have been little studied, despite their age-old ability to sustain human life. After fishing, the trade with the Japanese between 1600 and 1870 came under scrutiny, and we saw that there is still much controversy over basic questions. What is clear is that the trade linked Korea to global trading patterns, that the volumes of the private trade were enormous, and that these connections obviously attracted significant numbers of Korean merchants. Until much more work is done, we can only imagine that these merchants were more than their names. The names probably represent corporate bodies (with accounting, banking, and financial concerns), minor economies of production and transport, and far-flung connections that reached northwards to the Chinese border and penetrated many areas of the domestic Korean economy in between. In short, the maritime world was significant for Chosŏn Korea and the Japanese component was a significant element of that world.

Chapter 4 used the official trade with Japan to expose the economic structure governing the Japan House and looked at the economic cost of the Japan House to Korea. Chosŏn elites thought that the burden of supplying food and materials to the Japanese and the cost of engaging in trade with the Japanese were excessively heavy. The Japanese in the Japan House and the Tsushima interests they represented appeared to literate Koreans as a voracious horde of locusts dining on the national bounty. The *Yŏllyosil kisul*, a widely read encyclopedia of Korean history and culture, popular in the nineteenth century, includes authors who point out that the various costs associated with supporting the Japanese at the Japan House amounted to over half the taxes from Kyŏngsang Province. The close similarity of statements made over several centuries created a "rhetorical image" that dominated discussion on the subject. These statements constituted our internal evidence for proving the existence of a mentality associated with the cost of the Japanese connection. Tax records constituted our external evidence and showed the general accuracy of the assertions put forward by that mentality.[1]

When we examined the actual tax records, we saw that the amounts, at their greatest, for trade, receptions, and so on (i.e. all expenditures associated with the Japan House), possibly amounted to about 56 percent of Kyŏngsang Province's tax revenues for the later Chosŏn period. Whether for political or economic reasons, about one half of Kyŏngsang Province tax revenues were tied up in relations with Japan, specifically, Tsushima. Unmistakably then, we can say that relations with Tsushima had an enormous impact on the economy of Kyŏngsang Province. But if we assess "costs" at their lowest, that is, limit our survey to expenditures associated with reception costs only, without including accounts that were classified by the Chosŏn Kingdom as official trade, then we see that the total was no more than about 14 percent of tax revenues for the period after 1600. The contradiction between our internal evidence (individual statements) and external evidence (tax records) led us to the following conjectures and hypotheses.

Chosŏn-period Koreans did not disaggregate diplomatic receptions and official trade, considering these activities as one activity. Perhaps their views were born of an agrarianist predisposition to denigrate commerce, a physiocratic inclination to suspect any activity that might lead to economic dependency, or an incantatory approach that treated international relations as a secular activity with sacred connotations. All of these ideas have been associated with doctrinaire Confucianism. Our concern has not been to explain why Chosŏn-era Koreans viewed matters in an aggregate fashion, but to examine that holistic view and what prejudices and assumptions it produced about Korea's relation to Tsushima and Japan.

Since the Japanese connection "cost" so much, why did Koreans grant the Japanese access? The obvious reason was that Tsushima had to be placated to forestall piracy or it had to be fed for humanitarian reasons, since the island populace was completely dependent on Korea and hungry people will come and take food. Although not totally absent, there was little acceptance of the idea that the Japan trade was conducted as an activity that benefited Korea. With this institutionalized autarkic prejudice, we run up against the obvious limitations of government documents to tell us what we want to know about international trade and even economy. Herein lies a major difficulty in assessing the Japanese impact on the society and economy of Kyŏngsang Province, even on the economy and society of the entire country.

Chapter 5 used a survey of the Tongnae Magistracy to lay bare the structure of the political economy surrounding the Tongnae Magistrate. The Tongnae Magistracy's relative position among Magistracies in Kyŏngsang Province in terms of population and gross tax revenues was discussed in Chapters 3 and 4. Chapter 5 concerned itself with a statistical analysis of records on nearly 400 years of magistrates to isolate the significance of the Japanese connection as it affected careers.

Since the Japan House was self-administered, the Magistrate had to deal with his charges in an indirect fashion and was often unable to prevent problems or adjudicate over criminal Japanese. Nevertheless, the Magistrate was held responsible when incidents occurred. We examined a number of case studies for internal evidence and created a statistical analysis for external evidence. The case studies and statistics strongly corroborated each other: the post was dangerous and frustrating. In a survey of 285 Magistrates from 1506 to 1897, fully one in six was affected by an event involving Japanese. Two Magistrates lost their lives in war with the Japanese. One Magistrate was exiled while numerous others were promoted even after arrest and investigation. We have enough comparative data with other magistracies to hypothesize that the quality of Tongnae Magistrates was high. What this may finally mean is still open to question. Further comparisons with other counties are sorely needed. Was the post a high-risk posting for the talented but politically vulnerable or unwanted, or was the post a difficult provincial training ground for the promising?

Chapters 6 and 7 examined case studies of the Magistrates' struggles to impose their authority over the Japanese in the Japan House. The Japan House was often the site of economic crimes such as smuggling, thievery, or embezzlement, the site of social crimes such as prostitution, and the site of cultural-political incidents such as insults, fights, riots, and even murders. Chapter 6 concerned itself with controls over Japanese leaving the compound; Chapter 7 addressed controls over Koreans, particularly women, entering the compound. In the processes of developing controls, before and after the turn of the eighteenth century, Tongnae's authority was legally acceded to by Tsushima in formal agreements. Legalities gave the Magistrate legitimacy, but it was up to the man to enforce his authority. In Chapters 6 and 7 we employed Korean records as internal evidence and Japanese records on the same incidents as external evidence.

In Chapter 6 we saw that rioting or "storming out" of the Japan House was one negotiating tactic deployed against the local Korean authorities by the House Master, the *Saihan* (K: *Ch'aep'an*), and other Japanese officials. The Korean court and the Tongnae Magistrate were sufficiently shrewd to recognize the difference between spontaneous violations and the conscious employ of violence to put pressure on Korean authorities and so measured their responses accordingly. Spontaneous violators had no Japanese official in the lead, whereas any Japanese official present in the group was held by the Koreans to be responsible, and Korean authorities saw the unauthorized departure from the Japan House as a political gesture and test of their power. Since the Japanese were fully aware of their actions, we can only conclude that they had no ascriptive intentions. In other words, they did not see themselves as a part of Korean society. Chapter 7 showed that Korean officialdom had no intention of allowing them to become a part of Korean society.

Chapter 7 similarly used case studies to explore Korean–Japanese interaction and its significance in the formation of Korean attitudes towards the Japanese. Unauthorized exiting by groups of Japanese brandishing weapons was clearly understood by the Japanese as provocative towards Koreans, but the Japanese seemed genuinely puzzled by Korean concern with prostitution. From the Tsushima perspective, the Japan House was an economic umbilical cord that had been significantly shrunk from earlier years but which required the continuous residence of upwards of 500 men to conduct business. Being unable to establish domiciles and keep women, these men offered a ready market for prostitution. While they may have had no intention to reside permanently in Pusan, they did not consider the visits of Korean courtesans (however willing or unwilling) as a social, legal, or moral problem, but rather as a diplomatic problem. When Korean women violated Korean laws forbidding sexual contact with the Japanese and were punished, either voluntarily or by coercion, the men in the Japan House, including their superiors on Tsushima, did not wish to allow themselves to be similarly punished under Korean law. Punishment under Korean law meant almost certain decapitation; nor did the Japanese wish to enforce strictures against themselves or their subordinates governing sexual liaison. They consciously contrasted Korean unwillingness to allow them access to Korean women with Japanese treatment of Chinese and Dutch traders in Nagasaki, where special courtesans were legally recognized. Up until 1711, the general consensus on Tsushima was that Korean worries about prostitution could be easily dealt with by polite evasion and firm denial.

The Korean perspective grounded itself in a mixture of moral outrage and fear of Japanese immigration. Prior to the Riot of the Three Ports, Japanese boasted permanent residence in Korea and were generally free in the port areas to live among Koreans. The riots of 1510 demonstrated the folly of such permissiveness and thereafter Japanese in Korea were restricted to the reception centers and their movements and contacts were circumscribed. Hideyoshi's invasion was an outrage that confirmed Korea's worst fears about the Japanese. Japanese actions prior to Hideyoshi demonstrated their covetous desires towards what was to be had in Korea: grains, land, cultural riches, and women. Hideyoshi merely confirmed this on a grand scale. Furthermore, half-breed Korean/Japanese of dubious loyalty had aided the Japanese invasion, and the appearance of this fifth column had to be prevented. Post-Hideyoshi controls, therefore, were even more stringent: women who had sexual relations with Japanese men, either voluntarily or through coercion, were beheaded, as were those Korean men who acted as panderers. Korean authorities sought the Japanese involved for similar punishment but nearly always met with frustration. By the time of the Korean Embassy of 1711, a tactic was developed to broach this matter directly with the Tokugawa shogun. On learning of the Korean Embassy's intention, the elders of Tsushima backed down and conceded an agreement defining punishments for guilty Japanese.

The social burden of the Japan House on the society of Pusan Harbor is difficult to gauge, but from the case study of prostitution we can see that the burden was quite heavy for the victims. We still do not know answers to many other questions. Prostitution was often associated with the crime of smuggling, the most common crime mentioned in Korean records about the Japan House, so we can, at minimum, say that the Japan House was undoubtedly a breeding ground for various crimes that compromised the authority of the Korean state. Perhaps the Japan House acted as a regional magnet for criminals of various stripes. The upshot was that the Japanese in the Japan House had a most unsavory image, and their mingling with Korean women raised the threat of subversion and invasion.

Our enterprise has been two-fold. If importance can be measured by frequency and continuity of face-to-face dealings, we have sought information on the most important point of contact between pre-modern Korea and Japan, the Japan House in Pusan. We have also sought to identify Korean attitudes and ideas about the Japanese that grew from the direct experience of daily contact. The entire study has clung to the notion that the frontier was at least of equal importance with the cores in the conduct of international relations. Early inspiration was taken from Clifford

215

Geertz's "thick description" of culture as a public activity of "established structures of meaning in terms of which people do things."

> We are not, or at least I am not, seeking either to become natives . . . or to mimic them. Only romantics or spies would seem to find point in that. We are seeking, . . . to converse with them . . .[2]

And what have they told us? Late Chosŏn-period Koreans saw the Japan House as a severe economic drain with an inexhaustible appetite; a difficult administrative challenge that demanded, even occasionally consumed, good men; and a pernicious establishment that defied Korean authority, bred crime, and threatened to subvert the integrity of the society and polity. Why did Korea tolerate the connection? There were at least two obvious reasons: some form of licensed contact was less costly than military confrontation with pirates, and Korea was an advanced, great country that had a moral duty to be generous towards its inferiors. There was also a less obvious reason: Korea needed the Japanese trade. To address this last question thoroughly would take us far away from the ports, but offers ample opportunity for further study.

I hope that the study has a significance beyond the seventeenth to nineteenth centuries. Undoubtedly, the Japan House carried its baneful reputation with itself into the period after 1876 when it metamorphosed into the Japanese Consulate in Pusan. From 1876, Pusan became an open port into which Japanese and their capital started flowing. The location, security, and familiarity offered by Tsushima's former trading post, the Japan House, eventuated in a city springing literally from the site and environs of the old compound. Pusan was a city created, shaped, and suborned to Japanese mercantile and military interests, a city that became and still is Korea's largest port and its second largest city. The history of the Japan House from 1876 turns into the history of modern Pusan and the history of imperial Japan's first and most strategic foreign beachhead. From the early years of the twentieth century, when the first stage of the modern harbor was built and the rails were laid that connected to lines leading all the way to Europe, Pusan became imperial Japan's starting point for expansion on the continent. After 1876, Pusan was to take a more prominent place on the global stage, but its importance to Tsushima never disappeared. Throughout the colonial period, Pusan was where people from Tsushima shopped, went for medical treatment, and saw the latest movies; Hakata was far too distant. All that changed with Korean Liberation in 1945.

APPENDIX A

A bibliographical essay on Tongnae County documents and diplomatic correspondence

Introduction

Like the Tsushima officials, the various Tongnae County functionaries produced records and reports, but there were differences. For example, on the Japan side, the *Kanshu, Daikan*, and *Saihan* produced daily diaries focused on events associated with their official duties, but the coverage was broad and the audience left vague. These officers kept their separate records: the *Saihan kiroku* (Record of the *Saihan* or the Special Liaison) and the *Daikan mainikki* (Daimyo Deputy for Trade Affairs' Daily Diary). There is even a *Kanshu nikki* (House Master's Diary) by the chief Japanese official. The intended readers, aside from their own reference, were succeeding officials and superiors on Tsushima. The Japan House Master was the pivotal node for information; all business of the day on the Japanese side was recorded in the *[Wakan] mainikki* (Japan House Daily Diary). There are no separate records for business conducted with the *Hundo*, the Pusan Garrison Commander, and the Tongnae Magistrate.

By contrast, Tongnae County officials did not produce daily diaries in such a formal manner. When negotiations took place or an event occurred, reports were taken down from the *Hundo* and others and written up at the Magistrate's office. The intended readers were provincial and central government officials. Nevertheless, the Tongnae Magistrate had many worries associated with the Japanese, and for the sake of institutional memory and continuity of policy, he required some kind of categorization of records. The initial reports were later culled by topic, not by office. The multiple, primary records kept at Tongnae were synthesized by central authorities into annalistic-style synopses and eventually these were broken into general categories with their own chronologies for easy reference. The varieties of categories will become apparent below as we review the document base. Tsushima archivists as well eventually combed the individual office diaries for specific reports which they gathered by category in chronological fashion. Just as the culling and categorization of information coming from Tongnae was organized by central government officials, the *Bunrui kiji daikō* was produced on Tsushima. This collection mirrors a great deal of the Korean records discussed below, since it groups reports in an annalistic fashion by topic. However, most of what is left to us on the Japan side are predominately annalistic records taken down at the time of occurrence with a clear and explicit point of view. On the Korean side, we have records that have been edited and categorized. This process has homogenized viewpoints into one: the Tongnae Magistrate.

We might take a comparison of the character of record keeping between Tongnae and Tsushima as a comparison of bureaucratic style, but differences probably had more to do with complexity than style. The Tongnae Magistrate's post was much more complicated than any post at the Waegwan. The Japanese connection was but one of his duties, while the Korean connection dominated all matters for the Japanese at the Waegwan. Also, the size and organization of the Korean bureaucracy towered over anything Tsushima could mount. The Koreans were institutionally prepared to gather, categorize, and produce a variety of documents. In the end, both sides required the same kind of information: first-hand accounts of negotiations and the preservation of these accounts in accessible form to help create institutional memory. The simplicity of the Japanese bureaucratic arrangement meant that a good portion of institutional memory could be carried by individuals, so not much effort was put into culling and categorization. If we were to address style, then we would have to contrast the Japanese system with offices going to individuals for reasons of patronage and inheritance with the Korean system of rational bureaucracy and meritocratic appointments. We should not make too much of this, but it might help us to remember that certain Tsushima clans had near monopolies for long periods on certain offices.

There was one final complicating factor on the Japan side. We should recall that Tsushima officials also had to produce certain documents in duplicate: one set for themselves and one set for the *bakufu* and so we might expect this problem to interfere with Waegwan records. Apparently it did not, because the *bakufu* was unconcerned with the Waegwan. The *bakufu* was concerned with trade that supplied what it wanted and with diplomacy that used its name. Even the presence of the Gozan monks in Izuhara (*Iteian rinban*) had little or no impact on most of Tsushima's relations with Chosŏn, because the monk's remit was to pay attention when relations discussed the *bakufu*, and they never seemed to have concerned themselves with trade or the matters of the Waegwan.

Before proceeding directly to a brief overview of the Korean documents needed for research on Korea–Japan relations, we should note several qualifications at the outset. One, our concern is primarily with Tongnae County documents; other central government documents have been mentioned in the preceding chapters and will be only briefly mentioned here. Given this, our discussion will begin in Tongnae and will begin with what we have left of known primary records. We will then work our way from primary documents to secondary documents, and in so doing, we will also be working our way geographically from Tongnae through the Provincial Governor's office to the capital. Two, it goes without saying that we will not be able to discuss all and sundry documents; our concern will be with the major collections and most important examples. Three, our coverage will be limited almost entirely to documents preserved in the Kyujanggak collection, which was one of the two royal libraries and is currently housed at Seoul National University. The limitation is simply because most major Korean documents are preserved there. Many of the comments below were taken from bibliographic aids produced by the Kyujanggak librarians.[1]

Finally, four, our concern is the period after 1600 and before 1876, the year the Kanghwa Treaty was concluded with Japan. Before 1600, documents are exceedingly rare, and the researcher is generally limited to the *Sillok*. After 1876 and the Kanghwa Treaty, the status of the Waegwan officially changed from a Tsushima trading factory to Meiji Japan's first consulate, and we enter the modern period in Korean–Japanese relations. There were a vast number of Korean documents produced in Tongnae County, later Pusan City, in the late nineteenth and early twentieth centuries, but their concern is with a new and different world. Likewise, on the Japanese side, for the first time in history, the Meiji government introduces a direct, central Japanese concern into the daily affairs of the Japanese living in Pusan.

Primary documents

We will begin our discussion with the *tŭngnok* category of documents. *Tŭngnok* means "written records" and can be simply understood as daily record, such as the *Pibyŏnsa tŭngnok*, which is a collection of the Records of the Border Defense Command. These records are actual reports with a clearly indicated addressor and addressee and can be considered primary documents. Almost all the *tŭngnok* we will discuss here were compiled at the *Chŏn'gaeksa* or 'Office of the Custodian of Foreign Visitors of the Board of Rites' in the capital. The *Chŏn'gaeksa*'s duties were to receive foreign correspondence as well as manage provisions and banquets in connection with tribute from the provinces, an interesting comment on the view of the world from the capital. We will create sub-categories of *tŭngnok* to classify documents by the activity they describe: Regular Envoys, Irregular Envoys, Waegwan Facilities, Miscellaneous, and Political Economy. It may strike the reader as odd that miscellaneous is not the last category. The reason is that we will follow our consideration of *tŭngnok* with an examination of *saye*, another type of document devoted to economic matters. The discussion becomes clearer when we juxtapose documents with similar concerns, although they have different formats.

Tŭngnok for regular envoys

The *Sesŏn hangsik ch'ullae tŭngnok* ("Record of Standard Operating Procedure for the Arrival of Regular Envoys [from Tsushima]") is very short – only 22 folio leaves – but summarizes regulations for tribute trade with the regular envoys. The regular envoys were three Specially Dispatched Ships (*Tŭksongsŏn*), 17 Annual Ships (*Segyŏnsŏn*), and a few seal ships, bearing specially bestowed seals of permission from Korea. The last category varied over the period from 1609 to 1876 but never exceeded five. The Kyujanggak's annotated bibliography indicates that its date of compilation, judging from internal evidence, was probably the early to mid-eighteenth century.

The *Sesŏn chŏngt'al tŭngnok* ("Record of Rulings on Regular Envoys") gives us information on negotiations between Korea and Tsushima regarding the amalgamation of ship receptions in 1637 and changes in seal-holders. From 1637, the Korean government's provisions for the 17 Annual Ships were rationalized into annual, lump deliveries, no longer directly associated with actual arrivals. As a result of the Yanagawa Affair (1635), the Yanagawa clan's seal was commuted to the Sō; other seals were forfeited and awarded. This record also mentions banquets and the costs of goods given the Japanese in return for tribute goods.

The *Sesŏn ŭngyŏn tŭngnok* ("Record of Hawks [given] to Regular Envoys") includes information on hawks given to the Japanese in return for tribute and information on the kiln operated within the Waegwan.[2] Entries stretch from 1637 to 1683 on the trials of obtaining hawks from Kangwŏn Province and keeping them alive for delivery to the Japanese. Entries on the raw materials and occasional technical assistance for the Waegwan kiln cover the period from 1639 to 1678, although the kiln continued to operate up to the 1740s. The latter section on the kiln is perhaps best used in connection with another document to be discussed below, the *Waein kuch'ŏng tŭngnok* ("Record of Japanese Requests").

Tŭngnok for irregular envoys

We are very fortunate in regard to *tŭngnok* for irregular envoys in that we have the *Kagyang ch'awae tŭngnok mongnok* ("List of Records for Each Type of Irregular Envoy") and so are able to determine which documents we have and which are missing. As luck would have it, we seem to have some records for each document mentioned. The compilation date of the bibliography is unknown, but it appears to be during Yŏngjo's reign (1724–1776).

The *Pyŏlch'awae tŭngnok*[3] ("Record of the Tsushima Irregular Envoys") does not refer to the Korean official mentioned above, the *Pyŏlch'a*, who assisted the *Hundo* as interpreter, but rather refers to the irregular envoys sent from Tsushima and discussed in Chapter 4. The irregular envoys were called *ch'awae* (J: *sawa*), or *pyŏlch'awae* in a general sense, although each had a particular function indicated by particular names. In this record, we see the *Chŏbwigwan* ("Reception Official") receiving the various *ch'awae* ("irregular envoys") from Tsushima, although the entries are usually authored by the Tongnae Magistrate or the Provincial Governor.

The *Chaep'an ch'awae tŭngnok*[4] ("Record of the Tsushima Special Liaison") refers to a specific irregular envoy, the *Chaep'an ch'awae* (J: *Saihan Sawa*), whom we discussed in the main study. We should recall that the *Chaep'an* or *Saihan* was the Tsushima *daimyō*'s diplomatic troubleshooter and special liaison at the Waegwan. Authorship of the *Chaep'an ch'awae tŭngnok* reports varies between the Provincial Governor and the Tongnae Magistrate with the latter having written the bulk.

We also have *tŭngnok* for other Tsushima-dispatched envoys as well. We have records for the *Chinha ch'awae* ("Irregular Envoy to Express Congratulations [on royal ascensions]") in the *Chinha ch'awae tŭngnok*. Here we see records for particular Korean royal coronations. An envoy arrived in 1650 for Hyojong's coronation, in 1660 for Hyŏnjong's coronation, in 1675 for Sukjong's coronation, in 1720 for Kyŏngjong's coronation, and in 1725 for Yŏngjo's coronation.

We also have a composite record for a variety of congratulations and notifications in the *Ch'iha tŭngnok* ("Record of Dispatched Congratulations"). In 1637, the Tsushima *daimyō* sent congratulations on peace returning to the land after the *Pyŏngja Horan*, the 1636 Manchu invasion. In 1640, Tsushima notified Korea of the return of the Island lord to Tsushima from Edo and the birth of a son. In 1644, there was another envoy bearing a similar message. In 1653, a Gratitude Envoy (*Hoesa ch'awae*) arrived in return for condolences rendered at the death of Tachibana Narimasa. In 1678 and again in 1690, notifications of marriages were sent.

The *Chowi ch'awae tŭngnok* ("Irregular Envoy to Express Condolences") has records of condolences received on the occasions of Korean royal bereavement. We have similar records for the *Kwanbaek kobu ch'awae* ("Irregular Envoy to Notify Korea of the Death of the Shogun") and the *Toju kobu ch'awae* ("Irregular Envoy to Notify Korea of the Death of the Island Lord or of his immediate family member") gathered in the *Kobuch'a tŭngnok* ("Record of Irregular Envoy to Notify Korea of Deaths"). Although we have entries from 1645 to 1694, I have been unable as yet to confirm an inventory of which years. There are also extant records of 15 visits that occurred between 1637 and 1678 by a *Hoesa ch'awae* ("Gratitude Envoy") in the *Hoesa ch'awae tŭngnok* ("Record of Irregular Envoy to Communicate Gratitude"). Although this envoy is clearly an irregular envoy, there is no mention of him in our lists of irregular envoys. For the *Hoesa ch'awae* as well, I have as yet been unable to confirm an inventory of precise years. Finally, we have information on the *Toju kohwan ch'awae* ("Irregular Envoy to Notify Korea of the Island Lord's Return [from Edo]") found in the *Toju kohwan ch'awae tŭngnok*⁵ ("Record of the Irregular Envoy to Notify Korea of the Island Lord's Return from Edo"). A document with a similar title, the *Kohwan tŭngnok* ("Record of Returns"), is, according to the Kyujanggak's annotated bibliography, a record of reports from the Tongnae Magistrate on the departure of certain Japanese envoys from Korea between 1692 and 1716. Since I have been unable to examine the record first-hand, exactly what this document is remains unclear.

A common problem for Korean and Japanese fishermen was shipwrecks. The repatriation of Korean fishermen is recorded in the *P'yoin yŏngnae ch'awae tŭngnok*⁶ ("Records of the Repatriation of Castaways"). The corresponding record for the repatriation of Japanese castaways is the *P'yowae ipsong hoesa tŭngnok* ("Record of the Gratitude Envoy for the Repatriation of Japanese Castaways") which carries entries from 1637 to 1737. We have three detailed documents on Korean castaways in 1863 that describe the castaways individually by residence, profession, name, and age: *Kyŏngsang-do Tongnae-bu naep'yomin-dŭng yŏk – sŏng – myŏng – yŏnse – kŏju – sŏngch'ae* ("Book of Kyŏngsang Province, Tongnae County, Returned Castaways: Profession, Gender, Name, Age, and Residence").

Tŭngnok about Waegwan facilities

There are also two *tŭngnok* chronicling the negotiations to move the Waegwan from Tumo to Ch'oryang in 1678 and repairs of Waegwan facilities. The *Waegwan igŏn tŭngnok* ("Record of the Relocation of the Waegwan") begins with the first request from the Japanese in 1640 to move from Tumo and ends in 1723. It contains entries on the move in 1678 and later necessary repairs. The *Waegwan suri tŭngnok* ("Record of Repairs to the Waegwan") chronicles repairs to the Waegwan from 1724 to 1745. Finally, for repairs to the Ch'oryang Guest House – separate from the Waegwan – we can consult the *Ch'oryang kaeksa chungsu-rok*⁷ ("Record of Repairs to the Ch'oryang Guest House") but only for 1825–1826 and 1873.

Miscellaneous tŭngnok

The *Sŏgye wisik tŭngnok* ("Record of Form Violations in Diplomatic Correspondence") was compiled, like most other records, in the capital at the *Chŏn'gaeksa* office of the Board of Rites. Violations of form included: differences in the height of lines that would indicate unacceptable differences in status, no dates or incomplete dates, letters that are improperly addressed, and other irregularities. The Record of Form Violations has entries from 1637 to 1686. Also in connection with diplomatic affairs, we have the *Yŏkkwan sang'ŏn tŭngnok* ("Record of Interpreters' Petitions"), which is primarily composed of reports by the Interpreter Envoys to Tsushima by the *Hundo* under their charge. The Record of Interpreters' Petitions includes reports concerning those responsible for Chinese, Jurchen, and Manchu affairs, but the bulk is in reference to business with the Japanese. According to the annotated bibliographies for the Kyujanggak, this record includes reports from 1637 to 1692, but years are not specified.

There are also a few miscellaneous *tŭngnok* that carry entries related to the Waegwan and Tsushima. The *Kamdong ŏgi chŏnmal tŭngnok* ("Complete Records of Investigating and Enforcing [Regulations Concerning] Fishing") carries entries from the sixth month of 1828 to the third month of 1829 about Japanese fishing around the Waegwan.

The *Tojung silhwa tŭngnok* ("Record of Fires on Tsushima") reports fires on Tsushima and at the Waegwan. The Japanese pleaded for relief at these times and were given lumber, rice, and hempen cloth. This record has entries from 1660 to 1690.

Tŭngnok that show political economy

The *Nonsang sami tŭngnok* is actually composed of three documents. The *Nonsang sami* ("Weighing One's Merit and Making Appropriate Reward with Gifts of Rice") relates awards between 1637 and 1651 to two *Chaep'an* (J: *Saihan*) and to the *daimyō* of Tsushima. The *Aguk kuch'ŏng* ("Our Country's Requests") relates requests to Japan (Tsushima) for particular goods (sulfur, water buffalo horn, weapons, Chinese medicines, cotton plants, and others) between 1637 and 1645. The *Mu-noin* ("No Travel Permits") records the handling of Japanese ships without proper credentials between 1639 and 1646. The *Chapch'o* ("Miscellaneous Memoranda") records a variety of administrative irregularities and crimes connected with the Waegwan between 1638 and 1674.

The *Waein kuch'ŏng tŭngnok*[8] ("Record of Japanese Requests") is more comprehensive chronologically and its entries come from diverse offices. We see statements from the Tongnae Magistrate, the Provincial Governor, the Reception Officials, and the Board of Taxation in the capital. The last figures prominently in this record since the Japanese requested specific goods, often luxury goods, such as Chinese medicines or raw materials for the Waegwan kiln.

The *Waein kuch'ŏng tŭngnok* should be cross-referenced with the *Tongnae-bu chŏpdae tŭngnok*[9] ("Record of Tongnae Receptions"), which is a collection of records for certain *ch'awae* who came to discuss the dispatch of a *T'ongsinsa* ("[Korean] Embassy [to Edo]"). The authors were the *Chŏbwigwan*. We have records from 1643 to 1841.

The *Kongmok changmi tŭngnok's*[10] ("Record of Official Trade Cotton and Conversion to Rice") authorship also is dominated by the Tongnae Magistrate, but we find entries from the Korean Interpreters who periodically visited Tsushima for negotiations as well as entries from the Provincial Governor. This record is concerned with official trade: cotton and rice obtained as a substitute for certain portions of the cotton (see Chapter 4 for rice converted from cotton). This is the only record which is not dependent on the arrival of Japanese envoys, and that is apparent in the regularity of the entries. Most entries fall in the spring – third through sixth months – and the late winter – tenth and eleventh months – and indicate the delivery times of the official trade goods (rice and cotton) to the Japanese. Since permission to convert cotton to rice was granted in periodic installments (five years at a time), many of the entries discuss negotiations pertaining to the conversion. We also find records of Japanese ship arrivals to take deliveries.

At this point, we should mention a document that investigates the various provisions given to Japanese envoys in 1732. I have yet to investigate personally the

Chŏbwae sing'ye kae-kamjŏng tŭngnok ("Record of an Amended Appraisal of the Forms for Receiving Japanese") but the brief bibliographic description available mentions assessments of amounts of provisions given the Japanese in each category and should make a good snapshot from the early eighteenth century.

The *Chingch'ae tŭngnok* ("Record of Loan Collections") helps us understand the mechanics of private trade at the Waegwan. We have entries from 1637 to 1672 for the *Chingch'ae ch'awae* ("Collection Irregular Envoy"), a Japanese envoy who visited the Waegwan to ask for Tongnae mediation in settling outstanding debts incurred by Koreans. Since Japanese were forbidden to leave the Japan House to conduct business, they loaned capital to Korean partners for procurements, but some Korean partners defaulted or absconded and redress was sought directly with Tongnae. Osa Masanori explains in a study of the 1683 Agreement that offering and accepting loans was outlawed and classified as smuggling by the Korean government.[11] Part of his analysis rests on an examination of a late seventeenth century document, the *Waein changna tŭngnok* ("Record of Japanese [Wanted] for Investigation"). This record contains reports from the Tongnae Magistrate, the Provincial Governor, and central officials in the Board of Rites. The first part deals with prostitution, but the last part discusses the practice of Japanese offering loans to Korean merchants. The section on prostitution is used in Chapter 7.

Korean documents that reveal something of private trade at the Waegwan are rare. The two above discussing loans and smuggling tell us something about merchants at Tongnae dealing with the Japanese; we are fortunate to have another document that tells us something about Tongnae merchants dealing with each other. The *Kyŏngsang-do Tongnae-bu sangmae-tŭng kup'ye chŏlmok* ("Regulations to Eliminate Infringements [on] the Kyŏngsang Province, Tongnae County [official] Merchants") relates administrative directives issued at Tongnae in 1813. Permit-holding merchants (official merchants) were being forced out of the market by merchants without permits (private merchants) and faced ruin. The trade involved Korean sea cucumbers and Chinese medicines for Japanese cowhides, horn, copper, and iron. The directives declared that only official merchants could deal in hides and horn, and fixed prices on copper and iron to prevent public discontent. Since the official merchants were capital-deficient, they had been unable to deal in hides and horn and the private merchants had been trading by using official merchants' names. The policy decision was simply to end the dispute between the two groups, tax each hide at one *chŏn* (of cash), and subsidize the official merchants with increased government procurements.

Chŏngaeksa: the secretariat for information from Tongnae

Finally in the category of *tŭngnok*, we must take special note of the documents produced by the Chŏngaeksa. The Chŏngaeksa was responsible for processing nearly all of the *tŭngnok* discussed above. It was an office under the Board of Rites that oversaw matters related to both Japan and China. The *Kyŏngguk taejŏn* defines the duties of this unit in the following way: "[It is] in charge of receptions for Wae and Yain (Jurchen) envoys, banquets for provincial tribute, and the arrangement of royal grants."[12] We see no mention of China, per se, but the *Chŏngaeksa pang-mul tŭngnok* ("Record of provincial [tribute] in the Office of Custodian of Foreign Visitors") carries records of tribute sent to the Qing from Chosŏn. The most complete document produced by the Chŏngaeksa was the *Chŏngaeksa ilgi* ("Diary of the Office of Custodian of Foreign Visitors") in 99 volumes. Here we find information on tribute trade brought by nearly all of the Japanese envoys discussed in the main study. In addition, the Chŏngaeksa produced the *Chŏngaeksa pyŏl tŭngnok* ("Additional Record of the Office of Custodian of Foreign Visitors").

In the *Chŏngaeksa ilgi* and the *Chŏngaeksa pyŏl tŭngnok* we find records on the gamut of relations with Japan: arrival and circumstances of Irregular Envoys; problems with their letters; replies to those letters; correspondence with the Japan House Master; investigations of problems surrounding provisions, charcoal, and firewood; an overview of relations with the Waegwan; and rewards and punishments dispensed to Korean interpreters who visited Tsushima as well as military officials who had business with the Japanese. There are details on trade, the Waegwan market, problems associated with the use of precious metals for market exchange, matters pertaining to the silver values of official trade rice and cotton, and the circumstances of copper, tin, and iron. We find information on the export of official trade cotton, reed pipes, hawks, and ginseng (price, manufactured ginseng, and red ginseng). We also find information on sexual crimes and the training of interpreters in Japanese. In connection with China, we have information on the repatriation of Chinese castaways, and the arrival of Chinese ships. In addition, we have information on ginseng, medicine, and cotton production, and supplies to the Kwandong border region with China. The *Chŏngaeksa ilgi* covers the period from 1640 to 1886. The *Chŏngaeksa pyŏl tŭngnok* is less complete.[13] The first volume was lost, but the remaining eight cover 1699–1718 and 1720–1753. The problem with these records is that they are in annalistic form, like many of the Japanese documents, and so present serious problems to the researcher trying to gather information on specific problems. Of much greater use is the *Pyŏllye chibyo*, which will be discussed below. The contents of the *Pyŏllye chibyo* are drawn from the *Chŏngaeksa ilgi* and the *Chŏngaeksa pyŏl tŭngnok*, but the *Pyŏllye chibyo* presents information in annalistic form grouped by topics, and this gives the researcher an easy thematic approach to relations between Korea and Japan, but hinders cross-referencing to see the variety of issues that were being discussed at the same time.

Saye (ledgers)

We continue our discussion of the political economy of the Waegwan by examining the documents available for an economic study of Tongnae County and Kyŏngsang Province. Economic documents on the provincial and local level are often classified as *saye*, meaning "instance" or "case study" and are usually ledgers with or without elaborative prose.

The *Chŏpdae Waein saye* ("Instances of Receiving Japanese") is a collection of reports from all three levels of the bureaucracy: Tongnae County, Kyŏngsang Province, and central government offices in the capital, specifically the *Pibyŏnsa*. It begins in 1637 and abruptly terminates in 1687 for no apparent reason. Although the title refers to receptions, this should be considered as inclusive of trade (official trade, measures to control smuggling, market days at the Waegwan, fishing, special requests, and others) and diplomacy (repatriation of castaways, examples of official correspondence, regulations governing the arrival and treatment of Japanese envoys).

The earliest extant *saye* for the county of Tongnae – *Tongnae-bu saye* ("Ledger of Tongnae County") – dates from 1868, which means that the numbers probably refer to 1867. Most certainly there were earlier ledgers. The next version we have is in the *Yŏngnam ŭpchi* ("Kyŏngsang Province Gazette") for 1871 which contains the *Tongnae-bu ŭpchi saye taegae* ("Outline of the Tongnae-bu Gazette Ledger"). There also exists the *Naebu saye*[14] ("[Tong]nae County Ledger") from 1874. Chapter 4 uses the 1868 *Tongnae-bu saye* to calculate Waegwan expenses and compares the result with the *Mangi yoram* ("Detailed Regulations on Finances and the Military"), a central government document which also treats expenses related to the Japanese.

At the provincial level we have the *Yŏngnamch'ŏng saye*[15] ("Ledger of Kyŏngsang Province's Taedong Tax"). This document is composite, and its most recent section dates from about 1830, the probable date of its compilation. The sections referring to the Waegwan probably date from between 1811 and 1825. Since the *Yŏngnamch'ŏng saye* deals with the Taedong tax alone, we cannot rely on it for a complete view of provincial taxes. The *Yŏngnamch'ŏng saye* has a great deal of prose to explain its numbers, but the *Yŏngnam kamyŏng saye*[16] ("Ledger of the Provincial Governor's Office of Kyŏngsang Province") has scant prose to explain itself. It was compiled *c.*1870.

Ŭpchi (gazetteers)

Our survey of documents produced in Tongnae County would not be complete without a discussion of the document base – the Tongnae Gazetteers – used to compile the statistics on the Tongnae Magistrates for Chapter 5 and supply part of the economic and demographic data for Chapters 3 and 4.

The first national gazetteer of the Chosŏn kingdom was produced under King Sejong in 1432.[17] Sejong issued orders for a national geography to be compiled in 1424, the sixth year of his reign. In 1432, he was presented with the *Sinch'an p'aldo chiriji* ("Newly Compiled Geographic Treatise on the Eight Circuits"). With additions and corrections, this document became the *Sejong Sillok chiriji* ("King Sejong's Treatise on Geography"), published in its final form in 1454. The *Sinch'an p'aldo chiriji* is no longer extant. We do have the *Kyŏngsang-do chiriji*, finished in 1425 as one of the eight gazetteers covering the eight circuits for the *Sinch'an p'aldo chiriji*. In short, the *Kyŏngsang-do chiriji* is the oldest extant Chosŏn period gazetteer for Kyŏngsang Province. Here we find no economic data but more complete population data than that found in the *Sejong Sillok chiriji*. We also have extant the *Kyŏngsang-do sokch'an chiriji* from 1469. This document was a part of the 1477 *P'aldo chiriji*, the only part remaining. It contains scant economic data and no population data.

In short, a national gazetteer was produced under Sejong in 1432, went through slight modifications, and was edited down in 1481 (omitting demographic and economic information) into a new document with the title *Tongguk yŏji sŭngnam* ("Survey of the Geography of Korea"). Later efforts produced an updated version in 1531 under the title *Sinjŭng tongguk yŏji sŭngnam* ("Augmented Survey of the Geography of Korea").

Not until 1740 do we find another gazetteer for Tongnae, the *Tongnae-buji*,[18] compiled privately by Magistrate Pak Sa-ch'ang. The *Tongnae-buji* ("Tongnae County [Gazetteer]") was first compiled in 1611 but went through many revisions. Since it was compiled as a private document by the then Magistrate, it does not carry the word *ŭpchi* in its title. The text we have was finalized in 1740. The first official

Tongnae Gazetteer after 1600 was compiled in 1759 for the *Yŏji tosŏ*[19] ("Treatise [on Korea]"). Although the information on Tongnae is very general, it is the most detailed information available following the *Sejong Sillok chiriji* and contains demographic and economic data. The next survey of Kyŏngsang Province was conducted in 1786, but only some 30 counties have come down to us, Tongnae not among them. From the 1832 *Kyŏngsang-do ŭpchi*[20] ("Kyŏngsang Province Gazetteer"), we have the largest number of individual county reports (71) with decreasing numbers from the 1871 *Yŏngnam ŭpchi* ("Kyŏngsang Province Gazetteer," 63 counties) and the 1895 *Yŏngnam ŭpchi* ("Kyŏngsang Province Gazetteer," 66 counties). Therefore, we have official *Tongnae-bu ŭpchi* from 1759, 1832, 1871, 1895, and 1899, the last effort by the Chosŏn Kingdom to compile gazetteers before its extinction.

The province-wide gazetteers also form a comparative group for Tongnae's Gazetteers. Tongnae Gazetteers were produced for these collections, and although there are a few dissimilarities in organization and content between compilations, the other *ŭpchi* gathered in these sets can help us put Tongnae into a comparative context. A variety of specific comparative problems were mentioned in Chapters 3 and 4 and need not detain us again here. Of central importance, however, is the methodology of comparison. *Ŭpchi* for the same year in different places cannot simply be set side by side. According to the Kyujanggak's annotated bibliographies, the 1832 collection reports the economic figures from that time, but a large proportion of counties in the 1871 *ŭpchi* report population figures from the 1831 and the 1786 *ŭpchi*. Specifically for Tongnae, we see that the amount of arable land in *kyŏl* from the 1740 gazetteer, compiled privately by Pak Sa-ch'ang, was repeated as the baseline figure in the 1832 gazetteer and in the 1868 *Tongnae-bu saye*.

If population data was copied from earlier records, might other data have been copied? For example, the budget amounts for 1870 in Table 4.5, Chapter 4, may have been copied from earlier *ŭpchi* collections and may indicate nothing about the fiscal year 1870. However, when we examine Table 4.5 and see that the amounts for fiscal year 1870 differed from earlier years, we see that, at least for Tongnae, we probably do have actual economic information from 1870 since it is not from earlier years. Other county *ŭpchi* might not be so consistent. Demographic data as well, as examined in Chapter 3, differed from reference to reference and the accuracy is still in question.

Unlike the *tŭngnok* or other annalistic-type compilations, the gazetteers give us a snapshot of a county, a rather complete snapshot with a lot of background information, but nevertheless only a snapshot for the year of their compilation. We can find details on administrative offices, famous local people, buildings, natural features, and general tax information. The 1894–1895 *Yŏngnam ŭpchi* has a *saye* appended for each county. We also have maps appended to many counties; for example, the 1832, 1871, and 1895 Tongnae Gazetteers possess maps.

The Gazetteers or *ŭpchi* used in Chapters 3 and 4 were examined for notes on warehouse holdings. Within the same gazetteers we also find *Sŏnsaeng'an*, or Lists of Magistrates, with brief notes attached for each Magistrate. Notes for selected Tongnae Magistrates were translated from this record for Chapter 5, Table 5.3: "Transfers and removals of Tongnae Magistrates due to matters related to the Japanese" (in particular, the subsection on "Explanation of incident"). The *Sŏnsaeng'an* from *ŭpchi* were used to compile most of the statistical data on Magistrates for Chapter 5.

Kyerok (reports), memoranda, and notes

Other annalistic-style records exist for various offices in Tongnae County, and Kyŏngsang Province with entries on the Waegwan. One such is the *Tongnae-bu kyerok*[21] ("Reports from Tongnae," 1849–1889), whose authorship is clearly the Tongnae Magistrate's office. A similar document exists for the Left Naval Command for Kyŏngsang Province in the *Kyŏngsang chwasu-yŏng kyerok*[22] ("Reports from the Left Naval Command for Kyŏngsang Province"), but we have extant entries only for 1843 and 1844. As we recall, the Left Naval Command was based in Tongnae County. In addition, we also have the *Kyŏngsang kamyŏng kwanch'ŏp* ("Memoranda of the Kyŏngsang Provincial Governor's Office") with entries from 1785 to 1787. We also have the *Kyŏngsang chwasu-yŏng kwanch'ŏp*[23] ("Memoranda of the Left Naval Command for Kyŏngsang Province") with entries for 1863, 1866–1870. Yet another similar document is the *Tadaejin kongmun illok*[24] ("Journal of Official Documents of the Tadae Garrison") with entries from the twelfth month of 1856 to the third month of 1858. Thus far, I have been unable to locate any similar documents for the Pusan Garrison prior to 1876.

Finally, what appears to be a copy-book of notes and memoranda from the Tongnae Magistracy has come down to us as the *Naeyŏng munch'ŏp* ("Notes from the [Tong]nae Magistracy"). This collection of secondary writings only covers the years 1866-1867, but is largely taken up with matters concerning the Japanese.

Ilgi (diaries)

We have a few miscellaneous personal records as well. We are fortunate to have private diaries kept by two officials. The *Sulchŏngjip*[25] ("Collected Arbor Anecdotes") was kept by Ha Sŏng-tae, a *hyangni* ("Petty Town Official") who became the *Suyŏngni* ("Petty Official for the Naval Command") at the Left Naval Command for Kyŏngsang Province in the late 1700s. We also have the *Naebu ilgi*[26] ("Tongnae County Diary") kept by the Tongnae Magistrate Kim Sŏk (see Chapter 5, Table 5.3, No. 48) while he was Magistrate from the first month of 1859 to the sixth month of 1859.

Secondary documents

Here we should turn to a second level of documents – edited reports. These documents go under many names, but their form is the same. The entries in these collections lack the formal apparatus that identify actual field reports and have been excerpted from other reports, or are the gist of longer reports, or are verbatim from the original without certain bureaucratic addresses. Their coverage is broad and general, probably compiled with the intention of having handy a few easy references. They were compiled by central government authorities, most likely the Chŏngaeksa or the Sŭngmunwŏn or the Sayŏg'wŏn, all under the Board of Rites, and were based on reports received directly from Tongnae. The Sŭngmunwŏn was in charge of diplomatic correspondence. The Sayŏg'wŏn was the Koryŏ-era T'ongmun'gwan, simply renamed in 1392. It managed the training of interpreters and diplomatic correspondence and was the administrative heart of diplomatic affairs, together with the Sŭngmunwŏn, until the Kabo reforms of 1894. If there was any division of labor, then the Chŏngaeksa acted as a central secretariat, the Sayŏg'wŏn trained interpreters, and the Sŭngmunwŏn trained specialists in diplomatic documents. The chief advantage of these centrally-compiled documents is their chronological arrangement under topical headings. Because of this arrangement, the researcher can approach the document base via topics or problems and re-construct narratives related to issues. The narratives allow cross-referencing with Japanese records. We will look at three major documents in this group.

Although of uncertain date, the *Pongnae Kosa*[27] ("History of Pongnae," judging by its contents, taken to mean Tongnae County) was probably completed in the 1680s or 1690s, compiled from original records of the time, and reports Korean–Japanese relations following the Kiyu Agreement of 1609 up to about 1700.[28] The *Pongnae Kosa* is a mixture of annalistic records (first 75 percent) and explanatory notes (last 25 percent).

The *Tongnae-bu chŏpwae changgye tŭngnok kako samok-rok ch'och'aek*[29] ("A Copy Book of Excerpts from the Record of Reports from Tongnae on Entertaining the Japanese") is similar to the above two documents. It is excerpted in summary fashion, so its authorship is unclear. Clearly, it is not the original report as even the title indicates. The time period covered is from the first month of 1608 to the eighth month of 1694. That such a document as the *Tongnae-bu chŏpwae changgye tŭngnok* ("Record of Reports from Tongnae on Entertaining the Japanese") existed is natural, but it has yet to be re-discovered.

Finally, we come to an extraordinary collection of annalistic-style records collected thematically, by anonymous hands, and entitled the *Pyŏllye chibyo*[30] ("Collection of Border Precedents"). The *Pyŏllye chibyo* was edited by the Chŏngaeksa and undoubtedly based on the *Chŏngaeksa ilgi*, the *Chŏngaeksa pyŏl tŭngnok*, and others. The *Pyŏllye chibyo*'s chief advantage is its comprehensive thematic arrangement. Annalistic entries are arranged chronologically under the following themes: Irregular Envoys, Regular Envoys, Envoys for Castaways, [the Japan] House Master, Agreements [with Tsushima], Diplomatic Correspondence, Banquets and Tribute, Official Trade, [Waegwan] Markets, Provisions and Grants [to the Waegwan and the Japanese], [Wae]gwan Buildings, [Japanese] Requests, [Japanese] Recklessly Leaving [the Waegwan] Without Passes or Permission, Smuggling and Miscellaneous Crimes, Water and Land Routes to Repatriate [Japanese] Castaways, [Tongnae Officials'] Promotions and Punishments, Miscellaneous (including Ullŭng Island), Envoys to Edo, and Frontier Defense. Entries stretch from 1572 to 1841. The *Pyŏllye chibyo* is a handy reference that can be cross-referenced to other, secondary collections mentioned above; and then to the primary records (*tŭngnok*). It goes without saying that the next step would be to cross-reference dates, people, and events under investigation with the document bases of the central government so well known: *Chosŏn wangjo Sillok* ("Veritable Records of the Chosŏn Kingdom"), *Pibyŏnsa tŭngnok* ("Records of the Border Defense Command"), *Sŭngjŏngwŏn ilgi* ("Daily Records of the Royal Secretariat"), and the *Ilsŏngnok* ("Records for Daily Reflection"). Of course, finally, cross-reference should be made to the Japanese documents to obtain a full picture.

Diplomatic correspondence and handbooks

The most important and complete set of diplomatic correspondence for the late Chosŏn period can be found in the *Tongmun hwigo*. Here is a collection of diplomatic letters between Chosŏn Korea and China and Japan edited by the Sŭngmunwŏn.

The collection begins in 1607 with a stray item or two, becomes regular from 1636 and continues on to 1881. The 1788 extant text in lithographic reprint has broken up correspondence by topic, which helps in constructing narratives for single issues, but again, it becomes difficult to see the wide context of other issues.

Although collections of records on various issues existed in topical and annalistic formats, there must have been a need for an easy reference much like the *Kosa ch'walyo* (late sixteenth to early-mid seventeenth century) with its rough diplomatic narrative, important royal dates, distances in the country, and various other practical information. The *T'ongmun'gwanji* (1720) and the *Chŭngjŏng kyorinji* (1802 and 1865) were such two handbooks of the post-1600 period that summarized diplomatic and trade information with China and Japan. The *T'ongmun'gwanji* covered both China and Japan and the *Chŭngjŏng kyorinji* covered only Japan. They do not supply narrative information, but they do contain discussions that refer to the establishment of precedents and reforms. Both texts were condensed from the *Tongmun hwigo* and the *tŭngnok* mentioned above. Here one can find details on types of envoys, their receptions, lodgings, agreements controlling their access to Korea, and other information. The 1471 *Haedong chegukki*, edited by Sin Suk-chu, fulfilled this purpose in the pre-Imjin Waeran period and probably provided the model for the *T'ongmun'gwanji* and the *Chŭngjŏng kyorinji*.

The *T'ongmun'gwanji* is a collection of treatises on aspects of relations with China and Japan or the business conducted by the Sayŏg'wŏn, the Sŭngmunwŏn, and the Chŏngaeksa until the Kabo reforms of 1894. The *T'ongmun'gwanji* went through at least 11 editions that corrected typographical errors and added fascicles for periods following 1720.[31] There are two versions of the *Chŭngjŏng kyorinji*, the original that was produced in 1802 and an updated version produced in 1865. The updated version segregates additions at the end of sections so that they are clearly identifiable.

Conclusion

The Chosŏn bureaucracy was extensive and compartmentalized. Different units produced various document collections: some purely annalistic (e.g. *Chŏngaeksa ilgi*), some with annalistic content arranged thematically (e.g. *Pyŏllye chibyo*), some limited to very narrow timeframes such as a single year (e.g. *Tongnae-bu saye*), and some that appear timeless (e.g. *ŭpchi* or the *T'ongmun'gwanji*). In the case of relations with Japan, the first source of information was the frontier, so we started from that position and worked our way upwards to the capital offices. In the case of relations with China, a researcher might start with Ŭiju and follow the same route. The character of the documents reflects the character of the government organs that produced them, and in comparison with the Japanese documents, the point of view is much less individual and much more anonymous and institutional. The voice is almost always that of the Tongnae Magistrate as representative of the Chosŏn state, whereas on the Japanese side, there are different voices depending on the document and no input from the *bakufu*. The Tongnae Magistrate's office produced all of the information, but the officials in Tongnae were not as well equipped as the capital bureaucrats to maintain an institutional memory, analyze new developments thoroughly in light of precedents, nor make key decisions without consultation. Hence, the impression is one of an intimate and interactive connection between center and periphery.

APPENDIX B

Kyŏngsang-do Province Tax Assessments (in *kyŏl*) (original data for Figures 4.1 and 4.2)

Year	Arable land (wŏnjangbu)	Relief for misc. disasters (yunaejin chapt'al)	Exemptions (myŏnse)	Relief for weather (kŭpjae)	Actual assessment (ch'ulse silgyŏl)
1744	336,240			9,296	226,044
1745				32,140	196,850
1746				9,631	220,183
1747				16,779	213,508
1748				11,448	219,069
1749				6,370	224,953
1750				9,870	221,328
1751				8,324	221,986
1752				8,000	221,917
1753				11,000	218,490
1754	336,477			6,360	219,935
1755				45,883	183,733
1756				20,002	199,678
1757				3,648	214,271
1758				6,525	212,038
1759				14,488	207,515
1760				4,415	212,012
1761				25,707	190,659
1762				44,140	172,172
1763				13,715	202,911
1764	336,477			19,322	195,856
1765				14,306	200,697
1766				4,180	210,132
1767				10,500	203,490
1768				30,298	184,572
1769				16,400	199,547
1770				6,147	209,825
1771				24,000	193,028
1772				6,400	209,883
1773				20,033	196,616
1774	336,477			12,254	204,277
1775				21,700	194,292
1776		89,889	32,648	10,246	203,872
1777		91,188	31,651	17,360	196,705
1778		94,054	31,673	39,300	176,877

Year	Arable land (wŏnjangbu)	Relief for misc. disasters (yunaejin chapt'al)	Exemptions (myŏnse)	Relief for weather (kŭpjae)	Actual assessment (ch'ulse silgyŏl)
1779		94,941	31,519	5,793	204,663
1780		95,247	31,519	3,862	206,280
1781		94,302	31,519	29,852	181,235
1782		94,058	31,519	17,978	193,353
1783		94,497	31,519	15,176	195,715
1784	336,730	94,764	31,519	3,787	206,838
1785		94,605	31,539	4,877	205,887
1786		94,525	31,732	31,900	178,751
1787		94,524	31,742	10,000	200,642
1788		95,045	31,745	6,879	203,239
1789		94,782	31,756	8,382	202,000
1790		95,327	31,759	3,762	206,078
1791		95,085	31,801	17,308	192,934
1792		97,224	31,848	48,376	159,680
1793		97,704	31,860	7,632	199,932
1794	336,950	97,219	31,860	36,278	171,771
1795		97,009	31,860	9,765	198,494
1796		96,788	31,860	4,921	203,559
1797		97,332	31,860	26,928	181,006
1798		98,385	31,860	31,255	175,627
1799		99,750	31,860	6,918	198,600
1800		102,119	31,860	5,623	197,526
1801		101,807	31,860	14,617	188,844
1802		100,508	31,860	2,086	202,674
1803		100,305	31,860	2,486	202,477
1804	336,950	100,240	31,860	1,897	203,131
1805		100,118	31,860	8,638	196,512
1806		100,007	31,860	9,083	196,178
1807		99,964	31,860	3,751	201,553
1808		99,514	31,860	8,381	197,373
1809		99,447	31,920	39,096	166,665
1810		99,410	31,920	14,427	191,371
1811		99,418	31,920	2,995	202,795
1812		99,420	31,920	24,068	181,720
1813		99,374	31,920	13,500	192,334
1814	336,950	99,512	31,920	71,000	134,696
1815		100,804	31,920	30,717	173,687
1816		101,639	31,920	4,540	199,029
1817		102,448	31,847	17,764	185,067
1818		105,015	31,847	5,300	194,966
1819		105,104	31,847	7,721	192,456
1820		105,273	31,843	2,785	197,227
1821		105,243	31,843	13,200	186,842
1822		105,810	31,843	8,418	191,057
1823		105,732	31,055	7,000	193,341
1824	336,950	103,987	31,039	4,324	197,778
1825		104,093	31,037	2,900	199,098
1826		103,863	31,037	3,730	198,320
1827		104,184	31,037	3,900	198,005
1828		104,343	31,037	36,665	165,083

Year	Arable land (wŏnjangbu)	Relief for misc. disasters (yunaejin chapt'al)	Exemptions (myŏnse)	Relief for weather (kŭpjae)	Actual assessment (ch'ulse silgyŏl)
1829		105,742	31,037	3,554	196,795
1830		105,880	31,037	3,917	196,293
1831		105,973	31,037	4,843	195,275
1832		106,039	31,037	8,568	191,484
1833		107,618	31,037	15,000	183,473
1834	336,950	107,849	31,037	4,400	193,842
1835		106,144	31,037	3,168	196,779
1836		106,312	31,037	26,502	173,277
1837		107,287	31,037	13,000	185,804
1838		107,742	31,037	9,500	188,849
1839		107,340	31,037	8,200	190,550
1840		107,902	31,037	4,000	194,189

Source: T'akjijŏn pugo

GLOSSARY

Ae-gŭm   Korean personal name   愛今

Aguk kuch'ŏng   Korean book title   我國求請

Akamagaseki   Japanese place name   赤間馬関

Amenomori Hōshū   Japanese personal name   雨森芳洲

An Tong-jun   Korean personal name   安東晙

Ansŏng   Korean place name   安城

Arai Hakuseki   Japanese personal name   新井白石

aramugi   Japanese unhulled barley   荒麥

Ashikaga Yoshimochi   Japanese shogun's name   足利義持

Asō-wan   Japanese bay name   浅茅湾

bakufu   Japanese military government   幕府

bakuhan   Japanese military feudal regime (Tokugawa)   幕藩

bakumatsu   end period of a Japanese military government   幕末

Bangashira   Japanese term for "Captain of the Guard"   番頭

Bangorō   Japanese personal name   判五郎

Banshōin   personal posthumous name and Tsushima temple name   万松院

bu   Tsushima surface area measurement used to determine feudal stipend: kan, shaku, sun, bu, rin   分

bugyō   Japanese official title   奉行

bunbutsu   (K: *munmul*) Japanese term for "civilization"   文物

Bunrui kiji daikō   Japanese book title   分類記事大綱

Ch'abigwan   Special Officials, Sr. 3, who advised the Chŏbwigwan   差備官

Chaep'an   (J: *Saihan*) Tsushima's "Special Liaison" to Korea   裁判

Chaep'an Ch'awae   Korean term for Tsushima's "Special Liaison" to Korea   裁判差倭

Chaep'an ch'awae tŭngnok   Korean book title   裁判差倭謄錄

ch'ak   Korean measurement for grain: sŏk, tu, sŭng, hap, ch'ak   石

Ch'am'ŭi   Korean term for the capital official to whom the lord of Tsushima directed correspondence, Sr. 3, "Councillor"   參議

Ch'amp'an   Korean term for "Vice-minister" Jr. 2   參判

Changgi   Korean county name   長鬐

Changsŭng-p'o   Korean harbor name   長承浦

Chapch'o   Korean book title   雜抄

Chapŏm   Korean personal name   子範

Ch'awae   (J: *Sawa*) Korean term for Tsushima envoys   差倭

ch'ejik Korean official term for "transferral" 遞職

Cheng Tang Chinese personal name 成湯

Chep'o Korean harbor name, another name for Naeip'o 齋浦

chich'ak minjung Korean term for "constricted land, large population" 地窄
民衆

Ch'iha tŭngnok Korean book title 致賀謄錄

Chijŏp-ko Tongnae Reception Warehouse 支接庫

Chikuzen Japanese place name 筑前

Ch'ilgok Korean county name 漆谷

Chinhae Korean county name 鎭海

Chingbinok Korean book title 懲毖錄

Chingch'ae Ch'awae Korean term for "Collection Irregular Envoy" 徵債差倭

Chingch'ae tŭngnok Korean book title 徵債謄錄

chingong local Korean tribute goods to the court 進貢

Chinha Ch'awae Korean term for "Irregular Envoy to Express Congratulations
[on royal accessions]" 陳賀差倭

Chinha ch'awae tŭngnok Korean book title 陳賀差倭謄錄

chinsang offering up goods to a Korean domestic ruler as local tribute goods
進上

Chinsei Korean personal name as reported in Japanese text チンセイ

Chiye County in Kyŏngsang Province 知禮

Cho Hŭi Korean personal name 曹禧

Cho Kwang-wŏn Korean personal name 趙光瑗

Cho Si-jun Korean personal name 趙時俊

Chŏbwae sing'ye kae-kamjŏng tŭngnok Korean book title 接倭式例改監正
謄錄

Chŏbwigwan Korean term for "Reception Official: Capital or Provincial," Sr. 3
接慰官

choech'e Korean term for "transfer for violation" 罪遞

Ch'oe Ik-hyŏn Korean personal name 崔益鉉

Ch'oe Ŏk Korean personal name 崔檍

Ch'oe Sŏk-jŏng Korean personal name 崔錫鼎

Ch'ogye Korean county name 草溪

ch'ŏk or cha Korean linear measure, one tenth of a p'a, one sixth of a kan, or
0.303 meters 尺

Chŏlla-do Korean province name 全羅道

Chŏlyŏng-do Korean island name 絕影島

chŏn sub-unit of Korean cash 錢

ch'ŏn chŏng ch'ŏn Korean term to describe lower reaches of Naktong River 天
井川

Chŏn'gaeksa Korean term for "Office of the Custodian of Foreign Visitors of the
Board of Rites" 典客司

Chŏngaeksa ilgi Korean book title 典客司日記

Chŏngaeksa pang-mul tŭngnok Korean book title 典客司方物謄錄

Chŏngaeksa pyŏl tŭngnok Korean book title 典客司別謄錄

Chŏng Ch'a-tol-i Korean personal name 鄭次乧伊

Chŏng Ch'ŏk Korean personal name 鄭倜

Ch'ŏnggudo Korean map name 青邱圖

Ch'ŏngha Korean county name 清河

Chŏng Ho Korean personal name 鄭澔

Chŏng Hyŏn-dŏk Korean personal name 鄭顯德

ch'ŏngjoe Korean term for "confessions and pardons" 請罪

Chŏngjo Chosŏn king 正祖

Chŏng Kwang-jwa Korean personal name 鄭光佐

Chŏngmi Yakjo Chŏngmi Agreement of 1547 丁未約條

Chŏng Ŏn-sŏp Korean personal name 鄭彦燮

Chŏng Pu-hyŏn Korean personal name 鄭傅賢

Chŏng Sŏk Korean personal name 鄭哲

Chŏng Wŏn Korean personal name 鄭瑗

Chŏng Yang-p'il Korean personal name 鄭良弼

chŏngsa (J: *seishi*) Korean official title for head envoy 正使

chongsa ch'ugo Korean term for "enquiry on the performance of duty" 從事推考

Ch'ŏngsong Korean place name 青松

Chŏnju Korean place name 全州

chŏnse Korean land tax 田稅

Chŏn Yu-gwang Korean personal name 錢有光

Chŏpdae Waein saye Korean book title 接待倭人事例

Ch'ŏphae sinŏ (J: *Shōkai shingo*) Korean book title 捷解新語

Ch'oryang Korean place name 草梁

Ch'oryang kaeksa chungsu-rok Korean book title 草梁客舍重修錄

Ch'oryang Waegwan Ch'oryang Japan House 草梁倭館

Chōsen gorin ondomo no jinrui Japanese book title 朝鮮御隣御供之人類

Chōsen tsūko daiki Japanese book title 朝鮮通交大紀

Chōsen sho jirei Japanese book title 朝鮮諸事例

Chosŏn Korean dynasty 朝鮮

Chosŏn Taech'ŏng building name in Tongnae 朝鮮大廳

Chosŏn wangjo sillok Korean book title 朝鮮王朝實錄

Chowi ch'awae tŭngnok Korean book title 弔慰差倭謄錄

Chug'yŏng north Kyŏngsang Province area bordering Ch'ungch'ŏn Province 竹嶺

Chūka (K: *Chunghwa*) Japanese term for "Middle Kingdom" 中華

Ch'ulsa Ch'ŏng building name in Tongnae 出使廳

ch'ulse silgyŏl Korean term for "actual tax assessment" 出稅實結

chumu Korean term for "conjugal fashion" 綢繆

Chŭngbo munhŏn pigo Korean book title 增補文獻備考

Chungch'uwŏn Korean term for "Ministers without Portfolio" 中樞院

ch'unggun Korean term for "sent for military service in office" 充軍

Chunghwa (J: *Chūka*) Korean term for "Middle Kingdom" 中華

Chŭngjŏng kyorinji Korean book title 增正交隣志

Ch'ungnyŏl Koryŏ King 忠烈

Ch'un'gwanji Korean book title 春官志

Daikan (K: *Taegwan*) Sō *daimyō* deputy for trade affairs 代官

Daikan mainikki Japanese book title 代官每日記

daimyō Japanese official title 大名

235

Dai Nihon Kōkan (K: Tae-Ilbon Konggwan) name for Waegwan from 1873 大日本公館

Dazaifu Japanese place name 太宰府

Deshima Japanese term for "Dutch factory in Nagasaki" 出島

Edo Japanese city name and period name 江戸

eidai yakko Japanese term for "permanent enslavement" 永代奴

ema Japanese pictorial art form 絵馬

Ennin Japanese personal name 円仁

Fukami Danueimon or Enueimon, Japanese personal name 深見彈右衛門 or 深見圓右衛門

Fukuoka Japanese place name 福岡

fumie Japanese pictorial art used for inquisition 踏み繪

Fuzan-fu shi genkō Japanese book title 釜山府史原稿

Gaimushō Japanese Meiji government department 外務省

genmai Japanese term for "rice on hand" 現米

Genroku Japanese period name, 1688–1704 元禄

Genso Japanese monk's name 玄蘇

go kechū yakko Japanese term for "household slaves" 御家中奴

Gotōke reijō Japanese Tokugawa House Laws 御当家令条

Gozan Japanese leading Zen temples 五山

Haedong chegukki Korean book title 海東諸國記

haejang Korean term for "fishing grounds at sea" 海場

haejo Korean term for "sieve nets" 海條

Haenam Korean county name 海南

haengjang Korean term for "documents" 行狀

Haeundae Korean place name 海雲臺

haifuki Japanese term for "cupellation smelting technique" 灰吹

Hakata Japanese city name 博多

Hamgyŏng-do Korean province name 咸鏡道

han Japanese term for "feudal domain" 藩

Hansŏng Chosŏn dynasty capital name 漢城

Hanyang Chosŏn dynasty capital name 漢陽

hap Korean measurement for grain: sŏk, tu, sŭng, hap, ch'ak 合

Ha Sŏk-bŏm Korean personal name 河錫範

hatamoto direct vassal of the shogun 旗本

Heian Japanese city name and period name 平安

Hidaka Riuemon Japanese personal name 日高利右衛門

Hikomitsu Japanese personal name 彦滿

Hikozō Japanese personal name 彦三

Hirado Japanese city name 平戸

Hizen Japanese region name 肥前

Hizen koku, Kiyabu-gun amalgamated name from Kii-gun, 基肄郡, and Yabu-gun, 養父郡, Tsushima holding in northern Kyūshū, from 1896 it has been called Miyagi-gun, 三養基郡 肥前國基養父郡

Hizen, Matsuura, Chikuzen, Ito-gun Tsushima holdings in northern Kyūshū, from 1896 it has been called Itoshima-gun, 糸島郡 肥前松浦筑前怡土郡

Hizen Tashiro Tsushima holdings in northern Kyūshū 肥前田代

hoesa   Korean term for "return gifts from Korea in tribute trade"   回賜

Hoesa Ch'awae   Korean term for "Gratitude envoy"   回謝差倭

Hoesa ch'awae tŭngnok   Korean book title   回謝差倭謄錄

Hogu ch'ongsu   Korean book title   戶口總數

hogun   Korean official title   護軍

Hojŏk tŭnggwan-ch'aek   Korean book title   戶籍謄關冊

Hong Chung-hyo   Korean personal name   洪重孝

Hong Chung-il   Korean personal name   洪重一

Hong Mun-yŏng   Korean personal name   洪文泳

Honpō Chōsen ōfukusho   Japanese book title   本邦朝鮮往復書

Honshū   Japanese island name   本州

Hundo   Korean term for "liaison/interpreter official," Jr. 9   訓導

Hŭnghae   Korean county name   興海

hwa-chŏnse   Korean term for "cleared, dry field tax"   火田稅

hwa-i   Korean term for "civilized and barbarian"   華夷

hwanggŏp   Korean term for "funk"   惶怯

hwangjong ch'ŏk   Korean linear measurement   黃鍾尺

Hyang Chŏbwigwan   Korean term for "Provincial Reception Official"   鄉接慰官

hyangni   Korean official title   鄉吏

Hyōgo   Japanese region name   兵庫

Hyojong   Chosŏn king   孝宗

Hyŏllyŏng   Korean official title for "County Magistrate," Jr. 5   縣令

Hyŏn'gam   Korean term for "Small County Magistrate," Jr. 6   縣監

Hyŏnjong   Chosŏn king   顯宗

hyŏppak   Korean term for "threats"   脅迫

Ichiuemon   Japanese personal name   市右衛門

Ide Sōzaemon   Japanese personal name   井手惣佐衛門

idu   Korean term for scribal writing   吏讀

Ihon Chōsen monogatari   Japanese book title   異本朝鮮物語

Iki-shima   Japanese island name   壱岐島

Ilgi   diaries   日記

Ilsŏngnok   Korean book title   日省錄

Imgwan   Korean term for "Liaison Officers with the Waegwan"   任官

Imjin Waeran   Korean term for Hideyoshi's invasion   壬辰倭亂

Im Sang-wŏn   Korean personal name   林象元

Im Su-gan   Korean personal name   任守幹

inaka yakko   Japanese term for "country slaves"   田舍奴

Indong   Korean county name   仁同

ingsa   Korean term for "re-appointment in office"   仍仕

Injo   Chosŏn king   仁祖

Iteian rinban   Japanese term for "rotating system of priests from the Gozan temples dispatched to Tsushima"   以酊庵輪番

Izuhara   Tsushima city name   巌原

Jirō   Japanese personal name   次郎

jitō   Japanese term for "headman"   地頭

Kabaeryang   Korean place name   加背梁

kaek'in   (J: *kyakujin*) Korean term for "guest"   客人

Kaeksa Korean building name 客舍

Kaesŏng Korean city name 開城

Kagyang ch'awae tŭngnok mongnok Korean book title 各樣差倭贈錄目錄

Ka-i Korean personal name 加伊

kaikin Japanese term for "controls over foreign travel and contacts" 海禁

kaimai Japanese term for "rice received from Korea in official trade" 買米

Kamdong ŏgi chŏnmal tŭngnok Korean book title 監董漁基顛末贈錄

Kam-ok Korean personal name 甘玉

Kampaku (K: *Kwanbaek*) Korean term for the Japanese Shogun 關白

kan Korean linear measure, 6 ch'ŏk or cha, Tsushima surface area measurement used to determine feudal stipend: kan, shaku, sun, bu, rin 間

Kanbun Japanese period name, 1661–1672 寬文

kandaka Japanese term for "land yield as a function of quality grade and production" 間高

Kang Ko Korean personal name 姜浩

Kanggyebu ŭpchi Korean book title 江界府邑誌

Kanghwa-do Korean island name 江華島

kanjŏn Korean term for "reclaimed land or arable land" 墾田

kanme Japanese monetary unit and dead weight: 3.75 kg. of Japanese silver 貫目

kan nuhi Japanese term for "government slaves" 官奴婢

kano-kuni Japanese term for "that country" 彼國

kano-tokoro Japanese term for "that place" 彼所

kanshaku Japanese term for "land measurement as a function of quality grade and production" 間尺

Kanshu (K: *Kwansu*) Japanese term for "Master of the [Japan] House" 館守

Kanshu nikki Japanese book title 館守日記

Katō Kiyomasa Japanese personal name 加藤清正

Katsu Kaishū Japanese personal name 勝海舟

Keichō Japanese reign name, 1596–1615 慶長

kentai (K: *kyŏmdae*) Japanese term for "amalgamation of Tsushima envoy receptions" 兼帶

Kihaku Genpō Japanese monk's name 規伯玄方

Kijang Korean county name 機張

kijŏn ch'e Korean historical style 紀傳體

Kikuchi Japanese personal name 菊池

Kim Chin-gyu Korean personal name 金鎭圭

Kim Chŏn Korean personal name 金殿

Kim Ch'ung-min Korean personal name 金忠敏

Kim Chun-gye Korean personal name 金遵階

Kimhae Korean county name 金海

Kim Han-sei Korean personal name reported in Japanese text キミハンセイ

Kim Hong-su Korean personal name 金洪壽

Kim Kak-hyŏn Korean personal name 金珏鉉

Kim Kŭk-hae Korean personal name 金克諧

Kim P'aeng-jo Korean personal name 金彭祖

Kim Sang-jung Korean personal name 金尚重

Kim Sŏk Korean personal name 金鉐

kin   (K: *kŭn*) Japanese dead weight, 600 grams   斤

Kinai   Japanese regional name   機內

kisa ponmal ch'e   Korean historical style   記事本末體

Kiyabu   from Kii-gun and Yabu-gun, another name for Tsushima's Tashiro lands in northern Kyūshū   基養父（基肆郡 and 養父郡）

kiyu   (J: *kiyū*) sexagenary year name   巳酉

Kobuch'awae tŭngnok   Korean book title   告訃差倭謄錄

Kŏch'ilsan-gun   Korean county name   居漆山郡

kōeki yakko   Japanese term for "public service slaves"   公役奴

Ko'hwangsan-guk   Korean county name   古荒山國

Kohwan tŭngnok   Korean book title   告還謄錄

Kŏje-do   Korean island name   巨濟島

Koji ruien   Japanese book title   古事類苑

Kojong   Chosŏn king   高宗

kokudaka   Japanese term for "total possible yield"   石高

Kongbŏp   Korean term for "Tribute Tax Law"   貢法

kongch'ŏn   Korean term for "low-class corvée labor"   公賤

konggal   Korean term for "blackmail"   恐喝

kongjangmi   Korean term for "cotton converted to rice"   公作米

Kongmok changmi tŭngnok   Korean book title   公木作米謄錄

kono-tokoro   Japanese term for "this place"   此所

Kōrin teisei   Japanese book title   交隣提醒

Koryŏ   Korean dynasty   高麗

Koryŏng   Korean county name   高靈

Koryŏsa   Korean book title   高麗史

Kosa ch'walyo   Korean book title   攷事撮要

Kosŏng   Korean county name   固城

kuch'ŏng   Korean term for "requests"   求請

Kŭmsŏng   Korean county name   金成

kŭmtowae   Korean name for Japanese constables   禁徒倭

kŭn   (J: *kin*) Korean dead weight, 600 grams   斤

Kungbok   or Chang Po-go, Korean personal name   弓福 (or 張保皐)

Kun'gwan   Korean term for "Military Official"   軍官

Kunsu   Korean term for "Great County Magistrate," Jr. 4   郡守

kŭpjae   Korean term for "relief for weather disasters"   給災

Kuroda Kyotaka   Japanese personal name   黑田清隆

kut   Korean shaman exorcism   굿

Kwabang   Korean term for "Servants at the Tea Ceremony and Banquets"   果房

kwach'e   Korean term for "transfer after completion of tour"   瓜遞

Kwanbaek   (J: *Kampaku*) Korean term for the Japanese Shogun   關白

Kwanbaek kobu Ch'awae   Korean term for "Irregular Envoy to Notify Korea of the Death of the Shogun"   關白告訃差倭

Kwanch'alsa   Korean term for "Provincial Governor," Jr. 2   觀察使

Kwangju   Korean county name   光州

kwangŭp Wae   Korean term for "actual disbursement to Wae"   實給倭

Kwanjik   Korean term for "Attendants at Waegwan Banquets"   館直

Kwansu   (J: *Kanshu*) Korean term for "Master of the (Japan) House"   館守

Kwŏn I-jin   Korean personal name   權以鎮

Kwŏn Sang   Korean personal name   權詳

Kwŏn Se-ho   Korean personal name   權世豪

Kwŏn Su   Korean personal name   權燧

Kwŏn Tae-jae   Korean personal name   權大載

Kwŏn To   Korean personal name   權導

kyakujin   (K: *kaek'in*) Japanese term for "guest"   客人

Kyerim   Korean alternate name for Silla   鷄林

kyerok   Korean term for "reports"   啓錄

Kye-wŏl   Korean personal name   桂月

kyoch'e   Korean term for "transfer"   交遞

kyŏl   Korean term for "measuring land by its productive value"   結

kyŏlbu   Korean term for "measuring land by its productive value"   結負

kyŏlchak   Korean term for "Additional Tax on Land"   結作

kyŏmdae   (J: *kentai*) Korean term for "amalgamation of Tsushima envoy receptions 兼帶

Kyŏng Chŏbwigwan   Korean term for "Capital Reception Official," Sr. 3   京接慰官

Kyŏngdŏk   Sillan king   景德

Kyŏnggi   Korean province name   京畿

kyŏngja   sexagenary year name   庚子

Kyŏngju   Korean county name   慶州

Kyŏngguk taejŏn   Korean book title   經國大典

Kyŏngsang chwasu-yŏng kwanch'ŏp   Korean book title   慶尚左水營關牒

Kyŏngsang chwasu-yŏng kyerok   Korean book title   慶尚左水營啓錄

Kyŏngsang-do   Korean province name   慶尚道

Kyŏngsang-do chiriji   Korean book title   慶尚道地理志

Kyŏngsang-do kyebon tŭngnok   Korean book title   慶尚道啓本登錄

Kyŏngsang-do sokch'an chiriji   Korean book title   慶尚道續撰地理志

Kyŏngsang-do Tongnae-bu naep'yomin-dŭng yŏk – sŏng – myŏng – yŏnse – kŏju – sŏngch'aek   Korean book title   慶尚道東萊府來漂民等役姓名年歲居住成冊

Kyŏngsang-do Tongnae-bu sangmae-tŭng kup'ye chŏlmok   Korean book title   慶尚道東萊府商買等捄弊節目

Kyŏngsang-do ŭpchi   Korean book title   慶尚道邑誌

Kyŏngsang kamyŏng kwanch'ŏp   Korean book title   慶尚監營關牒

Kyŏngsang Namdo Tongnae-bu ŭpchi   Korean book title   慶尚南道東萊府邑誌

kyorin   Korean term for relations with Japan, "Neighborly relations"   交隣

kyosa   Korean term for "cunning"   狡詐

Kyōto   Japanese city name   京都

Kyujanggak   Korean royal library   奎章閣

Kyunyŏkbŏp   Korean term for "Equal-Service Law"   均役法

Kyūshū   Japanese island name   九州

Kyūshū Tandai   Japanese term for "Governor of Kyūshū"   九州探題

li   Korean linear measurement, 12,960 ch'ŏk or 3.927 km   里

Majik   Korean term for "Horse Attendants"   馬直

makidaka   Japanese term for "amount of seed grain required for a particular land parcel"   蒔高

makie   Japanese lacquer ware   蒔繪

Mangi yoram   Korean book title   萬機要覽

Masan   Korean city name   馬山

Meiji   Japanese period name, 1868–1911   明治

metsuke   Japanese constable   目付

Ming   Chinese dynasty   明

Min Ŭng-hyŏp   Korean personal name   閔應協

Min Yŏng-don   Korean personal name   閔泳敦

Mokp'o   Korean harbor name   木浦

Moksa   Korean term for "City/Island Magistrate," Sr. 3   牧使

mun'in   Korean term for "sealed documents of passage issued by the Tsushima *daimyō*"   文引

Munjŏnggwan   Korean term for "Foreign Ship Inspector from the Sayŏg'wŏn"   問情官

munmul   (J: *bunbutsu*) Korean term for "civilization"   文物

Mu-noin   Korean book title   無路引

Munwigwan   Korean official charged with greeting the Chinese ambassador at the Yalu and conducting him to the capital   問慰官

Munwihaeng   Korean term for Chosŏn Interpreter Embassies to Tsushima   問慰行

Muromachi bakufu   name of Japanese military government   室町幕府

myŏn   Korean term for "township"   面

myŏng   Korean term for "arrest in office and interrogation in the presence of the king"   命

myŏngmun   Korean term for "exchange agreements in the Japan House great market between Korean and Japanese merchants"   明文

myŏnjik   Korean term for "relieved of duty"   免職

myŏnse   Korean term for "tax exemption"   免稅

na   Korean term for "arrest in office"   拿

Naebu ilgi   Korean book title   萊府日記

Naebu saye   Korean book title   萊府事例

Naeip'o   Korean harbor name, another name for Chep'o   乃而浦

Naesan-guk   Korean place name   萊山國

Naesŏng-kang   Korean place name   乃城江

Naeyŏng munch'ŏp   Korean book title   萊營文牒

Nagasaki bugyō   Japanese term for *bakufu*-appointed Governor of Nagasaki   長崎奉行

Nagasaki kenshi   Japanese book title   長崎縣史

Naktong-kang   Korean river name   落東江

Namch'on-myŏn   Namch'on Township in Tongnae   南村面

Nam Hu   Korean personal name   南垕

nan   Korean term for "warm"   暖

nanch'ul   Korean term for "disorderly exiting" or "rioting and storming out" of the Japan House   闌出

nareru   Japanese term for "inured"   狃れる

nengiri yakko   Japanese term for "term-limit slaves"   年切奴

Nihon or Nippon (K: Ilbon) Japanese term for Japan 日本

Nihon kokuō-shi Japanese term for "Envoy from the king of Japan" 日本国王使

Ninjin-za Japanese name for the ginseng market 人參座

nobi Korean term for "unfree labor" or "slave" 奴婢

no-chŏnse Korean term for "Reed Field Tax on low-lying fields beside rivers" 蘆田稅

Nonsang sami tŭngnok Korean book title 論賞賜米謄錄

No Po-se Korean personal name 盧輔世

nuhi Japanese term for "unfree labor" or "slave" 奴婢

Ŏ Bu-dong Korean personal name 於夫同

oe-i Korean term for "foreign barbarian" 外夷

O Han-wŏn Korean personal name 吳翰源

ojikeru Japanese term for "fear" 怖じける

Ŏ Jin-ik Korean personal name 魚震瀷

Ok-p'o Korean harbor name 玉浦

Ŏm Sŏk-jŏng Korean personal name 嚴錫鼎

Ōnin Japanese period name, 1467–1468 応仁

Ōshima Tomonojō Japanese personal name 大島友之允

O Si-dae Korean personal name 吳始大

Ŏ Suk-kwŏn Korean personal name 魚叔權

Ōtomo Japanese clan name 大友

Ōuchi Japanese clan name 大內

p'a Korean linear measure, 10 ch'ŏk or 3.03 meters 把

P'aegwan chapki Korean book title 稗官雜記

p'ajik Korean term for "dismissal from office" 罷職

Pak Kwŏn Korean personal name 朴權

Pak Kyu-su Korean personal name 朴珪壽

Pak Shin Korean personal name 朴紳

Pak T'ae-hang Korean personal name 朴泰恒

Palgun Korean term for "Mounted Couriers" 撥軍

P'angwan Korean term for "Governor's Aide/Magistrate's Aide" 判官

pangyŏm Korean term for "river wiers" 防簾

P'anhyŏnsa Koryŏ civil official title 判縣使

P'ansa Korean official title 判事

pi Korean term for "bountiful" 肥

Pibyŏnsa Korean government organ 備邊司

Pibyŏnsa tŭngnok Korean book title 備邊司謄錄

Piguk tŭngnok Korean book title 備局謄錄

p'il Korean term for "bolt of cloth" 疋

Pinilhŏn Korean term for the Pyŏlch'a's domicile 賓日軒

po Korean linear measurement, "pace" 步

p'o Korean term for "harbor" 浦

Pokbyŏngso Korean guard houses for the Japan House 伏兵所

pŏmgan Korean term for "crimes of a sexual nature" 犯奸

Pŏm'ŏsa Korean temple name 梵魚寺

pongjin Korean term for "offering up of goods to a foreign ruler as tribute" 封進

Pongnae kosa Korean book title 蓬萊故事

Poŭn   Korean county name   報恩
Pu-gum   Korean personal name   夫金
Puk-myŏn   Tongnae's North Township   北面
Pukp'yŏnggwan   Korean term for "Hall of Northern Peace for Jurchen envoys"   北平館
Pulguk-sa   Korean temple name   佛國寺
Pusan Kaeksa   Korean term for the "Pusan Guest House"   釜山客舍
Pusan-myŏn   Tongnae's Pusan Township   釜山面
Pusanp'o   Korean harbor name   釜山浦
Puyŏk silch'ong   Korean book title   賦役實總
Puyun   Korean term for "Special Capital Magistrate," Jr. 2   府尹
P'yoin yŏngnae ch'awae tŭngnok   Korean book title   漂人領來差倭謄錄
p'yojun p'yŏnch'a   Korean term for "standard deviation"   標準偏差
Pyŏlch'a   Korean term for "liaison/interpreter official for the Japanese," no rank   別差
Pyŏlch'awae   Korean term for "Japanese irregular envoy"   別差倭
Pyŏlch'awae tŭngnok   Korean book title   別差倭謄錄
Pyŏllye chibyo   Korean book title   邊例集要
pyŏlp'ok   Korean term for "addendum to sŏgye that lists presents as tribute"   別幅
P'yomin taehwa   Korean book title   漂民對話
pyŏng   Korean area measurement, 0.3025 square meters   坪
P'yŏng'an-do   Korean province name   平安道
Pyŏngja Horan   1636 Manchu invasion   丙子胡亂
Pyŏngmasa   Koryŏ military official title   兵馬使
p'yŏnnyŏn ch'e   Korean historical style   編年體
Pyŏn Pak   Korean personal name   卞璞
P'yowae ipsong hoesa tŭngnok   Korean book title   漂倭入送回謝謄錄
Rekidai Hōan   Ryūkyūan book title   歷代寶案
rin   Tsushima surface area measurement used to determine feudal stipend: kan, shaku, sun, bu, rin   厘
Ritsuryō   Japanese administrative term   律令
ryō   Japanese term for unit of gold currency   両
Ryōkoku ōfuku kakiutsushi   Japanese book title   兩國往復書謄
sach'e   Korean term for "resignation"   辭遞
Sach'ŏn-myŏn   Tongnae's Sach'ŏn Township   沙川面
Saihan   (K: *Chaep'an*) Tsushima's "Special Liaison" to Korea   裁判
Saihan kiroku   Japanese book title   裁判記錄
sakeru   Japanese term for "avoid"   避ける
sakoku   Japanese term to describe Tokugawa foreign policy   鎖国
Samguk sagi   Korean book title   三國史記
Samguk yusa   Korean book title   三國遺事
Samsu-mi   Korean term for "Military Training Tax"   三手米
Sangju   Korean city name   尚州
sangp'i   Korean term for "avoidance of conflict of interest while in office"   相避
San'gun   Kyŏngsang Province area in the midlands or "inland counties in the mountains"   山郡
Sanpanshi   Japanese term for Tsushima's "Irregular Envoys"   参判使

Saryang   Korean place name   蛇梁

Saryŏng   Korean term for "Runners for the *Hundo* and *Pyŏlch'a*"   使令

Satsuma   Japanese domain name   薩摩

Sawa   (K: *Ch'awae*) Korean term for Tsushima envoys   差倭

saye   ledger   事例

Sayŏg'wŏn   Korean term for "Office of Interpreters" under the Board of Rites   司譯院

Segyŏnsŏn   Korean term for "17 Annual Ships"   歲遣船

Seikanron   Japanese foreign policy debate   征韓論

seishi   (K: *chŏngsa*) Japanese official title for head envoy   正使

seishin   (K: *sŏngsin*) Japanese term for "sincerity"   誠信

Sejong   Chosŏn king   世宗

Sejong sillok   Korean book title   世宗實錄

Sejong sillok chiriji   Korean book title   世宗實錄地理志

Sekijō   Korean alternative name for Hakata   石城

Sesŏn chŏngt'al tŭngnok   Korean book title   歲船定奪謄錄

Sesŏn hangsik ch'ullae tŭngnok   Korean book title   歲船恒式出來謄錄

Sesŏn ŭngyŏn tŭngnok   Korean book title   歲船鷹連謄錄

shaku   Tsushima surface area measurement used to determine feudal stipend: kan, shaku, sun, bu, rin   尺

Shang   Chinese dynasty   商

Shibukawa   Japanese clan name   渋川

Shikosamon   Japanese personal name   四古沙門

Shimazu   Japanese clan name   島津

Shimonoseki   Japanese place name   下関

Shiromizu Genshichi or Izumi Genshichi   Japanese personal name   白水源七 or 泉源七

shitsuji   Japanese official title   執事

Shōkai shingo   (K: *Ch'ŏphae sinŏ*) Korean book title   捷解新語

Shoku [Ji?]eimon   Japanese personal name   食只[次?]衛門

shomumai   Japanese term for "operating expenses"   所務米

Shōni   Japanese clan name   少弍

Shōtoku   Japanese period name, 1711–1716   正德

shugo   Japanese official title   守護

sigi-kyŏl   Korean term for "actual production"   時起結

Sihan   Korean term for "Woodcutters for the *Hundo* and *Pyŏlch'a*"   柴漢

sil-kyŏl   Korean term for "actual production"   實結

Silla   Korean dynasty   新羅

Sillok   Korean book title   實錄

Silsŏng   Silla king   實聖

Sim Pal   Korean personal name   沈撥

Sin'an   Korean place name   新安

Sinbo sugyo chimnok   Korean book title   新補受教輯錄

sinbyŏng   Korean term for "illness in office"   身病

Sinch'an p'aldo chiriji   Korean book title   新撰八道地理志

Sinjŭng tongguk yŏji sŭngnam   Korean book title   新增東國輿地勝覽

Sinsŏn p'aldo chiriji   Korean book title   新撰八道地理志

Sin Suk-chu   Korean personal name   申叔舟

Sin Wi   Korean personal name   申暐

Sin Yi   Korean personal name   辛曘

sirhak   Korean intellectual movement   實学

sit'an   Korean term for "firewood and charcoal"   柴炭

Sobaek-san   Korean mountain range name   小白山

Soch'awae   Korean term for Tsushima's "Minor Irregular Envoys"   小差倭

Sŏ Chong-t'ae   Korean personal name   徐宗泰

Sodong   Korean term for "Youths in Attendance" on the *Hundo*, *Pyŏlch'a*, *Munjŏnggwan*, and *Ch'abigwan*   小童

sogok   15-*tu sŏk*   小斛

sŏgye   Korean term for "diplomatic letter from Tsushima *daimyō*"   書契

Sŏgye wisik tŭngnok   Korean book title   書契違式謄錄

sŏk   Korean unit of weight measure, equivalent to 15 or 20 *tu*, Korean measurement for grain: sŏk, tu, sŭng, hap, ch'ak   石

sokhyŏn   Korean term for "subcounty"   屬縣

Sō Kin   Japanese personal name   宗金

Sok taejŏn   Korean book title   續大典

sŏlyŏnpi   Korean term for "banquet costs"   設宴費

Sŏmch'ŏn   Korean county name   陜川

Sŏ-myŏn   Tongnae's West Township   西面

Sŏn'am-sa   Korean temple name   仙菴寺

Son-da   Japanese personal name, Tadamasa?   孫多

Son In-gap   Korean personal name   孫仁甲

Sŏng Hyŏn   Korean personal name   成俔

Song Hŭi-gyŏng   Korean personal name   宋希璟

Sŏngjong   Chosŏn king   成宗

Sŏngjong   Koryŏ king   成宗

Sŏngju   Korean county name   星州

Sŏng Kwan   Korean personal name   成瓘

Song Sang-hyŏn   Korean personal name   宋象賢

Sŏng Su-yŏn   Korean personal name   成遂然

Sŏnsaeng-an   Korean term for "Role of Magistrates" in local gazetteers   先生案

sŏngsin   (J: *seishin*) Korean term for "sincerity"   誠信

Sŏngsindang   Korean building name in Tongnae: "Hall of Truth and Sincerity"   誠信堂

songsa   (J: *sōshi*) Korean and Japanese term for "envoy"   送使

Sŏnhyech'ŏng   Korean building name   宣惠廳

Sŏnsan   Korean county name   善山

Sŏnsaeng'an   Korean book title   先生案

Sŏnwisa   Korean term for "Reception Official," Sr. 3 before 1629   宣慰使

Sŏ Pu-sang   Korean personal name   徐富祥

Sōryō Wakan ezu   Japanese map name   草梁倭館繪圖

Sō Sadamori   *r.*?–1452, Japanese personal name   宗貞盛

sōshi   (K: *songsa*) Korean and Japanese term for "envoy"   送使

Sŏsŭngwae   (J: *Tōkōji*) Korean term for Zen monk scribe in Japan House   書僧倭

Sot'ongsa   Korean term for "Minor Interpreters at the Waegwan"   小通使

Sō Yoshinari   *r.*1615–1657, Japanese personal name   宗義成

Sō Yoshitoshi   *r.*1579–1615, Japanese personal name   宗義智

Sō Yoshizane   *r.*1657–1692, Japanese personal name   宗義真

Suan   Korean county name   守安

Sugun Chŏltosa   Korean term for "Commander of the Left Naval Headquarters," Jr. 2, stationed in Tongnae   水軍節度使

Sugun Ch'ŏmjŏlchesa   Korean term for "Navy Deputy Commander," Sr. 3, stationed in the Pusan Garrison   水軍僉節制使

Sugun Manho   Korean term for "Navy Sub-area Commander," Jr. 4   水軍萬戶

Sugun Tojŏlchesa   Korean term for "Deputy Provincial Naval Commander," Jr. 3   水軍都節制使

Sugun Uhu   Korean term for "Navy Inspector," Sr. 4   水軍虞侯

Sugun'yŏng   Korean term for "Left Naval Headquarters" in Tongnae   水軍營

sujik'in   Korean term for "appointee"   受職人

sujik'in-sŏn   Korean term for "Japanese envoy ship from Japan with Korean official title"   受職人船

Sukjong   Chosŏn king   肅宗

Sulchŏngjip   Korean book title   述亭集

Sumun   Korean term for Japan House "main gate"   守門

sun   Tsushima surface area measurement used to determine feudal stipend: kan, shaku, sun, bu, rin   寸

Sunch'alsa   Korean term for "Border Inspector," Jr. 2   巡察使

sŭng   Korean term for "promotion in office"   陞

sŭng   Korean dry weight measure, Korean measurement for grain: sŏk, tu, sŭng, hap, ch'ak   升

Sŭngjŏngwŏn   Korean term for "Royal Secretariat"   承政院

Sŭngjŏngwŏn ilgi   Korean book title   承政院日記

Sŭngmunwŏn   Korean term for the "Office of Diplomatic Correspondence" under the Board of Rites   承文院

Sunpu   Japanese place name   駿府

sup'yo   Korean term for "receipt for tribute goods delivered at the Japan House"   手標

suryŏng   general Korean term for "County Magistrate"   守令

Suyama Donō (Totsuan)   Japanese personal name   陶山鈍翁(訥庵)

Suyŏngni   Korean official title   水營吏

Tachibana Chishō   Japanese personal name   橘智正

Tadae   Korean place name in Tongnae   多大

Tadaejin kongmun illok   Korean book title   多大鎮公文日錄

T'aebaek-san   Korean mountain range name   太白山

Taech'awae   Korean term for Tsushima's "Great Irregular Envoys"   大差倭

Taech'i-ri   Taech'i Village in Tongnae   大峙里

Taech'ŏng   Korean building name   大廳

T'aedaekun   (J: *Taitaikun*) Japanese diplomatic title for shogun   太大君

Taedohobusa   Korean term for "Special City Magistrate," Sr. 3   大都護府使

Taedongbŏp   Korean term for "Uniform Land Tax Law"   大同法

Taedong-kang   Korean river name   大同江

taedong-mi   Korean term for "Taedong tax rice"   大同米

Taedongsaek Korean term within *Tongnae Saye* account book that refers to Taedongbŏp rice stores　大同色

taegok 20-*tu sŏk*　大斛

Taegu Korean county name　大邱

tae-guk hyul so-guk Korean term for policy towards Tsushima and Japan　大國恤小國

Taegwan (J: *Daikan*) Sō *daimyō* deputy for trade affairs　代官

T'aehwa-kang Korean river name　太和江

Tae-Ilbon Konggwan (J: *Dai Nihon Kōkan*) name for Waegwan from 1873　大日本公館

T'aejo Chosŏn king　太祖

Taejŏn t'ongp'yŏn Korean book title　大典通編

T'aejong Chosŏn king　太宗

T'aep'yŏnggwan Korean term for "Hall of Great Peace for Chinese envoys"　太平館

Taewŏngun Korean official title　大院君

Taikan zakki Japanese book title　對韓雜記

Taikun Japanese diplomatic title for shogun　大君

Taitaikun (K: *T'aedaekun*) Japanese diplomatic title for shogun　太大君

Takase Hachizaemon Japanese personal name　高瀬八左衛門

Takeshima Japanese island name　竹島

T'akjijŏn pugo Korean book title　度支田賦考

Tandai Shogunal deputy in Kyūshū, Governor of Kyūshū　探題

tangsang Korean term for "death in office"　當喪

Tashiro Tsushima land holding in northern Kyūshū, see Kiyabu　田代

Tōbō Shingorō Japanese personal name　唐坊新五郎

tohobu Korean local administrative division for "county"　都護府

Tohobusa Korean term for "Town Magistrate," Jr. 3　都護府使

tōjin Japanese term for Asian foreigners　唐人

Tōjin Yashiki Japanese term for "Chinese compound in Nagasaki"　唐人屋敷

Toju Kobu Ch'awae Korean term for "Irregular Envoy to Notify Korea of the Death of the Island Lord or of his immediate family member"　島主告訃差倭

Toju Kohwan Ch'awae Korean term for "Irregular Envoy to Notify Korea of the Island Lord's Return (from Edo)"　島主告還差倭

Toju kohwan ch'awae tŭngnok Korean book title　島主告還差倭謄錄

tojung Korean term for "large Korean merchants in the Japan House market"　都中

Tojung silhwa tŭngnok Korean book title　島中失火謄錄

Tōkai Yakkanshi Japanese term for "Korean envoy to Tsushima"　渡海譯官使

Tōkōji (K: *Sŏsŭngwae*) Japanese Zen monk scribe in Japan House　東向寺

Tokugawa Hidetada Japanese personal name　德川秀忠

Tokugawa Ieyasu Japanese personal name　德川家康

Tokugawa Tsunayoshi Japanese personal name　德川綱吉

t'omul or t'oŭi Korean terms for "domestic products"　土物

tong Korean unit for 50 bolts of cloth　同

Tongguk yŏji sŭngnam Korean book title　東國輿地勝覽

tongjŏng Korean term for "sympathy"　同情

T'ongmun'gwanji Korean book title 通文館志
Tongmun hwigo Korean book title 同文彙考
Tong-myŏn Tongnae's East Township 東面
Tongnae Korean county name 東萊
Tongnae-bu chŏpwae changgye tŭngnok kako samok-rok ch'och'a Korean book title 東萊府接倭狀啓謄錄可考事目錄抄冊
Tongnae-buji Korean book title 東萊府誌
Tongnae-bu kyerok Korean book title 東萊府啓錄
Tongnae-bu saye Korean book title 東萊府事例
Tongnae-bu ŭpchi Korean book title 東萊府邑誌
Tongnae-bu ŭpchi saye taegae Korean book title 東萊府邑誌事例大概
Tongnae-hyŏn Korean term for Tongnae County 東萊縣
Tongnae kiyŏnghoe Tongnae County's council of elites 東萊耆英會
Tongp'yŏnggwan Korean term for "Hall of Eastern Peace for Japanese envoys" 東平館
Tongp'yŏng-hyŏn Korean term for Tongp'yŏng County, later made a township within Tongnae 東平縣
Tongp'yŏng-myŏn Tongnae County's Tongp'yŏng Township 東平面
T'ongsa-ch'ŏng Korean term for the "Interpreter's Office" or the Minor Interpreters' domicile to the east of the Sŏngsin-dang 通使廳
t'ongsin Korean term occasionally used for "patent of identification required when Japanese landed in Korea" 通信
T'ongsinsa (J: *Tsūshinshi*) Korean title for "Communication Embassy to Edo" 通信使
T'ongsinsa tŭngnok Korean book title 通信使謄錄
Tongsa ilgi Korean book title 東槎日記
toridaka Japanese term for "actual production" 取高
Tosa Korean term for "Provincial Inspector," Jr. 5 都事
t'osan Korean term for "local products" 土產
tosŏ Korean term for "copper seals" 圖書
tosŏ-sŏn Korean term for "ship carrying a document impressed with a copper seal" 圖書船
t'oŭi or t'omul domestic products 土宜
Toyotomi Hideyoshi Japanese personal name 豐富秀吉
Tsushima Japanese island name 對馬
Tsūshinshi (K: *T'ongsinsa*) Korean title for "Communication Embassy to Edo" 通信使
tu or mal Korean sub-unit of dry weight measure, Korean measurement for grain: sŏk, tu, sŭng, hap, ch'ak 斗
t'ubi Korean term for "exile in office" 投畀
Tŭksongsŏn Korean term for "Specially dispatched ships" 特送船
Tumo Korean place name in Tongnae 豆毛
Tumo-p'o Waegwan Tumo port Japan House 豆毛浦倭館
tŭngnok annalistic records 謄錄
turak measure of land by amount of seed needed for planting 斗落
Uam-ri Uam Village 牛岩里
Ubusŭngji Korean term for "Censor of Criminal Activities" 右副承旨

Ŭiju   Korean county name   義州

Ukyō (Yoshitatsu)   Japanese personal name   右京(義龍)

Ulju   Korean place name   蔚州

Ullŭng-do   Korean island name   鬱陵島

Ulsan   Korean county name   蔚山

Umamawari   Japanese official title   馬廻

Uma-ōkami   Japanese personal name or official title   馬大守

Umeno Hisashiuemon   Japanese personal name   梅野久右衛門

Ungch'ŏn   Korean county name   態川

Ungsin   Korean sub-county name   熊神

ŭp   Korean term for "county"   邑

ŭpchi   Korean gazetteer for a county   邑誌

Waegu   (J: *Wakō*) Korean term for "Japanese pirates"   倭寇

Waegwan   (J: *Wakan*) Korean term for "Japan House"   倭館

Waegwan-do   Korean painting of the Waegwan   倭館圖

Waegwan igŏn tŭngnok   Korean book title   倭館移建登錄

Waegwan suri tŭngnok   Korean book title   倭館修理謄錄

Waehak   Korean term for "Japanese affairs"   倭學

Waehŏn   Korean term for "Wae presents"   倭獻

Waein   Korean term for "Japanese"   倭人

Waein changna tŭngnok   Korean book title   倭人作挈謄錄

Waein kuch'ŏng tŭngnok   Korean book title   倭人求請謄錄

Waenom   Korean term for "Japanese bastards"   倭奴

Wae ryomi   Korean term for "provisions for Wae"   倭料米

waga-kuni   Japanese term for "our country"   我國

Wakan   Japanese term for Japan House   和館

[*Wakan*] *mainikki*]   Japanese book title   [和館]每日記

Wakō   (K: *Waegu*) Japanese term for "Japanese pirates"   倭寇

Waniura   Tsushima harbor name   鰐浦

wataru-tokoro   Japanese term for "the place we cross to"   渡所

Wei shu   Chinese book title   魏書

wŏngongmok   Korean term for "gross official cotton"   元公木

wŏnjangbu kyŏl   Korean term for "registered land," or "total arable land"   元帳付結

Wŏn Man-sŏk   Korean personal name   元萬石

Xia   Chinese dynasty   夏

Xuan Wang   Zhou king   成湯

yakjo   Korean term for "Agreement" with Tsushima   約條

Yanagawa Kennosuke   Japanese personal name   柳川權之助

Yanagawa Shigenobu   Japanese personal name   柳川調信

Yanagawa Shigeoki   Japanese personal name   柳川調興

yang or ryang   Korean term for unit of copper and silver cash, one tael or unit of cash, equivalent to 10 *chŏn*   兩

yangban   general Korean term for scholar-bureaucrat   兩班

yangnyŏ   Korean term for "freeborn commoner woman"   良女

yasa   (J: *yashi*) Korean term for "unofficial history"   野史

yashi   (K: *yasa*) Japanese term for "unofficial history"   野史

yashiki Japanese term for daimyō residence 屋敷

yashū Tsushima holding in Tochigi-ken in the Kantō region, 栃木県 野州

Yedanjik Korean term for "Ceremonial Attendants" 禮單直

Yi Ch'ang-jŏng Korean personal name 李昌庭

Yi Chin-su Korean personal name 李進壽

Yi Chi-sŏk Korean personal name 李之石

Yi Chong-jik Korean personal name 李宗稙

Yi Chŏng-jung Korean personal name 李政中

Yi Ch'ŏn-wŏl Korean personal name 李賤月

Yi Hang Korean personal name 李沆

Yi Hong-mang Korean personal name 李弘望

Yi Hwang (T'oegye) Korean personal name 李滉(退溪)

Yi Kŭng-ik Korean personal name 李肯翊

Yi Maeng-hyu Korean personal name 李盟休

Yi Man-ung Korean personal name 李萬雄

Yi Myŏng-wŏn Korean personal name 李明元

Yi nae-gŭn-nae Korean personal name 李乃斤乃

Yi Pun-i Korean personal name 李紛伊

Yi Se-jae Korean personal name 李世載

Yi Si-man Korean personal name 李時萬

Yi Sŏ-chang Korean personal name 李恕長

Yi Sŏng-gye Korean personal name 李成桂

Yi Tŏk-p'il Korean personal name 李德弼

Yi To-nam Korean personal name 李圖南

Yi Wŏn-chŏng Korean personal name 李元禎

Yi Yang-jŏng Korean personal name 李養鼎

Yi Yu-sin Korean personal name 李裕身

Yi Yu-sŏng Korean personal name 李惟誠

yoi Japanese term for "lingering (martial) prowess or power" 余威

Yŏji tosŏ Korean book title 輿地圖書

Yŏkkwan Korean term for "Interpreters employed in the Sayŏg'wŏn' 譯官

Yŏkkwan sang'ŏn tŭngnok Korean book title 譯官上言謄錄

yokome Japanese constable 横目

yok'ong Korean term for "provisions-beans" 料太

Yŏllyŏsil kisul Korean book title 燃藜室記述

yomi Korean term for "provisions-rice" 料米

Yŏmp'o Korean harbor name 鹽浦

Yŏn[hyang] Taech'ŏng Banquet Hall outside the north wall of the Waegwan 宴[享]大廳

Yŏngdo-do Korean island name in Pusan harbor 影島島

Yŏngdŏk Korean county name 盈德

Yongdu-san Korean mountain name in Tongnae 龍頭山

Yŏnghae Korean county name 寧海

Yŏng'il Korean county name 迎日

Yongjae ch'onghwa Korean book title 慵齋叢話

Yŏngjŏ north Kyŏngsang Province area south of the mountains 嶺底

Yŏngjung ch'u pusa   Korean term for "First Minister, Sr. 1 rank, Office of Ministers Without Portfolio"   領中樞府事

Yŏngnam   Korean regional name   嶺南

Yŏngnamch'ŏng saye   Korean book title   嶺南廳事例

Yŏngnam kamyŏng saye   Korean book title   嶺南監營事例

Yŏngnam taedong samok   Korean book title   嶺南大同事目

Yŏngnam ŭpchi   Korean book title   嶺南邑誌

Yongsŏng   Korean county name   龍城

yŏng songno   Korean term for "permanent enslavement"   永屬奴

Yŏnhae   Kyŏngsang Province coastal counties that supported the Waegwan   沿海

Yotsuhō-gin   Japanese term for "20 percent purity silver"   四宝銀

yunaejin chapt'al   Korean term for "tax relief for miscellaneous disasters"   流來陳雜頉

Yun Chang-yŏl   Korean personal name   尹長烈

Yun Chi-wan   Korean personal name   君趾完

yungmul   Korean term for "sacks for rice and supplies for ship repairs"   陸物

Yun Haeng   Korean personal name   尹行

Yun In-bok   Korean personal name   尹仁復

Yunjung   Korean place name   允中

Yun Mun-kŏ   Korean personal name   尹文擧

Yu Sim   Korean personal name   柳頉

Yūtani Kōhiro   Japanese personal name   柚谷康廣

Yuwŏn'gwan   Korean building name   柔遠館

NOTES

1 INTRODUCTION

1 Amenomori Hōshū, "Kōrin teisei," in Izumi Chōichi *et al.*, ed., *Hōshū gaikō kankei shiryō kanshū, Amenomori Hōshū zenshū,* 3 (Suita: Kansai Daigaku), 1982: 82. Also see: Amenomori Hōshū, *Kōrin teisei,* folio 73b–75a, MS 15 in Amenomori Hōshū bunko (Amenomori Hōshū-an, Shiga-ken, Ika-gun, Takamatsuki-chō, Amenomori-mura); Amenomori Hōshū, *Kōrin teisei,* folio 42a–43a, cho 51, na 167, ko che 16859 ho 1 chaek in Hanguk kungnip tosŏgwan.

2 *Asahi shinbun,* 25 May 1990.

3 Kamigaito Kenichi, *Amenomori Hōshū: Genroku Kyōhō no kokusaijin* (Tōkyō: Chūkō Shinsho), 1989. Scholarship on Hōshū has significantly advanced since the early 1990s. For example, see: Yonetani Hitoshi, "Amenomori Hōshū no tai-Chōsen gaikō: 'seishin no kō' no rinen to jittai," *Chōsen gakuhō,* 148 (1993.7): 1–32, and Izumi Chōichi, *Tsushima han hanju Amenomori Hōshū no kiso-teki kenkyū* (Suita: Kansai daigaku shuppanbu), 1997.

4 Arthur O. Lovejoy, *The Great Chain of Being: A Study of the History of an Idea* (Cambridge, Massachusetts: Harvard University Press), 1936: 21.

5 Arthur O. Lovejoy, p. 19.

6 Jacob Burckhardt, *The Civilization of the Renaissance in Italy,* translated by S.G.C. Middlemore and revised and edited by Irene Gordon, (New York: The New American Library), 1960 (first published in German in 1860).

7 Lucien Febvre, *The Problem of Unbelief in the Sixteenth Century, the Religion of Rabelais,* translated by Beatrice Gottlieb, (Cambridge, Massachusetts: Harvard University Press), 1982 (first published in French in 1942).

8 Erwin Panofsky, *Gothic Architecture and Scholasticism* (New York: The World Publishing Company), 1957 (first published in 1951).

9 Ha U-bong, *Chosŏn hugi sirhakja ŭi Ilbon'gwan yŏn'gu* (Seoul: Iljisa), 1989.

10 Abe Yoshio, *Nihon Shūshi-gaku to Chōsen* (Tōkyō: Tōkyō Daigaku Shuppan Kai), 1965 (second edition, 1971). In English, see: Abe Yoshio, "Development of Neo-Confucianism in Japan, Korea, and China: A Comparative Study," *Acta Asiatica,* 19 (1970): 16–39. For a critique of Abe's arguments, see Willem Jan Boot, "The Adoption and Adaptation of Neo-Confucianism in Japan: The Role of Fujiwara Seika and Hayashi Razan" (Proefschrift, Rijksuniversiteit ti Leiden, Netherlands), 1982. See also Willem Jan Boot, "Yi T'oegye and Japan," *Korea Journal,* 22 (1982.2): 16–30. For a view on the question of intellectual exchange from Japan to Korea, see Mark Setton, "Chŏng Tasan and the 'Kogaku,'" *Oriens Extremus,* 33:2 (1990): 57–68; Mark Setton, *Chŏng Yagyong: Korea's Challenge to Orthodox Neo-Confucianism* (Albany: SUNY Press), 1997. For comparisons of societal responses to Neo-Confucianism, see Thomas Hosuck Kang, "The Making of Confucian Societies in Tokugawa Japan and Yi Korea: A Comparative Analysis of the Behavior Patterns in Accepting the Foreign Ideology, Neo-Confucianism" (unpublished Ph.D. dissertation at the American University), 1971, and Kang Chae-ŏn, "Chōsen no Jukyō – Nihon no Jukyō," *Sanzenri,* 19 (1979): 28–36.

11 Etsuko Hae-Jin Kang, *Diplomacy and Ideology in Japanese–Korean Relations: From the Fifteenth to the Eighteenth Century* (London: Macmillan Press Ltd.), 1997.

12 Wars of the twenty-first century will probably revert to a more common historical pattern and erupt over the control of natural resources or population or land, the pursuit of treasure, or sectarian or religious division. Technology may also obviate the need for mass mobilizations while mass populations will become the targets.

13 The latter are also called "modernists" for their argument that concern with identity is an invention of modernity and is designed to protect certain political and economic interests. For an overview of theories of ethnicity, see Marcus Banks, *Ethnicity: Anthropological Constructions* (New York: Routledge), 1996: 11–48. See also David A. Chappell, "Ethnogenesis and Frontiers," *Journal of World History*, 4:2 (Fall 1993): 268.

14 Anthony D. Smith, *The Ethnic Origin of Nations* (Oxford: Blackwell Publishers), 1986.

15 Ernest Gellner, *Nationalism* (London: Phoenix), 1997, and Benedict Anderson, *Imagined Communities, revised edition* (London: Verso), 1991.

16 Thongchai Winichakul, *Siam Mapped: A History of the Geo-Body of a Nation* (Honolulu: University of Hawai'i Press), 1994.

17 Liah Greenfeld, *Nationalism: Five Roads to Modernity* (Cambridge, Massachusetts: Harvard University Press), 1992.

18 Greenfeld's emphasis on the primacy of elite intellectuals as definers of identity has been employed rather successfully by JaHyun Kim Haboush who argues that the Korean intellectual elite became nationally mobilized in the 1650s and 1670s over questions of kingly legitimacy and Korea's place in the world. Haboush asserts that here we see the emergence of a "national identity" among the intelligentsia, the vanguard of the larger mentality. JaHyun Kim Haboush, "Constructing the Center: The Ritual Controversy and the Search for a New Identity in Seventeenth-Century Korea," in JaHyun Kim Haboush and Martina Deuchler, ed., *Culture and the State in Late Chosŏn Korea* (Cambridge, Massachusetts: Harvard University Press), 1999: 46–90.

19 The problem is apparent to a lesser extent in Thongchai Winichakul, since his concern is with the definition of boundaries, and he has given us a clear idea of pre-modern Siamese boundaries. Nevertheless, the boundaries are the objects on which the center acts.

20 Fredrik Barth, "Introduction" in *Ethnic Groups and Boundaries: The Social Organization of Culture Difference* (Oslo: Pensumtjeneste), 1994: 29 (first published in 1969).

21 For a concise survey of anthropological studies of borders, see: Thomas M. Wilson and Hastings Donnan, "Nation, state and identity at international borders" in Thomas M. Wilson and Hastings Donnan, ed., *Border Identities: Nation and State at International Frontiers* (Cambridge: Cambridge University Press), 1998: 1–30. See in particular p. 4.

22 Wilson and Donnan, p. 7.

23 For a history of the French word for frontier, see Lucien Febvre, "*Frontière*: The Word and the Concept" in Peter Burke, ed., *A New Kind of History: From the Writings of Lucien Febvre* (London: Routledge and Kegan Paul), 1973: 208–218.

24 Peter Sahlins, *Boundaries: The Making of France and Spain in the Pyrenees* (Berkeley: University of California Press), 1989. For a concise summation, see Peter Sahlins, "State Formation and National Identity in the Catalan Borderlands during the Eighteenth and Nineteenth Centuries" in Thomas M. Wilson and Hastings Donnan, ed., *Border Identities: Nation and State at International Frontiers* (Cambridge: Cambridge University Press), 1998: 31–61.

25 Sahlins in Wilson and Donnan, p. 33.

26 Sahlins in Wilson and Donnan, p. 42.

27 For a broad survey of borderland studies and their theoretical typologies, see Michiel Baud and Willem van Schendel, "Toward a Comparative History of Borderlands," *Journal of World History*, 8:2 (Fall 1997): 211–242. Baud and van Schendel argue that "[t]raditional, border studies have adopted a view from the center; we argue for a view from the periphery" (p. 212). The problem is defining the periphery.

28 The second part of their meaning seems related to Fredrik Barth and the postmodern metaphorical use of his work to indicate de-territorialized identities (e.g. Pakistanis in Britain).

29 Baud and van Schendel, p. 216. Here Baud and van Schendel outline typographies of border regions. They refer to Oscar Martínez's four models of borderlands: alienated

(no exchange), coexistent (contact but unfriendly state relations), interdependent (symbiosis with considerable flow of material and people), and integrated (all barriers eliminated). In this scheme, the border between Chosŏn Korea and Tsushima was most often an interdependent borderland. Borderlands come in various spatial dimensions: heartland, intermediate, and outer. The heartland and intermediate area in the present study would have been Tsushima and Pusan/Tongnae. The outer borderland would have been Kyūshū and Kyŏngsang Province. Finally, they describe borderlands over time: embryonic, infant, adolescent, adult, declining, defunct, and hidden. Over the period of this study, the borderland was fully developed, and, as will become apparent, differences were clearly etched.

30 Arai Hakuseki, "Oritaku shiba no ki" in Miyazaki Michio, ed., *Teihon Oritaku shiba no ki shakugi zoteihan* (Tōkyō: Kondō Shuppansha), 1985: 113–117. See also Joyce Ackroyd, trans., *Told Round a Brushwood Fire: The Autobiography of Arai Hakuseki* (Princeton: Princeton University Press), 1979: 62. Ackroyd's translation of the relevant passage is very accurate except: 1) the Chesulgwan was not a translator but a temporary appointment to the third highest office in the embassy responsible for formal or ceremonial writing for the envoy; rendered as "Auxiliary Envoy and Document Official" or "Counselor." For English translations of the various Korean officials, see Miao-Ling Tjoa, "Sakoku: The Full Range of Tokugawa Foreign Relations?" in Erika de Poorter, ed., *As the Twig is Bent . . . Essays in Honour of Frits Vos* (Amsterdam: J.C. Gieben), 1990: 220, and James B. Lewis, "Beyond Sakoku: The Cost of the Korean Envoy to Edo and the Diary of Shin Yu-han," (unpublished M.A. thesis, University of Hawai'i), 1983: 54. Also certain names in Ackryod's translation are mistaken and should be Sŏng Wan, Yi Tam-ryŏng, and Hong Se-t'ae.

31 Toshio G. Tsukahira, *Feudal Control in Tokugawa Japan: The Sankin Kōtai System* (Cambridge, Massachusetts: Harvard East Asian Monographs, No. 20), 1970: 75–80. Tsukahira mentions 4,000 in the Kaga-han retinue for the Genroku period (1688–1703) (p. 76), but no more than 1,500 typically appeared in the Kaga retinue by 1747 (p. 80).

32 Kim Hyŏn-ju, "Kinsei Ni-Chō bunka kōryūshi no kenkyū: Chōsen Tsūshinshi no bajōsai to kenjōuma" (unpublished M.A. thesis at Kyūshū University, Bungakubu, Chōsenshi Kenkyūshitsu), 1994.

33 Shin Ki-su, "Chōsen Tsūshinshi no atarashii shiryō: ema, eka, nikki . . . ," *Kankoku bunka*, 7:8 (1985.8): 21–27; Sin Ki-su "Mitsukatta Chōsen Tsūshinshi no ema: minshū dōshi no kōkan," *Mirai*, 227 (1985.8): 2–7, and Sin Ki-su "Matsuri no naka no Chōsen Tsūshinshi," *Kankoku bunka*, 7:11 (1985.11): 15–24. In English, see: Ronald P. Toby, "Carnival of the Aliens: Korean Embassies in Edo-period Art and Popular Culture," *Monumenta Nipponica*, 41:4 (1986): 443. That *ema* is in the Fukuhara Hachimangu of Otawara, painted in 1866. Toby considers the T'ongsinsa in the popular cultures of the *emaki*, *ema*, and festivals and concludes that, by the Genroku period (1688–1704), the T'ongsinsa motif had become ubiquitous. In the particular case of this *ema*, he argues that the date of its commission, 1866, indicates that the patron or patrons probably wished to recall a more stable international environment when the power of the *bakufu* was efficacious abroad. For a brief history of artistic exchange and a short bibliography of works in Korea and Japan see Yi Chin-hŭi, "Tōjin odori to Chōsen yama" and Yoshida Hiroyuki, "Chōsen Tsūshinshi no kaiga" in Eizō bunka kyōkai, ed., *Edo jidai no Chōsen Tsūshinshi* (Tōkyō: Mainichi Shinbunsha), 1979; Kim Tal-su, *Nihon no naka no Chōsen bunka*, 3 (Tōkyō: Kōdansha), 1972; An Hwi-jun, "Hanil hoehwa kwangye 1,500 nyŏn," in Kungnip chung'ang pangmulgwan, ed., *Chosŏn sidae T'ongsinsa* (Seoul: Kungnip Chung'ang Pangmulgwan), 1986: 125–147. See also Burglind Jungmann, "Confusing Traditions: Elements of the Korean An Kyon School in Early Japanese Nanga Landscape Painting," *Artibus Asiae*, 55:3–4 (1995): 303–318; Burglind Jungmann, "Ike Taiga's Letter to Kim Yusong and His Approach to Korean Landscape Painting," *The Review of Korean Studies*, 1 (September 1998): 180–195.

34 Yi Hun inaugurated the field in an article entitled, "Chosŏn hugi Taemado ŭi p'yoryumin songhwan kwa tae-Il kwangye," *Kuksa'gwan nonch'ong*, 26 (1991.10): 207–239. Recently, she consolidated much of her research in a monograph entitled *Chosŏn hugi p'yoryumin kwa Han-Il kwangye* (Seoul: Kukhak Charyowŏn), 2000.

35 Tashiro Kazui, *Kinsei Ni-Chō bōekishi no kenkyū* (Tōkyō: Sōbunsha), 1981. Ronald P. Toby, *State and Diplomacy in Early Modern Japan: Asia in the Development of the Tokugawa Bakufu* (Princeton: Princeton University Press), 1984. Arano Yasunori, *Kinsei Nihon to Higashi Ajia* (Tōkyō: Tōkyō Daigaku Shuppankai), 1988.

36 Yi Hun, "Chosŏn hugi Taemado ŭi p'yoryumin songhwan kwa tae-Il kwangye," pp. 218–219.

37 Yi Hun, "Chosŏn hugi Taemado ŭi p'yoryumin songhwan kwa tae-Il kwangye," pp. 218–219.

38 Yi Hun, "Chosŏn hugi Taemado ŭi p'yoryumin songhwan kwa tae-Il kwangye," p. 209.

39 For a similar description of how castaways were handled, see Kim, Yong-uk, "Pusan Waegwan ko," *Han-Il Munhwa*, 1:2 (1962.12): 113 ff. With no statistical evidence, however, Kim asserts that Japanese castaways outnumbered Korean castaways.

40 Kibe Kazuaki, "Chōsen hyōryūmin no kyūjo-sōkan ni miru Ni-Chō ryōkoku no sesshoku: Chōsen tsūshi no mondai to hyōryūmin no sōjō jiken o chūshin toshite," *Shikyō En Marge de l'Histoire*, 26 (1993.6): 36–54.

41 Kibe Kazuaki, "Chōsen hyōryūmin no kyūjo-sōkan ni miru Ni-Chō ryōkoku no sesshoku," p. 48.

42 J: *seishin*, K: *sŏngsin*. See Gaikō-bu 11, Chōsen 4, *Koji Ruien* (Tōkyō: Yoshikawa Kōbunkan), 1983: 809.

43 Nakada Yasunao and Nakamura Tadashi, ed., *Kiyō gundan* (Tōkyō: Kondō Shuppansha), 1974: 69–71. Kiyō is another name for Nagasaki.

44 Nakada Yasunao and Nakamura Tadashi, ed., *Kiyō gundan*, p. 70.

45 Kibe Kazuaki, "Chōsen hyōryūmin no kyūjo-sōkan ni miru Ni-Chō ryōkoku no sesshoku," p. 46.

46 More recently, a number of studies have been produced on aspects of the castaway question. In particular, see Ikeuchi Satoshi, *Kinsei Nihon to Chōsen hyōryūmin* (Tōkyō: Rinsen Shoten), 1998, and Han-Il kwangyesa hakhoe, ed., *Chosŏn sidae Han-Il p'yoryumin yŏn'gu* (Seoul: Kukhak Charyowŏn), 2001. Another promising approach to the problem of castaways and their impact on the Chosŏn world view is provided by Yun Ch'i-pu, *Hanguk haeyang munhak yŏn'gu* (Seoul: Hangmunsa), 1994. Yun approaches castaway records as a form of travel literature. His book offers analysis and a photolithographic reprint of the *P'yomin taehwa* (1845) by Pak Wŏn-ryang, a record in Korean and Japanese of the interrogation of the castaways in Japan.

47 Maurice Courant, "Un Établissement Japonais en Corée: Pusan depuis le XV siècle," *Annales Coloniales* (Paris) (15 Août-1 Octobre 1904), reprinted in Centre d'Études Coréennes, Collège de France, ed., *Cahiers d'Études Coréennes, 1, Études Coréennes de Maurice Courant* (Paris: Éditions du Léopard d'Or), 1983: 253–289. Later studies include: Takahashi Shōnosuke, *Sō-ke to Chōsen* (Keijō: Hokunai Insatsujo), 1920; Takeda Katsuzō, "Ni-Sen bōeki-shi jō no Sampo to Wakan," *Shigaku*, 1–3 (1911.5): 51–82; Oda Seigo, "Pusan no Wakan no setsumon ni tsuite," *Chōsen*, 125 (1926): 152–160; George McCune, "Korean Relations with China and Japan, 1800–1864," (unpublished Ph.D. thesis submitted to the University of California at Berkeley), 1941, especially "Chapter VIII: The Japanese Depot at Fusan and Trade," and George McCune, "The Exchange of Envoys between Korea and Japan during the Tokugawa Period," *Far Eastern Quarterly*, 5:3 (1946.5), reprinted in John A. Harrison, ed., *Japan, Volume 2, Enduring Scholarship selected from the Far Eastern Quarterly – The Journal of Asian Studies, 1941–1971* (Tucson: The University of Arizona Press), 1972: 83–100; Kim Yong-uk, "Pusan Waegwan ko," *Han-Il Munhwa*, 1:2 (1962.12): 53–116; Yi Wan-yŏng, "Tongnae-bu mit Waegwan ŭi haengjŏng sogo," *Hangdo Pusan*, 2 (1963): 11–75; Kim Ŭi-hwan, "Ri-Chō jidai ni okeru Fuzan no wakan no kigen to hensen," *Nihon bunkashi kenkyū*, 2 (Tezukayama Tanki Daigaku) (1977.12): 1–17; Kim Ŭi-hwan, "Fuzan wakan no shokkan kōsei to sono kinō ni tsuite: Ri-chō no tai Nichi seisaku no ichi rikai no tame ni," *Chōsen gakuhō*, 108 (1983): 111–145; Kim Ŭi-hwan, "Tsushima shima Sō-ke monjo *Wakan jikō* ni tsuite," *Nihon bunkashi kenkyū*, 5 (1983.5): 1–14; Kim Ŭi-hwan, "Fuzan wakan bōeki no kenkyū: 15 seki kara 17 seki ni kakete no bōeki keitai o chūshin ni," *Chōsen gakuhō*, 127 (1988): 43–72.

2 TSUSHIMA'S IDENTITY AND THE POST-IMJIN
WAERAN JAPAN HOUSE

1 Amenomori Hōshū, *Kōrin teisei*, folio 4a, MS 15 in Amenomori Hōshū bunko (Amenomori Hōshū-an, Shiga-ken, Ika-gun, Takatsuki-chō, Amenomori-mura).
2 "Dong yi chuan," *Wei shu*.
3 Gari Ledyard, "Galloping Along With the Horseriders: Looking for the Founders of Japan," *Journal of Japanese Studies*, 1:2 (Spring, 1975): 217–254.
4 Tanaka Takeo, *Wakō: Umi no rekishi* (Tōkyō: Kyoikusha), 1982; Benjamin H. Hazard, "Japanese Marauding in Medieval Korea: The Wakō Impact on Later Koryŏ" (unpublished Ph.D. dissertation, University of California, Berkeley), 1967.
5 Son Hong-yŏl, "Taemado chŏngbŏl," in Hanguk Chŏngsin Munhwa Yŏn'guwŏn, ed., *Hanguk minjok munhwa taepaekkwa sajŏn*, 6 (Sŏngnam: Hanguk Chŏngsin Munhwa Yŏn'guwŏn), 1991: 376.
6 Nakamura Hidetaka, *Ni-Sen kankeishi no kenkyū*, 1 (Tōkyō: Yoshikawa Kōbunkan), 1965: 227–310.
7 Kim Yong-uk, "Pusan Waegwan ko," *Han-Il munhwa*, 1:2 (1962.12): 53–116; Yi Hyŏnjong, *Chosŏn chŏngi tae-Il kyosŏpsa yŏn'gu* (Seoul: Hanguk Yŏn'guwŏn), 1964; Nakamura Hidetaka, *Ni-Sen kankeishi no kenkyū*, vol. 1, and Kenneth R. Robinson, "Policies of Practicality: The Chosŏn Court's Regulation of Contact with Japanese and Jurchens" (unpublished Ph.D. dissertation, University of Hawai'i), 1997.
8 Nakamura Hidetaka, *Ni-Sen kankeishi no kenkyū*, vol. 1, p. 231.
9 Nakamura Hidetaka, *Ni-Sen kankeishi no kenkyū*, vol. 1, p. 491.
10 Nakamura Hidetaka, *Ni-Sen kankeishi no kenkyū*, vol. 1, pp. 481–498. For a description in English, see: Kenneth R. Robinson, "From Raiders to Traders: Border Security and Border Control in Early Choson, 1392–1450," *Korean Studies*, 16 (1992): 101–108.
11 Kenneth R. Robinson, "Policies of Practicality: The Chosŏn Court's Regulation of Contact with Japanese and Jurchens" (unpublished Ph.D. dissertation, University of Hawai'i), 1997: 82–92.
12 For the texts of these agreements, see *T'ongmun'gwanji*, 5:24–25. Chapters 3 and 4 offer further discussion of these agreements in relation to trade.
13 Nakamura Hidetaka, *Ni-Sen kankeishi no kenkyū*, vol. 1, p. 491.
14 Nakamura Hidetaka, *Ni-Sen kankeishi no kenkyū*, vol. 1, pp. 494–495.
15 Nakamura Hidetaka, *Ni-Sen kankeishi no kenkyū*, vol. 1, p. 643; Murai Shōsuke, *Chūsei Wajin-den* (Tōkyō: Iwanami Shoten), 1993.
16 Nakamura Hidetaka, *Ni-Sen kankeishi no kenkyū*, vol. 1, p. 498.
17 Oda Seigo, "Rishi Chōsen jidai ni okeru Wakan no hensen: nakazuku Zetsueido Wakan ni tsuite," in *Chōsen Shina bunka no kenkyū* (Tōkyō: Toe Shoin), 1929: 107; Nakamura Hidetaka, *Ni-Sen kankeishi no kenkyū*, vol. 1, p. 498, and Kim Yong-uk, "Pusan Waegwan ko," p. 58. Kim reports that three officials and 30 sailors were killed. Kim also comments that Pusan was considered more defensible from Japanese pirates.
18 Tashiro Kazui, "Kanei roku nen (Jinso 7, 1629), Tsushima shisetsu no Chōsen koku *Gojōkyō no toki mainikki* to sono haikei," in three parts, *Chōsen gakuhō*, 96 (1980.7): 85–94; *Chōsen gakuhō*, 98 (1981.1): 63–76; *Chōsen gakuhō*, 101 (1981.10): 51–108; a transcript of the diary can be found in *Chōsen gakuhō*, 95 (1980.4): 73–115. See also Ronald Toby, *State and Diplomacy in Early Modern Japan: Asia in the Development of the Tokugawa Bakufu* (Princeton: Princeton University Press), 1984: 116–118.
19 Nakamura Hidetaka, *Ni-Sen kankeishi no kenkyū*, 3 (Tōkyō: Yoshikawa Kōbunkan), 1969: 253 ff. For a record of Ieyasu instructing Yanagawa in 1599 to begin negotiations, see Tanaka Takeo and Tashiro Kazui, ed., *Chōsen tsūkō daiki* (Tōkyō: Meicho Shuppan), 1978, fascicle 4, p. 147. This is a typeset version of Matsuura Masatada, *Chōsen tsūkō daiki*, MS in Nagasaki Kenritsu Tsushima Rekishi Minzoku Shiryōkan, Kiroku rui 1, Hyōsho satsugata, N Chōsen kankei, 3 Chōsen kankei shoseki, 1, 10 volumes. For a detailed discussion in English, based on these works, of the re-establishment of relations between Korea and Japan, see Ronald Toby, *State and Diplomacy in Early Modern Japan*, pp. 25–44. Also see *Tsūkō sōron*, Hanguk Kuksa P'yŏnch'an Wiwŏnhoe Chong-ka munsŏ kirok ryu,

cat. no. 4311, for a detailed record of the re-establishment of Korea–Tsushima relations from 1599 to 1609.

20 Nakamura Hidetaka, *Ni-Sen kankeishi no kenkyū*, vol. 3, p. 291 ff.; Tashiro Kazui, *Kinsei Ni-Chō tsūkō bōekishi no kenkyū*, p. 44 ff.; Ronald Toby, *State and Diplomacy in Early Modern Japan*, p. 39 ff.

21 Osa Setsuko, *Chūsei Ni-Chō kankei to Tsushima* (Tōkyō: Yoshikawa Kōbunkan), 1987 and, more recently, "Jūgoseiki kōhanno Ni-Ehō bocki no keitai", in Nakamura Tadshi, ed., *Sakoku to kokusai kankei* (Tokyo: Yoshikawa kōbunkan), 1997: 2–30, for a detailed examination of late fourteenth- and fifteenth-century Tsushima relations with Korea. For a discussion in English, see: Kenneth R. Robinson, "The Tsushima Governor and Regulation of Japanese Access to Chŏson in the Fifteenth and Sixteenth Centuries", *Korean Studies*, 20 (1996): 25–50 and "Policies of Practicality: The Chosŏn Court's Regulation of Contact with Japanese and Jurchens" (unpublished Ph.D. dissertation, University of Hawai'i), 1997. Osa examines in detail the political position of the lord of Tsushima between Korea and Japan. Robinson refigures medieval Northeast Asian relations by examining Tsushima's Korean contacts within a system of overlapping administrative zones through which envoys from the Japanese islands travel up to the Korean king's capital. Osa and Robinson demonstrate that state-to-state relations were but one form of contact between the Korean Peninsula and the Japanese archipelago, and by no means the most important form of contact. Their approach harkens back to discussions of "dual diplomacy" (national and sub-national), but their emphasis is to reverse the importance of the levels examined. They argue that local diplomacy was most critical to trade, and that even state-to-state relations were more affected by local diplomacy than the reverse. Although their frame of reference for Japanese envoys is post-Kamakura and pre-Tokugawa, their arguments hold true for the post-1600 period: the complex and irregular variety of Japanese envoys (some illegitimate), the Korea-centered structures devised to manage these envoys, and the primacy of Tsushima envoys.

22 *Chŭngjŏng kyorinji*, 4:1a–2a. The fascicle and folio numbers are for the 1998 edition.

23 Tashiro Kazui, *Kakikaerareta kokusho* (Tōkyō: Chūō Shinsho), 1983.

24 Tashiro Kazui, *Kakikaerareta kokusho*, 1983, for a description of the forgeries and the lawsuit between Kagenao and Yoshinari. For a description in English see: Ronald Toby, *State and Diplomacy in Early Modern Japan*, pp. 76–97. For information in the system of rotating priests, or the *Iteian rinban*, see Izumi Chōichi, "Tsushima Iteian rinbansō Egaku Gensaku ni tsuite," in Yokota Kenichi sensei kanreki kinenkai, ed., *Yokota Kenichi sensei kanreki kinen: Nihonshi ronsō* (Suita: Yokota Kenichi Sensei Kanreki Kinenkai), 1976: 753–766; Izumi Chōichi, "Tenryūji dai 209 sei: – Chūzan Genchu oshō ni tsuite: Tsushima Iteian rinban jidai o chūshin ni shite," in Osaka Rekishi Gakkai, ed., *Historia*, 63 (1973.6): 79–89; Izumi Chōichi, "Tenryūji 204 sei – Ranshitsu Genshin oshō ni tsuite – Empō 3–5 nen: Tsushima Iteian rinban jidai no kōjitsu," *Tsushima Fudoki*, 11 (1974.10): 29–51; Izumi Chōichi, "Tenryūji 216 sei – Zuigen Tōtei oshō ni tsuite: Tsushima Iteian rinban jidai no kōjitsu," *Tsushima Fudoki*, 12 (1975.10): 55–75; Izumi Chōichi, "Edo jidai, Ni-Chō gaikō no ichi sokumen: Tsushima Iteian rinban seido to Kankei shiryō ni tsuite," *Kansai Daigaku Tōzai Gakujutsu kenkyūjo kiyō*, 10 (1977.9): 23–44; Izumi Chōichi, "Iteian dai 2 sei – Kihaku Genpō oshō no bannen: Banji gan-Kanbun gannen, shamengo no Kyō-Ōsaka ni okeru nichinichi," in Tsuda Hideo sensei koki kinenkai, ed., *Tsuda Hideo sensei koki kinen: Hōken shakai to kindai* (Kyōto: Dōhōsha Shuppan), 1989: 340–360. Izumi has found that the priests generally stayed out of Korean matters.

25 Concerning the question of normalization, Ronald Toby and most others consider normal relations to have been re-established from the first Reply and Prisoner Repatriation Envoy of 1607. Toby, in particular, argues that since normalization occurred from this time and established the broad framework of relations between Korea and Japan, Tsushima was able to negotiate the 1609 Kiyu Agreement allowing the island people to trade with Korea once again. Toby's argument is essentially correct in that the 1607 envoy again regularized relations allowing for negotiation, but if we define normalization as a return to the status quo before the Imjin Waeran, we must await the dispatch of the first post-war Communication Envoy (T'ongsinsa) in 1636. All of the envoys prior to the Imjin Waeran

NOTES

were called by this term. Thus, from the Korean perspective, relations were not actually normalized until 1636. Logic might dictate then that the broad relationship between the *bakufu* and the Korean government was not particularly linked to Tsushima making Agreements with Korea. In fact, since the Ōnin War, Korea did not seem averse to making Agreements with Tsushima regardless of what relations Korea had with the Ashikaga *bakufu*. We should not expect the immediate post-Imjin Waeran period to have been too different. See: Toby, above, note 13, p. 41. For details and analysis of the 1636 envoy, see Miyake Hidetoshi, *Kinsei Ni-Chō kankeishi no kenkyū* (Tōkyō: Bunken Shuppan), 1986: 241–280. Miyake points out that the circumstances of the 1636 envoy were a good deal more complicated than depicted here. Principally, the Manchus posed a serious threat, and this weighed heavily on the Korean minds. Also, the envoys were commissioned to investigate the Japanese situation for military and political threats to Korea, and this illustrates the basic suspicions still harbored towards Japan.

26 Key-huik Kim, *The Last Phase of the East Asian World Order: Korea, Japan, and the Chinese Empire, 1860–1882* (Berkeley: University of California Press), 1980: 91–109. Ōshima's position paper to the Young Turks around Katsu Kaishū can be found in his *Chōsen koku goyōken kenbakusho* ("A White Paper Setting Forth His Majesty's Government's [*bakufu*] Business [regarding] Korea"), 1864.6 entry in Yamada Hōkoku zenshū kankōkai, ed., *Hōkoku sensei nenpu* (Tōkyō: Yamada Hōkoku Zenshū Kankōkai), 1951: 233–241. Here are enunciated the main points that will re-appear in the debates within the Meiji government over Korean policy. I would like to thank Ms. Kim Hyŏn-ju for bringing this important document to my attention.

27 *Samguk sagi*, 3:5a.

28 Inoue Hideo, trans., *Samguk sagi* (Tōkyō: Heibonsha), 1980: 90. Inoue Hideo argues that the name Tsushima could have been added to the passage in later centuries, so that Kim Pu-sik's transmission is of a corrupted tradition.

29 *Sejong sillok*, 4:14a–15a (1419/6/9).

30 *Sinjŭng tongguk yŏji sŭngnam*, 23:3, Tongnae, sanch'ŏn entry.

31 Ŏ Suk-kwŏn, *P'aegwan chapki* (Taepuk: Tongbang Munhwa Sŏguk), 1971, vol. 8, 11. Compare with: Peter H. Lee, trans., *A Korean Storyteller's Miscellany: The P'aegwan Chapki of O Sukkwon* (Princeton, N.J.: Princeton University Press), 1989: 81: "Tsushima formerly belonged to Korea. It is not known when it was occupied by the Japanese. The island is divided into eight counties."

32 *Yŏllyŏsil kisul*, pyŏljip, fascicle 18, pyŏnguk chŏngo, Waeguk entry, in *Kugyŏk Yŏllyŏsil kisul* (Seoul: Minjok Munhwa Ch'ujinhoe), 1967: vol. 11, p. 414 (Korean trans.), p. 768 (Chinese).

33 *Tongnae-bu ŭpchi* in Kim Tong-ch'ŏl et al., ed., *Tongnae saryo*, 2 (Seoul: Yŏgang Ch'ulp'ansa), 1989. 1759 *ŭpchi*: sanch'ŏn susan entry, p. 211. 1832 *ŭpchi*: tosŏ Chŏlyŏng-do entry, p. 276. 1871 *ŭpchi*: tosŏ Chŏlyŏng-do entry, p. 385.

34 Suyama Donō, *Taikan Zakki*, in *Nihon keizai sōsho*, fascicle 13, (Tōkyō: Nihon Keizai Sho Kankōkai), 1915: 373. See also Tashiro Kazui, *Kinsei Ni-Chō tsūkō bōekishi no kenkyū*, p. 142 for discussion of same.

35 For a discussion in English of Hakuseki's motives and arguments, see: Kate Wildman Nakai, *Shogunal Politics: Arai Hakuseki and the Premises of Tokugawa Rule* (Cambridge, Massachusetts: Harvard University Press), 1988: 190–201. For a summation of Hakuseki's intent by a leading Japanese scholar, see Miyazaki Michio, *Arai Hakuseki* (Tōkyō: Yoshikawa Kōbunkan), 1989: 208–215.

36 *Sŭngjŏngwŏn ilgi*, fascicle 461, p. 10d (1711/5/27). See also Ronald P. Toby, "Korean–Japanese Diplomacy in 1711: Sukchong's Court and the Shogun's Title," *Chōsen gakuhō*, 74 (1975.1): 247. The translation is Ronald Toby's.

37 *Tongnae-bu ŭpchi* (Kyujanggak cat.no. 666) (1832) Chingong entry, in *Tongnae saryo*, vol. 2. Here, we see a list of local "tribute" goods from Tongnae to the court. These *chingong* (local tribute) are usually local products, but the list from Tongnae is entirely made up of Japanese products.

38 *17 Segi Kug'ŏ Sajŏn* on *pongjin*, Ch'oganbon, 1676.

39 The following Korean documents take note of the change in terminology, but the response and rationale for the acceptance and use of the terms in this fashion is still unclear:
T'ongmun'gwanji, fascicle 5, kyorin sang, nyŏn'ye songsa, il t'ŭk songsa entry and *Tongnae-
bu chŏpdae samok-ch'o* (Kyujanggak cat. no. 9764), 1635/12 entry. See Nakamura Hidetaka,
Ni-Sen kankeishi no kenkyū, vol. 3, pp. 462–494 for a discussion of the changes made in
terminology and dating. For a discussion of the same, see Tashiro Kazui, *Kinsei Ni-Chō
bōekishi no kenkyū*, p. 149.

40 Kobayashi Hajime, *Tsushima ryō Tashiro baiyakushi* (Saga: Kobayashi Hajime), 1960: 8–11.

41 Tashiro Kazui, *Kinsei Ni-Chō tsūkō bōekishi no kenkyū*, pp. 154–155.

42 Nagasaki Kenshi Hensan Iinkai, ed., *Nagasaki Kenshi: Hansei hen* (Tōkyō: Yoshikawa
Kōbunkan), 1973: 861.

43 See Note 1 above.

44 Higaki Motokichi, "Tsushima ni okeru nuhi to hikan," in a collection by the same author
Kinsei hokubu Kyūshū shohan-shi no kenkyū (Fukuoka: Kyūshū Daigaku Shuppankai), 1991:
169.

45 *Chōsen koku kōbōeki aitodokori on kattemuki on nanjū no omomuki oyobi go naii sōrō tokoro
okane ichi man ryō on haishaku narabi nennen hannō kin on sashinobi no kiroku*, folio 3a–3b,
MS in Kyūshū daigaku bungakubu Kyūshū bunkashi kenkyū shitsu shisetsusō, folio numbers added by myself.

46 *Chōsen koku kōbōeki aitodokori on kattemuki on nanjū no omomuki*, folio 5b.

47 Nagasaki Kenshi Hensan Iinkai, ed., *Nagasaki Kenshi: Hansei hen*, pp. 856–859.

48 Tanaka Takeo, *Taigai kankei to bunka kōryū* (Tōkyō: Shibunkaku Shuppan), 1982: 235–
238, discusses the *kandaka* system, as well as slash-and-burn agriculture on Tsushima.
Tanaka also curiously raises no comparisons with Korean agriculture. Tanaka describes
the *kandaka* system briefly (p. 237):

> In ordinary *han*, following the land survey, the unit of production was the *koku*,
> but Tsushima adopted the *kandaka* system based on the peculiar *kanshaku* law.
> The *kanshaku* law took top grade fields and barley as the standard; the produc-
> tion of paddy and slash-and-burn fields was converted to this standard [barley
> being the chief grain produced on Tsushima]. One *kan* was not a unit of surface
> area. In the surface area of one *cho* (99.173 acres) of top grade land, a *kan* was
> the [surface area needed] to produce the basic production [unit] of 22 *koku* 8 *to*
> of harvested barley from 1 *koku* 5 *to* of seed grain. Taxes were one fourth of that
> or 5 *koku* 7 *to*. One *kan* was 4 *shaku* and below the *shaku*, the *sun*, *bun*, *rin*, and
> *mo* descended in a decimal system. Land ranged from top grade paddy to bottom
> grade slash-and-burn. The surface area of one *kan* and the amount [needed for]
> sowing were fixed [in accordance with the particular grade].

His description is strikingly similar to the Korean *kyŏlbu* system. See also Matsushita
Shirō, "Tsushima han no makidaka to kandaka," in *Keizaishi keieishi ronshū* (Ōsaka: Ōsaka
Keizai Daigaku Nihon Keizai-shi Kenkyūjo Hakkō), 1984: 37–67. Matsushita points out
that *makidaka* or the amount of seed grain required for a particular land parcel was, in the
end, the levying basis for annual grain taxes. The *makidaka* system used in other domains
(e.g. Satsuma *han*) was also employed on Tsushima in the system of cultivation. That is,
according to the amount of seed rice scattered on the fields and paddies, land was indicated
in grades by amounts needed to seed. The *kandaka* system, which appeared from 1625, was
limited only to the purpose of expressing the basis of retainer stipends. Matsushita argues
(p. 57) that the *kandaka* system was used jointly with the *makidaka* system and that "the
kandaka system was of no concern to the peasantry, and of course played no part in
establishing standards for the annual taxes." Korean peasants also measured land by the
amount of grain needed to seed it and even by the amount of time needed to seed and
harvest, but the Korean government measured land in the amount of surface area needed
to produce a fixed unit of production. Matsushita finds a similar socio-economic division
on Tsushima. The peasantry used seed grain and the *han* government used production.
But, like Tanaka, there is no consideration of just why the *kandaka* system was employed

by Tsushima. If, as the *Nagasaki Kenshi* authors (p. 881) argue, the purpose of Tsushima's *kanshaku* law (which established the *kandaka* system) and other cadastral surveys of the early Tokugawa period was to break the link between the *bushi* and the countryside, to achieve a complete separation of the warrior class from the peasantry, and to establish the absolute ascendancy of the domain's lord, the same objectives across almost all other *han* as well, what prompted Tsushima to adopt the *kanshaku* system in preference to the *kokudaka* system?

49 Susan S. Shin, "Some Aspects of Landlord-Tenant Relations in Yi Dynasty Korea," *Occasional Papers on Korea*, 3, ed. by James B. Palais and Margery D. Lang, ACLS-SSRC, (1975.6): 75 for a succinct description in English of a few basic Chosŏn-period measurements.

50 Yi Ki-baek, *A New History of Korea*, trans. by Edward W. Wagner with Edward J. Shultz, (Seoul: Ilchogak), 1984: 188.

51 Ellen Salem Unruh, "The Landowning Slave: A Korean Phenomenon," *Korea Journal*, 16:4 (1976.4): 27–28.

52 Higaki Motokichi, "Tsushima ni okeru nuhi to hikan," pp. 145–175.

53 Yasukōchi Hiroshi, *Tsushima han ni okeru nuhi seido no kenkyū* (Fukuoka: Kyūshū Daigaku Bungakubu Kokushi Kenkyū Shitsu), 1953: 162–192.

54 Higaki Motokichi, "Tsushima ni okeru nuhi to hikan," p. 153.

55 The Japanese term was *eidai yakko*, and the Korean term was *yŏng songno*.

56 Ellen Salem Unruh, "The Landowning Slave: A Korean Phenomenon," *Korea Journal*, 16:4 (1976.4): 27–34; and "The Utilization of Slave Labor in the Koryŏ Period: 918–1392," *Papers of the First International Conference on Korean Studies at the Academy of Korean Studies* (Songnam: The Academy of Korean Studies), 1979: 630–642.

57 Nakamura Tadashi, "Jinshin Waran ni kansuru shomondai," in *Che 2 hoe kukche haeyangyŏk shimp'ojium palp'yo munjip, chuje: Imjin Waeran kwa haeyangyŏk* (Chinhae: Taehan Minguk Haegun, Haegun Haeyang Yŏn'guso), 1991, p. 44 (Korean translation) or p. 63 (original Japanese). Also see *Chōsen gorin ondomo no jinrui*, folio 37, MS 363 in Naganuma bunko (Kyūshū daigaku bungakubu Kyūshū bunkashi kenkyū shitsu shisetsusō).

58 Ronald P. Toby, "Leaving the Closed Country: New Models for Early-Modern Japan," *Transactions of the International Conference of Orientalists in Japan*, 35 (1990): 213–226. Toby proposes that we consider Nagasaki, Tsushima, Satsuma, and Ezo (Hokkaido) as zones of contact with gradations of sovereignty and foreignness.

59 Murai Shōsuke, *Chūsei Wajin-den*, pp. 4–5.

60 David A. Chappell, "Ethnogenesis and Frontiers," *Journal of World History*, 4:2 (Fall, 1993): 274.

61 See *Kōrin teisei* (Note 1 above) for numerous examples of all these terms.

62 Kim Yong-uk, "Pusan Waegwan ko," p. 61; Oda Seigo, "Rishi Chōsen jidai ni okeru Wakan no hensen: nakazuku Zetsueido Wakan ni tsuite," p. 122. See also *Chŭngjŏng kyorinji*, 3:1b, which states 3 *li*.

63 Pak Hŭng-su, "Yijo ch'ŏkdo e kwan han yŏn'gu," *Taedong munhwa yŏn'gu*, 4 (1967.7): 215.

64 Oda Seigo, "Rishi Chōsen jidai ni okeru Wakan no hensen: nakazuku Zetsueido Wakan ni tsuite," p. 126.

65 Kim Yong-uk, "Pusan Waegwan ko," p. 61.

66 *Chŭngjŏng kyorinji*, 3:1b. The intensity of the negotiations is described below in Chapter 6.

67 Map 2.2 was adapted from Kim Ŭi-hwan, "Fuzan Wakan bōeki no kenkyū: 15 seki kara 17 seki ni kakete no bōeki keitai o chūshin ni," *Chōsen gakuhō*, 127 (1988): 49. Map 2.3 is from the Rikugun sanbō kyoku, mufuzō, *Chōsen zenkoku* (1875.11) cat. no. 242.1J 1 in Kyūshū daigaku bungakubu Chōsenshi kenkyū shitsu sozō.

68 Kim Ŭi-hwan, "Ri-Chō jidai ni okeru Fuzan no Wakan no kigen to hensen," *Nihon bunkashi kenkyū*, 2 (Nihon, Tezukayama tanki daigaku) (1977.12): 1–17.

69 Tashiro Kazui, *Kinsei tsūkō Ni-Chō bōekishi no kenkyū*, p. 172 for a comparative chart of recorded and estimated dimensions. In addition to this chart, the *Chōsen zenkoku* (1875.11) estimates the total area of the Waegwan in 1875 as 60,000 *pyŏng* or 198,600 square meters. The *T'ongmun'gwanji*, 5:18, gives the dimensions of the Ch'oryang Waegwan as: east to west was 372 *po* 4 *ch'ŏk* and from south to north was 256 *po*. Each *po* has 6 *ch'ŏk*

and each *ch'ŏk* is calculated at the length of a *hwangjong ch'ŏk*, the basic *ch'ŏk*, or 34.72 cm. This length yields 414,027.5 square meters. In 1750, the *hwangjong ch'ŏk* was shortened to 31.25 cm., and in 1820, again lengthened to 37.74 or 34.97 cm. where it roughly remained (34.72 cm., 34.82 cm., 34.26 cm.) until the end of the dynasty. Here calculations have been based on the more common measure of the period: 34.72 cm., although modern *ch'ŏk* are customarily measured at 33 centimeters. See Pak Hŭng-su, "Yijo ch'ŏkdo e kwan han yŏn'gu," *Taedong munhwa yŏn'gu*, 4 (1967.7): 221. The size of the Tumo Waegwan has yet to be verified in one possible reference, the *Waegwan igŏn tŭngnok* (Kyujanggak cat. no. 12892), but Oda reports it as 126 *po* by 63 *po* (reference unknown). See Oda Seigo, "Rishi Chōsen jidai ni okeru Wakan no hensen," p. 126. Kim Yong-uk also states the same dimensions referring to the *Kyŏngsang-do kyebon tŭngnok* (location unknown). Kim Yong-uk, "Pusan Waegwan ko," p. 66. From Pak Hŭng-su we know that one *ch'ŏk* was 34.72 cm. and there were six *hwangjong ch'ŏk* in a *po*, thus 126 *po* was 262.4832 meters and 63 *po* was 131.2416 meters. The area was 34,448.71514 square meters or one twelfth the size of the largest estimate for the Ch'oryang Waegwan. Osa Masanori gives us a smaller estimate for the Ch'oryang Waegwan. East was 278 *kan*; north was 289 *kan*; west 224 was *kan*; and south was 373 *kan*. If one *kan* was 1.82 meters (Japanese measure), then the area was 247,449.5296 square meters or only seven times the size of the Tumo Waegwan. See Osa Masanori, "Ni-Sen kankei ni okeru kiroku no jidai," *Tōyō gakuhō*, 50:4 (1968.3): 74. Osa refers to a 1780 report from the House Master.

70 Map 2.4 is the *Waegwan-do* by Pyŏn Pak, preserved in the National Museum of Korea. Map 2.5 is adapted from Oda Seigo, "Pusan no Wakan no setsumon ni tsuite," *Chōsen*, 125 (1926): 160. Map 2.6 is from Takahashi Shonosuke, *Sō-ke to Chōsen* (Keijō: Hokunai Insatsujo), 1920.

71 Map 2.7 is adapted from *Pusan chikhal-si kaepal chehan kuyŏk-do* (Seoul: Chung'ang chido Munhwa-sa), 1988.

72 See *Pyŏllye chibyo*, vol. 2, fascicle 11, 1678.3 entry, p. 157 for an initial estimate of 4,776 *sŏk* of rice. See the following pages (intercalary 3) for a detailed explanation of costs and final payments due: rice 4,254 *sŏk* 5 *tu* 8 *sŭng* and silver 6,223 *yang* 5 *chŏn* 5 *bun*. Payment was calculated at graded daily rates for master or apprentice artisans up to 680 days. Apparently these costs are only for payments to 150 Japanese artisans. Kim Yong-uk reports the following totals for construction: 9,000 *sŏk* of rice and grains, 16,000 *yang* of cash, 1,250,000 Koreans involved in the construction, and 2,000 Japanese. See Kim Yong-uk, "Pusan Waegwan ko," pp. 62–63 and 68. Yi Wan-yŏng repeats these same figures. See Yi Wan-yŏng, "Tongnae-bu mit Waegwan ŭi haengjŏng soko," *Hangdo Pusan*, 2 (1963): 68. I have, as yet, been unable to confirm these figures. More realistic numbers of workers involved appear in connection with reconstruction done on only the west side of the Tumo Waegwan between the spring of 1645 and the sixth month of 1647: 37,814 men (8,623 carpenters) were employed for 19 months at a cost of 2,169 bolts of cotton. The Japanese supplied 70 carpenters and 723 *yang* of cash. A more comprehensive assessment of the initial construction costs must await further research, but the long-term maintenance costs are hinted at in the following passage from the *Chŭngjŏng kyorinji*, 3:5a (kamdong):

> Maintenance: In 1678, when the [Wae]gwan was moved, the Wae brought many artisans from Tsushima, but they came and only wished to neglect their duty [while] three years passed. The first report on the settlement of accounts for [daily] provisions and wages was extreme. Those amounts were over 9,000 *sŏk* in rice and over 6,000 *yang* in silver. From this time, all costs for repairs were borne by our country. Since the [Wae]gwan sat at the seashore on swampy land, it was pre-disposed to collapse. Every 25 years, there are repairs styled "great maintenance" [made because] [buildings in] the East and West [ends] of the [Wae]gwan [compound] had become useless, or there would be repairs styled "minor maintenance" [made because] [buildings] were completely destroyed by fire and were rebuilt, including [routine] rebuilding done after a set number of years. Both [types of repairs] employed Wae artisans. For a "great maintenance," [we] dispatch three upper level interpreters (one for the East [Wae]gwan, and two for

the West [Wae]gwan) and three lower level [interpreters] (one for the east [Wae]gwan and two for the West [Wae]gwan). For a "minor maintenance," we [dispatch] one upper level [interpreter] and one lower level [interpreter]. (Following this passage are notes on fires and repairs from 1680 to 1801: five major fires and eight instances of major repairs.)

73 Ch'oe Yŏng-hŭi, "Ch'oryang Waegwan," *Chosŏn sidae T'ongsinsa* (Seoul: Kungnip Chung'ang Pangmulgwan), 1986: 120: "tae-guk hyul so-guk."

74 Yi Wan-yŏng, "Tongnae-bu mit Waegwan ŭi haengjŏng soko," p. 56.

75 Yi Wan-yŏng, "Tongnae-bu mit Waegwan ŭi haengjŏng soko," pp. 56–57.

76 Yi Wan-yŏng, "Tongnae-bu mit Waegwan ŭi haengjŏng soko," p. 58. See also Hong Sŏng-dŏk, "Chosŏn hugi 'Munwihaeng' e taehayo," *Hanguk hakpo*, 59 (1990): 120–128; Hong Sŏng-dŏk, "Chosŏn hugi tae-Il oegyo sachŏl Munwihaeng ŭi tohang inwŏn punsŏk," *Han-Il kwangyesa yŏn'gu*, 11 (1999): 61–81. Ōba Ikuyo, "Kinsei Ni-Chō kankei ni okeru Yakkanshi," (unpublished MA thesis, Keiō University), 1995.

77 For details on the wall, see Yi Wan-yŏng, "Tongnae-bu mit Waegwan ŭi haengjŏng soko," p. 53.

78 *Chŭngjŏng kyorinji*, 3:3a–3b (Kwansu). See also Kim Yong-uk, "Pusan Waegwan ko," pp. 68–70, for details on the guard houses, guard postings, and other details and locations of Waegwan structures. A similar argument is found in Son Sŭng-ch'ŏl, "*Waein changna tŭngnok* ŭl t'ong hayŏ pon Waegwan," *Hangdo Pusan*, 10 (1993): 78–79.

79 Tashiro Kazui, "Sakoku jidai no Nihon machi: Chōsen hantō no Wakan," *Sinica*, 4:12 (1993.12): 43.

80 Kim Yong-uk and Kim Ŭi-hwan state it was 454. Kim Yong-uk, "Pusan Waegwan ko," p. 67; Kim Ŭi-hwan, "Richō jidai ni okeru Fuzan no Wakan no kigen to hensen," p. 10. Both take their reference from *Waegwan igŏn tŭngnok* (Kyujanggak cat. no. 12892), vol. 2, folio 64. The *Pyŏllye chibyo* (vol. 2, fascicle 11, 1678.4 entry, p. 163) reports 489.

81 *Tsūkō ichiran*, fascicle 125, vol. 3, p. 463. Hayashi cites the *Ihon Chōsen monogatari* to the effect that usually about 500 from Tsushima went over. See also Tashiro Kazui, *Kinsei Ni-Chō tsūkō bōekishi no kenkyū*, p. 70. Tashiro refers to a court debate in 1624 about the Japanese in which Yi Yŏn-kwi and O Yun-kyŏm state that they heard that the number of Japanese in Tongnae was nearly 1,000. See *Injo sillok* 4:22a–22a (1624/2/10).

82 Nagasato Kazu, "Tsushima hachigyō no hitobito," in Nagasaki kenritsu Tsushima rekishi minzoku shiryōkan, ed., *Tsushima kurashi no shiryōten* (Nagasaki: Nagasaki Kenritsu Tsushima Rekishi Minzoku Shiryō Kan), 1988: 7. Nagasato gives us a table describing Tsushima's population from 1665 to 1862. He divides the population figures for 1699 into "[Island] Population" (32,725) and "Population from other *han*" (6,730). We assume these people from "other *han*" were Japanese, since Koreans would have probably been classified separately. We might also assume that people from other *han* were not qualified for dispatch to the Waegwan, and so the population of the Waegwan was probably a slightly higher proportion of the population or around 3.1 percent. If we further consider that only men could qualify for Waegwan service, about half of the population, then our percentage climbs to 6.1 percent. Tashiro Kazui points out that we should exclude the elderly as well, suggesting about 5 percent. In other words, about one man in 20, maybe even 10, of the active adult male population may have been in Pusan at any given time. See Tashiro Kazui, *Kinsei Ni-Chō tsūkō bōekishi no kenkyū*, p. 176–177. Before leaving the topic of Tsushima's population, we might note that 1699 was the peak year for the period from 1665 to 1862. When we break down the total for island population, we can see a definite urban concentration, indicating Tsushima's general dependence on the Korea trade. Izuhara had 16,138; the silver mine had 662; and the villages had 15,925. Nagasato also points out that Izuhara's population was 49.3 percent of the total in 1699. Some 20 years earlier, in 1677, the relationship was reversed with 49.2 percent of the population outside Izuhara. The population of the city surpassed the countryside from 1683 to 1703, which corresponds to the trading peak. As trade fell off in the latter part of the eighteenth century, Izuhara's population fell to below six-tenths of the peak of 1699 and less than half the rural population.

83 For more on the *Saihan*, see discussion below in main body.

84 Osa Masanori, "Ni-Sen kankei ni okeru kiroku no jidai," *Tōyō gakuhō*, 50:4 (1968.3): 70–124.

85 Osa's article carries a handy list of 105 House Masters (usual name, official name, and date of appointment) who served from 1637 to 1870. See Osa Masanori, "Ni-Sen kankei ni okeru kiroku no jidai," pp. 70–124.

86 The Nagasaki Kenritsu Tsushima Rekishi Minzoku Shiryō-kan in Izuhara on Tsushima, the National Diet Library in Tōkyō, the Kuksa P'yŏnch'an Wiwŏnhoe in Kwach'ŏn, Keio University Library in Tōkyō, and the Shiryō Hensanjo at Tōkyō University.

87 For a succinct description of Tsushima archives and their whereabouts, see Tashiro Kazui, *Kinsei Ni-Chō tsūkō bōekishi no kenkyū*, pp. 17–21.

88 For a detailed treatment of the Kwach'ŏn holdings, see Izumi Chōichi, "Taemado Chongka munsŏ ŭi bunsŏk yŏn'gu: Kuksa P'yŏnch'an Wiwŏnhoe sŏjang ŭi kirok-ryu (6592 chŏm) rŭl chungshim ŭ ro," *Kunsa-gwan nonch'ong*, 7 (1989): 127–156.

89 In Izuhara, we have records by *Daikan* for: 1702, 1797, 1820, 1864–1868, and *[Daikan] Mainikki* for: 1806–1808, 1812–1818, 1832, 1863–1865. In Kwach'ŏn, we have *Mainikki* for: 1739–1741, 1769–1770, 1773–1775, 1784–1785, 1810–1812, 1819, 1829–1833, 1836–1850, and 1862–1863. Many *Mainikki* in the Kwach'ŏn holdings are not clearly labeled in the bibliography, so these statements are tentative.

90 Many are unclear, but we have records with the following dates: 1655–1658, 1661–1663, 1678, 1705, 1744, 1747 (?), 1791, 1793 (?), 1809 (?), 1841 (?), 1863, and 1867–1868. There are no records in Korea.

91 Toby reports that there are 120 volumes in the Shiryō Hensanjo at Tōkyō University, and that the originals are in Kwach'ŏn. The *Kokusho sōmokuroku* (Tōkyō: Iwanami Shoten), 1970, lists records for: 1711–1718, 1730–1732, 1748–1750, 1784–1786, 1819–1821, 1860–1862 and mentions only six to nine volumes. In Kwach'ŏn, we have records for: 1634–1657, 1659–1661, 1663–1665, 1669–1672, 1681–1683, 1688–1690, 1694–1702, 1706–1708, 1716–1860, 1862–1864, and 1866–1867. The Korean complement to these records is the *Tongmun hwigo*, published in photolithographic reproduction by the Kuksa P'yŏnch'an Wiwŏnhoe in four volumes in 1978. This collection contains Korean letters to and from China and Japan from 1636–1881.

92 In Izuhara, we also have records from: 1708, 1738–1739, and 1845. In Kwach'ŏn, we have: 1707–1710, 1713–1714, 1716–1721, 1724–1727, 1733–1736, 1739–1740, 1742, 1744–1755, 1758, 1765, 1768–1769, 1771, 1773, 1775, 1779–1780, 1783–1785, 1788–1791, 1794–1795, 1799–1800, 1804–1805, 1807, 1809–1811, 1813, 1815, 1819–1820, 1824–1825, 1830, 1835, 1839, 1843–1844, 1849–1850, 1853–1855, 1858–1860, 1863–1864, and 1868–1869. Osa has also compiled an easy table for our reference of the usual name, the formal name, date of arrival at the *Waegwan*, commission title, and other miscellaneous information for *Saihan* from 1607 to 1870. See Osa Masanori, "Ni-Sen kankei ni okeru kiroku no jidai," pp. 70–124.

3 THE DEMOGRAPHIC SIGNIFICANCE OF THE JAPAN HOUSE

1 Arne Kalland, *Fishing Villages in Tokugawa Japan* (Honolulu: University of Hawaii Press), 1995. Kalland's study of Fukuoka domain fishing villages thoroughly dispels two mistaken assumptions about Tokugawa fishing villages. First, fishing villages were not isolated. Kalland demonstrates that the fishing villages served as small intermediate commercial centers between agricultural producers and urban markets. The villagers engaged in regional and national economies and certainly did more than just catch fish: they farmed, traded, shipped, and produced salt. The other mistaken assumption, often encountered in European and American studies of coastal societies, is that there was a "natural" access to the sea and coastal areas as "frontier zones giving landless farmers an opportunity in the last resort to make a living from fishing," or, in other words, that the sea and its resources were there for all to exploit (p. 307). In fact, access was governed by a matrix of formal and informal rights and licensing arrangements, and the only way to discern these is by close examination. Also see: John W. Dardess, *A Ming Society: T'ai-ho County, Kiangsi, Fourteenth to Seventeenth Centuries* (Berkeley: University of California Press), 1996. Dardess

creates a landscape and then peoples that landscape with intellectuals. His purpose is to examine reciprocity between national and local levels, and his main point is that the local has a character all its own and cannot be subsumed and dismissed.

2 In Chapter 4 we will see that trade and receptions for the Japanese from Tsushima involved supplies from all over Kyŏngsang Province.

3 Yi Ho-ch'ŏl demonstrates a wide regional diversity of crops and argues that agricultural management varied by region. See: Yi Ho-ch'ŏl, *Chosŏn chŏngi nong'ŏp kyŏngjae-sa* (Seoul: Han'gilsa), 1986: 531–570.

4 In Chapter 5 we will see that incidents involving Japanese had an extensive impact on the careers of Tongnae Magistrates.

5 Hermann Lautensach, translated by Katherine and Eckart Dege, *Korea: A Geography Based on the Author's Travels and Literature* (Berlin: Springer-Verlag), 1988: 484 (original German version, 1945).

6 Hermann Lautensach, *Korea*, p. 63.

7 Lautensach, *Korea*, pp. 330–331. Shannon McCune uses Lautensach's term. See: Shannon McCune, *Views of the Geography of Korea, 1935–1960* (Seoul: The Korean Research Center), 1980: 144–175.

8 Ch'a Mun-sŏng, "Chijil," in Pusan chikhal-si sa p'yŏnch'an wiwŏnhoe, ed., *Pusan-si sa* (Pusan: Pusan Chikhal-si), 1989: 81–82.

9 According to Chosŏn period geomantic theory, the "head" of the peninsula was Paektu Mountain and the two "feet" of this organic figure were in Cheju and Tsushima Islands. See: Yi Ik's quote in Pae U-Sŏng, *Chosŏn hugi kukt'ogwan kwa Ch'ŏnha'gwan ŭi pyŏnhwa* (Seoul: Iljisa), 1998: 38.

10 O Kŏn-hwan, "Chise," in Pusan chikhal-si sa p'yŏnch'an wiwŏnhoe, ed., *Pusan-si sa* (Pusan: Pusan Chikhal-si), 1989: 41–48.

11 Lautensach, *Korea*, p. 330.

12 O Kŏn-hwan, "Chise," pp. 56–57.

13 Lautensach, *Korea*, p. 335.

14 O Kŏn-hwan, "Chise," pp. 41–46 and 56–61.

15 "Traces" can be nearly any documentary or material source left behind that allows the compilation of quantitative chronological series. These can reflect social practices, but their interpretation is often full of difficulty. Silences in the series can mean either interiorization or disappearance: the life or death of an idea and a practice associated with it. For example, between 1730 and 1770, when religious clauses disappeared from French wills, did this mean "the beginnings of dechristianization" or a mere "change of convention"? See: Michel Vovelle, translated by Eamon O'Flaherty, *Ideologies and Mentalities* (Cambridge: Polity Press), 1990: 19–21.

16 For a succinct survey of Chosŏn period demographics in English, see: Tony Michell, "Fact and Hypothesis in Yi Dynasty Economic History: The Demographic Dimension," *Korean Studies Forum*, 5 (Winter–Spring 1979–1980): 65–93. In attempting to calculate an absolute total population, Michell dispenses with census population totals prior to 1681, preferring to multiply household totals by a constant. From the 1680s onward he relies on the series of household returns, the *Hogu ch'ongsu*, which was begun in 1639. Michell rightly emphasizes that his objective is not absolute totals but the "course of population change" (p. 66). In similar fashion, this study is not overly concerned with under-reporting, with favoring household figures over census figures, or with multiplying household figures by constants, since we are not concerned with absolute demographics but with the relative position of Tongnae vis-à-vis other counties in Kyŏngsang Province. Lautensach takes the same view regarding pre-modern census figures: "Of course we must not attach too much importance to the absolute figures even here, since they are obviously still much too low. But the degree of inaccuracy should be approximately the same in the different periods and provinces, so that by comparing the differences from region to region and from time to time we can obtain certain results." Lautensach, *Korea*, p. 151.

17 Yi Ho-ch'ŏl, *Chosŏn chŏngi nong'ŏp kyŏngjae-sa*, p. 662.

18 For a consideration of population growth in connection with the expansion of intensive, wet-field farming and the increasing hegemony of Neo-Confucian ideology, see:

Yi Tae-Jin, "The Influence of Neo-Confucianism on 14th–16th Century Korean Population Growth," *Korea Journal*, 37:2 (Summer 1997): 5–23.

19 A Chosŏn-era land use pattern of dry and paddy fields has been shown to support the country's greatest concentration of population. James Lewis and Seong-ho Jun, "Economic Perspectives on Korean History: Macroscopic Structures, Part 1," paper presented at a Biennial Conference of the Association for Korean Studies in Europe, April 2001.

20 Yi Ho-ch'ŏl, *Chosŏn chŏngi nong'ŏp kyŏngjae-sa*, pp. 660–687.

21 For serial data on arable land and actual taxation assessment in Kyŏngsang Province from 1744 to 1840, see Chapter 4.

22 Yi Ho-ch'ŏl, *Chosŏn chŏngi nong'ŏp kyŏngjae-sa*, p. 675.

23 *Sejong sillok chiriji* and the *Kyŏngsang-do chiriji*. The *Sejong sillok chiriji* was commissioned in 1424 and officially finished in 1454. There were at least two intermediate stages, and the *Kyŏngsang-do chiriji* is part of these intermediate stages. The *Kyŏngsang-do chiriji* may date from as early as 1425 and is the only surviving provincial gazetteer from this time. It was a part of the *Sinch'an p'aldo chiriji* of 1432, which we do not have, but which formed perhaps the most immediate basis for the *Sejong sillok chiriji*. See: Yi Sŏng-mu, "Haeche," in Hanguk-hak munhŏn yŏn'guso, ed., *Chŏnguk chiriji* (Seoul: Asea Munhwasa), 1983: 3–12, and Katsuragi Tomesada, "Kaisetsu," in Chūsūin chōsa kahen, *Keishōdō chiri shi – Keishōdō Zokusen chiri shi* (Keijō: Chōsen Sōtokufu Chūsūin), 1938: 1–21. Note that the *Kyŏngsang-do chiriji* (1425 or 1432), which contains detailed population data but no agricultural production data, has been used here for population data for Figures 3.1, 3.3, and 3.4. Agricultural production data comes from the 1454 *Sejong sillok chiriji*. Thus, the dates mentioned here, 1432 and 1454, indicate that the information being used is a composite of the 1432 (population) and the 1454 (agricultural) data. Often, exact dating is impossible and the documents contain some information from other years. For example, the last date mentioned for Tongnae in the *Sejong sillok chiriji* is 1428, while the foreword to the geography in the *Sillok* states that the text was submitted in 1432 and then extensively amended afterwards. See: *Sejong sillok chiriji*, 148:1a–1b. The date 1454 is taken merely for convenience sake to distinguish it from the *Kyŏngsang-do chiriji*. Yi Ho-ch'ŏl's analysis of the *Sejong sillok chiriji* refers to the data as coming from *c*.1432 to make the point that the data precedes the 1444 *Kongbŏp* which newly classified land by six grades of fertility and nine grades of yearly harvest. See: Yi Ho-ch'ŏl, *Chosŏn chŏngi nong'ŏp kyŏngjae-sa* (Seoul: Han'gilsa, 1986): 259. Below, we will address the matter of the significance of the data being pre-1444 and of comparing that with later periods.

24 The standard deviation was 0.38. "Standard deviation" in Korean is *p'yojun p'yŏnch'a*. I wish to thank Dr. Brian Buck, University Lecturer in Theoretical Physics and Fellow of Wolfson College, for helping me to understand the mysteries of standard deviation and for helping me prepare Figures 3.4, 3.8 and 3.12.

25 "Tongnae hyŏn" in *Sejong sillok chiriji*, 150:9b–10a (no date).

26 Yi Ho-ch'ŏl, *Chosŏn chŏngi nong'ŏp kyŏngjae-sa*, p. 269.

27 Only one case out of 71 was from a year other than 1759. Hadong County's data may have come from 1711, 1771, or it may have been a scribal error.

28 The Hanguk haeyang charyo sent'ŏ (Korea Oceanographic Data Center) in Pusan has available a collection of remote sensing images of the seas around the Korean peninsula and the Japanese archipelago. NOAA (National Oceanic and Atmospheric Administration, U.S. Government) provided these satellite images. They begin from 1997 and record sea surface temperatures (SST) for all months of the year. By comparing composite images over the four seasons, we can see the wintertime predominance of coldwater areas, the springtime entrance of the warm southern currents, and the summertime height of surface temperatures. See: Korea Oceanographic Data Center (http://www.nfrdi.re.kr/kodc/index.html) and the Sea Surface Temperature images from the Marine Remote Sensing Lab (http://www.nfrdi.re.kr/kodc/data/noaa/index.html).

29 Cho Kyu-tae, "Haeyang," in Pusan chikhal-si sa p'yŏnch'an wiwŏnhoe ed., *Pusan-si sa* (Pusan: Pusan chikhal-si), 1989: 152–157.

30 Lautensach, *Korea*, p. 443.

31 Cho Kyu-tae, "Haeyang," pp. 147–157.

32 Lautensach, *Korea*, p. 335.

33 Hong Sŏng-yun, "Haeyang saengmul sang," in Pusan chikhal-si sa p'yŏnch'an wiwŏnhoe ed., *Pusan-si sa* (Pusan: Pusan Chikhal-si), 1989: 262–326.

34 These petroglyphs are located in Taegŭng-ni, Ŏnyang-myŏn, Ulju-gun, Ulsan City.

35 According to the *Nihon kokugo daijiten*, the first literary reference to "Kuroshio" comes in the *Chinsetsu yumiharizuki*, a novel published between 1807 and 1811.

36 Chi Tu-hwan, "Chosŏn chŏngi sahoe-kyŏngje wa Pusan," in Pusan chikhal-si sa p'yŏnch'an wiwŏnhoe ed., *Pusan-si sa* (Pusan: Pusan Chikhal-si), 1989: 615.

37 Chi Tu-hwan, "Chosŏn chŏngi ŭi munhwa wa Pusan," in Pusan chikhal-si sa p'yŏnch'an wiwŏnhoe ed., *Pusan-si sa* (Pusan: Pusan Chikhal-si), 1989: 636. See also: *Tongnae-bu ŭpchi* (1832) in Kim Tong-ch'ŏl, ed., *Tongnae saryo*, 2 (Seoul: Yŏgang ch'ulp'ansa), 1989: 285 which lists old sites around Haeundae and notes that the Sillan state sacrificed to the God of the Southern Sea at Hyŏngpyŏn pugok.

38 The *ŭpchi* for 1740, 1759, 1832, and 1871 list 46 items as *t'osan* (local products) of which 32 are marine products; 11 items as *chinsang* (local tribute goods) of which all 11 come from the Japan trade; and 9 items as *chin'gong* (tribute goods to the court) of which four are marine products and one category is *Waehŏn* (Wae presents). See: Kim Tong-ch'ŏl, ed., *Tongnae saryo*, 2, p. 35 for 1740, pp. 217–218 for 1759, pp. 291–292 for 1832, and pp. 391–392 for 1871.

39 Chi Tu-hwan, "Chosŏn chŏngi sahoe-kyŏngje wa Pusan," pp. 614–617.

40 Underwood describes river skiffs as having a narrow flat bottom with extreme flaring sides. Perhaps this is what is meant by "wide" boats. Horace H. Underwood, "Korean Boats and Ships," *Transactions of the Korea Branch of the Royal Asiatic Society*, 23 (1933) (reprinted, Seoul: Yonsei University Press, 1979): 7. Lautensach describes fishing boats in the 1930s in the following way:

> The Korean fishing boats are flat-bottomed vessels without a keel and with low sides, 15 m long at the most. Most of the types originated in traditional Korea. To be able to move when it is calm they have one or several gigantic oars on which occasionally as many as ten men pull. The boats on the west coast which have to reckon with strong tidal currents, extremely shallow water at times and surging seas and surf, are built more sturdily than the ones on the east coast and have two large, rectangular cotton sails with horizontal bamboo poles, instead of the one that predominates on the coast of the Sea of Japan.
> (pp. 439–440)

Regarding length, Underwood reports that his survey of sea-going vessels found most to be under 10 meters (p. 13), but he reports sighting the occasional 23 meter boat (p. 18). Regarding design, flat-bottomed boats are notoriously difficult to sail, but Underwood reports that traditional designs, although flat-bottomed, contained a "long deep rudder" that extended beneath the boat and served as a centerboard. This allowed sailing close to the wind and rapid speeds (p. 15). Such a "false" centerboard could easily be taken in when sailing over shallows. The *Tongnae-bu saye* (1868) gives us information on the length of river boats: 9.09 meters (3 *p'a* or 30 *ch'ŏk*) was "small, small"; 12.12 to 18.18 meters (4–6 *p'a*) was "small"; 21.21 to 27.27 meters (7–9 *p'a*) was "middle"; and 30.3 to 45.45 meters (10–15 *p'a*) was "large." Riverboats of 12.12 meters and above that were merchant vessels and paid an additional tax. Not much detail is available for sea-going vessels, but they were taxed at nearly three times the rate, and merchant vessels also paid an additional tax. See: *Tongnae-bu saye* (1868) in Kim Tong-ch'ŏl, ed., *Tongnae saryo*, 2, p. 521.

41 For Tongpyŏng: Pusan Harbor had 30 "tribute" (officially managed) pans and seven "military" pans; there were two "private" pans, and Tadae Harbor had one "military" pan. For Tongnae: 23 "tribute" pans and one "military" pan each for the Left Naval Headquarters and the Haeun Harbor garrison. See: *Kyŏngsang-do chiriji* (1425/1432), in Hanguk-hak munhŏn yŏn'guso, ed., *Chŏn'guk chiriji* (Seoul: Asea Munhwasa), 1983: 139 and 157. The gazetteers from the later Chosŏn period do not distinguish the pans by private or military designations, only by geographic location.

42 Lautensach describes the salt operations he witnessed in the late 1930s:

> Along the coast of the Sea of Japan such old saltpans are still in operation today. Small canals have been dug through the narrow sandbars there to allow salt water to enter. They conduct it to level, firmly pounded surfaces about 1 are [100 square meters] in size with a layer of loose dirt about 5 cm thick spread out by means of an ox-drawn harrow. In summer when the weather is good men sprinkle water from the canals over the ground with gourd dippers twice a day. After 5 days enough salt has accumulated by evaporation. The dirt containing the salt is piled up in heaps and put in earthen kettles with permeable wooden bottoms. Here fresh salt water is poured over it, leaching the salt out of the dirt, so that a concentrated solution collects in the receiving vessels. This is evaporated over a wood fire. The Korean salt obtained in this manner still contains rather large residues of bittern salts and is therefore of poor quality.
>
> (p. 189)

43 Detailed information on taxation is available for 1868 in the *Tongnae-bu saye* (1868) in Kim Tong-ch'ŏl, ed., *Tongnae saryo*, 2, pp. 521–523.

44 *Tongnae-buji* (1740) in Kim Tong-ch'ŏl, ed., *Tongnae saryo*, 2, p. 62. Here, 113 official salt laborers are listed under the category of official slaves.

45 Chi Tu-hwan, "Chosŏn chŏngi sahoe-kyŏngje wa Pusan," pp. 621–622.

46 Chi Tu-hwan, "Chosŏn chŏngi sahoe-kyŏngje wa Pusan," pp. 615–616.

47 *Chiriji* in *Sejong sillok*, 150:28b–29b (no date), "Kimhae tohobu." Sub-counties had often been independent counties during the Silla or Koryŏ periods.

48 I wish to thank Professor Kenneth R. Robinson for raising this question.

49 I wish to thank Professor Yi T'ae-Jin and Professor Kenneth R. Robinson for raising this question. See: Kenneth R. Robinson, "Shaping Chosŏn: The Japanese Island of Tsushima in Chosŏn Korea, 1418–1592" (unpublished paper presented at a conference, "Critical Issues in Korean Studies: in the Millennium," 19 February 2000, Honolulu, Hawai'i) for a brief discussion of government policies regarding the re-population of islands. Part of the court's intention was to foreclose or pre-empt the possibility of Japanese colonization.

50 The connection with the Japanese is repeated in all *ŭpchi*. For example, see the *pusŏnsaeng[pyo]* in *Tongnae-bu ŭpchi* (1899) in *Tongnae saryo*, 3 (Seoul: Yŏgang Ch'ulp'ansa), 1989: 357–387, and Kim Yong'uk, "Pusan Waegwan ko," *Han-Il munhwa*, 1:2 (1962.12): 58.

51 Trading and fishing by Japanese around Kŏje Island were common prior to 1600, but tightly controlled afterwards. After 1600, Japanese continued to fish in the area, but that simply argues that the Japanese and the Kŏje Islanders were both engaged in a maritime economy.

52 John Sommerville, "Stability in Eighteenth Century Ulsan," *Korean Studies Forum*, 1 (1976–1977): 1–18, for a methodological discussion of the *hojŏk* for Ulsan County, just to the north of Tongnae. Similar *hojŏk* for Tongnae have not been found.

53 Yi Wan-yŏng, "Tongnae-bu mit Waegwan ŭi haengjŏng soko," *Hangdo Pusan*, 2 (1963): 17–21, for a description of Chosŏn-period Tongnae townships, the villages they contained, and their transformations into the modern period. From Yi we learn that the Tumo Japan House was in Tongp'yŏng-myŏn (Tongp'yŏng Township) Chwaja(ch'i)ch'ŏn i-ri or Chwaja(ch'i)ch'ŏn Village 2; that the market for the Ch'oryang Japan House was in Sach'ŏn-myŏn (Sach'ŏn Township) in Taech'i-ri (Taech'i Village) and that castaways were entertained in Namch'on-myŏn (Namch'on Township) in Uam-ri (Uam Village).

54 The demographic data was drawn from the *Hogu ch'ongsu* and that was correlated with the maps in the *Yŏji tosŏ*.

55 See Yi Ho-ch'ŏl, *Chosŏn chŏngi nong'ŏp kyŏngjae-sa*, p. 260, note 52, where he equates *kanjŏn* and *wŏnjangbu kyŏl* and states that all we have from the early Chosŏn period is the "*wŏnjangbu kyŏl.*"

56 This manuscript has been published in photolithographic reprint. Oda Seigo *et al.*, ed., *Fuzan-fu shi genkō*, in six volumes (Seoul: Kyŏng'in Munhwasa), 1989.

57 Yi Wan-yŏng, "Tongnae-bu mit Waegwan ŭi haengjŏng soko," p. 59.
58 Kim Ŭi-hwan (Kin Gikan), "Fuzan Wakan no shokkan kōsei to sono kinō ni tsuite: Ri-Chō no tai-Nichi seisaku no ichi rikai no tame ni," Chōsen gakuhō, 108 (July 1983): 113.
59 To estimate for dependents, we could consider each official as having a separate household. In 1789, the average household contained 4.15 people; in 1867, the average household contained 3.82 people. See Tables 3.5 and 3.6.
60 Kim Ŭi-hwan, "Fuzan Wakan no shokkan kōsei to sono kinō ni tsuite," p. 113.
61 See Table 3.5.
62 Yi Wŏn-kyun, "Chosŏn hugi ŭi Pusan," in Pusan chikhal-si sa p'yŏnch'an wiwŏnhoe ed., Pusan-si sa (Pusan: Pusan Chikhal-si), 1989: 720–727. Although Yi supplies no evidence for his assertion regarding the mercantile inclinations of local yangban, we will see evidence to support this assertion presented in the discussion below on Korean merchants. See ŭpchi for market locations and days of operation.
63 For example, see: Yi Hyŏn-jong, Chosŏn chŏngi tae-Il kyosŏpsa yŏn'gu (Seoul: Hanguk yŏn'guwŏn), 1964; Nakamura Hidetaka, Ni-Sen kankeishi no kenkyū (Tōkyō: Yoshikawa Kōbunkan), 1965–1969; Tanaka Takeo, Chūsei kaigai shishōshi no kenkyū (Tōkyō: Tōkyō Daigaku Shuppankai), 1959; and Tanaka Takeo, Chūsei taigai kankeishi (Tōkyō: Tōkyō Daigaku Shuppankai), 1975.
64 Tanaka Takeo, Chūsei kaigai shishōshi no kenkyū (Tōkyō: Tōkyō Daigaku Shuppankai), 1959: 59–65.
65 Tanaka Takeo, Chūsei kaigai shishōshi no kenkyū, p. 63.
66 The following discussion comes from Professor Saeki Kōji's lectures on Sō Kin and the following articles: Arimitsu Yasushige, "Hakata Sō Kin shōnin to sono kakei," Shien, 16 (1931): 201–237; Tanaka Takeo, "Ni-Sen bōeki ni okeru Hakata shōnin no katsudō," in Tanaka Takeo, Chūsei kaigai shishōshi no kenkyū (Tōkyō: Tōkyō Daigaku Shuppankai, 1959): 35–65; Ueda Junichi, "Myōrakuji to Hakata shōnin: Ōei no gaikō o megutte," in Chihōshi kenkyū kyōgi kaihen, ed., Ikoku to Kyūshū (Tōkyō: Yūsankaku), 1993: 99–113; Saeki Kōji, "Chūsei toshi Hakata to 'Sekijō Kanji' Sō Kin," [Kyūshū University] Shien, 133 (1996.2): 1–22.
67 Song Hŭi-kyŏng, Nosongdang Ilbon haengnok. See: Minjok munhwa ch'unjinhoe, ed., Kojŏn kukyŏk ch'ongsŏ Haehaeng Ch'ongjae, 8 (Seoul: Minmungo), 1967: 61 for Korean translation and p. 19, top left, for original Chinese (reprinted 1989). Murai Shōsuke has given us a modern Japanese translation. Murai Shōsuke, translator and editor, Rōmatsudō Nihon Kōroku: Chōsen shisetsu no mita chūsei Nihon (Tōkyō: Iwanami Shoten), 1987: 69 (for Japanese translation).
68 See Saeki for a discussion of the connection between changes in Sō Kin's titles and the fighting over control of Hakata. Saeki argues that from 1425 to 1429 Sō Kin was Hakata's "representative." Saeki prefers this characterization since other scholars have mistakenly imputed that Sō Kin "ruled" Hakata. Between 1425 and 1429, it was unclear which of the three regional warlords controlled Hakata: Shōni, Ōuchi, or Ōtomo. From 1429 to 1442, Saeki characterizes Sō Kin as something akin to a city magistrate operating under Ōtomo's rule, following on from Ōtomo's victory over Ōuchi and Shōni.
69 Sejo sillok, 1:38b–40a (1455/7/24).
70 Sejong sillok, 10:17b–17b (1420/11/25).
71 Honda Miho, "Muromachi jidai ni okeru Shōni shi no dōkai: Sadayori-Mitsusada ki," Kyūshū shigaku, 91 (1988.2): 27–41. Honda revises Kawazoe's date of 1423, as appeared in Kyūshū chūseishi kenkyū, 23 (1978).
72 Trip 1: Sejong sillok, 11:2a–2a (1421/1/6); trip 2: Sejong sillok, 12:22a–22a (1421/7/5) and Sejong sillok, 13:7b–7b (1421/8/27); trip 3: Sejong sillok, 14:8b–8b (1421/11/16); trip 4: Sejong sillok, 27:3b–3b (1425/1/6); trip 5: Sejong sillok, 30:3b–3b (1425/10/13), and Sejong sillok, 30:5a–5a (1425/10/18). On 1425/10/18, Sō Kin received his seal.
73 The early fifteenth century was still a time when seals were properly used more often than not. From the late fifteenth century through the sixteenth century, impostor envoys deluged the Chosŏn authorities with documents sporting seals fraudulently obtained or even manufactured in Japan. For a detailed description of seals and their abuse by impostor envoys, see: Kenneth R. Robinson, "Policies of Practicality: The Chosŏn Court's

Regulation of Contact with Japanese and Jurchens, 1392–1580s" (unpublished Ph.D. dissertation, University of Hawai'i), 1997: 127–180, 484–543, and "The Jiubian and Ezogachishima Embassies to Chosŏn, 1478–1482," *Chōsenshi kenkyūkai ronbunshū*, 35 (1997): 55–86 (203–234).

74 *Sejong sillok*, 41:4a–4a (1428/7/14).

75 *Sejong sillok*, 42:21b–21b (1428/12/14). Saeki believes that Sō Kin was instrumental in establishing Ōtomo's link to Korea in 1429. Saeki Kōji, "Chūsei toshi Hakata to 'Sekijō kanji' Sō Kin," p. 17.

76 *Sejong sillok*, 41:2b–2b (1429/7/4).

77 *Sejong sillok*, 47:8b–8b (1430/2/11).

78 *Sejong sillok*, 46:16b–17b (1429/12/9). For Sō Kin's visit requesting gifts, see: *Sejong sillok*, 44:24b–24b (1429/6/13). The request appears to be from the shogun's advisors, but the name and office do not appear in common references. The letter addresses the "*shitsuji*" (K: *chipsa*) of the Chosŏn court.

79 *Sejong sillok*, 84:34a–34b (1439/3/15).

80 For a discussion of the establishment of the Tsushima governor's control over Japanese access to Chosŏn and a discussion of the origins of the *mun'in* system as an outgrowth of policies to control the domestic travel of Chosŏn period Koreans, see: Kenneth R. Robinson, "From raiders to traders: border security and border control in early Chosŏn, 1392–1450," *Korean Studies*, 16 (1992): 94–115; Kenneth R. Robinson, "The Tsushima Governor and the Regulation of Japanese Access with Chosŏn in the Fifteenth and Sixteenth Centuries," *Korean Studies*, 20 (1996): 23–50, and Kenneth R. Robinson, "Policies of Practicality: the Chosôn Court's Regulation of Contact with Japanese and Jurchens, 1392–1580s" (unpublished dissertation, University of Hawai'i), 1997: 82–126. For a discussion of the usual early Chosŏn period envoy trip to the capital, protocol, and volumes of cargoes, see: Kenneth R. Robinson, "Policies of Practicality: The Chosŏn Court's Regulation of Contact with Japanese and Jurchens, 1392–1580s" (unpublished dissertation, University of Hawai'i), 1997: 44–81.

81 *Sejong sillok*, 116:19a–19b (1447/5/26).

82 *Sejo sillok*, 1:38b–40a (1455/7/24).

83 *Hogun chonggamu* from Ch'ukchŏnju (J: *Chikuzen shū*), a *sujik'in* or "appointee of the Chosŏn government." See: Appendix A, Table 3.2, original Japanese, Category 4 in James B. Lewis, "The Pusan Japan House (Waegwan) and Chosŏn Korea: early-modern Korean views of Japan through economic, political, and social connections" (unpublished dissertation, University of Hawai'i), 1994: 382. See also: Tanaka Takeo, "Richō Sejongcho ni okeru Ni-Sen kōtsū no shomondai" in Tanaka Takeo, *Chūsei kaigai shishōshi no kenkyū*, 66, interfolio chart.

84 *Sejong sillok*, 62:13b–13b (1433/11/5).

85 *Sŏngjong sillok*, 58:7b–9a (1475/8/14).

86 *Sŏngjong sillok*, 11:16a–16b (1471/8/26). Sō Kin's name often appeared in the *Sillok* preceded by "Sekijō," which referred to Hakata's role as a defender against Mongol attack. Saeki Kōji, "Chūsei toshi Hakata to 'Sekijō Kanji' Sō Kin," pp. 3–4.

87 Na Chong-u states that between 1392 and 1608, some 2,369 Japanese "envoys" visited Korea, while only 71 Korean envoys visited Japan. Na Chong-u, *Hanguk Chungse tae-Il kysŏpsa yŏn'gu* (Seoul: Wŏngwang Taehakkyo Ch'ulp'anguk), 1996: 189. Kenneth Robinson points out that Na does not explain how he got this figure and if missions arriving under the names of Ryukyuan elites are included, then the total would exceed 2,400. Kenneth R. Robinson, "Policies of Practicality: The Chosŏn Court's Regulation of Contact with Japanese and Jurchens, 1392–1580s" (unpublished dissertation, University of Hawai'i), 1997: 2.

88 For example, see: *Sejong sillok*, 41:4a–4a (1428/7/14) for alcohol; *Sejong sillok*, 17:22b–22b (1430/2/19) for various luxury goods including ginseng; *Sejong sillok*, 42:21b–21b (1428/12/14) for dogs; *Munjong sillok*, 5:10b–10b (1450/12/13) for the *Koreana Tripitaka*. See also Kenneth R. Robinson, "Treated as Treasures: The Circulation of Sutras in Maritime Northeast Asia from 1388 to the Mid-Sixteenth Century", *East Asian History*, 21 (June 2001): 33–54.

89 Calculation from table by Saeki Kōji, lecture given 20 January 1994.

90 *Sejong sillok*, 39:13a–13b (1428/1/25).

91 Kenneth R. Robinson, "Policies of Practicality: The Chosŏn Court's Regulation of Contact with Japanese and Jurchens, 1392–1580s" (unpublished dissertation, University of Hawai'i), 1997: 75.

92 Kenneth R. Robinson, "Policies of Practicality," p. 79.

93 See: Kenneth R. Robinson, "From raiders to traders: border security and border control in early Chosŏn, 1392–1450," *Korean Studies*, 16 (1992): 94–115; Kenneth R. Robinson, "The Tsushima Governor and the regulation of Japanese contact with Chosŏn in the fifteenth and sixteenth centuries," *Korean Studies*, 20 (1996): 23–50, and Kenneth R. Robinson, "Policies of Practicality: The Chosŏn Court's Regulation of Contact with Japanese and Jurchens, 1392–1580s" (unpublished dissertation, University of Hawai'i), 1997.

94 Tashiro Kazui, *Kinsei Ni-Chō tsūkō bōekishi no kenkyū* (Tōkyō: Sōbunsha), 1981: 269.

95 Gold had been presented to Korea from at least A.D. 804 or the fifth year of Silla King Aejang. See: *Chŭngbo munhŏn pigo*, 178:2b–2b in Hong Ponghan *et al.*, ed., *Chŭngbo munhŏn pigo*, 3 (Seoul: Myŏngmundang), 1977: 67. During the seventeenth century silver became a major Japanese export to Korea, but copper was, by bulk, far more important from the fifteenth to the nineteenth centuries.

96 Tashiro Kazui, *Kinsei Ni-Chō tsūkō bōekishi no kenkyū*, p. 272.

97 Chŏng Sŏng-il, *Chosŏn hugi tae-Il muyŏk* (Seoul: Tosŏ Ch'ulp'an Sinsŏwŏn), 2000: 66.

98 Tashiro Kazui, *Kinsei Ni-Chō tsūkō bōekishi no kenkyū*, p. 270.

99 Chŏng Sŏng-il dates the Japanese process to replace imported ginseng from its beginnings in 1719 to final success in 1733. Chŏng Sŏng-il, *Chosŏn hugi tae-Il muyŏk*, pp. 233–254.

100 For a discussion of these four goods see: Tashiro Kazui, "Bakumakki Ni-Chō shi bōeki to Wakan bōeki shōnin: yunyū yon hinmoku no torihiki o chūshin ni," in Hayami Tōru *et al.*, ed., *Tokugawa shakai kara no tenbō: hatten-kōzō-kokusai kankei* (Tōkyō: Dōbunkan), 1989: 304–312.

101 For a discussion of the jelly trade and mid- to late-nineteenth century Korean–Japanese trade in general, see: Kim Tong-ch'ŏl, "*Tongnae-bu sanggoan* ŭl t'onghaesŏ pon 19 segi huban ŭi Tongnae sang'in: *Tongnae muim sŏnsaeng'an* kwa ŭi pigyo," *Han-Il kwangyesa yŏn'gu*, 1 (1993.10): 115–144.

102 McCune counts 32. See: George McCune, "The Japanese Trading Post at Pusan," p. 11.

103 Robert Innes states that by the 1620s, Tsushima had expanded the number of ships beyond the need to transport cargo and that in 1635, Tsushima petitioned Korea to allow a reduction in the number of ships. He is referring to the consolidation known as the *kyŏmdae* system (to be discussed below), but he has confused two points: 1) the *kyŏmdae* system was a Korean proposal designed to curtail reception costs, and 2) the *kyŏmdae* system did not reduce the number of ships crossing; it reduced the number of ships requiring receptions. See: Robert L. Innes, "The Door Ajar: Japan's Foreign Trade in the Seventeenth Century" (unpublished Ph.D. dissertation, University of Michigan), 1980: 406.

104 Tashiro Kazui, *Kinsei Ni-Chō tsūkō bōekishi no kenkyū*, and in particular, the second chapter in part one: "Kinsei shotō no bōeki ninpō to torihiki hinmoku." For a comprehensive view of trade, based on a large archival document base and the sophisticated use of econometric theory, see: Chŏng Sŏng-il, *Chosŏn hugi tae-Il muyŏk* (Seoul: Tosŏ Ch'ulp'an Sinsŏwŏn), 2000. The following discussion is largely beholden to these two scholars, except where noted.

105 Chŏng Sŏng-il, *Chosŏn hugi tae-Il muyŏk*, p. 330. Attempts to abrogate the old system in the early 1870s led to the crises of the 1873 Seikanron and the 1876 Kanghwa Treaty.

106 *Shōkai shingo*, Robert Elvin Campbell, trans., "The Pusan Section of the Shōkai shingo: Study and Translation" (unpublished dissertation, University of California at Berkeley), 1994.

107 Tashiro Kazui, *Kinsei Ni-Chō tsūkō bōekishi no kenkyū*, p. 62. Fans and swords were transported to Korea by Sō Kin's ships in the early 1400s.

108 Tashiro Kazui, *Kinsei Ni-Chō tsūkō bōekishi no kenkyū*, p. 62. Tashiro glosses black linen as yellow lustrous cloth.

109 *Pyŏllye chibyo*, fascicle 8, entry 1608.1, p. 437 in Kuksa p'yŏch'an wiwŏnhoe, ed., *Pyŏllye chibyo*, 1 (Seoul: T'amgudang), 1969.

110 Tashiro Kazui, *Kinsei Ni-Chō tsūkō bōekishi no kenkyū*, p. 268.

111 Tashiro Kazui, *Kinsei Ni-Chō tsūkō bōekishi no kenkyū*, pp. 262–263 for a complete list.

112 Tashiro Kazui, *Kinsei Ni-Chō tsūkō bōekishi no kenkyū*, p. 268. Although Nakamura Tadashi questioned this re-export of cotton back to Korea, Chŏng concludes that Tashiro is correct. See: Chŏng Sŏng-il, *Chosŏn hugi tae-Il muyŏk*, p. 199.

113 Tashiro Kazui, "Bakumakki Ni-Chō shi bōeki to Wakan bōeki shōnin," p. 300.

114 Chŏng Sŏng-il, *Chosŏn hugi tae-Il muyŏk*, pp. 42–65.

115 Tashiro Kazui, *Kakikaerareta kokusho* (Tōkyō: Chūō Shinsho), 1983.

116 Tashiro Kazui, *Kinsei Ni-Chō tsūkō bōekishi no kenkyū*, p. 145 ff.

117 Kyŏmdae: *Chŭngjŏng kyorinji*, 1:23a–30a in Kim Kŏnsŏ, ed., *Chŭngjŏng kyorinji*, translated by Ha Woo Bong and Hong Sŏng-dŏk (Seoul: Minjok Munhwa Ch'ujinhoe), 1998.

118 *Chŭngjŏng kyorinji*, 1:29a–30a, (chapmul chŏlmi sik jo).

119 *T'ongmun'gwanji*, 5:4a–4a (nyŏnye songsa) in Kim Chi'nam, ed., *T'ongmun'gwanji* (Seoul: Kyŏng'in Munhwasa), 1974.

120 *Shōkai shingo*, Robert Elvin Campbell, trans., "The Pusan Section of the *Shōkai shingo*: Study and Translation" (unpublished dissertation, University of California at Berkeley, 1994): 34.

121 Tashiro (*Kinsei Ni-Chō tsūkō bōekishi no kenkyū*) gives us series from Japanese documents on the silver trade, 1684–1710 (pp. 256, 271, and 325), a general picture of the private trade (p. 259), details on various imports and exports from 1684–1710 (p. 267), details on copper for 1684–1710 (p. 274), Korean cotton exports for 1684–1710 (p. 277), Korean textiles for 1684–1710 (p. 284), and ginseng for 1674–1712 (pp. 286–287). Chŏng Sŏng-il's addenda contain data on the volume of Korean return gifts in the seventeenth century (pp. 366–373), Japanese silver exports in the private trade for 1687–1743 (pp. 383–384), Korean exports and imports for 1844–1849 (pp. 385–387), detailed information on Japanese exports and imports for 1695 (p. 390), and information on Japanese exports and imports for 1684–1710 (pp. 391–400).

122 Nakamura Tadashi, "Kinsei Ni-Chō shibōeki ron no saikentō," in Such'on Pak Yŏng-sŏk kyosu hwagap kinyŏm nonch'ong kanhaeng wiwŏnhoe, ed., *Such'on Pak Yŏng-sŏk kyosu hwagap kinyŏm Hanguk sahak nonch'ong*, 2 (Kwach'ŏn: Kuksa P'yŏnch'an Wiwŏnhoe), 1992: 774.

123 Chŏng Sŏng-il, *Chosŏn hugi tae-Il muyŏk*, p. 189.

124 Robert L. Innes, "The Door Ajar," pp. 426–427.

125 Chŏng Sŏng-il, *Chosŏn hugi tae-Il muyŏk*, pp. 177–200.

126 Chŏng Sŏng-il, *Chosŏn hugi tae-Il muyŏk*, pp. 191–194 and p. 360.

127 Chŏng Sŏng-il, *Chosŏn hugi tae-Il muyŏk*, pp. 188–190 and p. 360.

128 Robert Innes offers a broad and comprehensive picture of Japanese trade in the seventeenth century and includes Tsushima trade with Korea and Satsuma trade with the Ryūkyūs. He argues that Japanese silver flowed out and Chinese silk flowed in. If the flow was hampered in Nagasaki, then it would shift to Tsushima and Satsuma. See: Robert L. Innes, "The Door Ajar," pp. 193–198.

129 Chŏng Sŏng-il, *Chosŏn hugi tae-Il muyŏk*, p. 197.

130 Chŏng Sŏng-il, *Chosŏn hugi tae-Il muyŏk*, pp. 201–232.

131 Chŏng Sŏng-il, *Chosŏn hugi tae-Il muyŏk*, pp. 343 and 352.

132 Chŏng, Sŏng-il, *Chosŏn hugi tae-Il muyŏk*, p. 352.

133 Ronald P. Toby, *State and Diplomacy in Early Modern Japan: Asia in the Development of the Tokugawa Bakufu* (Princeton: Princeton University Press), 1984: xvii–xviii.

134 Dennis O. Flynn, "Comparing the Tokugawa Shogunate with Habsburg Spain: Two Silver-Based Empires in a Global Setting," in James D. Tracy, ed., *The Political Economy of Merchant Empires: State Power and World Trade, 1350–1750* (Cambridge: Cambridge University Press), 1991: 335. See also: Dennis O. Flynn and Arturo Giráldez, "Born with a 'Silver Spoon': The Origin of World Trade in 1571," *Journal of World History*, 6:2 (1995 Fall): 201–221. Flynn and Giráldez argue that "global trade" dates from 1571 with the founding of Manila and the establishment of the trans-Pacific silver trade that linked

China to the Americas to Iberia. Silver profits powered both Habsburg Spain and Tokugawa Japan. By the mid-seventeenth century, the profits were disappearing, because the price of silver was falling to meet the cost of production. The world-wide decline in the price of silver resulted in a global price inflation for those economies on a silver standard.

135 Robert L. Innes, "The Door Ajar," p. 24. Innes borrows a description of the *haifuki* (cupellation) process from Kobata Atsushi: The silver ore is melted with lead. The silver–lead alloy is then re-melted and poured into ash. The lead sinks into the ash, leaving the silver on top.

136 Forgery was not limited to the Yanagawa Incident of the 1630s, but was commonly practiced on the frontier with Korea. For example, see: Nakamura Hidetaka, *Ni-Sen kankeishi no kenkyū*, 2 (Tōkyō: Yoshikawa Kōbunkan), 1969: 250 for a brief explanation of how Konishi Yukinaga and Sō Yoshitoshi were faced with a dilemma over clearly expressing Hideyoshi's intention to conquer the Ming and obfuscated matters by opening negotiations with Korea over "borrowing a road to enter China."

137 Osa Masanori, "Ni-Sen kankei ni okeru kiroku no jidai," *Tōyō gakuhō*, 50:4 (1968): 117–121. Osa identifies a "period of record-keeping" beginning in the first half of the seventeenth century and extending through to the Meiji Restoration. The reasons he gives for the sudden interest in documents are: (1) the Tsushima daimyo centralized his power in the seventeenth century, finally displacing the power of local clans and bureaucratizing his domain government; (2) with the 1635 exposure of diplomatic forgery called the Yanagawa Incident, the Yanagawa clan, which had dominated appointments of *Daikan* (K: *Taegwan*, the Daikan was the *daimyō* deputy in charge of trade accounts) to the Japan House and had monopolized control over Korean trade and diplomacy, was finally displaced and their functions taken over by the *han* government; (3) Tsushima was responding to a new resolve in Korea to tighten control over Japanese relations, a resolve arising from a stabilization of relations with the new Manchu regime and increasing internal recovery.

138 See: *Chōsen koku kōbōeki aitodokori on kattemuki on nanjū no omomuki oyobi go naii sōrō tokoro okane ichi man ryō on haishaku narabi nennen hannō kin on sashinobi no kiroku*, MS B30/154 in Kyūshū daigaku bungakubu Kyūshū bunkashi kenkyū shitsu shisetsuso, and Ōba Ikuyo, "Kinsei Ni-Chō kankei ni okeru Yakkanshi" (unpublished M.A. thesis, Keiō University), 1994 and Ōba Ikuyo, "Tsushima han ni yoru Chōsen-gawa shōtsūji e no enjo," *Mita Chūseishi kenkyū*, 4 (October, 1997): 102–115.

139 Chŏng Sŏng-il, *Chosŏn hugi tae-Il muyŏk*, pp. 142–143.

140 Kim Tong-ch'ŏl criticizes Japanese scholarship on Korean–Japanese trade as being a mere extension of questions central to the Japanese economy. See: Kim Tong-ch'ŏl, "*Tongnae-bu sanggoan* ŭl t'onghaesŏ pon 19 segi huban ŭi Tongnae sangin: *Tongnae muim sŏnsaeng'an* kwa ŭi pigyo," *Han-Il kwangyesa yŏn'gu*, 1 (1993.10): 116.

141 Tashiro Kazui has given us an annual chart of private trade copper exports for the years 1684–1710. Care should be taken with the presentation here of an "average." Tashiro notes that from 1678 the Korean government began to mint coins and the Korean demand for Japanese copper soared. From 1698 the *bakufu* devalued its silver coinage and this presented serious problems for the Korea trade as copper was seen as an alternative. From 1701, the *bakufu* established a *dō-za* (administration for copper) in Nagasaki, and at about the same time, a peak was reached in the production of Japanese copper. The *dō-za* resulted in a radical decline in the private copper trade from 1703. All of these events resulted in fluctuations; therefore, to present her findings as an average is rather simplistic. The point is to show a rough annual estimate. See: Tashiro Kazui, *Kinsei Ni-Chō tsūkō bōekishi no kenkyū*, pp. 274–275. The figure for tin was given to me in personal correspondence.

142 Chŏng Sŏng-il, *Chosŏn hugi tae-Il muyŏk*, p. 171.

143 Chŏng Sŏng-il, *Chosŏn hugi tae-Il muyŏk*, pp. 385–387.

144 Kim Yŏng-ho, "Ansŏng hogi sanŏp e'gwan han chosa pogo," *Asea yŏn'gu*, 8:4 (1965:12): 158.

145 Kim Pyŏng-ha, *Yijo chŏngi tae-Il muyŏk yŏn'gu* (Seoul: Hanguk Yŏn'guwŏn), 1969: 153.

146 Kim Ok-kŭn, *Chosŏn hugi kyŏngchesa yŏn'gu* (Seoul: Sŏmundang, 1977): 71–72.

147 *Tongnae-buji* (1740) in Kim Tong-ch'ŏl, ed., *Tongnae saryo*, 2, p. 61. No other Tongnae gazetteer mentions craftsmen of any sort.

148 Tashiro Kazui, *Kinsei Ni-Chō tsūkō bōekishi no kenkyū*, pp. 331–334ff. and "Exports of Japan's silver to China via Korea and changes in the Tokugawa monetary system during the seventeenth and eighteenth centuries," in Eddy H.G. Van Cauwenberghe, ed., *Precious Metals, Coinage and the Changes of Monetary Structures in Latin-America, Europe and Asia: Late Middle Ages–Early Modern Times* (Leuven: Leuven University Press), 1989: 99–116.

149 The identity and activities of these merchants relate directly to questions of pre-modern capital accumulation and transport. See: Kim Tong-ch'ŏl, "Tongnae-bu," p. 116.

150 Tashiro Kazui, "Bakumakki Ni-Chō shi bōeki to Wakan bōeki shōnin: yunyū yon hinmoku no torihiki o chūshin ni" in Hayami Tōru *et al.*, ed., *Tokugawa shakai kara no tenbō: hatten-kōzō-kokusai kankei* (Tōkyō: Dōbunkan), 1989: 299–323; Kim Tong-ch'ŏl, "Chosŏn hugi su'ugak muyŏk kwa kung'gak kyegong'in," (Pusan taehakkyo, Hanguk munhwa yŏn'guso) *Hanguk munhwa yŏn'gu*, 4 (1991:12): 55–110; Kim Tong-ch'ŏl, *Chosŏn hugi kong'in yŏn'gu* (Seoul: Hanguk Yŏn'guwŏn), 1993; Kim Tong-ch'ŏl, "19 segi up'i muyŏk kwa Tongnae sang'in," (Pusan taehakkyo, Hanguk munhwa yŏn'guso) *Hanguk munhwa yŏn'gu*, 6 (1993:8): 399–440; Kim Tong-ch'ŏl, "*Tongnae-bu sanggoan* ŭl t'onghaesŏ pon 19 segi huban ŭi Tongnae sang'in: *Tongnae muim sŏnsaeng-an* kwa ŭi pigyo," *Han-Il kwangyesa yŏn'gu*, 1 (1993.10): 115–144; Kim Tong-ch'ŏl, "18 segi pinggye ŭi ch'angsŏl kwa togo hwaldong," *Pudae sahak* (1995:6): 383–414; Kim Tong-ch'ŏl, "Chosŏn hugi Waegwan kaesi muyŏk kwa Tongnae sang'in," *Minjok munhwa*, 21 (1998:12): 56–82. See also O Sŏng, *Chosŏn hugi sang'in yŏn'gu* (Seoul: Ilchogak), 1989 for a general description of ginseng merchants and their trade with Japan.

151 Kim Tong-ch'ŏl, "*Tongnae-bu sanggoan*," p. 116.

152 Oda Ikugoro made this observation in 1796. Chŏng Sŏng-il, *Chosŏn hugi tae-Il muyŏk*, p. 154.

153 Much of the following description is taken from Chŏng Sŏng-il, *Chosŏn hugi tae-Il muyŏk*, pp. 69–107, except where indicated.

154 Chŏng Sŏng-il, *Chosŏn hugi tae-Il muyŏk*, p. 73.

155 Chong Sŏng-il, *Chosŏn hugi tae-Il muyŏk*, pp. 83–84.

156 Although Chapter 5 will argue that the careers of Tongnae magistrates suffered from the outbreak of incidents involving Japanese and that magistrates would be pre-disposed to quelling activities in general, Chŏng Sŏng-il is correct in pointing to the profit motive that undoubtedly animated local officials and their society. Undoubtedly, trade with Japan was a Janus-faced proposition for the Koreans: on the one hand it created social and political disturbances, but on the other it brought goods and tax revenues.

157 Chŏng Sŏng-il, *Chosŏn hugi tae-Il muyŏk*, pp. 104–107 and, in particular, pp. 94–95 and p. 106 for the arguments regarding the correlation between the Japan House market days and Tongnae County market days. The primary evidence he provides are a 1796 note by a Waegwan Japanese indicating knowledge of the county's market days and a demonstration of concentration patterns in the monthly opening days for the 1720s, 1730s, 1810s, and 1840s. Clearly, more work needs to be done to establish the market connections, but comparable data from the Korean side has yet to be identified. Reasons for Waegwan great market cancellation were both economic and non-economic. About 60 percent of cancellations were due to merchants, both Korean and Japanese, being unable to deliver goods to market, indicating the overwhelming character of the market as driven by the supply of goods and their price. About 15 percent of closures were due to the absence of officials or official holidays such as state funerals. About 15 percent were due to bad weather.

158 *Ichi Daikan mainikki* and *Chōsen go Daikan kiroku*.

159 Chŏng Sŏng-il, *Chosŏn hugi tae-Il muyŏk*, pp. 145–173.

160 Kim Tong-ch'ŏl, "*Tongnae-bu sanggoan*," pp. 115–144.

161 For lists of local officials, see: Kim Tong-ch'ŏl, ed., *Tongnae saryo*, 1 (Seoul: Yŏgang Ch'ulp'ansa), 1989: 259–558.

162 The Kiyŏnghoe was founded in 1846 with 40 members and combined societies for former military and civil officials. See: Kim Tong-ch'ŏl, "*Tongnae-bu sanggoan*," p. 139.

163 Kim Tong-ch'ŏl, *"Tongnae-bu sanggoan,"* p. 143.
164 Chŏng Sŏng-il, *Chosŏn hugi tae-Il muyŏk*, pp. 385–387.
165 Chŏng Sŏng-il, *Chosŏn hugi tae-Il muyŏk*, pp. 162, 171.
166 Chŏng Sŏng-il, *Chosŏn hugi tae-Il muyŏk*, pp. 171–172. Chŏng identifies his source as the *Mainikki*. Whether this was the *Mainikki* (daily record) kept by the Master of the Japan House or the *Mainikki* kept by the daikan (*Ichi Daikan mainikki*) is unspecified.
167 Chŏng Sŏng-il, *Chosŏn hugi tae-Il muyŏk*, p. 169.
168 As above, the method for calculating the number of people in a single household is to take the average household size for 1867 (3.82) and 1789 (4.15) and multiply that by the number of household heads. Average size is taken from Tables 3.5 and 3.6.
169 Kim argues that "private" trade may not be the most useful term, since Japanese documents that record "private" trade also probably record smuggling within that category. To isolate this trade from other forms of non-official trade such as smuggling, he suggests calling private trade "market trade" to emphasize the site of the transaction – the market. Kim Tong-ch'ŏl, "Chosŏn hugi Waegwan kaesi muyŏk kwa Tongnae sang'in," (Pusan taehakkyo) *Minjok munhwa*, 21 (1998:12): 79–80.
170 These comments come from Kim Tong-ch'ŏl, "Chosŏn hugi Waegwan kaesi muyŏk kwa Tongnae sang'in," pp. 56–82.

4 THE ECONOMIC SIGNIFICANCE OF THE WAEGWAN

1 *Haedong chegukki*, Taemado. Virtually identical passages are repeated in the 1740 *Tongnaebuji*, sanch'ŏn and the 1832 *Tongnae-bu ŭpchi*, tosŏ Chŏlyŏng-do.
2 Baud and van Schendel, p. 231.
3 Yi Hyŏn-jong, *Chosŏn chŏngi tae-Il kyosŏpsa yŏn'gu* (Seoul: Hanguk Yŏn'guwŏn), 1964; Nakamura Hidetaka, *Ni-Sen kankeishi no kenkyū*, in three volumes, (Tōkyō: Yoshikawa Kōbunkan), 1965–1969; Kim Pyŏng-ha, *Yijo chŏngi tae-Il muyŏk yŏn'gu* (Seoul: Hanguk Yŏnguwŏn), 1969; and Tashiro Kazui, *Kinsei Ni-Chō tsūkō bōekishi no kenkyū* (Tōkyō: Sōbunsha), 1981.
4 A major component of *bakufu* legitimacy was its claim to be able to manage foreign relations and to defend the land from foreign threats. We know this to be true through hindsight. When the *bakufu* appeared unable to control foreigners from the 1850s, its legitimacy evaporated and it was destroyed.
5 Kenneth R. Robinson, "Policies of Practicality: The Chosŏn Court's Regulation of Contact with Japanese and Jurchens, 1392–1580s" (unpublished dissertation, University of Hawai'i), 1997. See also: Kenneth R. Robinson, "From Raiders to Traders: Border Security and Border Control in Early Chosŏn, 1392–1450," *Korean Studies*, 16 (1992): 94–115; Kenneth R. Robinson, "The Jiubian and Ezogachishima Embassies to Chosŏn, 1478–1482," *Chōsenshi kenkyūkai ronbunshū*, 35 (1997): 55–86 (234–203), and Kenneth R. Robinson, "The Tsushima Governor and Regulation of Japanese Access to Chosŏn in the Fifteenth and Sixteenth Centuries," *Korean Studies*, 20 (1996): 23–50.
6 There is no space to consider the other side of the equation: the functions and costs of Chosŏn envoys to Japan. In Japan, reception of the Korean Communication Embassy placed extraordinary burdens on the domains and the *bakufu*. By examining those costs in some detail, we find similar concrete and quantifiable expressions of Japan's engagement with Korea. This is the proper subject of another study.
7 Nakamura Hidetaka, *Ni-Sen kankeishi no kenkyū*, 3, p. 291 ff.; Tashiro Kazui, *Kinsei Ni-Chō tsūkō bōekishi no kenkyū*, p. 44 ff.; Ronald Toby, *State and Diplomacy in Early Modern Japan: Asia in the Development of the Tokugawa Bakufu* (Princeton: Princeton University Press), 1984, p. 39 ff.
8 *T'ongmun'gwanji*, 5:24a–26a and *Chŭngjŏng kyorinji*, 4:1a–2a for the Agreements of 1443, 1512, and 1609. The Agreement of 1443 allowed Sŏ to send 50 Annual Ships in addition to an unspecified number of Special Envoys and allotted him 200 sŏk of grains (rice and beans) a year. The Agreement of 1512 followed the 1510 Riot of the Three Ports. Its terms reduced the grain allotment to 100 sŏk and the number of Annual Ships to 25. In an attempt to forestall Japanese immigration, it forbade "receptions" for seal-holders,

effectively forbidding Japanese residency, and specified sizes and crew numbers for types of ships. It fixed the number of Special Envoys and stipulated that emergency communications be carried by Annual Ships. It limited those who had received commissions from the Chosŏn court to one ship a year and one envoy to visit the capital. Although not specified in the agreement, trading was limited to only one port. Amendments in the 1540s to the 1512 Agreement are not mentioned but can be found in the *Chōsen tsūkō daiki* by Matsuura Masatada (1676–1728). Matsuura was a Confucianist in the employ of Tsushima who compiled documents on Japanese (Tsushima)–Korean relations from the Muromachi period through the first century of Tokugawa rule. See: Matsuura, Masatada, *Chōsen tsūkō daiki*, ed. by Tanaka Takeo and Tashiro Kazui, (Tōkyō: Meicho shuppan), 1978: 108. Here we learn that Chep'o was closed and the Waegwan moved to Pusan in 1544. We also learn that the number of Annual Ships was increased to 30 in 1564–1565. Although based on these earlier agreements, the Kiyu Agreement of 1609 was the most elaborate and most restrictive to date. In addition to the limitations discussed in the text, it set limits on the number of days envoys from Tsushima and castaways could be in port drawing support; it specified procedures for certifying an envoy's authenticity; it limited envoys given receptions at the Waegwan to three types: envoys of the Japanese "king" (shogun), Special Envoys from Tsushima, and Tsushima men with Korean commissions.

9 See: Maurice Courant, "Un Établissement Japonais en Corée: Pusan depuis le XVe siècle," *Annales Coloniales* (Paris, 15 Août–1 Octobre 1904), reprinted in Centre d'Études Coréennes, Collège de France, ed., *Cahiers d'Études Coréennes, 1, Études Coréennes de Maurice Courant* (Paris: Editions du Léopard d'Or), 1983: 253–289. Maurice Courant explains these other ships as follows:

1   From 1611, Yanagawa Kagenao was allowed one ship, which, after his son was censured in the Yanagawa Incident of 1635, reverted to Sō as the Additional Special Envoy (40 man crew). The Three Special Envoys and Yanagawa's ship (later the Additional Special Envoy) were also allowed a support ship (30 man crew) and a ship for water and wood (20 man crew). The First Annual Ship was also permitted a ship for water and wood (15 man crew).

2   In recognition of Sō Yoshitomo's contribution to peace-making, a ship bearing his posthumous name, Banshōin, was permitted to land (40 man crew) with a water and wood ship (15 man crew).

3   A similar ship honoring the memory of Yanagawa Kagenao was briefly permitted from 1621 to the Yanagawa Incident in 1635.

4   Another, similar ship for the monk Gensō, the diplomat and peacemaker, was granted in 1609 and briefly terminated from 1636 to 1638 (40 man crew). It was also allowed a water and wood ship (15 man crew).

5   A seal was also issued to Yoshitoshi, bearing the childhood name for his son, Yoshinari or (Taira no) Hikosan, in 1610–1611 and was used until Yoshinari's death in 1657. In fact, there were at least two other similar cases (see below, case number 6 and 1823–1839) of a seal being issued for a minor; usually such was given to the island lord's heir apparent. The ship carried 40 men but was not allowed a water and wood ship.

6   A seal was issued with (Taira no) Yoshizane's name when be became heir apparent to Yoshinari and was returned at his death in 1702.

See also *Tongnae-bu saye*, Waegwan-cho, 1868 (Kyujanggak cat. no. 4272) in Kim Tong-ch'ŏl et al., ed., *Tongnae saryo*, 2 (Seoul: Yŏgang ch'ulp'ansa, 1989): 677. Although the envoy was terminated, we can see its costs in Table 4.6, "Envoy using the Island Lord's juvenile name." According to McCune's annotated bibliography attached to his dissertation ("Korean relations with China and Japan, 1800–1864," unpublished dissertation at the University of California, Berkeley, 1941), the following, more general, studies preceded Courant, but I have, as yet, been unable to investigate their contents: A. D. Heard, W. Stevens, and H. Martin, "China and Japan in Korea," *North American Review*, 159 (1894:9); Hattori Toru, *Nikkan Kōtsū-shi*, (Seoul), 1895; and J. H. Longford, "Japan's

Relations with Korea in the 19th century," *Nineteenth Century*, 55 (1904), 618–629. Also of interest from pre-WWII scholarship are: Yamagata Isoh, "Japanese–Korean relations after the Japanese Invasion of Korea in the 16th century," *Transactions, Korea Branch of the Royal Asiatic Society*, 4 (1913), 1–11, and Yoshi S. Kuno, *Japanese Expansion on the Asiatic Continent* (Berkeley: University of California Press), vol. 1 (1937) and vol. 2 (1940). As an aside, we should note that Courant states that the main result of Hideyoshi's invasion for Korea was to force it into isolation. He mentions a variety of other problems that have become subjects for modern scholars: the T'ongsinsa (including the Nikkō sojourns); Genpō's trip to Hanyang in 1629; the Yanagawa incident of 1635; and concludes from the terms used in the list of presents (*pyŏlp'ok* and *pongjin*) that the two parties (Korea and Japan) were viewing each other as equals (p. 274), anticipating an interpretation that has become popular in the last quarter of the twentieth century (e.g. Ronald Toby argues the same based on the forms of address used in state letters). Courant also takes note of Southeast Asian products in the lists of tribute goods and comments that we might compare the tribute goods lists for each country from the fifteenth and seventeenth centuries as a way to judge the development of manufactures.

10 Please see Note 21 on p. 277.

11 Tashiro Kazui, *Kinsei Ni-Chō tsūkō bōekishi no kenkyū*, and in particular, Chapter 2 of Part 1, "Kinsei shotō no bōeki ninpō to torihiki hinmoku."

12 *Chŭngjŏng kyorinji*, 4:1a–2a.

13 For the classic studies of the *taedongbŏp* in Ch'ungch'ŏng and Chŏlla Provinces, see: Han Yŏng-guk, "Ho-sŏ e silsi toen Taedongbŏp (part one): Taedongbŏp yŏn'gu ŭi ilch'ak," *Yŏksa hakpo*, 13 (1960.10): 77–107; Han Yŏng-guk, "Ho-sŏ e silsi toen Taedongbŏp (part two): Taedongbŏp yŏn'gu ŭi ilch'ak," *Yŏksa hakpo*, 14 (1961.4): 77–132; Han Yŏng-guk, "Ho-nam e silsi toen Taedongbŏp (part one): Ho-sŏ Taedongbŏp kwa ŭi pigyo mit ch'ŏmpo," *Yŏksa hakpo*, 15 (1961.9): 31–59; Han Yŏng-guk, "Ho-nam e silsi toen Taedongbŏp (part two): Ho-sŏ Taedongbŏp kwa ŭi pigyo mit ch'ŏmpo," *Yŏksa hakpo*, 20 (1963.4): 29–80; Han Yŏng-guk, "Ho-nam e silsi toen Taedongbŏp (part three): Ho-sŏ Taedongbŏp kwa ŭi pigyo mit ch'ŏmpo," *Yŏksa hakpo*, 21 (1963.8): 67–99; Han Yŏng-guk, "Ho-nam e silsi toen Taedongbŏp (part four and final): Ho-sŏ Taedongbŏp kwa ŭi pigyo mit ch'ŏmpo," *Yŏksa hakpo*, 24 (1964.7): 91–117. See also: Rokutanda Yutaka, "Yŏngnam Taedong Samok to Keishōdō Daidōhō," *Chōsen gakuhō*, 131 (1989.4): 1–56. Rokutanda Yutaka has done us a great service by reconstructing a document many thought lost, the *Taedong Samok* from 1678 for Kyŏngsang Province, thus giving us three case studies of the first years of the *taedongbŏp*. See also: Kim Ok-kŭn, *Chosŏn wangjo chaejŏngsa yŏn'gu*, 3 (Seoul: Ilchogak), 1988: 197–230. For a general outline in English, see: James Palais, *Confucian Statecraft and Korean Institutions: Yu Hyŏngwŏn and the Later Chosŏn Dynasty* (Seattle: University of Washington Press), 1996: 769–854.

14 Kim Ok-kŭn, *Chosŏn wangjo chaejŏngsa yŏn'gu* (Seoul: Ilchogak), 1984: 8.

15 Ruisu Jeimusu, "Kinsei Chōsenjin no Nihon-kan: Wakan ni okeru kōbōeki-settai no hiyō wo reiji toshite," *Nenpō Chōsengaku*, 2 (1992.3): 1–38.

16 There were three ways to measure land: area of seeding, area tilled in a day, and area based on the size of harvest or *kyŏlbu*.

17 Until recently, the dating of the records in the *T'akjijŏn pugo* had been unclear, but Jun Seongho has employed local data in comparison with the central records of the *T'akjijŏn pugo* to make a convincing case for the dates used here. His work shows a strong correlation between the actual assessments and relief for weather recorded in the *T'akjijŏn pugo* and the price of rice recorded in various areas in the three southern provinces. The correlation between the macro data (*T'akjijŏn pugo*, dating unclear) and the micro data (dating clear) allows him to date the macro data with greater certainty than has been the case so far. See: Jun Seong-ho, "Chosŏn hugi mi-gasa yŏn'gu, 1725–1875," unpublished Ph.D. dissertation (Sŏnggyungwan University, 1998): 122. According to Jun's dating, the last date in the *T'akjijŏn pugo* is 1900, so the compilation must have been completed soon thereafter. *T'akjijŏn pugo*, reprinted in *Sahoe kyŏngjesa saryo ch'ongsŏ 3, T'akjijŏn pugo* (Seoul: Yŏgang Ch'ulp'ansa), 1986. Original data for Figures 4.1 and 4.2 can be found in Appendix B.

18 E. P. Thompson, "The Moral Economy of the English Crowd in the Eighteenth Century", *Past and Present*, 50 (1971). Reprinted in E. P. Thompson, *Customs in Common: Studies in Traditional Popular Culture*, (New York: The New Press), 1993, 185–258. James C. Scott, *The Moral Economy of the Peasant: Rebellion and Subsistence in Southeast Asia* (New Haven: Yale University Press), 1976.

19 Standard deviation: 14,731.2107 *kyŏl*; minimum: 134,696; maximum: 226,044.

20 We can see a variety of magistracies in Kyŏngsang Province mentioned in the following documents. Records (a) and (b) represent central government plans, while (c) through (f) represent actual practice.

(a) We see 17 magistracies listed in *Mangi yoram*, (1807), chaeyong-p'yŏn, fascicle 5, Waeryang, ha'nap kaekŭp;

(b) We see 17 magistracies listed in *T'akjijŏn pugo*, (c.1900), saye, suse or page 7b in *T'akjijŏn pugo*;

(c) We see 50 magistracies which supplied rice, cotton, or other goods to Tongnae for the Japanese listed in the *Puyŏk silch'ong, vol. 2*, Kyŏngsang-do (compiled in 1794) (Kyujanggak cat. no. 252) (Seoul: Yŏgang Ch'ulp'ansa), 1984;

(d) We see 36 magistracies and transport costs from these locations listed in *Yŏngnamch'ŏng saye*, Waegwan soyong, ha'nap sŏn'ga (compiled between 1811 and 1825, Kyujanggak cat. no. 15233). This section of the document also offers a detailed budget for transport costs for grains and other items from selected places in Kyŏngsang Province. The indeterminate dating derives from the document's composite nature. The entire report in its present form probably dates from around 1830, but from internal evidence, this part was compiled between 1811, the last mentioned date, and 1825, the year a new envoy was added to the list of envoys from Tsushima (a special envoy arriving in Pusan under the juvenile name of the Lord of Tsushima from 1825 to 1839). There is no mention of this envoy among the other budgetary items indicating that the document predates 1825. The date 1830 is suggested by a note in an annotated bibliography for the Kyujanggak collection at Seoul National University Library: *Kyujanggak Hangukbon tosŏ haeje sabu*, vol. 4, (Seoul: Seoul Taehakkyo Tosŏgwan), 1987: 495: "The date of compilation is unclear, but it appears to have been around the final year of Sunjo or 1834." See: Rokutanda Yutaka, "*Yŏngnam taedong samok* to Keishōdō Daidōhō," pp. 35–38 for a general discussion of the *Yŏngnamch'ŏng saye*, "Waegwan soyong" section from the point of view of the *taedongbŏp*;

(e) We see no place names but simply the following comments mentioning 43 or 42 magistracies in *Pyŏllye chibyo*, (compiled after 1843), fascicle 8, 1789.4 entry: "This year the official trade rice and cotton from [Kyŏngsang] Province's Governor's Office was divided among 43 Magistracies." Also see the 1791.3 entry: "The official trade rice and cotton [as well as] the supply rice and soybeans this year from the Governor's Office were apportioned among 42 Magistracies within [Kyŏngsang] Province;"

(f) We also see no place names but simply the following comment mentioning 40 localities in *Tongnae-bu kyerok* (1849–1889) (Kyujanggak cat. no. 15105) 1849/12/27: "Since [supplies] came from the Governor's Office apportioned in [Kyŏngsang] Province among 40 Magistracies...."

21 The map is a digitized version of a Kyŏngsang Province map found in the *Ch'ŏnggu sŏnp'yŏ-do*, drawn by Kim Chŏng-ho during King Sunjo's reign (1800–1834).

22 The actual assessment or *sigi kyŏl* for Ulsan is not available, so the assessment of arable land or the *wŏnjangbu* is substituted. The assessment of arable land was always higher than the actual assessment in any given year. This is clear from the gap between the *wŏnjangbu* and the *ch'ulse silgyŏl* in Table 4.2. The substitution skews the calculation slightly, but the effect is not significant.

23 *Yŏngnamch'ŏng saye* (Kyujanggak cat. no. 15233).

24 *Tongnae-bu saye* (Kyujanggak cat. no. 4272).

25 *Tongnae-bu saye*'s Taedong accounts are found in *Tongnae-bu saye*, Taedong ŭp.

26 Table 4.4 has been prepared from *Tongnae-bu saye*, sŏgye ŭp, kongjangmi.

27 Jeimusu Ruisu, "Jinshin-Teiyŭ Waran ikō Koka jōyaku izen no Chōsen kara mita Tsushima," *Chihōshi kenkyū*, 41:4, vol. 232 (1991:8): 37–53. See Chapter 5.

28 *T'akjijŏn pugo*, saye, suse or page 6b–7a.

29 *Pongnae kosa*, 1651.4 entry. Traditionally, the Korean *sŏk* was composed of either 20 *tu* or 15 *tu*. Officially, the 20-*tu sŏk* was called a *taegok*, and the 15-*tu sŏk* was called a *sogok*. See: *Kyŏngguk taejŏn*, 6:1b–2a, kongjŏn, toyanghyŏng. The 15-*tu sŏk* was very common in Kyŏngsang Province and was used by the government as its standard *sŏk* for taxation purposes.

30 *T'ongmun'gwanji*, 5:3b–10a and *Chŭngjŏng kyorinji*, 1:6a–23a. The 1,120 *tong* is arrived at by adding up the return amounts for "official trade" (*kongmu-ka*) and "tribute trade" (*chinsang-ka*) for each ship listed in the *T'ongmun'gwanji*. In connection with each ship, cotton is mentioned only under official trade and tribute trade. The total for the *Chŭngjŏng kyorinji* (1802) is 1,104 and for the *T'ongmun'gwanji* (1720) is 1,120. The difference indicates a slight change in official and tribute trade between 1720 and 1802. The total for cotton in the *Tongnae-bu saye* (1867) is 664 *tong*, demonstrating a more significant fall. In other parts of the texts, there are separate totals given for the official trade (*Chŭngjŏng kyorinji* 1:32a–32a and *T'ongmun'gwanji* 5:10a–10a). Here, the totals are slightly different. The *Chŭngjŏng kyorinji* records 1,047 *tong* and the *T'ongmun'gwanji* records 1,148 *tong*. The totals for the individual ships have been used here, rather than the lump sums, because we are able to see all transactions involving cotton or both the tribute and the official trade. Within the total amount is 49 *p'il* 15 *ch'ŏk* 3 *ch'on* that was earmarked for the Hundo and the Pyŏlch'a, the Tongnae officials in charge of liaison with the Waegwan.

31 *Pyŏllye chibyo*, fascicle 8, kong muyŏk, (Seoul: Kuksa P'yŏnch'an wiwŏnhoe), 1969: 437 and 440.

32 *Chŭngjŏng kyorinji*, 1:34a.

33 For the conversion of Korean *sŏk* to Japanese *koku*, see: Tashiro Kazui, "Tsushima han no Chōsen komei yunyū to "Wakan masu": Sō-ke kiroku *Koku ikken oboegaki* kara mita Chōsen komei no keiryōhō," *Chōsen gakuhō*, 124 (1987.7): 25. According to Tashiro's interpretation of Amenomori Hōshū's text, one Korean *sŏk* was 0.54427 Japanese *koku*, or one Japanese *koku* was 1.84 Korean *sŏk*.

34 Amenomori Hōshū, *Kōrin teisei*, in Amenomori Hōshū bunko, Amenomori Hōshū-an, Shiga-ken, Ika-gun, Takatsuki-chō, Amenomori-mura, folio 57a–59b.

35 Kim Ok-kŭn, *Chosŏn wangjo chaejŏngsa yŏn'gu*, 3 (Seoul: Ilchogak), 1988: 226. See also Kim Ok-kŭn, *Chosŏn hugi kyŏngjaesa yŏn'gu* (Seoul: Sŏmundang, 1977): 72 and particularly note 42 where he points out that his earlier assertion of 80,752 *sŏk* was mistaken and corrects that to 70,866 *sŏk*.

36 Evidence of the problems that the local peasantry faced in supplying commodities for the Waegwan came to light in the early 1990s. In the summer of 1993, an unofficial report by Professor Chŏng Kyŏng-chu of Kyŏngsŏng University to the city authorities of Pusan reported on a cache of documents produced by the Tongha or Lower East Township of Tongnae found in 1992. The documents were collected, analyzed, translated, and published as a photolithographic reprint in 1994 by the Hyangt'o Munhwa Yŏn'guso (the Local Culture Research Institute of Kyŏngsŏng University) and the Munhwa Kongbo-sil (Cultural Information Unit) of the Haeundae Ward Office. The documents range from 1742 to 1982 with the vast bulk produced before 1910. They discuss the internal workings of the township, a particularly rare find and the first of its kind in Pusan. One of the documents, dated 1815, discusses the finances of supplying fish from the Lower East Township villages to the Waegwan. It suggests a way to finance current losses and produce a surplus whose rate of return would pay future costs. The villagers supplied fish for the Waegwan at an estimated value of a little over 8 *sŏk* 12 *tu* of rice (*kongjangmi*), which came from the county officials. Because sea produce was expensive and there were many Japanese envoys to supply, the additional costs had grown to 125 *yang* of cash annually that had to be borne by the coastal villages, in particular by Haeunjin. Land had been sold to raise funds, and in 1811, the county officials had supplied a subsidy of 150 *yang*, but these steps had not solved the problem. The costs had become a heavy burden on the

coastal villages, and many coastal villagers had absconded to inland areas. The document proposes setting taxes on those villagers who had moved from coastal villages inland to raise 60 *yang*. This would be combined with 57 *yang* from the sale of 8 *turak* of land, plus 150 *yang* from the county officials. The total capital raised would be 267 *yang*, which could then be lent at 30 per cent interest. If this had been done in 1815, when rice prices jumped, the income would have been 96 *yang* per annum. In addition, the original 8 *sŏk* 12 *tu* of rice supplied to pay for the fish would continue and this would be sold at market value. In 1815, the price of rice had spiked, so when the 8 *sŏk* 12 *tu* of rice was sold, it generally met the 125 *yang* cost overrun. Since this scheme would generate funds surpassing the cost of supplying fish, the surplus could be used to buy land that would add to the tax base. For the initial report, see: Chŏng Kyŏng-chu, "Tongnae-bu Tongha myŏn komunsŏ e tae hayŏ," *Pusan-si* (1993.8.26). I want to thank Mr. Tada Yukio for bringing this report to my attention. For the document in translation and facsimile, see: *Tongha-myŏn komunsŏ* (entries 1742–1982). Translation into modern Korean, annotation, and photolithographic reprint in *(Haeundae ŭi yet mosŭp-i tam'gin) Tongha-myŏn komunsŏ* (Pusan: Haeundae-ku ch'ŏng), 1994. In the area, similar documents came to light in 1993 in Kimhae, but I have yet to see these.

37 *Pongnae kosa*, 1634.2 entry. The *Pongnae kosa* in the Tenri University Library was reproduced in *Chōsen gakuhō*, 57–58 (1970.10). The most important difference between Kim Ok-kŭn's research and the present study is the documents used. For the purpose of calculating expenses associated with the Japanese for the *early* Chosŏn period (pre-1600), there is no other method presently known but to infer from the *Haedong chegukki* and the *Veritable Records* of the Chosŏn Dynasty, both of which are documents prepared by the central government. For a re-construction of accounts from the fifteenth century, see Ruisu Jeimusu, "Kinsei Chōsenjin no Nihon-kan: Wakan ni okeru kōbōeki-settai no hiyō o reiji toshite," *Nenpō Chōsengaku*, 2 (1992.3): 1–38 or James B. Lewis, "The Pusan Japan House (Waegwan) and Chosŏn Korea: early-modern Korean views of Japan through economic, political, and social connections" (unpublished dissertation, University of Hawai'i, 1994): 127–148. When we come to the *later* Chosŏn period (post-1600), since records about the finances of the Tongnae Magistracy remain for us, conjecture and supposition are unnecessary. The documents central to Kim Ok-kŭn's research for the *later* period are those prepared by the central bureaucracy: *Mangi yoram*, *Tongmun'gwanji*, and *Chŭngjŏng kyorinji*, or by the Provincial Governor: *Yŏngnamch'ŏng saye*. But the documents employed here are those prepared by the central bureaucracy (the above and the *T'akjijŏn pugo*), those prepared by the central bureaucracy but which report information directly from provincial officials (*Pyŏllye chibyo*, *Yŏngnamch'ŏng saye*), and documents prepared by county officials (*Tongnae-bu ŭpchi*, *Tongnae-bu kyenok*, and the *Tongnae-bu saye*). Among these county level documents, the *Tongnae-bu ŭpchi* (Tongnae County Gazetteers) and *Tongnae-bu saye* (Ledger of Tongnae County) deserve special mention. There are six extant *Tongnae-bu ŭpchi* prior to 1900: 1740, 1759, 1832, 1871, 1895, and 1899. Among these, the 1740 and 1759 gazetteers lack enough detailed economic information to be of any use. The 1895 and 1899 gazetteers post-date the Kanghwa Treaty of 1876 and so must be set to one side as materials to be used for the modern history of Pusan Harbor after it was opened to nineteenth-century trade. In what follows, we have made extensive use of the 1832 and 1871 gazetteers. Far surpassing gazetteers in their economic data is the *Tongnae-bu saye* (1868), the most detailed economic document on Tongnae County from the pre-modern period. It describes all aspects of government taxes and expenditures for Tongnae County. Below we contrast it to the *Mangi yoram*, an economic document prepared by the central government, and note that despite its detail, the *Tongnae-bu saye* does not include certain expenditures associated with the Japanese. In short, any discussion of expenses related to the Japanese must use the documents prepared by central officials as well as those prepared by provincial and local officials. A comparison of the micro with the macro is critical to understanding.

38 Tashiro Kazui, *Kinsei Ni-Chō tsūkō bōekishi no kenkyū*, pp. 276–278.

39 Kim Ok-kŭn's confusion probably stems from the following passage in the *Mangi yoram*: "Tax beans 7 *tu* 5 *sung*, tax rice 5 *tu*, military training tax rice 6 *tu*, each converts to one

bolt of official cotton; but when exchanging [cotton] for rice, one bolt of cotton obtains 12 *tu* of rice from the people." See also Table 4.5, note g.

40 Kim Ok-kǔn gives no citation for his datum, but I have been able to locate the passage in the *Sǔngjǒngwǒn ilgi*, fascicle 1500, 1781/12/28, (Kwach'ǒn: Kuksa p'yǒnch'an wiwǒnhoe): 879–880:

> The Governor of Kyǒngsang Province, Cho Si-jun's report reads: . . .' On the problem of the coastal and riverine towns seeking reductions in sequestered [tax grains] (under the Taedong tax law that keeps part of the taxes in the province). The Necessary Expenditure (*ǔng'yong*) for one year from the Sequestered Rice (*chǒch'imi*), at its greatest, reaches 60–70,000 *sǒk*, and at its smallest, does not drop below 40–50,000 *sǒk*. Thus the earliest Taedong [tax usage] scheme, with its 80,000 [*sǒk*] plan, possibly had a planned amount that was realistic. [But] in recent years, capital officials have expropriated [our taxes], and [there have been] calamities without number. [We] collect taxes and then plan their disbursement. [But we obtain only] 30,000 *sǒk* or 24–25,000 *sǒk*. Every appropriation is necessary, [but we] are unable to continue payments. Since the military controls the ever-normal granaries' rice, [we] request that [you] inform [them] to shift the registries. Two towns' rice [production] has slowly declined, therefore we have repeatedly shifted ever-normal tax grains into [those] registries, dividing it and disbursing it to the people. Tax rice is taken and used but the registries are shifted. At the time [we collect] tax rice, [we] have already passed the appointed time for [its] use. Thereby, the requirements to entertain the Wae at [Tong]nae year after year have a consistent form, coming to over 10,000 *sǒk*. If we put a value on the times when the *Pyǒlch'awae* (irregular envoys) come and go, then [we must] employ special criteria and dispense provisions. Assuredly, there is no fixed limit.

The passage indicates that Taedong tax rice was directed to the Waegwan and seems to imply this was for irregular envoys. For a discussion of "Sequestered Rice" and "Necessary Expenditure", see: Rokutanda Yutaka, "*Yǒngnam taedong samok* to Keishōdō Daidōhō," Illustration 2, p. 47, for a clear and graphic description of Kyǒngsang Province's taxes, their classifications, and destinations.

41 Kasuya Kenichi, "Naze Chōsen Tsūshinshi wa haishi sareta ka – Chōsen shiryō o chūshin ni," *Rekishi hyōron*, 355 (1979.11): 17.

42 Kim Yǒng-ho, "Ansǒng hogi sanǒp e'gwan han chosa pogo," *Asea yǒn'gu*, 8:4 (1965.12): 157–164. Kim Pyǒng-ha, *Yi Chosǒn chǒngi tae-Il muyǒk yǒn'gu* (Seoul: Hanguk Yǒn'guwǒn), 1969: 153. See: Kim Ok-kǔn, *Chosǒn hugi kyǒngjesa yǒn'gu* (Seoul: Sǒmundang), 1977: 71–72. For recent studies in Japan on assaying medieval Japanese coinage, see: Saito Tsutomo, Takahashi Teruhiko, and Nishikawa Yuichi, "Chemical Study of the Medieval Japanese *Mochu-sen* (Bronze Coins)," *Institute for Monetary and Economic Studies Discussion Paper*, Bank of Japan (Nov. 1998), Paper No. 98-E-13. I would like to thank Dr. Charlotte Horlyck of the Victoria and Albert Museum for bringing this study to my attention.

43 *Tongnae saryo*, 2, p. 260, *Tongnae-bu ǔpchi*, (1832) ch'anggo sach'ang, taedong ko.

44 *Tongnae saryo*, 2, p. 260, Pu-ch'ang.

45 See Note p, Table 4.5.

46 *Tongnae-bu saye*, taedong ǔp. From the data we cannot determine how much was used for the Irregular Envoys and how much for other purposes.

47 *T'ongmun'gwanji*, 5:12a. See: *Chǔngjǒng kyorinji*, 2:1a–1b for a nearly identical passage.

48 Kasuya Kenichi, "Naze Chōsen Tsūshinshi wa haishi sareta ka: Chōsen shiryō o chūsin ni," pp. 11–13. Kasuya, relying on a 1787 report by Yi I-sang, the Magistrate of Kanggye in P'yǒng'an Province, points out that Kanggye supplied 60 *kǔn* of ginseng for the purpose of the Japanese, and this became a great burden to the people of Kanggye. See: *Chǒngjo Sillok*, 24:6b–8b, (1787/7/18). According to the passage, the official price of ginseng was

672 cash per *kŭn* of ginseng, but the market price was 1600 cash per *kŭn*. Since the ginseng had to be supplied to the government at its price, any shortfalls in production had to be bought by the peasantry on the open market at an exorbitant price and then sold to the government at a great loss.

49 The "*Mangi yoram*'s Japan House cost" is taken from Table 4.8. "Kyŏngsang Province tax revenues" are calculated from Figure 4.2. "*Tongnae-bu saye*'s Japan House cost" is taken from Table 4.7.

50 James B. Lewis, "The Pusan Japan House (Waegwan) and Chosŏn Korea: Early-Modern Korean views of Japan through Economic, Political, and Social Connections" (unpublished Ph.D. dissertation, University of Hawai'i), 1994: 127–148.

51 *Mangi yoram*, chaeyong p'yŏn, fascicle 5, shinsam.

52 Tashiro Kazui "Tōkai Yakkanshi no mitsu bōeki: Tsushima han *Senshō giron* no haikei," *Chōsen gakuhō*, 150 (1994.1): 49.

53 Wŏlgan Sintonga p'yŏn chipsilp'yŏn,Yu Hong-yŏl, ed., *Hanguk ŭl umjikin kojŏn paeksŏn*, *Yŏllyŏsil kisul* by Yi Kŭng-ik (Seoul: Shintong'a po sa), 1978: 112.

54 *Yŏllyŏsil kisul*, pp. 110–112.

55 Ch'oe Yŏng-ho, "An Outline History of Korean Historiography," *Korean Studies*, 4 (1980): 1–27; especially p. 16.

56 Kwŏn O-ton, "*Yŏllyŏsil kisul*," in *Hanguk ŭi myŏngjo* (Seoul: Hyŏnamsa), 1969: 909–910.

57 Roger Chartier, "Intellectual History/History of Mentalities" in Roger Chartier, translated by Lydia G. Cochrane, *Cultural History: Between Practices and Representations* (Ithaca: Cornell University Press, 1988): 42.

58 *Yŏllyŏsil kisul*, volume 11, pyŏljip, fascicle 18, pyŏn'guk chŏngo, Waeguk cho, p. 415 (Seoul: Minjok Munhwa Ch'ujin hoe), 1967, p. 415 (Korean translation), p. 768 (Chinese). See: Nam Man-sŏng, "Yongjae ch'onghwa – haesŏl," in Sŏng Hyŏn, *Yongjae ch'onghwa*, Nam Man-sŏng, trans., (Seoul: Taeyang sŏjŏk), 1973: 23–25; for Sŏng Hyŏn's original passage, see same, pp. 351–353, fascicle 10, entry no. 19.

59 The *Sillok* reports on the Japanese permanent residents of the Three Ports have been collected and analyzed by Nakamura Hidetaka. See: Nakamura Hidetaka, *Ni-Sen kankeishi no kenkyū*, 1 (Tōkyō: Yoshikawa Kōbunkan), 1965: 661.

60 *Sŏngjong Sillok*, 48:19a–25a, (1474/10/28).

61 I wish to thank Professor Yoshida Mitsuo for emphasizing to me the point regarding "lower" Kyŏngsang Province via correspondence with Professor Tashiro Kazui.

62 *Yŏllyŏsil kisul*, pp. 419–420 (Korean translation), p. 770 (Chinese) from the *Ch'un'gwanji*.

63 Yonetani Hitoshi, "Amenomori Hōshū no tai-Chōsen gaikō: 'seishin no kō' no rinen to jittai," *Chōsen gakuhō*, 148 (1993.7): 1–32. Yonetani does an excellent job of probing Hōshū's attitudes toward Korea by examining his deployment of rhetoric to secure Tsushima's interests. One of the immediate problems facing Hōshū as *Saihan* (K: *Chaep'an*), or Special Liaison from the Tsushima *daimyō*, was the re-negotiation of the five-year cotton to rice conversion. See in particular page 5.

64 The lord was Sō Yoshimichi (r. 1694–1718). In 1705, a daughter was born to Yoshimichi, his first child. See: Izumi Chōichi, ed., *Sō shi Jitsuroku, vol. 2, Tsushima han shiryō* (Ōsaka: Seimundō shuppansha), 1988: 56. See also: Suzuki Tōzō, ed., *Sō shi-ke furyaku* (Tōkyō: Murata shoten), 1981: 73. However, the seal was requested for one Hikochiyo who was a child born to the man who would become the next lord of Tsushima, Yoshinobu (b. 1693–r. 1718–d. 1730), Yoshimichi's younger half-brother. See: Takayanagi Mitsunaga *et al.*, ed., *Shintei Kansei jūshū sho kafu*, 8 (Tōkyō: Zoku Gunruijū Kansei Kai), 1965: 264–265. Hence Yoshimichi was requesting a seal for his half-nephew. Hikochiyo died young.

65 Hikomitsu was Sō Yoshizane (r. 1615–1657)'s childhood name. Hikozō is unclear but may have been Hikozō Sadamitsu, Sō Yoshinari (r. 1615–1657)'s childhood name. See: *Sō shi-ke furyaku*, p. 56 and p. 48.

66 Ukyō Yoshitatsu was Sō Yoshitsugu's (r. 1692–1694) childhood name. Jirō was one of Sō Yoshimichi's (r. 1694–1718) childhood names. See: Suzuki Tōzō, *Sō shi-ke furyaku*, p. 66 and p. 69.

67 *Yŏllyŏsil kisul*, p. 426 (Korean translation), p. 773 (Chinese) from the *Piguk tŭngnok*. For information on the *Piguk tŭngnok*, see: Maema Kyōsaku, *Ko-Sen sappu* (Tōkyō: Tōyō Bunko),

1957. Since Yi Kŭng-ik's *Yŏllyŏsil kisul* is not clear, we do not know if the *Piguk tŭngnok* is a text prepared in 1781 based on the *Pibyŏnsa tŭngnok*, an excerpt from the *Pibyŏnsa tŭngnok*, or the *Pibyŏnsa tŭngnok* itself. The title is retained here as given in the source.

68 *T'ongmun'gwanji*, 5:11a–b (kyorin sang).

69 The letter is dated 1874, but the Taewŏngun was forced out of power in the eleventh month of 1873.

70 Yi Hong-chik, *Chŭngbo sae kuksa sajŏn* (Seoul: Ch'ŏng'a Ch'ulpa'nsa), 1983.

71 Yi Ki-baek, *A New History of Korea*, translated by Edward W. Wagner with Edward J. Shultz (Seoul: Ilchogak), 1984: 267–268.

72 *Hwanjaejip*, 11:2b in Hanguk-hak munhŏn yŏn'guso, ed., *Hanguk kŭndae sasang ch'ongsŏ*, *Pak Kyu-su chŏnjip*, 1 (Seoul: Asea Munhwasa), 1978: 752. I wish to thank Professor Kasuya Kenichi for pointing out this passage to me.

73 W. J. Boot, "Yi T'oegye and Japan," *Korea Journal*, 22:2 (1982.2): 18–19. The translation is by W. J. Boot.

74 *Yŏllyŏsil kisul*, p. 425 (Korean translation), p. 772 (Chinese) from the *Piguk tŭngnok*.

5 THE POLITICAL SIGNIFICANCE OF THE WAEGWAN

1 *Waein changna tŭngnok*, Kyujanggak cat. no. 12962, folio 4b. Note: there is no original folio enumeration. I have given each folio a number counting from the first folio.

2 Although the official rank of the Tongnae Magistrate varied over time, "Magistrate" will be used here to refer to the Korean government's chief executive officer (civil or military) stationed in Tongnae. For the translation of terms of office, see: Edward Willett Wagner, *The Literati Purges: Political Conflict in Early Yi Korea* (Cambridge: Harvard University Press), 1974: 128 and 129. Charles Hucker refers to *suryŏng*, a general Korean term for local, chief executive officer, as shou(3)-ling(4): "Prefect" or "District Magistrate," and to *Hyŏllyŏng* as "District Magistrate." See: Charles O. Hucker, *A Dictionary of Official Titles in Imperial China* (Stanford: Stanford University Press), 1985. For the hierarchy of civil command in Kyŏngsang Province, see: *Kyŏngguk taejŏn* (compilation date: 1460–1485) fascicle 1, ijŏn, oegwanjik. See: Ki-baik Lee, *A New History of Korea*, trans. Edward Wagner with Edward Shultz (Seoul: Ilchokak Publishers), 1984: 176 for a brief general description of local government.

3 An earlier version of the statistical analysis was published in Japanese under the title: "Jinshin-Teiyū Waran ikō Kōka jōyaku izen no Chōsen kara mita Tsushima," Ruisu Jeimusu *Chihō-shi kenkyū*, 41:4, vol. 232 (1991.8): 37–53.

4 Kang Chu-chin, "Kyŏngsang-do sŏnsaeng'an ŭi haechae mit sŏ," in Kukhoe Tosŏgwan, ed., *To sŏnsaeng'an* (Seoul: Seoul Taehakkyo Ch'ulp'anbu), 1970: 4.

5 The following hierarchy is taken from the *Kyŏngguk taejŏn* and the English translations are taken from Edward Wagner.

1 Jr. 2: *Kwanch'alsa*, Governor, one man in Kyŏngju; *Puyun*, Special Capital Magistrate, one person in Kyŏngju;

2 Sr. 3: *Taedohobusa*, Special City Magistrate, one man in Andong; *Moksa*, City/Island Magistrate, three people in: Sangju, Sŏngju, and Chinju;

3 Jr. 3: *Tohobusa*, Town Magistrate, seven men in: Ch'angwŏn, Kimhae, Yŏnghae, Milyang, Sŏnsan, Ch'ŏngsong, and Taegu;

4 Jr. 4: *Kunsu*, Great County Magistrate, 14 men;

5 Jr. 5: *Tosa*, Provincial Inspector, one man, *P'angwan*, Governor's Aide/Magistrate's Aide, five men, and *Hyŏllyŏng*, County Magistrate, seven men in: Yŏngdŏk, Kyŏngsan, Tongnae, Kosŏng, Kŏje, Ŭisŏng, and Namhae.

6 See: *Sejong sillok chiriji* and *Kyŏngsang-do ŭpchi* (Kyujanggak cat. no. 666). The *Sejong sillok chiriji* was commissioned in 1424 and officially finished in 1454. See Chapter 3, Note 23.

7 This administrative history is taken from the *Tongnae-buji* (1740), Kŏnch'i soch'o, except where indicated.

8 *Koryŏsa*, 19:30b–30b, (1176/12/1).

9 Yi Wan-yŏng, "Tongnae-bu mit Waegwan ŭi haengjŏng soko," *Hangdo Pusan*, 2 (1963): 14.

10 Yi Wan-yŏng, "Tongnae-bu mit Waegwan ŭi haengjŏng soko," pp. 14–17.

11 The *Kunsu* change is briefly explained in: Pŏpchech'ŏ, ed., *Kobŏpjon yong'ŏjip* (Seoul: Yukjisa), 1981 and Yi Wan-yŏng, "Tongnae-bu mit Waegwan ŭi haengjŏng soko," p. 16, refers to a *Kwanch'alsa*, not a *Kunsu*.

12 Yi Wan-yŏng, "Tongnae-bu mit Waegwan ŭi haengjŏng soko," p. 16.

13 Kim Ŭi-hwan, "Fuzan Wakan no shokkan kōsei to sono kinō ni tsuite: Richō no tai-Nichi seisaku no ichi rikai no tame ni," *Chōsen gakuhō*, 108 (1983.7): 111–145. This part of Kim's article is based on a summation of the information available in *Chŭngjŏng kyorinji*, 3:8a ff. (chŏp-Wae ch'ulsagwan). See also: Yi Wan-yŏng, "Tongnae-bu mit Waegwan ŭi haengjŏng soko," pp. 59ff.

14 *Chŭngbo munhŏn pigo*, 179:14 (po kyobing ko 9, Ilbon kyobing 2). Exactly which Irregular Envoy (*Ch'awae*) was greeted by which Reception Official: Capital or Provincial (*Chŏbwigwan*) is indicated.

15 See: Yi Wan-yŏng, "Tongnae-bu mit Waegwan ŭi haengjŏng soko," p. 59.

16 The change occurred with the interrogation and punishment of the Reception Official who allowed Kihaku Genpō to go to Hansŏng in 1629. See: Tashiro Kazui, "Kanei roku nen (Jinso 7, 1629), Tsushima shisetsu no Chōsen koku Go jōkyō no toki mainikki to sono haikei," *Chōsen gakuhō*, 95 (1980.4), 96 (1980.7); 98 (1981.1); and 101 (1981.10). See also: *Chŭngbo munhŏn pigo*, 179:14 (po kyobing ko 9, Ilbon kyobing 2).

17 *Chŭngjŏng kyorinji*, 3:8a (chŏp-Wae ch'ulsagwan, Chŏbwigwan).

18 See: Yi Wan-yŏng, "Tongnae-bu mit Waegwan ŭi haengjŏng soko," p. 59 and Kim Ŭi-hwan, "Fuzan Wakan no shokkan kōsei to sono kinō ni tsuite: Richō no tai-Nichi seisaku no ichi rikai no tame ni," pp. 113–114.

19 Robert Elvin Campbell, "The Pusan Section of the *Shōkai shingo*: Study and Translation" (unpublished Ph.D. dissertation, University of California at Berkeley), 1994. I wish to thank Dr. Campbell for his years of friendship and instruction and most directly for allowing me to read drafts of his dissertation. For bibliographic information on Korean texts used to study Japanese, see: Song Ki-joong, *The Study of Foreign Languages in the Chosŏn Dynasty (1392–1910)*, (Seoul: Jimoondang International), 2001. In particular, see pp. 142–151 for a discussion of extant versions of the *Ch'ŏphae sinŏ*.

20 Yi Wan-yŏng, "Tongnae-bu mit Waegwan ŭi haengjŏng soko," pp. 57–58.

21 Their domicile was called the Pinilhŏn. See: Yi Wan-yŏng, "Tongnae-bu mit Waegwan ŭi haengjŏng soko," pp. 57–58.

22 Yi Wan-yŏng, "Tongnae-bu mit Waegwan ŭi haengjŏng soko," pp. 38–39.

23 The following information on the military officials in Tongnae County comes from Yŏngjinbo chwasuyŏng, *Tongnae-bu ŭpchi* (1832) in Kim Tong-ch'ŏl, ed., *Tongnae-bu saryo*, 2 (Seoul: Yŏgang Ch'ulp'ansa), 1989 and Yi Wan-yŏng, "Tongnae-bu mit Waegwan ŭi haengjŏng soko," pp. 46–48. The 1832 Gazetteer (*ŭpchi*) mentions only two garrisons: Pusan and Tadae, but Yi Wan-yŏng mentions all three.

24 Yi Wan-yŏng, "Tongnae-bu mit Waegwan ŭi haengjŏng soko," p. 48.

25 Osa Masanori, "Ni-Sen kankei ni okeru kiroku no jidai," *Tōyō gakuhō*, 50:4 (1968.3): 75. See also: *Chŭngjŏng kyorinji*, 3:12a–12a (Ch'ayeŭi, Pusan Ch'ŏmsa).

26 Some degree of responsibility in extraordinary situations obviously accrued, however, since in 1710, the Commander of the Left Naval Headquarters (*Sugun chŏltosa*) was nearly ordered caned in connection with Japanese storming out of the Japan House. See: *Pyŏllye chibyo*, fascicle 13, entry 1710.3, (Seoul: Kuksa p'yŏnch'an wiwŏnhoe): 272.

27 *Tongnae-bu ŭpchi* (1899) in *Tongnae saryo*, 3 (Seoul: Yŏgang Ch'ulp'ansa), 1989.

28 Hangukhak munhŏn yŏn'guso, ed., *Hanguk chiriji ch'ongso ŭpchi Kyŏngsang-do*, (1832), (Seoul: Asea Munhwasa), 1982. Here we see gazetteers on 71 magistracies. Compare the same for 1895: 66 magistracies, and the *Sinjŭng tongguk yŏji sŭngnam* which also lists 66 magistracies. A brief survey of the 1832 Gazetteer reveals the following counties were at one time made military commandaries: Andong, Tongnae, Sangju, Ulsan, Nyŏnghae, Yŏngil, and Saju.

29 For a brief specification of duties in connection with the Japanese, see: *Chŭngjŏng kyorinji*, 3:12a–12a (Ch'ayeŭi, Tongnae Pusa).

30 Although the circumstances of two people listed in category 15 under section 12 of Table 5.1, and one person in category 27 are yet unclear, the possibility seems high that either Japanese caused the incidents or Japanese were involved in the incidents.

31 *Hyojong Sillok*, 9:17a–17b (1652/9/22).

32 *Pyŏllye chibyo*, fascicle 13, entry 1652.9, p. 254.

33 *Pyŏllye chibyo*, fascicle 16, entry 1652.9, p. 427.

34 Calculations are based on 292 appointments. These 292 include six re-appointments. The overall median appointment time was 15.51 months.

35 For example, No. 37, Sin Wi, was exiled (*t'ubi*), and No. 5, Ha Sŏk-bŏm, was sent for military service (*ch'unggun*). There was also one other large category not included here. "Administrative Enquiry Concerning the Performance of Duty" (*chongsa ch'ugo*) appears in a large number of cases recorded in the *Pyŏllye chibyo*, fascicle 16, pp. 405–426, but this reprimand did not lead to dismissal or transfer and is not recorded in the Gazetteers. Another category also not included, as it does not appear in the Gazetteers was "Confessions and Pardons" (*ch'ŏngjoe*). See also Note c in Table 5.3.

36 Yi Wŏn-kyun, "Chosŏn sidae ŭi suryŏngjik kyoch'e silt'ae: Tongnae busa ŭi kyŏngu," *Pusan Sahak*, 3 (1979.2): 61–86.

37 Amenomori Hōshū, "Kōrin teisei" in Izumi Chōichi, *et al.*, ed., *Hōshū gaikō kankei shiryō kanshū*, *Amenomori Hōshū zenshū*, 3 (Suita-shi: Kansai daigaku), 1982: 55.

38 *Hyŏnjong kaesu Sillok*, 24:46a–46b (1671/9/25).

39 *Hyŏnjong Sillok*, 20:4b–4b (1671/11/25).

40 Yi Wŏn-kyun, "Chosŏn sidae ŭi suryŏngjik kyoch'e silt'ae," Note 46.

41 Tabohashi Kiyoshi, *Kindai Ni-Sen kankei no kenkyū*, 1 (Keijō: Chōsen Sōtokufu Chūsūin), 1940: 167ff. for negotiations between Tongnae and representatives of the new Meiji government. See also p. 335 for An Tong-jun's execution in 1875.

42 See Table 5.3, No. 37.

43 *Pyŏllye chibyo*, fascicle 16, entry 1753.4, p. 471.

44 *Yŏngjo Sillok*, 79:18a–19a (1753/3/23). See the same record in the *Pibyŏnsa tŭngnok*, fascicle 125, p. 387a–387c, (1753/3/23). The account given here is a composite of the three documents.

45 The *Pyŏllye chibyo* records the second month, but the *Sillok* and *Pibyŏnsa tŭngnok* entries are dated as the third month. One wonders if the difference may have been indicative of the central government's bureaucratic delay. The date given in the *Pyŏllye chibyo* is preferred since those reports were closer to the origin.

46 *Yŏngjo Sillok*, 80:12a–12a (1753/9/16).

47 Tashiro Kazui, *Kinsei Ni-Chō tsūkō bōekishi no kenkyū* (Tōkyō: Sōmunsa), 1981, p. 298ff.

48 *Pyŏllye chibyo*, fascicle 9, entry 1699.8–10, pp. 15–16.

49 Tashiro Kazui, *Kinsei Ni-Chō tsūkō bōekishi no kenkyū*, p. 303.

50 See Table 5.3, No. 32.

51 *Sukjong Sillok*, 34 sang: 24a–24b (1700/4/29).

52 Fredrik Barth, "Introduction" in *Ethnic Groups and Boundaries: The Social Organization of Culture Difference* (Oslo: Pensumtjeneste), 1994: 14 (first published in 1969).

53 See Table 5.3, No. 20.

54 *Injo Sillok*, 49:40a–40a (1648/9/30). Evidently, the Commander of the Left Naval Headquarters was the ranking officer.

55 *Injo Sillok*, 49:42a–42a (1648/10/4/4).

56 *Injo Sillok*, 47:74a–76a (1646/12/22).

57 One of Tsushima's negotiating tactics was to mention petitioning the *bakufu* as a threat to enlarge whatever problem was under discussion. See *Hyŏnjong kaesu Sillok*, 24:40b–41a (1671/8/27) for the court's interpretation of involving the *bakufu* in discussions to move the Waegwan as "blackmail" (*konggal*) and "threats" (*hyŏppak*).

58 See Table 5.3, No. 25.

59 See Appendix A, "The Office of the Custodian of Foreign Visitors or the Chŏngaeksa."

60 *Pyŏllye chibyo*, fascicle 16, entry 1674.7, p. 407.

61 *Pyŏllye chibyo*, fascicle 16, entry 1674.7, p. 407. The *Chŭngjŏng kyorinji*, 3:13b–14a (Chinsang mulgŏn kanp'um sik), mentions the *Hundo* and the *Pyŏlch'a*, but no red umbrella. The *T'ongmun'gwanji*, 5:21b–22a, also describes the ceremony but there is no red umbrella. Both sources mention the two interpreters and that the tribute articles are laid out in the hall. Both texts explain the ceremony in the following way. The Japanese envoy, the ship captain, and a *Daikan* come to the Banquet Hall and line up facing the Commander of the Pusan Garrison. They exchange bows and then sit down. The *Hundo* and *Pyŏlch'a* then sit. Next, the tribute goods are brought in and the Commander of the Pusan Garrison sends a receipt for the goods to the Guest House (Waegwan). The receipt is most important, since it is that item that the *Daikan* uses to claim rice and cotton from the official trade. After the items have all been displayed in the hall, the chief envoy goes to the courtyard and offers a formal bow. There is no mention of a red umbrella, but it is possible that procedures had become different from those described here and that was the source of the Magistrate's sympathy for the Japanese argument.

62 There is also evidence to the effect that the Governor of Kyŏngsang Province was dismissed in 1647 for acceding to a Japanese request to increase official trade amounts. See: *Pyŏllye chibyo*, fascicle 16, entry 1647.6, p. 405.

6 LEAKY ROOFS AND OTHER MATTERS

1 *Chŏngjo Sillok*, 2:40a–41a (1776/9/22).

2 Peter Sahlins, *Boundaries: The Making of France and Spain in the Pyrenees* (Berkeley: University of California Press), 1989: 6–7.

3 Amenomori Hōshū, "Kōrin Teisei," in Izumi Chōichi, ed., *Hōshū bunshū, Amenomori Hōshū zenshū*, 3 (Suita: Kansai Daigaku), 1982: 81.

4 Amenomori Hōshū, "Kōrin Teisei," pp. 68–69.

5 Kuksa P'yŏnch'an Wiwŏnhoe, ed., "Nanch'ul" in *Pyŏllye chibyo* (Seoul: T'amyŏngdang), 1971, fascicle 13, pp. 254–275. Originally compiled by the Chŏn'gaeksa of the Board of Rites (Kyujanggak cat. no. 2089).

6 See: "Waesŏ yakjo" in the *Pongnae kosa*, reprinted in *Chōsen gakuhō*, 58 (1970.10): 93. There is no Pongnae in Tongnae County. Judging from the content, the title could be translated as "A History of Tongnae County."

7 *Chŭngjŏng kyorinji*, 4:2b (Waein sŏnap yakjo).

8 *Pyŏllye chibyo*, fascicle 13, entry 1652, p. 254; and *Tongmun hwigo*, vol. 3, 24:5a–b, p. 2236 ("yakjo" for 1652). See also: Kim Yong-uk, p. 105.

9 *Chŏpdae Waein saye*, Kyujanggak cat. no. 9763; Kuksa P'yŏnch'an Wiwŏnhoe, cat. no. B13J–82; set in modern type: *Pusan saryo ch'ongsŏ*, 2 (Pusan: Yŏngnam Inswaeso), 1963: 88.

10 Kim Yong-uk, pp. 107–111.

11 This is roughly indicated outside the northern wall on Map 2.6 in Chapter 2.

12 Directions are based on exiting the main gate (seaside, north of the jetties in Map 2.6). At the corner of the wall, west leads to the "banquet hall" and east is towards the Pusan Garrison.

13 *Chŭngjŏng kyorinji*, 4:2b–3a, and *Pongnae kosa*, same year, for a slightly less detailed version.

14 *Chŭngjŏng kyorinji*, 4:3a–3b.

15 *Chŭngjŏng kyorinji*, 4:4b. The major points raised are as follows:

> [Point:] Those "Waein" who come into the "new villages" to smuggle will be arrested and turned over to the House Master according to Agreement. In determining the guilt of those [Koreans] who received [the Japanese], we will act in accordance with the laws [governing] smuggling, report to the [relevant] officials and adjudicate [the case]. [Point:] The "Waein" are not permitted to guard the gates. Those [Japanese] who at other places jump the wall and secretly go to commoners' homes will [be] taken [by] the [Korean] gate guards and each

one will be searched. [Point:] The coming and going of the [Japanese] Interpreters and the Waegwan Wae [to] the residence of the *Hundo* and the *P'yŏlch'a* will all require [accompaniment] by two people and afterwards there will be no individual receptions for the [Japanese].

16 Kim Yong-uk, p. 111.
17 *Chŭngjŏng kyorinji*, 4:6b.
18 1626, 1637, 1646, 1652, 1653, 1658, 1659, 1665, 1671, 1672, 1673, 1680, 1695–1696, 1697–1698, 1708, 1710, 1736, 1807, and 1824.
19 *Pyŏllye chibyo*, fascicle 13, entry 1697.8, pp. 262–263.
20 Amenomori Hōshū, "Kōrin Teisei," p. 55.
21 *Pyŏllye chibyo*, fascicle 13, entry 1671.8, p. 257. The *Sillok* report on these incidents seems to combine them into one report (200 men) and gives an account of the Chŏbwigwan, Sin Hu-chae, being held and humiliated by Japanese. See: *Hyŏnjong kaesu Sillok*, 24:40b–41a (1671/8/27). See also: Kim Yong-uk, pp. 64–65.
22 *Pyŏllye chibyo*, fascicle 13, entry 1671.11, p. 257.
23 *Hyŏnjong kaesu Sillok*, 24:40b–41a (1671/8/27).
24 Kim Yong-uk, pp. 65–66.
25 *Pyŏllye chibyo*, fascicle 13, entry 1672.4, p. 258.
26 Kim Yong-uk, p. 66. See also: Kim Üi-hwan, "Ri-chō jidai ni okeru Fuzan no Wakan no kien to hensen," *Nihon bunkashi kenkyū*, 2 (1977.12): 7–8. See also: Yi Wŏn-kyun, "Chosŏn hugi ŭi Pusan," in Pusan chikhal-shi sa p'yŏnch'an wiwŏnhoe, ed., *Pusan shisa*, 1 (Pusan: Pusan chikhal-shi sa p'yŏnch'an wiwŏnhoe), 1989: 755–756.
27 Kim Yong-uk, p. 65.
28 *Hyŏnjong Sillok*, 20:4b–4b (1671/11/25).
29 Sŏn'am Temple appears in the *Tongnae-buji* of 1740 in *Tongnae saryo*, vol. 2, p. 30. Of unknown origin, it may have been erected in 1483. Sŏn'am was located on Kŭmyong mountain and is probably modern-day Kŭmsŏn'am in Pujŏn-dong in Pusanjin-gu. The location and frequency of appearance – it is the only Buddhist temple mentioned in connection with Japanese illegally leaving the Waegwan – suggest that it enshrined Japanese deceased from the Tumo Waegwan period and possibly earlier.
30 *Pyŏllye chibyo*, fascicle 13, entry 1695.1, p. 261.
31 See: Chapter 5, Table 5.3, No. 30. Hangukhak munhŏn yon'guso, ed., "Yŏk sŏnsaeng-jo" in "Tongnae," (1895), *Hanguk chiriji ch'ongsŏ ŭpchi Kyŏngsang-do*, (Kyujanggak cat. no. 12174), (Seoul: Asea munhwasa), 1982: 159–166. See also: *Tongnae-bu ŭpchi*, 1899, "Yŏk sŏnsaeng-jo," (Kyujanggak cat. no. 10877), in Kim Tong-ch'ŏl et al., ed., *Tongnae saryo*, 3 (Pusan: Yŏgang Ch'ulpansa), 1989: 372.
32 *Pyŏllye chibyo*, fascicle 17, entry 1697.1, p. 510. See also: Kawakami Kenzō, *Takeshima no rekishi chirigakuteki kenkyū* (Tōkyō: Koki shoin), 1966: 159.
33 *Pyŏllye chibyo*, fascicle 13, entry 1697.8, p. 262.
34 *Pyŏllye chibyo*, fascicle 13, entry 1697.8, pp. 262–263.
35 *Pyŏllye chibyo*, fascicle 13, entry 1697.8–11, pp. 263ff.
36 Tashiro Kazui, "Foreign Relations During the Edo Period: Sakoku Reexamined," *Journal of Japanese Studies*, 8:2 (Summer 1982): 297. See Magistrate Chŏng Ho's case in the discussion on "Promotions" in Chapter 5. Chŏng Ho was Magistrate when an agreement was reached on silver in 1699.
37 *Pyŏllye chibyo*, fascicle 13, entry 1697.8, p. 264.
38 Osa Masanori, "Ni-Sen kankei ni okeru kiroku no jidai," *Tōyō gakuhō*, 50:4 (1968.3): 98.
39 *Tōhei yuki ni tsuki Fuzan nite kenka tsunawachi migi no ishu onkuni e mōshiage kōjō Tōrai yori settai tsukamatsuri onkuni mōshiage sōrō jō hikae*, 1697.8, MS in Sō-ke monjo, kiroku-rui Chōsen kankei, P, 1 (1), Nagasaki kenritsu Tsushima rekishi minzoku shiryōkan (Nagasaki-ken, Izuhara-shi).
40 Michell reports "a severe mortality crisis" (which he defines as famine and/or epidemic) hit Korea between 1693 and 1695, reducing the total population from 12.3 million to 10.2 million. In fact, "the whole of the reign of Sukchong has been described as one of famine. . . ." See: Tony Michell, "Fact and Hypothesis in Yi Dynasty Economic

History: The Demographic Dimension," *Korean Studies Forum*, 5 (Winter–Spring, 1979 1980): 78.

41 *Tōhei yuki ni tsuki Fuzan nite kenka tsunawachi migi no ishu onkuni e mōshiage kōjō Tōrai yori settai tsukamatsuri onkuni mōshiage sōrō jō hikae*, folio 8a.

42 What happened to the reduced hours for the Tongnae merchants, requiring their departure from the Waegwan before sundown, is unknown.

43 *Tōhei yuki ni tsuki Fuzan nite kenka tsunawachi migi no ishu onkuni e mōshiage kōjō Tōrai yori settai tsukamatsuri onkuni mōshiage sōrō jō hikae*, folio 4a–b.

44 Amenomori Hōshū, "Kōrin teisei," pp. 79–80.

45 *Pyŏllye chibyo*, fascicle 13, entry 1710.3, p. 271.

46 *Pyŏllye chibyo*, fascicle 13, entry 1710.8, p. 273.

47 *Pyŏllye chibyo*, fascicle 13, entry 1710.3, p. 272.

48 Michiel Baud and Willem van Schendel, "Toward a Comparative History of Borderlands," *Journal of World History*, 8:2 (Fall 1997): 226–229.

49 Fredrik Barth, "Introduction" in *Ethnic Groups and Boundaries: The Social Organization of Culture Difference* (Oslo: Pensumtjeneste), 1994, 14–16 (first published in 1969).

7 *PÉNÉTRATION DU CORPS SOCIALE*

1 *Waein changna tŭngnok*, Kyujanggak cat. no. 12962, folio 2b–3a.

2 For "first mention," see Nakamura Hidetaka, *Ni-Sen kankeishi no kenkyŭ*, 1 (Tōkyō: Yoshikawa Kōbunkan), 1965: 492. For earlier mention of the capital Waegwan, see *T'aejong sillok*, 22:52b–52b (1411/intercalary 12/13); *T'aejong sillok*, 27:32a–32a (1414/5/9); and *T'aejong sillok*, 32:16b–16b (1416/9/13).

3 *T'aejong sillok*, 35:19a–19a (1418/3/2).

4 *Sejong sillok*, 41:13a–13b (1428/9/3). The highest Ming punishment was beheading, followed by strangulation, so the passage is not clear. See the "O-hyŏng-chi-do" before the preface to the *Tae-Myŏng yul chikhae* (Seoul: Pogyŏng Munhwa-sa), 1986: 25.

5 Murai Shōsuke, *Chūsei Wajin-den* (Tōkyō: Iwanami Shoten), 1993: 4–5.

6 *Haedong chegukki*, "Choch'ŏng ŭngjŏp-ki," and "Samp'o kŭmyak."

7 In the 1544 incident, three Korean officials and 30 Korean sailors were murdered. See: Nakamura Hidetaka, *Ni-Sen kankeishi no kenkyū*, 1 (Tōkyō: Yoshikawa Kōbunkan), 1965: 498; Oda Seigo, "Rishi Chōsen jidai ni okeru Wakan no hensen – nakanzuku Zetsueido (Chŏlyŏng-do) Wakan ni tsuite", in Keijō Teikoku Daigaku Hōbun Gakkai, ed., *Chōsen Shina bunka no kenkyū* (Tōkyō: Tōgō Shoin), 1929: 107; and Kim Yong-uk, "Pusan Waegwan ko," *Han-Il munhwa*, 1:2 (1962.12): 58.

8 *T'ongmun'gwanji*, 5:18a (Kyorin), and *Chŭngjŏng kyorinji*, 3:2a. The *T'ongmun'gwanji* accurately quotes the *Chingbinok* by Yu Sŏng-yong (pen-name Sŏae). See Taedong Munhwa Yŏn'guwŏn, Sŏnggyungwan Taehakkyo, ed., *Sŏae munjip*, 1:10a (Seoul: Tongguk Munhwasa), 1958: 496b.

9 Nakamura Hidetaka, *Ni-Sen kankeishi no kenkyū*, 1, pp. 627–728, for an examination of Japanese trade (and smuggling), fishing, and population growth in the Three Ports and Korean government attempts to extend controls. We are arguing that the Korean intention was to restrict Japanese residence to Pusan and put controls on Japanese movement in Pusan. We can also see this intent in policies that governed private trade following the Hideyoshi invasion. Korean officialdom worked to concentrate private Korean traders in Tongnae to help speed the Japanese on their way so that traders from Tsushima would not overstay their officially designated time limits claiming that they had to await contacts with distant traders or await the delivery of goods. See: Tashiro Kazui, *Kinsei Ni-Chō tsūkō bōekishi no kenkyū* (Tōkyō: Sōbunsha), 1981: 70–71.

10 *Sukjong sillok*, 4:2a–2b (1675/intercalary 5/3). See also: Kim Yong-uk, "Pusan Waegwan ko," *Hanil munhwa* 1:2 (1962.12): 111.

11 Murai Shōsuke argues that Korean society, based on Song Neo-Confucianism, thinking of the world in terms of a barbarian–civilized split, and with a focus on China, regarded the Jurchen in the north and the "Waein" who lived in south as lower than humans or like animals. There was perhaps such a view, but this would have derived from a lack of

education and civilized conduct, not from blood. Murai Shōsuke, *Chūsei Wajin-den* (Tōkyō: Iwanami Shoten), 1993: pp. 59 ff.

12 Ch'oe was a disciple of Yi Hangno. See Chai-sik Chung, *A Korean Confucian Encounter with the Modern World: Yi Hang-no and the West* (Berkeley: University of California Press), 1995: 63.

13 For a summary of the court debate and in particular Ch'oe Ikhyŏn's opposition, see James B. Palais, *Politics and Policy in Traditional Korea* (Cambridge, Massachusetts: Harvard University Press), 1975: 265–266, and Martina Deuchler, *Confucian Gentlemen and Barbarian Envoys: the Opening of Korea, 1875–1885* (Seattle: University of Washington Press), 1977: 43–44. For the original text of Ch'oe's memorial, see *Ilsŏngnok*, entry 1876.1.23, and Tabohashi Kiyoshi, *Kindai Ni-Sen kankei no kenkyū*, 1 (Keijō: Chōsen Sōtokufu Chūsūin), 1940: 514.

14 *Pongnae kosa*, 1678 entry, reprinted manuscript in *Chōsen gakuhō*, 57 (1970.11). Compare with the *T'ongmun'gwanji* (Seoul:Yŏngin Munhwasa), 1974: 5:19b (Kyorin,), which gives the length as 1,273 *po* and height as 6 *ch'ŏk* (1 *po* = 6 *ch'ŏk*, therefore about 2.314 kilometers). Permission to rebuild the wall higher and to move "Old Ch'oryang" village away from the compound had been given in 1697.7 to the Magistrate in connection with a case of illegal sexual relations. See: Kuksa P'yŏnch'an Wiwŏnhoe, ed., *Pyŏllye chipyo*, 2 (Seoul: T'amyŏngdang), 1971 (Kyujanggak cat. no. 2090), fascicle 14, entry 1697.7, p. 327.

15 Kim Yong-uk, "Pusan Waegwan ko," *Han-Il munhwa*, 1:2 (1962.12): 107. Kim describes "Waegwan Regulations" (Waegwan kŭmchae) issued in 1676, which, in article three, bans Korean women from the Waegwan. These "Waegwan Regulations" do not exist in either the *T'ongmun'gwanji* or the *Chŭngjŏng kyorinji*, but according to Kim, are to be found in the *Chōsen sho jirei*, not yet identified.

16 *Pyŏllye chibyo*, fascicle 13, entry 1710.3, p. 271.

17 *Pyŏllye chibyo*, fascicle 9, entry 1731.3, p. 53.

18 *Kōkan ikken*, folio 5b ff. in the *Bunrui kiji taikō* (MS 31 in Nihon Koku Kokkai Toshokan, Sōke monjo).

19 *Kōkan ikken*, folio 6b ff.

20 Taking a loan from a Japanese was declared to be smuggling and a capital offense for Koreans in 1653. See: *Chŭngjŏng kyorinji*, 4:2a (1653 Agreement, article 2), and *Pusansi-sa*, p. 722.

21 *Kōkan ikken*, folio 8a.

22 *Waein changna tŭngnok*, folio 16a–17a.

23 *Waein changna tŭngnok*, folio 16a–16b. Pun-i was 13 when she was first taken into the Japan House by her father. Ch'ŏn-wŏl was 21 when she first entered the Japan House.

24 Amenomori Hōshū, *Kōrin teisei*, MS 15 in Amenomori Hōshū bunko (Amenomori Hōshū-an, Shiga-ken, Ika-gun, Takatsuki-chō, Amenomori-mura; *Kōrin teisei*, MS 16859, cho 51, na 167, koche in Hanguk Kungnip Tosŏgwan; Izumi Chōichi, et al., ed., "Kōrin teisei" in *Hōshū gaikō kankei shiryō kanshū, Amenomori Hōshū zenshū*, 3 (Suita-shi: Kansai Daigaku), 1982.

25 *Waein changna tŭngnok*, folio 2b–3a. See also: Kim Ŭi-hwan, "*Waein changna tŭngnok* ni tsuite, fu: shiryō honbun," in Nara Teizukayama tanki daigaku Nihon bunka-shi gakkai, ed., *Nihon bunkashi kenkyū*, 16 (1992.1): 61. Although Kim Ŭi-hwan has appended to this article a printed transcription of the *Waein changna tŭngnok*, there are a few mistakes and the transcription must be used with caution. There is also a printed transcription of the two sections of the *Waein changna tŭngnok* dealing with smuggling in *Han-Il yŏn'gu*, 1 (1972.3): 239–245. The latter was kindly brought to my attention by Dr. Kenneth R. Robinson.

26 *Waein changna tŭngnok*, folio 2a–2b.

27 Pak Shin was appointed Tongnae Magistrate on 1689.4.19 and, because of this incident, was interrogated and replaced on 1690.7.16. See Chapter 5. The Provincial Governor at the time was O Shi-tae (1689.12.25–1690.8.6), and his Provincial Inspector (Jr. 5) was Shim Ch'oe-yang (1690.3–1690.7). See: Kukhoe Tosŏgwan, ed., *To sŏnsaeng'an* (Seoul: Seoul Taehakkyo Ch'ulp'anbu), 1970: 83–84.

28 *Waein changna tŭngnok*, folio 4b, entry 1690.4.12.

29 *Tongmun hwigo*, vol. 3, 24:14a, p. 2240 (pup'yŏn, yakjo) in Kuksa P'yŏnch'an Wiwŏnhoe, ed., *Tongmun hwigo* (Seoul: Hanjin Inswae Hoesa), 1978.

30 *Waein changna tŭngnok*, folio 4b, entry1690.4.12. Pak's superior, the Governor of Kyŏngsang Province, O Shi-tae, concurs with this assessment of why the House Master adamantly refused to acknowledge the crime: "What the *Ch'aep'an* (J: *Saihan*) has been saying, from the beginning to now, differs from the House Master. The truth is that the women in the [Japan] House have to emerge in the end. The House Master and his subordinates know they are plotting their own pardons, and do not consider the loss of sincerity (*sŏngshin*) to both sides." Ibid. folio 7a–7b.

31 The second report within the *Waein changna tŭngnok*, written by O Shi-tae, Governor of Kyŏngsang Province, states: "[In this matter of] extraditing the women from the [Wae]gwan, the Master of the Japan House protects [his] followers from a death sentence; he consistently dodges and stalls." Ibid. folio 7a.

32 *Waein changna tŭngnok*, folio 5a–5b.

33 *Pibyŏnsa tŭngnok*, fascicle 44, pp. 301–302 (1690/6/23 and 24); *Sŭngjŏngwŏn ilgi*, fascicle 341, pp. 161–162 (1690/6/23 and 24).

34 *Sŭngjŏngwŏn ilgi*, fascicle 341, p. 164 (1690/6/30).

35 *Tongnae-bu ŭpchi* (1899) in Kim Tong-ch'ŏl, ed., *Tongnae saryo*, 3 (Seoul: Yŏgang ch'ulp'ansa), 1989: 371.

36 *Sukjong sillok*, 22:39a–39a (1690/10/6).

37 *Sukjong sillok*, 46:2a–3a (1708/1/15).

38 *Tongmun hwigo*, vol. 3, 24:15b, p. 2241 (pup'yŏn, yakjo).

39 *Sukjong sillok*, 47:21b–22a (1709/4/13).

40 *Kōrin teisei*, folio 42–46; and "Kōrin teisei" in Izumi Chōichi, *et al.*, ed., *Hōshū gaikō kankei shiryō kanshū, Amenomori Hōshū zenshū*, 3, pp. 70–71:

> . . . There are many points of grievance by the Koreans against Tsushima. Among these, the first is that we did not turn over the Japanese involved in the illicit sexual relations' case. . . ." (folio 43 or p. 70) and ". . . When we consider our debt [to Korea], you should order that our people do not violate the strict prohibitions that [Korea] has laid down [to govern] our relations. . . .
>
> (folio 44 or p. 70)

41 As for "cunning," see:

> . . . [a report on the 1662 incident contained the following:] '[We] ordered the [Korean] interpreters to reproach the Master of the [Japan] House to settle the matter of the criminal Waein, but the Waein, never made a report to us as to how they settled it.' We find the details in a copied record, although we cannot discover what we need to know. In our failed [negotiations] to come up with a joint law, the Waein [pleaded] circumstances, repeatedly being cunning. Right off, [they objected], with a common law, do we restrict it to the extreme cases? Since that is calculated to do no more than protect the criminal. . . .

Waein changna tŭngnok, folio 8a.

42 *Waein changna tŭngnok*, folio 7b.

43 *T'ongsinsa tŭngnok*, vol. 2, fascicle 6, pp. 404–405 in Kyujanggak charyo ch'ongsŏ Kŭmho Shirijŭ [Series] Tae-oe kwangye p'yŏn, *T'ongsinsa tŭngnok*, 2 (Seoul: Seoul Taehakkyo Tosŏgwan), 1991. Corroborating entries can be found in *Pibyŏnsa tŭngnok*, fascicle 62, p. 171a–186c (particularly p. 177) (1711/5/20); and *Sŭngjŏngwŏn ilgi*, fascicle 460, p. 1012 (1711/5/15).

44 *Chŭngjŏng kyorinji*, 4:3b (1683 Agreement, article 2). See also Yi Wŏn-kyun, "Chosŏn hugi ŭi Pusan," in Pusan Chikhal-shi sa p'yŏnch'an wiwŏnhoe, ed., *Pusansi-sa*, 1 (Pusan: Pusan Chikhal-shi), 1989: 723; and Osa Masanori, "Nobuseikō – Shukusō chō kigai yakujō no ichi kōsatsu," *Chōsen gakuhō*, 58 (1971): 1–20.

45 Im Su-kan, *Tongsa ilgi* (Shinjŏng yakjo) by Im Su-kan in Minjok munhwa ch'ujinhoe, ed., *Haehaeng ch'ongjae sok*, 9 (Seoul: Minjok Munhwa Mungo Kanhang Hoe), 1977: 96 (reprinted 1986).

> Years ago, a Wae in the [Japan] House, Genshichi, had illicit relations with a Pusan woman, but Tsushima never punished him. Since the [Korean] court wished to establish a treaty on the present trip, while the envoys were in Edo, there were negotiations. The Island Lord (Sō) procrastinated rather too much, [although we] repeatedly sent missives to him. In the end, he did not heed [our overtures]. When it came time for [we] three envoys to have an audience [with the Shōgun], we [planned] to write a statement to present to the *Kampaku* (Shōgun) and that may [have produced] a [certain] flexibility. One [of us] pulled out paper for a draft and another spoke to the several *bugyō* (Tsushima officials). They fell into an extreme funk. [When we] proposed sending someone to the Island Lord's residence, the group of *bugyō* said, '[Any] agreement will, of course, treat rape and seduction as the same crime, [although] this differs from the *Da Ming Lu* (Ming Code). If we separate [the two] we can [better] ascertain guilt, [but our] handling of [affairs] will naturally not require going to the Island Lord's residence. [You can] come to a conclusion with us.' [This] made it possible to produce a written agreement. [We] sent a *bugyō* to the Island Lord's residence and he returned with a document bearing the [Island] Lord's seal.

46 *T'ongsinsa tŭngnok*, vol. 2, fascicle 6, p. 537; *Chōsen tsūkō daiki*, fascicle 8, p. 296–297 in Matsuura Masatada, *Chōsen tsūkō daiki*, Tanaka Takeo and Tashiro Kazui, ed., (Tōkyō: Meicho shuppan), 1978; *Tongmun hwigo*, vol. 3, 24:17–18, p. 2242 (pup'yŏn, yakjo). The agreement is also recorded in the *Pyŏllye chibyo*, fascicle 5, entry 1712.2, p. 275; the *Koji ruien*, Gaikōbu 11, Chōsen 4, p. 763. The *Tongsinsa tŭngnok* version, the *Pyŏllye chibyo* version, and the *Chōsen tsūkō daiki* version are identical to Im's version, not surprising since the *Chōsen tsūkō daiki* includes Im's diary as an appendix. The *Tongmun hwigo* version is slightly different but essentially the same in meaning. There is no significant difference between the Korean and Japanese records.

47 *Chŭngjŏng kyorinji*, 4:4b.

48 *Chŭngjŏng kyorinji*, 4:4b.

49 *T'ongsinsa Tŭngnok*, vol. 2, fascicle 6, pp. 563–564.

50 *Tae-Myŏng yul chikhae*, *chŏn*, 25:1a, p. 539 (Hyŏngnyul, pŏmgan), in Chūsūin, ed., *Tae-Myŏng yul chikhae, chŏn* (Seoul: Kyŏng'in Munhwa-sa), 1974; or *Tae-Myong yul chikhae* (Seoul: Pogyŏng Munhwasa, 1986): 559:

> Common adultery with consent is 80 strokes with a cane. In case the man is married, it is 90 strokes; if seduction is involved, the penalty is 100 strokes. Rapists [will be put to death by] strangulation. If attempted [rape], 100 strokes and banishment to 3,000 *li*.

51 *Pyŏllye chibyo*, fascicle 14, 1716.8 entry, p. 338.

52 *Pyŏllye chibyo*, fascicle 14, 1716.6 entry, p. 337.

53 *Sinbo sugyo chimnok*, 1717 entry, p. 467 (hyŏngjŏn, kŭmche), in Kyŏng'in munhwasa p'yŏnbu, ed., *Chosŏn wangjo pŏpjŏnjip*, 2 (Seoul: Kyŏng'in munhwasa), 1972.

54 *Pyŏllye chibyo*, fascicle 14, entry 1726.5, p. 342; entry 1738, pp. 344–347; entry 1786.12, pp. 353–354.

55 *Sok taejŏn* (1744), 5:12b–13a, vol. 3, p. 418 (hyŏngjŏn, kŭmche, Waegwan). This statute is repeated in the *Taejŏn t'ongp'yŏn* (1785), 5:19a–19b, vol. 3, p. 160 (Waegwan kŭm); and the *Taejŏn Hoet'ong* (c.1865), 5:20a–20b, vol. 4, p. 687 (hyŏngjŏn, kŭmche). All of these texts can be found in Kyŏng'in munhwasa pyŏnbu, ed., *Chosŏn wangjo pŏpjŏnjip*, vol. 1–4 (Seoul: Kyŏng'in Munhwasa), 1972. See also: Son Sŭng-ch'ŏl, "*Waein changna tŭngnok* ŭl t'onghayŏ pon Waegwan," *Hangdo Pusan*, 10 (1993): 96.

56 *Pyŏllye chibyo*, fascicle 14, entry 1786.12, pp. 353–354.

57 Hendrick Hamel, translated from the Dutch by Br. Jean-Paul Punys of Taizé, *Hamel's Journal and a Description of the Kingdom of Korea, 1653–1666* (Seoul: Royal Asiatic Society), 1994: 59.

58 *Sinbo sugyo chimnok*, 1717 entry, p. 467 (hyŏngjŏn, kŭmche).

59 Kim Ŭi-hwan, "*Waein Changna Tŭngnok* ni tsuite, fu: shiryō honbun," *Nihon bunkashi kenkyū*, 16 (Nara Teizukayama Tanki Daigaku Nihon Bunka-shi Gakkai), (1992.1): 66. Although Kim has attached a printed version of the *Waein Changna Tŭngnok*, since there are errors, it must be used with caution.

60 Son Sŭng-ch'ŏl, "*Waein changna tŭngnok* ŭl t'ong hayŏ pon Waegwan," *Hangdo Pusan*, 10 (1993): 70.

61 According to Jae-ŏn Kim, Korean society is perhaps "unique" among the societies of Korea, China, Japan, and Mongolia in its "obsession" with female chastity. Folk tales common to all four cultures acquire a chastity motif in Korea. Doubts about legitimacy denigrated the status of concubines and their offspring under T'aejong (r.1400–1418), which, by the end of Yongjo's reign (r.1724–1776), resulted in excluding from higher civil appointments the children of remarried women. See: Jae-ŏn Kim, "Chastity as a Social Ideal in Korea: Comparative and Historical Explanations," paper presented at the First Pacific Basin International Conference on Korean Studies, Honolulu, Hawaii, July 27–August 2, 1992. Actually, as Ch'oe Yŏng-ho pointed out long ago, the *Kyŏngguk taejŏn* (3:1–2, Yejŏn, Chegwa) of 1485 clearly discriminates against the children of remarried women: "Those who have been discharged for committing a crime, the children of corrupt officials, the children and grandchildren of remarried women and immoral wives, the children and grandchildren of concubines shall [all] be forbidden from sitting the lower examination. . . ." See: Yŏng-ho Ch'oe, "Commoners in early Yi Dynasty Civil Examinations: An Aspect of Korean Social Structure, 1392–1600," *The Journal of Asian Studies*, 33:4 (1974.8): 614.

62 The connection between sexual customs and political economy has a long theoretical history in the modern West. For example, Friederich Engels argued that monogamous marriage is imposed on women to establish a clear line for the inheritance of property:

> The overthrow of mother-right was the world historical defeat of the female sex (p. 59). . . . [Monogamous marriage] is based on the supremacy of the man, the express purpose being to produce children of undisputed paternity: such paternity is demanded because these children are later to come into their father's property as the heirs of his body (p. 65). . . . [Monogamy] was the first form of the family to be based, not on natural, but on economic conditions . . . on the victory of private property over primitive, natural communal property (p. 69).

See: Friederich Engels, *The Origin of the Family, Private Property and the State (Der Ursprung der Familie, des Privateigentums und des Staats) In the Light of the Researches of Lewis H. Morgan* (London: Lawrence and Wishart, Ltd.), 1940, first edition 1884. More recently, Martina Deuchler has asserted the Chosŏn-era ideological connection between sexual customs and the health of the polity:

> Confucianism . . . regards the union between man and woman as the root of all human relations . . . it holds this union to be the foundation of human morality and the mainspring of the socialization process . . . The administration of the household was likened to that of a state. . . . [T]he purity of the [domestic] customs . . . was directly correlated with the rise and fall of the dynasty.
> (pp. 231–232)

See: Martina Deuchler, *The Confucian Transformation of Korea: A Study of Society and Ideology* (Cambridge, Massachusetts: Harvard University Press), 1992. Sheila Jager finds the phrases: "woman – as nation . . . – body"; "miscegenation"; and "defense of the social body" to be useful for a metaphorical approach to the problem of Korean reunification. See: Sheila Miyoshi Jager, "Women, Resistance and the Divided Nation:

The Romantic Rhetoric of Korean Reunification," *Journal of Asian Studies*, 55:1 (1996.2): 3–21.

63 Foreign women are thought to have been forbidden entrance to Japan sometime in the 1630s when the so-called "Sakoku" edicts were promulgated. In 1634, the Japanese wives and children of Macao merchants were deported. In 1639, consanguineous children born of Japanese women and Dutch and English men were deported to Batavia. Also in 1639, Japanese women were forbidden from being employed as servants to the Dutch. In 1640, a Dutchman was executed for adultery with a married Japanese woman; soon thereafter capital punishment was decreed for any Dutchman having relations with married or unmarried Japanese women. Between the 1640 execution and the 1666 prohibition on women other than courtesans entering Dejima, the situation is unclear. We might hypothesize that a great distinction was made between courtesans and ordinary women, and that liaisons with the latter represented a controllable threat addressed by the earlier deportations and steps to seclude the Dutch and the Chinese. One exception to foreign women visiting Japan was made in 1661 when Cheng Ch'eng-kung or Koxinga attacked the Zeelandia Fortress (Dutch headquarters on Taiwan) and forced Dutch women and children to flee to Nagasaki. Their temporary admission was clearly an exception, since in 1817 and 1829, wives accompanying the *opperhoofd* were forbidden residence and repatriated. See: Morioka Yoshiko, "Dejima," in Nagasaki kenshi henshū iinkai, ed., *Nagasaki Kenshi Taigai Kōshōhen* (Tōkyō: Yoshikawa Kōbunkan 1985): 504–506. In 1817, the *opperhoofd* was not allowed to keep his wife, child, and Javanese nurse. The Japanese argued that there was no reason for his wife to accompany him, since she was not necessary to the conduct of trade. See H. and B. compilers, *Manners and Customs of the Japanese in the Nineteenth Century* (New York, 1841, 21–22 (reprinted by Charles E. Tuttle Company, Tōkyō, 1973). This volume is a compilation from other works, principally Philipp Franz von Seibold's account of his sojourn in Japan from 1823 to 1830, entitled *Nippon*. The story of a nineteenth-century "love child," born between a Japanese woman and one Doeff Hendrik remains to us in the *Dōfujō Kichiyū Shosho*. Other such children include the child born to von Siebold and Ms. Sonogi. See: Morioka Yoshiko, "Dejima," cited above. For a concise summation of the Chinese and the Dutch presence in Nagasaki in the 1600s, see: Robert L. Innes, "The Door Ajar: Japan's Foreign Trade in the Seventeenth Century" (unpublished Ph.D. dissertation, University of Michigan), 1980: 164–193. Dejima's size was about 600 feet long by 240 feet wide (about 144,000 square feet). Dutch were forbidden exit except with permission. Anyone going and coming was searched. In the 1820s, there were but 11 Europeans. All Japanese were required to leave the island by sunset, that is, all except "women who have forfeited the first claim of their sex to respect or esteem" (H. and B., p. 28). Children of these relations were considered Japanese and the paternal connection was strictly con-trolled (pp. 26–28). See: H. and B. compilers, *Manners and Customs of the Japanese in the Nineteenth Century*, cited above. In 1666, a prohibition board was erected outside Dejima; the first entry read: "Women other than courtesans are forbidden entrance." Thirty-five women at one time were permitted entrance. Legal provisions governing the birth, care, and disposition of children by a Japanese mother and Dutch or Chinese father are spelled out in a letter from the Nagasaki Bugyō to local officials dated 1715. See: *Tsūkō ichiran*, fascicle 244, p. 234 and 236 ff. In response to a rapid surge in the junk trade in the 1680s, construction of the Tōjin Yashiki, the Chinese Compound, began in 1688, and Chinese traders entered the compound in the first month of 1689. Construction costs reached almost 634 silver *kanme*, of which 400 *kanme* were supplied by the *bakufu* and the remaining 234 *kanme* came from Nagasaki City. The reasons usually given for the segrega-tion of the Chinese include: control of Christianity, control of smuggling, and control of precious metal exports. By 1760, the total size of the compound reached 9,373 *tsubo* (about 337,428 square feet), but this area was divided into an inner and outer area. The inner area contained apartments, bath, shrines, and a guardhouse and was 6,874 *tsubo* (about 247,464 square feet) in size. The Chinese paid a rent of, at first, a flat 160 *kanme* that was taken as a tax on ships and sales, but which was, from 1701, calculated only on silver transactions at 2.119 *kanme* for every 100 *kanme* of silver paid to the Chinese for

goods. There was an additional land tax of 3.970 silver *kanme*. In 1689, 4,888 Chinese used the compound. Unlike the Waegwan, local officials or the Japanese directly administered the Chinese Compound. From 1692, an entry pass was required; all Chinese leaving the compound had to be escorted. Certain merchants and prostitutes were the only people admitted. For example, in 1731, from New Year's to the last day of the year, 20,738 Japanese courtesans (J: *yūjo*) entered the compound for the "cheer" of the residents. The *bakufu* did not demand that criminal Chinese be subject to Japanese law, but granted a form of "extraterritoriality." See: Yamawaki Teijirō, "Tōjin Yashiki," in Nagasaki kenshi henshū iinkai, ed., *Nagasai Kenshi Taigai Kōshōhen* (Tōkyō: Yoshikawa Kōbunkan), 1985: 511–524. The most famous story of a Japanese courtesan being made available to a foreigner is that of Okichi who supposedly became courtesan to the first American Consul-General and Minister to Japan, Townsend Harris, when he was stationed at Shimoda. Okichi may be apocryphal, or according to Oliver Statler, at least her reputation as solicitous nurse to an ailing Harris is fantasy. Okichi, or her legend, has come to represent all the women supplied by the Japanese authorities to Western men, specifically American men, for the sake of the country. The Okichi legend has been the theme of novels, plays, movies, and songs, and is available in English translation in Yamamoto Yuzo's 1929 play, "Tōjin Okichi," which Glenn W. Shaw translated as "Chink Okichi." See: *Three Plays by Yamamoto Yuzo* (Tōkyō: Hokuseido Press), 1935. See also: Oliver Statler, *Shimoda Story* (Honolulu: University of Hawaii Press), 1986 (first published by Random House in 1969). Okichi, or women like her, may have inspired John Luther Long to write "Madam Butterfly," wherein we see the rogue Captain Pinkerton seduce the young Cio Cio san and then leave her.

64 For "foreigner" (J: *tōjin*, K: *tang'in*, composed of the character for the Chinese Tang dynasty and the character for person), see: *Pyŏllye chibyo*, fascicle 14, entry 1708.9, p. 330, where the House Master is negotiating with the Tongnae officials. The House Master reportedly stated,

> . . . Controlling Wae who had illegal sexual relations [with Koreans was done] before without protest; all the more so for those seized outside this compound. Foreigner (J: *tōjin*) relations with Wae women are so numerous as to be uncountable. In our country (Japan), we certainly do not take this as a criminal matter; so how, in short, can I put a law like yours into an Agreement, when it is not a crime? By dispatching [such] a letter to [Tsushima, I] will be threatened and scolded, and I am full of fear. . . .

The appearance of the word *tōjin* in a letter addressed to a Korean is curious. Jurgis Elisonas explains *tōjin* in the following way:

> . . . Tōjin Ikki (local Korean revolts against the Hideyoshi invasion). *Tōjin* being a term with an opprobrious connotation, the phrase might be translated as 'Chinamen's uprisings.' Naturally enough, those who came to conquer in the name of Jingu Kōgō could not worry themselves about such tenuous details as calling the Korean people by their proper name, Koreans.

See: Jurgis Elisonas, "Chapter 6, The Inseparable Trinity: Japan's Relations with China and Korea," in John W. Hall, ed., *The Cambridge History of Japan, Vol. 4, Early Modern Japan* (Cambridge: Cambridge University Press), 1991: 276. Nevertheless, as we can see here, at least Japanese from Tsushima seem to have used *tōjin* in a general fashion to mean 'Chinese and European foreigner.' Shin Yu-han, Secretary to the 1716 Korean Embassy to Japan, asked Amenomori Hōshū why Japanese referred to Koreans as *tōjin*, and Hōshū told him that the Japanese officially referred to Koreans as "guests" (J: *kyakujin*, K: *kaek'in*) or "Koreans"(J: *Chōsenjin*, K: *Chosŏn'in*), but that ordinary Japanese people had long taken Korean "civilization" (J: *bunbutsu*, K: *munmul*) as of the same character as that of the "Middle Kingdom" (J: *Chūka*, K: *Chunghwa*) and referring to Koreans as *tōjin* indicated love and respect. See: Sin Yu-han, "Haeyurok," in *Haehaeng ch'ongjae*, cat. no. yŏng ko cho, 90/2/6 in the Kungnip Chung'ang Tosŏgwan, vol. 6, folio 70a–70b. For a Japanese translation of the same, see: "Haeyurok" *Shin I-kan* (K: *Sin Yu-han*), "Kaiyūroku" (K: *Haeyurok*), translated by Kyō Zai-gen (K: *Kang Chae-ŏn*) in Tōyō bunko 252, *Kaiyūroku: Chōsen Tsūshinshi no Nihon kikō* (Tōkyō: Heibonsha), 1974: 318. The Nagasaki Bugyō, Ōoka Bizen-no-kami, used the term *tōkoku* (composed of the same *tō* from *tōjin* plus the character for country) in a general sense in 1716 when he wrote that Japanese "castaways in foreign lands (*tōkoku*) are subject to regulations forbidding residence in other domains and other lands and so must be investigated when repatriated." See: *Kiyō Gundan*, ed. by Nakada Yasunao and Nakamura Tadashi, (Tōkyō: Kondō Shuppansha), 1974: 71. In early twenty-first century Japan one finds *tōjin* used for place names. In the city of Hakata/ Fukuoka there is an area of the city called "Tōjin-machi," or quite literally, "China-town." When one considers the antiquity of the port of Hakata and its far-flung trade connections with the rest of Asia prior to 1600, then it should come as no surprise that there are numerous records of Chinese merchants having resided in the port. Hakata merchants also traded with Korea, but for sensitive political reasons originating in the Meiji period, that connection was ignored and the literalness of *tōjin* was probably stressed. In these circumstances, one might wonder if "China-town" was not also "Korea-town." Sin Ki-su also reports that, at the point where the Korean Envoy to Edo landed up the Yodo River from Osaka, there is a stone monument inscribed with the words meaning "*tōjin* stepped pier." See: Sin Ki-su, "Mitsukatta Chōsen Tsūshinshi no ema: minshū dōshi no kōkan –," *Mirai*, 227 (1985.8): 5. The use of *tōjin* to mean Korean person is also apparent in the festival traditions that grew up in villages along the Korean envoys' route to Edo. These festivals re-enact the processions and often carry the appellation *tōjin*. See: Yi Chin-hŭi, "Tōjin odori to Chōsen yama," in Eizō bunka kyōkai, ed., *Edo jidai no Chōsen Tsūshinshi* (Tōkyō: Mainichi Shinbunsha), 1979, pp. 51–68; and Sin Ki-su, "Matsuri no naka no Chōsen Tsūshinshi," *Kankoku bunka* 7:11 (1985.11): 15–24. The character for *tō* in *tōjin* was also known in sixteenth-century Japan as *kara*, as in *karamono*, which referred to the expensive, exotic, and beautiful luxury items imported from China that were so creatively put together by Sen no Rikyū to create a new Japanese aesthetic that we recognize in the tea ceremony. In this connection, Kang Jae-ŏn argues that the correct pronunciation of *tōjin* is *karabito*. He points out that from antiquity in the archipelago, when reference was made to Korean cultural items or place names, the term *han* as in Hanguk carried the pronunciation *kara* as did the character for the Tang dynasty, the character meaning spicy hot (K: *meul shin*), and the characters for sweet music/pleasure (K: *tal kam* and *p'ungnyu ak* or *chŭlgil ak*). This argument, however, risks pushing the nuance too far in the other direction towards the exotically interesting. See: Shin I-kan (K: Sin Yu-han), "Kaiyūroku" (K: *Haeyurok*), p. 318. In short, the word's "opprobrious connotation" and even whether or not its usage was limited to designating Koreans have yet to be clearly determined. By contrast, the Sino-Korean referent for Japanese people used consistently in late Chosŏn period documents is *Wae-in* or "Wae person," an ancient designation the islanders had hoped to dispel as early as the late seventh century, when they designated their land Nihon or Nippon (K: *Ilbon*). Sin Yu-han, in the same conversation with Hōshū in Ōsaka mentioned above, reports that Hōshū objected to Koreans using Wae to refer to Japan and the Japanese people. Sin countered that this is a traditional term. Hōshū argued that the name had been changed to "Nippon" as far back as the Tang dynasty and would Sin please use this designation. Hōshū was obviously referring to the *Xin Tang shu* (c.1072), which mentions an embassy in 670 that changed "Wa" (or "Yamato") to "Nihon" or "Nippon." The origins of the term Wae probably come from a character whose pronunciation resembled the pronunciation used by an archipelago envoy to the Chinese court and was written for phonetic value. The envoy identified his land as "Wa," and the Chinese or Korean scribe recorded a character with similar pronunciation. Since many Chinese characters could have served this purpose, we might ask if the character had other meanings that would have colored its reference to the islanders. It is questionable as to whether the character had a neutral meaning and was chosen merely for pronunciation. The *Zenrin kokuhōki* (1470) quotes from the *Yangwengong tanyuan* (mid-eleventh century by Yang Yi [974–1020], a Song statesman): "In my view, Nihon (or Nippon) is another name for

Wo [also read Yamato], because they disliked it as inelegant. Probably it was because they understood the [negative implication of the] Chinese character *wo*." See: Tanaka Takeo, trans. and ed., *Zenrin kokuhōki* [and] *Shintei zoku zenrin kokuhōki* (Tōkyō: Shūeisha), 1995: 60–61; and Charlotte von Verschuer, "Japan's foreign relations 600 to 1200 A.D. – a translation from *Zenrin kokuhōki*," *Monumenta Nipponica* 54(1): 30. The "negative implications" probably referred to the meanings "subservient" and "ugly," which are meanings, at least from the later Han period, carried by the character for Wae/Wa/Wo that we see in the *Sanguozhi, Weizhi, Dong yi chuan*, published in 1959 in Beijing by Zhonghua shuju chubanshe. Even setting this argument aside, any neutrality the term may have had was corrupted from as early as the first century A.D., when it was paired with the character for "slave" (K: *no* as in *nobi*). This pairing survives in Korea into the present (e.g. Waenom). Koryŏ and Chosŏn-period documents often couple Wae with characters meaning "pirate" (Waegu), regardless of the actual origins of the pirates. The association of Wae with slaves, pirates, and invaders (e.g. Hideyoshi's armies) was widespread from the fourteenth century into the twentieth century on the peninsula as well as the continent. Slave, pirate, and invader are not good company to keep, and for most of recorded history, and in particular for the period from the thirteenth to the twentieth century, the term cannot be considered a neutral rendering of pronunciation. By itself and by association, Wae was a term tainted with the image of either the lowborn or the criminal or both.

65 As the Governor of Kyŏngsang Province, O Shi-tae, put the matter, ". . . Without reservation I have done my duty. Under no circumstances have I condoned insult. The foreign barbarians' recourse to constant fabrication loses authority as soon as [our majesty's] dignity takes command. . . ." See *Waein changna tŭngnok*, folio 8a. The Governor's use of the words "foreign barbarian" (K: *oe-i*) was in a context explaining his frustration with the House Master's failure to extradite the Korean women.

66 For a complete list of House Masters and *Chaep'an* (J: *Saihan*, Special Liaison Official), see: Osa Masanori, "Ni-Sen kankei ni okeru kiroku no jidai," *Tōyō gakuhō*, 50:4 (1968): 78. Osa and Amenomori Hōshū render his name as Fukami Danueimon, but the *Kōkan ikken* renders the name as Fukami Enueimon.

67 Amenomori Hōshū, *Kōrin teisei*, folio 42–46 or the Kansai Daigaku printed version, pp. 70–71:

> During the tenure of House Master Fukami Danueimon [1688.8.6–1690.9.16], two or three Korean women kept inside the compound were discovered. Demands from Tongnae were ignored. When the women were secretly put out the compound gate, they were apprehended, not only tortured but also decapitated and their heads put on pikes. When the [Japanese] involved was named and the House Master called upon to be swift in his duty [and extradite the criminal], the House Master made excuses. Months and years passed in that state, and the matter of extradition was dropped. At that time, it was said on [Tsushima] that [Fukami] handled the matter reasonably well. . . .

68 Etsuko Hae-Jin Kang, *Diplomacy and Ideology in Japanese–Korean Relations: From the Fifteenth to the Eighteenth Century* (London: Macmillan Press, Ltd.), 1997.

8 CONCLUSION

1 "Internal" and "external" refers to Carlo Ginzburg's criteria for the formulation of a historical proof based on what he calls the "evidential paradigm" or Charles Pierce's idea of "abductive reasoning." Simply stated, abduction begins with facts and no theory and goes in search of a theory to relate and explain the facts. Abduction finally proves nothing but states conclusions in probable terms of maybe/maybe not. Abduction differs from induction in that the latter begins with a theory or hypothesis and goes in search of facts to prove or disprove the hypothesis. Deduction relies solely on reason without necessitating the introduction of facts. Abduction in Ginzburg's practice divides facts into "internal" and

"external" evidence; the only real difference being that internal evidence is produced by the subject and external evidence is produced by someone or something else. When the two agree, probability increases that the assertion by the subject is true. When the two disagree, as we found in Chapter 4, doubt is thrown on the subject's assertions. Ginzburg has done us the favor of restating traditional historiographical practice in a simple, eloquent, and sophisticated fashion. See: Carlo Ginzburg, "Clues: Roots of an Evidential Paradigm," in Carlo Ginzburg, *Clues, Myths, and the Historical Method*, trans. by John and Anne Tedeschi, (Baltimore: The Johns Hopkins Press, [1986] 1989): 96–125, and Edward Muir, "Introduction: Observing Trifles," in *Microhistory and the Lost Peoples of Europe*, ed. by Edward Muir and Guido Ruggiero, trans. by Eren Branch, (Baltimore: The Johns Hopkins Press), 1991: vii–xxviii.

2 Clifford Geertz, *The Interpretation of Cultures* (New York: Basic Books, Inc.), 1973: 13.

APPENDIX A

1 We will be referring to: 朴秉濠 (Pak Pyŏng-ho) ed., 奎章閣韓國本圖書解題 (Kyujanggak Hanguk-bon tosŏ haeje), 서울: 서울大學校出版部 (Seoul: Seoul taehakkyo ch'ulp'anbu), 1987, for many of the document descriptions that follow. All of the documents are located in the Kyujanggak unless indicated otherwise.

2 Izumi, Chōichi (泉澄一), 釜山窯の史的研究 (Pusan yō no shiteki kenkyū), 吹田市: 關西大學出版部 (Suita-shi: Kansai Daigaku Shuppanbu), 1986.

3 We have entries from the following years: 1637–1646, 1649, 1654, 1657–1661, 1667–1670, 1691–1693, 1699, 1702–1705, 1709–1714, 1716–1722, 1724–1727, 1731–1736, 1738, and 1752.

4 We have entries for: 1667–1670, 1689, 1691–1692, 1694–1696, 1698–1706, 1708–1710, 1712–1714, 1716–1721, 1724–1727, 1729–1730, 1734–1736, and 1739.

5 We have entries for: 1640, 1642, 1646, 1652–1655, 1660, 1662, 1664, 1666, 1668, 1670, 1672, 1675, 1700, 1716, 1720–1723, 1725–1727, 1730–1733, 1735–1736, 1739–1742, 1745–1747, and 1749–1751.

6 We have entries for: 1641–1709, 1711–1733, and 1737–1751.

7 Also available in 國史編纂委員會 (Kuksa P'yŏnch'an Wiwŏnhoe) ed., 各司謄錄 13, 慶尚道篇 3 (Kaksa tŭngnok, vol. 13, Kyŏngsang-do p'yŏn 3), 서울: 大光印刷公社 (Seoul: Taegwang Inswae Kongsa) 1984, pp. 503–515.

8 We have entries for: 1637–1687, 1689–1696, 1698–1701, 1703–1706, and 1708–1724.

9 Also available in 國史編纂委員會 (Kuksa P'yŏnch'an Wiwŏnhoe) ed., 各司謄錄 13, 慶尚道篇 3 (Kaksa tŭngnok vol. 13, Kyŏngsang-do p'yŏn 3), 서울: 大光印刷公社 (Seoul: Taegwang Inswae Kongsa), 1984, pp. 372–481. We have entries for: 1653–1654, 1681, 1717–1719, 1746–1747, 1762–1763, and 1841.

10 We have entries for: 1637–1638, 1640–1642, 1644–1645, 1648, 1650–1652, 1656, 1658–1661, 1665–1667, 1669–1670, 1672–1673, 1691–1692, 1695–1696, 1699–1702, 1704–1705, 1708, 1710, 1714–1715, 1720, 1724–1725, 1729, 1735, 1739–1740, 1744–1745, and 1749–1751.

11 Osa Masanori (長正統), 路浮税考: 肅宗朝癸亥約條の一考察 (Nobuseikō: Shukusō chō kigai yakujō no ichi kōsatsu), 朝鮮學報 (Chōsen gakuhō), 58 (1971): 1–20.

12 *Kyŏngguk taejŏn*, 1:10a–10b.

13 Photolithographically reprinted in 奎章閣資料叢書錦湖시리즈對外關係 (Kyujanggak charyo ch'ongsŏ kŭmho siriju [series] taeoe kwangye) ed., 典客司別謄錄 (Chŏngaeksa pyŏl tŭngnok) 서울: 서울大學校奎章閣 (Seoul: Seoul Taehakkyo Kyujanggak), 1992. I wish to thank Dr. Kenneth R. Robinson for arranging for me to obtain copies.

14 韓國國立中央圖書館 (Hanguk gungnip chungang tosŏgwan), cat. no. 한-38–43 (han 38–43).

15 Photolithographically reprinted in 國史編纂委員會 (Kuksa P'yŏnch'an Wiwŏnhoe) ed., 各司謄錄 51, 慶尚道篇 3 (Kaksa tŭngnok vol. 51, Kyŏngsang-do p'yŏn 3), 서울: 時事文化社 (Seoul: Sisa Munhwasa), 1991, pp. 367–444.

16 Photolithographically reprinted in 國史編纂委員會 (Kuksa P'yŏnch'an Wiwŏnhoe) ed., 各司謄錄 51, 慶尙道篇 3 (Kaksa tŭngnok vol. 51, Kyŏngsang-do p'yŏn 3), 서울: 時事文化社 (Sisa Munhwasa), 1991, pp. 445–469.

17 The *Sejong Sillok chiriji* or King Sejong's Treatise on Geography is fascicle 148 through 155 of the *Sejong Veritable Records* and was published separately by Gakushūin University in Japan in 1957 as a photolithographic reprint.

18 One can find a good photolithographic reprint in the 東萊史料 (Tongnae saryo), vol. 2, pp. 1–200.

19 Preserved in the 韓國教會史研究所 (Hanguk Kyohoesa Yŏnguso).

20 All of the *ŭpchi* mentioned here can be found in photolithographic reprint in 金東哲 (Kim Tong-ch'ŏl) *et al.* ed., 東萊史料 (Tongnae saryo), vols. 2 and 3, 서울: 驪江出版社 (Seoul: Yŏgang Ch'ulp'ansa), 1989. The 1832, 1871, and 1895 *ŭpchi* can also be found in photolithographic reprint in 韓國學文獻研究所 (Hangukhak munhŏn yŏn'guso) ed., 邑誌慶尙道編 (Ŭpchi Kyŏngsang-do p'yŏn), 서울: 亞細亞文化社 (Seoul: Asea Munhwasa), 1982, 1987.

21 We have entries for: 1849–1850, 1860–1865, 1867, 1869–1874, and 1883–1889.

22 Also available in 國史編纂委員會 (Kuksa P'yŏnch'an Wiwŏnhoe) ed., 各司謄錄 12, 慶尙道篇 2 (Kaksa tŭngnok, vol. 12, Kyŏngsang-do p'yŏn 2), 서울: 大光印刷公社 (Seoul: Taegwang Inswae Kongsa), 1984, pp. 698–745.

23 Also available in 國史編纂委員會 (Kuksa P'yŏnch'an Wiwŏnhoe) ed., 各司謄錄 13, 慶尙道篇 3 (Kaksa tŭngnok, vol. 13, Kyŏngsang-do p'yŏn 3), 서울: 大光印刷公社 (Seoul: Taegwang Inswae Kongsa), 1984, pp. 169–178.

24 Reprinted in 金東哲 (Kim Tong-ch'ŏl) *et al.*, ed., 東萊史料 1 (Tongnae saryo, vol. 1), 서울: 驪江出版社 (Seoul: Yŏgang Ch'ulp'ansa), 1989, pp. 113–257.

25 By 河聖大 (Ha Sŏng-tae). Reprinted in 金東哲 (Kim Tong-ch'ŏl) *et al.*, ed., 東萊史料 1 (Tongnae saryo, vol. 1), 서울: 驪江出版社 (Seoul: Yŏgang Ch'ulp'ansa), 1989, pp. 1–68.

26 By 金鉐 (Kim Sŏk). Reprinted in 金東哲 (Kim Tong-ch'ŏl) *et al.*, ed., 東萊史料 1 (Tongnae saryo, vol. 1), 서울: 驪江出版社 (Seoul: Yŏgang Ch'ulp'ansa), 1989, pp. 69–111.

27 Preserved in the 今西文庫天理圖書館 (Imanishi bunko, Tenri Toshokan, Japan). Photolithographic reprint in 朝鮮學報 (Chōsen gakuhō), 57 (1970.10) and 58 (1970.12). Although unrelated, the name resonates with Taoist overtones. 逢萊山 (K.: *Pongnae-san*) is the island of the immortals in the Eastern Sea.

28 中村榮孝 (Nakamura Hidetaka), 逢萊故事について: 十七世紀日鮮關係の一史料 (*Pongnae Kosa ni tsuite: jūnana seki Ni-Sen kankei no ichi shiryō*), 朝鮮學報 (Chōsen gakuhō), 57 (1970.10).

29 Also available in 國史編纂委員會(Kuksa P'yŏnch'an Wiwŏnhoe) ed., 各司謄錄 49, 慶尙道篇 1 (Kaksa tŭngnok, vol. 49, Kyŏngsang-do p'yŏn 3), 서울: 時事文化社 (Seoul: Sisa Munhwasa), 1991, pp. 54–143.

30 Typeset version in 國史編纂委員會 (Kuksa P'yŏnch'an Wiwŏnhoe) ed., 邊例集要 (Pyŏllye chibyo) in two volumes, 서울: 探求堂 (Seoul: T'amgudang), 1969, 1971.

31 Kim Ku-chin (김구진) and Yi Hyŏn-suk (이현숙), 通文館志의편찬과그간행에대하어 (T'ongmun'gwanji ŭi p'yŏnch'an kwa kŭ kanhaeng e taehayŏ) in 세종다항기념사업회 (Sejong Taewang Ki'nyŏm Saŏphoe) ed., 국역통문관지 (Kugyŏk T'ongmun'gwanji), vol. 1, 서울: 세종다항기념사업회 (Seoul: Sejong Taewang Ki'nyŏm Saŏphoe, 1998): 1–30.

BIBLIOGRAPHY

All primary sources are arranged by title; all secondary sources are arranged by author.

Primary sources

Chingbinok (懲毖錄) (first printed 1633). Yu Sŏng-yong (柳成龍) 西厓 (penname Sŏae). In 大東文化研究院, 成均館大學校 (Taedong Munhwa Yŏn'guwŏn, Sŏnggyungwan Taehakkyo), ed. 西厓文集 (Sŏae munjip). 서울: 東國文化社 (Seoul: Tongguk Munhwasa), 1958.

Chŏngjo sillok (正祖實錄).

Ch'ŏnggu sŏnp'yo-do (青邱線表圖) (1800–1834). Kim Chŏng-ho (金正浩).

Chŏpdae Waein saye (接待倭人事例) (Entries from 1637–1687). Kyujanggak cat. no. 9763 and 16024, and Kuksa P'yŏnch'an Wiwŏnhoe cat. no. B13J-82. Typeset from Kyujanggak text in 釜山市史編纂委員會 (Pusan-si-sa P'yŏnch'an Wiwŏnhoe) ed., 釜山史料叢書, 2 (Pusan saryo ch'ongsŏ, volume 2). 釜山: 嶺南印刷所 (Pusan: Yŏngnam Inswaeso), 1963.

Ch'ŏphae sinŏ (捷解新語) (J: Shōkai shingo) (completed 1618). Yi, T'ae-yŏng (李太永), trans. and ed. 譯註 捷解新語 (Yŏkju Ch'ŏp-hae sin-ŏ). 서울: 太學社 (T'aehaksa), 1997. 京都大學文學部國語學國文學研究室 (Kyōto Daigaku Bungakubu Kokugogaku Kokubungaku Kenkyūshitsu), ed. 改修捷解新語, 本文。國語索引。解題 (Kaishū Shōkai shingo, honbun-kokugo sakuin-kaidai). 京都: 京都大學國文學界 (Kyōto: Kyōto Daigaku Kokubun Gakkai), 1987.

Chōsen gorin ondomo no jinrui (朝鮮御隣御供之人類) (c.1591). MS 363, folio 37 in 長沼文庫 (Naganuma bunko), 九州大學文學部九州文化史研究室 (Kyūshū daigaku bungakubu Kyūshū bunkashi kenkyūshitsu).

Chōsen koku goyōken kenbakusho (朝鮮國御用件建白書) (1864.6 entry). Ōshima Tomonojō (大島友之允). In 山田方谷全集刊行會 (Yamada Hōkoku zenshū kankōkai), ed. 方谷先生年譜 (Hōkoku sensei nenpu). 東京: 山田方谷全集刊行會 (Tōkyō: Yamada Hōkoku Zenshū Kankōkai), 1951.

Chōsen koku kōbōeki aitodokori on kattemuki on nanjū no omomuki oyobi go naii sōrō tokoro okane ichi man ryō on haishaku narabi nennen hannō kin on sashinobi no kiroku (朝鮮國公貿易相滯御勝手向御難澁之趣及御內意候處御金壹萬兩御拜借竝年年返納金御差延之記錄) (dating obscure). In 九州大學文學部九州文化史研究室施設倉 (Kyūshū daigaku bungakubu Kyūshū bunkashi kenkyūshitsu shisetsusō), cat. no. B30/154.

Chōsen tsūkō daiki (朝鮮通交大紀) (dating obscure). Matsuura Masatada (松浦允任). In 長崎縣立對馬歷史民俗資料館 (Nagasaki kenritsu Tsushima Rekishi Minzoku Shiryōkan), cat. no. 記錄類 1, 表書札方, N 朝鮮關係, 3 朝鮮關係書籍, 1 (Kiroku rui 1, Hyōsho satsugata, N Chōsen kankei, 3 Chōsen kankei shoseki, 1), 10 volumes. Typeset version by

Tanaka, Takeo (田中建夫) and Tashiro, Kazui (田代和生), ed. 東京: 名著出版 (Tōkyō: Meicho Shuppan), 1978.

Chōsen zenkoku (朝鮮全國) (1875). 陸軍參謀局 (Rikugun sanbō kyoku), compiler. 武富藏 (mufuzō). In 九州大學文學部朝鮮史研究室 (Kyūshū daigaku bungakubu Chōsenshi kenkyūshitsu), cat. no. 242.1J 1.

Chŭngbo munhŏn pigo (增補文獻備考) (c.1907). Hong Ponghan (洪鳳漢) et al., ed. 서울: 明文堂 (Seoul: Myŏngmundang), 1977.

Chŭngjŏng kyorinji (增正交隣志) (1802 and 1865). Kim Kŏn-sŏ (金健瑞), ed. In 奎章閣 (Kyujanggak), cat. no. 古 (ko) 5710–1 (vols. 1–2); in 奎章閣貴 (Kyujanggak kwi), cat. no. 94-v.1–2; and 奎章閣 (Kyujanggak) cat. no. 15223 (vols. 1–2). The 1865 version is in 奎章閣 (Kyujanggak) cat. no. 5273 (vols. 1–3); in the 國立中央圖書館 (Kungnip chung'ang tosŏgwan), cat. no. han (한)-31–231; and in the 藏書閣 (Changsŏgak), cat. no. 2-3512. Photolithographic reprint versions from 설울: 亞細亞文化社 (Seoul: Asea Munhwasa), 1974 (reprint of a 1940 photolithographic reprint that contains the 1802 xylographic original in photolithographic form and the 1865 additions in typeset font). The 1865 text from the 國立中央圖書館 (Kungnip chung'ang tosŏgwan) is in Ha, Woo Bong and Hong, Sŏng-dŏk (하우봉 and 홍·성덕) trans. and ed. 국역중정교린지 (Kugyŏk Chŭngjŏng kyorinji). 설울: 민족문화추진회 (Seoul: Minjok Munhwa Ch'ujinhoe), 1998. This is the text used here.

Chungjong sillok (中宗實錄).

Dong yi chuan (東夷傳) (c.297). In Chen Shou (陳壽), ed. 魏志 (Wei shu), juan 30 in 三國志 (Sanguozhi). Beijing: Zhonghua Shuju Chubanshe, 1959.

Furukawa-ke oboegaki-utsushi (古川家覺書寫) (dating obscure). In 飯田家文書, 九州大學文學部國史研究室 (Iida-ke monjo, Kyūshū Daigaku Bungakubu Kokushi Kenkyūshitsu).

Haedong chegukki (海東諸國紀) (c.1471). Sin Suk-chu (申叔舟). Text used here is the photolithographic print 東京: 国畫刊行会 (Tōkyō: Kokusho kankōkai), 1975.

Haeyurok (海游錄) (1719). Sin Yu-han (申維翰). In Haehaeng ch'ongjae (海行摠載), in 國立中央圖書館 (Kungnip chung'ang tosŏgwan), cat. no. yŏng ko cho, 90/2/4–6. Modern Japanese translation: Haeyurok (海游錄) by Sin Yu-han (申維翰, J: Shin I-kan). In Kang Chae-ŏn (姜在彦, J: Kyō Zai-gen), trans. 東洋文庫 252, 海游錄, 朝鮮通信使の日本紀行 (Tōyō bunko 252, Kaiyūroku: Chōsen Tsūshinshi no Nihon kikō). 東京: 平凡社 (Tōkyō: Heibonsha), 1974.

Hangukhak munhŏn yŏn'guso (韓國學文獻研究所), ed. 韓國地理志叢書 邑誌 慶尚道 (Hanguk chiriji ch'ongsŏ ŭpchi Kyŏngsangdo) (1832). 서울: 亞細亞文化社 (Seoul: Asea Munhwasa), 1982, 1987.

Hogu ch'ongsu (戶口總數) (1789). In 奎章閣 (Kyujanggak), cat. no. 1602. 서울: 서울大學校出版部 (Seoul: Seoul Taehakkyo Ch'ulp'anbu), 1971.

Hwanjaejip (瓛齊集) (c.1911). Pak Kyu-su (朴珪壽). In 韓國學文獻研究所 (Hanguk-hak munhŏn yŏn'guso), ed. 韓國近代思想叢書 朴珪壽全集 (Hanguk kundae sasang ch'ongsŏ, Pak Kyu-su chŏnjip). 서울: 亞細亞文化社 (Seoul: Asea Munhwasa), 1978.

Hyŏjong sillok (孝宗實錄).

Hyŏnjong kaesu sillok (顯宗改修實錄).

Hyŏnjong sillok (顯宗實錄).

Ilsŏngnok (日省錄).

Injo sillok (仁祖實錄).

Kaksa tŭngnok, vol. 13, Kyŏngsangdo-p'yŏn 3 (各司謄錄 13, 慶尚道篇 3). In 國史編纂委員會 (Kuksa P'yŏnch'an Wiwŏnhoe) ed., 各司謄錄 13, 慶尚道篇 3 (Kaksa tŭngnok, vol. 13, Kyŏngsangdo-p'yŏn 3). 서울: 大光印刷公社 (Seoul: Taegwang Inswae Kongsa) 1984.

Kaksa tŭngnok vol. 51, Kyŏngsang-do p'yŏn 3 (各司謄錄 51, 慶尚道篇 3). In 國史編纂委員會 (Kuksa P'yŏnch'an Wiwŏnhoe) ed., 各司謄錄 51, 慶尚道篇 3 (Kaksa tŭngnok vol. 51, Kyŏngsang-do p'yŏn 3). 서울: 時事文化社 (Seoul: Sisa Munhwasa), 1991.

Kanggye-bu ŭpchi (江界府邑誌 全) (or 江界誌, Kanggye-chi). In 奎章閣 (Kyujanggak), cat.
no. 10948. Published photolithographic reprint in 私選邑誌 53, 平安道 9 (Sasŏn ŭpchi,
vol. 53, P'yŏng'an-do 9). 서울: 韓國人文科學院 (Seoul: Hanguk Inmun Kwahakwŏn), 1990.

Kiyō gundan (崎陽群談) (c.1717). Ōoka Yasunao (大岡清相). In Nakada Yasunao
(中田易直) and Nakamura Tadashi (中村 質), ed. 東京: 近藤出版社 (Tōkyō: Kondō
Shuppansha), 1974.

Koji ruien (古事類苑) (c.1896). 東京: 吉川弘文館 (Tōkyō: Yoshikawa Kōbunkan), 1983.

Kōkan ikken (交奸一件) (entries for 1672–1712). In 分類紀事大綱 (Bunrui kiji taikō), cat.
no. 31 in 日本國國會圖書館, 宗家文書 (Nihon Koku Kokkai Toshokan, Sōke monjo).

Kōrin teisei (交隣提醒) (1728/1729). Amenomori Hōshū (雨森芳洲). In Amenomori Hōshū
bunko (雨森芳洲文庫), 雨森芳洲庵, 滋賀縣, 伊香郡, 高月町, 雨森村 (Amenomori
Hōshū-an, Shiga-ken, Ika-gun, Takamatsuki-chō, Amenomori-mura), cat. no. 15. Also in
韓國國立圖書館 (Hanguk kungnip tosŏgwan), cat. no. 朝 51, 사 167, 古第 16859,
1 volume (cho 51, na 167, ko che 16859). Printed version in 芳洲外交關係資料翰集
雨森芳洲全書三 (Hōshū gaikō kankei shiryō kanshū, Amenomori Hōshū zenshū vol. 3).
泉 澄一 (Izumi Chōichi) ed. 吹田: 關西大學 (Suita: Kansai Daigaku), 1982.

Koryŏsa (高麗史).

Kyŏngguk taejŏn (經國大典) (c.1460–1485).

Kyŏngsang-do chiriji (慶尚道地理志) (1425?). In 韓國學文獻研究所 (Hanguk-hak munhŏn
yŏn'guso), ed. 全國地理志 (Chŏnguk chiriji). 서울: 亞細亞文化社 (Seoul: Asea
Munhwasa), 1983, pp. 99–291.

Kyŏngsang-do ŭpchi (慶尚道邑誌) (1832). In 奎章閣 (Kyujanggak), cat. no. 666. Kyŏngsang-
do ŭpchi (慶尚道邑誌) (1871). In 奎章閣 (Kyujanggak), cat. no. 12173. Kyŏngsang-do
ŭpchi (慶尚道邑誌) (1895). In 奎章閣 (Kyujanggak), cat. no. 12174. Kyŏngsang-do ŭpchi
(慶尚道邑誌) also in 韓國學文獻研究所 (Hanguk-hak munhŏn yŏn'guso) ed. 韓國地理
志叢書 邑誌 慶尚道編 (Hanguk chiriji ch'ongsŏ ŭpchi Kyŏngsang-do p'yŏn, 1–4).
서울: 亞細亞文化社 (Seoul: Asea Munhwasa), 1982, 1987.

Mangi yoram (萬機要覽) in two volumes (1808). 沈象圭 (Sim Sang-kyu) and 徐榮輔
(Sŏ Yŏng-bo) ed. 서울: 景仁文化社 (Seoul: Kyŏngin Munhwasa), 1972.

Munjong sillok (文宗實錄).

Nosongdang Ilbon haengnok (老松堂 日本行錄) (c.1420). Song Hŭi-kyŏng (宋希璟). In
민족문화추진회 (Minjok munhwa ch'unjinhoe), ed. 고전국역총서해행총재 (Kojŏn kukyŏk
ch'ongsŏ Haehaeng Ch'ongjae), vol. 8. 서울: 민문고 (Seoul: Minmungo, 1967, reprint
1989, Chinese and Korean). Xylographic version (1799) in 國立中央圖書館 (Kungnip
Chung'an Tosŏgwan), cat. no. 古 (ko) 2837-18. Typeset version (1799) in 國立中央圖書
館 (Kungnip Chung'an Tosŏgwan), cat. no. 한/古/朝45-가42 (han/ko/cho 45-ka 42).
Modern Japanese translation in Murai Shōsuke (村井章介), trans. and ed. 老松堂日本
行錄: 朝鮮使節の見た中世日本 (Rōmatsudō Nihon Kōroku: Chōsen shisetsu no mita
chūsei Nihon). 東京: 岩波書店 (Tōkyō: Iwanami Shoten), 1987.

Oritaku shiba no ki (折いたく柴の記) (c.1716). Arai Hakuseki (新井白石). In 官崎道生
(Miyazaki Michio). 定本 折いたく柴の記釋義 增訂版 (Teihon Oritaku shiba no ki shakugi
zōteihan). 東京: 近藤出版社 (Tōkyō: Kondō Shuppansha, 1985.

P'aegwan chapki (稗官雜記) (c.1554). Ŏ Suk-kwŏn (漁叔權). 臺北: 東方文化書局 (Taepuk:
Tongbang Munhwa Sŏguk), 1971.

Pibyŏnsa tŭngnok (備邊司謄錄).

Piguk tŭngnok (備局謄錄).

Pongnae kosa (蓬萊故事) (seventeenth century). 天理大學図書館 (Tenri Daigaku Toshokan).
In 朝鮮學報 (Chōsen gakuhō), 57 (1970.10): 87–168 and 58 (1971.1): 71–170.

Puyŏk silch'ong (in two volumes) (賦役實總 上下) (1794). In 奎章閣 (Kyujanggak), cat.
no. 252. Photolithographic reprint printed by 서울: 驪江出版社 (Seoul: Yŏgang Ch'ulp'ansa),
1984.

Pyŏlch'awae tŭngnok (別差倭謄錄) (Entries for 1637–1860). In 奎章閣 (Kyujanggak), cat. no. 12871.

Pyŏllye chibyo (in two volumes) (邊例集要 上下) (1592–1841). In 奎章閣 (Kyujanggak), cat. no. 2089 and 2090. Typeset version in 國史邊纂委員會 (Kuksa P'yŏnch'an Wiwŏnhoe) ed. 서울: 探求堂 (Seoul: T'amgudang), 1969 and 1971.

Samguk sagi (三國史記).

Samguk yusa (三國遺事).

Sejo sillok (世祖實錄).

Sejong sillok (世宗實錄).

Sejong sillok chiriji (世宗實錄地理志).

Shōkai shingo (捷解新語) (see above: Ch'ŏp-hae sin-ŏ).

Sinbo sugyo chimnok (新補受教輯錄) (1698–1743). In 景仁文化社編部 (Kyŏng'in munhwasa p'yŏnbu), ed. 朝鮮王朝法典集 (Chosŏn wangjo pŏpjŏnjip), volume 2. 서울: 景仁文化社 (Seoul: Kyŏng'in Munhwasa), 1972.

Sinch'an p'aldo chiriji (新纂八道地理志).

Sinjŭng tongguk yŏji sŭngnam (新增東國輿地勝覽).

Sok taejŏn (續大典) (c.1744). In 景仁文化社編部 (Kyŏng'in munhwasa p'yŏnbu), ed. 朝鮮王朝法典集 (Chosŏn wangjo pŏpjŏnjip), volume 3. 서울: 景仁文化社 (Seoul: Kyŏng'in Munhwasa), 1972.

Sŏngjong sillok (成宗實錄).

Sōryō Wakan ezu (草梁倭館繪圖). In 舊万松院宗家文庫, 對馬歷史民俗資料館藏 (Kyū Banshōin Sō-ke bunko, Tsushima Rekishi Minzoku Shiryōkan).

Sukjong sillok (肅宗實錄).

Sŭngjŏngwŏn ilgi (承正院日記).

Taejŏn hoet'ong (大典會通) (c.1865). In 景仁文化社編部 (Kyŏng'in munhwasa p'yŏnbu), ed. 朝鮮王朝法典集 (Chosŏn wangjo pŏpjŏnjip), volume 4. 서울: 景仁文化社 (Seoul: Kyŏng'in Munhwasa), 1972.

Taejŏn t'ongp'yŏn (大典統編) (c.1785). In 景仁文化社編部 (Kyŏng'in munhwasa p'yŏnbu), ed. 朝鮮王朝法典集 (Chosŏn wangjo pŏpjŏnjip), volume 3. 서울: 景仁文化社 (Seoul: Kyŏng'in Munhwasa), 1972.

T'aejong sillok (太宗實錄).

Tae-Myŏng yul chikhae (大明律直解 全) (in one volume, typeset). 中樞院編 (Chūsūin) ed. 서울: 景仁文化社 (Seoul: Kyŏng'in Munhwasa), 1974. Photolithographic reprint version in 大明律直解 (Tae-Myŏng yul chikhae). 서울: 保景文化社 (Seoul: Pogyŏng Munhwasa), 1986.

Taikan zakki (對韓雜記) (c.1732). Suyama Donō (陶山鈍翁). In 日本經濟叢書 (Nihon keizai sōsho), vol. 13. 東京: 日本經濟叢書刊行會 (Tōkyō: Nihon Keizai Sōsho Kankōkai), 1915.

T'akijŏn pugo (度支田賦考) (c.1900). In 奎章閣 (Kyujanggak), cat. no. 5470 (6 vols.); 5173 (3 vols.); 12208 (2 vols.); 2939 (1 vol.); 2940 (1 vol.). Photolithographic reprint in 社會經濟史 史料 總書 3, 度支田賦考 (Sahoe kyŏngjesa saryo ch'ongsŏ 3, T'akijŏn pugo). 서울: 驪江出版社 (Seoul: Yŏgang Ch'ulp'ansa), 1986.

Tanjong sillok (端宗實錄).

Tōhei yuki ni tsuki Fuzan nite kenka tsunawachi migi no ishu onkuni e mōshiage kōjō Tōrai yori settai tsukamatsuri onkuni mōshiage sōrō jō hikae (東平行に付釜山に而喧嘩則右之意趣御國へ申上口上東萊より接待仕御國申上候狀控) (1697). In 宗家文書 (Sō-ke monjo), cat. no. 記錄類, 朝鮮關係, P, 1 (1) (kiroku-rui Chōsen kankei, P, 1 [1]) in 長崎縣立對馬歷史民俗資料館, 嚴原, 長崎縣, 日本 (Nagasaki kenritsu Tsushima rekishi minzoku shiryōkan, Izuhara-shi, Nagasaki-ken).

Tongha-myŏn komunsŏ (東下面古文書) (entries 1742–1982). Translation into modern Korean, annotation, and photolithographic reprint in 文化公報室 (Munhwa Kongbo-sil) and 慶星大學校 鄕土文化硏究所 (Kyŏngsŏng Taehakkyo, Hyangt'o Munhwa Yŏn'guso), ed. 海雲臺의옛모습이담진束下面古文書 (Haeundae ŭi yet mosŭp-i tamjin Tongha-myŏn komunsŏ). 釜山: 海雲臺區廳 (Pusan: Haeundae-ku Ch'ŏng), 1994.

T'ongmun'gwanji (通文館志) (1720). Kim Chi-nam (金指南) and Kim Kyŏng-mun (金慶門), ed. Xylographic editions in 國立中央圖書館 (Kungnip chung'ang tosŏgwan), cat. no. 한古朝 (han ko-cho) 31–15; 한古朝 (han ko-cho) 31–24; and 古 (ko) 2107–58 (all three with publication date 1778); 古 (ko) 2107–59 (publication date 1888: generally held to be the most complete and correct edition); 古 (ko) 2150–46 (publication date 1944, which used the 1888 text, reprinted by 景仁文化社, Kyŏng'in Munhwasa in 1972). Photolithographic reprint from 서울: 景仁文化社 (Seoul: Kyŏng'in Munhwasa), 1972 used here. Photolithographic reprint and modern Korean translation from 세종대왕기념사엎회 (Sejong Taewang Ki'nyŏm Saŏphoe) ed. 국역통문관지 (Kugyŏk T'ongmun'gwanji) in four volumes. 서울: 세종대왕기념사엎회 (Seoul: Sejong Taewang Ki'nyŏm Saŏphoe), 1998, which also uses the 1888 edition.

Tongmun hwigo (同文彙考) (Entries for Japan 1607–1881). Edited by the offices of the 承文院 (Sŭngmunwŏn) and the 司譯院 (Sayŏg'wŏn). First edition produced in 1788 奎章閣 (Kyujanggak) cat. no. 660, vols. 1–60 and cat. no. 15331, vols. 1–60. Second extant edition produced in 1879 奎章閣 (Kyujanggak) cat. no. 1338, vols. 1 and 2. Third extant edition produced in 1907 (?) 奎章閣 (Kyujanggak) cat. no. 1338, vol. 5. Photolithographic reprint of the 1788 edition with an added 36 fascicles for the years following 1788 in 國史編纂委員會 (Kuksa P'yŏnch'an Wiwŏnhoe), ed. 서울: 翰印刷會社 (Seoul: Han Inswae Hoesa), 1978.

Tongnae-bu chŏpdae samok-ch'o (東萊府接待事目抄) (entries for 1608–1694). In 奎章閣 (Kyujanggak), cat. no. 9764. Photolithographic reprint in 國史編纂委員會 (Kuksa P'yŏnch'an Wiwŏnhoe), ed. 各司謄錄 (Kaksa tŭngnok), vol. 49. 서울: 國史編纂委員會 (Seoul: Kuksa P'yŏnch'an Wiwŏnhoe, 1991): 54–143.

Tongnae-buji (東萊府誌) (1740). In 奎章閣 (Kyujanggak), cat. no. 11904. Photolithographic reprint in Yi, T'ae-jin (李泰鎭) and Yi, Sang-t'ae (李相泰) ed. 朝鮮時代私撰邑誌 17 慶尙道 2 (Chosŏn sidae sach'an ŭpchi 17, Kyŏngsang-do 2). 서울: 韓國人文科學院 (Seoul: Hanguk Inmun Kwahakwŏn), 1989, pp. 484–681.

Tongnae-bu kyerok (東萊府啓錄) (1849–1889). In 奎章閣 (Kyujanggak), cat. no. 15105. Photolithographic reprint in 國史編纂委員會 (Kuksa P'yŏnch'an Wiwŏnhoe), ed. 各司登錄 12, 慶尙道篇 (Kaksa tŭngnok, vol. 12, Kyŏngsang-do p'yŏn). 서울: 大光印刷公社 (Seoul: Taegwang Inswae Kongsa), 1984, pp. 1–697.

Tongnae-bu saye (東萊府事例) (1868). In 奎章閣 (Kyujanggak), cat. no. 4272. Photolithographic reprint in Kim, Tong-ch'ŏl (金東哲) et al., ed. 東萊史料 2 (Tongnae saryo, volume 2). 서울: 驪江出版社 (Seoul: Yŏgang Ch'ulp'ansa), 1989, pp. 453–795. Also in O Yŏng-kyo (吳永教) ed., 韓國地方史資料叢書 事例篇 2 (Hanguk chibang-sa charyo ch'ongsŏ, saye-p'yŏn 2), 서울: 驪江出版社 (Seoul: Yŏgang Ch'ulp'ansa), 1987, pp. 195–287.

Tongnae-bu ŭpchi (東萊府邑誌) (1759). In 韓國敎會史硏究所 (Hanguk Kyohoesa Yŏn'guso) Tongnae-bu ŭpchi (東萊府邑誌) (1832). In 奎章閣 (Kyujanggak), cat. no. 666. Tongnae-bu ŭpchi (東萊府邑誌) (1871). In 奎章閣 (Kyujanggak), cat. no. 12173. Tongnae-bu ŭpchi (東萊府邑誌) (1895). In 奎章閣 (Kyujanggak), cat. no. 12174. All as photolithographic reprints in Kim, Tong-ch'ŏl (金東哲) et al., ed. 東萊史料 2 (Tongnae saryo, volume 2). 서울: 驪江出版社 (Seoul: Yŏgang Ch'ulp'ansa), 1989.

Tongnae-bu ŭpchi (東萊府邑誌) (1899). In 奎章閣 (Kyujanggak), cat. no. 10877. Photolithographic reprint in Kim, Tong-ch'ŏl (金東哲) et al., ed. 東萊史料 3 (Tongnae saryo, volume 3). 서울: 驪江出版社 (Seoul: Yŏgang Ch'ulp'ansa), 1989, pp. 319–401.

Tongsa ilgi (東槎日記) (1711). Im Su-kan (任守幹). Photolithographic reprint in 민족문화추진회 (Minjok munhwa ch'ujin hoe), ed. 海行總載 續 (Haehaeng ch'ongjae sok) vol. 9. 서울: 민족문화문고간행회 (Seoul: Minjok Munhwa Mungo Kanhaenghoe), 1986 (reprint).

T'ongsinsa tŭngnok (通信使謄錄). In 奎章閣 (Kyujanggak), cat. no. 12870, 1–3. Photolithographic reprint in 奎章閣資料叢書 錦湖시리즈對外關係篇 (Kyujanggak charyo ch'ongsŏ Kŭmho Shirijŭ [Series] Tae-oe kwangye p'yŏn), vol. 2. 서울: 서울大學校圖書館 (Seoul: Seoul Taehakkyo Tosŏgwan), 1991.

To sŏnsaeng'an (道先生案) (entries 1078–1970). In 國會圖書館 (Kukhoe Tosŏgwan), ed. 서울: 서울大學校出版部 (Seoul: Seoul Taehakkyo Ch'ulp'anbu), 1970.

Tsūkō ichiran (通航一覽) (c.1859). Hayashi Fukusai (林復斎) et al., ed., in 8 volumes. 東京: 國書刊行會 (Tōkyō: Kokusho Kankōkai), 1912–1913.

Tsūkō sōron (通交總論) (1599–1609). In 宗家文書記錄類 (Chong-ka munsŏ kirok ryu) in 韓國國史編纂委員會 (Hanguk Kuksa P'yŏnch'an Wiwŏnhoe), cat. no. 4311.

Waegwan igŏn tŭngnok (倭館移建登錄) (Entries from 1640–1723). In 奎章閣 (Kyujanggak), cat. no. 12892, 1–2.

Waein changna tŭngnok (倭人作拏謄錄) (Entries 1690–1692). In 奎章閣 (Kyujanggak), cat. no. 12962. Typeset version in Kim, Ŭi-hwan (金義煥). 倭人作拏謄錄について附: 史料本文 (Waein changna tŭngnok ni tsuite, fu: shiryō honbun). 日本文化史研究 (Nihon bunkashi kenkyū), 奈良帝塚山短期大學日本文化史學會 (Nara, Tezukayama Tanki Daigaku, Nihon Bunkashi Gakkai), 16 (1992.1): 59–82. A printed version of the two sections on smuggling can be found in 韓日研究 (Han-Il yŏn'gu), 1 (1972.3): 239–245.

Xin Tang shu (新唐書).

Yŏji tosŏ (輿地圖書) (1765). In 韓國教會研究所 (Hanguk Kyohoe Yŏn'guso). Photolithographic reprint in 國史編纂委員會 (Kuksa P'yŏnch'an Wiwŏnhoe), ed. 서울: 探求堂 (Seoul: T'amgudang), 1973.

Yŏllyŏsil kisul (國譯 燃黎室記述) (c.1806). Yi Kŭng-ik (李肯翊). In 國譯 燃黎室記述 (Kugyŏk Yŏllyŏsil kisul), vol. 11. 서울: 민족문화추진회 (Seoul: Minjŏk Munhwa Ch'ujinhoe), 1967.

Yongjae ch'onghwa (慵齋叢話) (c.1504). Sŏng Hyŏn (成俔). In 奎章閣 (Kyujanggak), cat. no. 7132, 1–3 and 6905, 1–3.

Yŏngjo sillok (英祖實錄).

Yŏngnamch'ŏng saye (嶺南廳事例) (dating obscure). In 奎章閣 (Kyujanggak), cat. no. 15233. Photolithographic reprint in 國史編纂委員會 (Kuksa P'yŏnch'an Wiwŏnhoe), ed. 各司謄錄 (Kaksa tŭngnok) v.51. 서울: 探求堂 (Seoul: T'amgudang), 1991, pp. 367–443.

Zenrin kokuhōki (善隣國宝記) (1470). Shūhō (周鳳). 田中健夫 (Tanaka, Takeo), trans. and ed. 善隣國宝記, 新訂続善隣國宝記 (Zenrin kokuhōki [and] Shintei zoku zenrin kokuhōki). 東京: 集英社 (Tōkyō: Shūeisha), 1995.

Secondary sources

17-segi kug'o sajŏn (17 세기국어사전). 홍윤표 (Hong Yun-p'yo) et al., ed. 서울: 太學社 (Seoul: T'aehaksa), 1995.

Abe, Yoshio. "Development of Neo-Confucianism in Japan, Korea, and China: A Comparative Study." Acta Asiatica, 19 (1970): 16–39.

Abe, Yoshio (阿都吉雄). 日本朱子學と朝鮮 (Nihon Shushi-gaku to Chōsen). 東京: 東京大學出版會 (Tōkyō: Tōkyō Daigaku Shuppankai), 1965 (second edition, 1971).

Ackroyd, Joyce, trans. Told Round a Brushwood Fire: The Autobiography of Arai Hakuseki (Princeton: Princeton University Press), 1979.

Anderson, Benedict. Imagined Communities, revised edition (London: Verso), 1991.

An, Hwi-jun (安輝濬). 韓日 繪畫關係1500年 (Han-Il hoehwa kwangye 1500 nyŏn). In 國立中央博物館 (Kungnip chung'ang pangmulgwan), ed. 朝鮮時代通信使 (Chosŏn sidae T'ongsinsa). 서울: 國立中央博物館 (Seoul: Kungnip chung'ang pangmulgwan), 1986: 125–147.

Arano, Yasunori (荒野泰典). 近世日本と東アジア (Kinsei Nihon to higashi Ajia). 東京: 東京大學出版社 (Tōkyō: Tōkyō Daigaku Shuppankai), 1988.

Arimitsu, Yasushige (有光保茂). 博多宗金商人とその家係 (Hakata Sō Kin shōnin to sono kakei). 史淵 (Shien), 16 (1931): 201–237.

Asahi Shinbun (朝日新聞).

Banks, Marcus. *Ethnicity: Anthropological Constructions* (New York: Routledge), 1996.

Barth, Fredrik. "Introduction." In Fredrik Barth, ed. *Ethnic Groups and Boundaries: The Social Organization of Culture Difference.* (Oslo: Pensumtjeneste), 1994: 9–38 (first published in 1969).

Baud, Michiel and Willem van Schendel. "Toward a Comparative History of Borderlands." *Journal of World History,* 8:2 (Fall 1997): 211–242.

Boot, Willem Jan. "The Adoption and Adaptation of Neo-Confucianism in Japan: The Role of Fujiwara Seika and Hayashi Razan." (Proefschrift, Rijksuniversiteit ti Leiden, Netherlands), 1982.

Boot, Willem Jan. "Yi T'oegye and Japan." *Korea Journal,* 22 (1982.2): 16–30.

Bŏpchech'ŏ (法制處) (Bureau of Legislation), ed. 古法典用語集 (Kobŏpjŏn yong'ŏjip). 서울: 育志社 (Seoul: Yukjisa), 1979.

Burckhardt, Jacob. *The Civilization of the Renaissance in Italy.* Translated by S. G. C. Middlemore, revised and edited by Irene Gordon. New York: The New American Library, 1960 (first published in German in 1860).

Burton, Donald. "Peasant Movements in Early Tokugawa Japan." *Peasant Studies,* 8:3 (Summer, 1979): 59–73.

Campbell, Robert Elvin. "The Pusan Section of the *Shōkai shingo*: Study and Translation." Unpublished Ph.D. dissertation, University of California, Berkeley, 1994.

Ch'a, Mun-sŏng (車文星). 지질 (Chijil). In 釜山直轄市史編纂委員會 (Pusan chikhal-si sa p'yŏnch'an wiwŏnhoe), ed., 釜山市史 (Pusan-si sa), vol. 1. 釜山: 釜山直轄市 (Pusan: Pusan Chikhal-si), 1989: 81–106.

Chang, Sun-sun (張舜順). 朝鮮時代倭館變遷史 研究 (Chosŏn sidae Waegwan pyŏnch'ŏn sa yŏn'gu). Unpublished Ph.D. dissertation, Chŏlla Pukdo Taehakkyo, 2001.

Chappell, David A. "Ethnogenesis and Frontiers," *Journal of World History,* 4:2 (Fall 1993): 267–275.

Chartier, Roger. *Cultural History: Between Practices and Representations.* Translated by Lydia G. Cochrane (Ithaca: Cornell University Press), 1988.

Chi, Tu-hwan (池斗煥). 조선전기사회경제와부산 (Chosŏn chŏngi sahoe-kyŏngje wa Pusan). In 釜山直轄市史編纂委員會 (Pusan chikhal-si sa p'yŏnch'an wiwŏnhoe), ed. 釜山市史 (Pusan-si sa), vol. 1. 釜山: 釜山直轄市 (Pusan: Pusan Chikhal-si), 1989: 606–632.

Chi, Tu-hwan (池斗煥). 조선전기의문화와부산 (Chosŏn chŏngi ŭi munhwa wa Pusan). In 釜山直轄市史編纂委員會 (Pusan chikhal-si sa p'yŏnch'an wiwŏnhoe), ed. 釜山市史 (Pusan-si sa), vol. 1. 釜山: 釜山直轄市 (Pusan: Pusan Chikhal-si), 1989: 632–636.

Ch'oe, Sŭng-hŭi (崔承熙). 韓國古文書研究 (Hanguk komunsŏ yŏn'gu). 城南: 韓國精神文化研究院 (Sŏngnam: Hanguk Chŏngsin Munhwa Yonguwŏn), 1981 (reprint, 1985).

Ch'oe, Yŏng-ho. "Commoners in early Yi Dynasty Civil Examinations: An Aspect of Korean Social Structure, 1392–1600." *The Journal of Asian Studies,* 33:4 (1974.8): 611–631.

Ch'oe, Yŏng-ho. "An Outline History of Korean Historiography." *Korean Studies,* 4 (1980): 1–27.

Ch'oe, Yŏng-hŭi (崔永禧). 초량왜관 (Ch'oryang Waegwan). In 國立中央博物館 (Kungnip Chung'ang Pangmulgwan), ed. 朝鮮時代通信使 (Chosŏn sidae T'ongsinsa). 서울: 國立中央博物館 (Seoul: Kungnip Chung'ang Pangmulgwan), 1986: 118–124.

Cho, Kyu-tae (曺圭大). 해양 (Haeyang). In 釜山直轄市史編纂委員會 (Pusan chikhal-si sa p'yŏnch'an wiwŏnhoe), ed. 釜山市史 (Pusan-si sa), vol. 1. 釜山: 釜山直轄市 (Pusan: Pusan Chikhal-si), 1989: 147–177.

Chŏng, Kwang (鄭光). 司譯院 倭學研究 (Sayŏkwŏn Waehak yŏn'gu). 서울: 太學社 (Seoul: T'aehaksa), 1988.

Chŏng, Kyŏng-chu (鄭景柱). 東萊府東下面古文書에대하여 (Tongnae-bu Tongha-myŏn komunsŏ e tae hayŏ). 釜山市 (Pusan-si) (1993.8.26).

Chŏng, Sŏng-il (鄭成一). 朝鮮後期對日貿易 (Chosŏn hugi tae-Il muyŏk). 서울: 圖書出版 新書苑 (Seoul: Tosŏ Ch'ulp'an Sinsŏwŏn), 2000.

Chung, Chai-sik. *A Korean Confucian Encounter with the Modern World: Yi Hang-no and the West* (Berkeley: University of California Press), 1995.

Courant, Maurice. "Un Établissement Japonais en Corée: Pusan depuis le XVe siècle." *Annales Coloniales.* (Paris), 15 Août–1 Octobre 1904, reprinted in Centre d'Études Coréennes, Collège de France ed. *Cahiers d'Études Coréennes, 1, Études Coréennes de Maurice Courant* (Paris: Editions du Léopard d'Or), 1983: 253–289.

Dardess, John W. *A Ming Society: T'ai-ho County, Kiangsi, Fourteenth to Seventeenth Centuries* (Berkeley: University of California Press), 1996.

Deuchler, Martina. *Confucian Gentlemen and Barbarian Envoys: The Opening of Korea, 1875– 1885* (Seattle: University of Washington Press), 1977.

Deuchler, Martina. *The Confucian Transformation of Korea: A Study of Society and Ideology* (Cambridge, Massachusetts: Harvard University Press), 1992.

Elisonas, Jurgis. "Chapter 6, The inseparable trinity: Japan's relations with China and Korea," in John W. Hall, ed. *The Cambridge History of Japan, Vol. 4, Early Modern Japan* (Cambridge: Cambridge University Press), 1991.

Engels, Friederich. *The Origin of the Family, Private Property and the State (Der Ursprung der Familie, des Privateigentums und des Staats) In the light of the researches of Lewis H. Morgan* (London: Lawrence and Wishart, Ltd.), 1940 (first edition 1884).

Febvre, Lucien. "*Frontière*: The Word and the Concept." In Peter Burke, ed. *A New Kind of History: From the Writings of Lucien Febvre* (London: Routledge and Kegan Paul), 1973: 208–218.

Febvre, Lucien. *The Problem of Unbelief in the Sixteenth Century, the Religion of Rabelais.* Translated by Beatrice Gottlieb (Cambridge, Massachusetts: Harvard University Press), 1982 (first published in French in 1942).

Flynn, Dennis O. "Comparing the Tokugawa Shogunate with Habsburg Spain: Two Silver-Based Empires in a Global Setting." In James D. Tracy, ed. *The Political Economy of Merchant Empires: State Power and World Trade, 1350–1750* (Cambridge: Cambridge University Press), 1991: 332–359.

Flynn, Dennis O. and Arturo Giráldez, "Born with a 'Silver Spoon': The Origin of World Trade in 1571." *Journal of World History*, 6:2 (1995 Fall): 201–221.

Geertz, Clifford. *The Interpretation of Cultures* (New York: Basic Books, Inc.), 1973.

Gellner, Ernest. *Nationalism* (London: Phoenix), 1997.

Ginzburg, Carlo. *Clues, Myths, and the Historical Method.* Trans. by John and Anne Tedeschi (Baltimore: The Johns Hopkins University Press), 1989.

Greenfeld, Liah. *Nationalism: Five Roads to Modernity* (Cambridge, Massachusetts: Harvard University Press), 1992.

H. and B., compilers. *Manners and Customs of the Japanese in the Nineteenth Century, from the Accounts of Dutch Residents in Japan and from the German Work of Dr. Philipp Franz von Siebald* (Tōkyō: Charles E. Tuttle), 1973 (reprint of first edition, New York, 1841).

Haboush, JaHyun Kim. "Constructing the Center: The Ritual Controversy and the Search for a New Identity in Seventeenth-Century Korea," in JaHyun Kim Haboush and Martina Deuchler, ed. *Culture and the State in Late Chosŏn Korea* (Cambridge, Massachusetts: Harvard University Press), 1999: 46–90.

Haeundae-ku (海雲臺區), ed., (海雲臺의옛모습이담긴) 東下面古文書: 譯注影印 (Haeundae ŭi yet mosŭp-i tamgin, Tongha-myŏn komunsŏ: yŏkju yŏng'in). 부산: 海雲臺區 (Pusan: Haeundae-ku), 1994.

Hamel, Hendrick. *Hamel's Journal and a Description of the Kingdom of Korea, 1653–1666.* Translated from the Dutch by Br. Jean-Paul Punys of Taizé, (Seoul: Royal Asiatic Society), 1994.

Hanguk Chŏngsin Munhwa Yŏn'guwŏn (한국정신문화연구원), ed. 한국민적문화대백과사전 (Hanguk minjok munhwa taepaekkwa sajŏn). 성남: 한국정신문화연구원 (Sŏngnam: Hanguk Chŏngsin Munhwa Yŏn'guwŏn), 1991.

Hanguk Haeyang Charyo Sent'ŏ (한국해양자료센터) (Korea Oceanographic Data Center) in Pusan. (http://www.nfrdi.re.kr/kodc/index.html).

Han-Il Kwangyesa Hakhoe (한일관계사학회), ed. 조선시대한일표류민연구 (Chosŏn sidae Han-Il p'yoryumin yŏn'gu). 서울: 國學資料院 (Seoul: Kukhak Charyowŏn), 2001.

Han, Yŏng-guk (韓榮國). 湖西에實施된大同法(上) — 大同法研究의一齣 – (Ho-sŏ e silsi toen Taedongbŏp (part one): Taedongbŏp yŏn'gu ŭi ilch'ak), 歷史學報 (Yŏksa hakpo), 13 (1960.10): 77–107.

Han, Yŏng-guk (韓榮國). 湖西에實施된大同法(下) — 大同法研究의一齣 – (Ho-sŏ e silsi toen Taedongbŏp (part two): Taedongbŏp yŏn'gu ŭi ilch'ak), 歷史學報 (Yŏksa hakpo), 14 (1961.4): 77–132.

Han, Yŏng-guk (韓榮國). 湖南에實施된大同法(上) — 湖西大同法과의比較및添補 – (Ho-nam e silsi toen Taedongbŏp (part one): Ho-sŏ Taedongbŏp kwa ŭi pigyo mit ch'ŏmpo), 歷史學報 (Yŏksa hakpo), 15 (1961.9): 31–59.

Han, Yŏng-guk (韓榮國). 湖南에實施된大同法 — (二) 湖西大同法과의比較및添補 – 」 (Ho-nam e silsi toen Taedongbŏp (part two): Ho-sŏ Taedongbŏp kwa ŭi pigyo mit ch'ŏmpo), 歷史學報 (Yŏksa hakpo), 20 (1963.4): 29–80.

Han Yŏng-guk (韓榮國). 湖南에實施된大同法 — (三) 湖西大同法과의比較및添補 – 」 (Ho-nam e silsi toen Taedongbŏp (part three): Ho-sŏ Taedongbŏp kwa ŭi pigyo mit ch'ŏmpo), 歷史學報 (Yŏksa hakpo), 21 (1963.8): 67–99.

Han Yŏng-guk (韓榮國). 湖南에實施된大同法 – (四, 完) 湖西大同法과의比較및添補 – (Ho-nam e silsi toen Taedongbŏp (part four and final): Ho-sŏ Taedongbŏp kwa ŭi pigyo mit ch'ŏmpo), 歷史學報 (Yŏksa hakpo), 24 (1964.7): 91–117.

Hattori, Tōru (服部徹). 日韓交通史 (Nikkan Kōtsū-shi). 東京: 博聞社 (Tokyo: Hakubunsha), 1894.

Ha, U-bong (河宇鳳). 朝鮮後期實學者의日本觀研究 (Chosŏn hugi Sirhakja ŭi Ilbon'gwan yŏn'gu). 서울: 一志社 (Seoul: Iljisa), 1989.

Hazard, Benjamin H. "Japanese Marauding in Medieval Korea: The Wakō Impact on Later Koryŏ." Unpublished Ph.D. dissertation, University of California, Berkeley, 1967.

Heard, A. D., W. Stevens, and H. Martin. "China and Japan in Korea." *North American Review,* 159 (1894:9).

Higaki, Motokichi (檜垣元吉). 對馬における奴婢と被官 (Tsushima ni okeru nuhi to hikan). In Higaki, Motokichi (檜垣元吉). 近世北部九州諸藩史の研究 (Kinsei hokubu Kyūshū shohan-shi no kenkyū). 福岡: 九州大學出版會 (Fukuoka: Kyūshū Daigaku Shuppankai), 1991.

Honda, Miho (本多美穂). 室町時代における少貳氏の動回: 貞賴。滿貞期 (Muromachi jidai ni okeru Shōni shi no dōkai: Sadayori, Mitsusada ki). 九州史學 (Kyūshū sahak), 91 (1988): 27–41.

Hong, Sŏng-dŏk (홍성덕). 조선후기問慰行에대하어 (Chosŏn hugi Munwihaeng e taehayo). 韓國學報 (Hanguk hakpo), 59 (1990): 120–128.

Hong Sŏng-dŏk (홍성덕). 조선후기對日와교사절問慰行의渡航人員분석 (Chosŏn hugi tae-Il oegyo sachŏl Munwihaeng ŭi tohang inwŏn punsŏk). 韓日關係史研究 (Han-Il kwangyesa yŏn'gu), 11 (1999): 61–81.

Hong, Sŏng-yun (洪性潤). 해양생물상 (Haeyang saengmul sang). In 釜山直轄市史編纂委員會 (Pusan chikhal-si sa p'yŏnch'an wiwŏnhoe), ed. 釜山市史 (Pusan-si sa), vol. 1. 釜山: 釜山直轄市 (Pusan: Pusan Chikhal-si), 1989: 260–328.

Hong, Yun-p'yo (홍윤표) *et al.*, ed. 十七世期國語辭典 (Sipch'il segi kug'ŏ sajŏn). 서울: 太學社 (Seoul: T'aehaksa), 1995.

Hucker, Charles. *A Dictionary of Official Titles in Imperial China* (Stanford: Stanford University Press), 1985.

Ikeuchi, Satoshi (池内敏). 近世日本と朝鮮漂流民 (Kinsei Nihon to Chōsen hyōryūmin). 東京: 臨川書店 (Tōkyō: Rinsen Shoten), 1998.

Innes, Robert L. "The Door Ajar: Japan's Foreign Trade in the Seventeenth Century." Unpublished Ph.D. dissertation, University of Michigan, 1980.

Izumi, Chōichi (泉 澄一). 天龍寺第二〇九世 — 中山玄中和尚について: 對馬以酉庵輪番時代を中心にして (Tenryūji dai 209 sei – Chūzan Genchū oshō ni tsuite: Tsushima Iteian rinban jidai o chūshin ni shite) in 大阪歴史學會 (Osaka Rekishi Gakkai), ed. ヒストリア (Historia), 63 (1973.6): 79–89.

Izumi, Chōichi (泉 澄一). 天龍寺第二〇四世 — 蘭室玄森和尚について — 延寶三. 五年: 對馬以酉庵輪番時代の行實 (Tenryūji 204 sei – Ranshitsu Genshin oshō ni tsuite – Empō 3–5 nen: Tsushima Iteian rinban jidai no kōjitsu), 對馬風土記 (Tsushima fūdoki), 11 (1974.10): 29–51.

Izumi, Chōichi (泉 澄一). 天龍寺第二一六世 — 瑞源等禎和尚について: 對馬以酉庵輪番時代の行實 (Tenryūji 216 sei – Zuigen Tōtei oshō ni tsuite: Tsushima Iteian rinban jidai no kōjitsu). 對馬風土記 (Tsushima fūdoki), 12 (1975.10): 55–75.

Izumi, Chōichi (泉 澄一). 對馬以酉庵輪番僧 江岳元策について (Tsushima Iteian rinbansō Egaku Gensaku ni tsuite). In Yokota Kenichi sensei kanreki kinenkai (橫田健一先生還曆記念會), ed. Yokota Kenichi sensei kanreki kinen: Nihonshi ronsō (橫田健一先生還曆記念, 日本史論叢). 吹田: 橫田健一先生還曆記念會 (Suita: Yokota Kenichi sensei kanreki kinenkai), 1976: 753–766.

Izumi, Chōichi (泉 澄一). 江戶時代, 日朝外交の一側面: 對馬以酉庵輪番制度と關係史料について (Edo jidai, Ni-Chō gaikō no ichi sokumen: Tsushima Iteian rinban seido to Kankei shiryō ni tsuite). 關西大學東西學術研究所紀要 (Kansai Daigaku Tōzai Gakujutsu Kenkyūjo kiyō), 10 (1977.9): 23–44.

Izumi, Chōichi (泉 澄一). 釜山窯の史的研究 (Pusan yō no shiteki kenkyū). 吹田市: 關西大學出版部 (Suita-shi: Kansai Daigaku Shuppanbu), 1986.

Izumi, Chōichi (泉 澄一), ed. 宗氏實錄(二): 對馬藩史料 (Sō shi Jitsuroku, vol. 2, Tsushima han shiryō). 大阪: 清文堂出版社 (Ōsaka: Seimundō shuppansha), 1988.

Izumi, Chōichi (泉 澄一). 對馬島宗家文書의分析研究: 國史編纂委員會所藏의記錄類 (6592점)를중심으로 (Taemado Chongka munsŏ ŭi bunsŏk yŏn'gu: Kuksa P'yŏnch'an Wiwŏnhoe sojang ŭi kirok-ryu (6592 chŏm) rŭl chungsim ŭ ro). 國史館論叢 (Kuksa'gwan nonch'ong), 7 (1989): 127–156.

Izumi, Chōichi (泉 澄一). 以酉庵第二世 — 規伯玄方和尚の晩年: 萬治元. 寬文元年, 赦免後の京. 大坂における日日 (Iteian dai 2 sei – Kihaku Genpō oshō no bannen: Banji gan–Kanbun gannen, shamengo no Kyō–Ōsaka ni okeru nichinichi). In 津田秀夫先生古稀記念會 (Tsuda Hideo sensei koki kinenkai), ed. 津田秀夫先生古稀記念: 封建社會と近代 (Tsuda Hideo sensei koki kinen: Hōken shakai to kindai). 京都: 同朋舍出版 (Kyōto: Dōhōsha Shuppan), 1989: 340–360.

Izumi, Chōichi (泉 澄一). 對馬藩藩儒: 雨森芳洲の基礎的研究 (Tsushima han hanju Amenomori Hōshū no kiso-teki kenkyū). 吹田: 關西大學出版部 (Suita: Kansai daigaku shuppanbu), 1997.

Izumi, Chōichi (泉 澄一). 對馬藩の研究 (Tsushima han no kenkyū). 吹田: 關西大學出版部 (Suita: Kansai Daigaku Shuppanbu), 2002.

Jager, Sheila Miyoshi. "Women, Resistance and the Divided Nation: The Romantic Rhetoric of Korean Reunification." *Journal of Asian Studies*, 55:1 (1996.2): 3–21.

Jungmann, Burglind. "Confusing Traditions: Elements of the Korean An Kyon School in Early Japanese Nanga Landscape Painting." *Artibus Asiae*, 55:3–4 (1995): 303–318.

Jungmann, Burglind. "Ike Taiga's Letter to Kim Yusong and His Approach to Korean Landscape Painting." *The Review of Korean Studies*, 1 (September 1998): 180–195.

Jun, Seong-ho (全成昊, Chŏn Sŏng-ho). 朝鮮後期米價史研究, 1725–1875 (Chosŏn hugi mi-gasa yŏn'gu, 1725–1875). Unpublished Ph.D. dissertation, Sŏnggyungwan Taehakkyo (成均館大學校), 1998.

Kalland, Arne. *Fishing Villages in Tokugawa Japan* (Honolulu: University of Hawaii Press), 1995.

Kamigaito, Kenichi (上垣外憲一). 雨森芳洲 元禄享保の國際人 (Amenomori Hōshū: Genroku Kyōhō no kokusaijin). 東京: 中蚣新書 (Tōkyō: Chūkō shinsho), 1989.

Kang Chae-ŏn (姜在彦) (J: Kan Jeon). 朝鮮の儒教—日本の儒教 (Chōsen no Jukyō – Nihon no Jukyō). 三千里 (Sanzenri), 19 (1979): 28–36.

Kang, Chu-chin (姜周鎭). 慶尚道先生案의解題및序 (Kyŏngsang-do sŏnsaeng'an ŭi haeche mit sŏ). In 道先生案 (To sŏnsaeng'an), 서울: 서울大學校出版部 (Seoul: Seoul Taehakkyo Ch'ulp'anbu), 1970.

Kang, Etsuko Hae-Jin. *Diplomacy and Ideology in Japanese–Korean Relations: From the Fifteenth to the Eighteenth Century* (London: Macmillan Press Ltd.), 1997.

Kang, Thomas Hosuck. "The Making of Confucian Societies in Tokugawa Japan and Yi Korea: A Comparative Analysis of the Behavior Patterns in Accepting the Foreign Ideology, Neo-Confucianism." Unpublished Ph.D. dissertation, American University, 1971.

Kasuya, Kenichi (糟谷憲一). なぜ朝鮮通信使は廢止されたか – 朝鮮資料を中心に – (Naze Chōsen Tsūshinshi wa haishi sareta ka: Chōsen shiryō o chūshin ni). 歷史評論 (Rekishi hyōron), 355 (1979.11): 8–23 (and 42).

Katsuragi, Tomesada (葛城末治). 解說 (Kaisetsu) in 中樞院調查課編 (Chūsūin Chōsa-kahen), 慶尚道地理志: 慶尚道續撰地理誌 (Keishōdō chiri shi: Keishōdō zokusen chiri shi). 京城: 朝鮮總督府中樞院 (Keijō: Chōsen Sōtokufu Chūsūin), 1938: 1–21.

Kawakami, Kenzō (川上健三). 竹島の歷史地理學的研究 (Takeshima no rekishi chirigakuteki kenkyū). 東京: 古今書院 (Tōkyō: Koku Shoin), 1966.

Kibe, Kazuaki (木部和昭). 朝鮮漂流民の救助 — 送還にみる日朝兩國の接觸: 朝鮮通詞の問題と漂流民の騷擾事件を中心として (Chōsen hyōryūmin no kyūjo-sōkan ni miru Ni-Chō ryōkoku no sesshoku: Chōsen tsūshi no mondai to hyōryūmin no sōjō jiken o chūshin toshite). 史境 En Marge de l'Histoire (Shikyō, En Marge de l'Histoire), 26 (1993.6): 36–54.

Kim, Chae-tŏk (金在德), ed. 古文獻用語例 (Komunhŏn yong'ŏye). 서울: 培英社 (Seoul: Paeyŏngsa), 1983.

Kim, Hyŏn-ju (金賢珠). 近世日朝文化交流史の研究: 朝鮮通信使の馬上才と獻上馬 (Kinsei Ni-Chō bunka kōryūshi no kenkyū: Chōsen Tsūshinshi no bajōsai to kenjō uma). Unpublished M.A. thesis, Kyūshū University, 1994.

Kim, Jae-on. "Chastity as a Social Ideal in Korea: Comparative and Historical Explanations." Paper presented at the First Pacific Basin International Conference on Korean Studies, Honolulu, Hawaii, July 27–August 2, 1992.

Kim, Key-huik. *The Last Phase of the East Asian World Order: Korea, Japan, and the Chinese Empire, 1860–1882* (Berkeley: University of California Press), 1980.

Kim, Ku-chin (김구진) and Yi Hyŏn-suk (이현숙). 通文館志의편찬과그간행에대하여 (T'ongmun'gwanji ŭi p'yŏnch'an kwa kŭ kanhaeng e taehayŏ). In 세종대왕기념사엎회 (Sejong Taewang Ki'nyŏm Saŏphoe) ed., 국역통문관지 (Kugyŏk T'ongmun'gwanji), vol. 1. 서울: 세종대왕기념사엎회 (Seoul: Sejong Taewang Ki'nyŏm Saŏphoe), 1998: 1–30.

Kim, Ok-kŭn (金玉根). 朝鮮後期經濟史研究 (Chosŏn hugi kyŏngjesa yŏn'gu). 서울: 瑞文堂 (Seoul: Sŏmundang), 1977.

Kim, Ok-kŭn (金玉根). 朝鮮王朝財政史研究 (Chosŏn wangjo chaejŏngsa yŏn'gu). 서울: 一潮閣 (Seoul: Ilchogak), 1984.

Kim, Ok-kŭn (金玉根). 朝鮮王朝財政史研究, 三 (Chosŏn wangjo chaejŏngsa yŏn'gu vol. 3). 서울: 一潮閣 (Seoul: Ilchogak), 1988.

Kim, Pyŏng-ha (金柄夏). 李朝前期對日貿易研究 (Yijo chŏngi tae-Il muyŏk yŏn'gu). 서울: 韓國研究院 (Seoul: Hanguk Yŏn'guwŏn), 1969.

Kim, Tal-su (金達壽). 日本の中の朝鮮文化3 (Nihon no naka no Chōsen bunka, volume 3). 東京: 講談社 (Tōkyō: Kōdansha), 1972.

Kim, Tong-ch'ŏl (金東哲). 朝鮮後期水牛角貿易과弓角契貢人 (Chosŏn hugi su'ugak muyŏk kwa kung'gak kyegong'in). 韓國文化研究 (釜山大學校韓國文化研究所) (Hanguk munhwa yŏn'gu, Pusan Taehakkyo, Hanguk Munhwa Yŏn'guso), 4 (1991:12): 55–110.

Kim, Tong-ch'ŏl (金東哲). 19세기牛皮貿易과東萊商人 (19 segi up'i muyŏk kwa Tongnae sang'in). 韓國文化研究 (Hanguk munhwa yŏn'gu), 6 (1993.8): 399–440.

Kim, Tong-ch'ŏl (金東哲). 東萊府商賈案을통해서본19세기후반의東萊商人: 東萊武任先生案과의비교 (Tongnae-bu sanggoan ŭl t'onghaesŏ pon 19 segi huban ŭi Tongnae sang'in: Tongnae muim sŏnsaeng'an kwaŭi pigyo). 韓日關係史研究 (Han-Il kwangyesa yŏn'gu), 1 (1993.10): 115–144.

Kim, Tong-ch'ŏl (金東哲). 17–18世紀對日公貿易에서의公作米문제 (17–18 segi tae-Il kong muyŏk esso ŭi kongjangmi munje). 港都釜山 (Hangdo Pusan), 10 (1993.11): 99–146.

Kim, Tong-ch'ŏl (金東哲). 朝鮮後期貢人研究 (Chosŏn hugi kong'in yŏn'gu). 서울: 韓國研究院 (Seoul: Hanguk Yŏn'guwŏn), 1993.

Kim, Tong-ch'ŏl (金東哲). 18 세기 氷契의창설과도고활동 (18 segi pinggye ŭi ch'angsŏl kwa togo hwaldong). 釜大史學 (Pudae sahak), 19 (1995:6): 383–414.

Kim, Tong-ch'ŏl (金東哲). 조선후기倭館開市貿易과東萊商人 (Chosŏn hugi Waegwan kaesi muyŏk kwa Tongnae sang'in). 民族文化 (Minjok munhwa), 21 (1998:12): 56–82.

Kim, Ŭi-hwan (金義煥) (J: Kin Gi-kan). 李朝時代に於ける釜山の倭館の起源と變遷 (Ri-Chō jidai ni okeru Fuzan no Wakan no kigen to hensen). 帝塚山短期大學日本文化史學會 (Tezukayama Tanki Daigaku Nihon Bunkashi Gakkai), ed. 日本文化史研究 (Nihon bunkashi kenkyū), 2 (1977.12): 1–17.

Kim, Ŭi-hwan (金義煥) (J: Kin Gi-kan). 對馬島宗家文書倭館事考について (Tsushima shima Sō-ke monjo Wakan jikō ni tsuite). 帝塚山短期大學日本文化史學會 (Nara Tezukayama Tanki Daigaku Nihon Bunkashi Gakkai), ed. 日本文化史研究 (Nihon bunkashi kenkyū), 5 (1983.5): 1–14.

Kim, Ŭi-hwan (金義煥) (J: Kin Gi-kan). 釜山倭館の職官構成とその機能について: 李朝の對日政策の一理解のために (Fuzan Wakan no shokkan kōsei to sono kinō ni tsuite: Ri-Chō no tai Nichi seisaku no ichi rikai no tame ni). 朝鮮學報 (Chōsen gakuhō), 108 (1983.7): 111–145.

Kim, Ŭi-hwan (金義煥) (J: Kin Gi-kan). 釜山倭館貿易の研究: 15世紀から17世紀にかけての貿易形態を中心に (Fuzan Wakan bōeki no kenkyū: 15 seki kara 17 seki ni kakete no bōeki keitai o chūshin ni). 朝鮮學報 (Chōsen gakuhō), 127 (1988.4): 43–72.

Kim, Ŭi-hwan (金義煥) (J: Kin Gi-kan). 倭人作拏謄錄について 附: 史料本文 (Waein changna tŭngnok ni tsuite, fu: shiryō honbun). 帝塚山短期大學日本文化史學會 (Nara Tezukayama Tanki Daigaku Nihon Bunkashi Gakkai), ed. 日本文化史研究 (Nihon bunkashi kenkyū), 16 (1992.1): 59–82.

Kim, Yŏng-ho (金泳鎬). 安城鍮器產業에관한調査報告 (Ansŏng hogi sanŏp e kwan han chosa pogo). 亞細亞研究 (Asea yŏn'gu), 8:4 (1965.12): 157–164.

Kim, Yong-uk (金容旭). 釜山倭館考 (Pusan Waegwan ko). 韓日文化 (Han-Il munhwa), 1:2 (1962.12): 53–116.

Kobayashi, Hajime (小林肇). 對馬領田代売藥史 (Tsushima ryō Tashiro baiyakushi). 佐賀: 小林肇 (Saga: Kobayashi Hajime), 1960.

Kuno, Yoshi S. *Japanese Expansion on the Asiatic Continent.* Berkeley: University of California Press, vol. 1 (1937) and vol. 2 (1940).

Kwŏn, O-ton (權五惇). 燃藜室記述 (Yŏllyŏsil kisul). In 朴鍾鴻 (Pak Chong-hong), ed. 韓國의名著 (Hanguk ŭi myŏngjo) vol. 3. 서울: 玄岩社 (Seoul: Hyŏnamsa), 1969: 248–256.

BIBLIOGRAPHY

Kyujanggak Hangukbon tosŏ haeje sabu (奎章閣 韓國本 圖書 解題 史部), vol. 4. 서울: 서울대학교규장각도서관 (Seoul: Seoul Taehakkyo Kyujanggak Tosŏgwan), 1987.

Lautensach, Hermann, translated by Katherine and Eckart Dege. *Korea: A Geography Based on the Author's Travels and Literature* (Berlin: Springer-Verlag), 1988 (original German version, 1945).

Ledyard, Gari. "Galloping Along With the Horseriders: Looking for the Founders of Japan." *Journal of Japanese Studies*, 1:2 (Spring, 1975): 217–254.

Lee, Ki-baik. *A New History of Korea*. Translated by Edward Wagner with Edward Shultz (Seoul: Ilchokak Publishers), 1984.

Lee, Peter H., trans. *A Korean Storyteller's Miscellany: the P'aegwan chapki of O Sukkwon* (Princeton: Princeton University Press), 1989.

Lewis, James B. "Beyond Sakoku: The Cost of the Korean Envoy to Edo and the Diary of Shin Yu-han." Unpublished M.A. thesis, University of Hawai'i, 1983.

Lewis, James B. "The Pusan Japan House (Waegwan) and Chosŏn Korea: Early-Modern Korean views of Japan through Economic, Political, and Social Connections." Unpublished Ph.D. dissertation, University of Hawai'i, 1994.

Lewis, James and Seong-ho Jun. "Economic Perspectives on Korean History: Macroscopic Structures, Part 1." Unpublished paper presented at a Biennial Conference of the Association for Korean Studies in Europe, April 2001.

Longford, J. H. "Japan's Relations with Korea in the 19th century." *Nineteenth Century*, 55 (1904): 618–629.

Lovejoy, Arthur O. *The Great Chain of Being: A Study of the History of an Idea* (Cambridge, Massachusetts: Harvard University Press), 1936.

Maema, Kyōsaku (前間恭作). 古鮮冊譜 (Ko-Sen sappu). 東京: 東洋文庫 (Tōkyō: Tōyō bunko), 1944–1957.

Matsushita, Shirō (松下志朗). 對馬藩の蒔高と間高 (Tsushima han no makidaka to kandaka). In 經濟史經營史論集 (Keizaishi keieishi ronshū). 大阪: 大阪經濟大學日本經濟史研究所發行 (Ōsaka: Ōsaka Keizai Daigaku Nihon Keizai-shi Kenkyūjo Hakkō), 1984: 37–67.

McCune, George. "Korean Relations with China and Japan, 1800–1864." Unpublished Ph.D. dissertation, University of California, Berkeley, 1941.

McCune, George. "The Exchange of Envoys Between Korea and Japan During the Tokugawa Period." *The Far Eastern Quarterly*, 5:3 (1946.5): 308–325. Reprinted in John A. Harrison, ed. *Japan, Volume 2, Enduring Scholarship selected from the Far Eastern Quarterly – The Journal of Asian Studies, 1941–1971.* (Tucson: The University of Arizona Press), 1972: 83–100.

McCune, George. "The Japanese Trading Post at Pusan." *Korean Review*, 1:1 (1948): 11–15.

McCune, Shannon. *Views of the Geography of Korea, 1935–1960* (Seoul: The Korean Research Center), 1980.

Michell, Tony. "Fact and Hypothesis in Yi Dynasty Economic History: The Demographic Dimension." *Korean Studies Forum*, 5 (1979–1980, Winter-Spring): 65–93.

Miyake, Hidetoshi (三宅英利). 近世日朝關係史の研究 (Kinsei Ni-Chō kankeishi no kenkyū). 東京: 文獻出版 (Tōkyō: Bunken Shuppan), 1986.

Miyazaki, Michiō (宮崎道生). 新井白石 (Arai Hakuseki). 東京: 吉川弘文館 (Tōkyō: Yoshikawa Kōbunkan), 1989.

Mori, Katsumi (森 克己). 近世に於ける對鮮密貿易と對馬島 (Kinsei ni okeru tai-Sen mitsu bōeki to Tsushima shima). 史淵 (Shien), 45 (1950): 49–73.

Mori, Katsumi (森 克己), ed. 體係 日本史叢書5 對外關係史. (Taikei Nihonshi sōsho 5 taigai kankeishi). 東京: 山川出版社 (Tōkyō: Yamakawa Shuppansha), 1978.

Morioka, Yoshiko (森岡美子). 山島 (Dejima). In 長崎縣史編集委員會 (Nagasaki kenshi henshū iinkai), ed. 長崎縣史 對外交渉編 (Nagasaki Kenshi Taigai Kōshōhen). 東京: 吉川弘文館 (Tōkyō: Yoshikawa Kōbunkan), 1985: 480–510.

Muir, Edward and Guido Ruggiero, ed. *Microhistory and the Lost Peoples of Europe*. Trans. by Eren Branch (Baltimore: The Johns Hopkins University Press), 1991.

Murai, Shōsuke (村井章介). アヅアのなかの中世日本 (Ajia no naka no chūsei Nihon). 東京: 倉書房 (Tōkyō: Sōshobō), 1988.

Murai, Shōsuke (村井章介). 中世倭人傳 (Chūsei Wajin-den). 東京: 巖波書店 (Tōkyō: Iwanami Shoten), 1993.

Moriyama, Tsuneo (森山恒雄) and Katayama, Naoyoshi (片山直義). 對馬藩 (Tsushima han). In 長崎縣史編纂委員會 (Nagasaki Kenshi Hensan Iinkai), ed. 長崎縣史: 藩政編 (Nagasaki kenshi: hansei hen). 東京: 吉川弘文館 (Tōkyō: Yoshikawa Kōbunkan), 1973: 806–1194.

Na, Chong-u (羅鐘宇). 韓國中世對日交涉史研究 (Hanguk Chungse tae-Il kyosŏpsa yŏn'gu). 서울: 圓光大學校 出版局 (Seoul: Wŏn'gwang Taehakkyo Ch'ulp'anguk), 1996.

Nagasaki Kenshi Hensan Iinkai (長崎縣史編纂委員會), ed. 長崎縣視: 藩政編 (Nagasaki Kenshi: Hansei hen). 東京: 吉川弘文館 (Tōkyō: Yoshikawa Kōbunkan), 1973.

Nagasato, Kazu (長鄉嘉壽). 對馬八鄉の人びと (Tsushima hachigyō no hitobito). In 長崎縣立對馬歷史民俗資料館 (Nagasaki kenritsu Tsushima rekishi minzoku shiryōkan), ed. 對馬くらしの資料展 (Tsushima kurashi no shiryōten). 長崎: 長崎縣立對馬歷史民俗資料館 (Nagasaki: Nagasaki Kenritsu Tsushima Rekishi Minzoku Shiryōkan), 1988: 6–14.

Nakai, Kate Wildman. *Shogunal Politics: Arai Hakuseki and the Premises of Tokugawa Rule* (Cambridge, Massachusetts: Harvard University Press), 1988.

Nakamura, Hidetaka (中村榮孝). 日鮮關係史の研究 上中下 (Ni-Sen kankeishi no kenkyū, three volumes). 東京: 吉川弘文館 (Tōkyō: Yoshikawa Kōbunkan), 1965–1969.

Nakamura, Tadashi (中村 質). 近世長崎貿易史の研究 (Kinsei Nagasaki bōekishi no kenkyū). 東京: 吉川弘文館 (Tōkyō: Yoshikawa Kōbunkan), 1988.

Nakamura, Tadashi (中村 質). 壬辰倭亂に關する諸問題 (Jinshin Waran ni kansuru shomondai). In 第二回 國際海洋力심포지움 發表文集, 主題: 壬辰倭亂 괴 海洋力 (Che 2 hoe kukche haeyangyŏk shimp'ojium palp'yo munjip, chuje: Imjin Waeran kwa haeyangyŏk). 鎭海: 大韓民國海軍, 海軍海洋研究所 (Chinhae: Taehan Minguk Haegun, Haegun Haeyang Yŏn'guso), 1991: 41–60 (Korean); pp. 61–78 (Japanese).

Nakamura, Tadashi (中村 質). 近世日朝私貿易論の再檢討 (Kinsei Ni-Chō shibōeki ron no saikentō). In 水邨朴永錫教授華甲紀念 韓國史學論叢 下 (Such'on Pak Yŏng-sŏk kyosu hwagap kinyŏm, Hanguk sahak nonch'ong), vol. 2. 果田: 國史編纂委員會 (Kwach'ŏn: Kuksa P'yŏnch'an Wiwŏnhoe), 1992: 771–785.

Nam, Man-sŏng (南晚星). 慵齋叢話: 解說 (Yongjae Ch'onghwa: haesŏl). In 成俔 (Sŏng Hyŏn), 慵齋叢話 (Yongjae Ch'onghwa). Translated by Nam Man-sŏng. 서울: 大洋書籍 (Seoul: Taeyang sŏjŏk), 1973: 23–25.

Nihon kokugo daijiten (日本國語大辞典). Edited in ten volumes by 日本大辞典刊行會 (Nihon daijiten kankōkai). 東京: 小學館 (Tōkyō: Shōgakkan), 1979–1981.

NOAA (National Oceanic and Atmospheric Administration) US Government. Surface Temperature images from the Marine Remote Sensing Lab, available through the Hanguk haeyang charyo sent'ŏ (한국해양자료센터) (Korea Oceanographic Data Center) in Pusan, (http://www.nfrdi.re.kr/kodc/data/noaa/index.html).

O Sŏng (吳星). 朝鮮後期商人研究 (Chosŏn hugi sang'in yŏn'gu). 사울: 一潮閣 (Seoul: Ilchogak), 1989.

Ōba, Ikuyo (大場生与). 近世日朝關係における譯官使 (Kinsei Ni-Chō kankei ni okeru Yakkanshi). Unpublished MA thesis, Keiō University (慶應大學), 1994.

Ōba, Ikuyo (大場生与). 對馬藩による朝鮮側小通事への援助 (Tsushima han ni yoru Chōsen-gawa shōtsūji e no enjo). 三田中世史研究 (Mita Chūseishi kenkyū), 4 (1997.10): 102–115.

Oda, Seigo (小田省吾). 釜山の倭館と設門に就て (Pusan no Wakan to setsumon ni tsuite). 朝鮮 (Chōsen), 125 (1926): 152–160.

Oda, Seigo (小田省吾). 李氏朝鮮時代に於ける倭館の變遷: 就中絶影島倭館に就て (Rishi Chōsen jidai ni okeru Wakan no hensen: nakanzuku Zetsueido Wakan ni tsuite). In 京城帝國大學法文學會 (Keijō Teikoku Daigaku Hōbun Gakkai), ed. 朝鮮支那文化の研究 (Chōsen Shina bunka no kenkyū). 東京: 刀江書院 (Tōkyō: Tōgō Shoin), 1929: 93–140.

Oda, Seigo (小田省吾) et al., ed. 釜山府史原稿 (Fuzan-fu shi genkō), in six volumes. 서울: 景印文化社 (Seoul: Kyŏng'in Munhwasa), 1989.

O, Kŏn-hwan (吳建煥). 지세 (Chise). In 釜山直轄市史編纂委員會 (Pusan chikhal-si sa p'yŏnch'an wiwŏnhoe), ed. 釜山市史 (Pusan-si sa), vol. 1. 釜山: 釜山直轄市 (Pusan: Pusan Chikhal-si), 1989: 41–78.

Osa, Masanori (長 正統). 日鮮關係における記錄の時代 (Ni-Sen kankei ni okeru kiroku no jidai). 東洋學報 (Tōyō gakuhō), 50:4 (1968.3): 70–124.

Osa, Masanori (長 正統). 路浮稅考: 肅宗朝癸亥約條の一考察 (Nobuseikō: Shukusō chō Kigai Yakujō no ichi kōsatsu). 朝鮮學報 (Chōsen gakuhō), 58 (1971): 1–20.

Osa, Setsuko (長 節子). 中世日朝關係と對馬 (Chūsei Ni-Chō kankei to Tsushima). 東京: 吉川弘文館 (Tōkyō: Yoshikawa Kōbunkan), 1987.

Osa, Setsuko (長 節子). 一五世紀後半の日朝貿易の形態 (Jūgoseiki kōhan no Ni-Chō bōeki no keitai). In 中村 質 (Nakamura Tadashi), ed. 鎖國と國際關係 (Sakoku to kokusai kankei). 東京: 吉川弘文館 (Tōkyō: Yoshikawa Kōbunkan), 1997: 2–30.

Pae, U-Sŏng (배우성). 조선후기국토관과천하관의변화 (Chosŏn hugi kukt'ogwan kwa Ch'ŏnha'gwan ŭi pyŏnhwa). 서울: 일지사 (Seoul: Iljisa), 1998.

Pak, Hŭng-su (朴興秀). 李朝尺度에關한研究 (Yijo ch'ŏkdo e kwan han yŏn'gu). 大東文化研究 (Taedong munhwa yŏn'gu), 4 (1967.7): 199–226.

Pak, Pyŏng-ho (朴秉濠), ed. 奎章閣韓國本圖書解題 (Kyuganggak Hanguk-bon tosŏ Haeje). 서울: 서울大學校出版部 (Seoul: Seoul Taehakkyo Ch'ulp'anbu), 1987.

Palais, James B. Politics and Policy in Traditional Korea (Cambridge, Massachusetts: Harvard University Press), 1975.

Palais, James B. Confucian Statecraft and Korean Institutions: Yu Hyŏngwŏn and the Later Chosŏn Dynasty (Seattle: University of Washington Press), 1996.

Panofsky, Erwin. Gothic Architecture and Scholasticism (New York: The World Publishing Company), 1957 (first published in 1951).

Pŏpchech'o (法制處), ed. 古法典用語集 (Kobŏpjŏn Yong'ŏjip). 서울: 育志社 (Seoul: Yukjisa), 1981.

Pusan chikhal-si kaepal chehan kuyŏk-do (釜山直轄市開發制限區域圖). 서울: 中央地圖文化社 (Seoul: Chung'ang Chido Munhwasa), 1988.

Robinson, Kenneth R. "From Raiders to Traders: Border Security and Border Control in Early Choson, 1392–1450." Korean Studies, 16 (1992): 94–115.

Robinson, Kenneth R. "The Tsushima Governor and Regulation of Japanese Access to Chosŏn in the Fifteenth and Sixteenth Centuries," Korean Studies, 20 (1996): 23–50.

Robinson, Kenneth R. "Policies of Practicality: The Chosŏn Court's Regulation of Contact with Japanese and Jurchens, 1392–1580s." Unpublished Ph.D. dissertation, University of Hawai'i, 1997.

Robinson, Kenneth R. "The Jiubian and Ezogachishima Embassies to Chosŏn, 1478–1482," 朝鮮史研究會論文集 (Chōsenshi kenkyūkai ronbunshū), 35 (1997): 55–86 (234–203).

Robinson, Kenneth R. "Treated as Treasures: The Circulation of sutras in maritime Northeast Asia from 1388 to the Mid-Sixteenth Century," East Asian History 21 (2001.6): 33–54.

Rokutanda, Yutaka (六反田豊). 慶南大同事目と慶尚道大同法 (Yŏngnam taedong samok to Keishōdō Daidōhō). 朝鮮學報 (Chōsen gakuhō), 131 (1989.4): 1–56.

Ruisu, Jeimusu (ルイス. ジェイムス, James Lewis). 壬辰 — 丁酉倭亂以降江華島條約以前の朝鮮からみた對馬 (Jinshin-Teiyū Waran ikō Koka jōyaku izen no Chōsen kara mita Tsushima). 地方史研究 (Chihōshi kenkyū) 41:4, vol. 232 (1991.8): 37–53.

Ruisu, Jeimusu (ルイス．ジェイムス, James Lewis). 近世朝鮮人の日本觀: 倭館における 公貿易 — 接待の費用を例示として (Kinsei Chōsenjin no Nihon-kan: Wakan ni okeru kōbōeki-settai no hiyō wo reiji toshite). 年報朝鮮學 (Nenpō Chōsengaku), 2 (1992.3): 1–38.

Saeki, Kōji (佐伯弘次). 中世都市博多と石城管事宗金 (Chūsei toshi Hakata to Sekijō Kanji Sō Kin). 史淵 (Shien, Kyūshū University), 133 (1996.2): 1–22.

Sahlins, Peter. Boundaries: The Making of France and Spain in the Pyrenees (Berkeley: University of California Press), 1989.

Sahlins, Peter. "State Formation and National Identity in the Catalan Borderlands during the Eighteenth and Nineteenth Centuries." In Thomas M. Wilson and Hastings Donnan, ed. Border Identities: Nation and State at International Frontiers (Cambridge: Cambridge University Press), 1998: 31–61.

Saito, Tsutomo, Takahashi Teruhiko and Nishikawa Yuichi. "Chemical Study of the Medieval Japanese Mochu-sen (Bronze Coins)." Institute for Monetary and Economic Studies Discussion Paper (Tōkyō: Bank of Japan), Paper No. 98-E-13, 1998.

Scott, James C. The Moral Economy of the Peasant: Rebellion and Subsistence in Southeast Asia (New Haven: Yale University Press), 1976.

Seoul Taehakkyo Tosŏgwan (서울大學校圖書館), ed. 奎章閣 韓國本 圖書 解題 史部 1–4 (Kyujanggak Hangukbon tosŏ haeje sabu 1–4). 서울: 서울大學校圖書館 (Seoul: Seoul Taehakkyo Tosŏgwan), 1987.

Setton, Mark. "Chŏng Tasan and the 'Kogaku.'" Oriens Extremus, 33:2 (1990): 57–68.

Setton, Mark. Chŏng Yagyong: Korea's Challenge to Orthodox Neo-Confucianism (Albany: SUNY Press), 1997.

Shaw, Glenn W., trans. "Chink Okichi." In Three Plays by Yamamoto Yuzo (Tōkyō: Hokuseido Press), 1935.

Shin, Susan S. "Some Aspects of Landlord–Tenant Relations in Yi Dynasty Korea." Palais, James B. and Margery D. Lang, ed. Occasional Papers on Korea 3. ACLS-SSRC, 1975, pp. 49–88.

Sin, Ki-su (辛基秀) (J: Shin Ki-shū). 朝鮮通信使の新しい資料: 繪馬, 繪畫, 日記 ... (Chōsen Tsūshinshi no atarashii shiryō: ema, eka, nikki ...). 韓國文化 (Kankoku bunka), 7:8 (1985.8): 21-27.

Sin, Ki-su (辛基秀) (J: Shin Ki-shū). みつかった朝鮮通信使の繪馬: 民衆同士の交歡 (Mitsukatta Chōsen Tsūshinshi no ema: minshū dōshi no kōkan). 未來 (Mirai), 227 (1985.8): 2–7.

Sin, Ki-su (辛基秀) (J: Shin Ki-shū). 祭の中の朝鮮通信使 (Matsuri no naka no Chōsen Tsūshinshi). 韓國文化 (Kankoku bunka) 7:11 (1985.11): 15–24.

Smith, Anthony D. The Ethnic Origins of Nations (Oxford: Blackwell Publishers), 1986.

Sommerville, John. "Stability in Eighteenth Century Ulsan." Korean Studies Forum, 1 (1976–1977): 1–18.

Song, Ki-joong. The Study of Foreign Languages in the Chosŏn Dynasty (1392–1910). Seoul: Jimoondang International, 2001.

Son, Sŭng-ch'ŏl (孫承喆). 倭人作挐謄錄을통하여본倭館 (Waein changna tŭngnok ŭl t'ong hayŏ pon Waegwan). 港都釜山 (Hangdo Pusan), 10 (1993): 67–98.

Statler, Oliver. Shimoda Story (Honolulu: University of Hawaii Press), 1986 (first published by Random House in 1969).

Suzuki, Tōzō (鈴木棠三), ed. 宗氏家譜略 (Sō shi-ke furyaku). 東京: 村田書店 (Tōkyō: Murata Shoten), 1981.

Tabohashi, Kiyoshi (田保橋潔). 近代日鮮關係の研究 上卷 (Kindai Ni-Sen kankei no kenkyū, vol. 1). 京城: 朝鮮總督府中樞院 (Tōkyō: Chōsen Sōtokufu Chūsūin), 1940.

Takahashi, Shōnosuke (高橋章之助). 宗家と朝鮮 (Sō-ke to Chōsen). 京城: 北內印刷所 (Keijō: Hokunai Insatsujo), 1920.

Takayanagi, Mitsunaga (高柳光壽) *et al.*, ed. 新訂 寬政重修諸家譜 (Shintei Kansei jūshū sho kafu), 8. 東京: 續群類從完成會 (Tōkyō: Zoku Gunruijū kansei kai), 1965.

Takeda, Katsuzō (武田勝藏). 日鮮貿易史上の三浦と倭館 (Ni-Sen bōeki-shi jō no Sampo to Wakan). 史學 (Shigaku), 1–3 (1911.5): 51–82.

Tanaka, Takeo (田中健夫). 中世海外支涉史の硏究 (Chūsei kaigai shishōshi no kenkyū). 東京: 東京大學出版會 (Tōkyō: Tōkyō Daigaku Shuppankai), 1959.

Tanaka, Takeo (田中健夫). 中世對外關係史 (Chūsei taigai kankeishi). 東京: 東京大學出版會 (Tōkyō: Tōkyō Daigaku Shuppankai), 1975.

Tanaka, Takeo (田中健夫). 對外關係と文化交流 (Taigai kankei to bunka kōryū). 東京: 思文閣出版 (Tōkyō: Shibunkaku Shuppan), 1982.

Tanaka, Takeo (田中健夫). 倭寇: 海の歷史 (Wakō: umi no rekishi). 東京: 教育社 (Tōkyō: Kyoikusha), 1982.

Tashiro, Kazui (田代和生). 寬永六年(仁祖七, 1629), 對馬使節の朝鮮國御上京之時每日記とその背景 (Kanei roku nen – Jinso 7, 1629 – Tsushima shisetsu no Chōsen koku *Go jōkyō no toki mainikki* to sono haikei). 朝鮮學報 (Chōsen gakuhō), 95 (1980.4): 73–115; 96 (1980.7): 85–94; 98 (1981.1): 63–76; 101 (1981.10): 51–108.

Tashiro, Kazui (田代和生). 近世日朝通交貿易史の硏究 (Kinsei Ni-Chō tsūkō bōekishi no kenkyū). 東京: 創文社 (Tōkyō: Sōbunsha), 1981.

Tashiro, Kazui. "Foreign Relations During the Edo Period: Sakoku Reexamined." *Journal of Japanese Studies*, 8:2 (1982 Summer): 283–306.

Tashiro, Kazui (田代和生). 書き替えられた國書 (Kakikaerareta kokusho). 東京: 中央新書 (Tōkyō: Chūō Shinsho), 1983.

Tashiro, Kazui (田代和生). 對馬藩の朝鮮米輸入と倭館升: 宗家記錄斛一件覺書からみた朝鮮米の計量法 (Tsushima han no Chōsen komei yunyū to Wakan masu: Sō-ke kiroku *Koku ikken oboegaki* kara mita Chōsen komei no keiryōhō). 朝鮮學報 (Chōsen gakuhō), 124 (1987.7): 1–47.

Tashiro, Kazui. "Exports of Japan's Silver to China via Korea and Changes in the Tokugawa Monetary System during the Seventeenth and Eighteenth Centuries." In Eddy H.G. Van Cauwenberghe, ed. *Precious Metals, Coinage and the Changes of Monetary Structures in Latin-America, Europe and Asia: Late Middle Ages – Early Modern Times* (Leuven: Leuven University Press), 1989, pp. 99–116.

Tashiro, Kazui (田代和生). 幕末期日朝私貿易と倭館貿易商人: 輸入四品目の取引を中心に (Bakumakki Ni-Chō shi bōeki to Wakan bōeki shōnin: yunyū yon hinmoku no torihiki o chūshin ni). In 速水融 (Hayami Akira) *et al.*, ed. 德川社會からの展望: 發展-構造-國際關係 (Tokugawa shakai kara no tenbō: hatten-kōzō-kokusai kankei). 東京: 同文館 (Tōkyō: Dōbunkan), 1989: 99–323.

Tashiro, Kazui (田代和生). 鎖國時代の日本町: 朝鮮半島の倭館 (Sakoku jidai no Nihon machi: Chōsen hantō no Wakan). しにか (Sinica), 4:12 (1993.12): 41–46.

Tashiro, Kazui (田代和生). 渡海譯官史の密貿易: 對馬藩潜商議論の背景 (Tōkai Yakkanshi no mitsu bōeki: Tsushima han *Senshō giron* no haikei). 朝鮮學報 (Chōsen gakuhō), 150 (1994.1): 29–84.

Thompson, E.P. "The Moral Economy of the English Crowd in the Eighteenth Century." *Past and Present* 50 (1971). Reprinted in E.P. Thompson. *Customs in Common: Studies in Traditional Popular Culture* (New York: The New Press), 1993: 185–258.

Tjoa, Miao-Ling. "Sakoku: The Full Range of Tokugawa Foreign Relations?" In Erika de Poorter, ed. *As the Twig is Bent . . . Essays in Honour of Frits Vos* (Amsterdam: J.C. Gieben), 1990: 209–236.

Toby, Ronald. "Korean–Japanese Diplomacy in 1711: Sukchong's Court and the Shogun's Title." 朝鮮學報 (Chōsen gakuhō), 74 (1975.1): 231–256.

Toby, Ronald P. *State and Diplomacy in Early Modern Japan: Asia in the Development of the Tokugawa Bakufu* (Princeton: Princeton University Press), 1984.

Toby, Ronald. "Carnival of the aliens: Korean Embassies in Edo-Period Art and Popular Culture." *Monumenta Nipponica*, 41:4 (1986 Winter): 415–456.

Toby, Ronald P. "Leaving the Closed Country: New Models for Early-Modern Japan." *Transactions of the International Conference of Orientalists in Japan*, 35 (1990): 213–226.

Tsukahira, Toshio G. *Feudal Control in Tokugawa Japan: The Sankin Kōtai System* (Cambridge, Massachusetts: Harvard East Asian Monographs, No. 20), 1970.

Ueda, Junichi (上田純一). 妙樂寺と博多商人: 應永の外寇をめぐって (Myōrakuji to Hakata shōnin: Ōei no gaikō o megutte). In 地方史研究協議會 (Chihōshi Kenkyū Kyōgikai), ed. 異國と九州: 歴史における國際交流と地域形成 (Ikoku to Kyūshū: Rekishi ni okeru kokusai kōryū to chiiki keisei). 東京: 雄山閣 (Tōkyō: Yūsankaku), 1993.

Underwood, Horace H. "Korean Boats and Ships." *Transactions of the Korea Branch of the Royal Asiatic Society*, 23 (1933) (reprinted, Seoul: Yonsei University Press, 1979).

Unruh, Ellen Salem. "The Landowning Slave: A Korean Phenomenon." *Korea Journal*, 16:4 (1976.4): 27–34.

Unruh, Ellen Salem. "The Utilization of Slave Labor in the Koryŏ Period: 918–1392." *Papers of the First International Conference on Korean Studies at the Academy of Korean Studies* (Sŏngnam: The Academy of Korean Studies), 1979: 630–642.

Verschuer, Charlotte von. "Japan's Foreign Relations 600 to 1200 A.D. – A Translation from *Zenrin kokuhōki*." *Monumenta Nipponica*, 54:1 (1999, spring): 1–39.

Vovelle, Michel. *Ideologies and Mentalities*. Translated by Eamon O'Flaherty (Cambridge: Polity Press), 1990.

Wagner, Edward Willett. *The Literati Purges: Political Conflict in Early Yi Korea* (Cambridge, Massachusetts: Harvard University Press), 1974.

Wilson, Thomas M. and Hastings Donnan. "Nation, State and Identity at International Borders." In Thomas M. Wilson and Hastings Donnan, ed. *Border Identities: Nation and State at International Frontiers* (Cambridge: Cambridge University Press), 1998: 1–30.

Winichakul, Thongchai. *Siam Mapped: A History of the Geo-Body of a Nation* (Honolulu: University of Hawai'i Press), 1994.

Yamagata, Isoh. "Japanese–Korean Relations after the Japanese Invasion of Korea in the 16th Century." *Transactions, Korea Branch of the Royal Asiatic Society*, 4 (1913): 1–11.

Yamamoto, Yuzo. *Three Plays by Yamamoto Yuzo*. Translated by Glenn W. Shaw (Tōkyō: Hokuseido Press), 1935.

Yamawaki, Teijirō (山脇悌二郎). 唐人屋敷 (Tōjin yashiki). In 長崎縣史編集委員會 (Nagasaki kenshi henshū iinkai) ed. 長崎縣史 對外交渉編 (Nagasaki Kenshi taigai kōshōhen). 東京: 吉川弘文館 (Tōkyō: Yoshikawa Kōbunkan), 1985: 511–524.

Yanai, Kenji (箭内健次), ed. 鎖國日本と國際交流 上下 (Sakoku Nihon to kokusai kōryū I, II). 東京: 吉川弘文館 (Tōkyō: Yoshikawa Kōbunkan), 1988.

Yasukochi, Hiroshi (安河內博). 對馬藩に於ける奴婢制度の研究 (Tsushima han ni okeru nuhi seido no kenkyū). 福岡: 九州大學文學部國史研究室 (Fukuoka: Kyūshū Daigaku Bungakubu Kokushi Kenkyūshitsu), 1953.

Yi, Chin-hŭi (李進熙) (J: Ri Shin-ki). 唐人踊いと朝鮮軸 (Tōjin odori to Chōsen yama). In 映像文化協會編 (Eizō bunka kyōkai), ed. 江戸時代の朝鮮通信使 (Edo jidai no Chōsen Tsūshinshi). 東京: 毎日新聞社 (Tōkyō: Mainichi Shinbunsha), 1979, pp. 51–68.

Yi, Ho-ch'ŏl (李鎬澈). 朝鮮前期農業經濟史 (Chosŏn chŏngi nong'ŏp kyŏngje-sa). 서울: 한길사 (Seoul: Han'gilsa), 1986.

Yi, Hong-chik (李弘稙). 增補새國史辭典 (Chŭngbo sae kuksa sajŏn). 서울: 청아출판사 (Seoul: Ch'ŏng'a Ch'ulp'ansa), 1983.

Yi, Hun (李薰). 朝鮮後期대마도의漂流民送還과對日관계 (Chosŏn hugi Taemado ŭi p'yoryumin songhwan kwa tae-Il kwangye). 國史館論叢 (Kuksa'gwan Nonch'ong), 26 (1991.10): 207–239.

Yi, Hun (李薰). 朝鮮後期 漂流民과 韓日關係 (Chosŏn hugi p'yoryumin kwa Han-Il kwangye). 서울: 國學資料院 (Seoul: Kukhak Charyowŏn), 2000.

Yi, Hyŏn-jong (李鉉淙). 朝鮮前期對日交涉史研究 (Chosŏn chŏngi tae-Il kyosŏpsa yŏn'gu). 서울: 韓國研究院 (Seoul: Hanguk Yŏn'guwŏn), 1964.

Yi, Ki-baek. *A New History of Korea*. Trans. by Edward W. Wagner with Edward J. Shultz (Seoul: Ilchogak), 1984.

Yi, Sŏng-mu (李成茂). 解題 (Haeche). In 韓國學文獻研究所 (Hanguk-hak munhŏn yŏn'guso), ed. 全國地理志 (Chŏnguk chiriji). 서울: 亞細亞文化社 (Seoul: Asea Munhwasa), 1983: 3–12.

Yi, Tae-Jin. "The Influence of Neo-Confucianism on 14th–16th Century Korean Population Growth." *Korea Journal*, 37:2 (1997, Summer): 5–23.

Yi, Wan-yŏng (李完永). 東萊府旻倭館의行政小考 (Tongnae-bu mit Waegwan ŭi haengjŏng soko). 港都釜山 (Hangdo Pusan) 2 (1963): 11–75.

Yi, Wŏn-kyun (李源鈞). 朝鮮時代의守令職交遞實態: 東萊府使의경우 (Chosŏn sidae ŭi suryŏngjik kyoch'e silt'ae: Tongnae busa ŭi kyŏngu). 釜山史學 (Pusan sahak), 3 (1979.2): 61–86.

Yi, Wŏn-kyun (李源鈞). 조선후기의부산 (Chosŏn hugi ŭi Pusan). In 釜山直轄市史編纂委員會 (Pusan chikhal-si sa p'yŏnch'an wiwŏnhoe), ed., 釜山市史 (Pusan-si sa), vol. 1. 釜山: 釜山直轄市 (Pusan: Pusan Chikhal-si), 1989: 699–772.

Yonetani, Hitoshi (米谷 均). 雨森芳洲の對朝鮮外交: 誠信之交の理念と實態 (Amenomori Hōshū no tai-Chōsen gaikō: seishin no kō no rinen to jittai). 朝鮮學報 (Chōsen gakuhō), 148 (1993.7): 1–32.

Yoshida, Hiroyuki (吉田宏志). 朝鮮通信使の繪畫 (Chōsen Tsūshinshi no kaiga). In 映像文化協會編 (Eizō bunka kyōkai, ed.). 江戸時代の朝鮮通信使 (Edo jidai no Chōsen Tsūshinshi), 東京: 毎日新聞社 (Tōkyō: Mainichi shinbunsha), 1979: 135–154.

Yu, Hong-yŏl (柳洪烈). 李肯翊, 燃藜室記述 (Yi Kŭng-ik Yŏllyŏsil kisul). In 月刊 新東亞 編輯室 (Wŏlgan Sintonga p'yŏnjipsil), ed. 韓國을움직인古典百選 (Hanguk ŭl umjikin kojŏn paeksŏn). 서울: 東亞日報社 (Seoul: Tong'a ilbo sa), 1985: 110–112.

Yun, C'hi-pu (尹致富). 韓國海洋文學研究 (Hanguk haeyang munhak yŏn'gu). 서울: 學文社 (Seoul: Hangmunsa), 1994.

INDEX

Lightning Source UK Ltd.
Milton Keynes UK
UKHW020826041019

350953UK00006B/1297/P

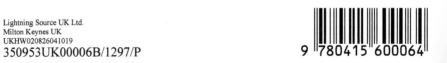